Macmillan/McGraw-Hill Edition

McGRAW-HILL READING

LCDSS LEARNING LAB

D1469215

McGraw-Hill
**McGraw-Hill
School Division**
New York   Farmington

Contributors

The Princeton Review, Time Magazine, Accelerated Reader

The Princeton Review is not
affiliated with Princeton
University or ETS.

McGraw-Hill School Division

A Division of The McGraw·Hill Companies

McGraw-Hill School Division
Two Penn Plaza
New York, New York 10121

Printed in the United States of America

ISBN 0-02-184770-3/4, U.6
1 2 3 4 5 6 7 8 9   006   04 03 02 01 00 99

McGRAW-HILL READING

McGraw-Hill School Division

New York   Farmington

Selected Quizzes Prepared by **Accelerated Reader**

McGraw-Hill Reading
Authors
Make the Difference...

Dr. James Flood

Ms. Angela Shelf Medearis

Dr. Jan E. Hasbrouck

Dr. Scott Paris

Dr. James V. Hoffman

Dr. Steven Stahl

Dr. Diane Lapp

Dr. Josefina Villamil Tinajero

Dr. Karen D. Wood

Contributing
Authors

Dr. Barbara Coulter

Ms. Frankie Dungan

Dr. Joseph B. Rubin

Dr. Carl B. Smith

Dr. Shirley Wright

iv

Part 1
START TOGETHER

Focus on Reading and Skills

All students start with the SAME:

- Read Aloud
- Pretaught Skills
  Phonics K–2
  Comprehension 3–6
- Build Background
- Selection Vocabulary

...Never hold a child back. Never leave a child behind.

Part 2
READ

Reading the Literature

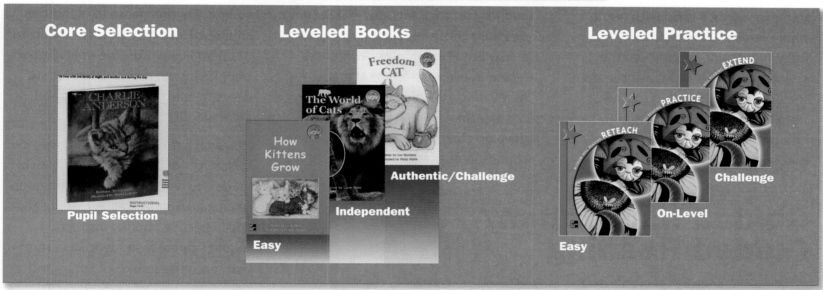

Core Selection

Pupil Selection

Leveled Books

How Kittens Grow

The World of Cats

Freedom CAT

Easy

Independent

Authentic/Challenge

Leveled Practice

RETEACH

PRACTICE

EXTEND

Easy

On-Level

Challenge

Examples Taken From Grade 2

Part 3
FINISH TOGETHER

Build Skills

All students finish with the SAME:

Phonics K–2
Comprehension
Vocabulary
Study Skills
Assessment

McGraw-Hill Reading Applying the Research

Phonological Awareness

Phonological awareness is the ability to hear the sounds in spoken language. It includes the ability to separate spoken words into discrete sounds as well as the ability to blend sounds together to make words. A child with good phonological awareness can identify rhyming words, hear the separate syllables in a word, separate the first sound in a word (onset) from the rest of the word (rime), and blend sounds together to make words.

Recent research findings have strongly concluded that children with good phonological awareness skills are more likely to learn to read well. These skills can be improved through systematic, explicit instruction involving auditory practice. McGraw-Hill Reading develops these key skills by providing an explicit Phonological Awareness lesson in every selection at grades K-2. Motivating activities such as blending, segmenting, and rhyming help to develop children's awareness of the sounds in our language.

Guided Instruction/ Guided Reading

Research on reading shows that guided instruction enables students to develop as independent, strategic readers. *The reciprocal-teaching model* of Anne-Marie Palincsar encourages teachers to model strategic-thinking, questioning, clarifying, and problem-solving strategies for students as students read together with the teacher. In McGraw-Hill Reading, guided instruction for all Pupil Edition selections incorporates the Palincsar model by providing interactive questioning prompts. *The guided-reading model* of Gay Su Pinnell is also incorporated into the McGraw-Hill Reading program. Through the guided-reading lessons provided for the leveled books offered with the program, teachers can work with small groups of students of different ability levels, closely observing them as they read and providing support specific to their needs.

By adapting instruction to include successful models of teaching and the appropriate materials to deliver instruction, McGraw-Hill Reading enables teachers to offer the appropriate type of instruction for all students in the classroom.

Phonics

Our language system uses an alphabetic code to communicate meaning from writing. Phonics involves learning the phonemes or sounds that letters make and the symbols or letters that represent those sounds. Children learn to blend the sounds of letters to decode unknown or unfamiliar words. The goal of good phonics instruction is to enable students to read words accurately and automatically.

Research has clearly identified the critical role of phonics in the ability of readers to read fluently and with good understanding, as well as to write and spell. Effective phonics instruction requires carefully sequenced lessons that teach the sounds of letters and how to use these sounds to read words. The McGraw-Hill program provides daily explicit and systematic phonics instruction to teach the letter sounds and blending. There are three explicit Phonics and Decoding lessons for every selection. Daily Phonics Routines are provided for quick reinforcement, in addition to activities in the Phonics Workbook and technology components. This combination of direct skills instruction and applied practice leads to reading success.

Curriculum Connections

As in the child's real-world environment, boundaries between disciplines must be dissolved. Recent research emphasizes the need to make connections between and across subject areas. McGraw-Hill Reading is committed to this approach. Each reading selection offers activities that tie in with social studies, language arts, geography, science, mathematics, art, music, health, and physical education. The program threads numerous research and inquiry activities that encourage the child to use the library and the Internet to seek out information. Reading and language skills are applied to a variety of genres, balancing fiction and nonfiction.

Integrated Language Arts

Success in developing communication skills is greatly enhanced by integrating the language arts in connected and purposeful ways. This allows students to understand the need for proper writing, grammar, and spelling. McGraw-Hill Reading sets the stage for meaningful learning. Each week a full writing-process lesson is provided. This lesson is supported by a 5-day spelling plan, emphasizing spelling patterns and spelling rules, and a 5-day grammar plan, focusing on proper grammar, mechanics, and usage.

Meeting Individual Needs

Every classroom is a microcosm of a world composed of diverse individuals with unique needs and abilities. Research points out that such needs must be addressed with frequent intensive opportunities to learn with engaging materials. McGraw-Hill Reading makes reading a successful experience for every child by providing a rich collection of leveled books for easy, independent, and challenging reading. Leveled practice is provided in Reteach, Practice, and Extend skills books. To address various learning styles and language needs, the program offers alternative teaching strategies, prevention/intervention techniques, language support activities, and ESL teaching suggestions.

Assessment

Frequent assessment in the classroom makes it easier for teachers to identify problems and to find remedies for them. McGraw-Hill Reading makes assessment an important component of instruction. Formal and informal opportunities are a part of each lesson. Minilessons, prevention/intervention strategies, and informal checklists, as well as student self-assessments, provide many informal assessment opportunities. Formal assessments, such as weekly selection tests and criterion-referenced unit tests, help to monitor students' knowledge of important skills and concepts. McGraw-Hill Reading also addresses how to adapt instruction based on student performance with resources such as the Alternate Teaching Strategies. Weekly lessons on test preparation, including test preparation practice books, help students to transfer skills to new contexts and to become better test takers.

McGraw-Hill School **TECHNOLOGY**

*inter***NET** **CONNECTION** For information on research that supports this program, visit ***www.mhschool.com/reading***

McGraw-Hill Reading

MULTI-AGE Classroom

Using the same global themes at each grade level facilitates the use of materials in multi-age classrooms.

GRADE LEVEL	Experience Experiences can tell us about ourselves and our world.	Connections Making connections develops new understandings.
Kindergarten	**My World** We learn a lot from all the things we see and do at home and in school.	**All Kinds of Friends** When we work and play together, we learn more about ourselves
Sub-theme 1	At Home	Working Together
Sub-theme 2	School Days	Playing Together
1	**Day by Day** Each day brings new experiences.	**Together Is Better** We like to share ideas and experiences with others.
2	**What's New?** With each day, we learn something new.	**Just Between Us** Family and friends help us see the world in new ways.
3	**Great Adventures** Life is made up of big and small experiences.	**Nature Links** Nature can give us new ideas.
4	**Reflections** Stories let us share the experiences of others.	**Something in Common** Sharing ideas can lead to meaningful cooperation.
5	**Time of My Life** We sometimes find memorable experiences in unexpected places.	**Building Bridges** Knowing what we have in common helps us appreciate our differences.
6	**Pathways** Reflecting on life's experiences can lead to new understandings.	**A Common Thread** A look beneath the surface may uncover hidden connections.

Themes: Kindergarten – Grade 6

Six Units IN EVERY GRADE

Expression	Inquiry	Problem-Solving	Making Decisions
There are many styles and forms for expressing ourselves.	By exploring and asking ques-tions, we make discoveries.	Analyzing information can help us solve problems.	Using what we know helps us evaluate situations.
Time to Shine We can use our ideas and our imagination to do many wonderful things.	**I Wonder** We can make discoveries about the wonders of nature in our own backyard.	**Let's Work It Out** Working as part of a team can help me find a way to solve problems.	**Choices** We can make many good choices and decisions every day
Great Ideas	In My Backyard	Try and Try Again	Good Choices
Let's Pretend	Wonders of Nature	Teamwork	Let's Decide
Stories to Tell Each one of us has a different story to tell.	**Let's Find Out!** Looking for answers is an adventure.	**Think About It!** It takes time to solve problems.	**Many Paths** Each decision opens the door to a new path.
Express Yourself We share our ideas in many ways.	**Look Around** There are surprises all around us.	**Figure It Out** We can solve problems by working together.	**Starting Now** Unexpected events can lead to new decisions.
Be Creative! We can all express ourselves in creative, wonderful ways.	**Tell Me More** Looking and listening closely will help us find out the facts.	**Think It Through** Solutions come in many shapes and sizes.	**Turning Points** We make new judgments based on our experiences.
Our Voices We can each use our talents to communicate ideas.	**Just Curious** We can find answers in surprising places.	**Make a Plan** Often we have to think carefully about a problem in order to solve it.	**Sorting It Out** We make decisions that can lead to new ideas and discoveries.
Imagine That The way we express our thoughts and feelings can take different forms.	**Investigate!** We never know where the search for answers might lead us.	**Bright Ideas** Some problems require unusual approaches.	**Crossroads** Decisions cause changes that can enrich our lives.
With Flying Colors Creative people help us see the world from different perspectives.	**Seek and Discover** To make new discoveries, we must observe and explore.	**Brainstorms** We can meet any challenge with determination and ingenuity.	**All Things Considered** Encountering new places and people can help us make decisions.

Sorting It Out

We make decisions that can lead to new ideas and discoveries.

written by **Peter Golenbock**
illustrated by **Paul Bacon**

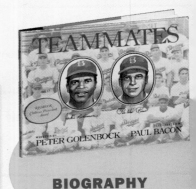

BIOGRAPHY

SKILLS			
Comprehension	**Vocabulary**	**Study Skill**	**Phonics**
• **Review** Cause and Effect	• **Review** Context Clues	• **Library/Media Center:** Use the Card Catalog: Subject Card	• **Review** Silent letters
• **Review** Make Judgments and Decisions			

written by **Alma Flor Ada**
illustrated by **Leonid Gore**

FAIRY TALE

SKILLS			
Comprehension	**Vocabulary**	**Study Skill**	**Phonics**
• **Review** Problem and Solution	• **Review** Antonyms and Synonyms	• **Library/Media Center:** Use the Card Catalog: Author and Title Cards	• **Review** /s/ and /f/
• **Review** Cause and Effect			

SKILLS			
Comprehension	**Vocabulary**	**Study Skill**	**Phonics**
• **Review** Make Judgments and Decisions	• **Review** Antonyms and Synonyms	• **Library/Media Center:** Conduct an Interview	• **Review** Silent Letters
• **Review** Problem and Solution			

PLAY

SKILLS			
Comprehension	**Vocabulary**	**Study Skill**	**Phonics**
• **Review** Compare and Contrast	• **Review** Context Clues	• **Library/Media Center:** Use an Encyclopedia Index	• **Review** Silent Letters
• **Review** Make Judgments and Decisions			

SCIENCE NONFICTION

SKILLS			
Comprehension	**Vocabulary**	**Study Skill**	**Phonics**
• **Review** Cause and Effect	• **Review** Context Clues	• **Library/Media Center:** Use the Internet	• **Review** Silent Letters /s/ and /f/
• **Review** Compare and Contrast	• **Review** Antonyms and Synonyms		

SCIENCE ARTICLE

Unit Planner

	WEEK 1 Teammates	**WEEK 2** The Malachite Palace
Leveled Books	**Easy:** *Doubles* **Independent:** *Me and Maya the Super Brain* **Challenge:** *Two Women Defying the Odds*	**Easy:** *King For A Day* **Independent:** *The Crown Jewels* **Challenge:** *A Most Exceptional Guest*
✓ **Tested Skills**	☑ **Comprehension** Cause and Effect, 616A–616B, 631E–631F Judgments and Decisions, 631G–631H ☑ **Vocabulary** Context Clues, 631I–631J ☑ **Study Skills** Library/Media Center, 630	☑ **Comprehension** Problem and Solution, 634A–634B, 663E–663F Cause and Effect, 663G–663H ☑ **Vocabulary** Antonyms and Synonyms, 663I–663J ☑ **Study Skills** Library/Media Center, 662
Minilessons	**Phonics and Decoding:** Silent Letters, 625 **Make Inferences,** 619 **Prefixes,** 621 **Main Idea,** 623	**Phonics and Decoding:** Words with /s/, 645 **Context Clues,** 643 **Draw Conclusions,** 651 **Summarize,** 657
Language Arts	**Writing:** Writing That Compares, 631K **Grammar:** Adverbs, 631M–631N **Spelling:** Words with Silent Letters, 631O–631P	**Writing:** Writing That Compares, 663K **Grammar:** Adverbs That Compare, 663M–663N **Spelling:** Homophones and Homographs, 663O–663P

Activities

Social Studies	Read Aloud: "Jackie Robinson," 614E	Read Aloud: "Windows of Gold," 632E
Mathematics	Stories in Art: *Daughters of the South,* 614/615	Stories in Art: *Lady Feeding a Bird,* 632/633
Science	Social Studies: Segregation and Integration, 618	Science: Malachite, 636
Curriculum Connections — **Music**	Social Studies: Life in the 1940s, 620	Social Studies: Medieval Palaces, 638
Art	Mathematics: Batting Averages, 624	Science: Deciduous and Evergreen Plants, 650
Drama		Mathematics: Bird Tally, 654
Language Arts		
🖐 **CULTURAL PERSPECTIVES**	An International Pastime, 622	Lullabies, 648

Easy: *Wolverine and White Elephant* **Independent:** *The Morningstar Sun* **Challenge:** *Super-Dupers*	**Easy:** *Saving the Black Rhino* **Independent:** *The Jaguar* **Challenge:** *Spring Break and Peaches*	**Self-Selected Reading of Leveled Books**	**Self-Selected Reading**

☑ **Comprehension** Judgments and Decisions, 666A–666B, 691E–691F Problem and Solution, 691G–691H ☑ **Vocabulary** Antonyms and Synonyms, 691I–691J ☑ **Study Skills** Library/Media Center, 690	☑ **Comprehension** Compare and Contrast, 694A–694B, 713E–713F Judgments and Decisions, 713G–713H ☑ **Vocabulary** Context Clues, 713I–713J ☑ **Study Skills** Library/Media Center, 712	☑ **Comprehension** Cause and Effect, 716A–716B Compare and Contrast, 723E–723F ☑ **Vocabulary** Context Clues, 723G–723H Antonyms and Synonyms, 723I–723J ☑ **Study Skills** Library/Media Center, 722	☑ **Assess Skills** Cause and Effect Judgments and Decisions Problem and Solution Compare and Contrast Context Clues Antonyms and Synonyms Library/Media Center ☑ **Assess Grammar and Spelling** Review Adverbs and Prepositions, 725G Review Spelling Patterns, 725H ☑ **Unit Progress Assessment** ☑ **Standardized Test Preparation**
Phonics and Decoding: Silent Letters, 677 **Character,** 673 **Suffixes,** 681 **Summarize,** 683	**Phonics and Decoding:** Silent Letters, 705 **Make Generalizations,** 699 **Context Clues,** 703 **Summarize,** 707		

Writing: Writing That Compares, 691K **Grammar:** Negatives, 691M–691N **Spelling:** Words with Suffixes, 691O–691P	**Writing:** Writing That Compares, 713K **Grammar:** Prepositions, 713M–713N **Spelling:** Words with Prefixes, 713O–713P	**Writing:** Writing That Compares, 723K **Grammar:** Sentence Combining, 723M–723N **Spelling:** Words from Math, 723O–723P	**Unit Writing Process:** Writing That Compares, 725A–725F

Read Aloud: "Super-Goopy Glue," 664E **Stories in Art:** *Scene from Modern Times, 1936,* 664/665 **Mathematics:** Millions and Millions, 670 **Science:** Baking Soda, 672 **Social Studies:** Population, 674 **Mathematics:** Gross, 678 **Social Studies:** Industry, 680 Views about Wealth, 668	**Read Aloud:** "When Whales Exhale," 692E **Stories in Art:** *Fighting Cows,* 692/693 **Mathematics:** Length and Weight, 696 **Science:** What Whales Eat, 700 **Social Studies:** Whale Migration, 702 Whales, 698	**Read Aloud:** "Birdfoot's Grampa," 714E **Stories in Art:** *Caribbean Jungle,* 714/715	 **Cooperative Theme Project** **Research and Inquiry:** Helping Hands, 725

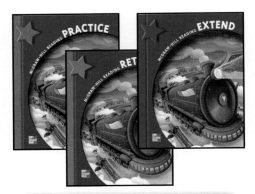

LITERATURE

LEVELED BOOKS

Easy:
- *Doubles*
- *King for a Day*
- *Wolverine and White Elephants*
- *Saving the Black Rhino*

Independent:
- *Me and Maya the Super Brain*
- *The Crown Jewels*
- *The Morning Star Sun*
- *The Jaguar*

Challenge:
- *Two Women Defying the Odds*
- *A Most Exceptional Guest*
- *Super-Dupers*
- *Spring Break and Peaches*

STUDENT LISTENING LIBRARY AUDIOCASSETTES
Recordings of the student book selections and poetry.

SKILLS

LEVELED PRACTICE

Practice Book: Student practice for phonics, comprehension, vocabulary, and study skills; plus practice for instructional vocabulary and story comprehension. Take-Home Story included for each lesson.

Reteach: Reteaching opportunities for students who need more help with assessed skills.

Extend: Extension activities for vocabulary, comprehension, story and study skills.

TEACHING CHARTS
Instructional charts for modeling vocabulary and tested skills. Also available as transparencies.

WORD BUILDING MANIPULATIVE CARDS
Cards with words and structural elements for word building and practicing vocabulary.

LANGUAGE SUPPORT BOOK
ESL Parallel teaching lessons and appropriate practice activities for students needing language support.

PHONICS AND PHONEMIC AWARENESS PRACTICE BOOK
Additional practice focusing on vowel sounds, phonograms, blends, digraphs, and key phonetic elements.

LANGUAGE ARTS

GRAMMAR PRACTICE BOOK
Provides practice for grammar and mechanics lessons.

SPELLING PRACTICE BOOK
Provides practice with the word list and spelling patterns. Includes home involvement activities.

DAILY LANGUAGE ACTIVITIES
Sentence activities that provide brief, regular practice and reinforcement of grammar, mechanics, and usage skills. Available as blackline masters and transparencies.

McGraw-Hill School
TECHNOLOGY

 **inter**NET **CONNECTION** extends lesson activities through Research and Inquiry Ideas.

Visit **www.mhschool.com/reading**

Resources for Meeting Individual Needs

	EASY	**ON-LEVEL**	**CHALLENGE**	**LANGUAGE SUPPORT**

UNIT 6

Teammates

Leveled Book: *Doubles*
Reteach, 186–192
Alternate Teaching Strategies, T60–T66
Writing: Sports Card, 631L

Leveled Book: *Me and Maya the Super Brain*
Practice, 186–192
Alternate Teaching Strategies, T60–T66
Writing: Dream Team, 631L

Leveled Book: *Two Women Defying the Odds*
Extend, 186–192
Writing: Dialogue, 631L

Teaching Strategies, 616C, 617, 621, 623, 625, 631A, 631B, 631C, 631L
Language Support, 201–208
Alternate Teaching Strategies, T60–T66
Writing: Compare Sports Heroes, 631K–631L

The Malachite Palace

Leveled Book: *King for a Day*
Reteach, 193–199
Alternate Teaching Strategies, T60–T66
Writing: Cartoon, 663L

Leveled Book: *The Crown Jewels*
Practice, 193–199
Alternate Teaching Strategies, T60–T66
Writing: Conversation, 663L

Leveled Book: *A Most Exceptional Guest*
Extend, 193–199
Writing: Design a Stage Set, 663L

Teaching Strategies, 634C, 635, 641, 652, 655, 663A, 663B, 663C, 663L
Language Support, 209–216
Alternate Teaching Strategies, T60–T66
Writing: Compare Characters, 663K–663L

The Toothpaste Millionaire

Leveled Book: *Wolverine and White Elephants*
Reteach, 200–206
Alternate Teaching Strategies, T60–T66
Writing: Comic Strip, 691L

Leveled Book: *The Morning Star Sun*
Practice, 200–206
Alternate Teaching Strategies, T60–T66
Writing: Interview, 691L

Leveled Book: *Super-Dupers*
Extend, 200–206
Writing: Sequel, 691L

Teaching Strategies, 666C, 667, 669, 675, 677, 682, 691A, 691B, 691C, 691L
Language Support, 217–224
Alternate Teaching Strategies, T60–T66
Writing: Write a Commercial, 691K–691L

Whales

Leveled Book: *Saving the Black Rhino*
Reteach, 207–213
Alternate Teaching Strategies, T60–T66
Writing: Compare and Contrast Pets, 713L

Leveled Book: *The Jaguar*
Practice, 207–213
Alternate Teaching Strategies, T60–T66
Writing: Classroom Mural, 713L

Leveled Book: *Spring Break and Peaches*
Extend, 207–213
Writing: Research Report, 713L

Teaching Strategies, 694C, 695, 697, 704, 707, 713A, 713B, 713C, 713L
Language Support, 225–232
Alternate Teaching Strategies, T60–T66
Writing: Write an Essay, 713K–713L

Saving the Everglades

Review:
Reteach, 214–220
Alternate Teaching Strategies, T60–T66
Writing: Picture of the Everglades, 723L

Review:
Practice, 214–220
Alternate Teaching Strategies, T60–T66
Writing: Comparisons, 723L

Review:
Extend, 214–220
Writing: Persuasive Speech, 723L

Teaching Strategies, 716C, 717, 723A, 723B, 723C, 723L
Language Support, 233–240
Alternate Teaching Strategies, T60–T66
Writing: Write an Encyclopedia Article, 723K–723L

INFORMAL

Informal Assessment

- Comprehension, 616B, 626, 627, 631F, 631H; 634B, 658, 659, 663F, 663H; 666B, 686, 687, 691F, 691H; 694B, 708, 709, 713F, 713H; 716B, 718, 719, 723F
    - Vocabulary, 631J, 663J, 691J, 713J, 723H, 723J

Performance Assessment

- Scoring Rubrics, 631L, 663L, 691L, 713L, 723L, 725F
- Research and Inquiry, 613, 725
- Writing Process, 631K, 663K, 691K–691L, 713K, 723K
- Listening, Speaking, Viewing Activities, 614E, 614/615, 616C, 616–629, 631D, 631L; 632E, 632/633, 634C, 634–661, 663D, 663L; 664E, 664/665, 666C, 666–689, 691D, 691L; 692E, 692/693, 694C, 694–711, 713D, 713L; 714E, 714/715, 716C, 716–721, 723D, 723L
- Portfolio
  Writing, 631K–631L, 663K–663L, 691K–691L, 713K–713L, 723K–723L, 725A–725F
- Cross Cumulative Activities, 618, 620, 622, 624, 636, 638, 648, 650, 654, 668, 670, 672, 674, 678, 680, 696, 698, 700, 702

Leveled Practice
Practice, Reteach, Extend

- **Comprehension**
  Cause and Effect, 186, 190, 198, 214
  Judgments and Decisions, 191, 200, 204, 212
  Problem and Solution, 193, 197, 205
  Compare and Contrast, 207, 211, 218
- **Vocabulary Strategies**
  Context Clues, 192, 213, 219
  Antonyms and Synonyms, 199, 206, 220
- **Study Skills**
  Library/Media Center, 189, 196, 203, 210, 217

FORMAL

Selection Tests

- **Skills and Vocabulary Words**
  Teammates, 51–52
  The Malachite Palace, 53–54
  The Toothpaste Millionaire, 55–56
  Whales, 57–58
  Saving the Everglades, 59–60

Unit 6 Assessment

- **Comprehension**
  Cause and Effect
  Judgments and Decisions
  Problem and Solution
  Compare and Contrast
- **Vocabulary Strategies**
  Context Clues
  Antonyms and Synonyms
- **Study Skills**
  Library/Media Center

Grammar and Spelling Assessment

- **Grammar**
  Adverbs and Prepositions, 165, 171, 177, 183, 189, 191, 192
- **Spelling**
  Words with Silent Letters, 166
  Homophones and Homographs, 172
  Words with Suffixes, 178
  Words with Prefixes, 184
  Math Words, 190
  Unit Review, 191–192

Diagnostic/Placement Evaluations

- Individual Reading Inventory, 5–6
- Running Record, 7–8
- Grade 4 Diagnostic/Placement
- Grade 5 Diagnostic/Placement
- Grade 6 Diagnostic/Placement

Test Preparation

- Test Power in Teacher's Edition, 631, 663, 691, 713, 723

Assessment Checklist

Student .... Grade ....

Teacher ....

	Teammates	The Malachite Palace	The Toothpaste Millionaire	Whales	Saving the Everglades	Assessment Summary
LISTENING/SPEAKING						
Participates in oral language experiences						
Listens and speaks to gain knowledge of culture						
Speaks appropriately to audiences for different purposes						
Communicates clearly						
READING						
Uses a variety of word identification strategies, including						
• Silent Letters						
• /s/ and /f/						
• Context Clues						
• Antonyms and Synonyms						
Reads with fluency and understanding						
Reads widely for different purposes in varied sources						
Develops an extensive vocabulary						
Uses a variety of strategies to comprehend selections						
• Cause and Effect						
• Judgements and Decisions						
• Problem and Solution						
• Compare and Contrast						
Responds to various texts						
Analyzes the characteristics of various types of texts						
Conducts research using various sources, including						
• Library/Media Center						
Reads to increase knowledge						
WRITING						
Writes for a variety of audiences and purposes						
Composes original texts using the conventions of written language such as capitalization and penmanship						
Spells proficiently						
Composes texts applying knowledge of grammar and usage						
Uses writing processes						
Evaluates own writing and writing of others						

+ Observed   − Not Observed

612H

Introducing the Theme

Sorting It Out

We make decisions that can lead to new ideas and discoveries.

PRESENT THE THEME Read the theme statement. Invite students to describe decisions people make that can change their lives and lead to new discoveries. They might mention decisions such as getting an after-school job, participating in an extracurricular activity, moving to a new community, or going to college.

READ THE POEM Read aloud the poem "Your World" by Georgia Douglas Johnson. Help students compare the eagle's metamorphosis with a person's decision to make a change in his or her life.

 Student Listening Library Audiocassettes

MAKE CONNECTIONS Have students preview the unit by reading the selection titles and looking at the illustrations. Then have them work in small groups to brainstorm a list of ways that the stories, poems, and the *Time for Kids* magazine article relate to the theme Sorting It Out.

Groups can then compare their lists as they share them with the class.

THEME SUMMARY

Each selection relates to the unit theme Sorting It Out as well as to the global theme Making Decisions. These thematic links will help students make connections across texts.

Teammates Three men change the face of baseball and our country.

The Malachite Palace A princess learns to embrace life.

The Toothpaste Millionaire A young entrepreneur meets challenges on the way to fame and fortune.

Whales The decisions we make affect our world and the creatures who share it with us.

Saving the Everglades Balancing the needs of humans and the environment can help save a natural wonder.

Sorting It Out

Your World

Your world is as big as you make it.
I know, for I used to abide
In the narrowest nest in a corner,
My wings pressing close to my side.

But I sighted the distant horizon
Where the sky line encircled the sea
And I throbbed with a burning desire
To travel this immensity.

I battered the cordons around me
And cradled my wings on the breeze
Then soared to the uttermost reaches
With rapture, with power, with ease!

by Georgia Douglas Johnson

613

LEARNING ABOUT POETRY

Literary Devices: Personification
Tell students that personification is giving human qualities to animals or objects. As you reread the poem aloud, have students listen for ideas that a person might have, but that an eagle could not, such as making a decision to leave the nest and fly around.

 Poetry Activity Ask students to imagine that they are an animal or object and to write a poem from the point of view of the object. Tell them to personify the object, and have them describe a decision the animal or object makes that leads to a new discovery.

 **Activity**

Research and *Inquiry*

 Theme Project: Helping Hands Let teams of students discuss decisions and changes that would improve your community. Students will plan a project to bring about a change.

List Action Groups Ask students to make a list of existing community groups or improvement projects.

Ask Questions and Identify Resources Have students list questions to help them choose a project, along with sources for finding the answers.

QUESTIONS	POSSIBLE RESOURCES
• What groups in our community need help? • Are there any existing projects we could help with? • What decisions made by local government affect us the most?	• Local newspapers • City Hall • Talk with a member of City Council or the Mayor • Internet

interNET CONNECTION For more information, students can also visit
www.mhschool.com/reading

Remind students to take notes about any important details.

Create a Presentation When their research is complete, have students present their proposals to the class. Students may wish to explore ways to make their project a reality. Encourage students to be creative. Encourage students to use visuals in their presentations. See Wrap Up the Theme, page 725.

613

Teammates

Selection Summary This selection gives students the information they need to sort out the facts about segregation. They will learn how the actions of just a few heroic men changed the face of Major League baseball forever.

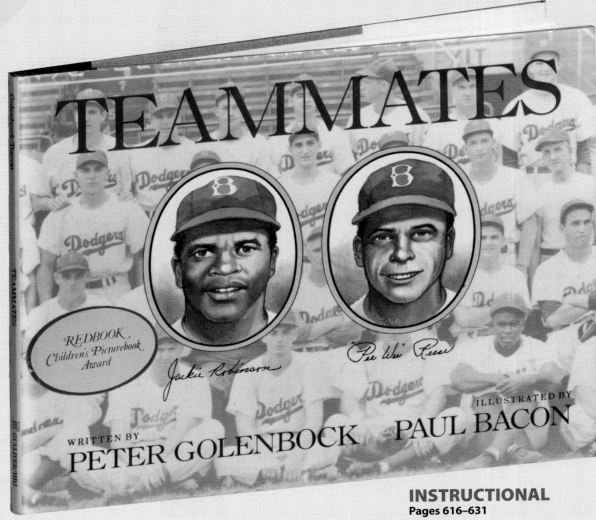

Student Listening Library Audiocassette

INSTRUCTIONAL
Pages 616–631

About the Author One of Peter Golenbock's most vivid childhood memories is of meeting the great Jackie Robinson. His early love of sports blossomed into a career as a sportswriter, and when he was asked to write a children's baseball book, he knew just who he wanted to write about.

About the Illustrator To illustrate *Teammates*, Paul Bacon chose to combine paintings with photographs. The combination allowed him to use his creativity to set the mood of the era, but the photographs still make the point that the story is a true one about real people who made real choices.

Resources for
Meeting Individual Needs

EASY
Pages 631A, 631D

INDEPENDENT
Pages 631B, 631D

CHALLENGE
Pages 631C, 631D

LEVELED PRACTICE

Reteach, 186–192

blackline masters with reteaching opportunities for each assessed skill

Practice, 186–192

workbook with Take-Home stories and practice opportunities for each assessed skill and story comprehension

Extend, 186–192

blackline masters that offer challenge activities for each assessed skill

ADDITIONAL RESOURCES

- **Language Support Book,** 201–208
- **Take-Home Story, Practice,** p. 187a
- **Alternative Teaching Strategies,** T60–T66

McGraw-Hill School
TECHNOLOGY

interNET CONNECTION Research and Inquiry Ideas. Visit **www.mhschool.com/reading**

Suggested Lesson Planner

 Available on CD-ROM

READING AND LANGUAGE ARTS	**DAY 1** *Focus on Reading and Skills*	**DAY 2** *Read the Literature*
○ **Comprehension** ○ **Vocabulary** ○ **Phonics/Decoding** ○ **Study Skills** ○ **Listening, Speaking, Viewing, Representing**	**Read Aloud and Motivate,** 614E *Jackie Robinson* **Develop Visual Literacy,** 614/615 ☑ **Review Cause and Effect,** 616A–616B **Teaching Chart 151** **Reteach, Practice, Extend,** 186	**Build Background,** 616C Develop Oral Language **Vocabulary,** 616D *circulated launched* *extraordinary opponents* *organizations teammate* **Teaching Chart 152** Vocabulary Cards **Reteach, Practice, Extend,** 187 **Read the Selection,** 616–627 ☑ Cause and Effect **Minilessons,** 619, 621, 623, 625 **Cultural Perspectives,** 622
○ **Curriculum Connections**	 Works of Art, 614/615	
○ **Writing**	**Writing Prompt:** Write about your favorite sports star in action. Describe what he or she does that makes the athlete a standout.	**Writing Prompt:** Write about an exciting sports event you watched or participated in. Tell when and where the event was held. **Journal Writing,** 627 Quick-Write

○ **Grammar**	**Introduce the Concept: Adverbs,** 631M
	Daily Language Activity
	1. The two friends talked _____.
	   (how?) quietly
	2. The runner moved _____. (how?)
	   quickly
	3. The crowd shouted _____.
	   (how?) loudly
	
	Grammar Practice Book, 161
		Teach the Concept: Adverbs, 631M
		Daily Language Activity
		1. We're going to a game _____.
		   (when?) now
		2. The batter swung _____. (how?)
		   slowly
		3. The catcher looked _____.
		   (where?) ahead
		
		Grammar Practice Book, 162

○ **Spelling**	**Pretest: Words with Silent Letters,** 631O **Spelling Practice Book,** 161,162	**Explore the Pattern: Words with Silent Letters,** 631O **Spelling Practice Book,** 163

DAY 3 — Read the Literature

Rereading for Fluency, 626

Story Questions, 628
  Reteach, Practice, Extend, 188

Story Activities, 629

Study Skill, 630
  ☑ Library/Media Center
  Teaching Chart 153
  Reteach, Practice, Extend, 189

Test Power, 631

 Read the Leveled Books, 631A–631D
  Guided Reading
  Silent Letters
  ☑ Cause and Effect
  ☑ Instructional Vocabulary

 Social Studies, 618

Writing Prompt: In one paragraph, explain who Jackie Robinson was to a person who never heard of him.

Writing Process: Write a Comparison, 631K
  Prewrite, Draft

Review and Practice: Adverbs, 631N
  Daily Language Activity
  1. Players arrived _____. (when?) yesterday
  2. A hotdog stand is _____. (where?) nearby
  3. Robinson batted _____. (how?) cautiously

Grammar Practice Book, 163

Practice and Extend: Words with Silent Letters 631P
Spelling Practice Book, 164

DAY 4 — Build Skills

 Read the Leveled Books and Self-Selected Books

☑ **Review Cause and Effect,** 631E–631F
  Teaching Chart 154
  Reteach, Practice, Extend, 190
  Language Support, 206

☑ **Review Make Judgments and Decisions,** 631G–631H
  Teaching Chart 155
  Reteach, Practice, Extend, 191
  Language Support, 207

 Social Studies, 620

Writing Prompt: Write a dialogue between Jackie Robinson and Pee Wee Reese telling about their friendship.

Writing Process: Write a Comparison, 631K
  Revise

Meeting Individual Needs for Writing, 631L

Review and Practice: Adverbs, 631N
  Daily Language Activity
  1. The pitcher threw the ball _____. (how?) easily
  2. Teams travel _____. (where?) everywhere
  3. Pee Wee fielded _____. (how?) expertly

Grammar Practice Book, 164

Proofread and Write: Words with Silent Letters 631P
Spelling Practice Book, 165

DAY 5 — Build Skills

 Read Self-Selected Books

☑ **Review Context Clues,** 631I–631J
  Teaching Chart 156
  Reteach, Practice, Extend, 192
  Language Support, 208

Listening, Speaking, Viewing, Representing, 631L
  Make a Sports Poster
  Give a Nominating Speech

Minilessons, 619, 621, 623

Phonics Review
  Silent Letters, 625

Phonics Workbook

 Math, 624

Writing Prompt: Imagine that your goal is to be an athlete who is also a role model for a younger brother, sister, or friend. Tell what you would do and how you would act.

Writing Process: Write a Comparison, 631K
  Edit/Proofread, Publish

Assess and Reteach: Adverbs, 631N
  Daily Language Activity
  1. My team bats _____. (when?) first
  2. We hope to play _____. (where?) there
  3. Our team wears our uniforms _____. (how?) neatly

Grammar Practice Book, 165, 166

Assess and Reteach: Words with Silent Letters 631P
Spelling Practice Book, 166

Read Aloud and Motivate

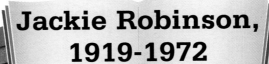

Jackie Robinson, 1919-1972

a poem by Susan Altman
and Susan Lechner

For many years,
Across the nation,
Baseball upheld
Segregation.

Black men couldn't
Make their mark
At Wrigley Field
Or Fenway Park.

The Brooklyn Dodgers
Changed all that
When they signed Robinson
To bat.

He hit 'em low.
He hit 'em high.

He made that baseball
Really fly!

With Robinson
On second base,
The Dodgers moved
Up to first place.

He scored the runs,
Was MVP,
And led the team
To victory.

With Brooklyn's Dodgers
(Now L.A.)
He paved the way
For blacks to play.

Continued on pages T2–T5

Oral Comprehension

LISTENING AND SPEAKING Use the poem to motivate students to find causes and effects. Read aloud the narrative poem that tells the story of Jackie Robinson and the integration of Major League baseball. When you have finished reading the poem, ask: "What caused African American players to be kept out of baseball stadiums such as Wrigley Field and Fenway Park? What effect did Jackie Robinson and his team, the Brooklyn Dodgers, have on the Major Leagues and on the game of baseball?"

Activity Organize the class into small groups, and have groups pantomime the poem as one group member reads it aloud. Suggest that besides choosing a narrator or narrators, other players and fans, each group should choose a student to play Jackie Robinson. Allow time for each group to rehearse its pantomime before presenting it. If possible, let groups present their work for another class. ▶ **Oral/Kinesthetic**

Develop Visual Literacy

Anthology pages 614–615

Stories in Art

Artists communicate through their art. Their paintings may express their feelings about people and places, family and friendship.

Look at this painting. What do you see? What can you tell about the two young women? How do you know they are friends? How does the artist show you they are "in step" with each other?

Close your eyes. What do you think has caused the women to take a walk by the water? What effect does the day have on them? What effect does the painting have on you? Explain.

Daughters of the South, by Jonathan Green, 1993

614

615

Objective: Identify Cause and Effect

VIEWING The artist who painted "Daughters of the South" used space and sensory details to show the closeness that the two friends enjoy. Ask students to imagine that they are in the painting with their best friend. Have them use sensory images to describe details that contribute to a feeling of togetherness.

Read the page with students, encouraging individual interpretations of the painting. Ask students to use details from the picture to explain what caused them to interpret the painting in a certain way. For example:

- The women look as if they are friends because they are close together, are dressed similarly, and are even walking "in step."

- Because they have chosen to take a walk by themselves, the young women might be telling secrets or just sharing the day without interference from others.

REPRESENTING Have partners role-play the scene between the two friends. Encourage them to think about cause and effect by mentioning why they are friends and how their friendship makes them feel.

614/615

OBJECTIVES

Students will identify cause-and-effect relationships.

TEACHING TIP

INSTRUCTIONAL Point out that stories don't always have cause-effect clue words such as *because, since,* and *in order to.* Suggest that students look for effects by asking themselves, "What happened?" Then they can find out cause by asking, "Why did it happen?"

Review Cause and Effect

PREPARE

Act Out Cause and Effect

Act out this scene: Leave a pile of books in a conspicuous, inconvenient place near your desk. Walk by and pretend to trip dramatically. Ask witnesses to tell what happened and why it happened.

TEACH

Define Cause and Effect

Explain that the tripping was *caused* by carelessness with books. Often, an event has a *cause.* Then the event is called an *effect.* Connecting causes and effects can help you understand the actions of characters and why the plot turns out the way it does.

A Real Friend

The score was tied in the bottom of the ninth, but the other team's best batter was at the plate. Just thinking about it made Marcie nervous.

Crack! The ball flew high into the air and headed for Marcie in right field. Marcie looked up, but the sun blinded her. She dropped the ball.

"Way to go, Marcie," her teammates jeered.

Keesha spoke up. "You know the sun made it impossible to see that ball. If we all play better, we'll win next time." Marcie smiled at Keesha. She knew a real friend when she saw one.

Teaching Chart 151

Read the Story and Model the Skill

Display **Teaching Chart 151.** Read the story and have students think about the major events and their causes.

MODEL Marcie was nervous. I wonder why. The score was tied. If anything went wrong, Marcie's team would lose. The effect on Marcie was nervousness. The cause was her fear of losing the game.

Find Cause and Effect

Have students circle each effect and underline each cause.

Create a Cause and Effect Chart

GROUP

Begin a Cause and Effect chart to help students make connections between story events and their causes. Then have small groups complete the chart. Have groups compare their finished charts and discuss any differences. ▶ **Logical/Visual**

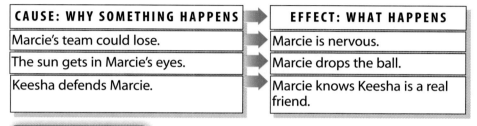

CAUSE: WHY SOMETHING HAPPENS	EFFECT: WHAT HAPPENS
Marcie's team could lose.	Marcie is nervous.
The sun gets in Marcie's eyes.	Marcie drops the ball.
Keesha defends Marcie.	Marcie knows Keesha is a real friend.

Identify Cause and Effect

Ask students to tell about something that happened to them and a friend. Afterwards, ask, "What happened?" to help students identify the effect, and "Why did it happen?" to help them identify the cause.

Students will apply cause and effect when they read *Teammates* and the Leveled Books.

ALTERNATE TEACHING
STRATEGY

CAUSE AND EFFECT

For a different approach to teaching this skill, see page T60.

Meeting Individual Needs for Comprehension

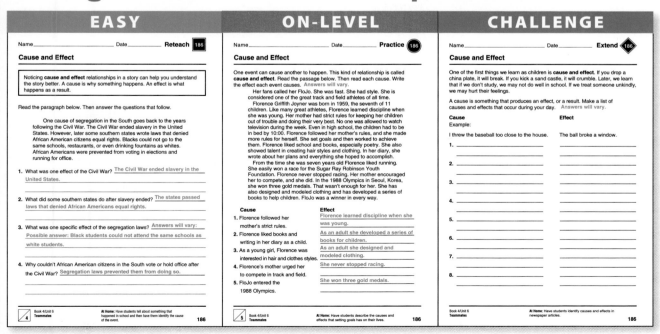

EASY	ON-LEVEL	CHALLENGE
Reteach, 186	Practice, 186	Extend, 186

Build Background

Anthology and Leveled Books

Evaluate Prior Knowledge

CONCEPT: FRIENDS TO THE END
These stories feature friends who stick together in tough times. Ask students to tell about characters from fiction or nonfiction books who were good friends.

TRUE FRIENDS Invite students to discuss ways they can tell when someone is a true friend. Then distribute copies of the word web. Have students write *A Real Friend* in the center circle and list characteristics of real friends around the outer edges.

▶ **Visual/Linguistic**

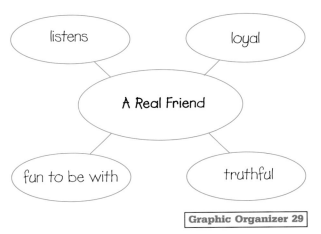

Graphic Organizer 29

PLAN A DAY Invite students to imagine that they can spend a day doing anything they choose with any friend they want. Have them write a journal entry about a perfect day with their friend.

 WRITING ONE

Develop Oral Language

ESL **TALK ABOUT TEAMWORK** Bring in and display pictures of different teams, from swimming to baseball. If possible, show other regalia, such as balls and jerseys. Invite students to tell about their experiences on teams.

Elicit vocabulary such as:
- teamwork
- losing
- teammate
- winning
- competition
- uniform

Students can work as a team to role-play a team event such as a touchdown or home run.

TEACHING TIP

MANAGEMENT Introduce the word web and the Plan a Day activity. As the class completes those activities, pull out a group to work on the Develop Oral Language activity.

If some students are unfamiliar with baseball, you may wish to incorporate a brief overview of the game in the teamwork discussion and to preview baseball-related terms, such as *shortstop* and *dugout*.

LANGUAGE SUPPORT

See **Language Support Book**, pages 201–204, for teaching suggestions for Build Background and Vocabulary.

Vocabulary

Key Words

1. All the (organizations) in town, from the Chamber of Commerce to the Crazy Quilt Club, backed baseball teams for county fair games. 2. Tran was a team captain, and he quickly chose Tim as his (teammate). 3. It would have been hard for the two best friends to play against each other as (opponents). 4. Mayor Downs (launched) the games by tossing out the first pitch. 5. The crowd was amazed when the two friends ended their game with an (extraordinary) double play. 6. The players (circulated) a petition through the crowd asking the umpires to name both boys Most Valuable Player.

Teaching Chart 152

Vocabulary in Context

IDENTIFY VOCABULARY WORDS
Display **Teaching Chart 152** and read the passage with students. Have volunteers circle each vocabulary word and underline other words that are clues to its meaning.

DISCUSS MEANINGS Ask questions like these to help clarify word meanings.

- Do you belong to any organizations?
- Who would you choose as a teammate?
- Are opponents always against each other?
- If you launched a rocket, would it be taking off or landing?
- Is it extraordinary for one person to hit four home runs in one game?
- How would you act if you circulated at a party?

Practice

DEMONSTRATE WORD MEANING Have students play "Password." One partner draws a vocabulary card and says clues. The other partner must say the word. The clues may be synonyms or examples, but not any form of the word. ▶ **Auditory/Linguistic**

Vocabulary Cards

WRITE A HEADLINE Ask students to choose three vocabulary words and use each one in a newspaper headline about a sports event.

WRITING

▶ **Linguistic/Intrapersonal**

Definitions

organizations (p. 623) groups of people with special aims

teammate (p. 618) a member of the same team

opponents (p. 620) persons who are against each other

launched (p. 620) started something

extraordinary (p. 619) very unusual; remarkable

circulated (p. 624) passed around

SPELLING/VOCABULARY CONNECTIONS

See Spelling Challenge Words, pages 6310–631P.

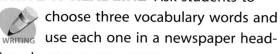
Take-Home Story 187a
Reteach 187
Practice 187 • Extend 187

Guided Instruction

Preview and Predict

Have a volunteer read the selection title aloud. Then have students look at the pictures to preview the selection and help them predict what the story is about.

- Do you think the story events happened recently or a long time ago?
- What will the story most likely be about?
- This selection tells about two real-life baseball players. What clues that this is nonfiction do you see? (There are photos, and the people and places seem real.) *Genre*

Have students record their predictions.

Set Purposes

Ask students to tell what they think they will learn from the selection. For example:

- Who are the two players?
  When did they play?

PREDICTIONS	WHAT HAPPENED
This story is about a baseball player.	
The two men on the cover become friends.	

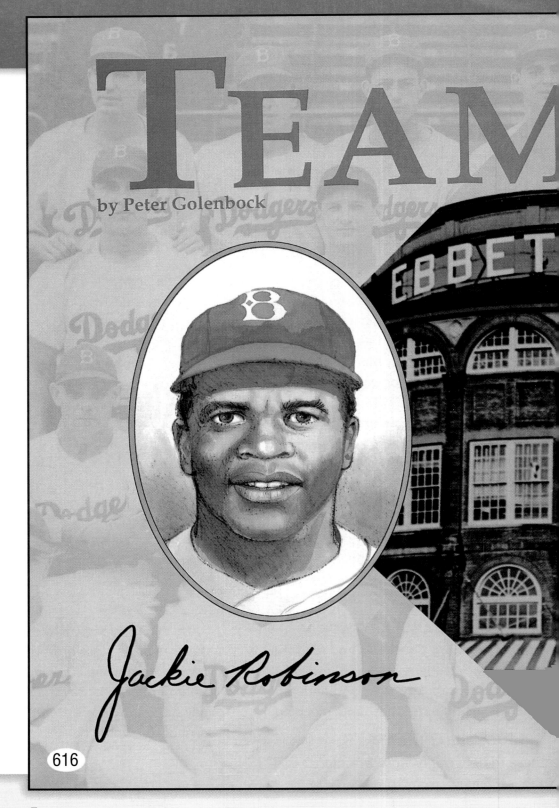

TEAM

by Peter Golenbock

Jackie Robinson

616

Meeting Individual Needs · Grouping Suggestions for Strategic Reading

EASY	ON-LEVEL	CHALLENGE
Read Together Let students follow along with the **Listening Library Audiocassette** or read the story aloud in a group. Use Guided Instruction and Intervention prompts as tools to help students decode unfamiliar words, review vocabulary, and increase comprehension. Stop after major story events to discuss cause and effect.	**Guided Reading** Introduce the story words on page 617. Then read the story with students or let them follow along with the **Listening Library Audiocassette.** Choose among the Guided Instruction questions. Have students make a Cause and Effect chart to help them understand how the story events changed baseball history.	**Read Independently** Make sure students understand the concepts of segregation and integration. Then let them read the selection on their own. Suggest that they make a Cause and Effect chart to help them analyze and remember information from the story. They can refer to the notes on their charts as they summarize the selection.

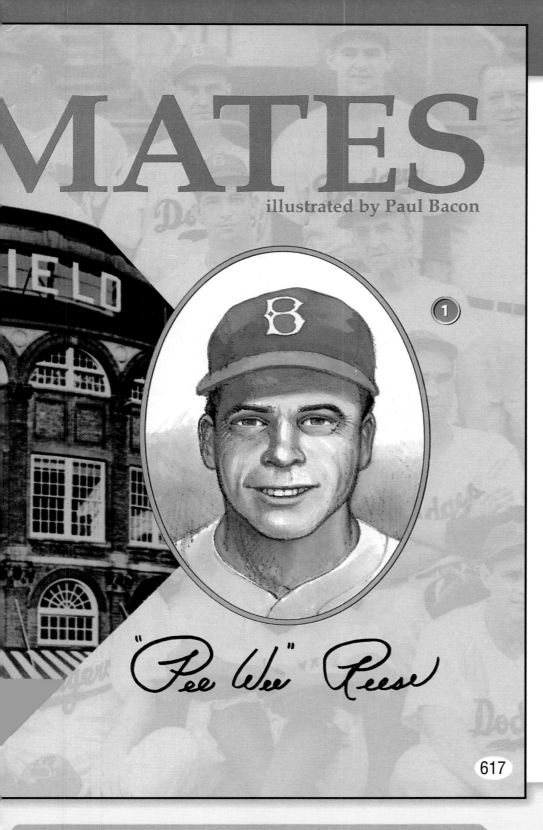

MATES

illustrated by Paul Bacon

(1)

"Pee Wee" Reese

617

Guided Instruction

✓ **Cause and Effect**

Strategic Reading This selection is a true story about an event that changed baseball forever. To understand the important events and the reasons they happened, we can use a Cause and Effect chart.

CAUSE: Why Something Happens	**EFFECT:** What Happens
	➡

(1) CAUSE AND EFFECT Look at the team portrait in the background. All the players seem to be white. Why do you think that is?

MODEL I know my favorite team doesn't look like that today, but years ago people of different races were segregated, or kept apart. Maybe baseball teams were segregated, too.

Story Words

The words below may be unfamiliar. Have students check their meanings and pronunciations in the Glossary beginning on page 726.

* leagues, p. 619
* segregation, p. 619
* prejudice, p. 620
* racial, p. 620
* vigilante, p. 620

LANGUAGE SUPPORT

A blackline master of the Cause and Effect chart is available in the **Language Support Book**.

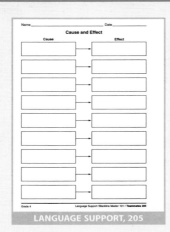

LANGUAGE SUPPORT, 205

617

Guided Instruction

② Look back at the picture of Jackie Robinson on page 616. Then read the quotation on this page. Did Jackie Robinson succeed as a baseball player? How do you know? (Yes, because the quotation is dated 1989, but the pictures show that the story happened long before that. By then, Pee Wee Reese knew how things had turned out.) *Draw Conclusions*

② Jackie Robinson was more than just my teammate. He had a tremendous amount of talent, ability, and dedication. Jackie set a standard for future generations of ball players. He was a winner.

Jackie Robinson was also a man.

PEE WEE REESE
October 31, 1989

618

Activity

Cross Curricular: Social Studies

SEGREGATION AND INTEGRATION Review some of the unfair policies and laws that supported segregation.

RESEARCH AND INQUIRY Brainstorm a list of ideas, people, and events involved in the battle for integration, such as the Freedom Riders and

Brown vs. Board of Education. Assign topics to small groups and have them research and report on their topics.

▶ **Linguistic/Interpersonal**

*inter***NET** **CONNECTION** Students can learn about segregation and integration at *www.mhschool.com/reading*

The Rosa Parks Story

Once upon a time in America, when automobiles were black and looked like tanks and laundry was white and hung on clotheslines to dry, there were two wonderful baseball leagues that no longer exist. They were called the Negro Leagues.

The Negro Leagues had extraordinary players, and adoring fans came to see them wherever they played. They were heroes, but players in the Negro Leagues didn't make much money and their lives on the road were hard.

Laws against segregation didn't exist in the 1940s. In many places in this country, black people were not allowed to go to the same schools and churches as white people. They couldn't sit in the front of a bus or trolley car. They couldn't drink from the same drinking fountains that white people drank from.

Back then, many hotels didn't rent rooms to black people, so the Negro League players slept in their cars. Many towns had no restaurants that would serve them, so they often had to eat meals that they could buy and carry with them.

619

Guided Instruction

③ CAUSE AND EFFECT Why would Negro League players, or an African American family for that matter, have needed to plan very carefully before making a long trip in the days of segregation? (In many towns, African Americans could not rent a hotel room, eat in a restaurant, or even get a drink of water or use the bathroom. Travelers would need to choose a route to avoid those towns or pack their own meals and water.)

P/i WORD STRUCTURE/CONTEXT CLUES Find the word *segregation* on this page. Do you know what the word means? Can you find any clues?

Minilesson

REVIEW
Make Inferences

Remind students that making inferences means understanding ideas or information that the author does not directly state. To make inferences, students use what they read in the text along with their own experiences to add meaning to the author's words.

- Have students list the rules that African Americans in segrated states had to live by during the 1940s.

- Ask students to recall a time when they felt they were treated unfairly and to think about how they felt.

Activity Invite students to take the role of an African American player on the Monarchs in the 1940s and write a journal entry that describes a typical day and tells how segregation makes him or her feel.

P/i PREVENTION/INTERVENTION

WORD STRUCTURE/CONTEXT CLUES Guide students in using structural and context clues to the meaning of *segregation*. Identify the *-tion* ending and ask what part of speech it usually signals. (noun) Then discuss clues in the third and fourth paragraphs that describe how segregation kept African American people separate.

Write *segregation* and *integration* on the board and explain that they are antonyms. Have students look at the beginning of each word and use this mnemonic device to remember the difference: *Segregation* begins like *separate*. *Integration* begins with *in*, as in *Everyone can come in*.

Guided Instruction

(4) CAUSE AND EFFECT Branch Rickey couldn't just hire the best player from the Negro Leagues. He needed a player with a special kind of personality. Why? (The first African American player would have to be able to stay calm even when people around him were being mean and unfair.) Let's add this to our chart.

CAUSE: Why Something Happens		EFFECT: What Happens
If the first African American player failed, it would be harder for others.	→	Branch Rickey had to recruit a very special person as well as a good player.
	→	

Life was very different for the players in the Major Leagues. They were the leagues for white players. Compared to the Negro League players, white players were very well paid. They stayed in good hotels and ate in fine restaurants. Their pictures were put on baseball cards and the best players became famous all over the world.

Many Americans knew that racial prejudice was wrong, but few dared to challenge openly the way things were. And many people were apathetic about racial problems. Some feared that it could be dangerous to object. Vigilante groups, like the Ku Klux Klan, reacted violently against those who tried to change the way blacks were treated.

The general manager of the Brooklyn Dodgers baseball team was a man by the name of Branch Rickey. He was not afraid of change. He wanted to treat the Dodger fans to the best players he could find, regardless of the color of their skin. He thought segregation was unfair and wanted to give everyone, regardless of race or creed, an opportunity to compete equally on ballfields across America.

To do this, the Dodgers needed one special man. Branch Rickey launched a search for him. He was looking for a star player in the Negro Leagues who would be able to compete successfully despite threats on his life or attempts to injure him. He would have to **(4)** possess the self-control not to fight back when opposing players tried to intimidate or hurt him. If this man disgraced himself on the field, Rickey knew, his opponents would use it as an excuse to keep blacks out of Major League baseball for many more years.

Rickey thought Jackie Robinson might be just the man.

620

Activity

Cross Curricular: Social Studies

LIFE IN THE 1940s To help students understand how times were different in the era when the story takes place, have them interview a person who remembers 1947, the year Jackie Robinson joined the Brooklyn Dodgers. Students can write a summary of their interview and include it in an oral history book about the '40s.

▶ **Interpersonal/Auditory**

 inter NET CONNECTION Students can learn about the 1940s by visiting **www.mhschool.com/reading**

The Forties: An Oral History

BRANCH RICKEY

621

Guided Instruction

5 **CAUSE AND EFFECT** What effect did excluding Negro League players have on the quality of play in the Major Leagues? (Excluding African American players meant that the Major Leagues were passing up some of the best baseball players. So Major League games may not have been as exciting as they could have been.) Let's add this information to our charts.

CAUSE: Why Something Happens	EFFECT: What Happens
If the first African American player failed, it would be harder for others.	Branch Rickey had to recruit a very special person as well as a good player.
African American players were not allowed in the Major Leagues.	The Major Leagues missed out on some star players.

Minilesson

REVIEW

Prefixes

Remind students that prefixes added at the beginning of a base word change the base word's meaning. The prefix *un-* means "not."

• Ask students to find a word in the third paragraph on page 620 that begins with *un-*. Write *unfair* on the board.

• Have a volunteer define *unfair*.

• Ask another volunteer to erase the prefix and define the word that remains.

Activity Give students a list of words and ask them to add *un-*. Then have them choose one pair of words and write a sentence for each word. Use words such as *successful*, *paid*, *afraid*, and *equal*.

621

Guided Instruction

6 Branch Rickey said he needed a player who had "the courage not to fight back." Why would *not* fighting take courage? (Often people who are treated unfairly feel like treating others the same way. It is harder to behave with dignity and self-control than to give in to anger.) *Make Inferences*

7 Who would like to act out the conversation between Jackie Robinson and Branch Rickey? Mr. Rickey, explain what might happen when Jackie Robinson walks onto the baseball field. Mr. Robinson, tell how you will act and why. *Role-Play*

> **TEACHING TIP**
>
> Explain that spectators often tire of sitting by the middle of the seventh inning of a baseball game. At that point fans stand, stretch, and sing a chorus of "Take Me Out to the Ball Game." Teach students to take a "seventh inning stretch" when they need a break during a long assignment.

622

CULTURAL PERSPECTIVES

AN INTERNATIONAL PASTIME Tell students that baseball was invented in Hoboken, New Jersey, USA in 1845 and is so popular it has been called the "national pastime." Discuss how baseball has recently become popular in Asia and Latin America. Today, many Major League teams include players from many countries.

Activity Have students research Major League baseball teams. Have them list each country that the players come from.

Jackie rode the train to Brooklyn to meet Mr. Rickey. When Mr. Rickey told him, "I want a man with the courage not to fight back," Jackie Robinson replied, "If you take this gamble, I will do my best to perform." They shook hands. Branch Rickey and Jackie Robinson were starting on what would be known in history as "the great experiment."

At spring training with the Dodgers, Jackie was mobbed by blacks, young and old, as if he were a savior. He was the first black player to try out for a Major League team. If he succeeded, they knew, others would follow.

Initially, life with the Dodgers was for Jackie a series of humiliations. The players on his team who came from the South, men who had been taught to avoid black people since childhood, moved to another table whenever he sat down next to them. Many opposing players were cruel to him, calling him nasty names from their dugouts. A few tried to hurt him with their spiked shoes. Pitchers aimed at his head. And he received threats on his life, both from individuals and from organizations like the Ku Klux Klan.

Despite all the difficulties, Jackie Robinson didn't give up. He made the Brooklyn Dodgers team. **8**

623

Guided Instruction

8 **CAUSE AND EFFECT** What did the players who tried to humiliate Jackie Robinson hope to accomplish? (They hoped that Jackie Robinson would quit and that would put an end to the idea of including African Americans on Major League teams.) **What do you think was the actual effect of the players' rude behavior?**

MODEL The players' rude behavior could have made Jackie Robinson so angry that he would quit. Or it could have made him feel more determined than ever to stay. Because I know that Branch Rickey hired Robinson in part for his strong personality, and because I know that Robinson became a great Major League player, I think the players' rudeness made Robinson feel tougher and determined.

PHONICS AND DECODING Look at the last word of the first sentence in paragraph 3. (humiliations) What words that you already know can you use to help sound out this word?

Minilesson

REVIEW

Main Idea

Remind students that the main idea of a paragraph tells what the paragraph is about. The other sentences give details that support, or tell more about, the main idea. The main idea is often, but not always, stated in the first sentence.

- Have students reread the third paragraph and identify the main idea sentence.
- Then ask volunteers to paraphrase sentences that tell about supporting details.

Activity For extra practice, have students repeat the activity with the first paragraph on page 620.

For extra practice, have students repeat the activity with the first paragraph on page 620.

PREVENTION/INTERVENTION

PHONICS AND DECODING Tell students that they can divide the a word into shorter parts and match the parts with parts of words they already know. Point out that they may need to try several times before they say a word that sounds familiar.

- Have students look at the first part of *humiliations* and name other words that begin the same way. (human, humor)

- Then have them look at the end of the word and do the same thing. (nations, organizations)
- Finally, have them look at *-ili-* and think of words that have similar sounds. (million)

Help students blend the parts of the word together.

623

Guided Instruction

9 **CAUSE AND EFFECT** Why do you think Pee Wee Reese refused to sign the petition? (Reese was loyal to his team. He wanted it to have the best players, and thought Robinson deserved a chance.) Let's add this to our charts.

CAUSE: Why Something Happens	EFFECT: What Happens
Reese was loyal to his team and wanted the best players.	Reese refused to sign the petition.

SELF-MONITORING

STRATEGY

VISUALIZE Remind students that readers can get more involved in a story by picturing the scene the author describes.

MODEL From the author's description, I can imagine what it would feel like to be at first base with angry, red, perspiring faces looking at me. Some people are shaking their fists in the air. I'm standing all alone.

But making the Dodgers was only the beginning. Jackie had to face abuse and hostility throughout the season, from April through September. His worst pain was inside. Often he felt very alone. On the road he had to live by himself, because only the white players were allowed in the hotels in towns where the team played.

The whole time Pee Wee Reese, the Dodger shortstop, was growing up in Louisville, Kentucky, he had rarely even seen a black person, unless it was in the back of a bus. Most of his friends and relatives hated the idea of his playing on the same field as a black man. In addition, Pee Wee Reese had more to lose than the other players when Jackie joined the team.

Jackie had been a shortstop, and everyone thought that Jackie would take Pee Wee's job. Lesser men might have felt anger toward Jackie, but Pee Wee was different. He told himself, "If he's good enough to take my job, he deserves it."

When his Southern teammates circulated a petition to throw Jackie off the team and asked him to sign it, Pee Wee responded, "I don't care if this man is black, blue, or striped"—and refused to **9** sign. "He can play and he can help us win," he told the others. "That's what counts."

Very early in the season, the Dodgers traveled west to Ohio to play the Cincinnati Reds. Cincinnati is near Pee Wee's hometown of Louisville.

The Reds played in a small ballpark where the fans sat close to the field. The players could almost feel the breath of the fans on the backs of their necks. Many who came that day screamed terrible, hateful things at Jackie when the Dodgers were on the field.

More than anything else, Pee Wee Reese believed in doing what was right. When he heard the fans yelling at Jackie, Pee Wee decided to take a stand.

624

Activity

Cross Curricular: Math

BATTING AVERAGES Show students how to figure batting averages by dividing the number of hits by the number of times at bat. Figure several averages, demonstrating how to insert the decimal point. Point out a batter who gets a hit every time would bat 1.000, which we read as "bat a thousand."

RESEARCH AND INQUIRY Have students research batting averages of their favorite players in almanacs, or on the Internet. ▶ **Mathematical**

 Students can learn more about baseball statistics by visiting **www.mhschool.com/reading**

World Series Batting Average				
Player	Year	AB	H	AVG
Babe Ruth	1927	15	6	.400
Ted Williams	1946	25	5	.200
Willie Mays	1954	14	4	.286

625

Guided Instruction

10 The tension is mounting in the Cincinnati ballpark. Do you think Jackie Robinson will be able to maintain his dignity? Or do you think he will finally break under the pressure? (Sample answer: Because Robinson has stood up so far under pressure from people who are much closer to him, including his own teammates, he will be able to keep his self-control now, too.) *Make Predictions*

Minilesson

REVIEW
Silent Letters

Say the word *might,* and have students name the sounds they hear. Write the letters that stand for the sounds on the chalkboard as students say them: *m-i-t,* and ask students if you have spelled the word correctly. Elicit that many English words have silent letters. In *might,* the *g* and *h* are silent, but different letters are silent in other words.

Activity Have students find the words *would, right, whole,* and *could* on page 624. Say each word slowly and have students identify the silent letter or letters.

LANGUAGE SUPPORT

ESL Draw a diagram of a baseball diamond and label the nine positions: pitcher, catcher, first base, second base, third base, shortstop, left field, center field, and right field. Have a volunteer point out Pee Wee Reese's position. (shortstop) Leave the chart in place so students will be able to trace the route of Reese's long walk as they read the selection's climactic event on page 626.

Guided Instruction

11 **CAUSE AND EFFECT** Let's review our Cause and Effect chart as we think about what we've read. We can add one more entry to explain the silence that fell on the crowd at the end of the story.

CAUSE: Why Something Happens	EFFECT: What Happens
If the first African American player failed, it would be harder for others.	Branch Rickey had to recruit a very special person as well as a good player.
African American players were not allowed in the Major Leagues.	The Major Leagues missed out on some star players.
Reese was loyal to his team and wanted the best players.	Reese refused to sign the petition.
The spectators were both shocked and humbled by Reese's support of his teammate.	The crowd fell silent.

RETELL THE STORY Ask students to relate the major events in the selection. Then have them write a brief summary of the selection, using their chart if they wish. Suggest that they focus on the causes and effects that changed baseball forever.
Summarize

STUDENT SELF-ASSESSMENT

- How did finding causes and effects help me understand the characters' actions?
- How did using the Cause and Effect chart help me remember what I read?

TRANSFERRING THE STRATEGY

- With what kinds of selections would this strategy be most helpful?

With his head high, Pee Wee walked directly from his shortstop position to where Jackie was playing first base. The taunts and shouting of the fans were ringing in Pee Wee's ears. It saddened him, because he knew it could have been his friends and neighbors. Pee Wee's legs felt heavy, but he knew what he had to do.

As he walked toward Jackie wearing the gray Dodger uniform, he looked into his teammate's bold, pained eyes. The first baseman had done nothing to provoke the hostility except that he sought to be treated as an equal. Jackie was grim with anger. Pee Wee smiled broadly as he reached Jackie. Jackie smiled back.

Stopping beside Jackie, Pee Wee put his arm around Jackie's shoulders. An audible gasp rose up from the crowd when **11** they saw what Pee Wee had done. Then there was silence.

Outlined on a sea of green grass stood these two great athletes, one black, one white, both wearing the same team uniform.

"I am standing by him," Pee Wee Reese said to the world. "This man is my teammate."

626

REREADING FOR *Fluency*

GROUP Have one student read page 626 aloud as other students pantomime the roles of Reese, Robinson, and audience members.

READING RATE You may want to evaluate a student's reading rate. Have the student read aloud from *Teammates* for one minute. Ask the student to place a self-stick note after the last word read. Then count the number of words he or she read.

Alternatively, you could assess small groups or the whole class together by having students count words and record their own scores.

Use the Reading Rate form in the **Diagnostic/Placement Evaluations** booklet to evaluate students' performance.

MEET *Peter Golenbock*

When Peter Golenbock was thirteen, he met one of his heroes. After a World Series game between the Dodgers and the Yankees, he was introduced to Jackie Robinson. Meeting the great baseball player was quite an experience. "I was in awe of him," Golenbock remembers. "Robinson was huge. When I shook his hand, mine disappeared in his." Years later, Golenbock became a sportswriter and learned more about Robinson. Rex Barney, who had pitched for the Dodgers when Robinson was a player, told the writer a true story about two teammates—Jackie Robinson and Pee Wee Reese, the Dodgers' shortstop. Peter Golenbock never forgot that story.

When he was asked to write about baseball for young people, he thought about Jackie Robinson. He remembered Robinson's courage—as an athlete and as the first African-American player in the major leagues. He also remembered the story that Rex Barney had told him. In Teammates, Peter Golenbock wrote about baseball and how Robinson changed it. It is a story you, like the author, may never forget.

627

LITERARY RESPONSE

QUICK-WRITE Students may use their journals to express their feelings, thoughts, and opinions about the selection. Start them off with questions like these:

- In what different ways did Jackie Robinson, Pee Wee Reese, and Branch Rickey all show courage?

- How would you have acted if you were in Jackie Robinson's situation?

ORAL RESPONSE Have students share their journal writings and discuss what part of the story they enjoyed most.

Guided Instruction

Return to Predictions and Purposes

Help students recall their predictions and purposes for reading. Have them compare their predictions with what actually happened in the selection.

PREDICTIONS	WHAT HAPPENED
This story is about a baseball player.	The story was about baseball players who had the courage to stand up for their beliefs.
The two characters on the cover become friends.	One character helps the other through a hard time and both players become role models for others.

INFORMAL ASSESSMENT

CAUSE AND EFFECT

HOW TO ASSESS

- Ask students to tell what effects they think the events in the selection had on the future of Major League baseball.

- Invite students to think about what effect the integration of Major League baseball had on the country as a whole.

Students should realize that after the events in the story, Major League baseball teams quickly became integrated. Today, players are judged on their talent and skill. The changes in baseball both reflected changes in American society as a whole and spurred on greater changes.

FOLLOW UP If students have difficulty connecting causes and effects, suggest that they look for effects first by asking "What happened?" and then ask "Why did it happen?" The answer to the first question will be the effect and the answer to the second will be the cause.

Story Questions

Have students discuss or write answers to the questions on page 628.

Answers:

1. African Americans played in the Negro Leagues, and whites played in the Major Leagues. *Literal/Details*

2. Branch Rickey was looking for a talented player who would be courageous enough to face hardship with grace. Rickey felt that Robinson was that person. *Inferential/Draw Conclusions*

3. Today, people of all races play baseball in the Major Leagues. *Inferential/Cause and Effect*

4. The main idea of the selection is that the courage of a few people can change the world for everyone. *Critical/Summarize*

5. Real teammates are people who stick together. The women would probably agree. *Critical/Reading Across Texts*

Compare Sports Lessons For a full writing process lesson related to this writing suggestion, see pages 631K–631L.

Story Questions & Activities

1. What were the names of the baseball leagues for African American and white players before the 1940s?

2. Why did Branch Rickey decide to hire Jackie Robinson?

3. What effect did Branch Rickey's decision to hire Jackie Robinson have on the game of baseball?

4. What is the main idea of this true story?

5. Imagine that Jackie Robinson became part of the painting on pages 614–615. What do you think he would say to the women about the real meaning of teammates? Do you think they would agree with him? Explain.

Compare Sports Heroes

Jackie Robinson was an American sports hero. Write a paragraph comparing Jackie Robinson with another sports star. List three qualities the two sports heroes share. Show how they are heroes in at least two other ways.

Meeting Individual Needs

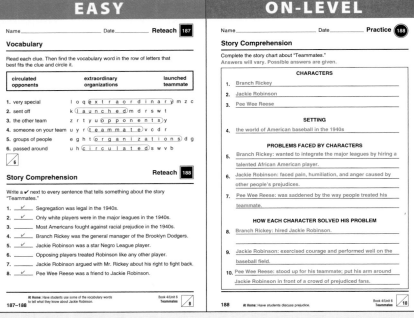

Reteach, 188

Practice, 188

Extend, 188

Create a Collage

Jackie Robinson was the first African American player in the Major Leagues. Plan a collage of other "firsts." Include people who were first, such as Amelia Earhart, who was the first woman to fly a plane across the Atlantic Ocean. Find pictures of these famous people. Then arrange them to make a collage. Be prepared to explain who each person was and what he or she did to be first.

Use Baseball Math

Use the Internet or a baseball almanac to solve these baseball math problems.

- How many years did Jackie Robinson play in the Major Leagues?

- How many home runs did he hit during his first five years as a Dodger?

- In his first eight years in the majors, how many bases did he steal?

Think of other baseball math problems. Try to stump your friends.

Find Out More

Jackie Robinson was the first African American to play in the National League. But who was the first African American to play in the American League? Which Negro League stars followed these two players into the Major Leagues? Find out the answers in a baseball encyclopedia or a baseball almanac. Then tell a friend what you learned.

629

Story Activities

Create a Collage

Materials: poster board, scissors, glue, drawing paper, and crayons (optional)

GROUP Suggest that students brainstorm a list of "famous firsts," consulting an almanac or encyclopedia if they wish. If photocopies of pictures of those people are not available, students may use photos in books as models for their own drawings.

Use Baseball Math

Materials: baseball almanacs, Internet access

PARTNERS Tell students to supply data from the reference books as they write their story problems. Compile the problems and give the whole class a baseball math quiz.

Find Out More

RESEARCH AND INQUIRY Suggest that students consult baseball books, African American history books, and the Internet to find information. After sharing what they learn, students can post interesting facts on a "Scoreboard" bulletin board in the classroom.

 _inter_**NET** **CONNECTION** For more information about African American baseball players, students can visit **www.mhschool.com/reading**

FORMAL ASSESSMENT

After page 629, see the Selection Assessment.

Study Skills

LIBRARY/MEDIA CENTER

OBJECTIVES Students will identify information on a catalog card.

PREPARE Ask a volunteer to read the introduction to the card catalog aloud. Then show **Teaching Chart 153**.

TEACH Explain that even when a library uses a computer catalog, the entry contains the same information as a catalog card. With students, read and discuss each entry on the card.

PRACTICE Have students answer questions 1–5. Review the answers. **1.** African Americans in baseball **2.** *Superstars of the Negro Leagues* **3.** Sandy Feller **4.** 333 **5.** You would go to the shelf that has the same call number.

ASSESS/CLOSE Take students to the library to locate a books about a few subjects they would like to read about.

STUDY SKILLS

Use the Card Catalog: Subject Card

Where would you look if you wanted to find a book about the Negro Leagues? The **card catalog** in the library is a good place to start. Each book in the library has an **author card**, a **title card**, and a **subject card**. Some libraries have card catalogs that are alphabetically arranged in drawers. Other libraries let you search the card catalog by computer. For a book about baseball, you would look at a subject card. The **call number** at the top of the card tells you where to find the book on the library shelf.

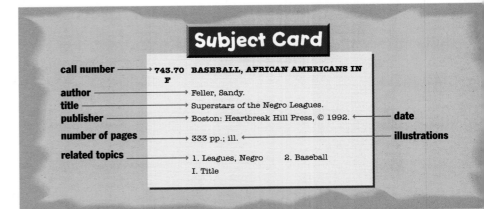

Subject Card

call number →	743.70 **BASEBALL, AFRICAN AMERICANS IN**
	F
author →	Feller, Sandy.
title →	Superstars of the Negro Leagues.
publisher →	Boston: Heartbreak Hill Press, © 1992. ← date
number of pages →	333 pp.; ill. ← illustrations
related topics →	1. Leagues, Negro 2. Baseball
	I. Title

Use the subject card to answer these questions.

1. What is the subject of the book?

2. What is the title?

3. Who is the author?

4. How many pages does the book have?

5. How would you use the call number at the top of the card?

Meeting Individual Needs

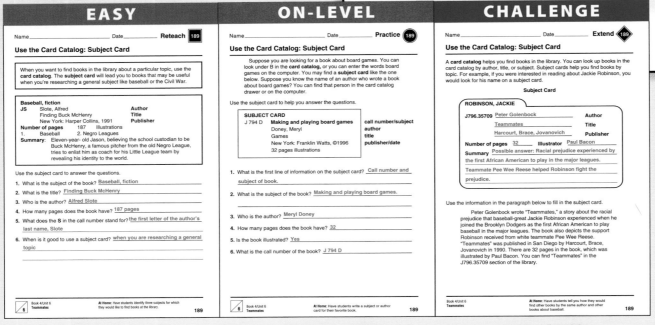

Reteach, 189   Practice, 189   Extend, 189

TEST POWER

DIRECTIONS

Read the sample story. Then read each question about the story.

SAMPLE

Time for New Trees

"Dad, must all the trees be cut down?" Barbara asked.

Barbara's father had just finished explaining why the trees would be cut down that day. They were all elm trees, and they all had Dutch elm disease. The disease would spread to all the other elm trees in the city if the infected trees were not removed right away.

"Unfortunately, there is nothing that can be done to save them," her father said.

"Maybe we'll feel better if we plant some new trees," Barbara suggested brightly. "How about if we go over to the university and ask for some recommendations from the tree specialist?"

1 Why were the elm trees being cut down?

○ They put in a sidewalk.

● The trees had a disease.

○ They planted new trees.

○ Barbara likes trees.

2 Which is an OPINION in this passage?

● Barbara will feel better if they plant new trees.

○ Barbara and her father will visit the university.

○ The infected trees will make the other trees sick.

○ The trees are elm trees.

631

Test Power

Read the Page

As students become more familiar with test taking, they should get in the habit of asking **why** or **how** when they come across questions in the text. In line 1 Barbara asks, "must all the trees be cut down?". Students should then be cued to look for the reason **why**?

Discuss the Questions

Question 1: This question requires students to locate information within the story. The 2nd paragraph explains that the trees have Dutch Elm disease and must be cut down.

Question 2: This question requires students to determine which of the four choices is an **OPINION**. Explain that an **OPINION** is how a person feels about something. Students must be able to distinguish between what is a **FACT** and what is an **OPINION**. Have students eliminate **FACTS**.

Leveled Books

EASY

Doubles

EASY

Doubles

Silent Letters

☑ **Cause and Effect**

☑ **Instructional Vocabulary:**
circulated, extraordinary, launched, opponents, organizations, teammate

Guided Reading

PREVIEW AND PREDICT Preview the book through page 11 and describe the action in the tennis pictures. Ask students to write in their journals predictions about what will happen to the girls' friendship.

SET PURPOSES Ask students to write in their journals a purpose for reading the story. For example, they may want to know why the girls look angry on page 11.

READ THE BOOK Guide a group reading with questions like these, or ask the questions after students read the story independently.

Pages 2–3: Why are the girls especially excited about summer tennis this year? (They are old enough to play in the tournament.) *Character*

Pages 5–6: The July 12 entries show that the girls' attitudes are beginning to differ. Which attitude seems wiser to you? (Answers will vary.) *Judgments and Decisions*

Page 10: What expression on this page means clumsy? (all thumbs) Which word

has a silent letter? (thumbs) *Phonics and Decoding*

Page 12: Mrs. Piers *circulated* on the courts. Did she yell, pace in circles, or walk around? (walk around) *Vocabulary*

Pages 13–16: What effect did changing partners have on Erin and Gracie's friendship? (It saved their friendship.) *Cause and Effect*

RETURN TO PREDICTIONS AND PURPOSES Have students review their predictions and purposes for reading. Were their predictions accurate? Did they find out what they wanted to know?

LITERARY RESPONSE Discuss these questions:

- How does the diary format make the story more interesting?

- What do you think would have happened if the girls had played in the tournament as partners?

Also see the story questions and activity in *Doubles*.

Answers to Story Questions

1. Erin cared mostly about winning, and Gracie wanted to enjoy herself also.
2. They began losing games because Gracie was angry at the way Erin was treating her on the court.
3. Answers may include: Friends are more concerned with one another than with the task at hand; friends might work better together because they know one another's strengths and weaknesses.
4. Two best friends who play tennis together have different feelings about competition and winning a big tournament.
5. Answers will vary.

Story Questions and Activity
Doubles

1. In what ways were Erin's and Gracie's attitudes about tennis different?
2. What effect did Erin returning balls from Gracie's side of the court have on their performance?
3. Gracie's mom tells her that it's common for best friends to have a hard time working together. Why might this be true? Can you think of examples in which it is not true?
4. What is the story mostly about?
5. If Gracie and Erin could speak with Pee Wee Reese and Jackie Robinson, what advice do you think the baseball players might have for the girls?

Dear Diary...

Think of another event or situation that might be experienced by Erin and Gracie. How would each of them record the events in their diaries? Write diary entries that describe what happened from each character's point of view.

from *Doubles*

Leveled Books

INDEPENDENT

Me and Maya, the Super Brain

☑ **Cause and Effect**

☑ **Instructional Vocabulary:** *circulated, extraordinary, launched, opponents, organizations, teammate*

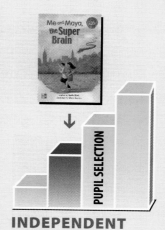

INDEPENDENT

Answers to Story Questions

1. Maya wants to win the prize—a trip to New York City—and go up to the top of the Empire State Building.
2. The contest makes Maya and Nick frustrated with each other.
3. Because Nick doesn't really want to participate in the contest, he doesn't study the flash cards Maya made for him. His attitude hurts his performance.
4. It is about two best friends who are teammates in a big contest.
5. Answers will vary but might include that both put a friend first and acted with the friend's best interests at heart.

Guided Reading

PREVIEW AND PREDICT Preview the book with students through page 11 to find out what kind of team Nick and Maya seem to be on. Have students write predictions in their journals about whether or not Nick and Maya will be friends by the end of the story.

SET PURPOSES Ask students to write a purpose for reading in their journals. For example, they may want to know why the girl looks sad on page 11 and whether the boy will help her.

READ THE BOOK Use questions like these to guide a group reading or in an after-reading discussion.

Page 2: Are *extraordinary* peanut butter cookies especially good, or are they not as good as usual? (especially good) *Vocabulary*

Pages 3–4: Why should Nick have known that the contest would cause trouble? (He knows Maya is good at memorizing facts and he is not.) *Cause and Effect*

Pages 7–11: Why do you think Maya refuses to speak to Nick? (Maya probably

thinks Nick did not try hard enough.) *Cause and Effect*

Pages 12–13: Do you think Emily's decision to drop out of the contest was a good one? (Sample answer: yes, because she was frightened; no, she'll never get over her stage fright unless she tries.) *Judgments and Decisions*

RETURN TO PREDICTIONS AND PURPOSES Have students review their predictions and purposes for reading. Invite volunteers to tell whether they correctly predicted that the contest would not ruin Nick and Maya's friendship. Encourage students to talk about whether their purposes for reading were met.

LITERARY RESPONSE Discuss these questions:

- Was Maya right or wrong to push Nick into entering the contest?

- If Emily did not want to drop out, what could Nick have done to become friends with Maya again?

Also see the story questions and activity in *Me and Maya, the Super Brain.*

Story Questions and Activity

1. How did Nick and Maya first become friends?
2. What does Nick feel about the Super Brain Challenge Contest?
3. Based on the evidence of the story, how does the Super Brain Challenge Contest challenge your brain?
4. How do you think Nick's attitude toward the Super Brain Contest effects his performance?
5. What is this story mostly about?

Design a Kite

In the story, Nick and Maya design and make a kite together. Alone or with a partner draw a picture of your dream kite. Get a book about kites or kite-making out of the library. Make a kite and fly it with your friend.

from Me and Maya, the Super Brain

Leveled Books

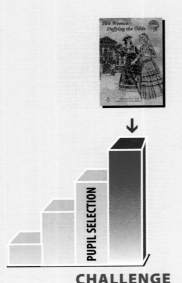

Two Women - Defying the Odds

written by Shelia Black
illustrated by Harold Henriksen

PUPIL SELECTION

CHALLENGE

Answers to Story Questions

1. Florence Nightingale asked Elizabeth Blackwell what inspired her to become the first woman doctor in England and America.

2. Young women did not work outside the home, and nursing was not a respectable profession.

3. Hospitals were so dirty and dangerous that only people who had no choice worked in them. Because of Miss Nightingale, nursing became a respected profession and hospitals much safer environments.

4. The main idea is the story of two women friends who made major contributions to the field of medicine.

5. Answers will vary.

Story Questions and Activity

1. At their first meeting what question did Florence Nightingale ask Elizabeth Blackwell?

2. Why did Florence's family object to her becoming a nurse?

3. What conditions prompted Miss Nightingale to want to be a nurse and improve nursing? What effect did she have on the health care?

4. What is the main idea of the book?

5. Compare and contrast the friendship of Pee Wee Reese and Jackie Robinson with that of Florence Nightingale and Elizabeth Blackwell. How were they alike and how were they different?

Write a Dialogue

Refer back to the story and write a dialogue between Florence Nightingale and Elizabeth Blackwell. Ask a partner to take the role of one of the characters, and you take the other. Then, together, put on an oral reading for your class.

from *Two Women Defying the Odds*

CHALLENGE

Two Women Defying the Odds

☑ **Cause and Effect**
☑ **Instructional Vocabulary:** *circulated, extraordinary, launched, opponents, organizations, teammate*

Guided Reading

PREVIEW AND PREDICT Preview the book with students through page 8, and have them use the pictures to predict the kinds of changes the two women brought about. Record students' predictions on a chart.

SET PURPOSES Ask students to write in their journals a purpose for reading. For example, they may want to know why these women were important.

READ THE BOOK Use questions like these to lead a group reading or as a follow-up to reading independently.

Pages 3–5: Why were female doctors and nurses unusual in the 1800s? (In those days, people thought it was "unladylike" for women to have jobs.) *Cause and Effect*

Page 8: Elizabeth thought hard about staying in London to work with Florence. Why did she decide to return to America? (Her family was there, and poor people in America needed medical help, too.) *Judgments and Decisions*

Page 10: During the Crimean War the British fought against Russia, but what were their real *opponents*? (disease, cold, and hunger) *Vocabulary*

Pages 10–13: What effect did Florence's work in the Crimea have on her later life? (It ruined her health.) *Cause and Effect*

RETURN TO PREDICTIONS AND PURPOSES Have students review their predictions and purposes for reading. Were their predictions accurate? Were their purposes met?

LITERARY RESPONSE Discuss these questions:

• Even though they spent most of their lives apart, the two women were still teammates. Why?

• What personal qualities do you think caused Elizabeth and Florence to set goals that were different from the goals of most women of their time?

Also see the story questions and activity in *Two Women Defying the Odds*.

Activities
Anthology and Leveled Books

Connecting Texts

FRIENDSHIPS CHART
Explain that all of the selections were about friendships that survived in spite of obstacles. Sometimes the friends had to make hard decisions to keep their friendships going. Have students use information from the selections they read to complete the chart.

Teamates	Doubles	Me and Maya the Superbrain	Two Women Defying the Odds
• Jackie Robinson • Pee Wee Reese • Working as teammates to win baseball games • Fighting racial prejudice	• Gracie • Erin • Working as teammates to win a tennis tournament • Having different attitudes about tennis	• Maya • Nick • Working as teammates to win an academic contest • Having different talents	• Elizabeth Blackwell • Florence Nightingale • Working as teammates to improve the practice of medicine • Fighting prejudice against professional women

Viewing/Representing

MAKE COMIC STRIPS Group students according to the Leveled Book they read. Have a few students from each group form a new group to make a presentation about the main selection. Ask the groups to locate the most important events in their selection and draw captioned pictures in comic strip form to summarize the story.

STAND UP COMICS After students present their comic strips, invite the audience to ask questions about story details and background information.

Research and Inquiry

MORE ABOUT FRIENDSHIP Ask students to research famous and not-so-famous friendships by

- reading about famous fictional friends like Tom Sawyer and Huckleberry Finn, or Frog and Toad.

- interviewing adult friends and family members about childhood friendships.

- making a scrapbook of captioned photos or drawings to share their research.

 *inter*NET **CONNECTION** For more information, have students log on to *www.mhschool.com/reading*.

Students will identify cause and effect.

LANGUAGE SUPPORT

ESL Have students act out things that could happen in the classroom, lunchroom, or schoolyard. After each event, have students talk about possible causes. Also discuss examples of cause and effect that occur during the day, such as illness causing a student to be absent.

Review Cause and Effect

PREPARE

Discuss Cause and Effect

Review: Making connections between events in a reading selection and their causes helps readers understand the logic of the selection. Some words and phrases, such as *since, because,* or *in order to* can be clues to identifying causes and effects.

TEACH

Read "Another First" and Model the Skill

Read the **Teaching Chart 154** passage with students. Ask students to think about causes and effects.

> **Another First**
>
> The Cincinnati game was only the beginning for Jackie Robinson. Some teams said they would not play against the Dodgers because Robinson was part of the team. They did play, though, since Ford Frick, the National League president, said they had to.
> The Dodgers were soon glad to have Robinson on their team. Partly because of his solid skills, the Dodgers won the National League pennant. In September of 1947, Jackie Robinson scored another first. He was the first African American to compete in a World Series.
>
> **Teaching Chart 154**

Model how to find one example of a cause and effect in the article on the chart.

MODEL I thought that maybe after Pee Wee Reese showed his support for his teammate Jackie Robinson, things would settle down. But apparently it took a while. One effect of having Jackie Robinson on the team was that some other teams threatened not to play against the Dodgers.

PRACTICE

Identify Causes and Effects

PARTNERS

Have volunteers circle the causes in the passage and underline the effects. Then, invite pairs of students to think of a funny incident from a television show or book and tell the cause or causes that led up to the incident.

ASSESS/CLOSE

Finish the Sentence

PARTNERS

Have pairs of students complete this sentence three different ways: I _____ because _____ .

Give this sentence as an example:

I <u>fell asleep in the movie</u> because <u>I couldn't sleep the night before.</u>

ALTERNATE TEACHING STRATEGY

CAUSE AND EFFECT

For a different approach to teaching this skill, see page T60.

SELF-SELECTED Reading

Students may choose from the following titles.

ANTHOLOGY

- **Teammates**

LEVELED BOOKS

- **Double**
- **Me and Maya the Super Brain**
- **Two Women Defying the Odds**

Bibliography, pages T76–T77

Meeting Individual Needs for Comprehension

EASY	ON-LEVEL	CHALLENGE	LANGUAGE SUPPORT
Reteach, 190	Practice, 190	Extend, 190	Language Support, 206

Review Judgments and Decisions

TEACHING TIP

INSTRUCTIONAL Explain that making judgments and making decisions are similar but slightly different skills. When you make a judgment, you apply your values to decide whether something is good, better, the best, or the worst. When you make a decision, you choose a course of action. Also explain that readers often apply these skills by analyzing the judgments and decisions characters make.

PREPARE

Discuss Making Judgments and Decisions

Review: When you make judgments or decisions, you use your own values and goals to evaluate choices. Every author has his or her own ideas. It is up to readers to decide how to react to those ideas.

TEACH

Read "Jackie Robinson's Choice" and Model the Skill

Read **Teaching Chart 155** with students. After reading, ask students to evaluate the options and tell what decision they would make if they were in Jackie Robinson's shoes.

Jackie Robinson's Choice

Jackie Robinson had to decide whether to stay in the Negro Leagues or move to the Majors. The Negro Leagues were friendly and familiar. Jackie and the fans liked each other and he was respected for his skill. But Jackie didn't choose the Negro Leagues; the color of his skin did.

> In the Major Leagues, Jackie would make more money. But many fans and teammates would dislike him on sight and treat him unfairly. Joining the Major Leagues, though, would be his own choice. It would also open the door for other Negro League players. Jackie knew he had the talent and personality to be first.

Teaching Chart 155

Have a volunteer draw a rectangle around the paragraph that tells reasons for joining the Major League and draw a circle around the reasons for staying with the Negro League.

MODEL Staying where he was would certainly be easier. It takes courage to leave something you know and like. But the opportunities for him and for others were too great to pass up. That's why he decided to give the Majors a try.

PRACTICE

Make a Pro and Con List

PARTNERS

Show students how to make a two-column Pro and Con list. Have them list the reasons for joining the Major League, or pros, and the reasons for not joining, or cons.

SHOULD HE JOIN THE MAJORS	
PRO	**CON**
more money	racial prejudice
chance to help others	leave friends and teammates

ASSESS/CLOSE

Analyze a Decision

PARTNERS

Have partners make a Pro and Con list for Branch Rickey's decision to hire Jackie Robinson, Pee Wee Reese's decision to support Robinson, or a personal decision they need to make about a situation at school.

ALTERNATE TEACHING STRATEGY
....

MAKE JUDGMENTS AND DECISIONS

For a different approach to teaching this skill, see page T62.

LOOKING AHEAD

Students will apply this skill as they read the next selection, *The Malachite Palace.*

Meeting Individual Needs for Comprehension

EASY	ON-LEVEL	CHALLENGE	LANGUAGE SUPPORT
Name_____ Date_____ Reteach 191	Name_____ Date_____ Practice 191	Name_____ Date_____ Extend 191	Name_____ Date_____
Make Judgments and Decisions	**Make Judgments and Decisions**	**Make Judgments and Decisions**	**Making Important Decisions**

EASY — Reteach, 191

Make Judgments and Decisions

Characters in stories **make judgments and decisions**. Readers make judgments and decisions about what characters decide to do or not do.

Read the paragraph. Then answer the questions. Student's answers may vary.

Jackie Robinson was a proud man who hated to lose. He was the kind of athlete who never gave up. That's what makes what he did in his first years with the Dodgers so unusual. Branch Rickey told Jackie he wanted him to promise he would not fight back. When people called Robinson, names, threw things at him, or tried to block him, Rickey wanted Robinson just to walk away. Rickey told Robinson that walking away would make the other fellow look bad. To Robinson, walking away felt like backing down. But he knew by not fighting back he would help the cause of black baseball players.

1. What decision did Jackie have to make? He had to decide if he could keep a promise to not fight back.

2. Was it fair of Branch Rickey to ask this of Robinson? Rickey probably felt strongly that Robinson could keep his promise, which would help all the players.

3. Why was the decision hard to make? Robinson was a proud man. Walking away felt like backing down to him.

4. Did Robinson's decision turn out to be a good one? Why? Yes. People saw Robinson as a wonderful athlete, not just an African American. He opened the doors for other African American players.

Book 4/Unit 6
Teammates
At Home: Have students discuss a difficult decision they have made.
191

ON-LEVEL — Practice, 191

Make Judgments and Decisions

Characters in stories **make judgments and decisions** based on what they see. Read each passage, and then answer each question. Answers will vary.

Mr. Garcia, the principal, brought the new student to the fourth grade classroom around 10:00. The class was in the middle of a math test. The whole class looked at Mr. Garcia when he said, "Please help me welcome your new classmate, Charlie Cable." Everybody turned back to their math test. The new student looked scared.

1. What judgment did the storyteller make about Charlie Cable? He was scared.

In gym, teams were chosen for baseball. Everyone was chosen except for Charlie. He went with the last team. Up at bat, Charlie looked nervous. It was obvious that Charlie had never held a bat before. To no one's surprise, Charlie struck out. Matt Carlson remembered when he was the new kid. After gym, he walked back with Charlie, but Charlie didn't talk.

2. What judgment did the storyteller make about Charlie's baseball abilities? He thought Charlie wouldn't be able to get a hit.

3. Why did Matt decide to walk back with Charlie? He remembered what is was like to be new and he wanted to show support for Charlie.

The next day, everyone chose partners for the field trip. Everyone wanted to be Matt Carlson's partner. Matt chose Charlie Cable. This time Charlie talked a little to Matt on the bus. Everyone could hear Matt laughing like crazy. Everyone was curious. What was so funny? A couple of the kids turned around to listen to Charlie. Pretty soon, they were laughing, too.

4. What judgment did Matt make about Charlie's humor? He thought Charlie was funny.

5. What decision did some of the kids make? to listen and talk with Charlie and Matt

Book 4/Unit 6
The Fox and the Guinea Pig
At Home: Write about a first impression of a friend and how your judgment changed.
191

CHALLENGE — Extend, 191

Make Judgments and Decisions

We make many **judgments and decisions** every day. Some are so easy we make them automatically. Others are more difficult and require careful thought.

Read the sentences or paragraphs below. Write what decision you would make in each situation. Be sure to explain your thinking. Answers will vary. Possible answers are given.

1. You see two classmates teasing and scaring a younger child on the playground.
If a parent is present, you alert the parent. If not, you go up to the child and help the child.

2. You promise you will rake the yard before dinner. You are halfway done when your best friend rides up on her bicycle and asks you to go for a ride.
You ask your friend to wait or help you. If the friend declines, you continue raking.

3. A friend tells a joke that makes fun of certain people. It makes you uncomfortable.
You tell your friend you don't like jokes that make fun of people.

4. You really want to buy a new baseball glove. You have saved $10 so far. You are invited to go to the video arcade for the afternoon. You know you'll spend at least $5 there, but it sounds like fun.
The decision depends on how soon you need the glove. If you need it soon, you don't go; if you won't need it for a while, you'll probably go and plan to continue saving.

Book 4/Unit 6
Teammates
At Home: Have students keep a list of some of the decisions they have to make in one day.
191

LANGUAGE SUPPORT — Language Support, 207

Making Important Decisions

1. Finish each sentence below. 2. Beneath the sentences draw a picture showing what is written about each person. Answers may vary.

Jackie chose to play baseball for the Brooklyn Dodgers
It was hard because his teammates were mean
It was good because it helped all people to be treated equally

Pee Wee chose to stand by Jackie
It was hard because he was scared
It was good because he made Jackie feel welcome

Grade 4
Language Support/Blackline Master 103 • Teammates 207

Reteach, 191　　　Practice, 191　　　Extend, 191　　　Language Support, 207

631H

Review Context Clues

TEACHING TIP

MANAGEMENT Pair students who are familiar with the game and rules of baseball with those who are not.

Pause occasionally as you work through the lesson to allow baseball savvy volunteers to define vocabulary and explain the rules of the game.

PREPARE

Discuss Context Clues

Review: Some familiar words may take on a different meaning when they are used to talk about a particular subject. If you're not sure what a word means, even if it looks familiar, you can use other words in the sentence or paragraph to determine the word's meaning.

TEACH

Read "Safe at Home" and Model the Skill

Read the **Teaching Chart 156** passage with students. Ask students to use context clues to understand the meaning of the baseball terms.

Safe at Home

Jackie walked toward the batter's box. He was new to the Major Leagues, and he hoped he wouldn't make an **out**. Jackie felt sweaty and nervous. He took a deep breath. Then he stepped up to the **plate** and faced the **pitcher**.

The first pitch was too low. Jackie was disappointed. He didn't want a **walk**. He wanted a solid hit. He swung at the next pitch. Oh, no! It looked like a high **fly** ball. But Jackie ran as fast as he could anyway and made it to second base. When the next batter singled, Jackie was **safe** at home. He had scored a **run** for his team!

Teaching Chart 156

Model using context clues to find the meaning of one of the baseball terms in dark type.

MODEL Of course I know what a plate is. I eat from one several times every day. But I don't think Jackie stepped up to that kind of plate. That would be silly! As I reread the surrounding sentences, I see the words *batter's box* and *pitcher*. These clues help me understand the writer must mean *home plate*, the base where batters stand to hit pitches.

PRACTICE

Find Baseball Words with Special Meanings

PARTNERS

Ask volunteers to underline words in the passage that are clues to the special meaning of the words in dark type. Then have partners write descriptions of definitions for each word.

ASSESS/CLOSE

Draw Definitions

ONE

Have students choose one of the words in dark type and think of another non-baseball meaning for the same word. Then have them fold a sheet of paper in half and draw two pictures to show the different meanings of the word. Tell them to draw a small baseball beside the picture of the meaning the word has when it is used as a baseball term.

ALTERNATE TEACHING STRATEGY

CONTEXT CLUES

For a different approach to teaching this skill, see page T63.

Meeting Individual Needs for Vocabulary

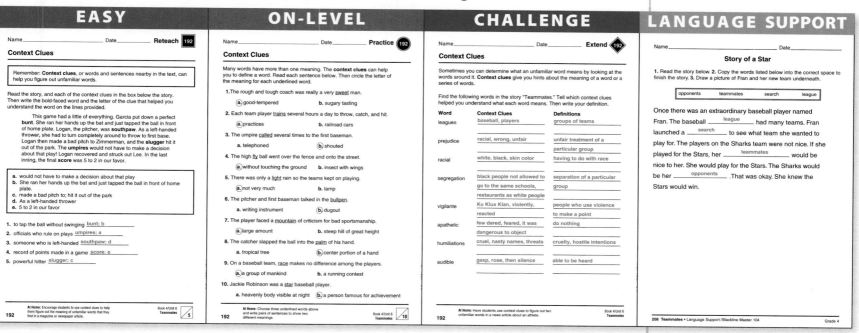

Reteach, 192   Practice, 192   Extend, 192   Language Support, 208

Writing That Compares

GRAMMAR/SPELLING CONNECTIONS

See the 5-Day Grammar and Usage Plan on adverbs, pages 631M–631N.

See the 5-Day Spelling Plan on words with silent letters, pages 6310–631P.

TECHNOLOGY TIP

Students working on computers can dress up their writing by trying out different type styles. Use a fancy font for the title. Choose a font that is easy to read for the text.

Prewrite

COMPARE SPORTS HEROES Present the following assignment: Jackie Robinson was an American sports hero. Write a paragraph comparing Jackie Robinson with another sports star. List three qualities the two sports heroes share. Show how they are heroes in at least two other ways.

EXPLORE THE TOPIC With the whole class, brainstorm a list of heroes in different sports. Have volunteers circle names of athletes that are heroes in several ways.

Strategy: Make a Character Traits Web
Give students two copies of the web.

- Have students write the name of one hero in the middle of each web.
- Then have them list four traits that are common to both characters and elaborate on each trait by giving an example of ways the character shows the trait

Draft

REHEARSE Suggest that students tell a partner about their ideas. Once they have formed an idea about what they will say, they can begin writing.

Revise

TAKE A BREAK If time allows, suggest that students put aside their work for a while before beginning to revise. Even a short break will help students see their writing with a more objective eye.

Have partners read each other's work and ask at least one question about it.

Edit/Proofread

CHECK FOR ERRORS Work with students to develop a proofreading checklist they can use as they check for grammar, punctuation, and spelling errors.

Publish

TAPE A RADIO SHOW Have students record their work. Make the tape available for all students in a listening area.

Jackie Robinson was a sports hero, and so is my sister. Jackie was the first African American to play baseball in the Major Leagues. Cindy was the first girl to make our junior high football team.

At first, fans and teammates gave both Jackie and Cindy a hard time. Like Jackie, my sister just kept quiet and worked hard. By the end of the season, both players were accepted.

My sister is my hero for other reasons, too. She is someone other girls who want to play sports can look up to. She spends her Saturdays teaching younger children to kick, pass, and run.

Presentation Ideas

MAKE A SPORTS POSTER Students can make sports posters that show both heroes playing their sport.

▶ **Viewing/Representing**

GIVE A NOMINATING SPEECH Have students nominate their hero for the Sports Hall of Fame, reading aloud their work to explain why their hero should be honored.

▶ **Speaking/Listening**

Two Great Heroes

Consider students' creative efforts, possibly adding a plus (+) for originality, wit, and imagination.

Scoring Rubric

Excellent	Good	Fair	Unsatisfactory
4: The writer	**3:** The writer	**2:** The writer	**1:** The writer
• begins with a sentence that compares two sports heroes.	• names both heroes early in the paragraph.	• does not begin with a clear topic sentence.	• tells about the hero, but fails to compare the hero to Jackie Robinson.
• includes a clear comparison of four traits the heroes share.	• lists three ways the heroes are alike.	• lists character traits but does not make a clear comparison.	• lists fewer than three character traits.
• clearly explains why the person is a hero.	• tells at least one thing the hero does besides play sports.	• tells one reason the person is a hero.	

0: The writer leaves the page blank or fails to respond to the writing task. The student does not address the topic or simply paraphrases the prompt. The response is illegible or incoherent.

For a 6-point or an 8-point scale, see pages T105–T106.

Meeting Individual Needs for Writing

EASY	ON-LEVEL	CHALLENGE
Sports Card Have students make a sports card that shows their hero and explain orally how the hero is like Jackie Robinson.	**Dream Team** Let students work together to make up a "dream team" of their favorite sports heroes, telling things that all the heroes have in common.	**Dialogue** Invite students to imagine that their hero is meeting Jackie Robinson and telling Robinson how he or she tries to be like him.

5 Day Grammar and Usage Plan

LANGUAGE SUPPORT

ESL Write adverbs such as *slowly*, *softly*, *quickly*, and *angrily* on cards. Have English learners choose one, act out the word, and write the adverb on the board after it has been guessed.

DAILY LANGUAGE ACTIVITIES

Write each day's activity on the board or use **Transparency 26.** Have students orally complete the sentences, using adverbs. Answers may vary.

Day 1
1. The two friends talked _____. (how?)
2. The runner moved _____. (how?)
3. The crowd shouted _____. (how?)

Day 2
1. We're going to a game _____. (when?)
2. The batter swung _____. (how?)
3. The catcher looked _____. (where?)

Day 3
1. Players arrived _____. (when?)
2. A hot dog stand is _____. (where?)
3. Robinson batted _____. (how?)

Day 4
1. The pitcher threw the ball _____. (how?)
2. Teams travel _____. (where?)
3. Pee Wee fielded _____. (how?)

Day 5
1. My team bats _____. (when?)
2. We hope to play _____. (where?)
3. Our team wears our uniforms _____. (how?)

Daily Language Transparency 26

DAY 1 — Introduce the Concept

Oral Warm-Up Have students suggest words that describe the way some people play sports, such as *well, badly, carelessly, professionally,* or *sloppily*.

Introduce Adverbs That Tell How Adverbs add details to a sentence.

Adverbs That Tell How

- An **adverb** is a word that tells more about a verb.
- Some adverbs tell *how* an action takes place.
- Most adverbs that tell *how* end in *-ly*. They are formed by adding *-ly* to an adjective.

Present the Daily Language Activity. Then have students write this sentence three times: *The man walked _____ to the dugout*, using different adverbs to complete it each time.

WRITING Assign the daily Writing Prompt on page 614C.

Name_____ Date_____ **LEARN Grammar 161**

Adverbs That Tell How

- An **adverb** is a word that tells more about a verb.
- Some adverbs tell how an action takes place.
- Most adverbs that tell how end in *-ly*. They are formed by adding *-ly* to an adjective.

A. Underline the adverb in each sentence.

1. In the 1940s, few Americans <u>openly</u> opposed racial segregation.
2. People were <u>generally</u> willing to let things stay as they were.
3. Many people believed that everyone should be treated <u>equally</u>.
4. They might have acted on their belief without stating it <u>publicly</u>.
5. There were groups that reacted <u>violently</u> to the idea of equality.

B. Add *-ly* to the bold faced word before each sentence to form an adverb that completes the sentence.

6. **significant** Branch Rickey changed baseball <u>significantly</u>.
7. **strong** He felt <u>strongly</u> that his team should have the best players, regardless of color.
8. **careful** He looked <u>carefully</u> for just the right player.
9. **exact** He found <u>exactly</u> the man he was looking for in Jackie Robinson.
10. **successful** He believed Jackie would <u>successfully</u> break the color barrier.

Grade 4/Unit 6 Teammates | EXTENSION: Ask students to write three sentences that include *-ly* adverbs. | 161

GRAMMAR PRACTICE BOOK, PAGE 161

DAY 2 — Teach the Concept

Review Common and Proper Nouns Ask volunteers to explain why adverbs can make their writing more interesting.

Introduce When and Where Adverbs Many adverbs end in *-ly*, however not all of them do. Present the following:

Adverbs That Tell When and Where

- Some adverbs tell *when* or *where* an action takes place.
- Adverbs that tell *when* include *first, always, next, after, tomorrow, soon, early, today, then, yesterday*.
- Adverbs that tell *where* include *there, outside, up, here, nearby, ahead, around, far, away, everywhere*.

Present the Daily Language Activity. Then have partners write five sentences with adverbs.

WRITING Assign the daily Writing Prompt on page 614C.

Name_____ Date_____ **LEARN & PRACTICE Grammar 162**

Adverbs That Tell When or Where

- Some **adverbs** tell *when* or *where* an action takes place.
- Adverbs that tell when include *first, always, next, after, tomorrow, soon, early, today, then, yesterday*.
- Adverbs that tell where include *there, outside, up, here, nearby, ahead, around, far, away, everywhere*.

A. Rewrite each sentence by adding an adverb that tells *when*, and then underline the adverb you include. Students' answers may vary.

1. Jackie Robinson played with the Dodgers' farm team, the Montreal Royals.
   Jackie Robinson <u>first</u> played with the Dodgers' farm team, the Montreal Royals.
2. He was moved up to play with the Brooklyn Dodgers.
   He was <u>then</u> moved up to play with the Brooklyn Dodgers.
3. No matter with happened, Jackie Robinson remained calm.
   No matter with happened <u>after</u>, Jackie Robinson remained calm.
4. He earned the respect of his fellow players.
   He <u>soon</u> earned the respect of his fellow players.

B. Rewrite each sentence by adding an adverb that tells *where*, and then underline the adverb you include. Students' answers may vary.

5. Negro League teams traveled in their own cars and buses.
   Negro League teams traveled <u>everywhere</u> in their own cars and buses.
6. Their fans were loyal and would travel to see a game.
   Their fans were loyal and would travel <u>around</u> to see a game.
7. Hotels would tell them they couldn't stay.
   Hotels would tell them they couldn't stay <u>there</u>.
8. At restaurants they would hear, "You can't eat."
   At restaurants they would hear, "You can't eat <u>here</u>."

162 | Extension: Ask students to identify and write three sentences from the selection that include adverbs. Have them decide if each adverb tells how, when, or where. | Grade 4/Unit 6 Teammates

GRAMMAR PRACTICE BOOK, PAGE 162

Adverbs

Learn from the Literature Review adjectives. Then read the second to last sentence in paragraph 2 on page 626 of *Teammates*.

> **Pee Wee smiled broadly as he reached Jackie.**

Ask students to identify the adverb and tell whether it answers the question *how, when,* or *where.*

Write a Journal Entry Present the Daily Language Activity. Then have students imagine that they were in the stands at the Cincinnati game from the story and write a journal entry about what happened. Suggest that they use adverbs to describe the scene in a way that will help them clearly remember the events.

 Assign the daily Writing Prompt on page 614D.

Review Adverbs Write *How?, When?,* and *Where?* on the board, and read the corrected sentences from the Daily Language Activities for Days 1–3. Have volunteers tell you in which column to list each adverb. Then present the Daily Language Activity for Day 4.

Mechanics and Usage Explain how to use *good* and *well.* Present:

> ### Using *Good* and *Well*
>
> • *Good* is an adjective and is used to describe nouns.
>
> • *Well* is an adverb that tells *how* about a verb.
>
> • Do not confuse the adjective *good* with the adverb *well.*

Present the following examples:
Jackie was a good player.
Pee Wee worked well with his team.

 Assign the daily Writing Prompt on page 614D.

Assess Use the Daily Language Activity and page 165 of the **Grammar Practice Book** for assessment.

Reteach Have students draw a picture of an action, and then write a caption using an adverb. (Example: *The dog ran quickly.*) Next use three large pieces of posterboard to create a chart. Label each column *How? When?* or *Where?* As a group, decide where to post each drawing on the chart, based on the adverbs contained in the captions.

Have students work together to make a word wall with adverbs.

Use page 166 of the **Grammar Practice Book** for additional reteaching.

 Assign the daily Writing Prompt on page 614D.

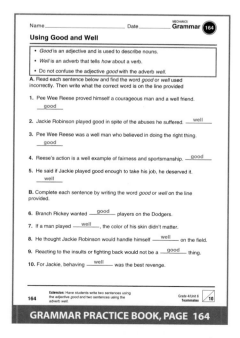

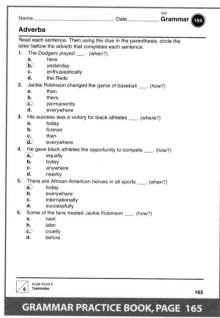

5 Day Spelling Plan

ESL Students who speak phonetic languages such as Spanish may be unfamiliar with the concept of silent letters. Help them make a visual connection by having them copy the Spelling Words and write the silent letter in another color.

DICTATION SENTENCES

Spelling Words

1. She <u>knew</u> him at her old school.
2. Don't <u>climb</u> too high up in the tree.
3. It was <u>calm</u> before the storm.
4. <u>Although</u> he is just six, he looks older.
5. The <u>knight</u> rode away on his white horse.
6. The <u>writer</u> knows how to tell a good story.
7. The <u>knob</u> on the door is broken.
8. His legs were <u>numb</u> after standing all day.
9. The baby laughed with <u>delight</u>.
10. The little <u>wren</u> has a pretty song.
11. You can <u>knead</u> the clay to make it soft.
12. The <u>plumber</u> cleaned up the spill.
13. Write the words with yellow <u>chalk</u>.
14. Have you ever been awake at <u>midnight</u>?
15. The room was a <u>wreck</u> after the party.
16. Corn grows on a long green <u>stalk</u>.
17. He had to <u>kneel</u> to look under the sofa.
18. She <u>sought</u> help from her father.
19. He made a <u>thorough</u> search for the missing toy.
20. The baby tigers like to <u>wrestle</u> together.

Challenge Words

21. The teacher <u>circulated</u> around the class-room.
22. The player made an <u>extraordinary</u> catch.
23. They <u>launched</u> their new boat in the water.
24. Our <u>opponents</u> won the game.
25. He belongs to four <u>organizations</u>.

DAY 1 — Pretest

Assess Prior Knowledge Use the Dictation Sentences at the left and **Spelling Practice Book** page 161 for the pretest. Allow students to correct their own papers. Students who require a modified list may be tested on the first ten words.

	Spelling Words		Challenge Words
1.	**knew**	11. knead	21. **circu-lated**
2.	climb	12. plumber	22. **extraor-dinary**
3.	calm	13. chalk	23. **launched**
4.	although	14. midnight	24. **oppo-nents**
5.	knight	15. wreck	25. **organiza-tions**
6.	writer	16. stalk	
7.	knob	17. kneel	
8.	numb	18. **sought**	
9.	delight	19. thorough	
10.	wren	20. wrestle	

*Note: Words in **dark type** are from the story.*

Word Study On page 162 of the **Spelling Practice Book** are word study steps and an at-home activity.

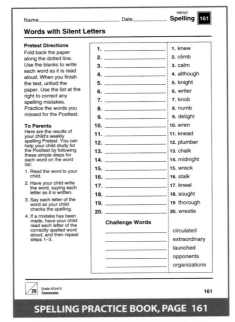

SPELLING PRACTICE BOOK, PAGE 161

WORD STUDY STEPS AND ACTIVITY, PAGE 162

DAY 2 — Explore the Pattern

Sort and Spell Words Say *numb*. Ask students to identify the letters they hear. Write *numb* on the board and have a volunteer circle the silent letter. Then have students read the Spelling Words aloud and sort them as below.

Words with silent letters

k	b	l
knew	climb	calm
knight	numb	chalk
knob	plumber	stalk
knead		
kneel		

gh	w
although	writer
delight	wren
midnight	wreck
sought	wrestle
thorough	

Word Wall Have students create a word wall based on the word sort and add more words from their reading.

Words with Silent Letters

Pattern Power!
Write the spelling words with these spelling patterns.

words with silent k		words with silent gh
1. knew	12.	although
2. knight	13.	delight
3. knob	14.	midnight
4. knead	15.	sought
5. kneel	16.	thorough

words with silent b		words with silent wr
6. climb	17.	writer
7. numb	18.	wren
8. plumber	19.	wreck
	20.	wrestle

words with silent l		
9. calm		
10. chalk		
11. stalk		

SPELLING PRACTICE BOOK, PAGE 163

Words with Silent Letters

Word Meaning: Synonyms Remind students that a synonym is a word that means almost the same thing as another word. Ask students to think of synonyms for as many spelling words as they can. (Examples: *calm/peaceful, delight/ happiness*)

If students need extra practice, have partners give each other a midweek test.

Glossary Ask a volunteer to locate and read the illustrative sentence for *circulated*. Remind students that these sentences show how a word is used. Have students:

- write each Challenge Word.

- look up the Challenge Words in the Glossary and read the illustrative sentences.

- write a new illustrative sentence for each Challenge Word.

Proofread Sentences Write these sentences on the chalkboard, including the misspelled words. Ask students to proofread, circling incorrect spellings and writing the correct spellings. There are two spelling errors in each sentence.

The ⃝nite ⃝climed onto the horse.
(knight, climbed)

The baker's hand grew ⃝num from ⃝neading so much bread.
(numb, kneading)

Have students create additional sentences with errors for partners to correct.

 Have students use as many Spelling Words as possible in the daily Writing Prompt on page 614D. Remind students to proofread their writing for errors in spelling, grammar, and punctuation.

Assess Students' Knowledge Use page 166 of the **Spelling Practice Book** or the Dictation Sentences on page 631O for the posttest.

Personal Word List If students have trouble with any words in the lesson, have them add the words to their personal word lists in their journals. Suggest that students say each letter as they write the words and then underline the silent letters.

Students should refer to their word lists during later writing activities.

SPELLING PRACTICE BOOK, PAGE 164

SPELLING PRACTICE BOOK, PAGE 165

SPELLING PRACTICE BOOK, PAGE 166

The Malachite Palace

Selection Summary Students will read a fairy tale about a princess who must make a decision about the importance of having friends.

Student Listening Library Audiocassette

INSTRUCTIONAL
Pages 634–663

About the Author Alma Flor Ada has written dozens of books for children. She transmitted her passion for writing to her daughter, with whom she collaborated on several books, often working together in both Spanish and English.

About the Illustrator Leonid Gore illustrated over fifty children's books in his homeland of Russia before moving to the United States. His style is the perfect complement to the fairy-tale genre of *The Malachite Palace.*

Resources for
Meeting Individual Needs

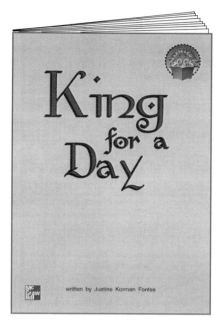

EASY
Pages 663A, 663D

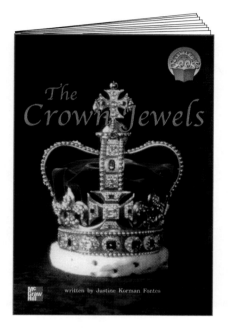

INDEPENDENT
Pages 663B, 663D

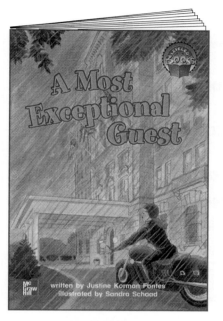

CHALLENGE
Pages 663C, 663D

LEVELED PRACTICE

Reteach, 193–199
blackline masters with reteaching opportunities for each assessed skill

Practice, 193–199
workbook with Take-Home stories and practice opportunities for each assessed skill and story comprehension

Extend, 193–199
blackline masters that offer challenge activities for each assessed skill

ADDITIONAL RESOURCES

- **Language Support Book,** 209–216
- **Take-Home Story, Practice,** p. 194a
- **Alternative Teaching Strategies,** T60–T66

McGraw-Hill School
TECHNOLOGY

interNET CONNECTION Research and Inquiry Ideas. Visit **www.mhschool.com/reading**

Suggested Lesson Planner

 Available on CD-ROM

READING AND LANGUAGE ARTS

 DAY 1 *Focus on Reading and Skills*

DAY 2 *Read the Literature*

- ● **Comprehension**
- ● **Vocabulary**
- ● **Phonics/Decoding**
- ● **Study Skills**
- ● **Listening, Speaking, Viewing, Representing**

Day 1

 Read Aloud and Motivate, 632E
Windows of Gold

Develop Visual Literacy, 632/633

☑ **Review Problem and Solution,** 634A–634B
  Teaching Chart 157
  Reteach, Practice, Extend, 193

Day 2

Build Background, 634C
Develop Oral Language

Vocabulary, 634D

cultured	*fragrance*	*resembled*
feeble	*mingled*	*scampered*

  Teaching Chart 158
  Vocabulary Cards
  Reteach, Practice, Extend, 194

Read the Selection, 634–659
  ☑ Problem and Solution
  ☑ Make Judgments and Decisions

Minilessons, 643, 645, 651, 657

Cultural Perspectives, 648

- ● **Curriculum Connections**

 Link Works of Art, 632/633

 Link Social Studies, 634C

- ● **Writing**

 Writing Prompt: Compare three ways you could make a new friend.

 Writing Prompt: Compare how two different birds look, act, and sound.

Journal Writing, 659
Quick-Write

- ● **Grammar**

Introduce the Concept: Adverbs That Compare, 663M
  Daily Language Activity
  1. This bird sings loud than all of them. loudest
  2. The princess caught the bird fast than the governess. faster
  3. The queen lived in the palace long than the princess. longer

Grammar Practice Book, 167

Teach the Concept: Adverbs That Compare, 663M
  Daily Language Activity
  1. The bird sang sweetly than before. more sweetly
  2. These windows are closed more tight than those. tightly
  3. Of all the ladies, the queen acted the more imperiously. most

Grammar Practice Book, 168

- ● **Spelling**

Pretest: Homophones and Homographs, 663O
Spelling Practice Book, 167, 168

Explore the Pattern: Homophones and Homographs, 663O
Spelling Practice Book, 169

 = **Skill Assessed in Unit Test**

DAY 3 — *Read the Literature*

Rereading for Fluency, 658

Story Questions, 660
Reteach, Practice, Extend, 195

Story Activities, 661

Study Skill, 662

☑ Library/Media Center
Teaching Chart 159
Reteach, Practice, Extend, 196

Test Power, 663

 Read the Leveled Books, 663A–663D
Guided Reading
/s/ and /f/
☑ Problem and Solution
☑ Instructional Vocabulary

 Activity Science, 636

✏ **Writing Prompt:** Compare how living in a palace would be different or similar to the way you live now.

Writing Process: Write a Comparison, 663K
Prewrite, Draft

Review and Practice: Adverbs That Compare, 663N
Daily Language Activity
1. I can climb high than the gates. higher
2. The princess listened to the children more sadlier than before. sadly

Grammar Practice Book, 169

Practice and Extend: Homophones and Homographs, 663P
Spelling Practice Book, 170

DAY 4 — *Build Skills*

 Read the Leveled Books and Self-Selected Books

☑ **Review Problem and Solution,** 663E–663F
Teaching Chart 160
Reteach, Practice, Extend, 197
Language Support, 214

☑ **Review Cause and Effect,** 663G–663H
Teaching Chart 161
Reteach, Practice, Extend, 198
Language Support, 215

 Activity Social Studies, 638

 Writing Prompt: Write about three special talents you have. Explain which are most and least important to you.

Writing Process: Write a Comparison, 663K
Revise

Meeting Individual Needs for Writing, 663L

Review and Practice: Adverbs That Compare, 663N
Daily Language Activity
1. The birdcage shone bright of all. brightest
2. The princess held the tools clumsily than a carpenter. more clumsily

Grammar Practice Book, 170

Proofread and Write: Homophones and Homographs, 663P
Spelling Practice Book, 171

DAY 5 — *Build Skills*

 Read Self-Selected Books

Vocabulary Strategy

☑ **Antonyms and Synonyms,** 663I–663J
Teaching Chart 162
Reteach, Practice, Extend, 199
Language Support, 216

Listening, Speaking, Viewing, Representing, 663L
Make a Poster
Listen Critically

Minilessons, 643, 651, 657

Phonics Review
/s/ and /f/, 645

Phonics Workbook

 Activity Math, 654

✏ **Writing Prompt:** Tell how you might try to help a friend who is lonely.

Writing Process: Write a Comparison, 663K
Edit/Proofread, Publish

Assess and Reteach: Adverbs That Compare, 663N
Daily Language Activity
1. The princess ran more fast to meet the other children. faster
2. This is the more frequently read story of all. most

Grammar Practice Book, 171, 172

Assess and Reteach: Homophones and Homographs, 663P
Spelling Practice Book, 172

Link

Language Arts

Read Aloud and Motivate

Windows of Gold

retold by Selma G. Lanes

Once upon a time at the bottom of a high hill, there lived a widow and her small son Harry. They were poor as church mice, but the mother did fine sewing and, in this way, earned money enough to keep a cottage roof over their heads and simple food on their table.

Whenever the sun shone, Harry played outside the cottage, while his mother worked at her sewing indoors. Though he had no toys, still Harry managed with sticks and stones to amuse himself quite well.

Best of all, Harry liked to gaze up to the top of the high hill.

There he saw a cottage much like his own. It had just one difference: the cottage at the top of the hill had windows all made of gold! How they gleamed in the mid-morning sunlight, and how Harry wished that he and his mother might live in such a grand place themselves.

One bright and cloudless day, when Harry and his mother were just finishing their lunch of bread and milk, the boy had an idea.

Continued on pages T2–T5

Oral Comprehension

LISTENING AND SPEAKING Motivate students to begin thinking about problems and solutions by reading this story aloud. First, have students listen as you read the story. When you have finished, ask, "What is the interesting problem in the story?" (Harry wishes he could live in a cottage with windows of gold.) Then ask, "How is the problem solved?" (Harry sees his cottage from another perspective and realizes he does live in a cottage with windows of gold.)

Activity Assign roles for the parts of Harry, his mother, and Sally. Ask these students to mime the actions of the story as you read it aloud again. Then have the actors describe what it felt like to be members of royalty for a few moments. ▶ **Kinesthetic/Visual/Spatial**

Develop Visual Literacy

Anthology pages 632–633

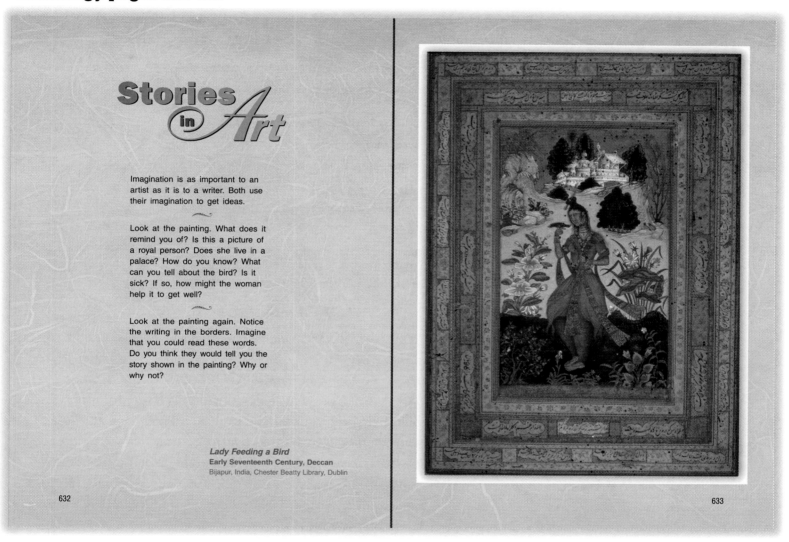

Stories in Art

Imagination is as important to an artist as it is to a writer. Both use their imagination to get ideas.

Look at the painting. What does it remind you of? Is this a picture of a royal person? Does she live in a palace? How do you know? What can you tell about the bird? Is it sick? If so, how might the woman help it to get well?

Look at the painting again. Notice the writing in the borders. Imagine that you could read these words. Do you think they would tell you the story shown in the painting? Why or why not?

Lady Feeding a Bird
Early Seventeenth Century, Deccan
Bijapur, India, Chester Beatty Library, Dublin

632

633

Objective: Identify Problem and Solution

VIEWING In this seventeenth century painting, the Indian artist has captured an idyllic scene between a lady and a bird. Have students compare this work with other older paintings they have seen, focusing on elements such as the two-dimensional quality of the figures and the landscape, the brilliant colors, and the decorative border.

Read the page with students, encouraging individual interpretations of the painting as they discuss their answers to these questions:

• What problem is suggested by the details of this painting?

• Can you think of ways that the lady might solve the problem?

REPRESENTING Have students write an imaginative translation of the text around the border of the painting. Encourage them to pose a problem and to solve it in the last lines.

OBJECTIVES

Students will identify problems and solutions.

TEACHING TIP

INSTRUCTIONAL Explain that in many stories the solution to one problem may create additional problems. Suggest to students that they watch for this type of chain as they look for problems and solutions.

Review Problem and Solution

PREPARE

Discuss Familiar Story Problems Have students think of a familiar character from a folktale such as *Hansel and Gretel*. Ask: What problem does this character face?

TEACH

Define Problem and Solution Tell students: In most stories, the main character wants something; this is the story problem. The actions of the plot show what happens as the character tries to solve this problem.

The Prince and the Tin Whistle

Once there was a prince (who was always bored.) He had so many toys that he didn't know which one to play with first, so he didn't bother with any of them. <u>One day he found a small tin whistle. By moving his fingers along it, he could play pretty tunes.</u> The prince had never heard music before and was enchanted by it. <u>Day after day, he made up new songs.</u> His mother the Queen said, "<u>You no longer seem bored.</u>" Her son answered, "How could anyone be bored with a whistle? I wish there were more hours in the day to play my music."

Teaching Chart 157

Read the Passage and Model the Skill Display **Teaching Chart 157.** Have students notice details that relate to the problem and solution in the passage.

MODEL The first sentence shows that the prince was always bored. I know many children complain about being bored, so I think that is the prince's problem. He finds that playing music keeps him from being bored, so he solves his problem.

Identify a Problem and Solution Have student volunteers circle the problem, and underline sentences that suggest the solution.

PRACTICE

Create a Problem and Solution Chart

Have students use a Problem and Solution chart to record information from the passage. Model how to fill it out and call on volunteers to complete the chart. ▶ **Logical/Visual**

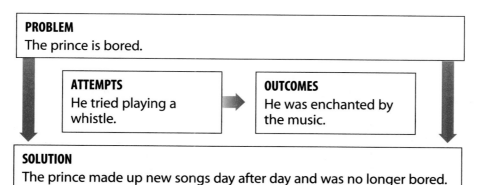

PROBLEM
The prince is bored.

ATTEMPTS
He tried playing a whistle.

OUTCOMES
He was enchanted by the music.

SOLUTION
The prince made up new songs day after day and was no longer bored.

ASSESS/CLOSE

Recognize Problem and Solution

Ask students what was different after the prince solved his problem.
(He was no longer bored.)

SELECTION Connection

Students will identify problems and solutions when they read *The Malachite Palace* and the Leveled Books.

ALTERNATE TEACHING STRATEGY

PROBLEM AND SOLUTION

For a different approach to teaching this skill, see page T64.

Meeting Individual Needs for Comprehension

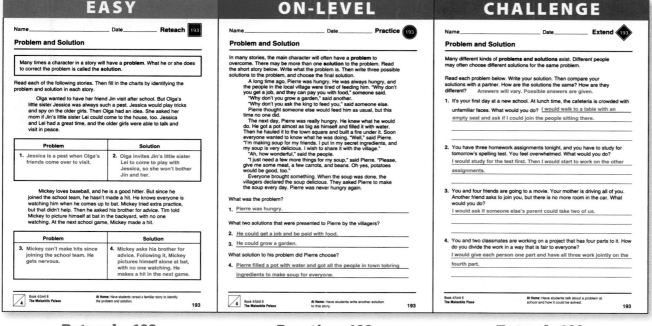

Reteach, 193   Practice, 193   Extend, 193

634B

Build Background

Social Studies

Anthology and Leveled Books

Evaluate Prior Knowledge

CONCEPT: ROYAL FAMILIES Royal families are the relatives of a monarch, usually a king or a queen. A monarch is a ruler of a country and the role of leader is inherited by his or her child, or another relative.

ROYAL CHILDREN Have students compare ways in which the child of a royal family is similar to or different from a child in an ordinary family. Create a Venn diagram.

▶ **Logical/Visual**

ROYAL CHILD		ORDINARY CHILD
Different	Alike	Different
has servants to perform chores	likes to play with friends	does own chores

Graphic Organizer 14

MAKE A SCHEDULE Have students
  imagine that they work for
WRITING **PARTNERS** the child of a royal family.
Their job is to plan a list of daily activities for a prince or princess. Partners can share their list with others.

Develop Oral Language

DISCUSS A PRINCESS'S DAY Ask

ESL students what kinds of things a prince or princess might do every day for entertainment. Remind students of movies they may have seen or fairy tales and cartoon strips they may have read that included characters who were members of a royal family. Also use photographs of real people, adding labels to show their titles, such as Queen, Princess, Lady-in-Waiting.

Have students role-play meeting a prince or princess. They can use some of the labels that are displayed as they have a conversation.

TEACHING TIP

MANAGEMENT To help keep students who are working independently focused on the task, give them checkpoints, such as a time of day by which they are expected to complete certain chunks of an assignment.

LANGUAGE SUPPORT

See the **Language Support Book**, pages 209–212, for teaching suggestions for Build Background and Vocabulary.

Vocabulary

Key Words

1. Once an old king had a cold and was feeling <u>weak</u> and feeble. 2. He lay in his bed, which resembled a <u>jewel box covered with fine gems</u>. 3. The king, whose voice was normally cultured and elegant, spoke in a <u>hoarse, cranky whisper</u>. "I want to feel better," he said.
4. The <u>scents of meats and vegetables</u> mingled in the air as the cook prepared a special soup for the king.
5. The fragrance <u>floated</u> up to the king's room.
6. He took a deep breath, jumped from his bed, and scampered <u>quickly</u> to the kitchen to taste the soup.

Teaching Chart 158

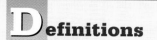

Definitions

feeble (p. 644) not strong, weak

resembled (p. 652) was alike or similar to something

cultured (p. 642) having good taste and an appreciation of the arts

mingled (p. 659) came together, mixed, or joined

fragrance (p. 644) a sweet or pleasing smell

scampered (p. 638) ran or moved quickly

SPELLING/VOCABULARY CONNECTIONS

See Spelling Challenge Words, pages 6630–663P.

Vocabulary in Context

IDENTIFY VOCABULARY WORDS
Display **Teaching Chart 158** and read it with students. Have students circle each vocabulary word and underline other words that provide clues to its meaning.

DISCUSS MEANINGS Use questions like the following to help clarify word meanings:

- When might your voice sound feeble?
- If you resembled your mother more than your father, how would you look?
- How does a cultured person behave?
- Have you ever mingled at a party?
- What is your favorite fragrance, hot apple pie or roses?
- If you scampered home, would you get there quickly or slowly?

Practice

PLAY CONCENTRATION Give pairs of students matching sets of vocabulary cards to mix up and lay face down. Have students challenge each other to find a specific word pair by giving a clue to the word.

▶ **Kinesthetic/Interpersonal**

Vocabulary Cards

WRITE AN AD Students can work with partners to use as many of the key words as possible to write an ad.

WRITING

▶ **Linguistic/Interpersonal**

ON-LEVEL

Andrew's Father

Everyone said Andrew's father was the most *cultured* man in town. He was a gentleman. Andrew's father had studied hard as a boy. He knew about music and paintings. He had read many books.
Andrew's father had something else he was known for. It was his beautiful flower garden. People could enjoyed the *fragrance* of his flowers as their scents *mingled* in the air. People brought their dying and *feeble* plants to Andrew's father. He told the people what to do. Soon the plants were strong again. As a small boy, Andrew *scampered* in and out of the garden as his father weeded and planted. Now that he was older, Andrew worked alongside his father, learning everything he could. When Andrew grew up, people remarked about how much he *resembled* his father. That made Andrew feel proud.

1. What makes a person *cultured*?
   Answers will vary, but may include that they are educated; that they enjoy the arts; or that they have manners.

2. What were the two things Andrew's father was known for?
   Possible answers: being cultured; growing a beautiful flower garden; bringing feeble plants back to help.

3. How did the *fragrance* of the flower garden affect people?
   The fragrance of the flowers mingled in the air and people enjoyed it.

4. What kinds of plants did people bring to Andrew's father?
   feeble and dying plants

5. How do you think Andrew felt about his father?
   Answers will vary, but may include that he felt pride and admiration.

Book4/Unit 6   At Home: Have students write a description of
The Malachite Palace   someone the consider to be cultured.   194a

Take-Home Story 194a
Reteach 194
Practice 194 • Extend 194

Guided Instruction

Preview and Predict

Have students read the title and preview the illustrations for clues to the story problem and solution.

- Who do you think is the main character?
- What kind of problem do you think the main character has?
- Do you think that the main character's problem will be solved?
- What kind of story do you predict this will be? How can you decide? (Sample answer: A fairy tale is about a royal family and takes place in a palace) *Genre*

Have students record their predictions about the story problem and solution.

PREDICTIONS	WHAT HAPPENED
I predict the story is about a princess whose bird won't sing.	

Set Purposes

What do students want to learn as they read the story? For example:

- What happens to the bird?
- How do the grown-ups in the palace act toward the princess?

Meet Alma Flor Ada

By the time she was in fourth grade, Alma Flor Ada knew that she would be a writer someday. She says, "I couldn't accept the fact that we had to read such boring textbooks while my wonderful storybooks awaited at home." As a result, she decided to devote her life to making schoolbooks that would be fun. "Since then," she says, she has been "having a lot fun doing just that!"

Ada was born in Cuba, but she has also lived in Spain and Peru. Today, she makes her home in San Francisco, California. She admits that her four children inspire her writing. They help in other ways, too. One of her greatest joys is that her daughter has translated many of her books, some into English and some into Spanish. For Ada, knowing two languages has made her world richer. She is happy that it has also enriched her daughter's life. In fact, Ada believes that all students should be given the chance to learn two or more languages.

Meet Leonid Gore

Leonid Gore is proud of his illustrations in *The Malachite Palace.* Although the work was a challenge, it wasn't much different from the work he had done on more than fifty children's books in his native country. Born and raised in the former Soviet Union, Gore moved to the United States in 1990. Over the years, he has developed a light and delicate style of painting. This style is perfect for the fairy-tale feeling in *The Malachite Palace.*

634

Meeting Individual Needs • Grouping Suggestions for Strategic Reading

EASY

Read Together Read the story with students or have them use the **Listening Library Audiocassette.** Have students use the Problem and Solution chart to record details about the main character's problem. Guided Instruction and Intervention prompts offer additional help with decoding, vocabulary, and comprehension.

ON-LEVEL

Guided Reading Preview the Story Words listed on page 635. You may want to have the students first read the story on their own. Then select from the Guided Instruction questions as you read the story with students or after they have played the **Listening Library Audiocassette.** Have students use the Problem and Solution chart.

CHALLENGE

Read Independently Have students begin a Problem and Solution chart as on page 635. Then have them read independently. After reading, students can use their chart to review the story events and summarize the problem and solution.

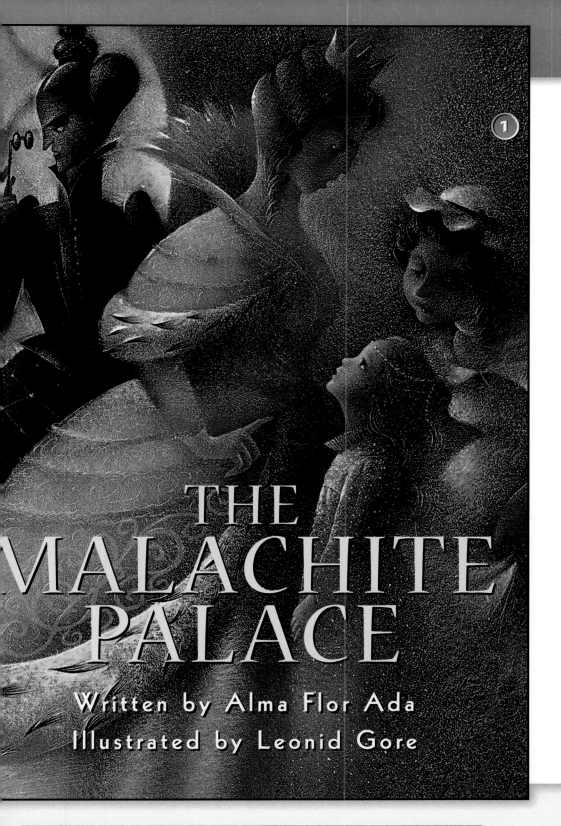

THE MALACHITE PALACE

Written by Alma Flor Ada

Illustrated by Leonid Gore

Guided Instruction

☑ **Problem and Solution**

☑ **Judgments and Decisions**

STRATEGIC READING Looking for details about the main problem and solution in a story helps you understand its plot. Let's prepare Problem and Solution charts so that we can follow the main character as she tries to solve her problem.

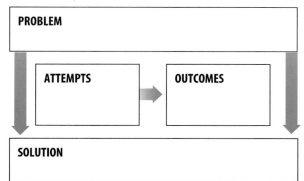

PROBLEM

ATTEMPTS → OUTCOMES

SOLUTION

1 **PROBLEM AND SOLUTION** Do you think the child in this picture usually gets to do as she pleases? (Sample answer: No; the adults don't look very pleasant.)

Story Words

The words below may be unfamiliar. Have students check their meanings and pronunciations in the Glossary beginning on page 726.

- malachite, p. 636
- governess, p. 637
- ignorant, p. 637
- gild, p. 643

LANGUAGE SUPPORT

A blackline master of the Problem and Solution chart is available in the **Language Support Book.**

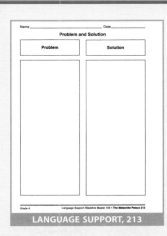

Name_____ Date_____
Problem and Solution

Problem	Solution

Grade 4   Language Support /Blackline Master 105 • The Malachite Palace 213

LANGUAGE SUPPORT, 213

635

Guided Instruction

② **PROBLEM AND SOLUTION** What is the princess's problem?

MODEL In trying to identify the problem, I look for something that the main character wants to change. The story says that the princess had everything she wanted except for a friend, so that must be the problem.

Let's fill this information in on our chart.

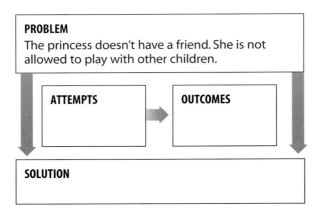

PROBLEM
The princess doesn't have a friend. She is not allowed to play with other children.

ATTEMPTS	→	OUTCOMES

SOLUTION

T here once was a princess who lived in a malachite palace. She had everything she could possibly want. **②** Everything, that is, except for a friend.

636

Activity

Cross Curricular: Science

MALACHITE Malachite is a semi-precious mineral, most often silky and greenish in appearance. It is usually found in copper deposits.

RESEARCH AND INQUIRY Have students work in small groups to choose different minerals to research and report on to the class. They can try to identify details such as the mineral's appearance, structure, color, hardness, and source.
▶ **Logical/Linguistic**

*inter***NET** **CONNECTION** Students can learn more about minerals by visiting *www.mhschool.com/reading*

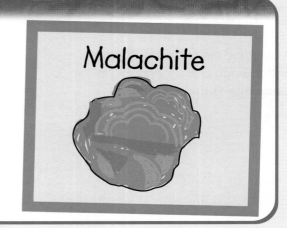

Malachite

On the other side of ornate iron gates, many children laughed and played in the fields beyond the palace. But neither the lady-in-waiting, all dressed in white, nor the governess, all dressed in black—and much less the queen, all dressed in gold—would have thought, even for a moment, that the princess could be allowed to play with the other children.

"Those children are rude!"

"Those children are ignorant!"

"Those children are common!" they would say, as if in a chorus.

637

(3) **Why isn't the princess allowed to play with the other children?** (The adults think that the other children are too common to play with the princess.)

Who would like to read the lines of the lady-in-waiting, the governess, and the queen? Let's hear you say your lines all together, like a chorus. *Cause and Effect/Role-Play*

Guided Instruction

(4) **JUDGMENTS AND DECISIONS**
Why do you think the princess keeps the windows closed? Explain your thinking.

MODEL When I make judgments and decisions about what I read, I use the information in the story as well as what I know from my own experience. If I were the princess, I might feel sad and lonely if I heard other children playing without me, so I think the princess might have closed the windows to avoid feeling sad.

And so the princess always kept the windows of her room in the malachite palace **(4)** tightly closed so that the voices of the children playing in the open fields would not reach her. Perhaps she had come to believe what her elders said about those children; or perhaps she just didn't want to be reminded of how happy the children sounded as they **(5)** scampered about.

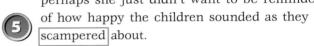

638

Activity

Cross Curricular: Social Studies

PALACES Explain to students that a palace is a large, grand building where a ruler lives. Have them use encyclopedias, magazines, or the Internet to find out about palaces around the world—for example, Buckingham Palace and the Palace of Versailles—and their uses today.

Students can work in small groups to make illustrations or models of an imaginary palace they might like to live in.

▶ **Spatial/Interpersonal**

639

Guided
Instruction

⑤ PROBLEM AND SOLUTION Do you think shutting the windows helped to solve the princess's problem? (Sample answer: No, she still does not have a friend. However, it may help keep the princess from thinking about how lonely she is.)

Guided Instruction

 6 Why do you think the princess wants to catch the bird? (She probably wants something to keep her from being lonely.)
Make Inferences

One windy morning in early spring, the princess heard a *tap, tap, tap* at her window. She looked and saw a cherry branch, heavy with blossoms. When she opened the window to reach the flowers, a little bird flew into the room.

 It was a tiny yellow bird, with bright black eyes. And when he opened his beak to sing, a light and joyful music filled the palace.

"Quickly, quickly!" cried the princess as she closed the window. "Come catch him, come catch him!"

640

640 *The Malachite Palace*

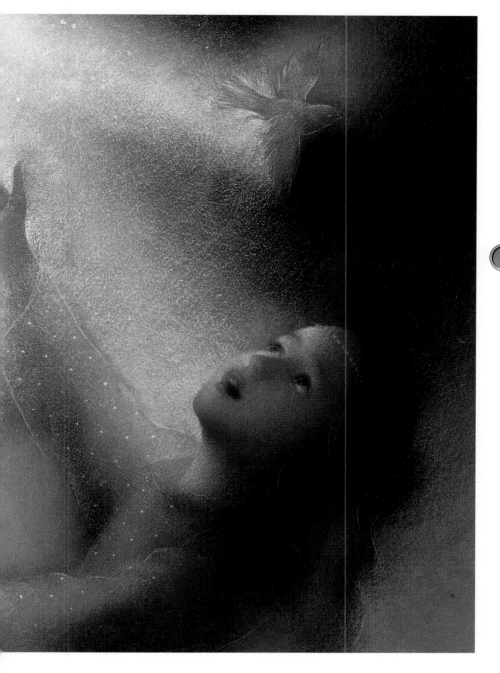

7

641

7 Do you think it is important for the author's purpose that the flowers and the bird come from outside the princess's window? Explain your answers. (Yes, this is one way that the author shows us that the princess wants to reach out beyond her palace walls.) *Author's Purpose*

LANGUAGE SUPPORT

ESL Help students understand the sequence of events that led to the capture of the bird. Explain that the princess did not open the window to catch the bird; instead she opened the window to reach the beautiful flowers that had brushed against the window, and the bird flew in. Have students pantomime the actions in this scene. Include one student to portray the bird.

Guided Instruction

⑧ PROBLEM AND SOLUTION Let's look at our charts and review the princess's problem. (She doesn't have a friend.) What is her first attempt to solve her problem? Let's add this information to our charts.

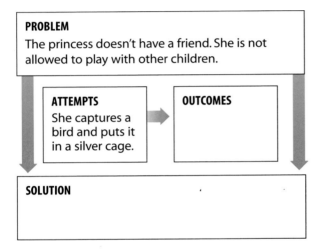

PROBLEM
The princess doesn't have a friend. She is not allowed to play with other children.

ATTEMPTS
She captures a bird and puts it in a silver cage.

OUTCOMES

SOLUTION

WORD STRUCTURE Reread the first sentence. Ask: What word ending means "in a certain manner"? (-*ly*) To which words has the ending been added? (immediate, immediately; hasty, hastily)

⑧   The lady-in-waiting appeared immediately with a towel in hand, while the governess hastily took off her black shawl. Between the two of them, they soon captured the tiny bird and locked him in a silver cage.

"What a rare and precious bird!" said the queen. "It's very fitting that he chose to come to my princess."

"How cultured," said the governess.

"How elegant," said the lady-in-waiting.

642

ⓟ/ⓘ PREVENTION/INTERVENTION

WORD STRUCTURE Write *immediately* and *hastily* on the chalkboard. Have students say the words aloud. Ask: What ending do these words have in common? (-*ly*)

Write the following on the chalkboard:

immediate + ly = immediately
hasty + ly = hastily

Point out that the spelling changes (*y* to *i*) when adding *ly* to *hasty*. Also, the long vowel sound at the end of *hasty* changes to a schwa sound when the –*ly* ending is added. Discuss the meaning of the base words. Then discuss the meaning of the new words that were formed by adding -*ly*: in an immediate manner; in a hasty manner. Explain that knowing the meaning of a base word and the meaning of a suffix can help them figure out the meaning of an unfamiliar word.

The princess wanted very much to hear the bird sing again. But many days went by, and the tiny bird did not let forth even a small warble.

"I'm sure that he knows how to sing," said the princess. "The day we caught him, he sang beautifully."

"Let's bring him chocolate," said the lady-in-waiting.

"Or caviar," suggested the governess.

"Let's gild his silver cage," ordered the queen. "He will certainly sing for us once he has a golden cage."

But in spite of all their efforts, the little bird remained silent.

643

Guided Instruction

9 What can you tell about the queen, the governess, and the lady-in-waiting from what they say and the way they speak? (Their language shows that they think they are very important and better than others.) *Character*

JUDGMENTS AND DECISIONS
10 Why do the women think that feeding the bird caviar will make it sing? What would you think of someone who fed chocolates and caviar to a bird? (Sample answer: They believe that expensive things—like caviar or a gilded cage—are better than common, everyday things. The women are foolish and filled with self-importance.)

Minilesson

REVIEW

Context Clues

Remind students that words in nearby sentences can provide clues to the meanings of unfamiliar words.

• Have students look for a word or words in the sentence in which *precious* appears which could give clues to the meaning of that word. (rare)

Activity Have students begin a web of words from the story that describe traits, beginning with the words *rare, precious, cultured,* and *elegant.* They can use a dictionary or thesaurus to look for other related words and add them to the web.

Guided Instruction

(11) **PROBLEM AND SOLUTION** Does setting the bird on the windowsill solve the problem of getting it to sing? Explain your answer. (No. The bird sings again, but its song is sad and feeble.)

TEACHING TIP

INSTRUCTIONAL Explain to students that the italicized text at the beginning of page 644 represents an interior monologue; it is the author's way of telling us what the princess is thinking to herself.

Fluency

READ FOR EXPRESSION Ask students how they would describe the mood on this page. (sad, subdued) Suggest that students practice rereading this page aloud to try to convey the mood in this section of the story.

Maybe he needs some air, thought the princess. *Perhaps he misses the* fragrance *of the flowers. . . .* So she opened the window and placed the birdcage on her balcony. When **(11)** she did this, the bird began to sing once more. But his song was sad and feeble, unlike the joyful song he had brought with him when he first arrived.

644

⑫

645

Guided Instruction

⑫ **What new problem could you predict opening the window may cause?**
(Sample answer: The open window may remind the princess of the other children.)
Make Predictions

Minilesson
REVIEW
/s/ and /f/

Remind students that the /s/ sound may be spelled with various letter combinations: *ss, s, c,* and *ce.*

Ask a volunteer to read aloud the word *fragrance* on page 644. Have another volunteer tell what letters represent the /s/ sound. (ce) Ask students to brainstorm other words with this letter pattern. (palace, Alice, lace, ice)

Also, remind studnets that the /f/ sound is sometimes spelled as /gh/ or /ph/, as in *laughed* on page 646 and *elephant* on page 649.

Activity Have students make word webs with the /s/ sound and with the /f/ sound, organizing the words by various spellings.

Guided Instruction

13 How does sitting by the open window make the bird feel? (Hearing the children through the open window makes the bird perk up and sing.) *Cause and Effect*

Since the window was now kept open, the little princess could once again hear the sounds of the children playing in the fields. **13** And she noticed that each time the children laughed, the bird would perk up a little, and his song became brighter. Sometimes when the bird sang, the children would peek into the palace gardens through the iron fence.

646

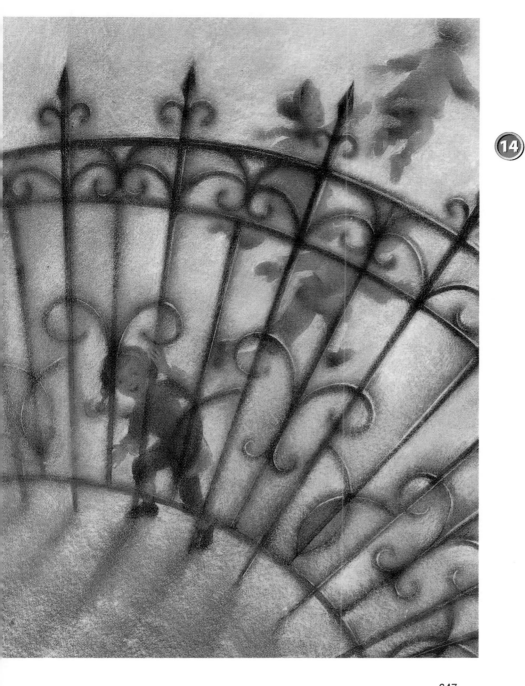

647

Guided Instruction

(14) How do you think the lady-in-waiting, the governess, and the queen will react when they see the children looking into the palace fence? (Sample answer: They will become angry.) *Make Predictions*

Guided Instruction

15 How did the queen react to the children looking in the palace fence? (She ordered vines planted to keep them out.) *Revise Predictions*

"How unseemly!" said the lady-in-waiting.

"How ill-mannered!" complained the governess.

15 "I'll put a stop to it!" announced the queen. And she ordered vines planted inside the iron fence. Soon the vines grew thick and tall, and the children's faces could no longer be seen, nor their laughter heard, from inside the palace.

When summer came, the vines grew even thicker. In the fall, the leaves changed color, and the palace seemed to be surrounded by walls of fire. Meanwhile, the tiny bird's song was becoming sadder and quieter every day. Finally, it stopped altogether.

648

CULTURAL PERSPECTIVES

LULLABIES Explain that in many families, lullabies—songs used to lull babies to sleep—are passed down from generation to generation. Have students share lullabies that were sung to them when they were small.

Activity Students can interview family members and neighbors to collect additional lullabies and other familiar folk music. Ask them to try to identify the cultural traditions in which the songs originate and teach them to a group of younger children.

▶ **Musical/Interpersonal**

Duérmete mi niño

Spanish: Duer-me-te mi ni-ño,
English: Sleep my lit-tle ba-by;

The princess tried everything she could think of to cheer him up. She told the bird the story of how his beautiful cage, a gift from a faraway emperor, had arrived at the palace balanced atop a tower of presents all carried by a white elephant. She hummed her favorite lullaby, and offered him dry dates and figs. But the bird remained silent.

649

Guided Instruction

 PROBLEM AND SOLUTION What things did the princess do to help solve the bird's problem? (She told him a story, sang to him, and fed him.) Did those things work? (No, the bird still didn't feel like singing.) Name some things you like to do when a friend or family member feels sad.

VOCABULARY/CONTEXT CLUES The lady-in-waiting calls the children's behavior *unseemly*. How might you figure out what this word means if it is unfamiliar to you?

Guided Instruction

(17) PROBLEM AND SOLUTION Why does the princess let the bird fly away? Will this solve the bird's problem? Will it affect the princess's problem in any way? (The princess loves the bird and wants it to be happy, so she lets it free. She solves the bird's problem, but now she is alone again.)

Let's add this information to the problem and solution chart.

PROBLEM
The princess doesn't have a friend. She is not allowed to play with other children.

ATTEMPTS
She captures a bird and puts it in a silver cage.

OUTCOMES
The bird is sad and will not sing. She lets the bird go.

SOLUTION

As the days grew colder, the princess moved the cage with the silent bird indoors. One morning, after all the leaves from the vines had fallen, the princess opened the door to the balcony. *Maybe if the bird sees the sky and fields again, he'll want to sing once more,* she thought. As she stood with the cage on the balcony, she heard the voices of the children playing outside the gates. They shouted and laughed as they slid over the snow with their sleds, and built a large snowman with a full, round face.

(17) The princess listened to the children's voices, longing to join them. Then without knowing quite why, she opened the door to the cage and let the tiny yellow bird fly away.

650

Activity

Cross Curricular: Science

DECIDUOUS AND EVERGREEN PLANTS Plants that drop their leaves in winter are *deciduous*. Those that keep them year round are *evergreens*.

RESEARCH AND INQUIRY Have students research and suggest evergreen plants that the queen could have had planted around the iron fence that would have blocked out the noises of the children outside the fence year round. ▶ **Logical/Linguistic**

651

18 Looking at this picture, how do you think the princess feels about letting the bird go? (Possible answers: She feels happy for him, but is sad to see him go. She wishes she could go out, too.) *Draw Conclusions*

Minilesson

REVIEW

Draw Conclusions

Remind students that when they draw conclusions they use facts and clues from a story, as well as their own knowledge, to figure things out.

- Have students look at the picture on page 651 and describe what has just happened. (The princess has just let the bird out of the cage.) Discuss how the princess looks. (happy)

- What conclusions can you draw about why the princess looks happy? (Answers will vary.)

Activity Have partners use story clues and background knowledge to develop a list to support the conclusion they made about why the princess let the bird out of the cage.

651

Guided Instruction

19 Why had the princess never used tools before? *(She has servants who do all of her chores for her.)* **Character**

For many days, the princess looked and looked at the empty cage, and listened to the sounds of the children as they played in the snow.

One morning, she woke up and saw frost covering the window. The princess called out for a lackey: "Quickly, quickly, I need some tools!"

And then the little princess, who had never before held a needle, a thimble, nor even a pair of scissors in her hands, began to work with the tools. Clumsily at first, and then more confidently, she managed to unhinge the delicate door of the cage. Next, she unfastened some of the bars from the other side. Now the cage resembled an

19 open archway.

652

LANGUAGE SUPPORT

ESL Bring in a needle, a thimble, and a pair of scissors. Pass them around, cautioning students on how to handle them correctly. Have a volunteer demonstrate how to use each one. Also show common tools such as wire cutters, a wrench, and a hammer that the princess might have used to transform the cage into a bird feeder.

653

Guided Instruction

WORD STRUCTURE Which words are used on page 652 to describe how the princess uses the tools? *(clumsily, confidently)* What is similar about many words like these that describe action?

PREVENTION/INTERVENTION

WORD STRUCTURE Explain that words that end with *-ly* are usually adverbs. Adverbs tell how an action is done. Have volunteers identify the words in the passage that describe how the princess works with the tools. (*clumsily* at first, and then more *confidently*) Write these words on the board and underline the *-ly* endings.

Have students brainstorm other *-ly* adverbs that could also describe how someone uses tools. (hurriedly, carefully, intently)

Guided Instruction

(20) **PROBLEM AND SOLUTION** How does the princess attempt to get the bird to return? What was the outcome?

Let's fill in the next line of our Problem and Solution chart.

PROBLEM
The princess doesn't have a friend. She is not allowed to play with other children.

ATTEMPTS
She captures a bird and puts it in a silver cage.

OUTCOMES
The bird is sad and will not sing. She lets the bird go.

She makes a bird feeder out of her bird cage.

The bird comes back with its friends.

SOLUTION

Then the princess said:

"Quickly, quickly, I want sunflower seeds, **(20)** and millet, and nuts!"

And she filled the open cage with food, and placed it on the balcony.

That afternoon, as the setting sun turned the snow into a crimson blanket, the princess saw many hungry birds pecking at the seeds. In the midst of the bright red cardinals, the feisty blue jays, the brown-and-white chickadees, and the soft gray sparrows stood the tiny yellow bird.

"You've come back!" she cried. "And you've brought your friends."

654

Activity

Cross Curricular: Science

BIRD TALLY Help students identify the birds pictured on page 655. (blue jay, cardinal, chickadee, sparrow, canary) Then use a bird identification book to identify birds that are commonly seen in your part of the country during this time of the year.

Display pictures of the most common birds and ask students to tally the different types of birds they see over a 24-hour period. Then have students compile the results of their observations into a bar graph.

▶ **Mathematical/Interpersonal**

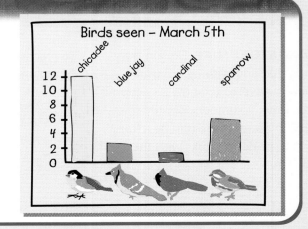

Birds seen – March 5th

655

Guided Instruction

Ⓢ ELF-MONITORING

STRATEGY

SEARCH FOR CLUES Searching for clues can help readers be sure that they understand the events of the plot in a story.

MODEL I think the bird's problem has been solved. Searching for clues can help me be sure. I notice in the picture that many birds are now in the birdcage. In the story, the princess says "You've come back! . . . And you've brought your friends." I know now that these are the bird's friends, so the bird must not be lonely any more.

LANGUAGE SUPPORT

ESL To help students understand that many of the terms on page 654 represent types of birds, show pictures of blue jays, cardinals, chickadees, and sparrows, along with a canary. Label these with the appropriate names and have students refer to the pictures as they read the text.

Guided Instruction

21 What do you think the princess is about to do to solve her own problem? (Students may predict that she will find a way to be with the other children.) *Make Predictions*

The yellow bird took a sunflower seed in his beak and flew back over the iron fence.

21 The princess watched him fly away. The laughter of the children playing outside seemed more joyful than ever. She ran to the palace fence and opened the ornate gates.

656

657

22 **JUDGMENTS AND DECISIONS**
What would you do at this point if you were the princess? (Possible response: I would go through the gates to find a friend.)

22

Minilesson

REVIEW

Summarize

Explain that a story summary includes only the important information and that it tells the story in the reader's own words.

• Ask students to summarize the story to this point in two or three sentences.

Activity Have students summarize other fiction and nonfiction selections they have read recently.

Guided Instruction

(23) **PROBLEM AND SOLUTION** Did you predict correctly how the princess would do to solve her problem? Let's have volunteers role-play the scenes on the last two pages of the story. *Role-Play*

Now let's add the final solution to the chart.

PROBLEM
The princess doesn't have a friend. She is not allowed to play with other children.

ATTEMPTS
She captures a bird and puts it in a silver cage.

→

OUTCOMES
The bird is sad and will not sing. She lets the bird go.

ATTEMPTS
She makes a bird feeder out of her bird cage.

→

OUTCOMES
The bird comes back with its friends.

SOLUTION
She disobeys the queen, the governess, and the lady-in-waiting and plays with the children.

RETELL THE STORY Have volunteers retell the story using their charts as guides. Have partners work together to write a short summary of the story. *Summarize*

STUDENT SELF-ASSESSMENT

- How did identifying problems and solutions help me understand the story?
- How did the Problem and Solution chart help me?

TRANSFERRING THE STRATEGY

- When might I try using this strategy again? In what other reading could a chart like this help me?

And when the lady-in-waiting, in her starched white coif, the governess, in her black silk dress, and the queen, in her gold evening gown, said:

"You can't play with those children. They are rude!"

"And ignorant!"

"And common!"

The little princess answered:

"That's not true! That's not true! That's not true!"

658

REREADING FOR *Fluency*

ONE Have students choose a section of the story to practice reading for expressiveness. Have them use a voice that helps convey the mood of the fairy tale.

READING RATE You may want to evaluate a student's reading rate. Have the student read aloud from *The Malachite Palace* for one minute; ask the student to place a self-stick note after the last word read. Then count the number of words he or she has read.

Alternatively, you could assess small groups or the whole class together by having students count words and record their own scores.

Use the Reading Rate form in the **Diagnostic/Placement Evaluations** booklet to evaluate students' performance.

Then she ran into the fields beyond the iron gates. There her laughter [mingled] with the laughter of the other children, while the yellow bird, perched on a leafless vine, sang louder and more sweetly than it ever had before.

659

LITERARY RESPONSE

QUICK-WRITE Have students write their thoughts about the selection. Use these prompts to get them started:

- What did you find that was surprising about the story?
- What would you have done if you were the princess?

ORAL RESPONSE Have students share their quick-write responses and discuss the sections of the story and the illustrations that they liked best.

Guided Instruction

Return to Predictions and Purposes

Review with students their story predictions and reasons for reading the story. Did they predict correctly? Did they find answers to what they wanted to learn?

PREDICTIONS	WHAT HAPPENED
I predict the story is about a princess whose bird won't sing.	Both the bird and the princess were lonely, but in the end, they both found friends.

INFORMAL ASSESSMENT

PROBLEM AND SOLUTION

HOW TO ASSESS

- Ask students to tell how the bird's problem was solved.
- Ask students to tell how the princess solved her problem at the end of the story.

Students should recognize that once the bird was free of the bird cage and the princess went out beyond the palace gates, they were both able to find friends. They both found the solution to their problem—loneliness.

FOLLOW UP If students have difficulty recognizing problems and solutions, help them brainstorm ways that they themselves might use to solve the problem that the princess faces in the story.

Story Questions

Have students discuss or write answers to the questions on page 660.

Answers:

1. in a malachite palace *Literal/Setting*

2. Both are caged up and lonely. *Inferential/Compare and Contrast*

3. The princess sets the bird free. She decides to play with the other children. Neither the bird nor the princess will be lonely any more. *Inferential/Judgments and Decisions*

4. the need for friends, freedom of choice, and love. *Critical/Summarize*

5. Sample answer: She might want to sing with the bird to show that they are both free and happy. *Critical/ Reading Across Texts*

Compare Characters For a full writing process lesson related to this suggestion, see the lesson on pages 663K–663L.

Story Questions & Activities

1. Where does the princess live?

2. How is the princess's problem like the bird's?

3. How does the princess solve the bird's problem? How does she solve her own loneliness? What makes them both good solutions?

4. What is this fairy tale about?

5. Imagine that the princess is the woman in the painting on pages 632–633. How do you think she would feel about the bird in the picture?

Compare Characters

The princess and the bird are alike in many ways. In one or more paragraphs, compare them. List at least three ways they are alike. Then list their differences.

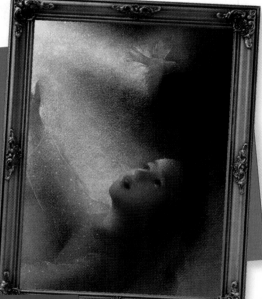

Meeting Individual Needs

EASY

Name_____ Date_____ **Reteach** 194

Vocabulary

Write a word from the list to complete each sentence.

| mingled   feeble   scampered   cultured   fragrance   resembled |

1. The girl is _cultured_ because she knows about art, music, and dance.
2. The woman was too _feeble_ to go out in the storm alone.
3. The _fragrance_ of the flowers in spring is wonderful.
4. The voices of the children _mingled_ with the music.
5. The children _scampered_ happily across the lawn.
6. The figure on the painting _resembled_ her father.

Story Comprehension **Reteach** 195

Write the answers to the following questions about "The Malachite Palace." You may look back at the story.

1. Why wasn't the princess allowed to play with the other children? _The adults around the princess thought the children were not good enough._
2. Why did the princess want the little bird caught? _She wanted a friend, or something to keep her company._
3. Why did the little bird stop singing? _Caged, the bird missed the outdoors, the children, and freedom._
4. What did the princess make the birdcage into? _She made it into a birdfeeder, a place where birds could eat and fly away._

At Home: Have students write about their favorite part of "The Malachite Palace."
194–195   Book 4/Unit 6
The Malachite Palace   4

Reteach, 195

ON-LEVEL

Name_____ Date_____ **Practice** 195

Story Comprehension

Read each statement. Write **T** if the statement describes "The Malachite Palace." Write **F** if it does not describe "The Malachite Palace."

1. _T_ The princess is the only child living in the palace.
2. _T_ The queen and the governess do not understand that the princess is lonely.
3. _F_ The princess has fun with her governess and the lady-in-waiting.
4. _F_ The governess admires the children who live near the palace.
5. _T_ The princess thinks the children sound happy as they play outside.
6. _F_ The bird only likes rich foods, caviar, and chocolate.
7. _F_ The bird can not sing because of an illness.
8. _T_ The princess turns the cage into a kind of bird feeder, and the birds come and go as they wish.

Refer to "The Malachite Palace" to help you answer each question.

9. How did the princess prove to be wiser than her governess and lady-in-waiting? _Answers may vary, but should include: The princess knew the bird needed to be free because it was lonely, just as she needed to play with the children._

10. Describe how the little bird and the princess are alike. _Possible answers: The bird wanted to have the freedom to be with other birds. The princess wanted to play with other children. Both the princess and the bird were lonely._

At Home: Have students retell the story to a family member.
195   Book 4/Unit 6
The Malachite Palace   10

Practice, 195

CHALLENGE

Name_____ Date_____ **Extend** 194

Vocabulary

| cultured   feeble   fragrance   mingled   resembled   scampered |

Work with a partner. Each of you choose three words from the vocabulary list and write down the definitions. Then make up false definitions for each of your three words. Read your partner both definitions for each word, and have him or her guess which is correct. Answers will vary.

Extend 195

Story Comprehension

After feeling lonely and frustrated for a long time, the princess in the story "The Malachite Palace" solved her problem for herself. What kinds of judgments or decisions did the princess make in order to solve her problem?
Answers will vary. Possible answer: After watching the bird and seeing that it wasn't happy being caged and isolated from the children, the princess realized that her own situation was the same. She decided to set the bird free and to end her loneliness by playing with the other children.

At Home: Have students talk about decisions they made today.
194–195   Book 4/Unit 6
The Malachite Palace

Extend, 195

Create a Pet-care Book

Write a short book explaining how to care for a pet. First, select the pet. Then include tips on diet, health, exercise, grooming, and other important pet-care "musts." Include a pet-care cartoon, a photograph, or a drawing of the pet.

Design a Bird Cage

The bird in the story became sadder and sadder and even stopped singing. Design and draw a bird cage that you think would make a bird happy. Use a piece of construction paper or oaktag. Include the perch, water dish, feeder, bird toys, and other special features.

Find Out More

The word *malachite* is used only in the title and in the first line of the story. What is *malachite*? What does it look like? Where is it found? What is it used for? Start by looking in an encyclopedia. Use the answers to these questions and others to make a list of facts about malachite.

661

Story Activities

Create a Pet-Care Book

Materials: resources on pet care, drawing paper, markers or crayons

PARTNERS Have partners first choose a pet. They can then brainstorm pet-care tips from personal experience or use resources such as library books and pamphlets from a veterinarian to add more information. Display the finished booklets after students present the information to the class.

Design a Bird Cage

Materials: construction paper or oak tag, pencils and markers

ONE If students are motivated, you might have them use their designs to construct actual models of bird cages.

Find Out More

RESEARCH AND INQUIRY Once students have completed their list of malachite facts, have them create a chart to display the information along with an illustration of malachite. Students might also choose another mineral to research. Then they can compare the qualities of the two minerals.

*inter*NET **CONNECTION** For more information on minerals, students can visit ***www.mhschool.com/reading***

FORMAL ASSESSMENT

After page 661, see the Selection Assessment.

Study Skills

LIBRARY/MEDIA CENTER

OBJECTIVES Students will use author and title cards from a library card catalog to find information.

PREPARE Point out that similar information is organized differently on author and title cards. Display **Teaching Chart 159.**

TEACH Review both types of cards. Have students identify when they would use each type of card.

PRACTICE Have students answer questions 1–5. Review the answers with them. **1.** the author card **2.** when you only know the title of the book **3.** It is not a new book; it was published in 1998. **4.** Yes. It lists illustrations on the cards. **5.** It helps you find books and gives information such as publication date.

ASSESS/CLOSE Display another book and have students suggest what information might appear on its title and author cards.

STUDY SKILLS

Use the Card Catalog: Author and Title Cards

A library **card catalog** helps you find books. The catalog includes title cards, author cards, and subject cards, all arranged alphabetically. **Author cards** help you find a book written by a certain author. **Title cards** help you find a book by the book's title. You can also find the card catalog on computer.

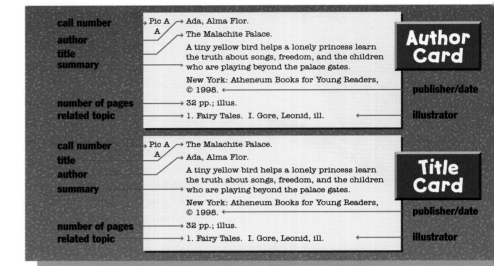

Use the cards above to answer these questions.

1 If you knew the book's author, which card would you use?

2 When would you use the title card?

3 Is *The Malachite Palace* a new book? Explain.

4 Does Alma Flor Ada's book have pictures? How do you know?

5 Why is it important to know how to use the card catalog?

Meeting Individual Needs

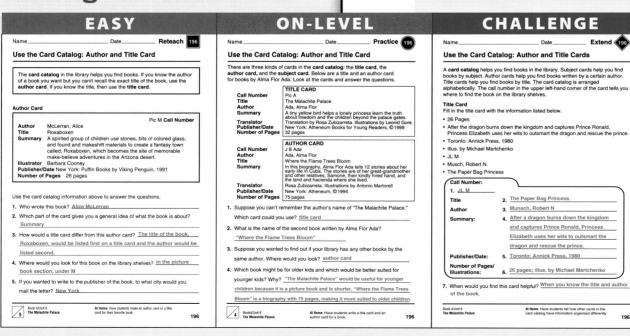

Reteach, 196   Practice, 196   Extend, 196

Test Tip

Read the directions first.

DIRECTIONS

Read the sample story. Then read each question about the story.

SAMPLE

Carlos Shovels Snow

Carlos stomped the snow off his boots. He was hot and frustrated. He came into the kitchen, tossed his hat onto the chair, and started removing his boots. His Aunt Teri finished pouring a cup of coffee and said, "Is something bothering you?"

"I'm already exhausted from shoveling snow, and I just started half an hour ago! I was supposed to walk to the movies to meet Doug, but now I'll never arrive there in time."

"Well, put your boots back on and I'll drive you to town. You can finish shoveling after the movie," said Aunt Teri.

1 Why was Carlos frustrated at the beginning of the story?

○ He doesn't like his Aunt Teri.

● He was going to be late for the movie.

○ He forgot to meet his friend Doug.

○ He did not want to see a movie.

2 The story takes place—

○ at school

○ in the driveway

● in the kitchen

○ at the mall

663

Read the Page

Have students read the story and pay attention to details in the story. Ask them to think about what is happening in the story.

Discuss the Questions

Question 1: This question requires students to understand the feelings of a character. Discuss the clues that tell how Carlos is feeling at the beginning of the story. The passage states that Carlos was "hot and frustrated." When his Aunt Teri asks if something is bothering Carlos, he explains why he is frustrated.

Question 2: This question requires students to determine where most of the story takes place. Have students recall the clues. The passage says that Carlos "came into the kitchen" and then talked with his Aunt Teri—he never left the kitchen.

For The Princeton Review test preparation practice for **TerraNova**, **ITBS**, and **SAT-9**, visit the McGraw-Hill School Division website. See also McGraw-Hill's *Standardized Test Preparation Book*.

EASY

Answers to Story Questions

1. Elsinore is threatening to go to war against Avalon; the King prepares a new treaty for the Queen of Elsinore and holds a banquet for the royal family of Valhalla.

2. A social gathering, such as a banquet, gives leaders a chance to get to know each other as people and hopefully develop friendships that will help them to understand each other's problems and needs.

3. Being King is a big job with a lot of responsibility. A king's decisions can lead his country into war or peace, prosperity or ruin.

4. Prince Paul learns what it's like to be King.

5. Answers will vary but should include that, although both were conscious of their rank, they came to appreciate the opportunity to maintain contact with the common folk.

Story Questions and Activity
King for a Day!

1. Which country is threatening war against Rune?

2. Why is Paul hesitant to be king?

3. How does a banquet or other social gathering serve to promote good relations between the leaders of various countries?

4. Why would a king commission an artist to paint his portrait?

5. What is the story mostly about?

Be Royal!

Pretend you are a king or queen. Draw or build a model of your palace. Write a constitution for your kingdom, listing the laws of the land.

from King for a Day

Leveled Books

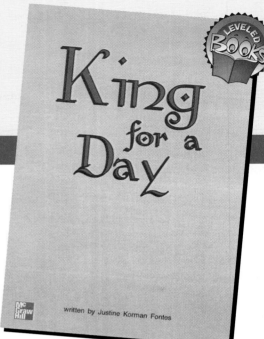

EASY

King for a Day!

Words with /s/

☑ **Problem and Solution**

☑ **Instructional Vocabulary:** *cultured, feeble, fragrance, mingled, resembled, scampered*

Guided Reading

PREVIEW AND PREDICT Preview the book through page 6. Have students record in their journals what they think the story will be about.

SET PURPOSES Ask students to write a few questions that they would like to have answered as they read the story. For example, they may want to know what country the king rules.

READ THE BOOK Use the questions that follow to guide students' reading or to reinforce reading strategies after they read the story independently.

Pages 2–3: What problem does Paul face as "King for a day"? (He doesn't know what to do as king.) What solution does his mother suggest? (Watch what his father does all day.) *Problem and Solution*

Pages 4–5: Have students find the word *ambassador* as you say it aloud. What letters stand for the /s/ sound? (ss) What other words on these pages contain the /s/ sound? What letter(s) represent the /s/ sound? *Phonics and Decoding*

Page 9: What does the author say the disputing noblemen *resembled*? (children fighting over a new toy) What does the word *resembled* mean? (looked like) *Vocabulary*

Pages 12–13: What is the effect of the king and Paul riding through the country? (The king gets to know the common people and their ideas.) *Cause and Effect*

RETURN TO PREDICTIONS AND PURPOSES Review students' predictions and questions. Were their predictions accurate? Did they make changes to their predictions as they read the story? Were their questions answered?

LITERARY RESPONSE Discuss these questions:

• What are some of the king's responsibilities?

• Is King Robert a good king? Explain.

Also see the story questions and activity in *King for a Day!*

Leveled Books

INDEPENDENT

The Crown Jewels

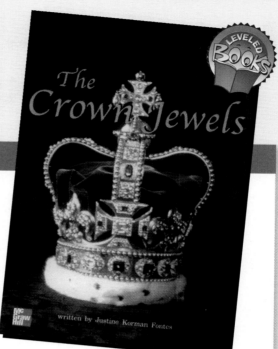

☑ **Problem and Solution**

☑ **Instructional Vocabulary:**
cultured, feeble, fragrance, mingled, resembled, scampered

written by Justine Korman Fontes

INDEPENDENT

Guided Reading

PREVIEW AND PREDICT Have students preview the text through page 7. Have students predict what the selection will be about. Have students record their ideas in their journals.

SET PURPOSES Have students write two questions in their journals that they would like answered as they read. For example, they may want to know who gets to wear the crown.

READ THE BOOK After students have read the selection independently, use the questions that follow to apply strategies.

Page 6: What does *fragrances* mean? (a sweet smell) What context clues help you know that the smell of the fragrances is sweet? (orange, roses) *Vocabulary*

Pages 6–9: Why are so many different symbols used during the King's or Queen's crowning ceremony? (to honor the past and to show the King's or Queen's relationship with England) What effect does this have on the people of England? (Their hearts fill with national pride.) *Cause and Effect*

Pages 10–11: Why does King Charles II order new Crown Jewels to be created? (He wants to return the crown to power.) *Make Inferences*

Pages 14–15: What problem does the King of Delhi have? (He needs to hide the Kohinoor, a special gem of the Crown Jewels, from his enemy.) How does he solve his problem? (He hides the gem in his turban because it is the custom not to remove the turban.) *Problem and Solution*

RETURN TO PREDICTIONS AND PURPOSES Review students' predictions and reasons for reading. Were their predictions accurate? Did they make changes to their predictions as they read the story? Were their questions answered?

LITERARY RESPONSE Discuss these questions with students:

- What is the most surprising fact that you learned in this selection?

- What is another possible title for this selection?

Also see the story questions and activity in *The Crown Jewels*.

Answers to Story Questions

1. Three crowns are involved in the coronation ceremony.
2. Goldsmiths recreated the original Crown Jewels.
3. He knew its folds contained the Kohinoor diamond.
4. This story is about how the history of England is reflected in the Crown Jewels.
5. Answers will vary.

Story Questions and Activity
The Crown Jewels

1. How many crowns are involved in the coronation ceremony?
2. What solution was found after Cromwell and the Puritans melted down the gold and sold the jewels from the Crown Jewels?
3. Why did the King of Persia exchange turbans with the King of Delhi?
4. What is this story mainly about?
5. If the bird from *The Malachite Palace* flew into Buckingham Palace today, what lesson might it teach the royal family?

Design Your Own Crown

From this story it is easy to see how a variety of symbols can be incorporated into an object such as a crown or a scepter. If you were to design a crown for yourself, what jewels would you choose? Would your crown have any symbolic designs, such as a dove, a hawk, or a dragon? Sketch and color in your crown. Then share your design with a classmate.

from *The Crown Jewels*

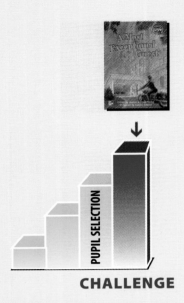

CHALLENGE

Answers to Story Questions

1. This is really a modern retelling of that fairy tale.

2. Answers may include that you have to be a good businessperson and be detail-oriented; you have to be friendly to customers even though you may not feel like it.

3. Albertís mother wanted her son to marry and knew he needed a fastidious wife for him to be happy. She thought that Elizabeth might be the right person for her son, so she put some chopped hazelnuts under Elizabethís mattress to see how sensitive she truly was.

4. This story is about how a modern day prince found his modern day princess within a hotel setting.

5. Answers will vary.

Story Questions and Activity

1. Why did Elizabeth Charming mention "The Princess and the Pea?"

2. What qualities are needed to run a big hotel?

3. What problem did Albert's mother have? How did she solve it?

4. What is this story mostly about?

5. If the princess from *The Malachite Palace* could give Albert some advice, what do you think she would tell him?

Be A Desk Clerk

Pretend you are a desk clerk at a big hotel. Write a short dialogue between yourself and a guest who has an unusual request. Maybe the guest has brought a pet and wants a special meal cooked for it. What would you say? Or maybe a guest has lost a piece of expensive jewelry. What would you say? How would you go about finding it? Share your dialogue with classmates.

from A Most Exceptional Guest

Leveled Books

CHALLENGE

A Most Exceptional Guest

☑ **Problem and Solution**
☑ **Instructional Vocabulary:**
cultured, feeble, fragrance, mingled, resembled, scampered

Guided Reading

PREVIEW AND PREDICT Have students preview the pictures up to page 5 and chart their ideas about what the story will be about based on these pictures.

SET PURPOSES Before they read the story, ask students to write down a few questions that they would like to have answered as they read the story.

READ THE BOOK After students have read the story independently, return to the text to apply these reading strategies.

Page 3: Reread paragraph 1. What problem causes Albert's unhappiness? (Hotel guests do not value their surroundings.) How might Albert solve this problem? (Sample answer: He might accept that people have different ways of appreciating the same thing.) *Problem and Solution*

Page 7: Why did Albert change his judgments about his guest? (When she spoke, she appeared to be different—more cultured and refined, more like the type of guest who would stay in the hotel.) What decision did Albert make then? (to let her use the honeymoon suite) *Judgments and Decisions*

Page 9: Why was the sauce *feeble*? (The spices had not blended.) What does *feeble* mean? (weak) *Vocabulary*

Page 16: What problem did Albert overcome? (never leaving his hotel to go on a vacation) How do you think he solved this problem? (He probably realized that he had trained his staff to be the best, so he had to let them have some responsibility. He probably listened to how Ms. Charming was able to travel.) *Problem and Solution*

RETURN TO PREDICTIONS AND PURPOSES Review students' predictions and reasons for reading. Were their predictions accurate?

LITERARY RESPONSE Discuss these questions:

• Why was Princess charming "a most exceptional guest"?

• How does the saying, "You can't judge a book by its cover!" apply to this story?

Also see the story questions and activity in *A Most Exceptional Guest.*

Activities
Anthology and Leveled Books

Connecting Texts

ROYALTY CHARTS Write the story titles on a chart. Discuss with students the problems faced by royalty and solutions they find in the books. Call on volunteers from all reading levels to present ideas for the selection *The Malachite Palace*. Call on volunteers from each reading level for the other selections. Write their suggestions on the chart.

Use the chart to discuss the problems and solutions in each selection. Invite students to tell how they might solve each problem using background knowledge and personal experiences.

Problem

The Malachite Palace	King for a Day	The Crown Jewels	A Most Exceptional Guest
The songbird stops singing.	Paul does not know what he must do when he is king.	The Crown Jewels were destroyed.	Albert does not want an unusual guest to stay at his hotel.

Solution

The Malachite Palace	King for a Day	The Crown Jewels	A Most Exceptional Guest
The princess lets the songbird out of the cage.	Paul spends a day with his dad, the king.	King Charles II has new Crown Jewels made.	Albert lets Ms. Charming stay and leans looks can be deceiving.

Viewing/Representing

MAKE STORYBOARDS Organize the class into groups, one for each of the four books read in the lesson. (For *The Malachite Palace*, combine students of different reading levels.) Have groups storyboard the main events in their stories. Then have groups use their storyboards to summarize their stories for the class.

COMPARE PROBLEMS AND SOLUTIONS As students listen carefully to each presentation, ask them to compare the problems and solutions presented with the problems and solutions in their own stories. Allow time for discussion and questions after each presentation.

Research and Inquiry

MORE ABOUT ROYALTY Invite volunteers to identify royal terms with which they are familiar. After discussion, have students ask themselves what else they would like to find out about royalty. Then invite them to do the following:

- Visit the school library and gather a collection of books about royalty. Use the resources to investigate royal titles, royal garments, royal ceremonies, and so on.

- Select a member of royalty to read about and then report on to the class.

- Create a class booklet about royalty.

 interNET CONNECTION Students can learn more about royalty by visiting **www.mhschool.com/reading**

OBJECTIVES

Students will recognize problem and solution.

TEACHING TIP

INSTRUCTIONAL

Students may have difficulty understanding that a solution to one problem may create another problem. In this case, use arrows to show how the solution to one problem can lead to another problem and so on.

Review Problem and Solution

PREPARE

Discuss Problem and Solution

Review: In most stories, the character's problem is what drives the plot of the story. Usually the problem is solved at the turning point of the story.

TEACH

Read "The Lonely Princess" and Model the Skill

Read the story "The Lonely Princess" on **Teaching Chart 160.** Focus students' attention on the problem and solution in the story.

The Lonely Princess

Once there was a princess just about your age. <u>She was the only child in the palace, and she felt very lonely.</u> She could hear the voices of other children outside the palace, but she had been told that she was too good to play with them. One day, the princess got tired of being alone. (She left the palace though the iron gates and ran to the field to find the other children.) To her surprise, she found out that they were every bit as nice as she.

Teaching Chart 160

Guide students to identify how to recognize problem and solution.

MODEL As I look for the problem, I try to find something that the main character wants to change. She is tired of being alone, so I know that is her problem. To find the solution, I look for an action that helps solve the problem.

Reread the chart and have students raise their hands when you read a sentence that states the problem or the solution.

PRACTICE

Recognize Problem and Solution

GROUP

Ask volunteers to underline the problem on the chart and circle the solution. Have them explain how they made these choices.

ASSESS/CLOSE

Recognize Problem and Solution of Other Characters

PARTNERS

Have students work with partners to brainstorm a list of problems and solutions in other stories they have read. Create a simple chart and let partners add to it.

STORY	PROBLEM	SOLUTION
A Place Called Freedom	living in slavery	starting a new life in Freedom
Mom's Best Friend	Mom's guide dog dies	getting and training a new guide dog

ALTERNATE TEACHING STRATEGY

PROBLEM AND SOLUTION

For a different approach to teaching this skill, see page T64.

SELF-SELECTED Reading

Students may choose from the following titles.

ANTHOLOGY

- The Malachite Palace

LEVELED BOOKS

- King for a Day
- The Crown Jewels
- A Most Exceptional Guest

Bibliography, pages T76–T77

Meeting Individual Needs for Comprehension

EASY	ON-LEVEL	CHALLENGE	LANGUAGE SUPPORT
Reteach, 197	**Practice, 197**	**Extend, 197**	**Language Support, 214**

OBJECTIVES

Students will identify causes and effects.

Review Cause and Effect

PREPARE

Discuss Cause and Effect

Review: A cause is what makes something happen. The effect is what happens, or the result.

TEACH

Read the Passage and Model the Skill

Have students read the passage on **Teaching Chart 161** and think about causes and effects that are included in the story.

The Princess's Surprise

A little princess missed her pet bird because she had set the bird free. Hoping to make the bird return, the princess took some tools and fashioned the cage into a bird feeder. Then she placed some birdseed inside the feeder. As soon as she opened the window, her feathered friend appeared. To the princess's surprise, the bird was not alone. It had invited several other pretty birds to come visit the princess and share the food she had for them.

Teaching Chart 161

Guide students to recognize causes and effects.

MODEL As I read, I look for causes and effects. Sometimes signal words are used to show causes and effects. Other times, I must add the cause and effect words myself.

Have students circle phrases or sentences that identify causes and underline any phrases or sentences that show the effects.

PRACTICE

Create a Cause and Effect Chart

GROUP

Have students create a Cause and Effect chart for **Teaching Chart 161.** Help them get started. ▶ **Linguistic/Logical**

CAUSE	EFFECT
A princess set her pet bird free.	She missed the bird.
She made a bird feeder out of a cage.	The bird came back to visit the princess.

ASSESS/CLOSE

Use the Chart for Other Stories

Have students work with partners to make similar Cause and Effect charts for a familiar fairy tale, such as *The Three Little Pigs,* or *Jack and the Beanstalk.*

ALTERNATE TEACHING STRATEGY

CAUSE AND EFFECT

For a different approach to teaching this skill, see page T60.

LOOKING AHEAD

Students will apply this skill as they read the next selection, *The Toothpaste Millionaire.*

Meeting Individual Needs for Comprehension

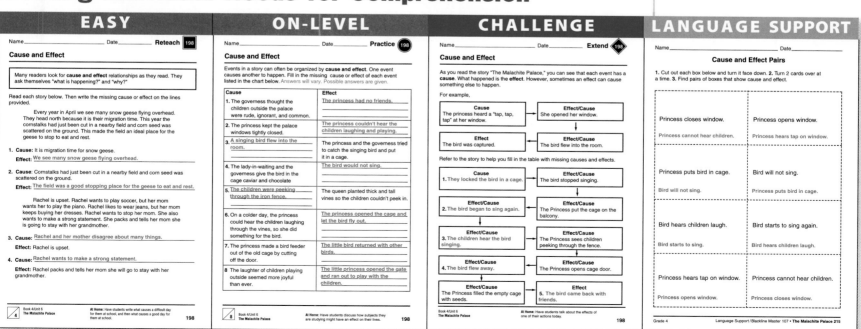

Reteach, 198   Practice, 198   Extend, 198   Language Support, 215

OBJECTIVES

Students will recognize antonyms and synonyms.

TEACHING TIP

INSTRUCTIONAL

If students have difficulty distinguishing synonyms and antonyms, provide flashcards for word pairs. Use the same color paper for words that are synonyms and different color papers for words that are antonyms.

Review Antonyms and Synonyms

PREPARE

Discuss Synonyms and Antonyms

Review: Synonyms are words that mean the same or nearly the same. Antonyms are words that have opposite meanings.

TEACH

Read the Passage and Model the Skill

Display and have students read **Teaching Chart 162.**

The Princess and the Children

The lonely princess listened (sadly) to the children who played (cheerfully) outside the palace gates. The governess and the lady-in-waiting insisted that those children were (ignorant.) The princess, they said, was unlike the other children; she was (cultured.) But the princess knew that she would be happy, if only she could play with those joyful children. One day she made a courageous decision. She decided to be brave and follow her heart. So she left the (solitude) of the palace for the (company) of the children.

Teaching Chart 162

Ask students to find antonyms that contrast the princess with the other children (ignorant/cultured), or synonyms that point out similarities between the princess and the other children (happy/joyful).

MODEL Looking for synonyms and antonyms helps me understand new words. For example, from the way the governess and the lady-in-waiting use the words ignorant and cultured to compare the princess and the children, I can tell the words have opposite meanings. Recognizing this helps me understand the meanings of both words.

PRACTICE

Identify Synonyms and Antonyms

GROUP

Have students circle the words on the chart that are antonyms and underline the words that are synonyms. Have students brainstorm other words that are synonyms or antonyms of these words. Remind students that they can use a thesaurus or dictionary to find additional synonyms. ▶ **Linguistic/Interpersonal**

ASSESS/CLOSE

Choose Synonyms and Antonyms

PARTNERS

Have students read these sentences and work with partners to add a synonym or antonym for the underlined word. Answers will vary.

- While the other children laughed _____cheerfully_____ the princess waited <u>sadly</u> to find a friend.

- Like her <u>happy</u> friends, the princess is also _____joyful_____.

- The little bird left the <u>solitude</u> of its cage for the _____company_____ of the other birds.

Meeting Individual Needs for Vocabulary

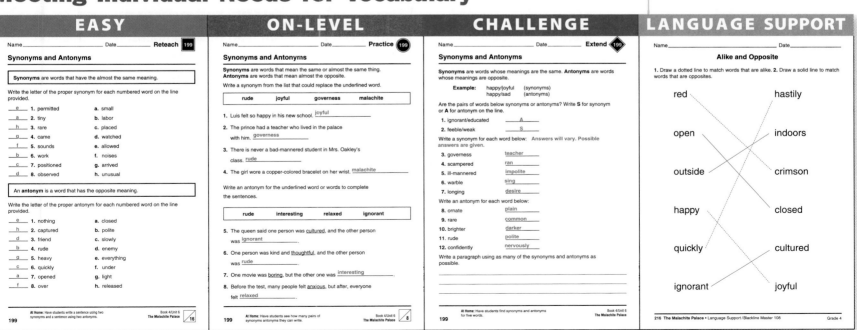

EASY	ON-LEVEL	CHALLENGE	LANGUAGE SUPPORT
Reteach, 199	Practice, 199	Extend, 199	Language Support, 216

663J

Writing That Compares

GRAMMAR/SPELLING CONNECTIONS

See the 5-Day Grammar and Usage Plan on adverbs that compare, pages 663M–663N.

See the 5-Day Spelling Plan on homophones and homographs, pages 663O–663P.

TECHNOLOGY TIP

Help students add frequently used proper nouns such as *malachite* to their own personal spelling dictionary in the software they use for the writing process.

TEACHING TIP

INSTRUCTIONAL Display pictures of characters that students might compare in their writing, such as the princess and the bird from *The Malachite Palace* or the woman in the painting *Lady and the Bird* pictured on pages 632 and 633.

Prewrite

COMPARE CHARACTERS Present the following assignment: The princess and the bird are alike in many ways. In one or more paragraphs, compare them. List at least three ways they are alike, then list their differences.

BRAINSTORM CHARACTER TRAITS Without editing their thoughts, allow students to create two lists of character traits, one for the bird and one for the princess.

Strategy: Use a Venn Diagram Have students organize their lists into a Venn diagram to make notes about similarities and differences between the princess and the bird.

Venn Diagram

princess	both	bird
has no friends in palace	lonely lives behind bars	sings until it is placed in a cage

Draft

USE THE GRAPHIC ORGANIZER Have students use their Venn diagrams to write their drafts. Remind them to organize the information in a logical way, for example, describing all similarities before moving on to differences.

Revise

SELF-QUESTIONING Ask students to evaluate their drafts for improvement.

- Did I include an introductory sentence?
- Did I include both similarities and differences?
- Are my ideas organized logically so that readers can follow them?

PARTNERS Partners can read their comparisons aloud both to hear how their own work sounds and to get input. Have partners help each other make the similarities and differences clear.

Edit/Proofread

CHECK FOR ERRORS Have students reread their comparisons and correct any errors in spelling, punctuation, and grammar.

Publish

SHARE THE COMPARISONS Students can read their comparisons in small groups. Listeners should identify the similarity or difference that they found most interesting or unusual.

Although a bird and a girl are quite different, there are many similarities between the princess and the bird in *The Malachite Palace*. The princess is a prisoner in a way, forbidden to go out beyond the palace gates to play with other children. When the bird is in the cage, it, too, is like a prisoner, and misses being free.

Once the bird and the princess go outside the palace gates or bars of the cage, they are happy and find new friends. Even though the girl speaks and runs and the bird sings and flies, they have a lot in common.

Presentation Ideas

MAKE A POSTER Students can make a poster to illustrate the similarities and differences between the princess and the bird. Have them label their drawings.
▶ **Viewing/Representing**

LISTEN CRITICALLY As students share their paragraphs aloud, instruct the audience to listen for similarities and differences between the speakers' comparison and their own. ▶ **Speaking/Listening**

Consider students' creative efforts, possibly adding a plus (+) for originality, wit, and imagination.

Scoring Rubric

Excellent	Good	Fair	Unsatisfactory
4: The writer	**3:** The writer	**2:** The writer	**1:** The writer
• writes a detailed comparison of the princess and the bird.	• compares the princess and the bird.	• compares the princes and another story character.	• lists traits of the princess, but may not clearly compare her with another character.
• lists three or more similarities and three or more differences.	• lists two similarities or differences or one of each.	• lists only one similarity or difference.	• identifies similarities or differences that are unfounded or confusing.
• writes one or more well-organized paragraphs.	• writes one reasonably well-organized paragraph.	• writes a brief paragraph with fair organization.	• writes a paragraph that lacks organization.

0: The writer does not provide a sample, does not respond to the task, or provides an incoherent response.

For a 6-point or an 8-point scale, see pages T105–T106.

Meeting Individual Needs for Writing

EASY

Make a Cartoon Students can draw a single cartoon frame showing the princess and another story character. They should include a speech balloon or caption to tell about the scene.

ON-LEVEL

Write a Conversation Have students write a conversation between the princess and a character from another story who shares a similar problem.

CHALLENGE

Design a Stage Set Have students design and construct a three-dimensional model of a stage set that could be used for a play production of *The Malachite Palace*.

5 Day Grammar and Usage Plan

Call on three students to act out a verb (*jump*) and an adverb (*high, higher, highest*). The rest of the group should say what each student did, using adverbs that compare.

DAILY LANGUAGE ACTIVITIES

Write each day's activity on the board or use **Transparency 27.** Have students correct the sentences orally.

Day 1

1. This bird sings loud of all of them.
2. The princess caught the bird fast than the governess.
3. The queen lived in the palace long than the princess.

Day 2

1. The bird sang sweetly than before.
2. These windows are closed more tight than those.
3. Of all the ladies, the queen acted more imperiously.

Day 3

1. I can climb high than the gates.
2. The princess listened to the children more sadlier than before.

Day 4

1. The birdcage shone bright of all.
2. The princess held the tools clumsily than a carpenter.

Day 5

1. The princess ran more fast to meet the other children.
2. This is the more frequently read story of all.

Daily Language Transparency 27

DAY 1 — Introduce the Concept

Oral Warm-Up Display three objects whose actions can be described by comparative adverbs. Hold up one and say, for example: *This car goes fast.* Ask students to compare the other objects in relation to the first. (This car goes faster. This car goes the fastest of all.)

Introduce Adverbs That Compare Explain that adverbs describe actions.

Adverbs That Compare

- An adverb can compare two or more actions.
- Add *-er* to short adverbs to compare two actions.
- Add *-est* to short adverbs to compare more than two actions.

Present the Daily Language Activity. Then have students name the three related comparative adverbs for each example, and use them in sentences.

 Assign the daily Writing Prompt on page 632C.

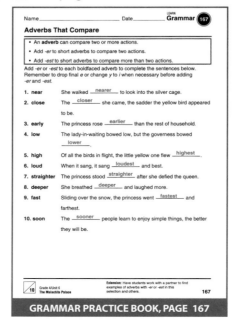

GRAMMAR PRACTICE BOOK, PAGE 167

DAY 2 — Teach the Concept

Review Comparative Adverbs Ask students how to change a short adverb to compare two or more actions.

More About Adverbs That Compare Longer adverbs use *more* or *most* to form comparisons. Present the following:

Adverbs That Compare

- Use *more* or *most* to form comparisons with adverbs ending in *-ly* or with longer adverbs.
- Use *more* to compare two actions.
- Use *most* to compare more than two actions.
- When you use *more* or *most*, do not use the ending *-er* or *-est*.

Present the Daily Language Activity. Then have students make up related sentences for different forms of each adverb, using *more* or *most*.

 Assign the daily Writing Prompt on page 632C.

GRAMMAR PRACTICE BOOK, PAGE 168

Adverbs that Compare

Learn from the Literature Review adverbs that compare. Then ask students to read the last sentence in the second paragraph on page 643 of *The Malachite Palace*:

> "The day we caught him he sang beautifully."

Focus their attention on the word *beautifully* and ask them to explain how the adverb would change if it compared two or more actions.

Use Adverbs that Compare Present the Daily Language Activity. Then have students make a chart with three columns. In the left-hand column, they can list short and long adverbs. Then in the next two columns, they should add the correct forms used when the adverbs compare two or more things.

 Assign the daily Writing Prompt on page 632D.

Review Adverbs that Compare Write the corrected adverbs from the Daily Language Activities for Days 1–3 on the chalkboard. Then ask students where on the three-column chart each adverb belongs. Ask them to explain their answer. Then present the Daily Language Activity for Day 4.

Mechanics and Usage Review the following:

Using *More* and *Most*

- Never add -*er* and *more* to the same adverb.
- Never add -*est* and *most* to the same adverb.

 Assign the daily Writing Prompt on page 632D.

Assess Use the Daily Language Activity and page 171 of the **Grammar Practice Book** for assessment.

Reteach Have students list each adverb from the Daily Language Activities for Days 1–4 on slips of paper. Then have them sort the words according to the different rules for forming adverbs that compare. Finally, each student should draw a slip and use it in a sentence.

Have students create a word wall of adverbs that follow each pattern.

Use page 172 of the **Grammar Practice Book** for additional reteaching.

 Assign the daily Writing Prompt on page 632D.

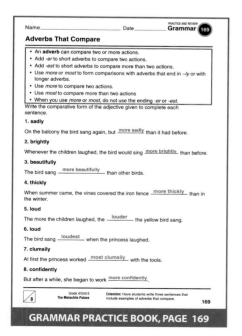

Name_____ Date_____ PRACTICE AND REVIEW **Grammar** 169

Adverbs That Compare

- An **adverb** can compare two or more actions.
- Add -*er* to short adverbs to compare two actions.
- Add -*est* to short adverbs to compare more than two actions.
- Use *more* or *most* to form comparisons with adverbs that end in –*ly* or with longer adverbs.
- Use *more* to compare two actions.
- Use *most* to compare more than two actions
- When you use *more* or *most*, do not use the ending -*er* or -*est*.

Write the comparative form of the adjective given to complete each sentence.

1. sadly
On the balcony the bird sang again, but ___more sadly___ than it had before.

2. brightly
Whenever the children laughed, the bird would sing ___more brightly___ than before.

3. beautifully
The bird sang ___more beautifully___ than other birds.

4. thickly
When summer came, the vines covered the iron fence ___more thickly___ than in the winter.

5. loud
The more the children laughed, the ___louder___ the yellow bird sang.

6. loud
The bird sang ___loudest___ when the princess laughed.

7. clumsily
At first the princess worked ___most clumsily___ with the tools.

8. confidently
But after a while, she began to work ___more confidently___

Grade 4/Unit 6 **The Malachite Palace** 8 Extension: Have students write three sentences that include examples of adverbs that compare. 169

GRAMMAR PRACTICE BOOK, PAGE 169

Name_____ Date_____ MECHANICS **Grammar** 170

Using *More* and *Most*

- Never add -*er* and *more* to the same adverb.
- Never add -*est* and *most* to the same adverb.

Write the correct adverbs on the lines provided.

1. Children live more happilier in the company of others. ___happily___

2. The princess spoke most confidentliest when she said, "That's not true!". ___confidently___

3. At the end, the yellow bird sang more louder than before. ___loudly___

4. She opened the window more wider, and the yellow bird flew in. ___wider___

5. When the children laughed, the bird sang more brightlier. ___brightly___

6. Nobody worked with tools more clumsilier than the princess. ___clumsily___

7. She developed her skills more sooner than most. ___sooner___

8. She removed the door so that the bird could come and go more freelier. ___freely___

9. Now the cage more closelier resembled an archway. ___closely___

10. The yellow bird returned most willingliest and brought his friends. ___willingly___

Extension: Have students write examples of comparative adverbs formed with *more* and *most* in the story *The Malachite Palace*. Grade 4/Unit 6 **The Malachite Palace** 10

170 **GRAMMAR PRACTICE BOOK, PAGE 170**

Name_____ Date_____ TEST **Grammar** 171

Adverbs That Compare

A. For each of the adverbs below, write the form you would use to compare two things. Then choose one of the adverbs you formed and use it in a sentence.

1. carefully ___more carefully___

2. soon ___sooner___

3. clumsily ___more clumsily___

4. patiently ___more patiently___

5. fast ___faster___

6. ___answers will vary___

B. For each of the following adverbs, write the form you would use to compare more than two things. Then choose one of the adverbs you formed and use it in a sentence.

7. loud ___loudest___

8. actively ___most actively___

9. soon ___soonest___

10. early ___earliest___

11. happily ___most happily___

12. ___answers will vary___

Grade 4/Unit 6 **The Malachite Palace** 12

171

GRAMMAR PRACTICE BOOK, PAGE 171

5 Day Spelling Plan

Help students remember the difference between *homophones* and *homographs* by telling them that these words come from the Greek; **homo-**, meaning "same," **-phone** meaning "sound," and **-graph** meaning "write."

DICTATION SENTENCES

Spelling Words

1. Have you <u>seen</u> my cat?
2. That was a <u>great</u> race.
3. The <u>light</u> was dimmed.
4. We <u>beat</u> that team.
5. I like <u>lean</u> meat.
6. The play has one <u>scene</u>.
7. Did the <u>beet</u> grow in the garden?
8. I want a <u>bowl</u> of soup.
9. Help me <u>grate</u> the cheese.
10. The <u>fan</u> made me cold.
11. How high is that <u>peak</u>?
12. Tie the horse to the <u>post</u>.
13. Fetch some water in this <u>pail</u>.
14. Be sure to <u>bury</u> the root of the plant.
15. Would you like some <u>punch</u>?
16. A <u>pale</u> light came through the window.
17. The coach had a <u>grave</u> look.
18. What kind of <u>berry</u> is that?
19. Hide your eyes and don't <u>peek</u>.
20. What are the <u>dates</u> of the test?

Challenge Words

21. The man gave a <u>feeble</u> call.
22. What is that sweet <u>fragrance</u>?
23. Students <u>mingled</u> in the classroom.
24. He <u>resembled</u> his father.
25. The mice <u>scampered</u> away.

DAY 1 — Pretest

Assess Prior Knowledge Use the Dictation Sentences at the left and **Spelling Practice Book** page 167 for the pretest. Allow students to correct their own papers. Students who require a modified list may be tested on the first ten words.

Spelling Words		Challenge Words
1. seen	11. peak	21. **feeble**
2. great	12. post	22. **fragrance**
3. light	13. pail	23. **mingled**
4. beat	14. bury	24. **resembled**
5. lean	15. punch	25. **scampered**
6. scene	16. pale	
7. beet	17. grave	
8. bowl	18. berry	
9. grate	19. peek	
10. fan	20. dates	

*Note: Words in **dark type** are from the story.*

Word Study On page 168 of the **Spelling Practice Book** are word study steps and an at-home activity.

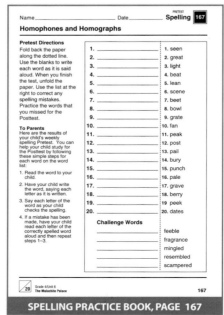

SPELLING PRACTICE BOOK, PAGE 167

WORD STUDY STEPS AND ACTIVITY, PAGE 168

DAY 2 — Explore the Pattern

Sort and Spell Words Have students sort the homophones into pairs; the remaining words are homographs. Have students think of two completely different meanings for each of the homographs.

Homophones

seen	beat	pail
scene	beet	pale
great	peak	bury
grate	peek	berry

Homographs

light	post
lean	punch
bowl	grave
fan	dates

Word Wall Have students create a word wall based on the word sort and add more words from their reading.

SPELLING PRACTICE BOOK, PAGE 169

Homophones and Homographs

DAY 3 **Practice and Extend**

Word Meaning: Synonyms Explain that students will have a better understanding of homophones and homographs if they can name a synonym for each Spelling Word. Make a chart of synonyms they suggest for each of the Spelling Words.

If students need extra practice, have partners give each other a midweek test.

Glossary Review how to find synonyms in the Glossary. Have partners:

- write each Challenge Word.

- use the Glossary to locate a synonym for the word *fragrance*.

- check the meanings of other Challenge words.

- list words that are synonyms or near synonyms of the Challenge words.

DAY 4 **Proofread and Write**

Proofread Sentences Write these sentences on the chalkboard, including the misspelled words. Ask students to proofread, circling incorrect spellings and writing the correct spellings. There are two spelling errors in each sentence.

> The last sceen in the play was graet.
> (scene, great)
>
> The lite on that posed burned out.
> (light, post)

Have students create additional sentences with errors for partners to correct.

 Have students use as many Spelling Words as possible in the daily Writing Prompt on page 632D. Remind students to proofread their writing for errors in spelling, grammar, and punctuation.

DAY 5 **Assess and Reteach**

Assess Students' Knowledge Use page 172 of the **Spelling Practice Book** or the Dictation Sentences on page 663O for the posttest.

Personal Word List If students have trouble with any words in the lesson, have them add the words to their personal word lists in their journals. Have students write pairs of sentences for each homograph or homophone pair.

Students should refer to their word lists during later writing activities.

SPELLING PRACTICE BOOK, PAGE 170

SPELLING PRACTICE BOOK, PAGE 171

SPELLING PRACTICE BOOK, PAGE 172

The Toothpaste Millionaire

Selection Summary Students will read about Rufus, an enterprising young man who develops a simple new formula for toothpaste. They will learn more about business as Rufus and his friends invest in a factory, machinery, and television advertising.

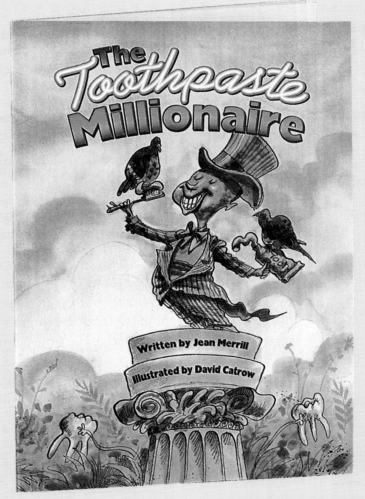

Student Listening Library Audiocassette

INSTRUCTIONAL
Pages 666–691

About the Author Jean Merrill is a well-known author of children's books. She likes to write about issues that are important to her, including recycling and animal rights, but also enjoys writing about common sense and respect for friends.

About the Illustrator David Catrow has illustrated more than 30 books for young people. He is also a cartoonist whose work is distributed in more than 900 newspapers.

Resources for
Meeting Individual Needs

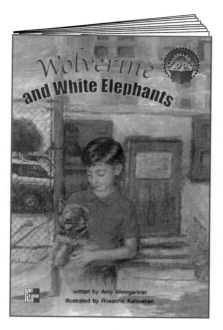

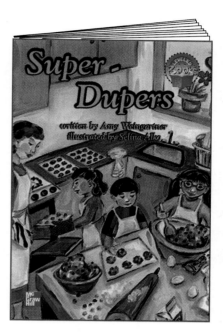

EASY
Pages 691A, 691D

INDEPENDENT
Pages 691B, 691D

CHALLENGE
Pages 691C, 691D

LEVELED PRACTICE

Reteach, 200–206

blackline masters with reteaching opportunities for each assessed skill

Practice, 200–206

workbook with Take-Home stories and practice opportunities for each assessed skill and story comprehension

Extend, 200–206

blackline masters that offer challenge activities for each assessed skill

ADDITIONAL RESOURCES

- **Language Support Book,** 217–224
- **Take-Home Story, Practice,** p. 201a
- **Alternative Teaching Strategies,** T60–T66

McGraw-Hill School
TECHNOLOGY

inter NET
CONNECTION Research and Inquiry Ideas. Visit
www.mhschool.com/reading

Suggested Lesson Planner

 Available on CD-ROM

READING AND LANGUAGE ARTS	DAY 1 *Focus on Reading and Skills*	DAY 2 *Read the Literature*

READING AND LANGUAGE ARTS

- **Comprehension**
- **Vocabulary**
- **Phonics/Decoding**
- **Study Skills**
- **Listening, Speaking, Viewing, Representing**

DAY 1 — Focus on Reading and Skills

Read **Read Aloud and Motivate,** 664E
Super-Goopy Glue

Develop Visual Literacy, 664/665

☑ **Review/Make Judgments and Decisions,** 666A–666B
Teaching Chart 163
Reteach, Practice, Extend, 200

DAY 2 — Read the Literature

Build Background, 666C
Develop Oral Language

Vocabulary, 666D

| brilliant | expensive | ingredient |
| commercials | gallon | successful |

Teaching Chart 164
Vocabulary Cards
Reteach, Practice, Extend, 201

Read **Read the Selection,** 666–687
☑ Make Judgments and Decisions
☑ Identify Cause and Effect

Minilessons, 673, 677, 681, 683

Cultural Perspectives, 668

- **Curriculum Connections**

 Works of Art, 664/665

 Social Studies, 666C

- **Writing**

 Writing Prompt: Imagine you are at the store shopping. Describe one product that leaves you dissatisfied. Tell why you would never buy it. Then tell how you might make it better.

 Writing Prompt: Describe a business someone you think might start in your neighborhood. Explain why anyone would want the business there. Then explain why no one would want their business there.

 Journal Writing, 687
Quick-Write

- **Grammar**

Introduce the Concept: Negatives, 691M
Daily Language Activity
1. We don't have no time. no
2. Ricky can't never go to the store. never
3. Nobody never asked Hector. never

Grammar Practice Book, 173

Teach the Concept: Negatives, 691M
Daily Language Activity
1. Nobody would not answer Mr. Conti. ever
2. Kate didn't see nothing. anything
3. Rufus won't go nowhere. anywhere

Grammar Practice Book, 174

- **Spelling**

Pretest: Words with Suffixes, 691O
Spelling Practice Book, 173, 174

Explore the Pattern: Words with Suffixes, 691O
Spelling Practice Book, 175

Meeting Individual Needs

☑ = **Skill Assessed in Unit Test**

Read EVERY DAY

DAY 3   *Read the Literature*

DAY 4   *Build Skills*

DAY 5   *Build Skills*

DAY 3

Rereading for Fluency, 686

Story Questions, 688
  Reteach, Practice, Extend, 202

Story Activities, 689

Study Skill, 690
  ☑ Library/Media Center
  Teaching Chart 165
  Reteach, Practice, Extend, 203

Test Power, 691

Read the Leveled Books, 691A–691D
  Guided Reading
  Silent Letters
    ☑ Make Judgments and Decisions
    ☑ Instructional Vocabulary

DAY 4

Read the Leveled Books and Self-Selected Books

☑ **Review Make Judgments and Decisions,** 691E–691F
  Teaching Chart 166
  Reteach, Practice, Extend, 204
  Language Support, 222

☑ **Review Problem and Solution,** 691G–691H
  Teaching Chart 167
  Reteach, Practice, Extend, 205
  Language Support, 223

DAY 5

Read Self-Selected Books

☑ **Review Antonyms and Synonyms,** 691I–691J
  Teaching Chart 168
  Reteach, Practice, Extend, 206
  Language Support, 224

Listening, Speaking, Viewing, Representing, 691L
  Present the Commercials
  Be an Announcer

Minilessons, 673, 681, 683

Phonics Review
  Silent letters, 677

Phonics Workbook

 Science, 672

 Social Studies, 674

 Math, 678

 Writing Prompt: Write a letter to Rufus. Tell him why you admire him for making something out of almost nothing. Give him some advice for his business too.

Writing Process: Write a Commercial, 691K
  Prewrite, Draft

Writing Prompt: Write a letter to Mr. Perkel persuading him that his policy toward children is unfair. Use *couldn't, wouldn't,* and *won't* to stress important points.

Writing Process: Write a Commercial, 691K
  Revise
Meeting Individual Needs for Writing, 691L

Writing Prompt: What did you learn from *The Toothpaste Millionaire* about businesses? How does this story support the statement "Never say *never!*"? Write a paragraph.

Writing Process: Write a Commercial, 691K
  Edit/Proofread, Publish

Review and Practice: Negatives, 691N
Daily Language Activity
1. Nobody can't help Rufus. can
2. Kate didn't never agree. ever
3. She would not say that to no one. anyone

Grammar Practice Book, 175

Review and Practice: Negatives, 691N
Daily Language Activity
1. Mr. Smiley can't go nowhere alone. anywhere
2. Customers never get nothing for free. anything
3. Nobody couldn't find Clem's math book. could

Grammar Practice Book, 176

Assess and Reteach: Negatives, 691N
Daily Language Activity
1. Mr. Conti couldn't find no one. anyone
2. Mr. Perkell never has no fun. no
3. Mr. Smiley won't never know. ever

Grammar Practice Book, 177, 178

Practice and Extend: Words with Suffixes, 691P

Spelling Practice Book, 176

Proofread and Write: Words with Suffixes, 691P

Spelling Practice Book, 177

Assess and Reteach: Words with Suffixes, 691P

Spelling Practice Book, 178

Read Aloud and Motivate

Super-Goopy Glue

a poem by Jack Prelutsky

Permit me to present to you
my famous SUPER-GOOPY GLUE,
by far the finest glue on earth,
one dollar for a penny's worth.

It's rumored that my glue adheres
for easily a thousand years,
my glue's the glue you surely seek,
it's guaranteed for one whole week.

My SUPER-GOOPY GLUE can glue
a carrot to a caribou,
a feather to a ferret's feet,
a pickle to a parakeet.

No other glue is half as good,
it works on metal, glass, and wood,
I'd demonstrate it for you, but
my glue has glued my gluepot shut.

Oral Comprehension

LISTENING AND SPEAKING Tell students that you are going to read a poem about a new product called Super-Goopy Glue. Ask students to listen and decide if they would like to buy this new product. After reading the poem, ask students, "What are some good things about Super-Goopy Glue? What are some bad things about the glue?"

Read the poem again, stopping after each stanza, and have students note the end-of-line rhymes. Ask students which lines in each stanza rhyme.

Activity Encourage students to work in pairs to draw their own advertisement for Super-Goopy Glue. Point out that the picture and the words in the ad should work together to say something important about the product. Alternatively, some pairs might like to write original advertising jingles for Super-Goopy Glue. After all partners have shared their advertisements or jingles, have them use information in the poem, the ads, and the jingles to judge the quality of Super-Goopy Glue.

▶ **Visual/Spatial**

Anthology pages 664–665

Stories in Art

This photograph shows a scene from an old silent film. Movies—old and new—often show characters making important decisions.

Look at this picture from the film *Modern Times*. What can you tell about the film? What is the character, played by Charlie Chaplin, deciding to do? Is he trying to help his coworker who is caught in the gears? Do you think Chaplin is trying to stop the machine? Explain your reasons. What might the film-maker be saying about "man and machine" in the modern world?

Look at the picture again. How can you tell that this movie was made a long time ago? If you were to make this movie today, what machine would you use? Explain why.

Scene from
Modern Times, 1936

664

665

Objective: Make Judgments and Decisions

VIEWING This scene from the 1936 movie *Modern Times* shows comedian Charlie Chaplin confronting a co-worker whose head is trapped in the gears of a piece of factory machinery. Chaplin is considering whether to jam the gears of the machine to stop it. Point out that Chaplin's film dramatized an important theme: people's complicated relationship to the machines that are part of our lives.

Read the page with students, encouraging individual interpretations of the still photographs from the film,

and have students make judgments about the proper role of machinery in our lives. For example:

- Machines should be our tools, not our masters.
- The man with his head in the gears shows how modern technology is crushing us.

REPRESENTING Have groups of students perform an interpretive dance that shows some of the ways in which different machines affect them on a typical day. Students should judge and express whether these machines are beneficial or harmful to an individual's creativity.

Students will identify and evaluate how characters in a story make judgments and decisions.

TEACHING TIP

INSTRUCTIONAL Point out that courtroom judges make an effort to find out the facts and details in a case. They are also aware of what is right and wrong. Explain that, like judges, strategic readers use facts and details, which they get from the story. Strategic readers also use their background knowledge to help them understand and evaluate how characters in a story make judgments and decisions.

Review Judgments and Decisions

PREPARE

Discuss Everyday Examples
Ask students about judgments and decisions they have already made today. Did they decide what to wear? What to eat? How did they decide?

TEACH

Read the Passage and Model the Skill
Tell students that making a decision involves judging choices, choosing one that fits their goals, needs, and values.

On-the-Job Judgments

Tom has a business taking care of people's lawns. He cuts grass, clips hedges, and does other yardwork. Last summer, Tom hired Ben and Maria to work for him. Tom told them he would pay them each $2.50 an hour. The first week, Ben and Maria each worked 10 hours. They worked hard, and the homeowners were happy with their yards. When Ben and Maria saw Tom, though, he said he could only pay them $1.00 an hour for their work. He said they hadn't done a good job. He also told them they would have to wait a few weeks for their money.

Teaching Chart 163

Display **Teaching Chart 163.** Have students make judgments about the situation and say whether or not they would work for Tom.

MODEL Tom promised to pay $2.50 an hour but after the work was done he changed his mind. He also said Ben and Maria's work was not good, yet the homeowners were happy with the work. In my judgment Tom is not a trustworthy person, I would not work for him.

Identify Story Evidence
Have students underline the evidence in the paragraph that led to this decision.

PRACTICE

Create a Judgment and Decision Chart

Have students make a Judgment and Decision chart. Then ask them to fill it out using evidence from the paragraph.

▶ **Spatial/Intrapersonal**

GROUP

JUDGMENT OR DECISION	EVIDENCE FROM STORY
Tom is not trustworthy or a good person to work for.	Tom broke his promise to pay $2.50.
I would not work for him.	Tom lied when he said Ben and Maria did bad work.
	Tom puts off paying Ben and Maria for no good reason.
	He doesn't appreciate the work they did, even though the homeowners liked the work.

ASSESS/CLOSE

Make Judgments and Decisions

Give students an example of a judgment and a decision, such as, *Welles Department Store is a very pleasant place to shop and I'll go there again.* Then have students make up some evidence that might lead to this judgment and decision. Alternatively, students might suggest some judgments or decisions they have made in their own lives recently and cite the evidence they used to make these judgments or decisions.

ALTERNATE TEACHING STRATEGY

JUDGMENTS AND DECISIONS

For a different approach to teaching this skill, see page T62.

Meeting Individual Needs for Comprehension

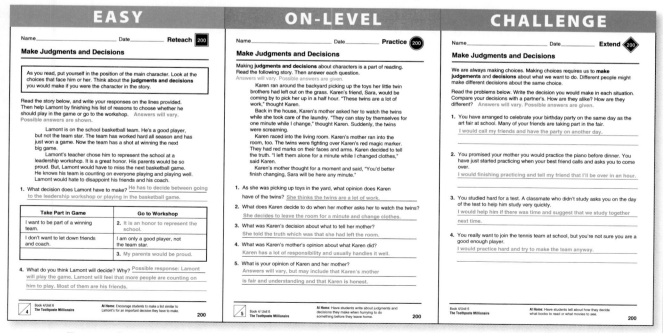

Reteach, 200   Practice, 200   Extend, 200

Build Background

 **Link**

Social Studies

Anthology and Leveled Books

Evaluate Prior Knowledge

CONCEPT: KIDS MAKING MONEY

These stories present young people who work hard to earn money for things they consider important. Have students share their ideas about how kids can make money.

LIST STEPS IN THE JOB PROCESS

Help students create a chart like the one shown that shows the steps in the process of getting and performing a job.

▶ Logical/Visual

```
┌─────────────────────────────────┐
│        THE JOB PROCESS          │
└─────────────────────────────────┘
             ↓
┌─────────────────────────────────┐
│     Read a job advertisement     │
└─────────────────────────────────┘
             ↓
┌─────────────────────────────────┐
│       Interview for the job      │
└─────────────────────────────────┘
             ↓
┌─────────────────────────────────┐
│          Report to work          │
└─────────────────────────────────┘
             ↓
┌─────────────────────────────────┐
│        Follow instructions       │
└─────────────────────────────────┘
             ↓
┌─────────────────────────────────┐
│           Do your best           │
└─────────────────────────────────┘
```

Graphic Organizer 17

JOB WATCH Have students create a list of   the different types of jobs they see people doing. For example, they might see a police officer on their way to work or an admnistrative assistant in the school office. Have them choose a job that interests them and find out more about it. Then, have them write a paragraph telling how a kid could bring something special to that job or do it in a different way than an adult.

Develop Oral Language

DISCUSS KIDS MAKING MONEY

ESL Brainstorm a list of ways that kids make money. For example, if possible, bring in pictures of kids doing work. Discuss the meanings of the words and phrases and ask volunteers to use them in sentences.

- babysitting
- selling flowers
- selling lemonade
- mowing lawns
- an allowance for household chores
- delivering newspapers
- collecting returnable bottles

TEACHING TIP

MANAGEMENT Many students may not have had experience working or earning money. To help students understand the concept of kids working for money, ask volunteers to speak about the work experiences of older siblings.

LANGUAGE SUPPORT

See **Language Support Book**, pages 217–220, for teaching suggestions for Build Background and Vocabulary.

Vocabulary

Key Words

1. The best job I had as a kid was acting in television commercials. 2. In my first television ad, which was for a rug cleaner, I had to spill a gallon of grape juice on a white rug. (That was fun!) 3. Then I had to use the rug cleaner, which had a special ingredient, to get the stain out. 4. By the way, you don't have to be brilliant to make television ads: my only line was, "So easy, a kid can use it!" 5. This rug cleaner was never very successful. 6. Not many people bought it since it was so expensive, and no one wanted to pay that much money.

Teaching Chart 164

Vocabulary in Context

IDENTIFY VOCABULARY WORDS
Display **Teaching Chart 164** and read the passage with students. Have volunteers circle each vocabulary word and underline other words/phrases that are clues to its meaning.

DISCUSS MEANINGS Ask questions like these to help clarify word meanings:

- Which television commercials are your favorites these days?

- Does your family buy milk by the quart or by the gallon?

- What is the main ingredient in your favorite dish or meal?

- Have you ever had a brilliant idea?

- Are you more successful in English or math?

- If an item is too expensive, do you buy it anyway?

Practice

DEFINITION RIDDLES Write the vocabulary words on the chalkboard. Have volunteers choose vocabulary word cards and then make up riddle-like questions about the words. For example, "My word is something you see all the time on television." Listeners then answer the riddle.

▶ **Linguistic/Oral**

Vocabulary Cards

WRITE CONTEXT SENTENCES Have students write context sentences using a synonym for each vocabulary word. Have them exchange papers and write each vocabulary word above its synonym. Have students refer to their glossary as needed. ▶ **Linguistic/Oral**

Definitions

commercials (p. 684) paid advertising messages on radio or television

gallon (p. 671) a unit of liquid measure equal to four quarts

ingredient (p. 672) a component part of a mixture

brilliant (p. 670) splendid or outstanding; magnificent

successful (p. 668) having wealth or status

expensive (p. 671) involving great cost

SPELLING/VOCABULARY CONNECTIONS

See Spelling Challenge Words, pages 000–P.

ON-LEVEL

The Never-Ending Pudding

Shanny saw several television *commercials* for instant pudding. "Who needs that," said Shanny. "I can make pudding from my own recipe."

Shanny poured a *gallon* of milk into a big pot. Beginning with cocoa, she added each *ingredient* she thought should be in a pudding. Once she had added them all, Shanny cooked the pudding over low heat for half an hour. Then she poured it in a bowl and put it in the refrigerator until dinner time.

Shanny's efforts were quite *successful*, and her family said that Shanny's pudding recipe was *brilliant*. "It wasn't very expensive to make either," said Shanny, feeling very pleased with herself.

ANNO: Answers may vary.

1. Where did Shanny get the idea for making pudding?
   from instant pudding commercials on television

2. Which two ingredients in pudding are mentioned in the story?
   milk, cocoa

3. What does it mean that Shanny's recipe was brilliant?
   It means her recipe made a good pudding; it was a smart recipe.

4. Do you think Shanny was successful?
   Answers will vary, but may include that she is successful because she is creative, making up her own recipe.

5. Think of one of your favorite foods for lunch or dinner. Describe the ingredients and how you could make that food in a way that is not expensive. Use as many vocabulary words as you can.
   Answers will vary.

Book 4/Unit 6
The Toothpaste Millionaire
At Home: Have students use the vocabulary words in a conversation.
201a

Take-Home Story 201a
Reteach 201
Practice 201 • Extend 201

Guided Instruction

Preview and Predict

Have students read the title and preview the illustrations to page 678. Ask them to predict what the play will be about.

- How do you know that this selection is a play? (The story is set up as dialogue for characters to read; there are stage directions.) *Genre*

- Who do you think will be the main character in this play?

- What do you think the play will tell about?

Have students record their predictions about the play on a chart.

PREDICTIONS	WHAT HAPPENED
The play will tell about a boy who makes toothpaste.	
I will learn about how new products come onto the market.	

Set Purposes

What do students want to find out by reading the play? For example:

- Does the kid really make a million dollars from toothpaste?

- Why is this a play and not a story?

Meet Jean Merrill

Jean Merrill is known as a writer of unusual books for young people. As an author, she is not afraid to take chances and to write about issues that matter to her. Some of these issues are recycling, animal rights, and solving problems between people. Her most famous book is *The Pushcart War*.

Friendship is also important to Merrill. In *The Toothpaste Millionaire*, not only does she teach simple lessons about business and math, she also encourages good common sense and respect for friends. Originally a novel, *The Toothpaste Millionaire* has been made into a play. It has also been shown on television. The book appears as a play in this selection.

Meet David Catrow

David Catrow is a man of many interests. As a young man, he wanted to be a doctor, but he took up drawing instead. Later, he became an illustrator of medical books. Tired of drawing bones, Catrow moved on to becoming a children's book illustrator. He has now drawn pictures for more than 30 books for young people. Also a cartoonist, Catrow creates cartoons for more than 900 newspapers in the United States and Canada.

666

Meeting Individual Needs • Grouping Suggestions for Strategic Reading

EASY

Read Together Assign different students to read aloud the lines of the characters. Or, invite students to use the **Listening Library Audiocassette.** Present the Judgment and Decision chart, and demonstrate how to complete it. For additional help with comprehension use the Guided Instruction and Intervention prompts.

ON-LEVEL

Guided Reading Before reading, have students review the story words on page 667. You may want to have the students read the play first on their own. Or, read with the students, using Guided Instruction prompts as needed. Encourage students to use the Judgment and Decision chart to keep tracks of Rufus's major decisions.

CHALLENGE

Read Independently As students read, let them work with a Judgment and Decision chart like the one on page 667. Remind them to use facts from the play as well as their own background knowledge in filling out the chart. After they finish the play, suggest that they use their charts to summarize the play.

The Toothpaste Millionaire

Written by Jean Merrill

Illustrated by David Catrow

LANGUAGE SUPPORT

A blackline master of the Judgment and Decision chart is available in the **Language Support Book.**

Guided Instruction

☑ **Judgments and Decisions**

☑ **Cause and Effect**

Strategic Reading Before we begin reading, let's make Judgment and Decision charts. Paying attention to causes and effects will also help you understand the play.

JUDGMENT OR DECISION	EVIDENCE FROM STORY

(1) JUDGMENTS AND DECISIONS
Why do you think a town might erect a statue of a millionaire?

MODEL This statue is holding a toothbrush. The town must have made a judgment that the toothpaste millionaire deserved a great honor. They decided to honor him with a statue.

Story Words

The words below may be unfamiliar. Have students check their meanings and pronunciations in the Glossary beginning on page 726.

- enterprise, p. 668
- downstage, p. 670
- portable, p. 670
- toothpaste, p. 670
- tube, p. 671
- sterilized, p. 675
- certificate, p. 676
- stockholder, p. 676

Guided Instruction

2 **CAUSE AND EFFECT** According to the description, why did Rufus become a millionaire?

MODEL In the opening sentence, I read that Rufus is a millionaire. Right away I wonder what caused a young man to become a millionaire. As I read on, I find out that he is a millionaire because he had ideas and because he had the initiative to put his ideas, himself and his friends to work.

Rufus Mayflower was a young man with ideas who became a millionaire. He didn't set out to build a successful enterprise. He just had the initiative to put his ideas, himself, and his friends to work. Rufus became quite a celebrity. In this play, he is being interviewed by talk-show host Joe Smiley.

668

CULTURAL PERSPECTIVES

VIEWS ABOUT WEALTH Explain that different peoples and cultures have held different views and attitudes toward wealth. Not all people have viewed wealth as uniformly positive.

RESEARCH AND INQUIRY Have students interview adults about their views on wealth. Suggest that they compile a chart of quotations that show varying views toward wealth. Students can also research distribution of wealth in cultures of the past, such as the Maya culture. ▶ **Interpersonal**

World Money		
Country	Currency	value (=1dollar)
USA	Dollar	$1.00
England	Pound	£.625
Japan	Yen	Y 120
Mexico	Peso	MX$9.5

CHARACTERS

Joe Smiley
Rufus Mayflower
Kate MacKinstrey
Mr. Conti
Clem
Josie
Lee Lu
James
Auctioneer
Customer #1
Customer #2
Customer #3
Hector
Josh
Sharon
Members of the Class
Mr. Perkell
Mr. Perkell's Secretary

Guided Instruction

3 What might you infer about the play based on the list of characters? (There are a great many characters for such a short play; many of the characters will have small parts.) *Make Inferences*

Visual Literacy

VIEWING AND REPRESENTING

Encourage students to study the cartoonlike illustrations on these and preceding pages. Based on the style of the drawings, what might you conclude about the play? (Sample answers: The play will be high-spirited and fun; this is a light-hearted look at the process of becoming a millionaire.)

LANGUAGE SUPPORT

ESL Some students may have a hard time telling the difference between a judgment and a decision. Share the definitions then use examples to give students practice identifying judgments and decisions:
judgment—opinion or conclusion
decision—making up one's mind, especially to do something

- I will take a well-lighted way. (D)
- Toothpaste is expensive. (J)
- The weather is perfect for skiing. (J)
- I will go to school today. (D)
- That road looks dangerous. (J)
- I will not buy toothpaste. (D)
- Sam is kind. (J)
- I will make friends with Sam. (D)

Guided Instruction

4 Why do you think the stage directions call for a chalkboard, a long table, and bowls? (During the interview, Rufus and his friends might enact how they came to discover and produce toothpaste.) *Make Predictions*

5 Think about Joe Smiley's question and Rufus's answer. How does this show that Joe and Rufus have different ideas about what is important? (Joe asks Rufus about the money part of his business. Rufus wasn't thinking about the money. He wanted to make toothpaste.) *Character*

A long bench is set up across the center of the stage. A large portable chalkboard is behind the bench. Downstage left is a long table with several bowls on it. Downstage right is a smaller table and two chairs. As the curtain opens, **4** *JOE SMILEY and RUFUS are seated at the small table.*

JOE: Welcome to the Joe Smiley Show! Today we have a fantastic young guest who has used his fantastic young brain to become a millionaire! Meet Rufus Mayflower of East Cleveland, Ohio. *(to Rufus)* Welcome, Rufus!

RUFUS: Thank you, Mr. Smiley.

JOE: Now, Rufus, my first question is one that I know everyone wants to ask. How did you figure out how to make so much money?

RUFUS: Well, I wasn't trying **5** to make money, just to make toothpaste.

JOE: All right, Rufus. What gave you that brilliant idea?

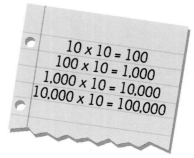

Activity

Cross Curricular: Math

MILLIONS AND MILLIONS Invite students to write the figure that represents one million—1,000,000. Ask them to express the amount one million in different terms, such as "one thousand thousand." Also have students write the figures that represent one billion and one trillion.

Have groups of students continue a chart similar to the one shown here to show a million, a billion, or a trillion. Have students talk about what patterns they see on the chart.

▶ **Mathematical/Visual**

$$10 \times 10 = 100$$
$$100 \times 10 = 1,000$$
$$1,000 \times 10 = 10,000$$
$$10,000 \times 10 = 100,000$$

RUFUS: It all started when I was doing some shopping for my mother at the Cut-Rate Drugstore with my friend Kate.

(KATE comes out and stands in the middle of the stage. RUFUS joins her. KATE pantomimes pushing a shopping cart, while RUFUS pulls out a list.)

RUFUS: Now, let's see. I need toothpaste.

KATE: Here it is.

(She pretends to hand him a tube.)

RUFUS: One dollar and thirty-nine cents for a six-inch tube of toothpaste? That's crazy!

KATE: It's better than this other one for a dollar and eighty-nine cents.

RUFUS: That's even crazier! What can be in those tubes, anyway? Just some peppermint flavoring and some paste.

KATE: Maybe the paste is expensive to make.

RUFUS: Who knows? I never tried, but I bet it isn't hard. Put that tube back.

KATE: But Rufus, your mother said to get toothpaste. You can't help it if it's expensive.

RUFUS: I'll make her some. I bet I can make her a gallon for less than a dollar.

6

671

Guided Instruction

COMPOUND WORDS Look at the word *toothpaste*. What is toothpaste? How can the word itself help you figure out its meaning?

6 **JUDGMENTS AND DECISIONS** What judgment has Rufus made here? What decision has he made?

MODEL Making judgments involves making choices based on one's values. Rufus judges both tubes of toothpaste to be too expensive for what they contain. Making a decision involves choosing a course of action. Rufus makes an unusual decision—he will make his own toothpaste to save money. Let's place this information on our chart.

JUDGMENT OR DECISION	EVIDENCE FROM STORY
Rufus says it's "crazy" to buy toothpaste.	Tubes of toothpaste cost $1.39 and $1.89.
Rufus decides to make his own cheaply.	Rufus says, "I can make a gallon for less than a dollar."

PREVENTION/INTERVENTION

COMPOUND WORDS Write *toothpaste* on the chalkboard. Ask students what two words they see in the word *toothpaste.* (tooth, paste) Have students tell more about each of these words. Then have students use this information to draw the conclusion that toothpaste is a paste used on teeth.

You might also call students' attention to the fact that *Toothpaste* on page 676 is capitalized and written in italic type. Elicit that it is used here as a proper noun because it is the name that Rufus gave to his toothpaste. Explain that brand names of products are sometimes printed in italic type.

671

Guided Instruction

7 Based on Rufus's answer to Joe Smiley's question, how would you describe Rufus? (Sample answer: He is bright, practical and down-to-earth.) *Character*

(KATE goes and sits on the bench. RUFUS returns to the small table to continue the interview with Joe Smiley.)

JOE: Fantastic! I suppose you stayed up day and night creating your secret formula.

RUFUS: No, I just used some stuff anybody can buy for a few cents and mix up in a few minutes. The main ingredient was plain old baking soda.

JOE: What happened next?

RUFUS: The next morning, Kate stopped by on the way to school.

672

Activity

Cross Curricular: Science

BAKING SODA Ask students to find out more about baking soda, or sodium bicarbonate, and why cooks often add it to breads, biscuits, and pastries before baking.

Invite students to mix a small amount of vinegar and baking soda together in a cup. Then have volunteers describe the chemical reaction that occurs. Some students might try brushing their teeth with baking soda and then evaluate whether they would like to use this as their regular toothpaste.

▶ Spatial

(RUFUS goes over to the long table with the bowls. KATE joins him.)

KATE: What are you making?

RUFUS: I already made it.

(He hands KATE a spoonful.)

Don't eat it. Rub a little on your teeth.

(KATE tries some.)

KATE: What's in here?

RUFUS: A drop of peppermint oil. I've got enough for forty tubes of toothpaste here!

KATE: Wow! Wait until we tell the kids at school! Come on, Rufus.

673

Guided Instruction

8 How do you know that the scene on page 673 happened long before Rufus's interview with Joe Smiley? (Joe Smiley interviewed Rufus after he became a millionaire; the scene on page 673 occurred on the morning Rufus made his very first batch of toothpaste.) Invite volunteers to show the sequence of events by role-playing Rufus as he makes his first batch of toothpaste. *Role-Play*

TEACHING TIP

INSTRUCTIONAL Make sure students understand that the scenes in the play are like flashbacks. That is, Rufus is recounting to Joe Smiley how he invented the toothpaste. To do so, Rufus and Kate, and later other characters, will re-enact scenes and events from the past.

Minilesson

REVIEW

Character

Remind students that authors reveal a great deal about characters through their actions. Instead of telling us what the character is like, they show us.

• What can we infer about Rufus from the fact that he is up before school perfecting his recipe for toothpaste? (Sample answer: He is highly-motivated and hardworking.)

Activity Students can create character webs for Rufus, Kate, and the other main characters in the play. As they read, ask them to list the characters' traits on the webs.

Guided Instruction

9 **CAUSE AND EFFECT** What causes Mr. Conti to read aloud the word problem about toothpaste? (Mr. Conti read it aloud because it was a note being passed in math class.)

(KATE and RUFUS hurry to the bench and sit down. CLEM, JOSIE, and LEE LU come out and join them. They face MR. CONTI, their math teacher, at the chalkboard.)

MR. CONTI: All right, class, take out your math books.

(RUFUS passes a note to CLEM, who hands it to JOSIE, who hands it to LEE LU, who hands it to KATE. KATE opens the note.)

MR. CONTI: Kate MacKinstrey, would you please bring me that note?

KATE: Well, it's not exactly a note, Mr. Conti.

MR. CONTI: I see. I suppose it's a math problem.

KATE: It looks like a math problem, Mr. Conti.

MR. CONTI: *(reading)* There are about 226 million people in the United States. Each one buys about ten tubes of toothpaste a year. That's two billion two-hundred-sixty million tubes of toothpaste a year! If an inventor made a new toothpaste, sold only *one* billion tubes, and made a one-cent profit on each tube, how much would he make? *(looking up)* Well, class, what would you do to figure it out?

CLEM: You'd have to take one billion times one cent or .01. That comes out to . . .

674

Cross Curricular: Social Studies

POPULATION Point out that today there are far more than 226 million people in the United States.

RESEARCH AND INQUIRY Invite students to track the American population over the last 50 years or so. Ask them to decide when the population was about 226 million. Invite students to create a bulletin-board display that shows population trends in the United States.

▶ **Logical/Visual**

*inter*NET **CONNECTION** Students can learn more about population growth by visiting **www.mhschool.com/reading**

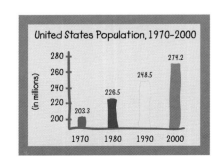

United States Population, 1970-2000

(in millions)

1970	1980	1990	2000
203.3	226.5	248.5	274.2

ALL: Ten million dollars!

JOSIE: Did you invent a toothpaste, Rufus?

CLEM: What's it called?

LEE LU: How much does it cost?

MR. CONTI: All right, class, quiet down.

(RUFUS gets up and goes back to sit at the small table with JOE SMILEY.)

RUFUS: I called it *Toothpaste*.

JOE: Not *Sparkle* or *Shine*?

RUFUS: No. Just plain *Toothpaste*. Kate and I packed it into sterilized baby jars, and we delivered them to customers on our bikes.

JOE: How much did you charge?

RUFUS: It cost me two cents to make, so I charged three cents unless I had to mail it somewhere out of town. Then I included postage. In a couple of months, I had so many customers that my math class had to help me out.

675

Guided Instruction

10 **JUDGMENTS AND DECISIONS** What judgments or decisions did Rufus make in naming and marketing his first toothpaste? Let's add this information to our chart.

JUDGMENT OR DECISION	EVIDENCE FROM STORY
Rufus says it's "crazy" to buy toothpaste.	Tubes of toothpaste cost $1.39 and $1.89.
Rufus decides to make his own cheaply.	Rufus says, "I can make a gallon for less than a dollar."
Rufus thinks it best to keep his toothpaste as simple and inexpensive as he can.	He names his product "Toothpaste"; he packs it in used jars; he charges only 3 cents instead of $1.39 or $1.89, which is what it cost at the store.

SELF-MONITORING

STRATEGY

SEARCH FOR CLUES Looking for clues in a story can help a reader clear up something that may seem unclear at first.

MODEL When I first read page 675, I thought the events took place the same day Rufus invented the toothpaste. So I reread the passage and searched for clues. The clues about packing the toothpaste into baby jars and delivering it to customers suggest that some weeks have passed. Also, the clue that he had so many customers he had to ask his math class for help tells me enough time has passed that his business has grown.

675

Guided Instruction

CONTEXT CLUES Find the word *stock* on page 676. Do you know what *stock* means? Can you figure it out by reading the rest of the page?

11 CAUSE AND EFFECT Why can't Rufus use the money he makes selling toothpaste to pay his friends? (He needs that money to buy more stuff for *Toothpaste*.)

12 JUDGMENTS AND DECISIONS If you were Kate or Clem, would you rather be paid by the hour or receive shares of stock? How would you decide? (Sample answer: I would take stock in the company because I know it will be successful.)

(RUFUS, KATE, CLEM, JOSIE, and LEE LU go over to the long table with the bowls. They pantomime filling the jars with toothpaste.)

CLEM: Rufus, what would you do if you had to pay us to do all this work?

JOSIE: We spend hours washing out baby jars and filling them with *Toothpaste*.

RUFUS: I don't have any profits to pay anybody yet. I've got to use the money I'm making to buy more stuff for *Toothpaste*. But I'll tell you what. I'll give **11** you stock in my company.

CLEM: Stock? What good is that?

RUFUS: At the end of the year, every stockholder will get a share of the year's profits.

KATE: Like in that game you have called "Stock Market"?

RUFUS: Right. Anybody who puts in a hundred hours helping me make *Toothpaste* gets a stock certificate, which will entitle him or her to a share of the company's profits. I'll use the stock **12** certificates from my game.

KATE: Well, I've already worked here more than two hundred hours.

676

P/i **PREVENTION/INTERVENTION**

CONTEXT CLUES Remind students that they can come to understand the meaning of an unfamiliar word by reading the sentences nearby. Have students reread the second column of page 676 to figure out the meaning of *stock* by using context clues. Ask them to explain the meaning of *stock* and to say which context clues they found.) A stock is a share of a business's profits .... every stockholder will get a share of the year's profits.)

RUFUS: So you are the first stockholder.

(RUFUS returns to JOE SMILEY to continue the interview.)

JOE: This is mind-boggling! What happened next?

RUFUS: The next part of the story belongs to Kate.

(KATE talks to LEE LU, CLEM, and JOSIE who are still working at the long table.)

KATE: You know, I wish we had real tubes instead of these baby jars.

LEE LU: It sure would look better.

KATE: I wonder if I can find any.

CLEM: I bet they'd be expensive even if you could.

KATE: I'm going to start looking around. *(She looks at her watch.)* Oh, oh, I have to get home for supper. See you tomorrow.

677

ESL Help students understand the term *mind-boggling* that Joe Smiley uses to describe Rufus's account. Bring out that it is a compound word formed from *mind* and *boggling*, which means "overwhelming." Point out that people sometimes say, "It boggles the mind," which means, "It's hard to imagine."

Guided Instruction

(13) When Clem says, "I'll bet they'd be expensive," does that remind you of any strategic reading skill? Which one? (Make Predictions) What do you think will happen next? (They will find the tubes somehow) *Make Predictions*

TEACHING **TIP**

INSTRUCTIONAL Authors don't always state all the reasons a decision is made. The author expects a reader to bring background knowledge to the reading. Suggest that students give some other reasons why Rufus might want to use tubes instead of baby jars. (Tubes might be more sterile, less breakable, more familiar to customers, and easier to fill.)

Minilesson

R E V I E W

Silent Letters

Remind students that many English words have silent letters. Point out the word *know* in the last line of the first column on page 677.

- Have students identify the silent letter in the word *know*. (k)
- Write the following words on the chalkboard and have students identify the silent letter in each: *limb* (b), *calf* (l), *night* (gh), *write* (w), *yolk*(l), *doubt* (b), and *knot* (k).

Activity Have partners work together to write a sentence that contains five or more silent letters. Students may refer to the words on the chalkboard or they may identify and use additional words with silent letters.

Guided Instruction

14 **CAUSE AND EFFECT** Why are the tubes being sold at an auction? (A company that packaged something in tubes went out of business before using the tubes.)

(KATE leaves the long table and goes back to the bench. Her brother, JAMES, comes out reading a newspaper and sits on the bench.)

KATE: Hi, James.

JAMES: Don't bother me, I'm reading.

KATE: Well, excuse me! I don't call that reading. It's just another list of companies going out of business.

JAMES: It can be very informative. Now, let's see . . . *(reads)* . . . Complete furnishings of ice cream parlor . . . Ferris wheel swings . . . 15 trailer trucks . . . 50 gross high-quality aluminum tubes . . .

KATE: Did you say *tubes*? Let me see. *(She looks at the paper.)* It doesn't give the price.

JAMES: Of course not. You have to go to the auction and bid on them.

KATE: An auction? Where?

JAMES: At Pulaski Brothers Warehouse. Somebody with a lot of tubes just went out **14** of business.

(JAMES walks off. KATE goes behind the bench. Several CUSTOMERS come on stage and stand near KATE at the auction. The AUCTIONEER comes out and faces the CUSTOMERS and KATE.)

678

Cross Curricular: Math

GROSS Grocers got their name because they bought food in very large quantities—by the gross. Point out that a gross is a unit of measurement equal to 12 dozen. Have students multiply 12 by 12 to find out how many items are in a gross. Then ask them to multiply their total by 50 to find out how many tubes are available for sale at the auction. Point out that Kate eventually buys the tubes for 10 cents a gross. How much does she pay in all? How much does she pay per tube?

▶**Mathematical/Logical**

50 gross
at 10 cents is
50
x.10
$5.00

AUCTIONEER: Item Number 76: aluminum tubes, 50 gross. How much am I bid by the gross? Bidder takes the lot.

KATE: How much is a gross? I can't remember. Let's see 50 dozen is 600 and that's already a lot. *(to AUCTIONEER)* Excuse me, sir. Can I just bid on a couple of dozen?

293

AUCTIONEER: The bid is for the whole lot. Who'll bid five cents a gross?

CUSTOMER #1: Five cents!

KATE: Six cents!

AUCTIONEER: Six cents for the lady.

CUSTOMER #2: Seven cents!

KATE: Eight! We really need those tubes.

AUCTIONEER: Anyone for nine?

KATE: TEN!

CUSTOMER #1: I give up.

CUSTOMER #2: Me, too.

AUCTIONEER: Sold to the lady for ten cents a gross.

KATE: Oh, well, I guess we'll use up six hundred tubes.

CUSTOMER #3: Six hundred? You just bought seven thousand two hundred tubes.

KATE: Seven thousand two hundred!

187

679

Guided Instruction

MULTIPLE-MEANING WORDS Draw students' attention to the word *gross* in the second line from the top in the first column. What is a common meaning for *gross*? What do you think the word means here?

15 **JUDGMENTS AND DECISIONS** Do you think Kate made a good decision when she bought the tubes? (Sample answer: The tubes were a bargain if there is a way to fill them with *Toothpaste*.)

16 This is an exciting scene. Let's read it again with volunteers playing the different parts. *Role-Play*

PREVENTION/INTERVENTION

MULTIPLE-MEANING WORDS
Bring out some common meanings of *gross*. Suggest that students use them in phrases. For example, "the overall sum," as in *gross pay*, "very obvious" as in *gross injustice*, or "coarse or unpleasant," as in a *gross meal*. Bring out that *gross* as used here, however, refers to a numerical amount, specifically, 12 dozen.

Guided Instruction

17 Why is Kate going to the Happy Lips Lotion Company? (She wants to find out about machines that fill tubes.) *Main Idea*

18 What do you predict will happen next in the plot? (Rufus, Kate, and the others will acquire a machine to fill toothpaste tubes.) *Make Predictions*

TEACHING TIP

INSTRUCTIONAL Tell students that they will better appreciate the action in this play if they imagine they are viewing a performance of it in a theater. In particular, ask them to visualize the actions described in the stage directions. Or, have a few students follow the stage directions to perform a scene.

(The CUSTOMERS and the AUCTIONEER exit. KATE goes back to the long table with JOSIE, LEE LU, and CLEM.)

KATE: I forgot that a gross is a dozen dozen. Twelve times twelve times fifty is what I bought.

LEE LU: Isn't there some kind of machine for filling tubes?

CLEM: What about the place that all these tubes came from?

KATE: Let's see if there's a name on the box. *(She pantomimes looking at a box and reads:)* Happy Lips Lotion Company. I am going to the Happy Lips Lotion Company to check it out.

17

(HECTOR comes out on stage. He moves away the bench and brings the chalkboard downstage. He flips the chalkboard around to display a diagram of a complicated machine.)

18

680

Activity

Cross Curricular: Social Studies

INDUSTRY Ask students to find out the names of some current or historical companies or industries in their region and the products they make.

RESEARCH AND INQUIRY Ask student groups to find out more about one of these industries. Encourage them to create a chart of one aspect of the industry, such as production, or employment.

▶ **Logical/Spatial**

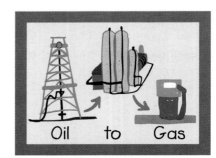

Oil to Gas

(KATE comes up to HECTOR.)

HECTOR: Can I help you?

KATE: No thank you. I'm just looking.

HECTOR: Oh?

KATE: For a machine. I have a friend who needs a certain kind of machine for filling toothpaste tubes.

HECTOR: Did you say toothpaste tubes?

KATE: Like this.

(She pulls out a tube and shows it to him.)

HECTOR: Oh. Sure, that's the Number 5 aluminum round-end.

KATE: Are you in the toothpaste business?

HECTOR: No. I was a mechanic for the Happy Lips Lotion Company. Is *your* friend in the toothpaste business? **19**

KATE: Yes. Is there a tube-filling machine still in there?

HECTOR: Is there! It's the most beautiful piece of machinery you ever saw.

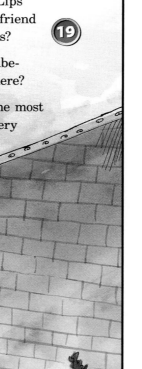

681

Guided Instruction

19 Why might Hector be interested in working with Rufus and Kate? (His employer, the Happy Lips Lotion Company, has just gone out of business, so Hector may be looking for another job.) *Make Inferences*

Minilesson

REVIEW

Suffixes

Remind students that suffixes are syllables that are added to the end of a base word to make a new word with a new meaning.

- Point out the word *beautiful* in the last sentence on page 681.
- Have students identify its base word. (beauty)
- Explain that the suffix *-ful* means "filled with." Then have students express the meaning of *beautiful*. (filled with beauty)

Activity Invite students to think of other common words formed with the suffix *-ful*. Possibilities include *wonderful*, *skillful*, *artful*, and *plentiful*.

Guided Instruction

20 **CAUSE AND EFFECT** Why did the Happy Lips Lotion Company leave the machine behind in the factory? (because it owed the owner of the factory building so much rent)

21 What decision do you think Kate and the stockholders will make? What will they need to consider as they make the decision? (Sample answer: After considering the costs and benefits of the deal I think the stockholders will go for it) *Make Predictions*

(HECTOR shows KATE the machine on the chalkboard.)

HECTOR: The Happy Lips Lotion Company owed the owner of the building so much rent that they had to leave him this machine. The owner is paying me a small salary to **20** keep an eye on the factory.

KATE: It looks like a wonderful machine.

HECTOR: Yes, ma'am. If your friend rented the place and hired me to look after the machinery, we could be in full production tomorrow. Have you got a lot of orders?

KATE: More than five thousand.

HECTOR: Do you think you can swing it? The rent's about three-hundred dollars a month.

KATE: The rent? Oh. I forgot about that. And how much would *you* want, Hector?

HECTOR: I was getting eight dollars an hour from Happy Lips. I guess that much would be fine.

KATE: Hmm. I think we better **21** have a stockholders' meeting.

682

LANGUAGE SUPPORT

ESL Call students' attention to the phrase "be in full production." Bring out that *production* is formed from the verb *produce*. Elicit that being in "full production" means "producing as much as possible."

Also explain that Hector's question, "Do you think you can swing it?" is slang for "Do you think you can afford it?" Students may want to practice reading these lines aloud using an appropriate tone and the correct inflection.

(The interview continues. RUFUS is talking with JOE SMILEY.)

RUFUS: So we all got together and discussed it. By now, we had a lot of other kids working with us, too.

(22)

(CLEM, JOSIE, and LEE LU remove the bowls from the table. They bring in chairs. KATE and RUFUS each sit at one end of the long table. CLEM, JOSIE, LEE LU, JOSH, SHARON, and other MEMBERS OF THE CLASS sit around the sides.)

RUFUS: Let's see, I'd say we need about $15,000.

LEE LU: Well, where do we get that? Just walk into a bank and ask for it?

RUFUS: Why not? Isn't that what other business people do? I'll just go down to Everybody's Friendly Bank and borrow the money!

(23)

Guided Instruction

(22) **CAUSE AND EFFECT** Why do you think Rufus had to hire a lot of other kids? (He needed more workers because he was selling more *Toothpaste*.)

(23) **JUDGMENTS AND DECISIONS** What decision has Rufus made? (He has decided to borrow money from a bank to expand his business.) What facts helped Rufus and the stockholders make this decision? (They need money to rent the factory and machine and to hire Hector; toothpaste sales are booming; packaging their toothpaste in tubes will improve their business even more.)

Minilesson
REVIEW
Summarize

Remind students that stopping from time to time to summarize what they've read will help them remember and appreciate a story better.

Ask students to sum up why it is necessary for Rufus to go to a bank to borrow money when his toothpaste company already seems successful.

Activity Have students choose one of the following topics to summarize:

- How Rufus has been producing toothpaste up to now without machinery.
- Why Rufus's toothpaste seems to be quite popular.

Guided Instruction

(24) **JUDGMENTS AND DECISIONS**
What decision does Mr. Perkell make when he realizes that Rufus is a kid? (He decides not to lend Rufus any money.) Do you think he judged Rufus fairly? (No; Mr. Perkell judged Rufus unfairly; he assumes that kids cannot borrow or repay money.)

Let's have volunteers role-play the scene on page 684 to understand how Rufus feels after his conversation with Mr. Perkell. *Role-Play*

Fluency

READ WITH EXPRESSION
GROUP Have groups read this page aloud. Explain that it's important to read the lines of a play in a way that expresses the characters' feelings. Point out that the word *You're* at the top of the second column is italicized for emphasis. It should be read louder to show how surprised the secretary is that Rufus is a kid. Similarly, *everybody* near the bottom of the second column is italicized to suggest that Mr. Perkell is distinguishing between kids and adults. The final lines of Kate and Rufus should express their anger at being denied the loan.

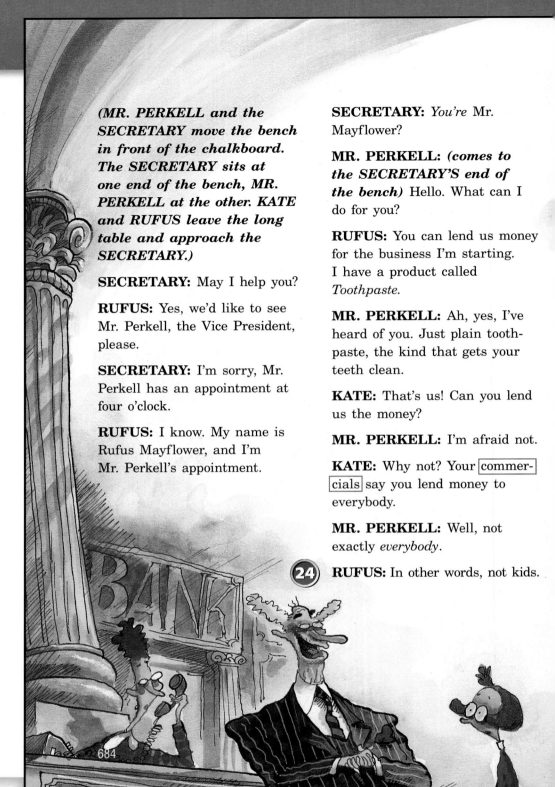

(**MR. PERKELL** and the **SECRETARY** move the bench in front of the chalkboard. The **SECRETARY** sits at one end of the bench, MR. PERKELL at the other. KATE and RUFUS leave the long table and approach the SECRETARY.)

SECRETARY: May I help you?

RUFUS: Yes, we'd like to see Mr. Perkell, the Vice President, please.

SECRETARY: I'm sorry, Mr. Perkell has an appointment at four o'clock.

RUFUS: I know. My name is Rufus Mayflower, and I'm Mr. Perkell's appointment.

SECRETARY: *You're* Mr. Mayflower?

MR. PERKELL: *(comes to the SECRETARY'S end of the bench)* Hello. What can I do for you?

RUFUS: You can lend us money for the business I'm starting. I have a product called *Toothpaste.*

MR. PERKELL: Ah, yes, I've heard of you. Just plain toothpaste, the kind that gets your teeth clean.

KATE: That's us! Can you lend us the money?

MR. PERKELL: I'm afraid not.

KATE: Why not? Your commercials say you lend money to everybody.

MR. PERKELL: Well, not exactly *everybody*.

(24) **RUFUS:** In other words, not kids.

RUFUS: I'll hire you as manager of the toothpaste factory. The money you borrow will be used to pay your first year's salary, to pay the rent, and to buy more tubes. I'll also give you shares of stock in the company.

HECTOR: You mean I'd own part of the business? That would be beautiful!

(RUFUS goes back and sits with JOE SMILEY.)

JOE: Absolutely fantastic! And did you get the money?

RUFUS: We sure did. Then we had to find more customers. So we decided to advertise. My friend Lee Lu had a movie camera, so we all got together and decided to create the Absolutely Honest Commercial.

(MR. PERKELL and the SECRETARY walk off. RUFUS and KATE go back to the long table. HECTOR brings a chair and joins them.)

HECTOR: I can't believe it! Just because you're under age, they turn you down! We have the machine. We have the product. We can make it big!

RUFUS: I believe you, Hector. I believe you would even lend me the money, if you had it.

HECTOR: You bet I would!

RUFUS: Great! Hector, you can go to Mr. Perkell and ask him to lend you the money.

HECTOR: Me?

685

Guided Instruction

25 How does Hector help Rufus get around the bank's policy against lending to kids? (Hector borrows the money from the bank and lends it to Rufus.) Why do you think Hector decided to do this? (Sample answer: Hector would become the factory manager and receive a salary and stock) *Character*

26 **CAUSE AND EFFECT** Why did Rufus have to make commercials? (After borrowing the money, he needed to find more customers.)

Guided Instruction

(27) JUDGMENTS AND DECISIONS
Rufus had to make decisions in order to keep his product inexpensive. Let's add this final information about those decisions to our chart.

JUDGMENT OR DECISION	EVIDENCE FROM STORY
Rufus says it's "crazy" to buy toothpaste.	Tubes of toothpaste cost $1.39 and $1.89.
Rufus decides to make his own cheaply.	Rufus says, "I can make a gallon for less than a dollar."
Rufus thinks it best to keep his toothpaste as simple and inexpensive as he can.	He names his product "Toothpaste"; he packs it in old jars; he charges only 3 cents instead of $1.39 and $1.89, which is what it cost at the store.
Rufus keeps his product *Toothpaste* as inexpensive as possible.	They make it cheaply; they package it in a plain cardboard box to keep prices low.

RETELL THE STORY Ask partners to use their charts to write a paragraph that summarizes the plot of the play. *Summarize*

STUDENT SELF-ASSESSMENT

- How did my Judgment and Decision chart help me keep track of events in the play?
- How did understanding the judgments and decisions that were made help me better understand and appreciate the action?

TRANSFERRING THE STRATEGY

- How might I use a Judgment and Decision chart to help me better understand events in a social studies article or a science article?

(CLEM and JOSIE and KATE move stage center. LEE LU is on his knees in front of them pantomiming shooting a movie camera.)

LEE LU: Okay, action!

CLEM: No fancy names.

JOSIE: No fancy promises.

KATE: All *Toothpaste* claims to do is clean your teeth.

CLEM: We make it as cheaply as possible so we don't have to charge you very much.

KATE: That's why *Toothpaste* comes in a plain cardboard box. **(27)** All to keep the prices low.

686

REREADING FOR *Fluency*

PARTNERS Have students choose a favorite section of the play to read aloud with a partner. Urge students to choose a section that originally gave them some difficulty.

READING RATE You may want to evaluate a student's reading rate. Have the student read aloud from *The Toothpaste Millionaire* for one minute; ask the student to place a stick-on note after the last word read.

Then count the number of words he or she has read.

Alternatively, you could assess small groups or the whole class together by having students count words and record their own scores.

Use the Reading Rate form in the **Diagnostic Placement Evaluation** booklet to evaluate students' performance.

JOSIE: We only make a one-cent profit on a tube, but we think it does the job as well as the more expensive kinds.

LEE LU: CUT!

(JOE SMILEY continues the interview with RUFUS.)

JOE: How big is this business now?

RUFUS: Let's put it this way. We had to order three more machines and hire ten people to work full time.

JOE: Fantastic! Well, Rufus, it looks like you really are a *Toothpaste* Millionaire. What's your next step? Do you have any new ideas up your sleeve?

RUFUS: *(smiles)* Not yet. But I'm not worried. All I have to do is walk into another store, or take a ride on my bike, or just keep my eyes and ears open and my brain working. Something will come to me.

JOE: Isn't he *fantastic?*

THE END

687

LITERARY RESPONSE

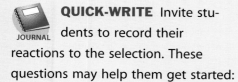
QUICK-WRITE Invite students to record their reactions to the selection. These questions may help them get started:

- What type of person was Rufus Mayflower? What traits helped him succeed?

- What did you learn in this selection about starting a business?

- What did you like about the combined play and interview format?

ORAL RESPONSE Have students share their journal writings and discuss what they liked most about the play.

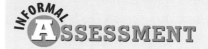

Guided Instruction

Return to Predictions and Purposes

Review with students their reasons for reading the story. Did they find out what they wanted to know?

PREDICTIONS	WHAT HAPPENED
The play will tell about a boy who makes toothpaste.	Rufus Mayflower became a millionaire making *Toothpaste*.
I will learn about how new products come onto the market.	Rufus had to come up with an idea, market it, hire workers, borrow money, and set up a factory.

INFORMAL ASSESSMENT

JUDGMENTS AND DECISIONS

HOW TO ASSESS

- Have students review the judgments and decisions they noted while reading the story.

- Then ask students to make some judgments about Rufus's toothpaste business based on details in the story. Would they like to become stockholders of his company too? Why?

Students should judge Rufus to be a very successful businessperson who made wise decisions about marketing, hiring, and borrowing.

FOLLOW UP If students have trouble making judgments and decisions about Rufus and his company, have them look back at their charts to review details from the story.

687

Story Questions

Have students discuss or write answers to the questions on page 688.

Answers:

1. Rufus thinks the cost of store-bought toothpaste is too high. *Literal/Main Idea*

2. Students should realize that his toothpaste is cheaper and more natural than others. *Literal/Draw Conclusions*

3. Sample answer: He succeeded because he had a good idea that he got others excited about. *Inferential/Draw Conclusions*

4. Answers will vary. *Critical/Summarize*

5. Possible answer: Rufus likes to solve problems. He would want to play the character. *Critical/Reading Across Texts*

WRITE A HOW-TO GUIDE For a full writing process lesson related to this writing suggestion, see the lesson on writing that persuades on pages 691K–691L.

Story Questions & Activities

1. Why does Rufus decide to make his own toothpaste?

2. Why is Rufus's company so successful?

3. How do you know that Rufus is a good businessman? Explain.

4. What did you think of this play? Give reasons.

5. Imagine that Rufus had a chance to act in the movie shown on pages 664–665. Do you think he would want to play the "Charlie Chaplin" character in the picture? Why or why not?

Write a Commercial

Do you remember when Rufus and his friends created the Absolutely Honest Commercial? Advertising is an important way to sell a product. Write a television or a radio commercial for Rufus's Toothpaste. Compare it to another major brand. Tell people why Rufus's is better. Then record your commercial and play it for the class.

Meeting Individual Needs

Brush Up on Your Math

Rufus charged three cents for each tube of Toothpaste. How much would he have to charge if he wanted to double his profits? Triple them? If Rufus wanted to mark up Toothpaste by 100%, how much would he charge? By 1000%?

Take a Poll

Toothpaste comes in many different sizes, packages, flavors, and brands. Take a poll of 10 people. Ask them which brand of toothpaste they buy, and why. Report your findings in the form of a graph or a chart.

Find Out More

In the story, the math teacher figures out that two billion two-hundred-sixty million tubes of toothpaste are sold in the United States each year. What makes people buy so much toothpaste? Why do people need to brush their teeth? Start by asking your dentist.

Then look in an encyclopedia or a dentist's pamphlet. Create a poster of toothpaste facts.

689

Story Activities

Brush Up On Your Math

PARTNERS Pair mathematical learners with partners in need of brushing up on their math.

Take a Poll

Materials: graph paper

PARTNERS Review the different types of graphs and bring out that a bar graph or a circle graph would allow students to express their findings more easily. Students may want to widen their polls to include friends outside the classroom and family.

Find Out More

RESEARCH AND INQUIRY If possible, arrange for a dentist, dental hygienist, or school nurse to speak to the class about dental care. In addition to the handouts available in dental offices, students might find facts in toothpaste ads in magazines. After researching the topic, suggest that students create a classroom chart that includes information and tips for keeping their teeth healthy.

*inter***NET CONNECTION** For more information on dental hygiene, students can visit **www.mhschool.com/reading**

FORMAL ASSESSMENT

After page 689, see the Selection Assessment.

Study Skills

Library/Media Center

OBJECTIVES Students will identify techniques for conducting an interview.

PREPARE Read the opening paragraph and discuss the questions with students. **Display Teaching Chart 165.**

TEACH Point out that the note card on the teaching chart lists helpful tips for conducting an interview. Have volunteers read the tips aloud.

PRACTICE Have students answer questions 1–5. Review the answers with them. **1.** make a note card of questions **2.** *Who? What? When? Where? Why?* and *How?* **3.** simply, clearly, and politely **4.** to make notes about it; to ask follow-up questions **5.** if you wanted more information about an answer; if a new question occurred to you

ASSESS/CLOSE Have students write five questions they might ask a dental hygienist during an interview for an article.

STUDY SKILLS

Conduct an Interview

Joe Smiley, the talk-show host, interviews Rufus during the play. What makes a good interview? Why is it important to know the right questions to ask? Here are some interviewing tips for you to follow.

TIPS

- Make a note card of questions before the interview.
- State the purpose of your interview.
- Begin questions with these words: Who? What? When? Where? Why? How?
- Be polite. Ask clear, simple questions.
- Listen closely to the answers and take notes about them.
- Prepare for follow-up questions.

Use the interviewing tips to answer these questions.

1 What should you do before you interview someone?

2 With what words should most of your questions begin?

3 How should you ask questions?

4 Why is it important to listen closely to the answer?

5 Why might you ask a follow-up question?

Meeting Individual Needs

EASY	ON-LEVEL	CHALLENGE

EASY — Reteach 203 — Conduct an Interview

The purpose of an **interview** is to gather information about a person. The person who asks the questions is the *interviewer*. The person who answers the questions is the *interviewee*.

Below are some words to remember when preparing to interview someone.

Key Words for Conducting an Interview:
Purpose—Know It
Prepare
Questions: *Who? What? Where? When? Why? How?*
Listen
Take Notes

A famous Olympic skating champion is coming to your school. You have been chosen to interview her at a school assembly. Answer the following questions about your interview with the champion.

1. How would you begin the interview? Introduce myself and the skater to the audience. Tell the purpose of the interview.

2. What would be the purpose of the interview? Possible responses: to learn how the skater became a champion; to learn about her training and experience; to inspire others to work towards their goals.

3. Write three questions you could ask in the interview. Possible responses: When did you start to skate? Who has helped you in your career? What is the most important thing you have learned from skating?

4. If the skater mentions the jumps and turns she does, but you don't understand the skating terms, what should you do? Possible answer: Ask her to explain more in a follow-up question.

Book 4/Unit 6
The Toothpaste Millionaire
At Home: Have students think of someone they would like to interview, and then have them write four questions for the interview.
203

ON-LEVEL — Practice 203 — Conduct an Interview

An **interview** is a meeting between an interviewer who asks questions and a person who is being interviewed. That person has information or an interesting story that the interviewer wants to know more about.

Read the interview plan below. Then answer the questions.
Answers will vary but should be in the correct context.

a. Choose a person to interview who you think is interesting.
b. Think about the person you will interview and what he or she knows. Write good questions to ask that person.
c. Begin the interview by stating your purpose for interviewing.
d. Ask polite, clear questions that use words such as *what? why? where? when? how?*
e. Listen carefully to the answers to your questions and take good notes.

1. On each blank line below write the name of someone you would like to interview:
   Family member: _____ Famous person: _____
   Neighbor: _____ Owner of a business: _____

2. Choose one person from above. Write what you think would be the most interesting question you could ask that person.
   Person: _____
   Question: _____

3. Write three questions you would like to ask this person in your interview.

4. State your purpose for interviewing this person.

Book 4/Unit 6
The Toothpaste Millionaire
At Home: Have students write a list of questions for an interview with a family member or a neighbor.
203

CHALLENGE — Extend 203 — Conduct an Interview

In an **interview** usually one person asks another person questions to gain information. To conduct a good interview, it is important to plan carefully before you begin. It's also important to be polite and listen carefully during the interview. Taking notes during it will help you organize what you learn from the interview.

Work with a partner. Suppose you were a talk show host who wanted to do a profile, or a short biography, of a guest. What would you want to know? Write a list of questions on an index card. Then interview your partner in the role of guest. Take notes on a separate sheet of paper. Use the notes to write a paragraph telling what you found out about your guest.

Questions:
Answers will vary but should give a clear biographical profile.

Paragraph:
Answers will vary.

Book 4/Unit 6
The Toothpaste Millionaire
At Home: Have students listen to an interview. Discuss whether or not the interview was a success.
203

Reteach, 203   Practice, 203   Extend, 203

TEST POWER

Test Tip

Read all answer choices.
Then pick the best one.

DIRECTIONS

Read the sample story. Then read each question about the story.

SAMPLE

The Toucan's Feathers

Even though Tanya was a toucan, her feathers looked like those of all the other birds in the jungle.

For fun, Tanya would squawk and then hide among the other birds. The other animals couldn't tell who was making the awful sound.

"Who's making that *hideous* racket?" the animals asked. Tanya let out another tremendous *squawk*! She tried to hide, but the jungle animals saw her. Like other toucans, Tanya's feathers had become brightly colored.

The jungle animals said to Tanya, "With those silly colored feathers you will stand out. Now we will know who makes the awful noise!"

1 In this passage, the word *hideous* means—

○ loud
● horrible
○ weird
○ clever

2 Why did Tanya squawk?

● She did it for fun.
○ She wanted everyone to see her.
○ Many birds made noise.
○ She wanted to talk to her friends.

691

Read the Page

As students read the story, remind them to note when events take place. Remind students to read all of the answer choices.

Discuss the Questions

Question 1: This question asks students to define a word in context. Ask students to find the clues that will help them answer this question. The passage provides two clues "who was making the awful sound" and "Tanya let out another tremendous squawk." Have students eliminate choices that are not supported by the information found near the italicized word.

Question 2: This question requires students to locate information within the story. Explain to students the importance of finding exactly where the author gives a clue about why Tanya squawked.

For The Princeton Review test preparation practice for **TerraNova**, **ITBS**, and **SAT-9**, visit the McGraw-Hill School Division website. See also McGraw-Hill's *Standardized Test Preparation Book*.

EASY

Answers to story questions

1. The animal shelter did not have enough money to keep its doors open.
2. A "white elephant" is an object that someone wants to get rid of.
3. Answers may include: Ms. Suarez had nothing to lose by letting the three children try to help.
4. The three children volunteer to help save the town animal shelter where one of them had hoped to adopt a puppy.
5. Answers will vary but should include the fact that the children's motivation in this story was for charity rather than profit.

Story Questions and Activity

1. Why did the animal shelter close?
2. What do you think a "white elephant" is?
3. Do you think Ms. Suarez made the right decision in allowing three children she didn't know organize a flea market for the shelter? Explain your answer.
4. What is the story mostly about?
5. In what ways were the children in this story similar to the boy in Toothpaste Millionaire? In what ways were they different?

Helping Out

Think of an organization in your community that might need some help. It could be a school, religious organization, homeless shelter, or any other nonprofit group. How could you help this organization? Could you hold a fundraiser? Could you organize a volunteer clean-up effort? Come up with a plan and write out the steps you will take. Then create a poster advertising your plan and encourage people to participate.

from Wolverine and White Elephants

Leveled Books

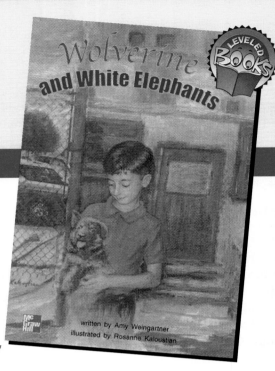

EASY

Wolverine and White Elephants
Silent Letters

☑ **Judgments and Decisions**

☑ **Instructional Vocabulary:**
brilliant, commercials, expensive, gallon, ingredient, successful

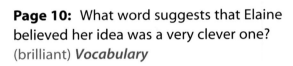

Guided Reading

PREVIEW AND PREDICT Preview the selection to page 6. Have students discuss the illustrations and predict what problem the characters in the story will face. Have students note their responses in their journals.

SET PURPOSES Ask students why they would like to read this story. Ask them to set purposes for reading by writing a few questions that they hope the story will answer.

READ THE BOOK Have students read the story independently. Then use the questions that follow to emphasize reading strategies.

Page 3: Reread paragraph 2. Which word has a silent *l*? (chalk) What word in paragraph 4 has a silent *l*? (couldn't) *Phonics and Decoding*

Pages 6–7: What problem does James face when he gets to the animal shelter to adopt Wolverine? (The animal shelter has closed so he can't get the puppy he wants.) *Problem and Solution*

Page 10: What word suggests that Elaine believed her idea was a very clever one? (brilliant) *Vocabulary*

Pages 12–15: How does the group make sure the flea market is successful? (They post flyers, tell people about it, and sell food.) *Problem and Solution*

Page 16: Do you think giving money to the shelter was better than giving white elephants? Explain. (Sample answer: Giving money was the fastest way to open the shelter again.) *Judgments and Decisions*

RETURN TO PREDICTIONS AND PURPOSES Review students' predictions. Were they accurate? Why or why not? Review their purposes for reading. Did they find out what they wanted to know?

LITERARY RESPONSE Discuss these questions with students:

• Which character in the story did you like the most? Why?

• Why do you think the author chose to write this story about an animal shelter?

Also see the story questions and activity in *Wolverine and White Elephants*.

Leveled Books

INDEPENDENT

The Morningstar Sun

☑ **Judgments and Decisions**

☑ **Instructional Vocabulary:**
brilliant, commercials, expensive, gallon, ingredient, successful

Guided Reading

PREVIEW AND PREDICT Preview the selection to page 7. Have students discuss the illustrations and make predictions about what the play will be about. Have students write their responses in their journals.

SET PURPOSES Ask students what they want to learn by reading this play. Ask them to set purposes for reading by writing questions that they hope the play will answer.

READ THE BOOK After students have read the play, use the following questions to emphasize reading strategies.

Pages 2–3: What problem do the members of the newspaper staff face? (They don't have enough money to publish a school paper and will have to think of a way to raise funds.) *Problem and Solution*

Page 7: With what does Bethany *compare* newspaper advertisements? (commercials on television) Why are they similar? (Both give information about a product.) *Vocabulary*

Pages 12–13: What two pieces of information does Mr. Johnson use to make his decision to not advertise in the paper? (He can't afford to but advertising; even without advertising, students can buy ice cream at his shop) *Judgments and Decisions*

Page 16: What do the children still have to do in order to solve their problem? (They still have to persuade at least two more businesses to pay for ads in their newspaper.) *Problem and Solution*

RETURN TO PREDICTIONS AND PURPOSES Discuss students' predictions. Were their predictions accurate? Also ask them to review their purposes for reading. Did they find out what they wanted to know?

LITERARY RESPONSE Discuss these questions:

* How might this selection have been different if it had been written in story form?

* What main idea, do you think the author wanted to get across to her readers?

Also see the story questions and activity in *The Morningstar Sun*.

Answers to Story Questions

1. The kids visited Mr. Wolfe at the Springfield Bugle to get advice about raising money for their school newspaper.
2. The newspaper club targeted businesses that offered goods and services kids their age would want.
3. At first, Mr. Johnson told the kids he couldn't afford to advertise.
4. A school newspaper learns how to raise enough money to publish their newspaper.
5. Answers will vary but include printing the newspaper themselves.

Story Questions and Activity

1. Why did the kids in *The Morningstar Sun* newspaper club go visit Mr. Wolfe at the *Springfield Bugle*?
2. What kind of businesses does the newspaper club target to sell advertising space?
3. **At first,** why did Mr. Johnson decide not to take out an ad in the newspaper?
4. What is the story mostly about?
5. If Rufus from *The Toothpaste Millionaire* were brainstorming ideas for funding publication of the school newspaper with the kids in the club, what ideas do you think he would come up with?

Advertisers Wanted!

Think about "Two Scoops," "Market Street Cycle," and "Village Books." Create an advertisement for one of these businesses. How will you describe it in the ad? Will you offer any discounts or special offers? First, list the major points you want to feature in the ad; then do the writing and illustrate your advertisement with a picture or a logo.

from The Morningstar Sun

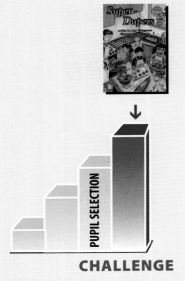

PUPIL SELECTION

CHALLENGE

Answers to Story Questions

1. The student who raised the most money at the fundraiser would win a bicycle, and Rachel wanted to win it.
2. Accept all reasonable responses. Answers might include Rachel's decision to ask others for help.
3. Answers may vary but might include that she was thinking about making brownies the following year.
4. It is about a girl who baked cookies as a fundraiser and, in the process, learned a bit about profit and loss and delegating tasks.
5. Answers will vary.

Story Questions and Activity

1. Why did Rachel want to bake so many cookies for the fundraiser?
2. What was the best decision Rachel made?
3. Why did Rachel have a glint in her eye when she praised Becky Winters' brownies?
4. What is the story mostly about?
5. If Rufus Mayflower had advised Rachel before she approached her mother, what might the master plan have included from the start?

Refreshments for Sale

Pretend you want to start a lemonade or iced tea business for the summer. Use these figures to answer the following questions:

Lemons	2/$1.00
Box of tea bags	$1.50
Pound of sugar	$1.00
Gallon of spring water	$1.50
Paper cups (100)	$2.50
Paper napkins (250)	$3.50
Plastic Pitcher	$4.50

• How many pitchers of lemonade or iced tea do you think you could sell in one day?
• How much will you charge for a glass?
• Will it be enough to cover your costs?
• How many days will your refreshment stand need to be open for you to make a profit?

from Super-Dupers

Leveled Books

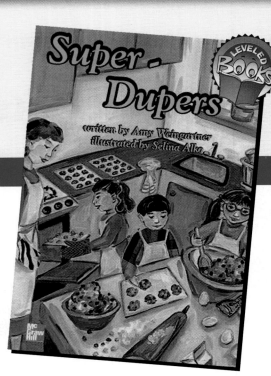

Super-Dupers
written by Amy Weingartner
illustrated by Selina Alko

CHALLENGE

Super-Dupers

☑ **Judgments and Decisions**
☑ **Instructional Vocabulary:**
brilliant, commercials, expensive, gallon, ingredient, successful

Guided Reading

PREVIEW AND PREDICT Preview the text to page 7. Have students discuss the illustrations. Have students predict what they think Rachel and her mother will do in the story. They may want to note their predictions in their journals.

SET PURPOSES Ask students to set purposes for reading by writing a few questions that they hope the story will answer. For example, they may want to know why the story is called *Super-Dupers*.

READ THE BOOK Have students read the story independently. Then use the questions that follow to emphasize reading strategies.

Page 4: What decision does Rachel hope students will make after tasting her mother's cookies? (to buy the cookies because they are so good) *Judgments and Decisions*

Page 5: What decision does Rachel make that might get her into trouble? (to take the cookies to school without asking for permission) *Judgments and Decisions*

Page 8: Why doesn't Mrs. Crossfield want to buy Rachel's cookies? (They are too expensive.) What does *expensive* mean? (having a high price) *Vocabulary*

Page 12: How does Rachel's mother help solve part of the problem? (She donates the ingredients and offers to help bake.) *Problem and Solution*

RETURN TO PREDICTIONS AND PURPOSES Discuss students' predictions. Ask them to describe how close they were to the actual story events. Also ask them to review their purposes for reading. Did they find out what they wanted to know?

LITERARY RESPONSE Discuss these questions:

• What words would you use to describe Rachel as a story character?

• What is another good title for this story?

Also see the story questions and activity in *Super-Dupers*.

Activities
Anthology and Leveled Books

Connecting Texts

MONEY-RAISING CHARTS
Write the story titles on a chart. Discuss with students how in each story characters must make money to solve a problem. Point out that these characters find successful ways to make money to solve their problem. Help them create a four-column chart that shows how the main characters of the stories raise money and solve problems.

The Toothpaste Millionaire	Wolverine and White Elephants	The Morningstar Sun	Super Dupers
• Rufus needs money to buy a machine to fill toothpaste tubes. • Hector agrees to sign for a loan at the bank.	• James and Elaine have to raise money to reopen an animal shelter. • They organize a flea market as a fund-raiser.	• The newspaper club needs to raise money to publish a school paper. • The students decide to sell ads in their paper.	• Rachel wants the fourth-grade to raise more money than the fifth-grade class. • Rachel organizes teams to bake cookies.

Viewing/Representing

GROUP PRESENTATIONS Organize the class into groups, one for each of the four stories read in the lesson. (For *The Toothpaste Millionaire*, combine students of different reading levels.) Have each group create a storyboard by drawing pictures of the main events. Have group members take turns orally summarizing the book, explaining how the main characters managed to solve their problems.

AUDIENCE RESPONSE Ask students to mentally compare the problems and solutions presented by each group with their own story's problems and solutions.

Allow time for questions after each group's presentation.

Research and Inquiry

MORE ABOUT KIDS AND MONEY-RAISING Have students find out about real-life situations in which kids have played a part in raising money to solve problems. Suggest that they do the following:

• Interview family members, neighbors, and friends.

• Look for information in the school library.

• Create a graphic to show how the kids raised money, as well as how much money they raised.

Students might create Young Money Makers posters to display the information they find.

*inter*NET **CONNECTION** Students can learn more about kids making money to solve problems by visiting
www.mhschool.com/reading

OBJECTIVES

Students will identify the judgment and decision a story character makes.

TEACHING TIP

INSTRUCTIONAL Remind students that in everyday life they have to make judgments and decisions. Be sure students understand that making a judgment involves applying criteria such as a person's goals and values to determine the best, worst, and so forth, and that making a decision involves identifying a course of action. Explain that making judgments about situations allows them to make better decisions.

Review Judgments and Decisions

PREPARE

Discuss Making Judgments and Decisions

Review: Making a decision involves judging various choices in a situation and choosing the one that best fits one's goals, needs, and values. Usually a decision will include making judgments after evaluating pieces of information.

TEACH

Read "Rufus and Hook" and Model the Skill

As you read the passage on **Teaching Chart 166,** ask students to pay attention to the judgment Rufus must make.

Rufus and Hook

Last week Rufus Mayflower got a call from Hook Freefro. Hook is one of the biggest basketball stars in the country. "I'll do television ads for *you*," Hook offered, "and you can put my face on every tube of *Toothpaste*. Sales will skyrocket! In return, you pay me $1 million a year."

Rufus thought it over. Hook Freefro would increase sales. Rufus, however, wanted to keep things simple. Paying Hook would force up the price of *Toothpaste*. Besides, what did basketball stars have to do with toothpaste? "Thanks Hook," said Rufus, "but our company won't be using big-name athletes to advertise its products."

Teaching Chart 166

Guide students to identify the judgment and decision that Rufus made.

MODEL As I read this passage, I realize that Rufus has to make a decision about whether or not to hire Hook Freefro. I notice that Rufus weighs his various goals, needs, and values before making his decision. For example, he remembers that he wants to keep his company simple and he wants to keep the price down.

PRACTICE

Identify a Judgment and Decision

GROUP

Have students underline on the chart the sentences that show the judgment and circle on the chart the sentence that shows the decision that Rufus made. Have them explain in their own words why Rufus made this judgment and decision. ▶ **Linguistic/Kinesthetic**

ASSESS/CLOSE

Describe Judgments

ONE

Have each student create a short paragraph that tells about a judgment he or she has made. Tell students to include a decision, that is, a course of action, which is a direct result of the judgment they made. Have partners exchange papers and identify the judgment and decision described in the paragraph.

ALTERNATE TEACHING STRATEGY

JUDGMENTS AND DECISIONS

For a different approach to teaching this skill, see page T62.

SELF-SELECTED Reading

Students may choose from the following titles.

ANTHOLOGY
- The Toothpaste Millionaire

LEVELED BOOKS
- Wolverine and White Elephants
- The Morningstar Sun
- Super-Dupers

Bibliography, pages T76–T77

Meeting Individual Needs for Comprehension

EASY	ON-LEVEL	CHALLENGE	LANGUAGE SUPPORT

EASY

Name_____ Date_____ Reteach **204**

Make Judgments and Decisions

Characters make **judgments and decisions**. You do, too, every day.

Circle the letter beside what you would do in each of the following situations. Then explain your decision.

1. You see smoke coming from a building. You are in a part of the neighborhood your parents have told you to stay away from.
   (a) You call the fire department.
   b. You return home, hoping someone will call about the fire.
   Reason: possible answer: I would rather get in trouble than risk someone getting hurt.

2. It is your little sister's birthday. For at least a month, she has been playing practical jokes on you and your family.
   a. You plan a special birthday joke to get even.
   (b) You make her a card and a little gift.
   Reason: possible answer: Birthdays are special, and I would want my sister to give me a card and a present if it was my birthday.

3. You know you can't have a pet dog. Your mom is allergic to dogs. You see a cute stray on your street.
   (a) You put up signs to find the dog's owner and call a shelter.
   b. You think the dog is small enough to hide and take it home.
   Reason: possible answer: I would make sure the dog was safe until its owner was found.

4. You find an empty wallet, except for a name and address card. It is the kind you always wanted.
   a. You keep the wallet, since it is empty anyway.
   (b) You call the owner and return it.
   Reason: possible answer: I wouldn't want someone to lose such a nice wallet, and if I lost my wallet, I would want someone to return it to me.

At Home: Have students explain the reasons for deciding what they did in a situation.
204   The Toothpaste Millionaire   **8**

ON-LEVEL

Name_____ Date_____ Practice **204**

Make Judgments and Decisions

Making judgments and decisions about characters is an important part of reading a story.
Think about "The Toothpaste Millionaire" as you answer the questions below. Answers may vary. Accept all reasonable responses.

1. What did you think of Rufus's decision to make his own toothpaste while he was talking with Kate in the drugstore? Some students may feel that Rufus was getting in over his head before even finding out how to make toothpaste.

2. Was Rufus right? Is toothpaste very simple to make? Yes, it has very few ingredients, and the main one is baking soda.

3. What did you think of Mr. Conti's decision to devote time to Rufus's business in the math class? Students may say that it made the class interesting and realistic, and it helped Rufus.

4. What did you think of Rufus's idea to get his math class involved? Students may note that it was a good idea because the class already knew about the business and they were interested in it.

5. Why did Rufus's friends deserve to be stockholders? They worked hard and should enjoy some of the profits.

6. It was the intention of the author, Jean Merrill, to entertain readers but also to help them understand how some businesses are run. In your judgment, do you think the author helped you understand how a business can be run? Explain your answer. Answers will vary.

At Home: Have students decide what they might like to do for a living when they grow up.
204   The Toothpaste Millionaire   **6**

CHALLENGE

Name_____ Date_____ Extend **204**

Make Judgments and Decisions

Everyone looks at problems differently. People bring their own values and experiences with them when they **make judgments and decisions**.

Suppose that you were Rufus in "The Toothpaste Millionaire." Choose one decision in the story that you would make differently. Explain your choice, and tell why you would do things in a different way. How does your choice affect the outcome of the story?

Answers will vary but should include a judgement or decision with supporting arguments.

At Home: Talk about a decision students made today. How could they have made it differently? What might have happened differently?
204   The Toothpaste Millionaire

LANGUAGE SUPPORT

Name_____ Date_____

How We Feel, What We Do

1. Read the sentences. 2. Cut out the art. 3. Put the pieces together to match judgments with decisions.

Judgement	Decision
Toothpaste is too expensive.	Rufus gives Hector a job.
Rufus is a good boss.	Workers take stock instead of money from Rufus.
Hector is good with machines.	Rufus makes his own toothpaste.

222 The Toothpaste Millionaire • Language Support/Blackline Master 110   Grade 4

Reteach, 204   **Practice, 204**   **Extend, 204**   **Language Support, 222**

OBJECTIVES

Students will identify the problem and solution in a story.

TEACHING TIP

INSTRUCTIONAL Tell students that the problem in a story is often called the conflict. Explain that the main problem or conflict usually appears early in the story while the solution does not come until near the end. Bring out that many of the plot events in a story show how the characters deal with a problem or conflict.

Review Problem and Solution

PREPARE

Discuss Story Problems and Solutions

Review: In many stories, the characters' actions center on a main problem. Identifying the problem and following what the characters do to solve it can make story events easier to understand.

TEACH

Read the Story and Model the Skill

Read the newspaper article "Boy Overcomes Bank's Loan Policy" on **Teaching Chart 167.** Focus students' attention on Rufus's problem and how he solves it.

Boy Overcomes Bank's Loan Policy

Rufus Mayflower, the wealthy young owner of the Toothpaste Company, faced a serious problem early in his career. Local banks refused to lend him money because he was a kid. "I went down to Everybody's Friendly Bank to borrow $15,000," Rufus recalled. "But Mr. Perkell refused to loan me a dime." Mayflower explained that he was fortunate to have an adult, Hector Ruiz, working for him. "Hector went and borrowed the money," Rufus recalled, "and then gave it to me. So we were able to rent the factory and machines." The rest, as they say, is history!

Teaching Chart 167

Ask a volunteer to find and underline a sentence that tells what Rufus's problem is. Help students think about Rufus's problem and how he solved it.

MODEL Rufus needed money so his business could grow, but he couldn't borrow money from the bank because of his age. That was a serious problem. Rufus asked Hector to borrow the money from the bank. That ended up being a good solution.

PRACTICE

Create a Problem and Solution Chart

GROUP

Have students create a Problem and Solution chart for *The Toothpaste Millionaire*. Encourage them to look back at the story as needed. Help them get started.

PROBLEM	SOLUTION
Rufus didn't have money to pay his employees.	He gave them stock instead.
The bank wouldn't lend Rufus money because he was a kid.	Hector borrowed the money and gave it to Rufus.

ASSESS/CLOSE

Use a Chart to Summarize

Have students create a Problem and Solution chart for a familiar story or show. Have them use their charts to summarize the story.

PROBLEM	SOLUTION
Cinderella has no way to get to the ball.	Her fairy godmother turns a pumpkin and mice into a coach and horses.
The Prince does not know the name of the girl who wore the glass slipper.	The Prince visits every home in the kingdom to find out whose foot fits the glass slipper.

ALTERNATE TEACHING STRATEGY

PROBLEM AND SOLUTION

For a different approach to teaching this skill, see page T64.

LOOKING AHEAD

Students will apply this skill as they read the next selection, *Whales*.

Meeting Individual Needs for Comprehension

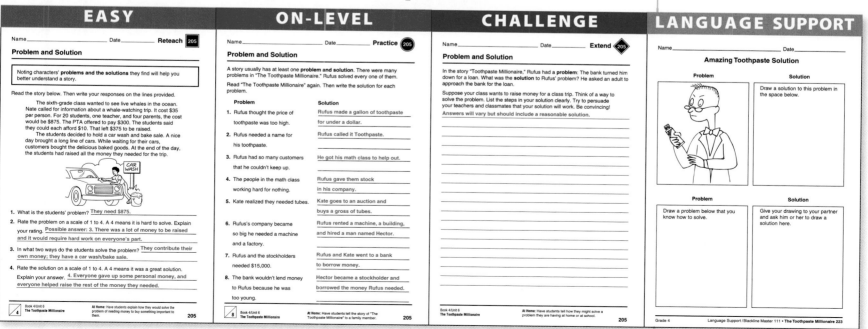

EASY	ON-LEVEL	CHALLENGE	LANGUAGE SUPPORT
Reteach, 205	Practice, 205	Extend, 205	Language Support, 223

691H

OBJECTIVES

Students will identify synonyms and antonyms.

Review Synonyms and Antonyms

PREPARE

Discuss Meaning of Synonyms and Antonyms

Review: Synonyms are words that have similar meanings. The words *chilly, nippy,* and *frosty* are synonyms since they all mean "cold." Antonyms are words with opposite meanings. The words *hot, warm,* and *steamy,* for example, are antonyms of *cold.*

TEACH

Read the Passage and Model the Skill

Have students read the passage on **Teaching Chart 168.**

Performing the Play

Our class presented the play *The Toothpaste Millionaire* last week. The dramatization was a great success! We placed Joe Smiley's interview table at the center of the stage. Most of the action took place near the middle of the stage. The actors usually entered from stage left and exited from stage right. Pantomiming the actions on-stage was fun. It was like role-playing. It was fun being off-stage too, behind the curtain.

Teaching Chart 168

Discuss the paragraph, asking students if they notice any pairs of synonyms or antonyms.

MODEL As I read this paragraph, I notice a few pairs of synonyms and antonyms. For example I see the phrase "stage left," which means the left side of the stage. That's an antonym for "stage right," which is the right side of the stage. I also see "pantomiming" which is a synonym for "role-playing." These two words have similar meanings.

ALTERNATE TEACHING STRATEGY

SYNONYMS AND ANTONYMS

For a different approach to teaching this skill, see page T65.

PRACTICE

Identify Other Pairs of Synonyms and Antonyms

GROUP

Have students circle pairs of words that are synonyms in the paragraph. Have them underline pairs of words that are antonyms. Then have students brainstorm original sentences that contain pairs of synonyms or antonyms.

ASSESS/CLOSE

Supply Synonyms or Antonyms

Ask students to complete each sentence below by suggesting a word that is either a synonym or antonym for the underlined word.

- Making such simple toothpaste was a <u>brilliant</u> idea; rarely do we get such _____ ideas. (synonym)

- The bank would lend to <u>adults</u> but not to _____. (antonym)

- Joe Smiley thought Rufus used <u>secret</u> ingredients; actually the ingredients were _____. (antonym)

- Rufus became quite <u>wealthy</u>; his Toothpaste Company made him _____. (synonym)

Meeting Individual Needs for Vocabulary

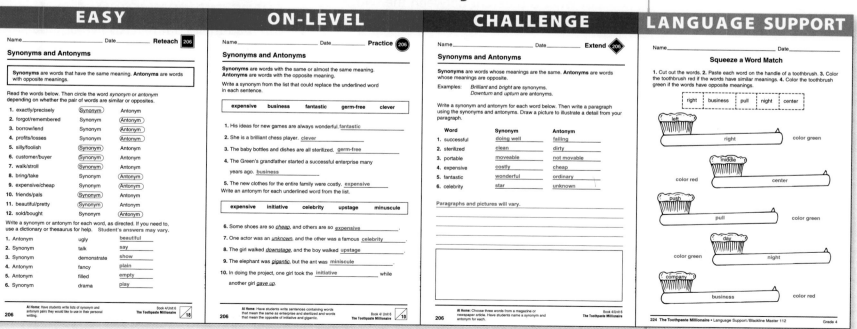

Reteach, 206   Practice, 206   Extend, 206   Language Support, 224

GRAMMAR/SPELLING
CONNECTIONS

See the 5-Day Grammar and Usage Plan on negatives, pages 691M–691N.

See the 5-Day Spelling Plan on words with suffixes, pages 6910–691P.

TECHNOLOGY TIP

Many word-processing programs come with a variety of font sizes and styles. Demonstrate or have a volunteer show how to change the font style of selected text for emphasis when creating printed advertisements.

Persuasive Writing

Prewrite

WRITE A COMMERCIAL Present this writing assignment: Do you remember when Rufus and his friends created the Absolutely Honest Commercial? Advertising is an important way to sell a product. Write a television or radio commercial for Rufus's toothpaste. Compare it to another major brand. Tell people why Rufus's is better. Then perform your commercial for the class.

BRAINSTORM IDEAS Have students brainstorm features of Rufus's toothpaste that might compare favorably with competing toothpastes.

Strategy: Make a Venn Diagram Have students create a Venn diagram to note similarities and differences between *Toothpaste* and another brand. Suggest the following:

- List what is similar between *Toothpaste* and another major brand.
- List what is different between the two.
- To create the lists, compare such features as taste, cost, effectiveness, or type of container.
- Do not limit yourself to what is in the text. Use your imagination.

Draft

USE THE VENN DIAGRAM Help students identify features of Rufus's toothpaste to mention in their ads. Also have them decide whether to write a radio or TV commercial. Point out that many TV commercials are written as scripts for actors and include stage directions, which describe the action that appears on the screen.

Revise

SELF-QUESTIONING Ask students to assess their drafts.

- Did I clearly compare the two brands, showing why *Toothpaste* is better?
- Did I use persuasive language to show why *Toothpaste* is better?
- How can I elaborate on my ideas? What would make my commercial more colorful or memorable?

PARTNERS Have partners trade commercials and conference on ways they can clarify and enrich their writing.

Edit/Proofread

CHECK FOR ERRORS Students should reread their commercials for spelling, grammar, and punctuation.

Publish

SHARE THE COMMERCIALS Students can read their commercials live or tape record them and play them for the class. Have the class identify the features of *Toothpaste* that are compared with another brand.

Radio Commercial for Toothpaste

All toothpastes are the same, right? Wrong! The all-new *Toothpaste* toothpaste beats the competition hands-down and leaves you smiling. Take price, for example. You might shell out $2.50, $3.50, or more for a tube of Brighten. A tube of all-new *Toothpaste*, however, only costs you twenty cents. Then there's ingredients. Brighten contains eight chemicals with names so long you can't read them. The all-new *Toothpaste* has only a few pure and simple ingredients, like good old baking soda and flavorful peppermint. For a healthy, economical, and effective toothpaste, you can't beat *Toothpaste!*

Presentation Ideas

PRESENT THE COMMERCIALS Students can perform their commercials live for the class or videotape them at home and play them at school. ▶ **Viewing/Representing**

BE AN ANNOUNCER Have students suppose they are radio announcers reading to a large audience. Have the class note how announcers use their voices to make the ad more effective. ▶ **Speaking/Listening**

COMMUNICATION TIPS

REPRESENTING Students might sketch a series of diagrams or a storyboard to show exactly what will happen in their commercial.

SPEAKING Students might listen to well-known radio and TV announcers. Students can attempt to imitate the tone, rate, and pitch of these speakers.

Consider students' creative efforts, possibly adding a plus (+) for originality, wit, and imagination.

Scoring Rubric

Excellent	Good	Fair	Unsatisfactory
4: The writer	**3:** The writer	**2:** The writer	**1:** The writer
• clearly compares *Toothpaste* with another brand.	• compares *Toothpaste* with another brand.	• compares *Toothpaste* with another brand.	• does not compare *Toothpaste* with another brand.
• contrasts two or more features of the two tooth-pastes.	• contrasts at least one feature of the two brands.	• does not compare specific features of the two brands.	• does not focus on specific features of *Toothpaste*.
• uses persuasive language effectively.	• uses persuasive language.	• uses little or no persuasive language.	• does not use language persuasively.

0: The writer leaves the page blank or fails to respond to the writing task. The student does not address the topic or simply paraphrases the prompt. The response is illegible or incoherent.

For a 6-point or an 8-point scale, see pages T105–T106.

LANGUAGE SUPPORT

Ask students to look over newspaper and magazine ads for toothpaste or other personal care items. Suggest that they highlight words and phrases that seem particularly persuasive. After students check the meaning of these words and phrases, suggest they use them in their commercials.

PORTFOLIO Invite students to include their commercials or another writing project in their portfolios.

Meeting Individual Needs for Writing

EASY

Comic Strip Have students create a comic strip with captions showing how Rufus started and built his toothpaste business. The last frame of the comic strip might be an ad for *Toothpaste*.

ON-LEVEL

Interview Have students write an imaginary interview with Rufus. Ask them to use a Question and Answer format to explore how Rufus started and built his successful company.

CHALLENGE

Sequel Have students write a short sequel to the play in which Rufus and his coworkers branch out and produce a new line of products. Rufus should continue making sound judgments and good decisions to make the new business a success.

5 Day Grammar and Usage Plan

ESL Ask English learners to suggest some simple phrases and body gestures that they use to indicate "no." These might include shaking the head, waving a hand, or saying "no way."

DAILY LANGUAGE ACTIVITIES

Write each day's activity on the board or use **Transparency 28.** Have students correct the sentences orally by deleting one negative or changing a negative to a positive. Answers may vary.

Day 1
1. We don't have no time.
2. Ricky can't never go to the store.
3. Nobody never asked Hector.

Day 2
1. Nobody would not answer Mr. Conti.
2. Kate didn't see nothing.
3. Rufus won't go nowhere.

Day 3
1. Nobody can't help Rufus.
2. Kate didn't never agree.
3. She would not say that to no one.

Day 4
1. Mr. Smiley can't go nowhere alone.
2. Customers never get nothing for free.
3. Nobody couldn't find Clem's math book.

Day 5
1. Mr. Conti couldn't find no one.
2. Mr. Perkell never has no fun.
3. Mr. Smiley won't never know.

DAY 1 Introduce the Concept

Oral Warm-Up Say: *None of my friends eats spinach. We don't serve it.* Ask students to find a "no" word in each.

Introduce Negatives Several words in English mean the same as "no."

Negatives

- A negative is a word that means "no," such as, *not, never, nobody, nowhere,* and contractions with *-n't.*
- Do not use two negatives in the same sentence.
- You can fix a sentence with two negatives by removing one.

Example: *My friends don't have no money./My friends have no money.*

Present the Daily Language Activity. Students should remove the extra negatives. Then have them form new sentences, using negatives correctly.

 Assign the daily Writing Prompt on page 664C.

GRAMMAR PRACTICE BOOK, PAGE 173

Name _____ Date _____ **Grammar 173**

Negatives

- **A negative** is a word that means "no," such as *not, never, nobody, nowhere,* and contractions with *n't.*
- Do not use two negatives in the same sentence.
- You can fix a sentence with two negatives by removing one.

Correct each sentence by removing one of the negatives. Then rewrite the sentence. Student's answers may vary

1. "I wouldn't never pay a dollar and eighty-nine cents for toothpaste."
"I would never pay a dollar and eighty-nine cents for toothpaste."

2. "Toothpaste isn't made of no expensive ingredients."
"Toothpaste isn't made of expensive ingredients."

3. Rufus wasn't trying to make no money.
Rufus wasn't trying to make money.

4. He thought people shouldn't never have to pay a lot for toothpaste.
He thought people should never have to pay a lot for toothpaste.

5. He didn't use no secret ingredients.
He didn't use secret ingredients.

6. His toothpaste didn't have no special name.
His toothpaste didn't have a special name.

7. He didn't put no printing on the box.
He didn't put printing on the box.

8. "I don't have no profits to pay you yet."
"I don't have any profits to pay you yet."

DAY 2 Teach the Concept

Review Negatives Ask students to name some words that mean "no."

Introduce Making Negatives Positive A sentence can't have two negatives.

Positives and Negatives

- You can correct a sentence with two negatives by changing one negative to a positive word.

Share these word pairs of negatives and positives: *no/any; never/ever; nothing/anything; nobody/anybody; no one/anyone; nowhere/anywhere.*
Incorrect: *Nobody never used toothpaste.*
Correct: *Nobody ever used toothpaste.*

Present the Daily Language Activity. Then have students list the negatives from each sentence, along with positive words they could use to replace them.

 Assign the daily Writing Prompt on page 664C.

GRAMMAR PRACTICE BOOK, PAGE 174

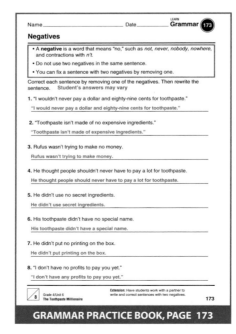

Name _____ Date _____ **Grammar 174**

Negatives

- You can correct a sentence with two negatives by changing one negative to a positive word.

no —— any   nothing —— anything   no one —— anyone
never —— ever   nobody —— anybody   nowhere —— anywhere

Correct these sentences by changing one negative word to a positive word.

1. "I don't think nobody should pay a lot for toothpaste."
"I don't think anybody should pay a lot for toothpaste."

2. The main ingredient isn't nothing but baking soda.
The main ingredient isn't anything but baking soda.

3. No one would never think three cents was too much for toothpaste.
No one would ever think three cents was too much for toothpaste.

4. You can't find cheaper toothpaste nowhere.
You can't find cheaper toothpaste anywhere.

5. No one never turned down a chance to be a stockholder.
No one ever turned down a chance to be a stockholder.

6. Kate had never seen nothing more beautiful than that machine.
Kate had never seen anything more beautiful than that machine.

7. "We don't exactly lend money to just nobody," said Mr. Perkell.
"We don't exactly lend money to just anybody," said Mr. Perkell.

8. Our toothpaste doesn't have nothing like a fancy name or a fancy box.
Our toothpaste doesn't have anything like a fancy name or a fancy box.

Negatives

DAY 3 — Review and Practice

Learn from the Literature On page 671 of *The Toothpaste Millionaire*, read Rufus's lines midway down the second column:

> "Rufus: Who knows? I <u>never</u> tried, but I bet it <u>isn't</u> hard. Put that tube back."

Ask students to identify the two negatives in Rufus's lines. (*never* and the *-n't* in *isn't*)

Correct Negatives in Sentences
Present the Daily Language Activity. Then have students make a two-column chart, with the headings *Negative* and *Positive*. After writing a negative word on the left, have them list its corresponding positive word, if there is one, on the right. Students should use the words to form sentences.

 Assign the daily Writing Prompt on page 664D.

DAY 4 — Review and Practice

Review Negatives Review how to change a negative to a positive. Then present the Daily Language Activity.

Mechanics and Usage Before students begin the daily Writing Prompt on page 664D, review the rules for contractions.

Contractions

- A **contraction** is a shortened form of two words.

- A contraction may be formed by combining a verb with the word *not*.

- An apostrophe (') shows where one or more letters have been left out.

List on the board: *can't/cannot, don't/do not, doesn't/does not, didn't/did not, couldn't/could not, wouldn't/would not, shouldn't/should not.* Note that in *can't* two letters are left out.

 Assign the daily Writing Prompt on page 664D.

DAY 5 — Assess and Reteach

Assess Use the Daily Language Activity and page 177 of the **Grammar Practice Book** for assessment.

Reteach Have students write each rule about negatives on index cards. Then have them pick five sentences from the Daily Language Activities, and re-write them two different ways. (For example, *We don't have no time,* could be corrected as *We don't have time,* or *We have no time.*)

Have students create a word wall with negative words and their accompanying positives.

Use page 178 of the **Grammar Practice Book** for additional reteaching.

 Assign the daily Writing Prompt on page 664D.

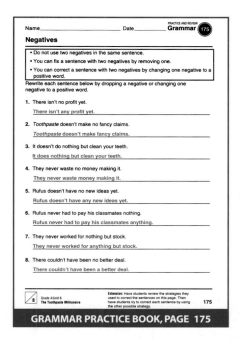

GRAMMAR PRACTICE BOOK, PAGE 175

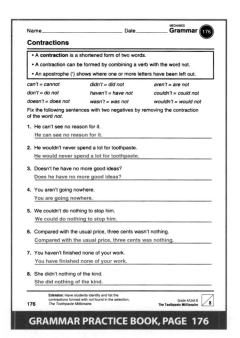

GRAMMAR PRACTICE BOOK, PAGE 176

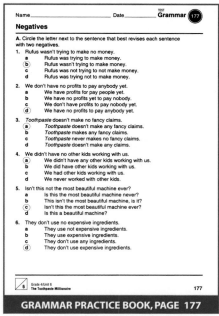

GRAMMAR PRACTICE BOOK, PAGE 177

5 Day Spelling Plan

WORD STUDY STEPS AND ACTIVITY, PAGE 174

LANGUAGE SUPPORT

Write the word *motionless* on the chalkboard. Show students how to divide the word into its suffix and base (root). Define the word with and with out the suffix. Make suffix and base (root) word flashcards for extra practice.

DICTATION SENTENCES

Spelling Words

1. The broken lock was <u>useless</u>.
2. We sing and dance for <u>entertainment</u>.
3. A new school is under <u>construction</u>.
4. The playground swings are <u>adjustable</u>.
5. We could not see in the <u>darkness</u>.
6. A deer stood <u>motionless</u> on the hill.
7. I have a <u>description</u> of your costume.
8. Use this ruler for the <u>measurement</u>.
9. The baby raccoon was <u>adorable</u>.
10. We were <u>breathless</u> after the race.
11. Our teacher talked about <u>fairness</u>.
12. The <u>government</u> takes care of its citizens.
13. We needed <u>protection</u> from the rain.
14. Is your bicycle <u>dependable</u>?
15. The germ can cause <u>sickness</u>.
16. He was sad and <u>hopeless</u>.
17. The farm was for hog <u>production</u>.
18. The show was <u>enjoyable</u>.
19. The <u>greatness</u> of his speech remains.
20. He needed <u>encouragement</u> to make a speech.

Challenge Words

21. It was a <u>brilliant</u> plan to make money.
22. The <u>commercials</u> sell bicycles.
23. The butter was too <u>expensive</u> to buy.
24. One <u>ingredient</u> in bread is water.
25. The plan was <u>successful</u> in the end.

DAY 1 — Pretest

Assess Prior Knowledge Use the Dictation Sentences and **Spelling Practice Book** page 173 for the pretest.

Spelling Words		Challenge Words
1. useless	11. fairness	21. **brilliant**
2. entertainment	12. government	22. **commercials**
3. construction	13. protection	23. **expensive**
4. adjustable	14. dependable	24. **ingredient**
5. darkness	15. sickness	25. **successful**
6. motionless	16. hopeless	
7. description	17. **production**	
8. measurement	18. enjoyable	
9. adorable	19. greatness	
10. breathless	20. encouragement	

*Note: Words in **dark type** are from the story.*

Word Study On page 174 of the **Spelling Practice Book** are word study steps and an at-home activity.

DAY 2 — Explore the Pattern

Sort and Spell Words Say *adjustable* and *useless*. Ask students what suffix they hear in each word. (*-able, -less*) Have students read the Spelling Words aloud and sort them by their suffixes, as below.

Words with Suffixes

-less	-ness	-ment
useless	darkness	entertainment
motionless	fairness	measurement
hopeless	sickness	government
breathless	greatness	encouragement

-ion	-able	
construction	adjustable	
description	dependable	
protection	enjoyable	
production	adorable	

Word Wall Have students create a word wall based on the word sort and add more words from their reading.

SPELLING PRACTICE BOOK, PAGE 173

SPELLING PRACTICE BOOK, PAGE 175

Words with Suffixes

Practice and Extend

Word Meaning: Base Words Point out that suffixes are added to base (root) words to form new words. Have students read aloud each Spelling Word and find the base word from which it is formed. Ask them to write sentences using the base words.

If students need extra practice, have partners give each other a midweek test.

Glossary Review that Glossary entries include syllabication—how the words are broken into syllables. Have students:

• write each Challenge Word.

• look up each Challenge Word.

• note how the entry shows the syllables of the word.

• write the Challenge Words, leaving a space between each syllable.

Proofread and Write

Proofread Sentences Write these sentences on the chalkboard, including the misspelled words. Ask students to proofread, circling incorrect spellings and writing the correct spellings. There are two spelling errors in each sentence.

> We all want protecton and fairnes from the government. (protection, fairness)
>
> This measuremint is not dependible and may be useless.
> (measurement, dependable)

Have students create additional sentences with errors for partners to correct.

 Have students use as many Spelling Words as possible in the daily Writing Prompt on page 664D. Remind students to proofread their writing for errors in spelling, grammar, and punctuation.

Assess and Reteach

Assess Students' Knowledge Use page 178 of the **Spelling Practice Book** or the Dictation Sentences on page 691O for the posttest.

 Personal Word List If students have trouble with words in the lesson, have them add the words to their personal lists of troublesome words in their journals. Have students write each word and its base (root) word next to it.

Students should refer to their word lists during later writing activities.

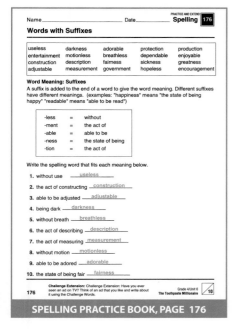

SPELLING PRACTICE BOOK, PAGE 176

SPELLING PRACTICE BOOK, PAGE 177

SPELLING PRACTICE BOOK, PAGE 178

Whales

Selection Summary Students will read about several kinds of whales to discover how they are alike and different. Students will also learn about the efforts of the International Whaling Commission to help preserve whales.

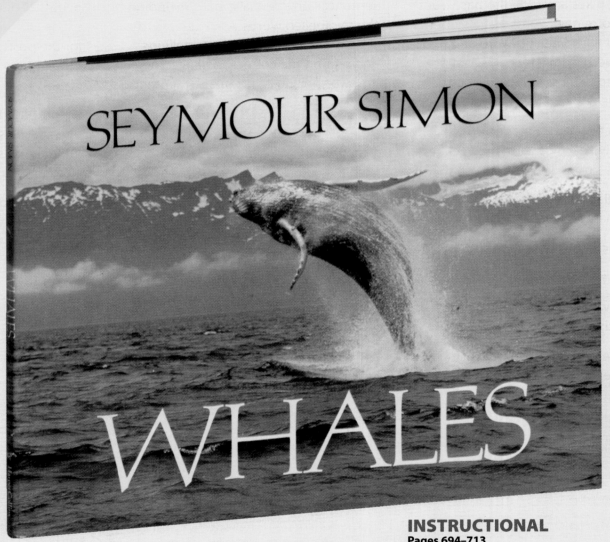

SEYMOUR SIMON

WHALES

INSTRUCTIONAL
Pages 694–713

Student Listening Library Audiocassette

About the Author Seymour Simon loves whales, and he loves telling students about them. He travels to the ends of the earth in order to learn more about these animals. Reading this selection is almost like following the author on one of his whale-watching expeditions. A former teacher, Mr. Simon writes to entertain as well as educate. In many of his books, he presents science projects for young readers to explore. Through his work, he hopes to lead students to develop an interest in science.

Resources for Meeting Individual Needs

EASY
Pages 713A, 713D

INDEPENDENT
Pages 713B, 713D

CHALLENGE
Pages 713C, 713D

LEVELED PRACTICE

Reteach, 207–213

blackline masters with reteaching opportunities for each assessed skill

Practice, 207–213

workbook with Take-Home stories and practice opportunities for each assessed skill and story comprehension

Extend, 207–213

blackline masters that offer challenge activities for each assessed skill

ADDITIONAL RESOURCES

- **Language Support Book,** 225–232
- **Take-Home Story, Practice,** p. 208a
- **Alternative Teaching Strategies,** T60–T66

McGraw-Hill School
TECHNOLOGY

interNET CONNECTION Research and Inquiry Ideas. Visit **www.mhschool.com/reading**

Suggested Lesson Planner

READING AND LANGUAGE ARTS	**DAY 1** *Focus on Reading and Skills*	**DAY 2** *Read the Literature*
● **Comprehension** ● **Vocabulary** ● **Phonics/Decoding** ● **Study Skills** ● **Listening, Speaking, Viewing, Representing**	**Read Aloud and Motivate,** 692E *When Whales Exhale* **Develop Visual Literacy,** 692/693 ☑ **Review Compare and Contrast,** 694A–694B **Teaching Chart 169** **Reteach, Practice, Extend,** 207	**Build Background,** 694C Develop Oral Language **Vocabulary,** 694D *identify marine preserve* *mammals pods related* **Teaching Chart 170** Vocabulary Cards **Reteach, Practice, Extend,** 208 **Read the Selection,** 694–709 ☑ Compare and Contrast ☑ Problem and Solution **Minilessons,** 699, 703, 705, 707 **Cultural Perspectives,** 698
● **Curriculum Connections**	**Link** Works of Art, 692/693	**Link** Science, 694C
● **Writing**	**Writing Prompt:** Research one type of whale you would like to know more about. Write a paragraph to tell where it lives, feeds, and migrates.	**Writing Prompt:** You are a newspaper reporter. Write a report on a beached sperm whale. Use the 5W's of good reporting as you answer questions a reader might have in mind. **Journal Writing,** 709 Quick-Write
● **Grammar**	**Introduce the Concept: Prepositions,** 713M Daily Language Activity 1. Whales live _____ the sea. by 2. A baby whale stays _____ its mother. with 3. Some whales migrate _____ Alaska. to **Grammar Practice Book,** 179	**Teach the Concept: Prepositions,** 713M Daily Language Activity 1. The whale spouted water _____ its blowhole. out 2. An orca swam _____ the pool. around 3. The dolphin slid _____ the ride at the marine park. by **Grammar Practice Book,** 180
● **Spelling**	**Pretest: Words with Prefixes,** 713O **Spelling Practice Book,** 179, 180	**Explore the Pattern: Words with Prefixes,** 713O **Spelling Practice Book,** 181

DAY 3 — Read the Literature

Rereading for Fluency, 708

Story Questions, 710
Reteach, Practice, Extend, 209

Story Activities, 711

Study Skill, 712
 Library/Media Center
Teaching Chart 171
Reteach, Practice, Extend, 210

Test Power, 713

 Read the Leveled Books, 713A–713D
Guided Reading
Silent Letters
 Compare and Contrast
Instructional Vocabulary

 Activity Math, 696

Writing Prompt: Describe a scene on a passenger ship that encounters a baby gray whale and its mother. Write the conversation that takes place among the passengers.

Writing Process: Essay That Compares, 713K
Prewrite, Draft

Review and Practice: Prepositions, 713N
Daily Language Activity
1. Gray whales migrate _____ winter. in
2. They swim _____ the coast from Alaska. along
3. The sky hangs _____ the sea. over

Grammar Practice Book, 181

Practice and Extend: Words with Prefixes, 713P
Spelling Practice Book, 182

DAY 4 — Build Skills

 Read the Leveled Books and Self-Selected Books

 Review Compare and Contrast, 713E–713F
Teaching Chart 172
Reteach, Practice, Extend, 211
Language Support, 230

 Review Make Judgments and Decisions, 713G–713H
Teaching Chart 173
Reteach, Practice, Extend, 212
Language Support, 231

 Activity Science, 700

Writing Prompt: Write a letter to the Humane Society comparing the ocean to a marine park.

Writing Process: Essay That Compares, 713K
Revise
Meeting Individual Needs for Writing, 713L

Review and Practice: Prepositions, 713N
Daily Language Activity
1. The baby swam _____ its mother. to
2. Whales can swim _____ an entire island. around
3. Whales stay _____ the water's surface for an hour. near

Grammar Practice Book, 182

Proofread and Write: Words with Prefixes, 713P
Spelling Practice Book, 183

DAY 5 — Build Skills

Read Self-Selected Books

 Review Context Clues, 713I–713J
Teaching Chart 174
Reteach, Practice, Extend, 213
Language Support, 232

Listening, Speaking, Viewing, Representing, 713L
Illustrate the Likenesses and Differences
Discuss the Art

Minilessons, 699, 703, 707

Phonics Review
Silent Letters, 705

Phonics Workbook

Activity Social Studies, 702

Writing Prompt: You are a member of a conservation group that has videotaped whales migrating from Mexico to Alaska. Write a script narrating the video.

Writing Process: Essay that Compares, 713K
Edit/Proofread, Publish

Assess and Reteach: Prepositions, 713N
Daily Language Activity
1. Whales stir up sediment _____ the ocean floor. from
2. Whales feed _____ different ways. in
3. Did you like reading _____ whales? about

Grammar Practice Book, 183, 184

Assess and Reteach: Words with Prefixes, 713P
Spelling Practice Book, 184

Language Arts

Read Aloud and Motivate

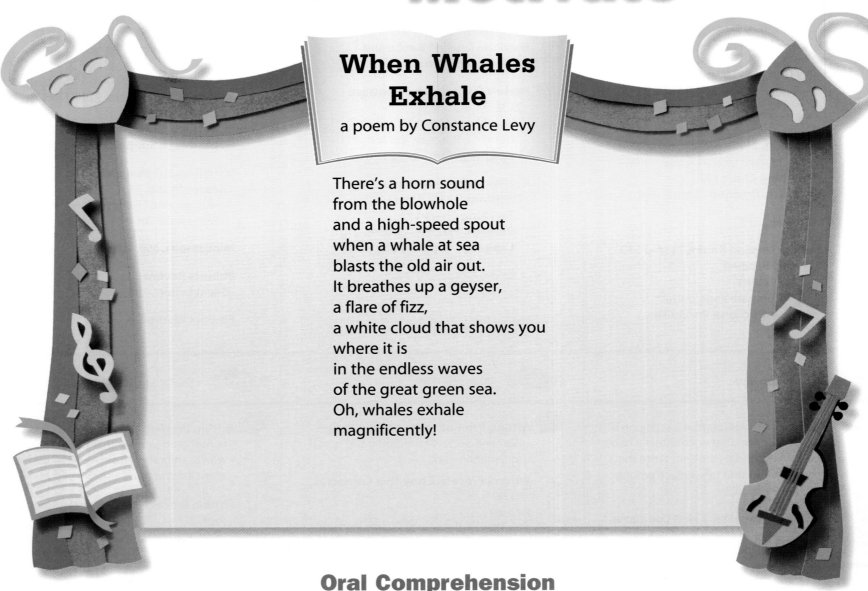

When Whales Exhale
a poem by Constance Levy

There's a horn sound
from the blowhole
and a high-speed spout
when a whale at sea
blasts the old air out.
It breathes up a geyser,
a flare of fizz,
a white cloud that shows you
where it is
in the endless waves
of the great green sea.
Oh, whales exhale
magnificently!

Oral Comprehension

LISTENING AND SPEAKING Motivate students to think about the similarities and differences between whales and other large sea animals as you read this poem aloud. When students have finished listening to the poem, ask them to name some whale traits they can identify from the poem. Ask students, "Based on your knowledge of sea animals as well as on the information in this poem, how does a whale differ from other large sea creatures?" (It has a blowhole through which it exhales.) "What colorful words and phrases describe this trait?" (blowhole, high-speed spout, geyser, flare of fizz)

Activity Tell students that the poem describes how a whale-watcher can identify a whale at sea. Have students compare and contrast other large sea creatures with whales by finding out how those sea animals can be recognized by their special traits. Invite volunteers to share their findings orally. (Examples: A shark has a visible fin; an octopus may spread inky fluid in the water; dolphins do flips and tricks as they follow boats.)
▶ **Visual/Linguistic/Oral**

Anthology pages 692–693

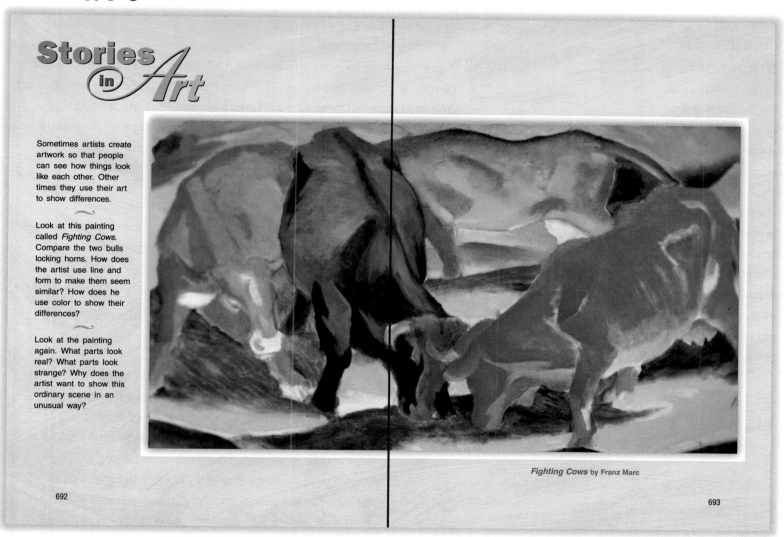

Stories in Art

Sometimes artists create artwork so that people can see how things look like each other. Other times they use their art to show differences.

Look at this painting called *Fighting Cows*. Compare the two bulls locking horns. How does the artist use line and form to make them seem similar? How does he use color to show their differences?

Look at the painting again. What parts look real? What parts look strange? Why does the artist want to show this ordinary scene in an unusual way?

692

693

Fighting Cows by Franz Marc

Objective: Compare and Contrast

VIEWING In his painting, Franz Marc has used line and form to make the animals seem similar. He has used color, however, to show their differences. Encourage students to notice the other animals in the picture and to compare and contrast them with the two animals in the foreground.

Read the page with students, encouraging individual interpretations of the painting. Ask students to support the comparisons and contrasts they make about the animals. For example:

- The blue bull appears to be meaner than the others because its eyes look angry.

- The cow with a white nose and ears seems younger because it doesn't have any horns. It seems too timid to fight, but it looks as if it is trying to copy the movements of the blue bull.

REPRESENTING Have students paint two of the same animals such as two pigs or two dogs. Encourage them to show through their paintings the similarities and differences between the two animals.

692/693

OBJECTIVES

Students will identify similarities and differences among things.

Review Compare and Contrast

PREPARE

Discuss Extinct, Endangered, and Common Animals
Have students discuss the meaning of extinct *(died off)* and endangered *(in danger of being destroyed)*. Have them identify one extinct, one endangered, and one common animal that are all related. *(Examples: saber-toothed tiger, Siberian tiger, house cat)* Ask them how these animals are alike and how they are different.

TEACH

Read the Passage and Model the Skill
Review that the previous discussion compared and contrasted animals because it focused on similarities and differences.

Whale Report

"I'm Captain McGee, and I've studied both killer and sperm whales for many years. The two types of whales are ⟨alike⟩ in several ways. ⟨Both⟩ are mammals; that is, their babies drink milk. A sperm whale has big teeth and a blowhole; a killer whale does ⟨too.⟩ There are also ways that they are ⟨different.⟩ Sperm whales are big enough to sink a ship, ⟨while⟩ killer whales are much ⟨smaller.⟩ Sperm whales swim in a relaxed manner, ⟨but⟩ killer whales speed through the seas. I think killer whales might be ⟨smarter than⟩ sperm whales. After all, I've never met a sperm whale that could do tricks, have you?"

Teaching Chart 169

Display **Teaching Chart 169.** Have students pay attention to clue words that signal comparisons and contrasts.

MODEL From the first sentence, I see that the speaker, Captain McGee, intends to discuss two kinds of whales—sperm whales and killer whales. The words *alike* and *both* indicate similarities between the two whales. The words *different* and *while* tell me that the speaker will now contrast the whales.

Identify Clue Words
Have students identify the similarities and differences between the two kinds of whales and circle clue words in the passage.

SELECTION
Connection

Students will apply sequence of events when they read *Whales* and the Leveled Books.

PRACTICE

Create a Compare and Contrast Chart

Have partners create a Similarities and Differences chart in order to identify the similarities and differences between killer whales and sperm whales. Students can refer to the passage on **Teaching Chart 169** to complete their charts. ▶ **Linguistic/Interpersonal**

SIMILARITIES	DIFFERENCES
Both are mammals.	Sperm whales are huge, but killer whales are smaller.
Both have teeth.	Sperm whales swim in a relaxed manner; killer whales speed through the water.
Both have blowholes.	Killer whales seem to be smarter than sperm whales.

ASSESS/CLOSE

Make Comparisons and Contrasts

Have students recall stories with animal characters such as "Mom's Best Friend," or "The Fox and the Guinea Pig," identifying similarities and differences among the animals. As students share, ask others to jot down any clue words they hear that signal comparisons or contrasts are being made. Have listeners state one similarity and one difference they heard.

ALTERNATE TEACHING
STRATEGY

COMPARE AND CONTRAST

For a different approach to teaching this skill, see page T66.

Meeting Individual Needs for Comprehension

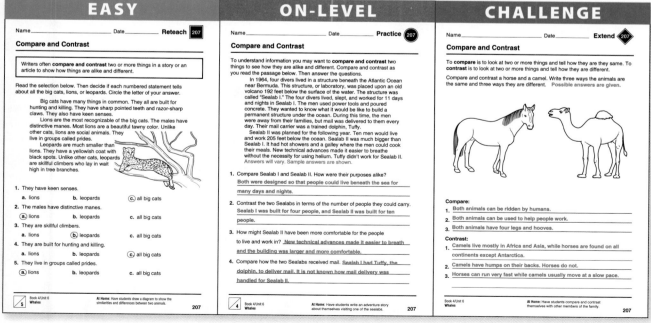

Reteach, 207   Practice, 207   Extend, 207

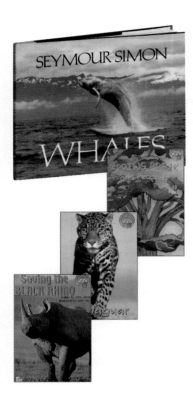

Build Background

 **Link**

Science

Anthology and Leveled Books

Evaluate Prior Knowledge

CONCEPT: ENDANGERED ANIMALS
Over 200 animal species in the United States alone are classified as endangered, or in danger of becoming extinct. Among them are some species of whales.

CAUSE AND EFFECT Tell students they will read about whales. Discuss why some whales are endangered. Write some of the causes of this problem on the chart.

▶ **Logical/Scientific**

CAUSE
People have polluted the oceans, killing the whales' food sources.

↓

Whalers have hunted whales for years.

↓

Some people kill whales for their tusks.

↓

People in some lands still eat whale meat.

↓

RESULT
Whales have become endangered.

Graphic Organizer 25

SAVE A WHALE Have students
  brainstorm ways they could
WRITING GROUP volunteer to save a whale
from an oil spill. For example, they and their friends might go out after breakfast, to throw straw into the water to soak up the oil. In what other ways could they help? Help students organize their ideas into lists.

Develop Oral Language

DISCUSS WHALE BEHAVIOR Share with
ESL students some pictures of whales, and elicit action words that describe what the whales are doing, such as diving, swimming, leaping, breathing, jumping, and playing. Together, brainstorm words that describe whale behavior, and write student suggestions on word cards.

Invite volunteers to select cards and act out the whale behaviors written on the cards. For students who have difficulty recognizing a word or understanding the concept, help match the words on the cards to the appropriate pictures.

TEACHING TIP

MANAGEMENT Students who participate in the Develop Oral Language Activity may not be able to create a Cause and Effect chart, but they may be able to create a word web about whales after completing the activity.

LANGUAGE SUPPORT

See the **Language Support Book**, pages 225–228, for teaching suggestions for Build Background and Vocabulary.

Vocabulary

Key Words

1. Everglades City in Florida is a wonderful place to view (marine) animals in their natural surroundings—the rivers, salt marshes, and Gulf of Mexico waters. 2. Park rangers help tourists recognize and (identify) these animals. 3. In the swamps, one can observe alligators, lizards, and other (related) members of the reptile family. 4. Passengers on tour boats are delighted by the tricks of family groups, or (pods,) of dolphins and whales. 5. However, one of the world's rarest (mammals,) the Florida panther, and its furry young are seldom seen by visitors. 6. It is the job of the rangers to (preserve) these endangered animals and to save them from being wiped out.

Teaching Chart 170

Definitions

marine (p. 698) having to do with or living in the sea

identify (p. 701) to find out or tell exactly who a person is or what a thing is; recognize

related (p. 696) belonging to the same family

pods (p. 699) family groups of whales or dolphins

mammals (p. 699) kinds of animals that are warm-blooded and have backbones

preserve (p. 708) to keep from being lost, damaged, or decayed; protect

SPELLING/VOCABULARY CONNECTIONS

See Spelling Challenge Words, pages 713O–713P.

Vocabulary in Context

IDENTIFY VOCABULARY WORDS
Display **Teaching Chart 170** and read it with students. Have students circle each vocabulary word and underline other words that are clues to its meaning.

DISCUSS MEANINGS Ask questions like these to help clarify word meanings:

- Do marine parks have dolphins or zebras?
- Which birds can you identify by their call?
- Name a person who is related to you.
- Which animals live and travel in pods?
- Name some mammals that make good pets.
- What are some ways people can preserve wildlife?

Practice

MAKE A SENTENCE Have students take turns drawing vocabulary cards from a stack of inverted cards and using each word correctly in a sentence. Invite volunteers to use another meaning of the word, if applicable.

▶ **Kinesthetic/Linguistic**

Vocabulary Cards

WRITE A HAIKU Tell students that a haiku is a three-line poem whose lines contain 5, 7, and 5 syllables, respectively. Have them use as many vocabulary words as possible to write haiku about whales. Encourage students to write more than one haiku. ▶ **Linguistic**

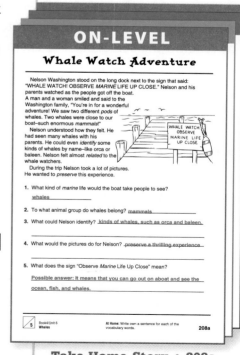

ON-LEVEL

Whale Watch Adventure

Nelson Washington stood on the long dock next to the sign that said: "WHALE WATCH! OBSERVE *MARINE* LIFE UP CLOSE." Nelson and his parents watched as the people got off the boat.
A man and a woman smiled and said to the Washington family, "You're in for a wonderful adventure! We saw two different *pods* of whales. Two whales were close to our boat—such enormous *mammals!*"
Nelson understood how they felt. He had seen many whales with his parents. He could even *identify* some kinds of whales by name—like orca or baleen. Nelson felt almost *related* to the whale watchers.
During the trip Nelson took a lot of pictures. He wanted to *preserve* this experience.

1. What kind of *marine* life would the boat take people to see?
   whales

2. To what animal group do whales belong? mammals

3. What could Nelson identify? kinds of whales, such as orca and baleen

4. What would the pictures do for Nelson? preserve a thrilling experience

5. What does the sign "Observe *Marine* Life Up Close" mean?
   Possible answer: It means that you can go out on a boat and see the ocean, fish, and whales.

Book4/Unit 6
Whales   At Home: Write own a sentence for each of the vocabulary words.   208a

Take-Home Story • 208a
Reteach 208
Practice 208 • Extend • 208

694D

Guided Instruction

Preview and Predict

Have students read the title and preview the photographs.

- Does the reading deal with facts or made-up details? Explain.
- In which textbook might you find a reading like this one? Explain. (Science; science textbooks present nonfiction articles about topics such as animals.) *Genre*
- What do you think will be the main idea of this selection?
- What sort of facts about whale behavior do you think the selection will contain?

Have students prepare a Predictions chart telling what they expect to learn.

PREDICTIONS	WHAT HAPPENED
I will learn about many different whales.	
I will learn the similarities and differences among whales.	

Set Purposes

What questions do students want to answer by reading the selection? For example:

- What are the names of some whales?
- How are whales alike, and different?

WHA
By Seymour Simon

Meeting Individual Needs · Grouping Suggestions for Strategic Reading

EASY	ON-LEVEL	CHALLENGE
Read Together Read the story with students or have them use the **Listening Library Audiocassette.** Have students use the Comparison and Contrast chart to record comparisons and contrasts they make as they read. Guided Instruction and Prevention/Intervention prompts offer additional help.	**Guided Reading** Preview the story words listed on page 695. You may want to have students read the selection first on their own. Then choose from the Guided Instruction questions as you read the story with students or after they have played the **Listening Library Audiocassette.**	**Read Independently** Have students read independently. Remind them that identifying comparisons and contrasts will help them understand the story. Have students set up a Comparison and Contrast chart as on page 695. After reading, they can use their charts to summarize the selection.

Guided Instruction

☑ **Compare and Contrast**
☑ **Problem and Solution**

Strategic Reading Comparing and contrasting information in a selection can help you understand similarities and differences among groups discussed in the selection. Before we begin, let's prepare a Similarities and Differences chart.

TITLE:

SIMILARITIES	DIFFERENCES

 COMPARE AND CONTRAST Is there enough information on the title page for you to understand the similarities and differences among kinds of whales? (no) Explain. (The title is too general; it does not name the kinds of whales, and the illustration shows only one kind of whale.)

Story Words

The words below may be unfamiliar. Have students check their meanings and pronunciations in the Glossary beginning on page 726.

- captivity, p. 699
- blowhole, p. 700
- frayed, p. 700
- skim, p. 700
- flippers, p. 701
- sediment, p. 703

LANGUAGE SUPPORT

A blackline master of the Similarities and Differences chart is available in the **Language Support Book.**

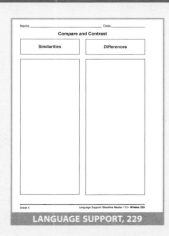

Guided Instruction

2 **PROBLEM AND SOLUTION** How do scientists tell the whales apart?

MODEL Keeping track of ninety whales is a big project, but scientist know how to tackle it. They divide them into two main groups, then they compare and contrast the groups to tell them apart.

3 **COMPARE AND CONTRAST** Name some similarities and differences between a male and a female sperm whale.

MODEL Both are sperm whales, so they will look similar. Each has a huge head, small eyes, and teeth along the lower jaw. But their lengths and weights differ.

TEACHING TIP

INSTRUCTIONAL Look at the word *squarish*. **What is its base word?** (square) **Point out that the suffix-*ish* means "like" or "similar to." Ask: If you read that a sperm whale has a squarish head, is its head exactly square?** (no) **How would you describe the shape of his head?** (somewhat square)

Sperm Whale

2 There are about ninety kinds of whales in the world. Scientists divide them into two main groups: toothed whales and baleen whales.

Toothed whales have teeth and feed mostly on fish and squid. They have only one blowhole and are closely related to dolphins and porpoises.

3 The **sperm whale** is the only giant among the toothed whales. It is the animal that comes to mind when most people think of a whale. A sperm whale has a huge, squarish head, small eyes, and a thin lower jaw. All the fist-sized teeth, about fifty of them, are in the lower jaw. The male grows to sixty feet long and weighs as much as fifty tons. The female is smaller, reaching only forty feet and weighing less than twenty tons.

A sperm whale's main food is squid, which it catches and swallows whole. A sperm whale is not a very fast swimmer, but it is a champion diver. It dives to depths of a mile in search of giant squid and can stay underwater for more than an hour.

696

Activity

Cross Curricular: Math

LENGTH AND WEIGHT The sperm whale is the giant among toothed whales. Apparently, the male is larger than the female, but by how much?

Activity As students reread the information about the size of sperm whales, have them:

• figure the difference in length.
• figure the difference in weight.

Working on the playground, help partners use a tape measure to measure the lengths of male and female sperm whales. ▶ **Mathematical/Spatial**

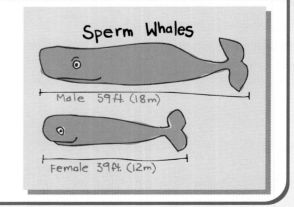

Sperm Whales
Male 59ft. (18m)
Female 39ft. (12m)

There are smaller and less familiar kinds of toothed whales. The **narwhal** is a leopard-spotted whale about fifteen feet long. It is sometimes called the unicorn whale, because the male narwhal has a single tusk. The tusk is actually a ten-foot-long front left tooth that grows through the upper lip and sticks straight out. No one knows for sure how the narwhal uses its tusk. Narwhals live along the edge of the sea ice in the Arctic.

④

Narwhals

697

Guided Instruction

④ **COMPARE AND CONTRAST** How is a narwhal like a sperm whale? (Both are toothed whales.) How is a narwhal different from a sperm whale? (A narwhal is smaller and less familiar to humans than a sperm whale. It also has a large tusk, which a sperm whale doesn't have.)

LANGUAGE SUPPORT

ESL To help students understand why the narwhal is sometimes called a unicorn whale, display a picture of a unicorn. Have students point to the horn on the unicorn and the tusk-like tooth of the narwhal.

To help students get a sense of how long this tooth actually is, choose an object that is about two feet long, and then if possible place five of these objects end to end to show the length of a narwhal's tooth.

Guided Instruction

⑤ PROBLEM AND SOLUTION Some people are afraid of killer whales because of their scary name. How could these people solve this problem? (Answers will vary. Possible responses: Read to find out more about killer whales. Go to a marine park and watch the killer whales do tricks. Use the term *orcas* instead of *killer whales*.)

⑥ What can you infer from the phrase "killer whales perform in theme parks"? (Answers will vary. They are intelligent, they are social, they can be trained.) *Make Inferences*

⑤

⑥

*P*erhaps the best known of the toothed whales is the killer whale, or **orca**. That's because there are killer whales that perform in marine parks around the country. A killer whale is actually the largest member of the dolphin family. A male can grow to over thirty feet and weigh nine tons.

698

CULTURAL PERSPECTIVES

WHALES Explain that people from many different countries have an interest in whales. How do different cultures view whales? Has that view changed?

RESEARCH AND INQUIRY Have students work in small groups to identify a culture, such as Norwegian or Inuit.

Have them research how whales are viewed and if whaling was an important aspect of the culture. Invite each group to make its own poster display.

▶ **Linguistic/Intrapersonal**

Whales and American Colonists

Orcas are found in all of the world's oceans, from the poles to the tropics. They hunt for food in herds called pods. Orcas eat fish, squid, and penguins, as well as seals, sea lions, and other sea mammals, including even the largest whales. Yet they are usually gentle in captivity, and there is no record that an orca has ever caused a human death.

7

Orcas

699

Guided Instruction

7 **COMPARE AND CONTRAST** We have been reading about different types of whales. Let's review what we have learned so far and put it on our charts.

SIMILARITIES	DIFFERENCES
Both toothed and baleen whales live in oceans.	Some whales have teeth and others have baleen.
Toothed whales eat mostly fish and squid.	The sperm whale is the largest of the toothed whales.
	The Narwhal has a tusk and leopard spots.
	Orcas are members of the dolphin family.

 WORD STRUCTURE Find the word *largest* in line 7. What is being described? (a group of whales) What does the word *largest* tell you about the whales? (They are the biggest ones.)

Minilesson

REVIEW

Make Generalizations

Remind students that when they make a generalization, they first read details then use them to write a broad statement.

- Ask them to look for the specific names of foods eaten by an orca.
- Ask them to suggest a general statement they could make about the orca's diet. (Orcas eat fish and sea animals)

Activity Have students draw small pictures of the orca's favorite foods, then label the whole group with a generalized term. (Example: sea creatures)

 PREVENTION/INTERVENTION

WORD STRUCTURE Tell students that the suffix *-est* can be added to a word to show comparison. Write on the board: *large, larger, largest*. Circle the endings *-er* and *-est*. Have students use the words in sentences. Point out that *larger* is used to com-pare two things, and *largest* is used to compare three or more things. Have students reread page 697 to find a word used to compare. (smaller)

699

Guided Instruction

8 **COMPARE AND CONTRAST** Read the first two sentences on this page. What clue words signal that two groups are being compared? (differ from, instead of) Use these clue words in sentences of your own. How do baleen whales differ from toothed whales? Let's add this information to our charts.

SIMILARITIES	DIFFERENCES
Both toothed and baleen whales live in oceans.	Some whales have teeth and others have baleen.
Toothed whales eat mostly fish and squid.	The sperm whale is the largest of the toothed whales.
	The narwhal has a tusk and leopard spots.
	Orcas are members of the dolphin family.
	Toothed whales have one blowhole; baleen whales have two-part blowholes.

Baleen Whale

8 **B**aleen whales differ from toothed whales. They have a two-part nostril or blowhole; and, instead of teeth, they have food-gathering baleen plates. Each whale has several hundred baleen plates, which hang down from the whale's upper jaw. The plates can be two to seven feet long and hang about one quarter of an inch apart. The inside edge of each plate is frayed and acts like a filter.

Baleen whales are the biggest whales of all, yet they feed on small fish and other very small sea animals, such as the shrimplike animals called krill. Krill, which are only as big as your little finger, occur in huge amounts in the Antarctic Ocean. In northern waters, baleen whales eat different kinds of small shrimplike animals.

Some baleen whales, such as the right whale, skim open-mouthed through the water. The frayed inner edges of the baleen trap the food animals while the water pours out through the gaps. In this way a right whale can filter thousands of gallons of seawater and swallow two tons of food each day.

700

Activity

Cross Curricular: Science

WHAT WHALES EAT You have read that some whales eat krill and other shrimplike creatures. Point out that *shrimplike* means "like a shrimp."

RESEARCH AND INQUIRY Have small groups research krill and other creatures in a whale's diet. The groups should make oral presentations with pictures. ▶ **Linguistic/Interpersonal**

 inter NET CONNECTION Students can learn more by visiting **www.mhschool.com/reading**

The **right whale** was once very common in the North Atlantic Ocean. It was given its name by early whalers who regarded it as the "right whale" to catch, because it swam slowly, had lots of baleen and blubber, and floated when dead. So many right whales were killed that they are now quite rare.

Right whales may reach more than fifty feet and weigh more than seventy tons. They have large flippers and a long lower lip that covers and protects their baleen plates. Each right whale has its own pattern of strange bumps along its head called callosities. Scientists sometimes identify individual whales by the patterns of their callosities.

Right Whale

701

Guided Instruction

9 PROBLEM AND SOLUTION The right whale faces a very critical problem. What is it? (It is very rare. It could become extinct.) What are some possible solutions to this problem? (Answers will vary. Possible answers: Protect the right whale as an endangered species. Educate people about the right whale.)

 WORD MEANING Look at the word *callosities*. What does it mean? (hardened skin) What other word does *callosities* look or sound like that might help you figure out its meaning?
(callus)

PREVENTION/INTERVENTION

WORD MEANING Help students who need further instruction to understand the word *callosities*. Remind students that callosities are bumps on a right whale's head. Explain that the words *callus* and *callosities* are related.

Ask students if they know anyone who has calluses on their hands or feet. Tell them they might get calluses from doing yard work, wearing tight shoes, or even from using a pencil. Ask them to define *callus*. (hardened skin) Discuss the similarities between human calluses and whale callosities.

Guided Instruction

10 **COMPARE AND CONTRAST** Point out some similarities and differences between the pictures at the top and bottom of the page. (Both pictures show very large whales. The top picture shows a whale swimming or diving underwater. The bottom picture shows a whale using its blowhole and swimming on the surface.) *Use Graphic Elements*

10

702

Activity

Cross Curricular: Social Studies

WHALE MIGRATION Display a world map. Ask students:

- To locate and point out the places mentioned on page 703.
- Which season do gray whales spend in Arctic waters? (summer)

Activity Have students draw on bulletin board paper a map of the west coast of North America, from the Arctic to Baja. Have them trace the summer and winter routes of the gray whales in different colors and label nearby states and countries. ▶ **Logical/Spatial**

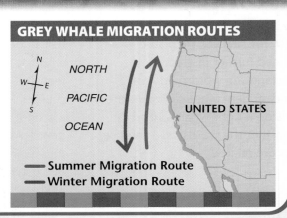

GREY WHALE MIGRATION ROUTES

NORTH PACIFIC OCEAN

UNITED STATES

—— Summer Migration Route
—— Winter Migration Route

he **gray whale** feeds differently from the way any other whale does. It swims on its side on the ocean bottom and pushes water out of its mouth between its baleen plates, stirring up sediment from the ocean floor. Then the whale draws back its tongue and sucks the sediment, and any living things around, into its mouth. As the whale rises to the surface, it rinses its mouth with fresh seawater and swallows the catch. This method of bottom feeding is sometimes called "grubbing."

Gray whales once swam, in both the North Atlantic and North Pacific oceans, in the shallow waters along the coasts. Now, because of whaling in the Atlantic, they live only in the North Pacific and Arctic seas.

In the summer, the gray whales feed in the cold waters of the Arctic. In the winter, they travel about ten thousand miles to Mexican waters. There, the females give birth in the warm, protected lagoons along the Baja California peninsula. The journey of the gray whales is the longest known yearly migration for any mammal.

(703)

Guided Instruction

(11) **COMPARE AND CONTRAST** How is a gray whale like other baleen whales? (It has baleen plates.) How is it different? (It catches food by "grubbing.")

Ⓢ ELF-MONITORING

STRATEGY

ASK QUESTIONS Questions help readers express what they want to know.

MODEL As I read, I find out that the whale sucks in sediment when it feeds. Sediment contains mud and sand. So I ask: Does the whale swallow the sediment? As I read on I find out that the whale rinses its mouth, which tells me that it does not swallow the sediment.

Have students write questions they would like to answer as they read further.

Minilesson

REVIEW

Context Clues

Review that context clues can be used to figure out the meaning of an unknown word. Direct students to the word *lagoons* on page 703. Point out that the context clues help them to figure out that a lagoon is a body of water.

Have students use context clues to figure out the meaning of *migration* on this page.

Activity Have partners write then exchange context-rich sentences using the words *lagoon* and *migration*.

703

Guided Instruction

(12) Rorquals are one group of whales. What is unique about them? (They have grooves on their throats.) How did this group of whales get its name? (from the Norwegian word for groove or furrow) Provide modeling clay and plastic knives. Invite students to mold the clay into a whale and then make grooves to show rorquals. *Supporting Details/Nonverbal Response*

(13) **COMPARE AND CONTRAST** To what animal does the author compare a blue whale? (dinosaur) Why does the author use this comparison? (to show how huge the blue whale really is)

Fin Whale

(12) With its long, streamlined body, its pointed head, and its thin flukes, the **fin whale** has the right shape to be a fast and nimble swimmer—and it is. The long grooves on its throat allow the throat to expand while the whale is feeding. Whales that have these grooves, such as the fin, minke, humpback, and blue, are called rorquals, from the Norwegian word for groove or furrow.

Fin whales often work in pairs to round up and eat schools of fish. Fin whales are second only to blue whales in size. They can reach seventy to nearly ninety feet in length and weigh eighty tons.

(13) The **blue whale** is bigger than the largest dinosaur that ever lived. The largest known dinosaur may have been 100 feet long and weighed 100 tons. But the biggest blue whales are over 110 feet long and weigh more than 150 tons. That's the weight of twenty-five full-grown elephants. The heart of a blue whale is the size of a small car.

A blue whale swims along the surface of the ocean up to a cloud of krill, opens its mouth wide, and sucks in fifty or more tons of water in one gulp. Then it opens its lips and strains out the krill through its baleen plates. In one day a blue whale eats more than four tons of krill, about forty *million* of these animals.

Blue whales have been hunted for many years. Even though they are now protected, only small numbers of blue whales are found in the Antarctic or anywhere else in the world.

Blue Whale

704

LANGUAGE SUPPORT

ESL Students may be overwhelmed by all the information presented in this selection. To help them organize it, provide them with a sheet of paper and have them fold it in half. Ask: What are the two main groups of whales? (tooth whales and baleen whales)

Have students use these group names as column heads. Then work with students as they look back and record the names of the different whales under the appropriate heads. Encourage them to write one interesting fact about each whale.

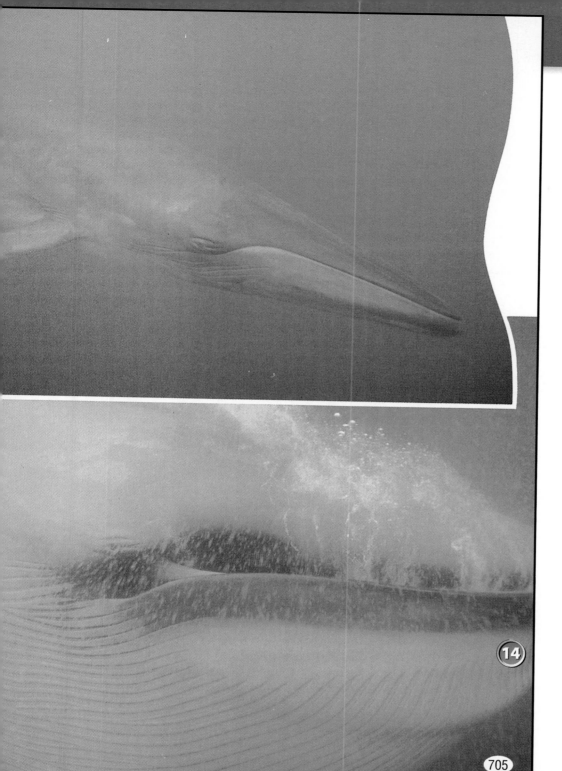

(14)

(705)

Guided Instruction

(14) Look back at the pictures, and think about what you have read so far about whales. What generalization can you make about the size of whales? (Whales are very large.) *Form Generalizations*

(p/i) MULTIPLE MEANING WORDS
Read the first sentence of the second paragraph on page 704. What do you think *round up* means? (bring together) Can you think of another meaning for the word *round* when it stands alone, without *up*? (shaped like a circle)

(p/i) PREVENTION/INTERVENTION

MULTIPLE MEANING WORDS
Write *round* on the board. Point out that the word can be used as an adjective when it stands alone, or as a verb with *up*. Ask students to describe a *round* object. (circular, curved) Then ask them how they might *round up* some friends. (Possible answer: Call them up and invite them over.)

Have students look up the two meanings in a dictionary. Then have them draw two pictures: one of a *round* object, and the other of a whale *rounding up* a school of small fish. They should label the drawings "round" or "round up" and note which one is the verb and which is the adjective.

Minilesson

PHONICS

Words with Silent Letters

Write the following words from page 704 on the board: *right, weigh, eighty, known, weight, through,* and *though.* Have students pronounce each word.

- Ask them what these words have in common. (silent letters)

- Ask students to underline the silent letters in the words. (gh, k, or w (known))

Activity Write the following letters on the board: *k, b, l, gh,* and *w.* Point out that in some words these letters can be silent. Ask students to work with partners to make a five-column chart, find other words in the selection with the silent letters listed on the board, and write the words on their charts in the appropriate column.

Guided Instruction

15 Read paragraphs 2 and 3 on this page. How would you express the main idea of these paragraphs in one sentence? (Possible answer: The male humpback whale is famous for its strange and beautiful songs.) *Inferential/Main Idea*

16 Describe "bubble netting." (Humpbacks send out clouds of bubbles. Small fish get trapped in the bubbles. Humpbacks go inside the circle of bubbles to eat the fish.) *Literal/Sequence of Events*

Fluency

REPEATED READINGS

PARTNERS Students can practice reading fluently using the paragraphs on page 706. Have students listen to the **Listening Library Audiocassette** and then practice reading independently, with smoothness and appropriate emphasis on surprising facts about whales. Partners can take turns reading aloud paragraphs until their reading is fluent.

*H*umpback whales appear to be curious and seem to be accustomed to whale-watching boats. The whales show no hostility to the boats and are careful to avoid collisions.

15 Many whales make sounds, but the most famous are the songs of the humpbacks. They are sung only by the males. Some scientists think the songs may help to attract females or to keep other males from coming too close.

Whatever the reasons the whales have for singing them, the songs are strange and beautiful. Each one lasts as long as twenty or thirty minutes and is sung over and over again. The songs have patterns that repeat, but are different from one whale to another and from one year to the next. The song of a humpback can be heard from miles away.

Humpbacks feed in different ways. One way is called "bubble netting." A humpback sends out clouds of bubbles in a circle beneath a school of small fish or other food animals. When the fish are trapped by the bubbles, the whale lunges up inside the circle with its mouth open, swallowing huge amounts of water and food. A humpback's throat expands to make lots of room for the food and water. Sometimes

16 several humpbacks feed together in the circle of bubbles.

Humpback Whales

706

17

707

Guided Instruction

17 Look at the photographs on this page. What is the author trying to express by the images he chose? (Answers will vary. Whales are majestic; breathtaking, magnificent, powerful, awesome) *Author's Purpose*

Minilesson

REVIEW

Summarize

Review that good readers often stop and summarize, or sum up, key ideas they have read so far. Remind them that a summary is always brief and only contains main ideas.

- Have students think over the parts of the story they have read so far.
- Ask them what the key ideas are.

Activity Have students choose one of the following topics to summarize in one sentence:

- The Characteristics of Toothed Whales
- The Characteristics of Baleen Whales

LANGUAGE SUPPORT

ESL Define *hump* for students who are unfamiliar with this word. Tell students that the name of the humpback whale is a compound word. What two words are combined to make *humpback*? (hump, back)

Encourage students to study the pictures on this page and other pictures of humpback whales. Do you think the name of this whale fits its appearance? (probably yes) Explain your opinion. (Example: The humpback whale seems to have a rounded or humped back.)

Guided Instruction

(18) **COMPARE AND CONTRAST** On this page, the author provides one more similarity among the whales. What is it? Let's complete our charts with this.

SIMILARITIES	DIFFERENCES
Both toothed and baleen whales live in oceans.	Some whales have teeth and others have baleen.
Toothed whales eat mostly fish and squid.	The sperm whale is the largest of the toothed whales.
Baleen whales eat mostly krill.	The narwhal whale has a tusk and spots.
The number of whales is growing smaller.	The Orcas are members of the dolphin family.
	Toothed whales have one blowhole; baleen whales have two-part blowholes.
	Fin whales are fast swimmers.
	Blue whales are the largest whales.
	Humpbacks feed using "bubble netting."

STUDENT SELF-ASSESSMENT

- How did the strategy of comparing and contrasting help me understand the selection better?
- How did the Similarities and Differences chart help me?

TRANSFERRING THE STRATEGY

- When might I try using this strategy again?

708 *Whales*

(18) In 1946, the International Whaling Commission (IWC) was set up to establish rules to limit whaling. Despite the rules, the numbers of whales steadily shrank. Some kinds of whales may be about to become extinct. Because of a worldwide movement to save the whales, the IWC banned all commercial whaling, beginning in 1985. But the governments of a few countries still allow their citizens to hunt whales.

Whales are one of the few wild animals that are commonly friendly to humans they encounter. Many people feel that we have an obligation to preserve these intelligent and special animals.

Will whales be allowed to remain to share the world with us? The choice is ours.

708

REREADING FOR *Fluency*

PARTNERS Have students choose a favorite section of the selection to read to a partner. Encourage them to read with expression, especially to emphasize interesting and amazing facts about whales.

READING RATE You may want to evaluate a student's reading rate. Have the student read aloud from *Whales* for one minute; ask the student to place a stick-on note after the last word read. Then count the number of words he or she has read.

Alternatively, you could assess small groups or the whole class together by having students count words and record their own scores.

Use the Reading Rate form in the **Diagnostic/Placement Evaluations** booklet to evaluate students' performance.

Meet Seymour Simon

From a very young age, Seymour Simon has been fascinated by whales. Simon's interest in the giant creatures has led him on whale watching expeditions from New York to Hawaii, and even to Alaska. "Whales are the greatest things going," he says.

The author of more than one hundred books, Simon has had more than forty of his books named as Outstanding Science Trade Books for Children. To Simon, a former teacher, science is a way of finding out about the world. Many of his books contain projects and questions that help readers find things out for themselves.

Simon enjoys receiving letters from readers who have answered a question using one of his books. For him, sharing a reader's experience is "as much fun as the first time I found out something myself."

709

LITERARY RESPONSE

QUICK-WRITE Invite students to record their thoughts about the selection. These questions may be used to help them get started:

- Which kind of whale would you most like to see? Why?

- What are some things you could do to help save the whales?

ORAL RESPONSE Have students share their journal writings. Encourage them to discuss which illustrations they found the most interesting and why.

Guided Instruction

Return to Predictions and Purposes

Review with students their reasons for reading the selection. Did they find out what they wanted to know? Were their predictions correct?

PREDICTIONS	WHAT HAPPENED
I will learn about many different whales.	I learned about the narwhal has a ten-foot-long front tooth.
I will learn the similarities and differences among whales.	I learned that whales are big animals that live in water and are becoming fewer in number.
	I learned there are differences among the whales. For example: toothed whales have teeth, eat fish and squid, have only one blowhole. Baleen whales have baleen in their mouths, eat mostly krill, and have a two-part blowhole.

STUDENT SELF-ASSESSMENT

COMPARE AND CONTRAST

HOW TO ASSESS

- Have students use their charts to review the comparisons and contrasts they made based on their reading.

- Ask students to tell the main differences between toothed and baleen whales.

They should remain aware that all whales are similar in some ways, too.

FOLLOW UP If students have trouble pinpointing similarities and differences among whales, choose a few details about two whale types in the selection. Then model identifying similarities and differences.

Story Questions

Have students discuss or write answers to the questions on page 710.

Answers:

1. Toothed whales and baleen whales.
   Literal/Compare and Contrast

2. Both groups live in oceans and eat fish. Toothed whales have teeth and one blowhole. Baleen whales have baleen plates and two-part blowholes.
   Inferential/Compare and Contrast

3. Possible response: Some whales are almost extinct. *Inferential/Compare and Contrast*

4. Whales are splendid animals that are endangered. *Critical/Summarize*

5. Possible response: This selection tells that orcas are not dangerous and the movie "Free Willy" shows this is true.
   Critical/Reading Across Texts

WRITE AN ESSAY For a full writing process lesson related to this suggestion, see the lesson pages 713K–713L.

Story Questions & Activities

1 What are the two main groups of whales?

2 How are the two main groups of whales alike? What are the differences?

3 Why do we need to save the whales?

4 What is the main idea of this selection?

5 Compare this selection with a movie or a television program about another endangered animal. How are these animals alike? What are people trying to do to help them?

Write an Essay

The author of this selection is fascinated by these giant creatures. Write a short essay that compares a whale with another large sea animal, such as a dolphin, a manatee, or a shark. First, describe the whale in as much detail as possible. Then describe the other animal. List at least three things the two animals have in common. Then list at least three differences.

Meeting Individual Needs

EASY

Name_____ Date_____ **Reteach** 208

Vocabulary

Unscramble each word by using the clues for help. Then write the unscrambled word on the line provided.

| identify | mammals | marine | pods | preserve | related |

1. MALMASM	warm blooded animals	mammals
2. SDOP	whale herd	pods
3. ENIRAM	relating to the oceans	marine
4. DLEATRE	connected to in some way	related
5. YFITNEDI	to name	identify
6. ERESRPVE	save	preserve

Story Comprehension **Reteach** 209

Circle the letter of the words that complete each statement about the story "Whales."

1. Whales are
   a. fish.   (b.) mammals.
2. Baleen whales have
   (a.) no teeth.   b. teeth.
3. The blue whale is bigger than the biggest
   (a.) dinosaur.   b. woolly mammoth.
4. Baleen, or toothless, whales eat.
   a. giant squid.   (b.) tiny fish.
5. There are not many gray whales because of.
   (a.) over hunting.   b. air pollution.
6. The goal of the International Whaling Commission is to.
   (a.) limit the hunting of whales.   b. tag whales for identification.

At Home: Have students recall what they have learned about whales.
208–209   Book 4/Unit 6 Whales 6

Reteach, 209

ON-LEVEL

Name_____ Date_____ **Practice** 209

Story Comprehension

Think about what you've learned about whales. Then complete the outline. Refer to "Whales" for help. Some parts of the outline are already filled in.
Answers will vary.

I. TOOTHED WHALES

A. Three features of toothed whales

1. feed mostly on fish and squid
2. have only one blowhole
3. are closely related to dolphins and porpoises

B. Three kinds of toothed whales

4. sperm whale
5. narwhal
6. orca

II. BALEEN WHALES

A. Three features of baleen whales

7. have a two-part nostril or blowhole
8. have food-gathering baleen plates
9. are the biggest whales of all

B. Three kinds of baleen whales

10. gray whale
11. fin whale
12. blue whale and humpback whale

At Home: Have students draw a picture of the whale they find most interesting. Label the picture.
209   Book 4/Unit 6 Whales 12

Practice, 209

CHALLENGE

Name_____ Date_____ **Extend** 208

Vocabulary

| identify | mammals | marine | pods | preserve | related |

Suppose you went on a whale-watching trip with your family. Using at least four of the vocabulary words above, write a diary entry about what you saw. Answers will vary, but should include at least four vocabulary words.

Dear Diary,

_____

_____

_____

_____

_____

Extend 209

Story Comprehension

Write a paragraph comparing and contrasting two of the types of whales mentioned in the story. Look back at "Whales" for help.

Answers will vary but should cite examples of similarities and differences from the story.

_____

_____

_____

At Home: Have students compare two rooms in the house or apartment.
208–209   Book 4/Unit 6 Whales

Extend, 209

Create a Time Line

Today, laws prevent whaling in most places. Yet whaling played a large role in American history. Create a "history of American whaling" time line. Include these dates and facts.

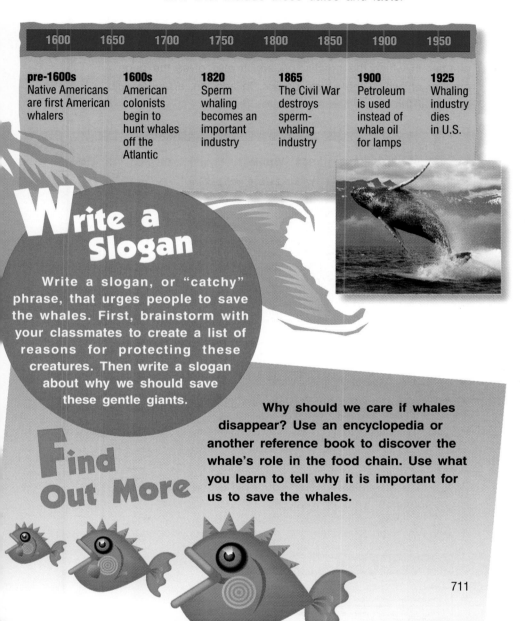

1600	1650	1700	1750	1800	1850	1900	1950

pre-1600s	**1600s**	**1820**	**1865**	**1900**	**1925**
Native Americans are first American whalers	American colonists begin to hunt whales off the Atlantic	Sperm whaling becomes an important industry	The Civil War destroys sperm-whaling industry	Petroleum is used instead of whale oil for lamps	Whaling industry dies in U.S.

Write a Slogan

Write a slogan, or "catchy" phrase, that urges people to save the whales. First, brainstorm with your classmates to create a list of reasons for protecting these creatures. Then write a slogan about why we should save these gentle giants.

Find Out More

Why should we care if whales disappear? Use an encyclopedia or another reference book to discover the whale's role in the food chain. Use what you learn to tell why it is important for us to save the whales.

711

Story Activities

Create a Time Line

Materials: bulletin-board paper, markers, yarn, thumbtacks

GROUP Have students make a time line by stretching a piece of yarn the width of the bulletin board, fastening it with tacks to represent the dates in the history of whaling, and labeling each date. Students might include illustrations corresponding to each date on the time line.

Write a Slogan

Materials: meter sticks, poster board, markers, glue or tacks

PARTNERS Have students paint save-the-whales slogans on their poster boards and then tack or glue their posters to sticks. Invite students to practice chanting their slogans as they march in a classroom parade.

Find Out More

RESEARCH AND INQUIRY Have students check the encyclopedia or a nature **PARTNERS** magazine to learn why whales are important. Students can role-play, as one student tries to convince a "whaler" to stop hunting whales. Then the "whaler" can present his or her reasons for hunting.

 For more information on endangered species, students can visit *www.mhschool.com/reading*

ASSESSMENT

After page 711, see the Selection Assessment.

Study Skills

Library/Media Center

OBJECTIVES Students will use an encyclopedia index.

PREPARE Point out that if students want to find an article, the index tells them the volume and page where the article appears. Display **Teaching Chart 171.**

TEACH Review how to read and understand the information presented in the index. Where would you find an article about the whaling industry? (vol. 21, page 284)

PRACTICE Have students answer questions 1–5. Review the answers with them. **1.** Whale **2.** volume 6 **3.** page 282 **4.** the main entry, volume 21, beginning on page 260 **5.** To find information quickly; to get a listing of topics; for volume and page numbers.

ASSESS/CLOSE Have students list the articles that might tell them how they can help whales survive. (Conservation 4:733; Endangered species (table) 6:225; Greenpeace 8:430)

STUDY SKILLS

Use an Encyclopedia Index

Where would you go to find more information about whales? You might start by checking the index of an encyclopedia. The **encyclopedia index** is the last book, or volume. It helps you find your topic quickly. The index gives you the volume number in which the article appears. It also gives the page number on which the article begins. In addition, an index will tell you if the article has any pictures or tables.

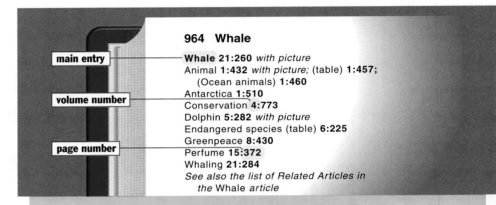

964   Whale

main entry

Whale 21:260 *with picture*
Animal **1:432** *with picture;* (table) **1:457;**
    (Ocean animals) **1:460**
Antarctica **1:510**
Conservation **4:773**
Dolphin **5:282** *with picture*
Endangered species (table) **6:225**
Greenpeace **8:430**
Perfume **15:372**
Whaling **21:284**
*See also the list of Related Articles in
    the* Whale *article*

volume number

page number

Use the sample index to answer these questions.

1 What is the main entry?

2 In which volume would you find special information about endangered animals?

3 On which page of Volume 5 would you begin to read about dolphins?

4 In which volume would you look to find general information about whales?

5 Why would you use the index of an encyclopedia?

Meeting Individual Needs

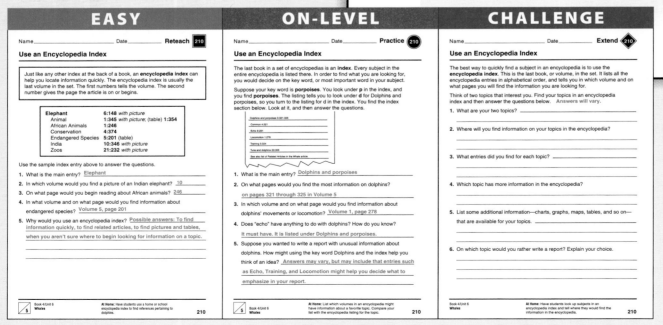

Reteach, 210

Practice, 210

Extend, 210

TEST POWER

Test Tip

Answer the question in your own words before looking at the choices.

DIRECTIONS

Read the sample story. Then read each question about the story.

SAMPLE

The Essay

"How I spent my summer vacation" was the topic for Rita's first essay when school resumed. Her two best friends did exciting things during the summer. Shana went to Mexico, and Juan went to Montana. Since Rita didn't go anywhere, she thought that her vacation would sound dull.

During Rita's summer vacation, her Aunt Marta came to visit after Marta had surgery on her wrists. It took several weeks before Marta could even do simple jobs. Rita helped her aunt whenever she could. When Aunt Marta was ready to go home, she gave Rita a silver dollar for all her help. Remembering this gave Rita an excellent idea for her essay.

1 How did Rita feel about Marta?
   ○ Angry
   ○ Jealous
   ● Caring
   ○ Miserable

2 What does Rita probably do next?
   ○ Writes about her dog
   ○ Calls her Aunt Marta
   ○ Goes back to school
   ● Writes about her silver dollar

713

Read the Page

Have students read the story. Ask students to pay attention to what happens in the story and to how characters interact with each other.

Discuss the Questions

Question 1: This question requires students to understand how Rita felt about her Aunt Marta. Discuss what information is a clue as to how Rita feels. The clue is "Rita helped her Aunt whenever she could." Ask which of the following matches that information: *angry*? *jealous*? *caring*? or *miserable*?

Question 2: This question requires students to determine what Rita will *probably* do next based on what has just happened. Have students tell you what kind of experience Rita had and upon what information in the story they would base their answers. Have students eliminate wrong answers.

For The Princeton Review test preparation practice for **TerraNova**, **ITBS**, and **SAT-9**, visit the McGraw-Hill School Division website. See also McGraw-Hill's *Standardized Test Preparation Book*.

EASY

Answers to Story Questions

1. Black rhinos in Africa face possible extinction because they are considered an endangered species.

2. The horn of the black rhino is used by some people to make medicine or household articles. Because of this, people kill black rhinos just to get their horns.

3. It means that people cannot live, or live well, without animals on the Earth. Very often animals become endangered or extinct because of the actions of people, so all people can learn a lesson about protecting animals by thinking about this saying.

4. The black rhino is an endangered species that some people are trying to protect.

5. Answers will vary.

Story Questions and Activity

1. What problem do black rhinos in Africa face?

2. Why do the horns of the black rhinos cause it trouble?

3. What do you think the saying on page 14 means? How does this saying include all endangered animals on earth?

4. What is the main idea of this book?

5. Compare and contrast the black rhino with the marine mammals discussed in *Whales*? How are they similar? How are they different?

Save the Animals

Choose another endangered animal, such as the elephant or the cheetah. Do some research on this animal, and write a paragraph or two explaining why it is endangered and what, if anything, is being done to protect it.

from Saving the Black Rhino

Leveled Books

EASY

Saving the Black Rhino

Silent Letters

☑ **Compare and Contrast**

☑ **Instructional Vocabulary:**
identify, mammals, marine, pods, preserve, related

Guided Reading

PREVIEW AND PREDICT Ask students to scan the Table of Contents and have students predict what this book will be about. Have them record their ideas.

SET PURPOSES Have students suggest questions using the *5Ws* (who, what, when, where, why) that they want to have answered. For example: Who is the Rhino Man?

READ THE BOOK Have students read on their own. Then use the Guided Reading questions for further teaching.

Page 4: Whales gather in groups called *pods*. Can you think of other group names for animals? (Sample answers: packs, flocks, herds.) *Vocabulary*

Page 4: Find the words *fighting, calf,* and *calves*. Which letter or letters are silent in each word? (gh, l, l) *Phonics*

Page 7: How is a rhino horn different from an elephant tusk? (A rhino horn is made up of thick, tangled hairs. An elephant tusk is made of ivory.) *Compare and Contrast*

Pages 9–11: Compare and contrast the ways Namibia and Zimbabwe have tried to save black rhinos. (In Namibia, rhino horns are cut off so poachers won't kill rhinos. Zimbabwe keeps rhinos in parks or tracks them.) *Compare and Contrast*

Page 16: How was Ms. Phanton's rescue different from the methods used in Zimbabwe? (Ms. Phanton's rescue was different because she was moved by airplane.) *Compare and Contrast*

RETURN TO PREDICTIONS AND PURPOSES Review students' predictions and reasons for reading this story. Which ones were accurate? Which questions were answered in the selection?

LITERARY RESPONSE Discuss these questions:

• Is this selection fact or nonfact? How do you know?

• Which parts of the reading would you like to research further? Where would you look for information?

Also see the story questions and activity in *Saving the Black Rhino*.

Leveled Books

INDEPENDENT

The Jaguar

☑ **Compare and Contrast**

☑ **Instructional Vocabulary:**
identify, mammals, marine, pods, preserve, related

Guided Reading

PREVIEW AND PREDICT Have students preview the pictures up to page 8. Have students write their predictions about the book in their journals.

SET PURPOSES Have students decide what they would like to learn about jaguars when they read the selection. Ask them to write a few questions they would like answered on index cards.

READ THE BOOK Have students read the book independently. Then use the guided reading questions below for further teaching.

Pages 4–5: How are jaguars similar to pet cats? (Both are mammals, eat meat, and have sharp claws.) *Compare and Contrast*

Page 6: If you see a jaguar and a leopard, how can you tell them apart? (A leopard's spots look like clumps, but the jaguar's are outlined. The jaguar is larger.) *Compare and Contrast*

Page 13: Find the word *preserve*. In this book, what endangered animal are people trying to preserve? (the jaguar) Can you name ways that people try to preserve

endangered animals? (Sample answers: enact laws; protect living areas; raise awareness) *Vocabulary*

Page 13: What decision did the Kolla Indians make regarding the gas pipeline, which was to run through the rainforest? (They decided to protest its construction.) What judgments helped the Kolla Indians make that decision? (Sample answers: They value the jaguars. They believed the pipeline would hurt the jaguars.) *Judgments and Decisions*

RETURN TO PREDICTIONS AND PURPOSES Have students share predictions and questions they wrote earlier.

LITERARY RESPONSE Discuss these questions:

- How does the author's use of compare and contrast help the reader better understand jaguars?

- Is this selection mostly fact or nonfact? How do you know?

Also see the story questions and activity in *The Jaguar*.

INDEPENDENT

Answers to Story Questions

1. So many jaguars have been killed for their fur or because ranchers felt they were a threat to their animals that now their populations are very low.
2. Possible answers: Jaguars are large, strong, and fast; they have good hearing, sight, and smell; they watch their prey, stalk them, then pounce and kill them quickly.
3. Jaguars and leopards both have spots, and both jaguars and snow leopards make a coughing sound. Jaguars and leopards have different patterns of spots; jaguars are larger and wider than leopards; jaguars live in the western hemisphere, and leopards live in Africa or Asia.
4. Jaguars are an endangered species, and people can work together to save them from extinction.
5. Answers will vary.

Story Questions and Activity

1. Who is Peaches?
2. Describe a situation in which you or someone you know might feel bored? What could you or that person do to stop feeling the big "B"?
3. Compare and contrast Peaches with wild birds you see in your community.
4. What is the story mostly about
5. Compare and contrast the animals in *Whales* with the African gray parrot in this story. How are they similar and how are they different?

Rescue Missions

Find out about organizations or groups that rescue animals in your community. If possible, arrange a telephone interview with a representative of this group. Make up five questions before the interview and then take notes on the responses. Report your findings to the class in an oral report.

from *The Jaguar*

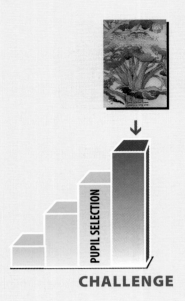

PUPIL SELECTION

CHALLENGE

Leveled Books

CHALLENGE

Spring Break and Peaches

☑ **Compare and Contrast**

☑ **Instructional Vocabulary**
identify, mammals, marine, pods, preserve, related

Answers to Story Questions

1. Peaches is an African gray parrot that showed up in Ana's backyard.
2. Answers will vary.
3. Answers will vary but may include: parrots are bigger, have brighter colors, eat fruit and nuts instead of worms or seeds, and speak words.
4. It is about three children who discover an African gray parrot and what was done to rescue it.
5. Answers will vary.

Story Questions and Activity
Spring Break and Peaches

1. Who is Peaches?
2. Describe a situation in which you or someone you know might feel bored? What could you or that person do to stop feeling the big "B"?
3. Compare and contrast Peaches with wild birds you see in your community.
4. What is the story mostly about?
5. Compare and contrast the animals in Whales with the African gray parrot in this story. How are they similar and how are they different?

Rescue Missions

Find out about organizations or groups that rescue animals in your community. If possible, arrange a telephone interview with a representative of this group. Make up five questions before the interview and then take notes on the responses. Report your findings to the class in an oral report.

from Spring Break and Peaches

Guided Reading

PREVIEW AND PREDICT Preview the book to page 8. Have students use the pictures to predict what the selection is about and then record their predictions in their journals.

SET PURPOSES Ask students to write questions they want to have answered as they read. For example, they may want to know the meaning of *Peaches* in this context.

READ THE BOOK After students have read on their own, use the questions that follow to apply reading strategies.

Page 2: Using a context clue on this page, tell where *marine* mammals live. (in the ocean; context clue is "Ocean World Park") What would you expect to find at a marine park? (water, water animals) *Vocabulary*

Page 5: How are Miami and Chicago different? (Miami is warm, even in March. Chicago is cold and may even have snow in March.) *Compare and Contrast*

Pages 10–11: How does the parrot in the tree present a problem to the children? (It might die if it isn't rescued.) How do they plan to solve the problem? (They ask Carlos from the pet store to help.) *Problem and Solution*

Page 15: Making Peaches come down from the tree is a problem for the rescuers from Bird Haven. Describe their solution. (They hold out their arms for a perch and offer her fruit to gain her confidence.) *Problem and Solution*

RETURN TO PREDICTIONS AND PURPOSES Discuss which predictions were accurate. If some of the students' questions weren't answered, where could they research the answers?

LITERARY RESPONSE Discuss these questions:

- How are other endangered animals rescued?
- In addition to making flyers, how could you find the owner of a lost pet?
- How could Anna have kept from being bored?

Also see the story questions and activity in *Spring Break and Peaches*.

Activities
Anthology and Leveled Books

Connecting Texts

ENDANGERED ANIMALS CHARTS Write the four book titles on a chart. Discuss the differences between two animals or places in each of the selections. Write the contrasts on the chart as students make suggestions. Then expand the chart by comparing the two animals or places. Talk about how the animals or places are similar.

Whales	Saving the Black Rhino	The Jaguar	Spring Break and Peaches
• Baleen whales have rows of soft plates in their mouths. Toothed whales have teeth. • Baleen whales eat small sea animals. Some toothed whales eat much larger animals.	• A black rhino is smaller than a white rhino. • A black rhino eats trees and shrubs. A white rhino eats grass.	• A jaguar is larger than a leopard. • A leopard's spots look like clumps. A jaguar's spots are outlined.	• Miami is very warm. Chicago is cold. • It seldom snows in Miami. It snows often in Chicago.

Viewing/Representing

MAKE A MURAL Divide the class into groups, one for each of the four books. (For *Whales*, combine students of various reading levels.) Have each group make a mural to represent the differences between places or animals in the selection. Mount the murals on the walls, and have groups explain their art.

AUDIENCE RESPONSE Encourage students to pay close attention to each presentation. Leave time for a question-and-answer session.

Research and Inquiry

MORE ABOUT ENDANGERED ANIMALS Have students write a list of interview questions for someone who helps endangered animals, like a marine biologist, vet, zookeeper, park ranger, or Greenpeace volunteer. Then have students do the following:

- Find the answers to their interview questions on the internet, in the encyclopedia, or other reference source.

- Invite someone who works with animals to come to class and answer their questions.

Have students write what they've learned in their journals.

interNET CONNECTION Students can find out more about endangered animals by visiting **www.mhschool.com/reading**

OBJECTIVES

Students will make comparisons and contrasts.

TEACHING TIP

INSTRUCTIONAL To have students practice identifying clue words that signal a comparison, write these sentences on the board, and have volunteers circle the clue words:

- A shark is a fish, (but) a whale is a mammal.
- (Although) the male gray whale sings, the female doesn't.
- (Both) fin whales and orcas are great swimmers.

Review Compare and Contrast

PREPARE

Discuss Comparisons and Contrasts

Review: We compare and contrast objects to determine how they are similar and how they are different. Words like *but, although,* and *both* provide clues that comparisons and contrasts might be being made.

TEACH

Read the Passage and Model the Skill

Share this comparison: Both Greenpeace and whalers are interested in whales. Then ask students to listen for ways both groups are compared and contrasted, as you read aloud **Teaching Chart 172.**

Greenpeace and the Whalers

Many countries still allow whaling, which is the practice of hunting and killing whales. (But) the members of Greenpeace are working to stop it. (Like) the whaling industry, Greenpeace owns many ships, and (both) groups have expert sailors. Whalers say whaling is important for many reasons. For example, whale meat is still eaten in some countries, (although) Greenpeace members feel that it is not necessary to eat whales. Whalers say they can make a living only by hunting whales. (However,) Greenpeace believes whalers could find other jobs.

Teaching Chart 172

Help students identify comparisons and contrasts.

MODEL The title suggests to me that this selection is going to be about two groups of people: members of an organization called Greenpeace and whalers. The rest of the selection will show how these two groups are similar and how they are different.

Reread the chart, and have students raise their hands when they hear a comparison or a contrast being made.

PRACTICE

Identify Comparisons and Contrasts

GROUP

Have volunteers circle words in the passage that signal a comparison or contrast. Discuss what is being compared and contrasted. Have them make a list of the signal words they found, and then as a group, brainstorm other signal words to add to their lists.

▶ **Kinesthetic/Linguistic**

ASSESS/CLOSE

Compare and Contrast

PARTNERS

Have students work in pairs to make a collage using magazine pictures of two animals. Have them present an oral report on the similarities and differences between the two animals. Suggest that students organize their presentations so that they present all the similarities and then all the differences.

ALTERNATE TEACHING STRATEGY

....

COMPARE AND CONTRAST

For a different approach to teaching compare and contrast, see page T66.

SELF-SELECTED Reading

....

Students may choose from the following titles.

ANTHOLOGY

• Whales

LEVELED BOOKS

• Saving the Black Rhino

• The Jaguar

• Spring Break and Peaches

Bibliography, pages T76–T77

Meeting Individual Needs for Comprehension

EASY	ON-LEVEL	CHALLENGE	LANGUAGE SUPPORT

EASY

Name_____ Date_____ Reteach 211

Compare and Contrast

Jotting down likenesses and differences in a chart can make **comparing and contrasting** two or more things easier.

Read the chart below, and then answer the questions.

Crocodiles	Whales
reptiles/cold-blooded	mammals/warm-blooded
good swimmers	good swimmers
air-breathers	air-breathers
swim mostly in fresh water	swim in salty ocean water
can move on land	cannot move on land
lay eggs that will hatch on land	bear live young in water

1. What are two things crocodiles and whales have in common? They are good swimmers; they are air-breathers.

2. What is different about where the animals swim? Crocodiles swim mostly in fresh water. Whales swim in salty ocean water.

3. Which animals cannot move on land? whales

4. What is different about where the animals give birth? Crocodiles lay eggs that will hatch on land. Whales give birth to live babies under water.

5. If the crocodile is cold-blooded, which means its body temperature changes according to the temperature of the surrounding air or water, what do you think the body temperature of the mammal does? Stays the same if the temperature changes.

At Home: Have students compare and contrast two kinds of trees.

211   Book 4/Unit 6 Whales 5

ON-LEVEL

Name_____ Date_____ Practice 211

Compare and Contrast

When you **compare and contrast** you tell how things are alike and how they are different. You have read about two main types of whales, toothed whales and baleen whales. To see how these whales are alike and different, complete each box below. Look back through "Whales" if you need help. Answers will vary.

What do the toothed whales and baleen whales have in common?

1. They are mammals.

2. Their population is shrinking.

3. They live in oceans.

4. They seem friendly to humans they meet.

How would you describe toothed whales?

5. They have teeth.

6. They have only one blowhole.

7. They feed mostly on squid and fish; but can eat larger sea animals.

How are you different from toothed whales?

8. They have food-gathering baleen plates.

9. They have two-part blowhole.

10. They feed mostly on small fish and very small sea animals.

At Home: Have students list ways in which pet dogs and cats are alike and ways in which they are different.

211   Book 4/Unit 6 Whales 10

CHALLENGE

Name_____ Date_____ Extend 211

Compare and Contrast

Comparing two or more things tells how the things are alike.

Example: Whales and dolphins are both sea creatures.

Contrasting two or more things tells how the things are different.

Example: Whales are mammals, and sharks are fish.

Think about yourself and a friend. How are you alike? How are you different? Write a paragraph that compares and contrasts the two of you. Then draw a picture of yourself and your friend.

Answers will vary but should draw appropriate comparisons and contrasts.

At Home: Have students compare and contrast themselves as they were at the age of 6 with themselves today.

211   Book 4/Unit 6 Whales

LANGUAGE SUPPORT

Name_____ Date_____

Comparing Whales

Name		What I Learned About the Whale
Toothed	**Baleen**	
Sperm Whale		The male grows to sixty feet long. The female to only 40 feet. It is a slow swimmer, champion diver and likes to eat squid. It can stay underwater for over an hour.
Narwhal		A leopard-spotted whale approximately 15 feet long. The male has a 10 foot long tooth that grows through the upper lip and sticks out. They live along the edge of the sea ice in the Arctic.
Orca		It is the largest member of the dolphin family. It can grow over 30 feet and weigh 9 tons. They are found all over the world. They eat fish, squid, seal and other mammals.
	Right	They can grow to 50 feet and weigh as much as 70 tons. They have large flippers and a long lower lip. They each have their own pattern of small bumps on their heads.
	Gray	It swims on its side on the bottom of the ocean to catch food. They live only in the North Atlantic. The females give birth in the warm lagoons of Baja California.
	Fin	It has a long body, a pointed head and thin flukes. The Fin whale is a fast swimmer. They work in pairs to catch food. They can grow to become nearly 90 feet long.
	Blue	The blue whale is bigger than the largest dinosaur that ever lived. In one day a blue whale eats more than 4 tons of Krill. Only a few can be found in the Antarctic.
	Humpback	The males sing songs that might attract female humpbacks. The songs last up to 30 minutes.

230 Whales • Language Support/Blackline Master 114   Grade 4

Reteach, 211   Practice, 211   Extend, 211   Language Support, 230

713F

TEACHING TIP

INSTRUCTIONAL Show students a picture or a painting of someone who is experiencing a problem—for example, a child with a flat bike tire, a person who has fallen on a patch of ice, or an animal in trouble. Have students study the picture and make judgments and decisions by answering questions such as these:

- **What is the problem?**
- **What should be done to solve this problem?**

Review Judgments and Decisions

PREPARE

Discuss Judgments and Decisions

Review: Making a judgment involves evaluating a situation based on one's personal goals, priorities, and values. Making a decision involves choosing what action you will take.

TEACH

Read the Passage and Model the Skill

Read the passage "Jackie's Decision" with students. Have students think about what judgments and decisions Jackie makes.

Jackie's Decision

Jackie often walked along the shore. He <u>enjoyed watching the whales splash</u> in the harbor. One day, he saw a horrible sight. A baby whale lay gasping on the beach. <u>Jackie was scared</u> and knew <u>he was too small</u> to push the whale back into the sea. He <u>imagined how he would feel if he were lying helpless on a beach</u>. Jackie made the decision to (run to the fire department and ask for help). The rescuers hopped into their trucks and radioed for help. Soon people from all over town arrived on the beach. Together, they pushed and tugged until the baby whale was safely back in the sea with his family.

Teaching Chart 173

Ask a volunteer to identify the judgment Jackie makes about the whale. What causes him to make this judgment?

MODEL I read that Jackie first thinks the beached whale is a horrible, scary sight. He also knows he is too weak to push the whale by himself. But when he thinks about how he would feel if he were helpless, Jackie makes the judgment that he must do something for the baby whale. His decision is to run to the fire department for help.

Create a Judgment and Decision Chart

GROUP

Have students create a Judgment and Decision chart for "Jackie's Decision," using evidence from the passage.

JUDGMENT/DECISION	EVIDENCE FROM THE STORY
Jackie likes whales.	He walked along the shore to watch the whales splash in the harbor.
He couldn't help the beached whale.	He is too small to help.
He decides to help.	He runs to the fire department and asks for help.
We should not allow whales to become extinct.	Whales are friendly to humans.
The IWC set up rules to limit whaling.	In 1985, the IWC banned all commercial whaling.

ASSESS/CLOSE

Use the Chart for Whales

Have students create a similar chart for the information about the International Whaling Commission on page 708.

ALTERNATE TEACHING STRATEGY

MAKE JUDGMENTS AND DECISIONS

For a different approach to teaching this skill, see page T62.

LOOKING AHEAD

Students will apply their knowledge of making predictions as they read the next selection, *Saving the Everglades.*

Meeting Individual Needs for Comprehension

EASY

Name_____ Date_____ Reteach **212**

Make Judgments and Decisions

As you read, try to use what you know to be right and wrong, wise and unwise from your own experience to help you understand a character's **judgments and decisions.**

Read the following story and then answer the questions. Answers will vary: Possible answers are shown.

The royal princess complained to the king. She had requested that the royal carpenter adjust her throne. She had asked that the silver at the top be changed to gold and that the gold at the bottom be changed to silver. The legs of the throne needed to be made shorter, and the arm rests had to be padded with blue velvet. Now her throne was ruined. The carpenter had made the whole throne red velvet and the legs twice as long. She insisted that the old, hard-of-hearing carpenter did everything wrong on purpose. She wanted him put in jail.

The king asked if she had made a list of her requests, so the carpenter would have a record of what to do. "No," she said. "It is not the work of a princess to make lists!"

1. What must the king decide? whether to jail the carpenter

2. Why do you think the king asked if the princess had given the carpenter a list? Possible answers: The king probably knew the carpenter was hard-of-hearing. He could see that he was old.

3. How do you think the king responded to the princess's statement that lists were not her work? It may have made him more sympathetic to the carpenter and less to the princess.

4. In whose favor will the king decide? Possible response: the carpenter's favor

Book 4/Unit 6
Whales

At Home: Have students explain why they think the king favored who he said he did.

212

ON-LEVEL

Name_____ Date_____ Practice **212**

Make Judgments and Decisions

Making **decisions and judgments** about characters in a story is an important part of reading. Read the passage below. Think about what the characters are doing and why. Then answer the questions.

A fourth-grade class was asked to think about their favorite school subject and then make a suggestion for a related field trip. Mrs. Canby said the subject could not be recess or lunch.

The students had lots of ideas. Benjamin wanted to go to the natural history museum to observe carpenter ants. Every other person in the class started groaning. Several students who like reading wanted to go to a play. Other kids had never been to a play, and they weren't interested. They would, however, go to a movie. Soon everyone started arguing. So Mrs. Canby made the decision to go to the natural history museum. Almost everyone enjoyed the field trip.

1. Mrs. Canby decided recess and lunch classes could not be used as ideas for a field trip. Why do you think she decided this? Possible answer: She wanted students to take the field trip seriously.

2. What would you say to someone who said bugs are boring? Answers will vary, but may include examples of bugs that are interesting.

3. What do you think about going to a movie for a field trip? Can you think of any movie that might make a good learning experience? Tell why. Answers will vary.

4. Are you surprised that everyone enjoyed the museum? Why or why not? Answers will vary.

5. Do you think Mrs. Canby should refrain from having students make suggestions for field trips in the future? What are your reasons for thinking as you do? Answers will vary.

Book 4/Unit 6
Whales

At Home: Have students write about a decision they have made recently.

212

CHALLENGE

Name_____ Date_____ Extend **212**

Make Judgments and Decisions

The Makah live in the state of Washington. This Native American group has been trying to bring back their ancient tradition of whale hunting. The United States government has decided to allow Makah people to hunt up to 20 gray whales for only two years, however protesters are afraid that this will pave the way for whale hunting all over the world.

Suppose you were the one who had to decide whether Makah should be allowed to hunt gray whales or not. Use your **judgment**. What **decision** would you make and why? Be sure to explain your thinking. Be convincing! Answers will vary but should include a judgment or decision with supporting arguments.

Book 4/Unit 6
Whales

At Home: Have students tell about difficult decisions they have made recently. Why were the decisions hard to make?

212

LANGUAGE SUPPORT

Name_____ Date_____

What Will We Do?

1. Cut out each picture. 2. Paste each picture to a stick to make a puppet. 3. Make a play to tell about the future of whales.

Grade 4

Language Support/Blackline Master 115 • Whales 231

Reteach, 212   Practice, 212   Extend, 212   Language Support, 231

713H

✓**OBJECTIVES**

Students will use context clues to figure out meanings of marine words.

TEACHING TIP

INSTRUCTIONAL Tell students context clues can help them figure out the meaning of an unknown word. Ask students to use context clues to identify the meaning of the italicized words:

- The giant squid tried to tangle up a baby whale in its long, armlike *tentacles*.
- If we do not stop killing whales, they may become as *extinct* as the dinosaur.

Review Context Clues

PREPARE

Discuss Using Context Clues

Review: A good way to figure out the meanings of science words is to use context clues. Some context clues to look for are synonyms, opposites, definitions, or examples.

TEACH

Read the Passage and Model the Skill

Have students read **Teaching Chart 174** with you.

Whales and the Arctic People

The Natives of the Arctic, the Inuit, or Eskimos, depended on gray whales, which they hunted in the shallow lagoons and bays on the coast. Whales were very useful to the Inuit. The meat from a whale could feed a whole village. "Eskimo Ice Cream" was made by mixing a whale's yellow, buttery, fatty blubber with blueberries and snow. The pointed tusks from toothed whales were carved into jewelry and tools. The tough, waterproof whale skin provided clothing and boot material that protected against salty seawater. When the Inuit hunted, they made sure to never waste a single part of the gray whale.

Teaching Chart 174

Write the following list of words on the board: *Inuit, lagoons, blubber, tusks, waterproof.* Ask volunteers to circle these words in the passage.

MODEL I am not sure what the word *Inuit* means. However, as I read, I find the context clues "natives of the Arctic" and "Eskimos." These clues help me to know that *Inuit* is the name for native people of the Arctic region.

PRACTICE

Identify Context Clues and Word Meanings

GROUP

Have students underline the words and phrases that help them figure out the meanings of the circled words. Discuss each word's meaning.

ASSESS/CLOSE

Create Context Sentences

PARTNERS

Have partners create new sentences using the circled words and then challenge each other to figure out from the context the meanings of the list words.

Students might also reread the selection, writing unfamiliar words and the page numbers on which these words can be found. Partners can then compare lists and help each other use context clues from the selection to determine the meanings of the words on their lists.

ALTERNATE TEACHING STRATEGY

CONTEXT CLUES

For a different approach to teaching this skill, see page T63.

Meeting Individual Needs for Vocabulary

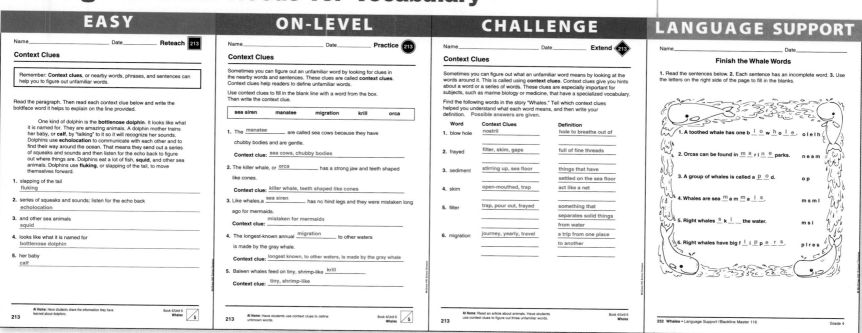

Reteach, 213   Practice, 213   Extend, 213   Language Support, 232

Writing That Compares

GRAMMAR/SPELLING CONNECTIONS

See the 5-Day Grammar and Usage Plan on prepositions, pages 713M–713N.

See the 5-Day Spelling Plan on words with prefixes, pages 7130–713P.

TECHNOLOGY TIP

Demonstrate how to set the line spacing feature in a word-processing program. Discuss that double-spaced copy is easier to read than single-spaced copy and that it makes it easier to mark corrections when they proofread their essays.

TEACHING TIP

INSTRUCTIONAL Remind students that an essay that compares is written in paragraph form and contains a beginning, middle, and end. It is used to tell the similarities and differences between two people, places, or things. Show students examples of writing that compares, such as magazine ads that compare products.

Prewrite

WRITE AN ESSAY Present this assignment: The author of this selection is fascinated by these giant creatures. Write a short essay that compares a whale with another large sea animal, such as a dolphin, a manatee, or a shark. First, describe the whale in as much detail as possible. Then describe the other animal. List at least three things the two animals have in common. Then list at least three differences.

READ AND ORGANIZE Give students an opportunity to research and take notes on the animal that they want to compare with a whale.

Strategy: Create a Venn Diagram Have students complete a Venn diagram that shows at least three ways in which the animal they chose is similar to and different from a whale.

Draft

USE THE VENN DIAGRAM Students may refer to the reading selection *Whales*, as well as the Venn diagram, for the information about whales as they write their essays. Encourage them to discuss the traits of the whale first then those of the other animal.

Revise

SELF-QUESTIONING Ask students to assess their drafts for improvement.

- Did I include three similarities and three differences?
- Does my essay have a beginning, a middle, and an end?
- Did I use appropriate transition words?

PARTNERS Have partners exchange papers to check for differences and similarities.

Edit/Proofread

CHECK FOR ERRORS Have students reread their essays for correct spelling, grammar, mechanics, and punctuation.

Publish

SHARE THE ESSAYS Encourage students to include illustrations of the two animals in their essays.

The Whale and the Manatee

Whales and manatees are two sea mammals that can be seen near the shores of our country. Though similar in some ways, whales and manatees also have many differences.

A whale lives underwater and eats krill, fish, and other sea creatures. Some whales live as far north as the Arctic Ocean. Whales are famous for the long distances they migrate. Because whales have been hunted for years, many species are now endangered.

Unlike the whale, the manatee, likes to keep close to shore. They must live in warm, coastal waters, and only migrate if weather conditions force them to move to warmer water. Manatees eat mostly sea plants that grow in the shallow waters of inlets.

Even though both whales and manatees are sea mammals, they differ in where they live, what they eat, and whether they migrate. Both of these fascinating animals, however, are endangered.

Presentation Ideas

ILLUSTRATE THE ESSAYS Have students make clay models of a whale and the animal to which they compared it.
▶ **Viewing/Representing**

DISCUSS THE ART Have students show their art to the class, and encourage class members to identify the similarities and differences between the two sea creatures in the clay models. ▶ **Speaking/Listening**

Scoring Rubric

Excellent	Good	Fair	Unsatisfactory
4: The writer • has presented a vivid, elaborate, and clear comparison that includes three similarities and three differences. • has followed through with a logical sequence, linked by appropriate transition words.	**3:** The writer • has presented a well-researched comparison with two similarities and two differences. • has followed through with a logical sequence of ideas.	**2:** The writer • includes only one similarity and one difference. • may exhibit organizational difficulty, such as disconnected facts with no comparisons or transitions.	**1:** The writer • has made an unsuccessful attempt at comparing two animals. • has not used comparison terms, or may not have stated a main idea. • has provided little or no information about the topic.

0: The writer leaves the page blank or fails to respond to the writing task. The student does not address the topic or simply paraphrases the prompt. The response is illegible or incoherent.

For a 6-point or an 8-point scale, see pages T105–T106.

Meeting Individual Needs for Writing

EASY

Compare and Contrast Pets Invite students to cut out magazine pictures of two common pets and mount them on a sheet of art paper. Under each picture, have them list the traits of the pet. Then ask them to identify the similar and different traits by writing either the letter *S* for "similar" or *D* for "different" beside each trait.

ON-LEVEL

Classroom Mural Encourage students to form groups that focus on studying different sea creatures. Cover a bulletin board with seawater-colored paper and have each group mount a display of the animal they are depicting. Students should write facts specific to their animals and include a visual aid.

CHALLENGE

Social Studies Research Report Have students research two different careers that are related to sea animals, such as fishing, marine biology, or whale or dolphin training. Have them write a report that compares and contrasts the two careers, include a bibliography, and bind their reports into a booklet for the classroom library.

Ask volunteers to move about the room, choose a position, and announce their location, using a preposition. (Example: *I am near the door.*)

DAILY LANGUAGE ACTIVITIES

Have students orally complete the sentences with prepositions. Answers may vary.

Day 1

1. Whales live _____ the sea.
2. A baby stays _____ its mother.
3. Some migrate _____ Alaska.

Day 2

1. The whale spouted water _____ its blow hole.
2. An orca swam _____ the pool.
3. The dolphin slid _____ the ride at the marine park.

Day 3

1. Gray whales migrate _____ winter.
2. They swim _____ the coast of Alaska.
3. The sky hangs _____ the sea.

Day 4

1. The baby swam _____ its mother.
2. Whales can swim _____ an entire island.
3. Whales stay _____ the water's surface for an hour.

Day 5

1. Whales stir up sediment _____ the ocean floor.
2. Whales feed _____ different ways.
3. Did you like reading _____ whales?

DAY 1 — Introduce the Concept

Oral Warm-Up Hold up a cutout of a whale and a boat. As you move the whale around, ask students where it is. Elicit answers such as *in the boat, under the boat,* or *behind the boat.*

Introduce Prepositions Some prepositions show location.

> ### Prepositions
>
> - A **preposition** comes before a noun or pronoun and relates that noun or pronoun to another word in a sentence.
> - Common prepositions are *about, above, across, after, around, at, behind, down, for, from, in, near, of, on, over, to, under,* and *with.*

Present the Daily Language Activity. Then have students use the following in sentences: *in, to,* and *with.*

 Assign the daily Writing Prompt on page 692C.

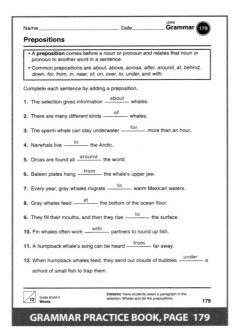

Prepositions

- A **preposition** comes before a noun or pronoun and relates that noun or pronoun to another word in a sentence.
- Common prepositions are *about, above, across, after, around, at, behind, down, for, from, in, near, of, on, over, to, under,* and *with.*

Complete each sentence by adding a preposition.

1. The selection gives information ___about___ whales.
2. There are many different kinds ___of___ whales.
3. The sperm whale can stay underwater ___for___ more than an hour.
4. Narwhals live ___in___ the Arctic.
5. Orcas are found all ___around___ the world.
6. Baleen plates hang ___from___ the whale's upper jaw.
7. Every year, gray whales migrate ___to___ warm Mexican waters.
8. Gray whales feed ___at___ the bottom of the ocean floor.
9. They fill their mouths, and then they rise ___to___ the surface.
10. Fin whales often work ___with___ partners to round up fish.
11. A humpback whale's song can be heard ___from___ far away.
12. When humpback whales feed, they send out clouds of bubbles ___under___ a school of small fish to trap them.

GRAMMAR PRACTICE BOOK, PAGE 179

DAY 2 — Teach the Concept

Review Prepositions Ask students to explain why prepositions are needed in our reading and writing. Have them name some prepositions while you write their suggestions on the board.

Introduce Prepositional Phrases A prepositional phrase is a group of words that often answers the question *where* or *when.* Present the following:

> ### Prepositional Phrases
>
> - A **prepositional phrase** is a group of words that begins with a preposition and ends with a noun or pronoun.

Present the Daily Language Activity. Then state a direction that contains a prepositional phrase. (Examples: Walk to the board. Sit on the floor.) Have volunteers follow the directions. Repeat by giving new directions.

 Assign the daily Writing Prompt on page 692C.

Prepositional Phrases

- A **prepositional phrase** is a group of words that begins with a preposition and ends with a noun or pronoun.

Underline the prepositional phrases in the following sentences.

1. Every year, gray whales travel about ten thousand miles.
2. Blue whales strain krill through their baleen plates.
3. Toothed whales are closely related to dolphins and porpoises.
4. A narwhal has a tooth that sticks through its upper lip.
5. Orcas, or killer whales, perform in marine parks around the country.
6. Orcas eat fish and other sea mammals, but they are gentle in captivity.
7. Orcas are found in all the world's oceans.
8. Right whales used to be common in the North Atlantic Ocean.
9. In the summer, gray whales feed in cold Arctic waters.
10. In the winter, they travel ten thousand miles to warmer waters.
11. The journey of the gray whales is the longest migration of any mammal.
12. The International Whaling Commission was established in 1946.

GRAMMAR PRACTICE BOOK, PAGE 180

Prepositions

DAY 3

Learn from the Literature Review prepositions and prepositional phrases. Read the second sentence in the last paragraph on page 703 of *Whales*:

> **In the winter, they travel about ten thousand miles to Mexican waters.**

Ask students to identify the prepositions and the prepositional phrases. Have them identify which prepositional phrase tells when (in the winter) and which ones tell where. (about ten thousand miles, to Mexican waters)

Use Prepositions Present the Daily Language Activity. Then ask students to write any five prepositional phrases from page 704 of the selection.

 Assign the daily Writing Prompt on page 692D.

DAY 4

Review Prepositions Write a list of prepositions used to complete the Daily Language Activities for Days 1–3 on the board. Challenge students to tell a group story using each of the prepositions. Then present the Daily Language Activity for Day 4.

Mechanics and Usage Before students begin the daily Writing Prompt on page 692D, review letter punctuation.

Letter Punctuation

- Begin the greeting and closing in a letter with a capital letter.
- Use a comma after the greeting and the closing in a letter.
- Use a comma between the names of a city and a state.
- Use a comma between the day and year in a date.

 Assign the daily Writing Prompt on page 692D.

DAY 5

Assess Use the Daily Language Activity and page 183 of the **Grammar Practice Book** for assessment.

Reteach Have students place a small box, such as an empty crayon box, and a rubber eraser on their desks. Using prepositions from the Daily Language Activities and the selection, have students take turns giving instructions on where partners should place the eraser or the box. (Example: Put the eraser *on* the box.)

Have students create a word wall with a list of prepositions.

Use page 184 of the **Grammar Practice Book** for additional reteaching.

 Assign the daily Writing Prompt on page 692D.

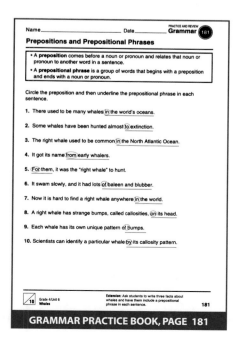

GRAMMAR PRACTICE BOOK, PAGE 181

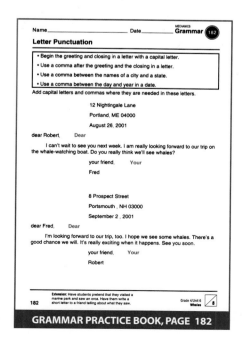

GRAMMAR PRACTICE BOOK, PAGE 182

GRAMMAR PRACTICE BOOK, PAGE 183

5 Day Spelling Plan

LANGUAGE SUPPORT

ESL Write the word *reread* on the chalkboard. Show students how to divide the word into its prefix and base (root). Define the word, with and without the prefix. Then explain that in English, adding a prefix does **not** change the spelling of the base (root) word. Make prefix and base (root) word flashcards for extra practice.

DICTATION SENTENCES

Spelling Words

1. I should redo my work.
2. We are not unkind to animals.
3. When the storms disappear, the sun comes out.
4. When words are too hard, reread them.
5. You might eat nonfat cheese.
6. Many animals are inactive in winter.
7. Would you like to take international trips?
8. I was unlucky when my toy broke.
9. Children often dislike snakes.
10. Did you unpack my books?
11. She rode a nonstop bus to town.
12. Should I refill the baby bottle?
13. I'm uncertain of his first name.
14. My uncle drives his truck on the interstate road.
15. Finish the incomplete experiment.
16. I'll rewind the clock.
17. I'm unsure of the right street.
18. The boys disagree with their sisters.
19. Reheat the cold soup.
20. The bird would talk nonsense.

Challenge Words

21. Can you identify the animals?
22. Cats are mammals.
23. We saw fish at the marine park.
24. We should preserve wildlife.
25. A cat and a tiger are related.

7130 *Whales*

DAY 1 — Pretest

Assess Prior Knowledge Use the Dictation Sentences at the left and **Spelling Practice Book** page 179 for the pretest. Allow students to correct their own papers. Students who require a modified list may be tested on the first ten words.

Spelling Words		Challenge Words
1. redo	11. nonstop	21. **identify**
2. unkind	12. refill	22. **mammals**
3. disappear	13. uncertain	23. **marine**
4. reread	14. interstate	24. **preserve**
5. nonfat	15. incomplete	25. **related**
6. inactive	16. rewind	
7. **international**	17. unsure	
8. unlucky	18. disagree	
9. dislike	19. reheat	
10. unpack	20. nonsense	

*Note: Words in **dark type** are from the story.*

Word Study On page 180 of the **Spelling Practice Book** are word study steps and an at-home activity.

DAY 2 — Explore the Pattern

Sort and Spell Words Say *unkind* and *nonsense*. Have students identify each prefix. Remind students that adding prefixes does **not** require spelling changes to base (root) words. Have them read the Spelling Words aloud and sort them as below.

Words with

re-	un-	inter-
redo	unkind	international
reread	unlucky	interstate
refill	unpack	**non-**
rewind	uncertain	nonfat
reheat	unsure	nonstop
dis-	**in-**	nonsense
disappear	inactive	
dislike	incomplete	
disagree		

Word Wall Have students create a word wall based on the word sort and add more words from their reading.

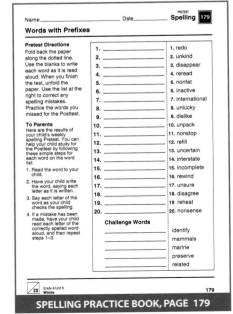

SPELLING PRACTICE BOOK, PAGE 179

WORD STUDY STEPS AND ACTIVITY, PAGE 180

SPELLING PRACTICE BOOK, PAGE 181

Words with Prefixes

Word Meaning: Prefixes Write the following on the chalkboard: *re-* "again"; *un-, dis-, in-* "the opposite of; not"; and *non-* "the opposite of; without". Have students use the meanings of the prefix and the base (root) word to define *nonfat*. (without fat) Repeat with other Spelling Words. Then have students write the meanings.

If students need extra practice, have partners give each other a midweek test.

Glossary Review that a Glossary entry may contain one or more sentences to illustrate word meanings. Have partners:

- write the Challenge Words.

- find the Challenge Words in the Glossary.

- find and copy each example sentence.

- write the meaning of each word as used in its example sentence.

Proofread Sentences Write these sentences on the chalkboard, including the misspelled words. Ask students to proofread, circling incorrect spellings and writing the correct spellings. There are two spelling errors in each sentence.

> My homework is ~~incompleet~~, so I'll ~~redue~~ it. **(incomplete, redo)**
>
> She's ~~unsertan~~ of the answer, so she'll ~~rered~~ the question. **(uncertain, reread)**

Have students create additional sentences with errors for partners to correct.

WRITING Have students use as many Spelling Words as possible in the daily Writing Prompt on page 692D. Remind students to proofread their writing for errors in spelling, grammar, and punctuation.

Assess Students' Knowledge Use page 184 of the **Spelling Practice Book** or the Dictation Sentences on page 713O for the posttest.

JOURNAL **Personal Word List** If students have trouble with any words in the lesson, have them add these to their personal lists in their journals. Have students define each prefix to aid in word meaning.

Students should refer to their word lists during later writing activities.

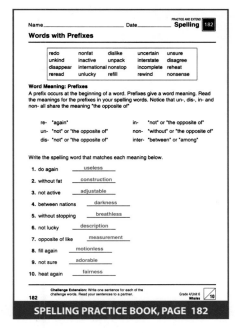

SPELLING PRACTICE BOOK, PAGE 182

SPELLING PRACTICE BOOK, PAGE 183

SPELLING PRACTICE BOOK, PAGE 184

Saving the Everglades

Selection Summary Students will read about efforts to preserve the plants and animals of Florida's Everglades, severely damaged by pollution and decades-long efforts to make the area habitable for humans.

TIME FOR KIDS
SPECIAL REPORT

SAVING THE
EVERGLADES

Cleaning up pollution in Florida's Everglades means a better future for wildlife there, including baby alligators like this one.

**Student
Listening
Library
Audiocassette**

INSTRUCTIONAL
Pages 716–723

Resources for Meeting Individual Needs

LEVELED BOOKS

EASY
Pages 723A, 723D

INDEPENDENT
Pages 723B, 723D

CHALLENGE
Pages 723C, 723D

LEVELED PRACTICE

Reteach, 214–220

blackline masters with reteaching opportunities for each assessed skill

Practice, 214–220

workbook with Take-Home stories and practice opportunities for each assessed skill and story comprehension

Extend, 214–220

blackline masters that offer challenge activities for each assessed skill

ADDITIONAL RESOURCES

- **Language Support Book,** 233–240
- **Take-Home, Practice,** p. 215a
- **Alternative Teaching Strategies,** T60–T66

McGraw-Hill School
TECHNOLOGY

interNET CONNECTION Research and Inquiry Ideas. Visit **www.mhschool.com/tfk**

READING AND LANGUAGE ARTS

 DAY 1 *Focus on Reading and Skills*

 DAY 2 *Read the Literature*

- ● **Comprehension**

- ● **Vocabulary**

- ● **Phonics/Decoding**

- ● **Study Skills**

- ● **Listening, Speaking, Viewing, Representing**

DAY 1

 Read Aloud and Motivate, 714E
Birdfoot's Grampa

Develop Visual Literacy, 714/715

☑ **Review Cause and Effect,** 716A–716B
Teaching Chart 175
Reteach, Practice, Extend, 214

DAY 2

Build Background, 716C
Develop Oral Language

Vocabulary, 716D

| compares | instance | soggy |
| importance | lurk | wildlife |

Teaching Chart 176
Vocabulary Cards
Reteach, Practice, Extend, 215

 Read the Selection, 716–719
☑ Cause and Effect
☑ Make Judgments and Decisions

- ● **Curriculum Connections**

Link Works of Art, 714/715

Link Science, 716C

- ● **Writing**

 Writing Prompt: Write a first-person account from an alligator's point of view explaining why it needs to have its home in the Everglades protected.

 Writing Prompt: Write a postcard to a friend describing your trip to the Everglades. What did you see and do?

 Journal Writing, 719
Quick-Write

- ● **Grammar**

Introduce the Concept: Sentence Combining, 723M
Daily Language Activity
1. Felix walked home. He walked quickly. Felix walked home quickly.
2. The frog has spots. The spots are black. The frog has black spots.
3. I have a bicycle. My bicycle is red. I have a red bicycle.

Grammar Practice Book, 185

Teach the Concept: Sentence Combining, 723M
Daily Language Activity
1. Chemicals are dangerous. They are dangerous to plants and people. Chemicals are dangerous to plants and people.
2. The crocodile has teeth. Its teeth are sharp. The crocodile has sharp teeth.

Grammar Practice Book, 186

- ● **Spelling**

Pretest: Words from Math, 723O
Spelling Practice Book, 185, 186

Explore the Pattern: Words from Math, 723O
Spelling Practice Book, 187

Meeting Individual Needs

 ✓ = **Skill Assessed in Unit Test**

DAY 3 — Read the Literature

Rereading for Fluency, 718

Story Questions, 720
Reteach, Practice, Extend, 216

Story Activities, 721

Study Skill, 722
 Library/Media Center
Teaching Chart 177
Reteach, Practice, Extend, 217

Test Power, 723

 Read the Leveled Books, 723A–723D
Guided Reading
✓ Cause and Effect
✓ Instructional Vocabulary

 Activity Music, 721

 Writing Prompt: Write a short paragraph describing three things that you can do every day to help control pollution.

Writing Process: Write an Encyclopedia Article, 723K
Prewrite, Draft

Review and Practice: Sentence Combining, 723N
Daily Language Activity
1. The ibis flew. It flew past the clouds.
   The ibis flew past the clouds.
2. The Everglades are full of water.
   The water is fresh. The Everglades is full of fresh water.

Grammar Practice Book, 187

Practice and Extend: Words from Math, 723P
Spelling Practice Book, 188

DAY 4 — Build and Review Skills

 **Read the Leveled Books and Self-Selected Books**

✓ **Review Compare and Contrast,** 723E–723F
Teaching Chart 178
Reteach, Practice, Extend, 218
Language Support, 238

Vocabulary Strategy
✓ **Review Context Clues,** 723G–723H
Teaching Chart 179
Reteach, Practice, Extend, 219
Language Support, 239

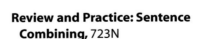 **Writing Prompt:** Write a discussion between you and a friend about a plan to build canals to stop flooding.

Writing Process: Write an Encyclopedia Article, 723K
Revise
Meeting Individual Needs for Writing, 723L

Review and Practice: Sentence Combining, 723N
Daily Language Activity
1. Builders drained the swamp. They drained it for hours. Builders drained the swamp for hours.
2. The owl hooted. It hooted loudly. The owl hooted loudly.

Grammar Practice Book, 188

Proofread and Write: Words from Math, 723P
Spelling Practice Book, 189

DAY 5 — Build and Review Skills

 Read Self-Selected Books

✓ **Review Antonyms and Synonyms,** 723I–723J
Teaching Chart 180
Reteach, Practice, Extend, 220
Language Support, 240

Listening, Speaking, Viewing, Representing, 723L
Display Drawings
Give a Talk

 Writing Prompt: Write a letter from a farmer to an environmentalist defending her or his use of pesticides.

Writing Process: Write an Encyclopedia Article, 723K
Edit/Proofread, Publish

Assess and Reteach: Sentence Combining, 723N
Daily Language Activity
1. The city was built. It was built where alligators used to roam. The city was built where alligators used to roam.
2. Sugar cane is a crop of the Everglades. It is an important crop. Sugar cane is an important crop of the Everglades.

Grammar Practice Book, 189, 190

Assess and Reteach: Words from Math, 723P
Spelling Practice Book, 190

Read Aloud and Motivate

Birdfoot's Grampa

a poem by Joseph Bruchac

The old man
must have stopped our car
two dozen times to climb out
and gather into his hands
the small toads blinded
by our lights and leaping,
live drops of rain.

The rain was falling,
a mist about his white hair
and I kept saying

you can't save them all,
accept it, get back in
we've got places to go.

But, leathery hands full
of wet brown life,
knee deep in the summer
roadside grass,
he just smiled and said
*they have places to go to
too.*

Oral Comprehension

LISTENING AND SPEAKING Motivate students to think about comparing and contrasting characters' speech and actions by reading them this poem. Before you read, encourage them to visualize the mental pictures, or images, that the words create. When you have finished reading, point out that the poem sounds almost like everyday language. Ask students, "What are some phrases that tell you that this is a poem and not everyday speech? How do these phrases help you know more about the 'old man' as he tries to save toads from being run over?" Ask students to listen for poetic language as you reread the poem.

Activity Encourage students to write a poem in this style. First let them brainstorm a list of events from their lives that they would like to write as a poem. Then encourage them to write about one of these events using a conversational voice. Finally, help them decide how to shape their writing into lines and stanzas. Let volunteers read their poems to the class.

▶ **Intrapersonal/Auditory**

Develop Visual Literacy

Anthology pages 714–715

Stories in Art

Like scientists, artists observe and study nature. They may even use the natural world to get their message across.

Look at the painting. What causes your eye to move around the picture? What effect does this have? How does it help you take in the whole scene?

Study the painting. How does the artist balance the picture? Does the wildlife seem to fit right into the landscape? What does this say about harmony in nature? What would happen if this balance were disturbed? Could saving the environment be the artist's message? Why or why not?

Caribbean Jungle
by Hilary Simon
Private Collection

714

715

Objective: Identify Cause and Effect

VIEWING   In her vibrant painting, Hilary Simon uses bright colors to suggest the lushness of the Caribbean jungle. How do these colors suggest harmony in the scene? Discuss with students how the jungle's canopy causes their eye to move around the pasture. Afterward, ask students why they think the artist placed animals in pairs.

Read the page with students, encouraging individual interpretations of the painting. Ask students to support cause-and-effect statements based on what they observe. For example:

- The border-like areas of blue at the top cause the eye to move around the painting.

- The strong central placement of the water within borders gives the scene a complete effect, as if it were a framed picture.

REPRESENTING   Ask students to use paints or pastels to show what the scene in the painting would look like if loggers or developers moved in and took over. Have them consider the effect on the scene and on the balance of nature.

OBJECTIVES

Students will identify cause-and-effect relationships.

TEACHING TIP

INSTRUCTIONAL

Point out to students that clue words often indicate cause and effect links. For example, the word *because* is often found before a "cause phrase." The word *so* is often found before an "effect phrase."

Review Cause and Effect

PREPARE

Discuss Cause and Effect

Have a volunteer tell about a time he or she broke something. Ask: *What happened? Why did it happen?* Write *cause* and *effect* on the chalkboard, and write students' answers to the questions under the appropriate headings.

TEACH

Review the Passage and Model the Skill

Point out that when reading, it is important to identify and understand cause-and-effect relationships—to find out what happened and why it happened.

Our Changing Earth

The search for new places for homes and work often hurts Earth. For instance, rain forests are being cut down to make room for farms and cattle ranches. When forests go, animals lose their homes, rare plants disappear, and our air is affected. Likewise, factories provide jobs but also pollute our air. This pollution thins the layer of gas that protects Earth from harmful sun rays.

As we continue to change Earth, many plants and animals are in danger of dying out. If this continues, humans may one day be in danger also.

Teaching Chart 175

Read the Passage and Model the Skill

Display **Teaching Chart 175.** Ask students to think about the questions *What happened?* and *Why did it happen?* as they read.

MODEL As I read the first paragraph, I ask myself, "What happened and why?" The answer is *Earth has been hurt because people are trying to make places for new homes and work.*

Identify Cause

Ask students, "Why have rain forest animals lost their homes?" Then ask a volunteer to circle the cause.

Identify and Chart Causes and Effects

GROUP

Have student groups use the information in the passage to make a Cause and Effect chart like the one shown. Ask them to record causes on the left side of the chart, then add "so" at the end. Have students record effects on the right side to make complete cause-and-effect statements. ▶ **Linguistic/Visual**

CAUSE	EFFECT
The rain forests are being cut down, so	animals are losing their homes, rare plants are dying off, and the air we breathe is affected.
Our air is becoming polluted, so	the layer of gas that protects Earth is thinning, which can let in harmful sun rays.
Many animals are dying off, so	other plants and animals either overmultiply or die off.

ASSESS/CLOSE

Make Cause-and-Effect Statements

Ask each student to make a cause-and-effect statement about an environmental issue. Have small groups discuss the statements.

SELECTION Connection

Students will apply cause and effect when they read *Saving the Everglades* and the Leveled Books.

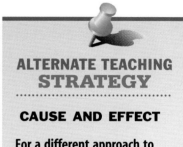

ALTERNATE TEACHING STRATEGY

CAUSE AND EFFECT

For a different approach to teaching this skill, see page T60.

Meeting Individual Needs for Comprehension

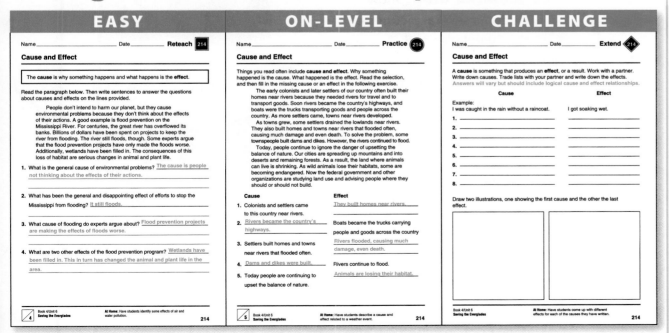

Reteach, 214   Practice, 214   Extend, 214

Build Background

Science

Evaluate Prior Knowledge

CONCEPT: CONSERVATION Many people think it is important for humans to preserve and protect Earth and its living creatures.

RECORD INFORMATION Have students complete a K-W-L chart to record what they know and want to know about conserving the Florida Everglades. Ask students to leave the L column blank and complete it after they read the selection. ▶ **Logical/Visual**

K	W	L
The Everglades has alligators.	Why does the Florida Everglades need to be saved?	
The Everglades is swampy.	How can the Everglades be saved?	

Graphic Organizer 27

EVERGLADES AIRBOAT RIDE Show
  students several pictures of
GROUP   WRITING   the Everglades and, if possible, of the airboats that take people on tours there. Ask student groups to write a description of what they might see on an airboat ride, and explain why it might be important to preserve the things they see.

Develop Oral Language

DISCUSS CONSERVATION Display
ESL posters and magazines showing pictures of endangered plants and animals that students can recognize. Write the words *conservation, endangered,* and *habitat* on the chalkboard. Discuss what the words mean. Add words such as *recycle, garbage,* and *compost*. Let students add words to the list. Help students form sentences using the new vocabulary.

Ask student groups to brainstorm ways that they can have a positive effect on the environment. Have groups share their ideas with the class.

TEACHING TIP

MANAGEMENT Have student groups add to the K-W-L charts as they work on their descriptive and persuasive "airboat" paragraphs.

While groups work on their "airboat" paragraphs, present visual aids that help students who need help with oral language skills discern the different usages of the word *conservation*.

LANGUAGE SUPPORT

See **Language Support Book,** pages 233–236, for teaching suggestions for Build Background and Vocabulary.

Vocabulary

Key Words

1. Some animals make their (soggy) homes in the watery Everglades. 2. What dangers (lurk) in the damp Everglades? 3. Many people might think the dangers are the (wildlife,) such as alligators, crocodiles, snakes, and the Florida panther. 4. But in this (instance,) the case of people versus the Everglades, scientists believe people are the real danger. 5. Scientists want people to understand the (importance) and meaning of preserving the Everglades. 6. No other place in the world (compares) to it.

Teaching Chart 176

Definitions

soggy (p. 717) very wet or damp

lurk (p. 717) lie hidden, especially to attack

wildlife (p. 717) wild animals that live naturally in an area

instance (p. 719) an example; case

importance (p. 718) having great value or meaning

compares (p. 718) to say or think something is like something else

SPELLING/VOCABULARY CONNECTIONS

See Spelling Challenge Words, pages 7230–723P.

Vocabulary in Context

IDENTIFY VOCABULARY WORDS Display **Teaching Chart 176** and read it with students. Have volunteers circle each vocabulary word and underline words that are clues to its meaning.

DISCUSS MEANINGS Ask questions like these to help students understand each word:

• How do you feel about eating soggy cereal?

• Do robbers lurk?

• What wildlife can you find in the desert?

• In what instance might you go to the doctor?

• Which is of more importance to you, playing sports or watching them?

• How do you think an apple compares with a banana in flavor?

Practice

SORT THE CARDS Have students sort the vocabulary cards into two or three categories such as: silent *e*/no silent *e*; nouns/verbs/adjectives; more than two syllables/two syllables or less; and so on.

▶ **Auditory/Linguistic**

Vocabulary Cards

WRITE VOCABULARY WORDS Ask students to use vocabulary words in the "speech bubbles" of a four- to six-frame comic strip they create. Have students refer to the Glossary as needed.

▶ **Linguistic/Oral**

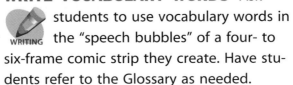

Take-Home Story 215a
Reteach 215
Practice 215 • **Extend 215**

Guided Instruction

Preview and Predict

Have students read the title and preview the article, looking at the photographs, section headings, and captions for clues about causes and effects in the article.

- What clues about problems do the photographs and section headings give?

- What might be some causes, or reasons, for the problems suggested by the photos and title?

- What do you think this article might be about? Why do you think so?

- How can you tell this is a nonfiction selection? (It contains factual information, discusses a real-life environmental problem, and includes photos of real places.) *Genre*

Have students record their predictions about the article and the cause-and-effect relationships it will discuss.

Set Purposes

What do students think they will learn from this article? For example:

- What might be wrong in the Everglades?

- Why does the Everglades need to be saved?

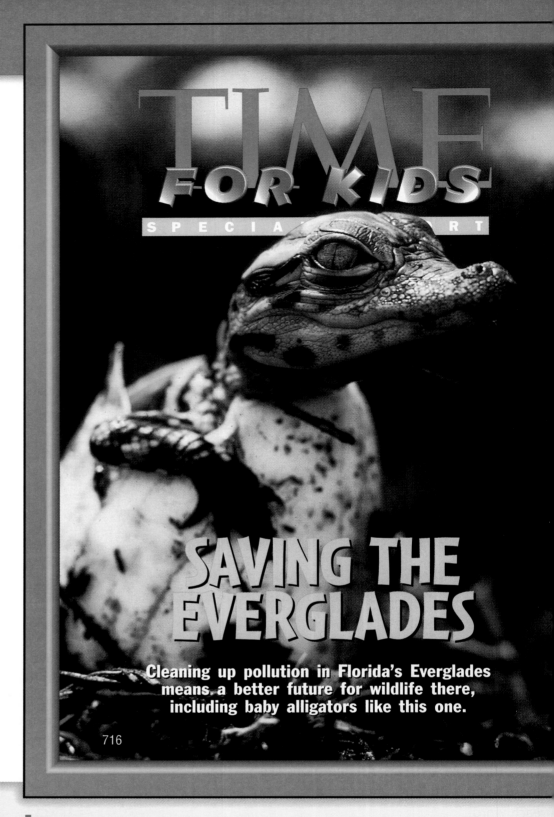

TIME FOR KIDS
SPECIAL REPORT

SAVING THE EVERGLADES

Cleaning up pollution in Florida's Everglades means a better future for wildlife there, including baby alligators like this one.

716

Meeting Individual Needs • Grouping Suggestions for Strategic Reading

EASY	ON-LEVEL	CHALLENGE
Read Together Read the article with students, or have them read along with the **Listening Library Audiocassette.** Have students use the Cause and Effect chart to record problems in the Everglades and their causes. Guided Instruction prompts offer additional help with vocabulary and comprehension.	**Guided Reading** Introduce the story word listed on page 717. Have students read the article together first, or, if you choose, have them read the article independently. Use the Guided Instruction questions to aid in comprehension. Have students use the Cause and Effect chart to record notes as they read.	**Read Independently** Have students read the article independently. Remind them that identifying cause-and-effect relationships will help them understand how events in the article are linked. Have students create a Cause and Effect chart as shown on page 718B.

Looking Out for 'Gators

Many of Florida's animals are being protected as the Everglades gets help from humans

Everglades National Park in Florida doesn't look like much from an airplane. A flat, soggy field of tall grass stretches toward the horizon. A few trees dot the landscape under the Florida sun.

But a closer look shows a busy natural world. Hundreds of kinds of animals live in the Everglades. Birds such as egrets and white ibis fly above the water. Lime-green tree frogs croak. Alligators lurk below the swamp's surface.

It's all very beautiful. But the Everglades is in serious trouble. After years of bad planning, the Everglades is dying. Dozens of its many kinds of animals are threatened. Some of its plants and flowers are disappearing. But help for the Everglades and its animals is under way. Humans are rescuing the Everglades and its wildlife from death by pollution.

GEORGIA
Atlantic Ocean
FLORIDA
Gulf of Mexico
Lake Okeechobee
EVERGLADES
Everglades National Park

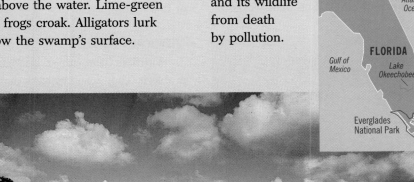

The swamplike Everglades has been called a "river of grass."

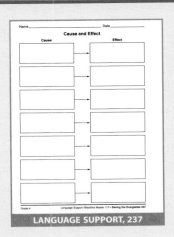

LANGUAGE SUPPORT

A blackline master of the Cause and Effect chart is available in the **Language Support Book.**

Name_____ Date_____
Cause and Effect
Cause | Effect

Grade 4   Language Support/Blackline Master 117 • Saving the Everglades 237

LANGUAGE SUPPORT, 237

Guided Instruction

☑ **Cause and Effect**

☑ **Judgments and Decisions**

Strategic Reading As we read, let's make a Cause and Effect chart to help us trace what is happening in the article and why.

1 **CAUSE AND EFFECT** What is happening in the Everglades? Why is it happening? (The Everglades is dying because of years of bad planning and pollution.)

2 **JUDGMENTS AND DECISIONS** Based on what you've read so far, do you think humans have taken good care of the Everglades? Explain. (Sample answer: No, because they have caused many of the Everglades' problems.)

Story Words

The word below may be unfamiliar. Have students check its meaning and pronunciation in the Glossary beginning on page 726.

• swamps, p. 717

717

Guided Instruction

3 **JUDGMENTS AND DECISIONS** Do you think the engineers should have straightened Florida rivers, even though this caused problems for the Everglades? (Sample answer: Yes, because they solved many problems for farms and cities.)

4 **CAUSE AND EFFECT** Use the Cause and Effect chart. Under which heading should we place the problems in the Everglades? (effects) What causes are behind these problems? Under which heading should we place people's attempts to solve the problems of the Everglades? (causes) What solutions have been found?

CAUSE	EFFECT
Engineers straightened rivers, so	fresh water and animals disappeared.
Farmers used dangerous fertilizers, so	cattails grew and pushed out plants that animals eat.
Farmers learned of fertilizer dangers, so	native plants can grow again.
Engineers are straightening out rivers, so	the Everglades can have the water it needs.

ORGANIZE INFORMATION Ask volunteers to tell what they have learned about the Everglades. Challenge them to restate the article's main idea. Then have volunteers add to the K-W-L charts they created in Build Background and complete the L column. *Summarize*

PEOPLE CAUSED THE PROBLEM

3 When large numbers of people first moved to Florida more than a century ago, the Everglades was thought to be nothing but swampland. No one paid much attention to the beauty of the area or **4** its importance to the wildlife living there. Builders tried to drain the swamp. Farms and cities sprang up where alligators used to run freely.

In the 1920s, engineers straightened rivers. They built thousands of miles of canals and dikes. They hoped to stop flooding and keep water supplies stable for farms and cities. The plan worked.

RIGHT: TONY ARRUZA/CORBIS; FAR RIGHT: KEVIN FLEMING/CORBIS
Canals keep flooding under control.

718

But the changes also harmed the Everglades. The area shrank in size by half. Much of the fresh water disappeared. And the numbers of birds, alligators, and other animals shrank, too.

"Everything depends on the water," says Sandy Dayhoff, who works for Everglades National Park. "Not only having enough water, but the right amount at the right time." Dayhoff compares the Everglades to a giant bathtub. In the rainy season, the tub is full. In the dry season, it slowly drains. But humans are getting in the way of both parts of this natural cycle.

CHEMICALS POLLUTE
Farmers have caused another problem. They use fertilizers that help crops grow. But the fertilizers contain chemicals that have changed the balance of park plants. Cattails,

Sugar cane is an important Everglades crop.

REREADING FOR *Fluency*

PARTNERS Have pairs alternate reading paragraphs aloud. Encourage students to read with expression and feeling.

READING RATE You may want to evaluate a student's reading rate. Have the student read aloud from *Saving the Everglades* for one minute; ask the student to place a self-stick note after the last word read. Then

count the number of words he or she has read.

Alternatively, you could assess small groups or the whole class together by having students count words and record their own scores.

Use the Reading Rate form in the **Diagnostic/Placement Evaluations** booklet to evaluate students' performance.

Alligator or Crocodile?

American alligators and crocodiles are close cousins. They are both related to 50-foot reptiles that lived millions of years ago. And they look very much alike.

But there are some differences. The easiest way to tell whether the reptile you are looking at is a crocodile or an alligator is to look at the face. The alligator has a broader snout. The crocodile's is pointier. And when a crocodile's mouth is closed, you can see a long tooth sticking out. You can't see that tooth in an alligator when its mouth is closed.

The American crocodile, but not the alligator, is on the endangered list. The Everglades is the only place in the U.S. where alligators and crocodiles live together.

American crocodile

American alligator

for instance, absorb the chemicals easily. So they are growing like mad. And they are pushing out some native plants, which provide food for the Everglades' animals.

Now everyone is aware of the importance of the Everglades. Farmers are aware of the dangers of the chemicals they are using. And engineers are putting rivers back on their old winding courses. It's a huge project that won't be finished until 2003 or later. In all, billions of dollars will be spent to help the Everglades.

For most people, that is money well spent. "There's no other place like this on Earth," says Dayhoff.

Based on an article in *TIME FOR KIDS*.

FIND OUT MORE
Visit our website:
www.mhschool.com/tfk

interNET
CONNECTION

Guided Instruction

Return to Predictions and Purposes

Review with students their predictions about the article. Were their predictions correct? Did they find out what they wanted to know?

INFORMAL ASSESSMENT

CAUSE AND EFFECT

HOW TO ASSESS

- Have students make a "cause statement" and an "effect statement" about Everglades problems.

- Have students make a "cause statement" and an "effect statement" about efforts to solve Everglades problems.

Students should recognize human changes to the land and water as causes and lack of water and dying wildlife as effects. Responsible farming and land use are causes, and Everglades recovery is an effect.

FOLLOW UP If students have trouble determining cause and effect, say a "cause phrase" such as *Engineers straightened rivers in the Everglades to make way for farms and cities, so . . .* and have students complete the sentence.

LITERARY RESPONSE

JOURNAL

QUICK-WRITE Invite students to record their thoughts about the selection. This question may help them get started:

- What did you learn about the effect of human actions on nature?

ORAL RESPONSE Have students share their journal responses with a group. Have groups discuss which Everglades problems they found most complicated.

interNET **CONNECTION** Have students go to *www.mhschool.com/tfk* for more information about the Everglades. Then have groups research to learn about an animal or plant that is native to the Everglades.

Story Questions

Have students discuss or write answers to the questions on page 720.

Answers:

1. The Everglades is in Florida. *Literal/Setting*

2. draining swamps; building roads, canals, dikes; straightening of rivers; fertilizer pollution *Inferential/Cause and Effect*

3. The Everglades will be destroyed. *Inferential/Make Predictions*

4. The Everglades is in serious trouble. People are working to rescue it. *Critical/Summarize*

5. Both articles discussed human impact on the environment. "Whales" focused on a species, while "Saving the Everglades" focused on habitat. *Critical/Reading Across Texts*

Write an Encyclopedia Article For a full writing process lesson related to this suggestion, see pages 723K–723L.

Story Questions & Activities

1. Where is the Everglades?

2. What is causing the Everglades to "die"?

3. What might happen to the Everglades if steps aren't taken to fix its problems?

4. How would you sum up this article in two sentences?

5. Compare this article with "Whales." How are the articles alike? What are the differences?

Write an Encyclopedia Article

Crocodiles and alligators are cousins. Yet like cousins, they are a little bit different. Write an encyclopedia article about alligators. Compare them with crocodiles. Show at least two ways they are alike. Then show their differences. Include a drawing that highlights their size, shape, scales, mouth, and teeth.

Meeting Individual Needs

EASY	ON-LEVEL	CHALLENGE

Reteach, 216

Practice, 216

Extend, 216

Create a Mural

The Everglades is home to "a busy natural world." Make a mural of some of the Everglades' most interesting animals. Find pictures of the animals in magazines or on the Internet. Paste them on a long sheet of paper. Then label each animal under its picture to create a mural of the Everglades.

Write a Song

Write a song about the Everglades. Include lines about what happened to the area and what can be done to save it. Set your words to a tune you know.

Find Out More

The article says that the American crocodile is on the endangered list. What does this mean? Start by doing some research. Find out which other animals in your part of the country are threatened or in danger of disappearing. Share what you learn in a news broadcast to your class.

721

Story Activities

Create a Mural

Materials: long sheets of paper, pictures from magazines or the Internet, glue, crayons or markers, scissors

GROUP Have each group map out its mural in pencil before gluing or coloring. Then have students add drawings of plants, water, animal homes, and sky to their murals for decoration.

Write a Song

Materials: writing paper

PARTNERS Have pairs of students write songs and perform them for the class. If possible, tape-record or videotape the performances.

Find Out More

GROUP **RESEARCH AND INQUIRY** Have students brainstorm questions they would like answered about endangered animals in their part of the country. Students can use nature videos and magazines, local conservation groups, encyclopedias, or the Internet as resources.

 **inter**NET **CONNECTION** For more information on endangered species, students can visit *www.mhschool.com/reading*

FORMAL ASSESSMENT

After page 721, see the Selection Assessment.

721

Study Skills

LIBRARY/MEDIA CENTER

OBJECTIVES Students will:

• understand elements of the Internet.

PREPARE Preview the computer screens, and point out elements such as the menus and icons. Display **Teaching Chart 177.**

TEACH Review the goal of Internet research: to find information quickly and easily.

PRACTICE Have students answer questions 1–5. Review the answers with them. **1.** the Everglades home page **2.** the Everglades Ecosystem entry on the Everglades home page. **3.** the History entry on the Everglades Ecosystem page. **4.** Click on the Endangered Animals entry on the Everglades Ecosystem page. **5.** The Internet provides fast access to information. Some Web pages are linked, making it easy to explore your topic.

ASSESS/CLOSE Ask students what they would click on for a menu about activities in the park today. (Current Events)

Study Skills

Use the Internet

When you want more information about a topic, you can search for it on the **Internet**. There is a **home page** on the Internet for the Everglades and other national parks. The home page will direct you to different topics that you can read by moving your pointer to the topic and clicking. Each topic will lead you to other topics until you find the one you want.

Use the screens above to answer these questions.

1 Which screen gives you the most general information about the park?

2 What would you click on to learn about the Everglades ecosystem?

3 If you wanted to know more about Native Americans in the Everglades, where would you look?

4 How would you find out more about the park's endangered animals?

5 Why would you use the Internet to learn about a topic?

Meeting Individual Needs

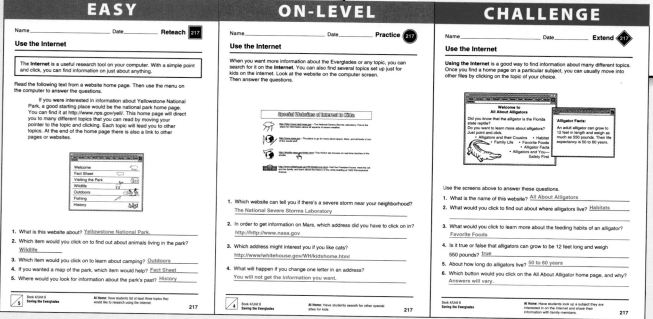

EASY	ON-LEVEL	CHALLENGE
Reteach, 217	Practice, 217	Extend, 217

TEST POWER

DIRECTIONS

Read the sample story. Then read each question about the story.

SAMPLE

How to Make a Lion Mask

What you need: paper plate, scissors, glue, crayons, yarn, and 4 pipe cleaners

Step 1: Place the plate over your face and ask a grown-up to mark where your eyes are under the plate. Take the plate away from your face and cut holes for your eyes.

Step 2: Use crayons to draw the nose, mouth, and eyebrows.

Step 3: Glue the pipe cleaners to the mask for the lion's whiskers.

Step 4: To make the lion's mane, glue yarn around the lion's face.

Step 5: Fasten a piece of yarn to each side of the plate so that you can tie the two pieces together to wear the mask.

1 According to this passage, which of these objects is NOT used in making the lion mask?

● Colored paper
○ Glue
○ Paper plate
○ Pipe cleaners

2 According to the steps, which of the following should be done first?

○ Punch holes in the mask
○ Glue on the whiskers
● Cut holes for the eyes
○ Color the mask

723

Test THE PRINCETON REVIEW
Power

Read the Page

Have students read **all** of the information in the directions

Discuss the Questions

Question 1: This question requires students to locate in the form of directions. Because the question asks which item is **not** used in making the mask, make sure students read each answer choice and eliminate items that **are** used.

Question 2: This question requires students to follow directions. Direct students back to the directions. As a group, read each answer choice. As you discuss each answer choice, remind students that they are **not necessarily** looking for what is done in the first step, but rather which of the answer choices is done first. Have students eliminate answers that come later in the instructions.

For The Princeton Review test preparation practice for **TerraNova**, **ITBS**, and **SAT-9**, visit the McGraw-Hill School Division website. See also McGraw-Hill's *Standardized Test Preparation Book*.

EASY

✓ **Phonics**

- silent letters *k, b, l, gh, w*
- /s/ and /f/

✓ **Comprehension**

- cause and effect
- problem and solution
- judgments and decisions
- compare and contrast

Answers to Story Questions

Answers will vary and should include examples and details from the stories students have read.

EASY

Story Questions for Selected Reading

1. When do the events in this story take place?

2. Why do you think the author wrote the book?

3. What is your favorite part of the story?

4. What is this story mainly about?

5. Have you read other books that described similar problems? Explain.

Draw a Picture

Draw a picture of the most interesting part of the book.

Self-Selected Reading
Leveled Books

EASY

UNIT SKILLS REVIEW

Phonics

✓ **Comprehension**

Help students self-select an Easy Book to read and apply phonics and comprehension skills.

Guided Reading

PREVIEW AND PREDICT Discuss the book's title, illustrations, and table of contents, if present. Have students look at the illustrations in the beginning of the story. Then ask them to predict what the book is about. Chart their suggestions.

SET PURPOSES Have students write in their journals why they want to read the book. Ask them to share their purposes.

READ THE BOOK Use questions like the following to guide students' reading or as discussion points after they have read the story independently.

- What was the cause of the problem described in the story? *Cause and Effect*

- How was the main character in this story different from other main characters you have read about? *Compare and Contrast*

- Do you think the problem in the story was handled well? Explain. *Judgments and Decisions*

- Can you think of a better solution? Explain why your solution is better than the story's solution. *Problem and Solution*

- Look back through the story. Can you find words with /s/ spelled *ss, s, c,* or *ce*? *Phonics and Decoding*

RETURN TO PREDICTIONS AND PURPOSES Discuss students' predictions. Were they accurate? Why or why not? Have students review their purposes for reading. Did they find out what they wanted to know?

LITERARY RESPONSE Have students discuss questions like the following:

- Were there parts of the story that made you laugh or feel angry or sad? Explain.

- Would you like to be friends with any of the characters in or the narrator of the story? Why?

- What would be another good title for this story? Why?

Self-Selected Reading
Leveled Books

INDEPENDENT

UNIT SKILLS REVIEW

 Comprehension

Help students self-select an Independent Book to read and apply comprehension skills.

Guided Reading

PREVIEW AND PREDICT Have students read the table of contents, if present, and look at the illustrations in the beginning of the book. Then have them predict what the story will be about. Ask them to record their predictions in their journals.

SET PURPOSES Have students write a few questions they hope will be answered as they read the book. Encourage them to write their questions in their journals. Ask them to share their purposes.

READ THE BOOK Use questions like the following to guide students' reading or as discussion points after they have read the book independently.

- Think about one event that directly caused another event in the story. What was the event? What was the outcome? *Cause and Effect*

- How was the problem in this story solved? *Problem and Solution*

- Do you think that the solution to the problem was the best one possible? Explain. *Judgments and Decisions*

- Compare and contrast two events in the book. How were they alike? How were they different? *Compare and Contrast*

RETURN TO PREDICTIONS AND PURPOSES Have students review and discuss their predictions. Were they accurate? What helped them the most in making their predictions? Ask students whether their purposes were met. Help them resolve any unanswered questions.

LITERARY RESPONSE The following questions will help focus students' responses:

- Would you like to invite the author to speak to your class? What questions would you ask?

- What was your favorite part of the book?

- Would you like to read other books like this one? Why?

Comprehension

- cause and effect
- problem and solution
- judgments and decisions
- compare and contrast

Answers to Story Questions

Answers will vary and should include examples and details from the stories students have read.

INDEPENDENT

Story Questions for Selected Reading

1. Where does this story take place?

2. Would you like to participate in the events in the book? Why?

3. Did you feel that the problem in the book was solved by the end of the book? Explain.

4. What was this story mainly about?

5. Did the book make you want to read other books on the same topic or by the same author? Why?

Write a Summary

Write a summary for the book you just read.

PUPIL SELECTION

CHALLENGE

☑ **Comprehension**

- cause and effect
- problem and solution
- judgments and decisions
- compare and contrast

Answers to Story Questions

Answers will vary and should include examples and details from the stories students have read.

Story Questions for Selected Reading

1. How would you describe the main character in this story?

2. Who was the most admirable character in the story? Explain.

3. Which event in the story surprised you the most? Why?

4. What was this story mainly about?

5. Did the story remind you of another story or film you have read or seen? Explain how.

Write a Review

Write a review of the book you just read. Would you advise others to read it?

Self-Selected Reading
Leveled Books

CHALLENGE

UNIT SKILLS REVIEW

☑ **Comprehension**

Help students self-select a Challenge Book to read and apply comprehension skills.

Guided Reading

PREVIEW AND PREDICT Discuss the book cover and the illustrations in the beginning of the book. Have students predict what the book will be about. Ask them to write their predictions in their journals.

SET PURPOSES Have students write a few sentences in their journals about why they want to read the book. Invite them to share their purposes.

READ THE BOOK Use questions like the following to guide students' reading or to motivate discussion after they have read the book independently.

- Compare and contrast two characters in the story. How are they alike? How are they different? *Compare and Contrast*

- How did the actions of characters affect the outcome of the story? *Cause and Effect*

- Would you like to be friends with the main character in the story? Why or why not? *Judgments and Decisions*

- How did the characters solve their problem? *Problem and Solution*

RETURN TO PREDICTIONS AND PURPOSES Discuss students' predictions. Ask which were closest to the book's contents and why. Have students review their purposes for reading. Did they find out what they wanted to know?

LITERARY RESPONSE Have students discuss questions like the following:

- Which character in the book would you most like to have a conversation with? Why?

- What would be another good title for the book?

- If you were to write this story how might it be different?

Activities
Anthology and Leveled Books

Connecting Texts

CLASS DISCUSSION Have students discuss connections between the stories. For example, write these story titles horizontally across the top of a chart: *The Morningstar Sun, Super-Dupers, Spring Break and Peaches, Wolverine and White Elephants.* Write a goal and some steps taken to achieve the goal for each story. Discuss with students the goals of the characters in each story and the steps they take to accomplish the goals. Write students' suggestions on the chart.

Goals and Steps

The Morningstar Sun	Spring Break and Peaches	Super-Dupers	Wolverine and White Elephants
• raise money to start a newspaper • get advice about raising money • sell ads	• find parrot's home • distribute posters • capture bird • take bird to aviary	• win a fund-raiser • give out sample cookies • organize baking teams • sell cookies individually	• get Wolverine from shelter • organize a flea market • raise money so shelter can stay open

Viewing/Representing

DRAMATIZE A SCENE Have students who have read the same book organize into groups. Have each group agree on a favorite scene from the book to dramatize. Have the groups practice their dramatizations and present them to the class.

AUDIENCE RESPONSE After each dramatization, encourage students in the audience to ask questions about the scene and the book.

Research and Inquiry

CHOOSE A TOPIC Have students choose a topic to research. Then have them:

- list a few questions about their topics.

- find information in encyclopedias, library books, magazines, organizations, or on the Internet.

- make notes on index cards.

- organize their notes to create an outline.

- make a short illustrated presentation of the information they gathered.

 *inter*NET **CONNECTION** For links to Web pages have students log on to ***www.mhschool.com/reading***

Students will make compar-
isons and contrasts based
on text.

LANGUAGE SUPPORT

ESL Before present-
ing the lesson,
have students compare and
contrast two familiar objects.
For instance, they might compare and contrast a softball and
a globe. Work together to
develop compare and contrast
statements about these or
other classroom objects.

Review Compare and Contrast

PREPARE

Discuss Comparisons and Contrasts

Explain: A comparison tells how two or more things are alike. A contrast tells how two or more things are different. Good readers make
comparisons and contrasts as they read to get meaning from text.

TEACH

Read "Gators!" and Model the Skill

Have students compare and contrast the Chinese alligator to the
American alligator as they listen to you read **Teaching Chart 178**.

Gators!

There are only two types of alligators in the world: the
Chinese alligator and the American alligator. The Chinese alligator is much smaller than the American alligator. It grows to
be about 8 feet (2.5 m) long. The American alligator can grow
up to 20 feet (6 m) long.

The Chinese alligator lives in the Yangtze River Basin of
China. The American alligator lives mainly in southeastern
United States in freshwater swamps and lakes.

Neither the Chinese alligator nor the American alligator
attacks humans much, as long as they are left alone.

Teaching Chart 178

Help students compare and contrast the Chinese and American
alligator.

MODEL: Chinese and American alligators live far apart, so they probably have important differences. The second sentence tells me
one contrast between the two alligators: Chinese alligators are
much smaller than American alligators.

PRACTICE

Identify Comparisons and Contrasts

ONE

Have students underline phrases that show how Chinese and American alligators are different. Have them circle phrases that show how the alligators are the same. ▶ **Linguistic/Logical**

ASSESS/CLOSE

Make Comparisons and Contrasts

If possible, show students pictures of both a Chinese alligator and an American alligator or of both an alligator and a crocodile. Have them compare and contrast the physical features of the two animals.

ALTERNATE TEACHING STRATEGY

COMPARE AND CONTRAST

For a different approach to teaching this skill, see page T66.

SELF-SELECTED Reading

Students may choose from the following titles.

ANTHOLOGY
• Saving the Everglades

LEVELED BOOKS
All titles for the unit

Bibliography, pages T76–T77

Meeting Individual Needs for Comprehension

EASY	ON-LEVEL	CHALLENGE	LANGUAGE SUPPORT

EASY

Name_____ Date_____ Reteach 218

Compare and Contrast

Writers often **compare and contrast** two or more things. They point out how the things are alike and different.

Read the paragraphs below. Then write your responses on the lines provided.

Some people call lemons the sunny fruit. The bright yellow color reminds them of the sun. Lemons have a thick skin that protects the juice and pulp inside. The zesty tart flavor of lemons is just perfect in cakes, candies, and drinks. Lemons ship well and are available throughout our country.

Peaches are an orange pink color. They have a soft, fuzzy skin. The flesh of a ripe peach is soft, and the flavor is sweet. People often eat peaches out of their hands. They make a great snack. Peaches often turn up in pies in the summertime. Peaches bruise easily and must be shipped with care.

List four ways in which lemons and peaches differ.

1. Lemons are yellow. Peaches are an orange pink color.

2. Lemons have a thick skin. Peaches have a soft, fuzzy skin.

3. Lemons are tart. Peaches are sweet.

4. Lemons ship well. Peaches bruise and must be shipped with care.

5. Although it is not stated, what is one way lemons and peaches are alike? Lemons and peaches are both fruits; they are both juicy.

At Home: Have students compare and contrast themselves with another family member.

218

Book 4/Unit 6
Saving the Everglades 5

ON-LEVEL

Name_____ Date_____ Practice 218

Compare and Contrast

In "Saving the Everglades," the author **compares and contrasts** what this vast wetland was like at the end of the 1800s with what it is like now. Think about how the Everglades are the same and how they are different. Then answer the questions below.
Students' answers will vary. Possible answers are shown.

1. Compare the feelings many nature lovers of long ago had about the Everglades to the feelings many scientists and nature lovers have today. How are those feelings the same? Both could see and appreciate the wild beauty.

2. Contrast peoples' understanding of what building farms and cities would do to the Everglades. Long ago people did not realize the value of the Everglades. To them it was just swampland. They had part of it drained to build farms and cities. Today, people know that draining part of the land and polluting it destroy a valuable area for animals, plants, and people.

3. Why are scientists today putting rivers back on their winding courses? Straightening the rivers by draining land and building dikes has harmed the Everglades. Scientists are returning the rivers to what they once were.

4. The Everglades used to be huge, but now the area has been reduced to half its size. Why? Land was drained for farms and cities. People thought the Everglades was a useless swamp area.

5. The Everglades has huge numbers of wild plants, cattails, compared to what there used to be. Why is that? Cattails easily absorb the chemicals found in farm fertilizers so they increase in number and strength.

6. How did the animal population change between the 1800s and the 1900s? Animals have less land to live on and find food. Some of the Everglades animals are now threatened and may possibly disappear.

At Home: Have students draw and label a two-part picture illustrating the Everglades long ago and today.

218

Book 4/ Unit 6
Saving the Everglades 6

CHALLENGE

Name_____ Date_____ Extend 218

Compare and Contrast

Comparing two or more things tells how the things are alike.
Example: Alligators and crocodiles are both reptiles.
Contrasting two or more things tells how the things are different.
Example: Alligators have broader snouts than crocodiles.

Compare and contrast an environmental issue in your community to the disappearance of the Everglades. Do some research on your topic on the Internet or in newspapers. How are the issues alike? How are they different? How are the solutions to your environmental problem and the problem of the Everglades alike? How are they different? Write your findings in the appropriate section of the chart below. Answers will vary.

	Community Issue	Everglades
Comparisons		
Contrasts		

At Home: Have students compare and contrast two animals that live in their region.

218

Book 4/Unit 6
Saving the Everglades

LANGUAGE SUPPORT

Name_____ Date_____

Change and Stay the Same

1. Color a picture for each scene. 2. Write a sentence about each scene.
The Everglades long ago.

The Everglades in the 1920's.

The Everglades today.

238 Saving the Everglades • Language Support /Blackline Master 118

Grade 4

Reteach, 218   Practice, 218   Extend, 218   Language Support, 238

OBJECTIVES

Students will learn how to recognize and use context clues to determine the meaning of specialized vocabulary.

> **TEACHING TIP**
>
> **INSTRUCTIONAL**
>
> - To use context clues, readers need to adjust their reading rates to reread sentences and words carefully.
>
> - Context clues can be used to decode words as well as to make meaning.
>
> - If efforts to use context clues as well as semantic and structural clues fail, readers should consult a dictionary to define unfamiliar words.

Review Context Clues

PREPARE

Discuss Context Clues and Specialized Vocabulary

Explain: Some reading selections use special words that relate to the selection's topic. For example, an article about the human body might contain special words such as the names for bones. If you come across a special word you don't understand, try to find clues to its meaning in the words or sentences around it. If that doesn't work, check a glossary or dictionary.

TEACH

Read the Passage and Model the Skill

Have students silently read the passage on **Teaching Chart 179.**

More Problems for the Everglades

Water-shrinking canals and <u>farmers'</u> fertilizers aren't the only problems facing the Florida Everglades. Two big high-ways cut across the area, disturbing the <u>homes of animals and birds</u> such as alligators and egrets. Also, Melaleuca <u>trees from Australia</u> have spread out of control. Farmers planted these trees hoping one day to harvest them. But they proved too hard to cut down. Today they are pushing out other plants and using lots of water.

It seems like it took only a short time to cause all the prob-lems in the Everglades. How long will it take to fix them?

Teaching Chart 179

MODEL If I don't know the word *canals,* I can read the words before it to help me figure out what it means. *Water-shrinking* tells me that canals must be used to control or stop the flow of water.

PRACTICE

Identify and Use Context Clues for Specialized Vocabulary

Have volunteers underline context clues for *fertilizers, egrets,* and *Melaleuca.* Then have groups write definitions based on those clues.

▶ **Linguistic/Interpersonal**

GROUP

ASSESS/CLOSE

Use Context Clues to Define Specialized Vocabulary

Write the following sentence on the chalkboard and have students read it silently. Ask groups to suggest meanings for the underlined word and explain how context clues support that meaning.

All the changes in the Everglades have created problems for the plants and animals in this rich <u>ecosystem</u>.

ALTERNATE TEACHING STRATEGY

CONTEXT CLUES

For a different approach to teaching this skill, see page T63.

SELF-SELECTED Reading

Students may choose from the following titles.

ANTHOLOGY

• Saving the Everglades

LEVELED BOOKS

All titles for the unit

Bibliography, pages T76–T77

Meeting Individual Needs for Vocabulary

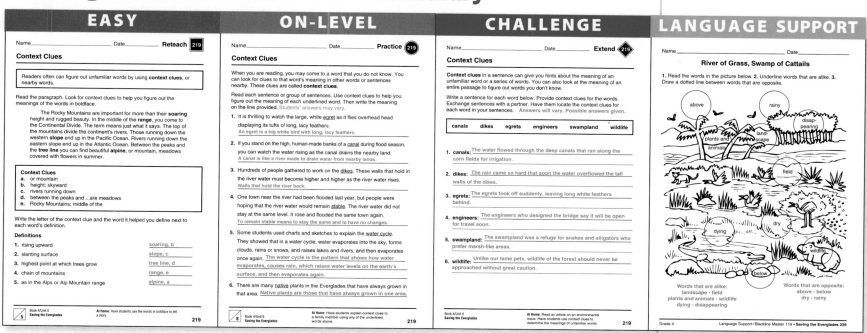

Reteach, 219   **Practice, 219**   **Extend, 219**   **Language Support, 239**

Students will identify antonyms and synonyms.

Review Antonyms and Synonyms

PREPARE

Discuss Antonyms and Synonyms

Explain: An *antonym* is a word or phrase that means the opposite of another word. A *synonym* is a word or phrase that has the same or almost the same meaning as another word. Sometimes you can find an antonym or a synonym to help you figure out the meaning of an unfamiliar word.

TEACH

Read the Passage and Model the Skill

Have students silently read the passage on **Teaching Chart 180**.

How the Everglades Was Formed

  Scientists believe the Everglades was created, or made, 8,000 to 10,000 years ago. They think that when glaciers melted, new water caused the sea to rise. The extra water from these giant ice blocks overflowed into Florida and turned the land into a swamp.
  Another cause might be the thousands of years of heavy rains that caused Lake Okeechobee to flood, not slowly leak, into the Everglades area.

Teaching Chart 180

Model using a synonym to figure out what an unfamiliar word means.

MODEL The signal word *or* tells me that *created* is another word for made. Knowing that synonym makes it easy to figure out the meaning of the unfamiliar word.

PRACTICE

Find Synonyms and Antonyms

GROUP

Have volunteers read the text and underline a synonym for *glaciers* and an antonym for *flood*. Then have groups brainstorm two synonyms and two antonyms for other words in the passage.

▶ Linguistic/Logical

ASSESS/CLOSE

Use Synonyms and Antonyms to Determine Meaning

GROUP

Write the following sentence on the chalkboard and have students read it silently. Ask groups to define the underlined words and explain how they used a synonym or antonym to build that meaning.

The <u>climate</u>, or weather pattern, in the Everglades includes hot, humid summers and warm, dry winters.

ALTERNATE TEACHING STRATEGY

ANTONYMS AND SYNONYMS

For a different approach to teaching this skill, see page T65.

SELF-SELECTED Reading

Students may choose from the following titles.

ANTHOLOGY
• Saving the Everglades

LEVELED BOOKS
All titles for the unit

Bibliography, pages T76–T77

Meeting Individual Needs for Vocabulary

EASY

Name_____ Date_____ **Reteach** 220

Synonyms and Antonyms

Synonyms have almost the same meaning. **Antonyms** have opposite meanings.

Choose one of the synonyms below to replace the underlined word in each sentence. Write your answer on the line provided.

correct	vanishing	wet	huge	hurt

1. Swamps are <u>soggy</u> places. wet
2. Fertilizers have <u>harmed</u> the environment. hurt
3. The Everglades is a <u>large</u> swamp. huge
4. Swamps need the <u>right</u> amount of water at the right time. correct
5. Some plants and flowers in the Everglades are <u>disappearing</u>. vanishing

Choose one of the antonyms below to replace the underlined word in each sentence.

awareness	vast	soggy	shrinking	harmed

1. All across the country, wetland areas are <u>growing</u>. shrinking
2. There is widespread <u>ignorance</u> of the importance of wetlands. awareness
3. The Everglades is a <u>tiny</u> swamp. vast
4. Fertilizers have <u>helped</u> the environment. harmed
5. Swamps are <u>dry</u> places. soggy

At Home: Have students use some of the words above to make a synonym and antonym chart.
220 | Book 4/Unit 6 Saving the Everglades 10

Reteach, 220

ON-LEVEL

Name_____ Date_____ **Practice** 220

Synonyms and Antonyms

Choose a word from the list that means the same thing as the underlined word. Write your answer on the line provided.

saline	immense	wetlands	migrating	reside

1. <u>Swamps</u> are a kind of wetlands that contain trees, shrubs, and bushes.
2. The <u>huge</u> Everglades make up an immense freshwater marsh measuring at 4,000 square miles.
3. Marshes and swamps can be important rest areas for birds traveling great <u>distances</u>, such as ducks and other migrating birds.
4. Alligators and crocodiles <u>live</u> side-by-side in the Everglades and reside there year around.
5. The <u>salt-filled</u> lands near the ocean are home to animals that need a saline element in their foods.

Choose a word from the list that means the opposite of the underlined word or words. Write your answer on the line provided.

finite	saltwater	nutrients	enhance	endangered

1. Some areas of the wetlands have <u>fresh water</u> while others have saltwater.
2. Changing the course of rivers can enhance the land, or it can <u>take away</u> important aspects of the area.
3. The Florida Everglades receive many of their nutrients or vitamins from rain water, but they also receive <u>poisons</u>.
4. Some wetland species are endangered while others are already <u>protected</u> by law.
5. Some rivers of grass seem <u>endless</u>, but they are finite and growing smaller.

At Home: Have students use antonyms and synonyms in ten sentences.
220 | Book 4/Unit 6 Saving the Everglades 10

Practice, 220

CHALLENGE

Name_____ Date_____ **Extend** 220

Synonyms and Antonyms

Synonyms are words whose meanings are the same. **Antonyms** are words whose meanings are opposite.

Are these pairs of words synonyms or antonyms? Write **S** or **A** on the line.

1. surface/depth — A
2. threatened/protected — A
3. rescuing/saving — S

Write two synonyms for each word below: Possible answers given.

4. soggy — wet; dripping
5. dikes — dams; walls
6. stable — barn; unchanged

Write two antonyms for each word below:

7. native — foreign; tourist
8. winding — straight; unbending
9. flood — drought; dryness
10. broader — narrower; tighter

Write a poem using as many of the synonyms as possible.

_____
_____
_____
_____
_____
_____
_____

At Home: Have students replace words in a magazine article with synonyms and antonyms.
220 | Book 4/Unit 6 Saving the Everglades

Extend, 220

LANGUAGE SUPPORT

Name_____ Date_____

A Swampy Story

1. Read the story below. 2. Fill in words in the blanks to finish the story. 3. Draw a picture of the swamp.

wildlife	egrets	canals	swamp	dikes

Two egrets were flying in the sky. They flew over the swamp where the alligator lived. Then they saw two men with machines. They were building canals and tall dikes to help stop flooding. They told the men that crocodiles, plants and other wildlife would soon not be able to survive here. The men said they were sorry and would be sure not to destroy the Everglades.

240 Saving the Everglades • Language Support/Blackline Master 120 | Grade 4

Language Support, 240

723J

TECHNOLOGY TIP

Demonstrate or have a volunteer show how students can use the *restore* function on their computers to retrieve material that they have accidentally deleted.

Writing That Compares

Prewrite

WRITE AN ENCYCLOPEDIA ARTICLE
Present the following writing assignment: Crocodiles and alligators are cousins. Yet, like cousins, they are a little bit different. Write an encyclopedia article about alligators. Compare them with crocodiles. Show at least two ways they are alike. Then show how they are different. Include a drawing that highlights their size, shapes, scales, mouth, and teeth.

ORGANIZE INFORMATION Have students use a Venn diagram to list crocodiles' and alligators' similarities and differences.

Strategy: Work with a Partner Have students compare their diagrams with a partner's. They can discuss how to use their points of comparison to write an interesting encyclopedia article.

SIMILARITIES	DIFFERENCES
• Reptiles • Use tails to swim • Lay eggs • Have extra long fourth tooth	• Alligators have a rounded snout, crocodiles a pointed one • Crocodiles are more aggressive.

Draft

USE THE GRAPHIC ORGANIZER Help students identify the strongest points of comparison and contrast in their diagrams. Encourage them to elaborate each point with vivid, descriptive details and facts. Remind them to provide their articles with a clear introduction and conclusion.

Revise

SELF-QUESTIONING Ask students to assess their drafts.

• What are the strongest examples of similarities and differences in my article?

• Do I give a clear introduction and conclusion?

• Do I use appropriate transition words to connect ideas in my comparison?

Have students reread their articles and create a second draft. Conference with students on ways they can clarify and elaborate their writing.

Edit/Proofread

CHECK FOR ERRORS Have students revise once more for word use and elaboration.

Publish

SHARE THE ARTICLES Have students read their articles aloud or share them with partners. Encourage them to notice key similarities and differences in each other's articles.

Crocodiles and Alligators

To many people, crocodiles and alligators may seem very much alike. For one thing, they are both large reptiles. Another similarity is that they both live in the water.

But despite their similarities, crocodiles and alligators have important differences. One difference is in their snouts. The crocodile's snout is broader and blunter than an alligator's. Also, the crocodile's lower fourth tooth sticks out when its mouth is closed. The alligator's does not.

So while alligators and crocodiles have many similarities, you don't have to be an expert to tell them apart.

Presentation Ideas

DISPLAY DRAWINGS Make a bulletin board display of the drawings students have made illustrating crocodiles' and alligators' likenesses and differences.

▶ **Viewing/Representing**

GIVE A TALK Using their pictures as a starting point, have students present a short talk comparing alligators and crocodiles.

▶ **Speaking/Listening**

Alligators have rounded noses

Crocodiles have longer, skinnier noses

Consider students' creative efforts, possibly adding a plus (+) for originality, wit, and imagination.

Scoring Rubric

Excellent	Good	Fair	Unsatisfactory
4: The writer • clearly introduces the topic. • provides vivid and effective comparisons on at least two points. • presents a strong conclusion. • provides an accurately labeled drawing.	**3:** The writer • states the topic of comparison. • provides comparative material on two points. • presents a conclusion. • provides an accurately labeled drawing.	**2:** The writer • states the intent to compare. • provides sparse material for comparison. • presents only a vague conclusion. • provides a drawing that is inaccurately labeled.	**1:** The writer • has stated the main idea, but only vaguely. • provides no similarities or differences. • does not present a conclusion. • provides no drawing or one that is inaccurate.

0: The writer leaves the page blank or fails to respond to the writing task. The response is illegible or incoherent.

For a 6-point or an 8-point scale, see pages T105–T106.

Meeting Individual Needs for Writing

EASY

Picture of the Everglades Remind students that the Everglades has been called a "river of grass." Have them draw a picture of the Everglades. Then have them write a paragraph comparing the Everglades to a river.

ON-LEVEL

Comparisons Have students write a few paragraphs comparing two animals (other than crocodiles and alligators) that live in the Everglades or any other part of the United States. Include their differences as well as their similarities.

CHALLENGE

Persuasive Speech Have students write a speech explaining why alligators and crocodiles should be protected. Have them learn about conservation efforts in the Everglades and include information about how students can help.

5 Day Grammar and Usage Plan

Read aloud: *Juan has a book.* Ask two students to add a description to the sentence, such as *Juan has a red book. Juan has a big book.* Then combine the two sentences. *Juan has a big, red book.*

DAILY LANGUAGE ACTIVITIES

Have students combine the sentences orally.

Day 1
1. Felix walked home. He walked quickly.
2. The frog has spots. The spots are black.
3. I have a bicycle. My bicycle is red.

Day 2
1. Chemicals are dangerous. They are dangerous to plants and people.
2. The crocodile has teeth. Its teeth are sharp.

Day 3
1. The ibis flew. It flew past the clouds.
2. The Everglades is full of water. The water is fresh.

Day 4
1. Builders drained the swamp. They drained it for hours.
2. The owl hooted. It hooted loudly.

Day 5
1. The city was built. It was built where alligators used to roam.
2. Sugar cane is a crop of the Everglades. It is an important crop.

Daily Language Transparency 30

DAY 1 — Introduce the Concept

Oral Warm-Up Read this sentence aloud: *The tall man walked quickly.* Have students identify an adjective and an adverb. Remind students that an adjective describes a noun and an adverb tells more about a verb.

Combining with Adjectives/Adverbs When you write two sentences that tell about the same person, place, or thing, or about the same action, you can sometimes combine them. Leave out the words that repeat. Discuss:

> **Sentence Combining**
> - Two sentences can be combined by adding an adjective or adverb to one sentence.

Present the Daily Language Activity. Then say: *I have a hat. The hat is red.* Ask students to combine these sentences.

 Assign the daily Writing Prompt on page 714C.

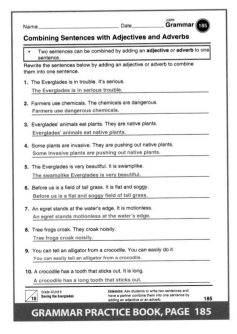

GRAMMAR PRACTICE BOOK, PAGE 185

DAY 2 — Teach the Concept

Review Combining Sentences Ask students to combine these sentences into one: *I see an ibis. The ibis is white.*

Introduce Combining with Prepositions Another way to combine sentences is to add a prepositional phrase. Present the following:

> **Combining with Prepositions**
> - Two sentences can be combined by adding a prepositional phrase to one sentence.

Offer this example: *The train left the station. The train left at noon. The train left the station at noon.*

Present the Daily Language Activity. Then have students write a sentence that combines these two sentences: *Come home. Come in the morning.*

 Assign the daily Writing Prompt on page 714C.

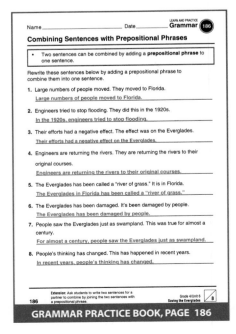

GRAMMAR PRACTICE BOOK, PAGE 186

Sentence Combining

Learn from the Literature Read the last sentence in the first paragraph on page 717 of *Saving the Everglades*:

> **A few trees dot the landscape under the Florida sun.**

Ask students to tell two sentences that might have been combined to make this one. Answers may vary.

Combine Sentences Present Daily Language Activity 3. Then write the following in two columns on the chalkboard:

Column 1: *Look at the alligator.*

The ibis flew.

Column 2: *It flew toward the sun.*

The alligator is green.

Have students combine the appropriate sentences.

 Assign the daily Writing Prompt on page 714D.

Review Combining Sentences Write:

1. The Everglades is dying. It is dying after years of bad planning.

Have students find the sentence on page 717 that combines them. Then present the Daily Language Activity.

Mechanics and Usage Before students begin the daily Writing Prompt on page 714D, display and discuss:

Using Punctuation Marks

- Every sentence begins with a capital letter.
- Use the correct end mark for each sentence.
- Use a comma to set off a person's name when the person is spoken to directly.
- Use a comma after introductory words such as *yes, no,* and *well*.

 Assign the daily Writing Prompt on page 714D.

Assess Use the Daily Language Activity and page 189 of the **Grammar Practice Book** for assessment.

Reteach Organize the class into small groups. Have each group write two pairs of sentences onto slips of paper, each of which can be combined into one. Then have the groups exchange sentences and combine them.

Have students display the individual sentences and the resulting combined sentences on the class bulletin board.

Use page 190 of the **Grammar Practice Book** for additional reteaching.

 Assign the daily Writing Prompt on page 714D.

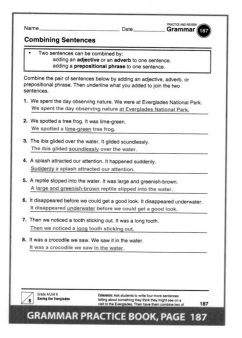

GRAMMAR PRACTICE BOOK, PAGE 187

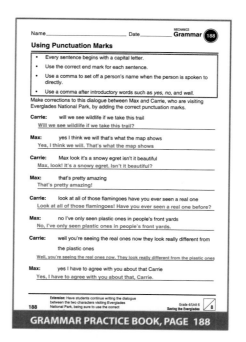

GRAMMAR PRACTICE BOOK, PAGE 188

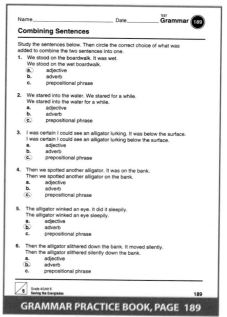

GRAMMAR PRACTICE BOOK, PAGE 189

5 Day Spelling Plan

LANGUAGE SUPPORT

Display pictures or objects of Spelling Words for students. Have students draw and label the following: *cone, cylinder,* and *rectangle.*

DICTATION SENTENCES

Spelling Words

1. She knows every person in the area.
2. We will drive for hundreds of miles.
3. What is the size of your foot?
4. The stars are billions of miles away.
5. The scale will tell you your weight.
6. I'll be there in just a minute.
7. The sun is hot at noon.
8. Put the ice cream in a cone.
9. There are three feet in a yard.
10. The marble rolled off the edge.
11. Can you drink a large amount of water?
12. A tree trunk is a cylinder.
13. Zero is one less than one.
14. He skated in a figure eight.
15. Check the date on the calendar.
16. A quart is less than a gallon.
17. A decade is ten years.
18. He drew a circle and a rectangle.
19. It was an era of hard times.
20. The snake was five feet in length.

Challenge Words

21. She compares dolphins to whales.
22. Water is of great importance.
23. In this instance, he is right.
24. Don't lurk there in the shadows.
25. The ground was soggy after the rain.

DAY 1 — Pretest

Assess Prior Knowledge Use the Dictation Sentences at the left and **Spelling Practice Book** page 185 for the pretest. Allow students to correct their own papers. Students who require a modified list may be tested on the first ten words.

Spelling Words		Challenge Words
1. **area**	11. **amount**	21. **compares**
2. **hundreds**	12. cylinder	22. **importance**
3. **size**	13. zero	23. **instance**
4. **billions**	14. figure	24. **lurk**
5. weight	15. calendar	25. **soggy**
6. minute	16. quart	
7. noon	17. decade	
8. cone	18. rectangle	
9. yard	19. era	
10. edge	20. length	

*Note: Words in **dark type** are from the story.*

Word Study On page 186 of the **Spelling Practice Book** are word study steps and an at-home activity.

DAY 2 — Explore the Pattern

Sort and Spell Words Ask students what the word *hundreds* tells about. (numbers) Then ask what the word *minute* tells about. (time) Then have students read the Spelling Words and sort them according to what they tell about, as below.

Words that tell about		
Numbers	**Shapes**	**Time**
hundreds	area	minute
billions	size	noon
amount	cone	calendar
zero	edge	decade
Measurement	cylinder	era
weight	figure	
yard	rectangle	
quart		
length		

Word Wall Have students create a word wall based on the word sort and add more words from their reading.

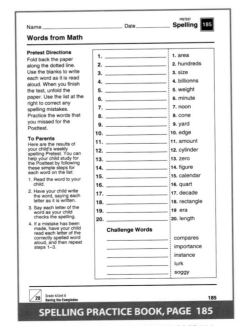

SPELLING PRACTICE BOOK, PAGE 185

WORD STUDY STEPS AND ACTIVITY, PAGE 186

SPELLING PRACTICE BOOK, PAGE 187

Words from Math

Word Meaning: Analogies Remind students that an analogy shows the relationship between things. Have students choose the two Spelling Words that complete each analogy.

_____ is to gallon as foot is to _____.
(quart, yard)

_____ is to clock as month is to _____.
(minute, calendar)

If students need extra practice, have partners give each other a midweek test.

Glossary Review the pronunciation key in the Glossary. Have partners:

- write each Challenge Word.

- look up the respelling in the Glossary.

- find the symbol that stands for the first vowel sound in the word.

- write the word from the pronunciation key that contains the same vowel sound.

Proofread Sentences Write these sentences on the chalkboard, including the misspelled words. Ask students to proofread, circling incorrect spellings and writing the correct spellings. There are two spelling errors in each sentence.

> There are hunnerds of bilyuns of stars in the sky. (hundreds, billions)
>
> Meet me five minnits before nune. (minutes, noon)

Have students create additional sentences with errors for partners to correct.

WRITING Have students use as many Spelling Words as possible in the daily Writing Prompt on page 714D. Remind students to proofread their writing for errors in spelling, grammar, and punctuation.

Assess Students' Knowledge Use page 190 of the **Spelling Practice Book** or the Dictation Sentences on page 723O for the posttest.

JOURNAL **Personal Word List** If students have trouble with any words in the lesson, have them add the words to their personal lists of troublesome words in their journals. Have students draw and label the Spelling Words.

Students should refer to their word lists during later writing activities.

Wrap Up the Theme

Sorting It Out

We make decisions that can lead to new ideas and discoveries.

REVIEW THE THEME Reread the theme statement. Ask how decisions the characters in the selections made changed their lives. Ask students to name stories, movies, and television shows that could also be included in this theme.

READ THE POEM Read aloud "Decisions" by Angela Shelf Medearis, and ask students to tell how it relates to the theme. Ask how people know when they are hearing "the clear, soft sound of a heart that is true."

 Student Listening Library Audiocassettes

MAKE CONNECTIONS Have students work in small groups to brainstorm a list of ways that the stories, poems, and the *Time for Kids* magazine article relate to the theme Sorting It Out.

Groups can then compare their lists as they share them with the class.

LOOKING AT GENRE

Review *Teammates* and *The Toothpaste Millionaire* with students. Are both selections realistic? How is the form of the two selections different? Have students create a Genre chart to compare the two selections. Ask students to name favorite stories and books and tell whether they are fiction or nonfiction.

BIOGRAPHY *Teammates*	PLAY *The Toothpaste Millionaire*
• Tells about real people. • Tells a story that really happened.	• Tells about a made-up character. • Tells a made-up story.

Decisions

Sometimes I have hard
  decisions to make.
I must decide the road I
  should take.
I must do the right thing
  for me,
even if no one else agrees.

Sometimes the pathway
  is dark and unclear,
  and the crowd's angry
  shouts make it hard
  to hear,
the clear, soft sound of a
  heart that is true,
I must decide the right
  thing to do.

Now is the time to face
  my fears,
and leave behind all I
  hold dear,
to throw open the gates
  and fly away,
to discover new ideas
  and a better day.

by Angela Shelf Medearis

725

Research and Inquiry

Complete the Theme Project Have students prepare a proposal to explain their goal and their plan for accomplishing it. Suggest that they use charts, graphs, and other appropriate visual aids.

Present the Proposal Have teams present their proposal to a group of students taking the roles of community members who would approve the project. Teams can take turns acting as the panel members. Encourage that panel members ask questions of the student presenters.

Draw Conclusions Help students draw conclusions about planning their project. Did they use the resources they expected to use? What other sources were helpful? What obstacles did they encounter while developing their proposal? How did they overcome these obstacles?

Ask More Questions What did students learn from planning the project? Would it be harder or easier to carry out than they thought? Do they still think it would help the community?

LEARNING ABOUT POETRY

Literary Devices: Rhyme Pattern
Have students number a sheet of paper from 1 to 12, leaving spaces between lines 4 and 5 and lines 8 and 9. Then slowly reread "Decisions." Have students write the word from the end of each line beside the appropriate number and then find the *aabb* rhyme pattern of each verse.

Response Activity Give students drawing paper and have them fold it into three equal panels. Ask students to draw three pictures, one to represent each verse of the poem.

Writing that compares

CONNECT TO LITERATURE In the story *The Malachite Palace,* a young princess learns to reach out to the world around her. Invite students to discuss and compare the princess's life before and after she met the yellow bird.

Frogs and carp living in fresh water ponds have a lot in common. Frogs lay eggs that turn into baby tadpoles. Carp reproduce by laying eggs, too. Carp and frogs are both cold-blooded. Sometimes, they even eat the same kind of bugs.

Once tadpoles grow into frogs, the differences between frogs and carp become more clear. Adult frogs have legs and can breathe air, which allows them to move around on land. Carp, which have gills rather than lungs, must stay in the water, so they don't have as many food sources as frogs.

Prewrite

PURPOSE & AUDIENCE Students will write reports that compare two animals who live in the same ecosystem. Have them focus on how each animal is affected by, or affects, its environment.

STRATEGY: RESEARCH THE TOPIC Make a research table with animal books, encyclopedias, and nature magazines. If possible, show a videotape of an ecosystem you'd like students to focus on. Help them set up comparison charts to organize the differences and similarities between their topic animals.

Use **Writing Process Transparency 6A** to model a Venn Diagram.

FEATURES OF WRITING THAT COMPARES

- presents similarities and differences, of two topic items
- clearly introduces the main idea, and elaborates on it with facts
- organizes facts and ideas in a logical pattern of comparison
- may have a conclusion based on factual comparative information

---

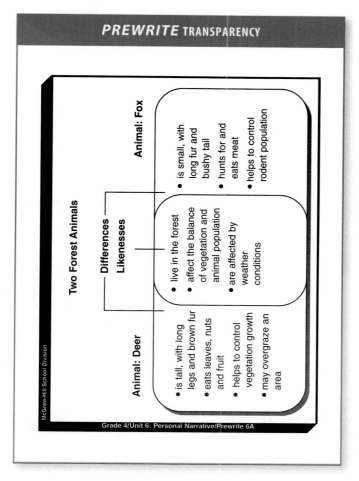

PREWRITE TRANSPARENCY

Two Forest Animals

Animal: Fox
- is small, with long fur and bushy tail
- hunts for and eats meat
- helps to control rodent population

Differences
Likenesses
- live in the forest
- affect the balance of vegetation and animal population
- are affected by weather conditions

Animal: Deer
- is tall, with long legs and brown fur
- eats leaves, nuts and fruit
- helps to control vegetation growth
- may overgraze an area

McGraw-Hill School Division

Grade 4/Unit 6: Personal Narrative/Prewrite 6A

Writing that Compares

Draft

STRATEGY: CONSULT THE VENN DIAGRAM Have students use their diagrams to guide the structure for their first drafts. Invite them to use rich descriptive language to clarify and enliven their factual information. Encourage them to consider whether their essays should have a final conclusion.

Use **Writing Process Transparency 6B** to model a first draft.

LANGUAGE CONTROL Have students start collecting a word bank of adjectives that apply to their topic. Then, guide them to construct descriptive phrases using the articles a, an, and the; for example: a young bear, or, the swift falcon. They can save the adjective banks in their writing portfolios.

LANGUAGE SUPPORT

Some students may need help identifying animal traits. Have students close their eyes and imagine how the animal looks and acts. A partner can help them write lists of descriptive words.

DRAFT TRANSPARENCY

Our team has been watching two forest animals. deer and foxes. Obviously, they look very diffrent. Deer are tall, with long legs and short brown fur, while foxes are small with reddish fur and bushy tails. Deer walk and leap with their heads high. Foxes creep slow, or scurry close to the ground.

Deer roam the forest looking for things to eat. They live on leaves, nuts, and sometimes fruit. Foxes have very different tastes. They were meat eaters who hunt for small animals like rodents, birds and sometimes lizards or snakes. They are most cunning than deer.

These animals affect the environment in their own way. Deer help to keep forest plants from overgrowth. Their grazeing allows sunlight to reach the forest. But sometimes, too many deer will graze in the same area and use up too much plant life. This can cause problem for other animals who rely on vegetation for its shelter and food.

Foxes help to keep the number of smaller animals under control. This helps to make sure that there is enough food and space for other species.

Deer and foxes both show us that all plants and animals play a role in creating the balanced environment.

McGraw-Hill School Division

Grade 4/Unit 6: Writing That Compares/Draft 6B

Revise

Have students review their own essays for accuracy and clarity. Remind them to be sure that their comparisons are arranged in paragraphs. Ask them to consider whether a reader will have enough facts and details to learn something about their animals.

Use **Writing Process Transparency 6C** for classroom discussion on the revision process. Ask students to comment on how revisions may have improved this writing example.

STRATEGY: ELABORATION Have students examine their first drafts for elaboration on their comparison points, such as environmental challenges, life span, and natural enemies. Ask them to reflect on the following questions:

- Did I show how each animal looks and acts?

- Did I show how each animal affects its environment?

- How should I end my essay? Do I need a conclusion?

REVISE TRANSPARENCY

Two Animals That Affect the Forest

Our team has been watching two forest animals. deer and foxes. Obviously, they look very diffrent. Deer are tall, with long legs and short brown fur, while foxes are small with reddish fur and bushy tails. Deer walk and leap with their heads high. Foxes creep slow, or scurry close to the ground. *but they always stay*

Deer roam the forest looking for things to eat. They live on leaves, nuts, and sometimes fruit. Foxes have very different tastes. They were meat eaters who hunt for small animals like rodents, birds and sometimes lizards or snakes. They are most cunning than deer. *grasses* *twigs in the winter months.*

These animals affect the environment in their own way. Deer help to keep forest plants from overgrowth. Their grazeing allows sunlight to reach the forest. But sometimes, too many deer will graze in the same area and use up too much plant life. This can cause problem for other animals who rely on vegetation for its shelter and food. *each* *all life forms in*

Foxes help to keep the number of smaller animals under control. This helps to make sure that there is enough food and space for other species.

Deer and foxes both show us that all plants and animals play a role in creating the balanced environment. *help us see*

McGraw-Hill School Division

Grade 4/Unit 6: Writing That Compares/Revise 6C

Writing that Compares

Proofread

After students finish revising their texts, have them proofread for final corrections and additions.

GRAMMAR/SPELLING CONNECTIONS

See the 5-day Grammar and Usage Plans on adverbs, pp. 631M–631N, 663M–663N, 691M–691N, 713M–713N, and 723M–723N.

See the 5-day Spelling Plans, pp. 631O–631P, 663O–663P, 691O–691P, 713O–713P, and 723O–723P.

GRAMMAR, MECHANICS, USAGE

- correct use of adverbs
- correct use of possessive pronouns
- pronoun-verb agreement
- using adverbs *more* and *most* to compare

Publish

TEACHER FOR A DAY Volunteers can read their work aloud to the class. Invite them to pretend they are guest nature professors for a day.

Use **Writing Process Transparency 6D** as a proofreading model, and **Writing Process Transparency 6E** to discuss presentation ideas for their writing.

PROOFREAD TRANSPARENCY

Two Animals That Affect the Forest

Our team has been watching two forest animals, deer and foxes. Obviously, they look very diffrent. Deer are tall, with long legs and short brown fur, while foxes are small with reddish fur and bushy tails. Deer walk and leap with their heads high. Foxes creep slow, or scurry close to the ground.

Deer roam the forest looking for things to eat. They live on leaves, nuts, and sometimes fruit. Foxes have very different tastes. They were meat eaters who hunt for small animals like rodents, birds, and sometimes lizards or snakes. They are most cunning than deer.

These animals affect the environment in their own way. Deer help to keep forest plants from overgrowth. Their grazing allows sunlight to reach the forest. But sometimes, too many deer will graze in the same area and use up too much plant life. This can cause problems for other animals who rely on vegetation for its shelter and food.

Foxes help to keep the number of smaller animals under control. This helps to make sure that there is enough food and space for other species.

Deer and foxes both show us that all plants and animals play a role in creating the balanced environment.

Grade 4/Unit 6: Writing That Compares/Proofread 6D

PUBLISH TRANSPARENCY

Two Animals That Affect The Forest

Our team has been observing two forest animals, deer and foxes. Obviously, they look very different. Deer are tall, with long legs and short brown fur, while foxes are small with long reddish fur and bushy tails. Deer walk and leap with their heads high. Foxes creep slowly or scurry, but they always stay close to the ground.

Deer roam the forest looking for things to eat. They live on leaves, grasses, and sometimes twigs in the winter months. Foxes have very different tastes. They are meat eaters who hunt for small animals like rodents, birds, and sometimes lizards or snakes. They are more cunning than deer.

These animals each affect the environment in their own way. Deer help to keep forest vegetation from overgrowth. Their grazing allows sunlight to reach all life forms in the forest. But sometimes, too many deer will graze in the same area and use up too much plant life. This can cause problems for other animals who rely on vegetation for their shelter and food.

Foxes help to keep the population of smaller animals under control. This helps to make sure there is enough food and space for other species.

Deer and foxes both help us see that all plants and animals play a role in creating a balanced environment.

Grade 4/Unit 6: Writing That Compares/Publish 6E

Presentation Ideas

MAKE A NATURE SHOW Have students create a TV-style nature show on the animals they've written about. "Nature Reporters" can also show pictures of the animals and their environments.
▶ **Speaking/Listening**

MAKE A MENAGERIE Have students make animal models from self-drying clay. Make a display of their sculptures, with labels naming each animal and telling where they live. ▶ **Representing/Viewing**

Assessment

- Ask students to self assess their writing. Present the writing that compares features, page 725B, in question form on a chart.

- For a 6-point or an 8-point scale, see pages T105–T106.

COMMUNICATION TIPS

REPRESENTING Have students use nature photos to model their clay animals. They can make shoebox bases painted to show the animal's environment.

SPEAKING Students can create "reporter" personalities. Encourage them to watch a nature reporter on TV.

Scoring Rubric: 6-Trait Writing

4 Excellent	**3** Good	**2** Fair	**1** Unsatisfactory
Ideas & Content	**Ideas & Content**	**Ideas & Content**	**Ideas & Content**
• crafts a well-constructed factual comparison of two animals; carefully-selected details clarify each comparison point.	• crafts a solid, well-thought-out comparison; details show knowledge of the topic; may make some fresh observations about the animals and their habitat.	• has some control of the comparison task, but may offer limited or unclear facts and details; makes obvious or predictable observations.	• does not successfully compare two animals; it is hard to tell what the writer intends to say about the topic.
Organization	**Organization**	**Organization**	**Organization**
• careful strategy moves the reader smoothly through each point, from beginning to end; well-placed observations and details strengthen the logic.	• presents a capable, easy-to-follow strategy; reader can follow the logic from beginning to end; details fit and build on each other.	• tries to structure a comparison, but has trouble sequencing ideas; may not present distinct comparison categories; reader may be confused by poorly-placed facts and details.	• extreme lack of organization makes the text hard to follow; ideas, facts, and details are not connected, out of order, and may not fit the purpose.
Voice	**Voice**	**Voice**	**Voice**
• originality and deep involvement with the topic enlivens the content; writer reaches out to share ideas with an audience.	• clearly shows who is behind the words; personal style matches the purpose; reaches out to the reader effectively.	• communicates a main idea, with some hint of who is behind the words; writer may seem personally uninvolved with the topic and an audience.	• does not connect with the topic; is not involved in sharing ideas with a reader.
Word Choice	**Word Choice**	**Word Choice**	**Word Choice**
• makes imaginative use of precise, sophisticated words to describe distinct differences and similarities.	• uses a range of precise words to present facts and observations; explores new words, or uses everyday words to state ideas in a fresh way.	• gets the argument across, but experiments with few new words; may not use words intended to create a clear picture for the reader.	• does not use words that show differences or similarities; some words may detract from the purpose to compare; words do not fit, or are overused.
Sentence Fluency	**Sentence Fluency**	**Sentence Fluency**	**Sentence Fluency**
• varied, effective sentences flow naturally; uses both simple and complex sentences creatively; varied beginnings, lengths, and patterns add appeal to the comparisons.	• crafts careful sentences that make sense, and are easy to read and understand; sentence lengths and patterns vary, and fit together well.	• sentences are understandable, but may be choppy, rambling, or awkward; some writing is difficult to follow or read aloud, or may interfere with meaning.	• uses choppy, rambling, or confusing sentences; does not understand how words and sentences fit together; writing doesn't follow natural sentence patterns, and is hard to read aloud.
Conventions	**Conventions**s	**Conventions**	**Conventions**
• has strong skills in most writing conventions; proper use of the rules of English enhances clarity and cohesion of the comparisons; editing is largely unnecessary.	• uses most conventions correctly; some editing may be needed; errors are few and don't make the paper hard to understand.	• makes frequent noticeable mistakes which prevent an even reading of the text; extensive need for editing and revision.	• has repeated errors in spelling, word choice, punctuation and usage; some parts are impossible to read or understand.

0: This piece is either blank, or fails to respond to the writing task. The topic is not addressed, or the student simply paraphrases the prompt. The response may be illegible or incoherent.

VOCABULARY

PARTNERS To review vocabulary, have students sort the words according to their part of speech (noun, verb, etc.) and make up a sentence for each word. Suggest that students include a category for words that can be more than one part of speech.

Unit Review

Teammates

circulated   launched   organizations
extraordinary opponents   teammate

The Malachite Palace

cultured   fragrance   resembled
feeble   mingled   scampered

The Toothpaste Millionaire

brilliant   expensive   ingredient
commercials   gallon   successful

Whales

identify   marine   preserve
mammals   pods   related

Saving the Everglades

compares   instance   soggy
importance   lurk   wildlife

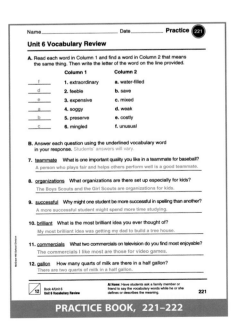

PRACTICE BOOK, 221–222

GRAMMAR

PARTNERS Have students write a paragraph on a topic of their choice and exchange it with a partner who will edit it, paying special attention to adverbs, adverbs that compare, negatives, prepositions, and sentences that could be combined.

Unit Review

Teammates
Adverbs

The Malachite Palace
Adverbs That Compare

The Toothpaste Millionaire
Negatives

Whales
Prepositions

Saving the Everglades
Sentence Combining

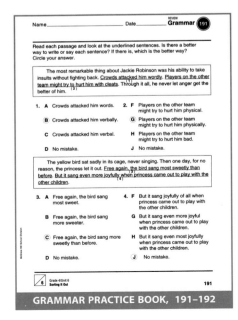

GRAMMAR PRACTICE BOOK, 191–192

SPELLING

GROUP Organize the class into small groups. Give each group twelve note cards and have students cut six of them in half. Group members can take turns building word shapes with the cards. The remaining students can name the spelling word the shape represents.

Unit Review

Silent Letters
knead
numb
calm
delight
wreck

Prefixes
rewind
unsure
disagree
inactive
nonstop

Homophones and Homographs
grate
great
bury
berry
dates

Math Words
hundreds
billions
cylinder
era
weight

Suffixes
breathless   protection
darkness   adjustable
encouragement

SPELLING PRACTICE BOOK, 191–192

☑ SKILLS & STRATEGIES

Comprehension
☑ Cause and Effect
☑ Judgments and Decisions
☑ Problem and Solution
☑ Compare and Contrast

Vocabulary Strategies
☑ Context Clues
☑ Antonyms and Synonyms

Study Skills
☑ Library/Media Center

Writing
☑ Writing That Compares

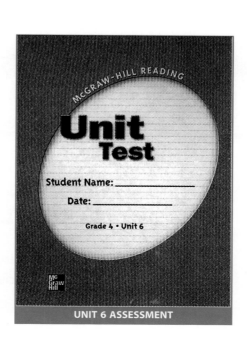

UNIT 6 ASSESSMENT

Assessment
Follow-Up

Use the results of the informal and formal assessment opportunities in the unit to help you make decisions about future instruction.

SKILLS AND STRATEGIES	Reteach Blackline Masters	Alternate Teaching Strategies
Comprehension		
Cause and Effect	186, 190, 198, 214	T60
Judgments and Decisions	191, 200, 204, 212	T62
Problem and Solution	193, 197, 205	T64
Compare and Contrast	207, 211, 218	T66
Vocabulary Strategy		
Context Clues	192, 213, 219	T63
Antonyms and Synonyms	199, 206, 220	T65
Study Skills		
Library/Media Center	189, 196, 203, 210, 217	T61

Writing	Alternate Writing Project—Easy	Unit Writing Process Lesson
Writing That Compares	631L, 663L, 691L, 713L, 723L, 725A	

McGraw-Hill School
TECHNOLOGY

interNET CONNECTION Research and Inquiry Ideas.
Visit **www.mhschool.com/reading**

Glossary

Introduce students to the Glossary by reading through the introduction and looking over the pages with them. Encourage the class to talk about what they see.

Words in a glossary, like words in a dictionary, are listed in **alphabetical order.** Point out the **guide words** at the top of each page that tell the first and last words appearing on that page.

Point out examples of **entries** and **main entries.** Read through a simple entry with the class, identifying each part. Have students note the order in which information is given: entry words(s), definition(s), example sentence, syllable division, pronunciation respelling, part of speech, plural/verb/adjective forms.

Note that if more than one definition is given for a word, the definitions are numbered. Note also the format used for a word that is more than one part of speech.

Review the parts of speech by identifying each in a sentence:

inter.	*adj.*	*n.*	*conj.*	*adj.*	*n.*
Wow!	A	dictionary	and	a	glossary

v.	*adv.*	*pron.*	*prep.*	*n.*
tell	almost	everything	about	words!

Explain the use of the **pronunciation key** (either the **short key,** at the bottom of every other page, or the **long key,** at the beginning of the glossary). Demonstrate the difference between **primary** stress and **secondary** stress by pronouncing a word with both.

Point out an example of the small triangle signaling a homophone. **Homophones** are words with different spellings and meanings but with the same pronunciation. Explain that a pair of words with the superscripts **1** and **2** are **homographs**—words that have the same spelling, but different origins and meanings, and in some cases, different pronunciations.

The **Word History** feature tells what language a word comes from and what changes have occurred in its spelling and/or meaning. Many everyday words have interesting and surprising stories behind them. Note that word histories can help us remember the meanings of difficult words.

Allow time for students to further explore the Glossary and make their own discoveries.

Glossary

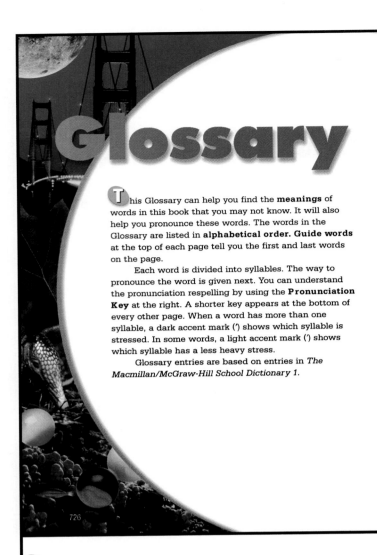

The Glossary can help you find the **meanings** of words in this book that you may not know. It will also help you pronounce these words. The words in the Glossary are listed in **alphabetical order. Guide words** at the top of each page tell you the first and last words on the page.

Each word is divided into syllables. The way to pronounce the word is given next. You can understand the pronunciation respelling by using the **Pronunciation Key** at the right. A shorter key appears at the bottom of every other page. When a word has more than one syllable, a dark accent mark (′) shows which syllable is stressed. In some words, a light accent mark (′) shows which syllable has a less heavy stress.

Glossary entries are based on entries in *The Macmillan/McGraw-Hill School Dictionary 1.*

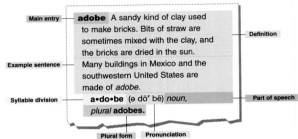

adobe/banner

First word on the page · Last word on the page

Sample Entry

Main entry — **adobe** A sandy kind of clay used to make bricks. Bits of straw are sometimes mixed with the clay, and the bricks are dried in the sun. Many buildings in Mexico and the southwestern United States are made of *adobe.* — Definition

Example sentence

Syllable division — **a•do•be** (ə dō′ bē) *noun, plural* **adobes.** — Part of speech

Plural form · Pronunciation

a	at, bad	d	dear, soda, bad
ā	ape, pain, day, break	f	five, defend, leaf, off, cough, elephant.
ä	father, car, heart		
âr	care, pair, bear, their, where	g	game, ago, fog, egg
e	end, pet, said, heaven, friend	h	hat, ahead
ē	equal, me, feet, team, piece, key	hw	white, whether, which
i	it, big, English, hymn	j	joke, enjoy, gem, page, edge
ī	ice, fine, lie, my	k	kite, bakery, seek, tack, cat
îr	ear, deer, here, pierce	l	lid, sailor, feel, ball, allow
o	odd, hot, watch	m	man, family, dream
ō	old, oat, toe, low	n	not, final, pan, knife
ô	coffee, all, taught, law, fought	ng	long, singer, pink
ôr	order, fork, horse, story, pour	p	pail, repair, soap, happy
oi	oil, toy	r	ride, parent, wear, more, marry
ou	out, now	s	sit, aside, pets, cent, pass
u	up, mud, love, double	sh	shoe, washer, fish, mission, nation
ū	use, mule, cue, feud, few	t	tag, pretend, fat, button, dressed
ü	rule, true, food	th	thin, panther, both,
ů	put, wood, should	th	this, mother, smooth
ûr	burn, hurry, term, bird, word, courage	v	very, favor, wave
		w	wet, weather, reward
ə	about, taken, pencil, lemon, circus	y	yes, onion
b	bat, above, job	z	zoo, lazy, jazz, rose, dogs, houses
ch	chin, such, match	zh	vision, treasure, seizure

726

727

Aa

abandon 1. To leave and not return; desert. The sailors *abandoned* the sinking ship. **2.** To give up completely. Because of heavy rain, we *abandoned* our picnic.
▲ **Synonym:** leave
a•ban•don (ə ban′ dən) *verb,* **abandoned, abandoning.**

> **Language Note**
> A **synonym** is a word with the same meaning as another word. A synonym for *abandon* is *desert.*

absorb 1. To soak up or take in. A towel *absorbed* the spilled water. **2.** To hold the interest of. The book about animals *absorbed* me.
ab•sorb (ab sôrb′ *or* ab zôrb′) *verb,* **absorbed, absorbing.**

accidental Not planned or expected; happening by chance. We did not know we would see each other; our meeting was *accidental.*
ac•ci•den•tal (ak′si den′təl) *adjective; adverb* **accidentally.**

admit 1. To make known that something is true; confess. They *admitted* that they had broken the lamp. **2.** To allow to enter; let in. We were *admitted* to the club last week.
ad•mit (ad mit′) *verb,* **admitted, admitting.**

affection A feeling of tenderness, fondness, or love. I have deep *affection* for my sister.
▲ **Synonym:** liking
af•fec•tion (ə fek′shən) *noun, plural* **affections.**

amazement Great surprise or wonder; astonishment. The people watching the whales swim by were filled with *amazement.*
a•maze•ment (ə māz′mənt) *noun.*

ancestor A person from whom one is descended. Your grandparents and great-grandparents are among your *ancestors.*
an•ces•tor (an′ses tər) *noun, plural* **ancestors.**

728

assure 1. To give confidence to. We *assured* the child that the dog was friendly. **2.** To state positively. I *assure* you that I won't be late.
as•sure (ə shûr′) *verb,* **assured, assuring.**

attendant A person who takes care of someone or provides service to other people. The *attendant* at the park showed us where we could rent a canoe.
at•ten•dant (ə ten′dənt) *noun, plural* **attendants.**

available 1. Possible to get. There are still a few seats available for the game. Strawberries become *available* in early summer. **2.** Ready for use or service. The telephone is now *available.*
a•vail•a•ble (ə vā′lə bəl) *adjective.*

awkward 1. Difficult or embarrassing. It was an *awkward* moment when the teacher found out that I hadn't done my homework. **2.** Lacking grace or poise in movement or behavior; clumsy or uncomfortable. The *awkward* colt had trouble standing up.
▲ **Synonym:** troublesome
awk•ward (ôk′wərd) *adjective; adverb,* **awkwardly.**

Bb

background 1. A person's experience or learning. Her *background* is in physics. **2.** The part of a picture that appears in the distance.
back•ground (bak′ground′) *noun, plural* **backgrounds**

ballerina A woman or girl who dances ballet.
bal•le•ri•na (bal′ə rē′ nə) *noun, plural* **ballerinas.**

barracks The building or buildings where soldiers live. The *barracks* are inspected every week. The word **barracks** may be used with a singular or a plural verb.
bar•racks (bar′əks) *plural noun.*

> at; āpe; fär; câre; end; mē; it; īce; pîerce; hot; ōld; sông; fôrk; oil; out; up; ūse; rūle; půll; tûrn; chin; sing; shop; thin; this; hw in white; zh in treasure. The symbol ə stands for the unstressed vowel sound in about, taken, pencil, lemon, and circus.

729

beloved Loved very much. The dog was *beloved* by the whole neighborhood.
be•lov•ed (bi luv′id *or* bi luvd′) *adjective.*

bid To offer to pay. We *bid* thirty-five dollars for the old desk at the auction. *Verb.*— An offer to pay money. The rug was sold to the person who made the highest *bid. Noun.*
bid (bid) *verb,* bid, *or* bidden, bidding; *noun, plural* bids.

biscuit 1. A small cake of baked dough. For breakfast, he had eggs, bacon, juice, and a *biscuit.* **2.** A cracker. Every afternoon, she has tea and *biscuits.*
bis•cuit (bis′kit) *noun, plural* biscuits.

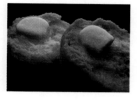

Word History
Cuit is the French word for "cooked." *Biscuit* comes from a 14th-century French word *bescuit,* meaning "twice-cooked bread."

brand-new Completely new. My aunt just bought a *brand-new* car.
brand-new (brand′nü *or* brand′nü) *adjective.*

brilliant 1. Very intelligent. That woman is a *brilliant* scientist. **2.** Very bright; sparkling. The North Star is a *brilliant* light in the sky.
bril•liant (bril′yənt) *adjective.*

brisk 1. Quick and lively. She walked at a *brisk* pace. **2.** Refreshing; keen; bracing. We walked in the *brisk* winter air.
brisk (brisk) *adjective,* brisker, briskest.

broad 1. Large from one side to the other side; wide. The side of the red barn is so *broad* that you can see it from a mile away. **2.** Wide in range; not limited. We have a *broad* knowledge of U.S. history.
broad (brôd) *adjective,* broader, broadest.

bulge To swell out. Because he put so many clothes in it, the suitcase *bulged. Verb.*— A rounded part that swells out. The rag made a *bulge* in the mechanic's back pocket. *Noun.*
bulge (bulj) *verb,* bulged, bulging; *noun, plural* bulges; *adjective,* bulging.

730

canoe To paddle or ride in a canoe. During the summer, they liked to go *canoeing* on the lake. *Verb.*— A light narrow boat, usually pointed at both ends and moved and steered with a paddle. The *canoe* tipped over when Eddie stood up. *Noun.*
ca•noe (kə nü′) *verb,* canoed, canoeing; *noun, plural* canoes.

captive A person or animal captured and held by force; prisoner. The police kept the *captive* in jail. *Noun.*—Held prisoner. The *captive* lion was kept in a cage. *Adjective.*
▲ **Synonym:** prisoner
cap•tive (kap′tiv) *noun, plural* captives; *adjective.*

captivity The state of being captive. Wolves live longer in *captivity* than in the wild.
cap•tiv•i•ty (kap ti′ və tē) *noun.*

celebration 1. The festivities carried on to observe or honor a special day or event. The wedding *celebration* is usually shared by friends and family. **2.** The act of celebrating. We went to the *celebration* of my cousin's graduation.
cel•e•bra•tion (sel′ ə brā′ shən) *noun, plural* celebrations; *adjective,* celebratory.

century A period of one hundred years. The time from 1651 to 1750 is one *century.*
century (sen′ chə rē) *noun, plural* centuries

challenge 1. Something calling for work, effort, and the use of one's talents. Chemistry is a real *challenge.* **2.** A call to take part in a contest or fight. In the days of duels, only a coward would refuse a *challenge. Noun.*—To question the truth or correctness of. They *challenged* my claim that bats are mammals. *Verb.*
chal•lenge (chal′ənj) *noun, plural* challenges; *verb,* challenged, challenging.

at; āpe; fär; câre; end; mē; it; īce; pîerce; hot; ōld; sông; fôrk; oil; out; up; ūse; rüle; pùll; tûrn; chin; sing; shop; thin; this; hw in white; zh in treasure. The symbol ə stands for the unstressed vowel sound in about, taken, pencil, lemon, and circus.

731

---

chant A singing or shouting of words over and over. *Chants* usually have a strong rhythm. *Noun.* — To sing or shout in a chant. At the election rally, the group *chanted* the name of their favorite candidate. *Verb.*
chant (chant) *noun, plural* chants; *verb,* chanted, chanting.

Word History
Chant, as it is spelled today, is based on the Middle English word *chaunten.* The Latin word *cantare,* which means "to sing," is the original basis of the word.

circulate 1. To pass from person to person. Bills and coins have *circulated* in the United States since Colonial times. **2.** To move around widely among different places. The window fan *circulates* air around the room.
cir•cu•late (sûr′kyə lāt′) *verb,* circulated, circulating.

climate The average weather conditions of a place or region through the year. Climate includes average temperature, rainfall, humidity, and wind conditions. Southern California has a warm, mild *climate.*
cli•mate (kli′mit) *noun, plural* climates.

cling To stick closely. The wet pants were *clinging* to her legs.
cling (kling) *verb,* clung, clinging.

clipper 1. A tool used for cutting. Use *clippers* to cut your fingernails. **2.** A fast sailing ship. American *clippers* sailed all over the world.
clip•per (klip′ər) *noun, plural* clippers.

clover A small plant with leaves of three leaflets and rounded, fragrant flowers of white, red, or purple.
clo•ver (klō′vər) *noun, plural* clovers.

cluster To grow or group in a cluster. We all *clustered* around the campfire. *Verb.*— A number of things of the same kind that grow or are grouped together. Grapes grow in *clusters. Noun.*
clus•ter (klus′tər) *verb,* clustered, clustering; *noun, plural* clusters.

732

---

combine To join together; unite. We *combined* eggs, flour, and milk to make the batter. *Verb.* — A farm machine that harvests and threshes grain. *Noun.*
com•bine (kəm bin′ *for verb;* kom′bin *for noun*) *verb,* combined, combining; *noun, plural* combines.

commercial An advertising message on radio or television. *Noun.*— Relating to business or trade. I plan to take *commercial* subjects in high school. *Adjective.*
com•mer•cial (kə mûr′shəl) *noun, plural* commercials.

communicate To exchange or pass along feelings, thoughts, or information. People *communicate* by speaking or writing.
com•mu•ni•cate (kə mū′ni kāt′) *verb,* communicated, communicating.

compare 1. To say or think that something is like something else. The writer *compared* the boom of big guns to the sound of thunder. **2.** To study in order to find out how persons or things are alike or different. We *compared* our watches and saw that your watch was five minutes ahead of mine.
com•pare (kəm pâr′) *verb,* compared, comparing.

compass 1. An instrument for showing directions; it has a magnetic needle that points to the north. Pilots, sailors, and many other people use compasses. The camper was able to get home because his *compass* showed him which way was west. **2.** An instrument for drawing circles or measuring distances, made up of two arms joined together at the top. One arm ends in a point and the other holds a pencil. Using a *compass,* the student was able to create a perfect circle on her drawing paper.
com•pass (kum′pəs) *noun, plural* compasses.

at; āpe; fär; câre; end; mē; it; īce; pîerce; hot; ōld; sông; fôrk; oil; out; up; ūse; rüle; pùll; tûrn; chin; sing; shop; thin; this; hw in white; zh in treasure. The symbol ə stands for the unstressed vowel sound in about, taken, pencil, lemon, and circus.

733

Glossary

G3

complicated Hard to understand or do. The directions for putting together the bicycle were too *complicated* for me to follow.
▲ **Synonym:** difficult
com•pli•ca•ted (kom′pli kā′tid) *adjective.*

confusion 1. The condition of being confused; disorder. In my *confusion*, I gave the wrong answer. 2. A mistaking of one person or thing for another. Mistaking John for his twin brother Tom is a common *confusion*.
con•fu•sion (kən fū′zhən) *noun, plural* **confusions.**

connect 1. To fasten or join together. *Connect* the trailer to the car. 2. To consider as related; associate. We *connect* robins with spring.
con•nect (kə nekt′) *verb,* **connected, connecting.**

contain 1. To include as a part of. Candy *contains* sugar. 2. To hold. The jar *contains* candy.
con•tain (kən tān′) *verb,* **contained, containing.**

coral A hard substance like stone, found in tropical seas. Coral is made up of the skeletons of tiny sea animals. *Coral* is beautiful when growing underwater, and it is very pretty as a decoration out of the water, too. *Noun.*— Having the color coral; pinkish red. She decided to use a *coral* nail polish. *Adjective.*
cor•al (kôr′əl) *noun, plural* **corals;** *adjective.*

county 1. One of the sections into which a state or country is divided. The longest bridge in the whole state is in that *county*. 2. The people living in a county. Most of the *county* came to the fair.
coun•ty (koun′tē) *noun, plural* **counties.**

crate A box made of slats of wood. We broke up the old apple *crates* to use in our bonfire. *Noun.*—To pack in a crate or crates. The farmer *crated* the lettuce. *Verb.*
crate (krāt) *noun, plural* **crates;** *verb,* **crated, crating.**

734

crate

Dd

damage Harm that makes something less valuable or useful. The flood caused great *damage* to farms. *Noun.*— To harm or injure. Rain *damaged* the young plants. *Verb.*
dam•age (dam′ij) *noun, plural* **damages;** *verb,* **damaged, damaging.**

dart To move suddenly and quickly. The rabbit *darted* into the bushes. *Verb.*— A thin, pointed object that looks like a small arrow. He hit the target with each *dart* that he threw. *Noun.*
dart (därt) *verb,* **darted, darting;** *noun, plural* **darts.**

desire A longing; wish. I have always had a great *desire* to travel. *Noun.*—To wish for; long for. My sister *desires* a basketball more than anything. *Verb.*
de•sire (di zīr′) *noun, plural* **desires;** *verb,* **desired, desiring.**

crumple 1. To press or crush into wrinkles or folds. He *crumpled* up the letter and threw it into the trash can. 2. To fall down or collapse. The old shack *crumpled* when the bulldozer rammed it.
crum•ple (krum′pəl) *verb,* **crumpled, crumpling.**

culture An appreciation of the arts, knowledge, and good taste and manners that are the result of education. The literature professor is a very *cultured* woman. *Adjective.* —The arts, beliefs, and customs that make up a way of life for a group of people at a certain time. We are studying the *culture* of the Inuit. *Noun.*
cul•ture (kul′chər) *noun, plural* **cultures;** *adjective,* **cultured.**

at; āpe; fär; câre; end; mē; it; īce; pîerce; hot; ōld; sŏng; fôrk; oil; out; up; ūse; rūle; pull; tûrn; chin; sing; shop; thin; this; hw in white; zh in treasure. The symbol ə stands for the unstressed vowel sound in about, taken, pencil, lemon, and circus.

735

destroy To ruin completely; wreck. The earthquake *destroyed* the city.
▲ **Synonym:** ruin
de•stroy (di stroi′) *verb,* **destroyed, destroying.**

disaster 1. An event that causes much suffering or loss. The flood was a *disaster*. 2. Something that does not go right. My birthday party was a *disaster* because it rained.
▲ **Synonym:** catastrophe
dis•as•ter (di zas′tər) *noun, plural* **disasters.**

display To show or exhibit. The art museum is now *displaying* some of Monet's paintings. *Verb.* —A show or exhibit. A hug is a *display* of affection. *Noun.*
dis•play (dis plā′) *verb,* **displayed, displaying;** *noun, plural* **displays.**

ditch A long, narrow hole dug in the ground. Ditches are used to drain off water. After the rain shower, the *ditch* was full. *Noun.*— To make an emergency landing in water. No pilot wants to have to *ditch* an airplane. *Verb.*
ditch (dich) *noun, plural* **ditches;** *verb,* **ditched, ditching.**

downstage Toward the front of a theatrical stage. The prop was supposed to land *downstage* left. *Adverb* or *adjective.*
down•stage (doun′stāj′) *adverb; adjective.*

Ee

editor 1. A person who edits. The *editor* made changes in the book after talking with its author. 2. A person who writes editorials. The newspaper *editor* wrote an article in favor of raising city taxes.
ed•i•tor (ed′i tər) *noun, plural* **editors.**

eerie Strange in a scary way; making people frightened or nervous. Walking through that abandoned house was an *eerie* experience.
▲ **Synonym:** creepy
ee•rie (îr′ē) *adjective,* **eerier, eeriest.**

736

eldest Born first; oldest. I am the *eldest* of three children.
el•dest (el′dist) *adjective.*

elegant Rich and fine in quality. The museum has a major display of *elegant* costumes.
▲ **Synonym:** tasteful
el•e•gant (el′i gənt) *adjective; noun,* **elegance;** *adverb,* **elegantly.**

Word History
The word *elegant* first appeared in the English language in the 15th century. The word comes from the Latin *eligere*, which means "to select."

endanger 1. To threaten with becoming extinct. Pollution is *endangering* many different species of animals. 2. To put in a dangerous situation. The flood *endangered* the lives of hundreds of people.
▲ **Synonym:** risk
en•dan•ger (en dān′jər) *verb,* **endangered, endangering.**

endless 1. Having no limit or end; going on forever. The drive across the desert seemed *endless*. 2. Without ends. A circle is *endless*.
end•less (end′lis) *adjective.*

enterprise Something that a person plans or tries to do. An *enterprise* is often something difficult or important. The search for the treasure was an exciting *enterprise*.
en•ter•prise (en′tər prīz′) *noun, plural* **enterprises.**

entertain 1. To keep interested and amused. The clown *entertained* the children. 2. To have as a guest. They often *entertain* people in their house in the country.
en•ter•tain (en′tər tān′) *verb,* **entertained, entertaining.**

at; āpe; fär; câre; end; mē; it; īce; pîerce; hot; ōld; sŏng; fôrk; oil; out; up; ūse; rūle; pull; tûrn; chin; sing; shop; thin; this; hw in white; zh in treasure. The symbol ə stands for the unstressed vowel sound in about, taken, pencil, lemon, and circus.

737

Glossary

errand 1. A short trip to do something. I have to run several *errands* this morning. 2. Something a person is sent to do; the purpose of such a trip. Our *errand* was to buy the newspaper.
er•rand (er′ənd) *noun, plural* **errands.**

exist 1. To be found. Outside of zoos, polar bears *exist* only in arctic regions. 2. To be real. I do not believe that ghosts *exist.*
ex•ist (eg zist′) *verb,* **existed, existing.**

expensive Having a high price; very costly. The town bought an *expensive* new fire engine.
▲ **Synonym:** costly
ex•pen•sive (ek spen′siv) *adjective.*

extinct 1. No longer existing. The dodo became *extinct* because people hunted it for food. 2. No longer active. The village is built over an *extinct* volcano.
ex•tinct (ek stingkt′) *adjective; noun,* **extinction.**

extraordinary Very unusual; remarkable. The teacher said my friend had *extraordinary* talent.
ex•tra•or•di•nar•y (ek strôr′də ner′ē *or* ek′strə ôr′də ner′ē) *adjective.*

738

Ff

fang A long, pointed tooth. When trying to look threatening, a wolf shows its *fangs.*
fang (fang) *noun, plural* **fangs.**

feeble Not strong; weak. That is a *feeble* excuse.
fee•ble (fē′bəl) *adjective,* **feebler, feeblest;** *noun,* **feebleness;** *adverb,* **feebly.**

festival 1. A program of special activities or shows. We saw a foreign film at the film *festival.* 2. A celebration or holiday. There were plenty of delicious foods to try at the street *festival.*
fes•ti•val (fes′tə vəl) *noun, plural* **festivals.**

---

foggy 1. Full of or hidden by fog; misty. Driving is dangerous on *foggy* days and nights. 2. Confused or unclear. The ideas were *foggy* and the project needed more research to clear things up.
fog•gy (fôg′ē *or* fog′ē) *adjective,* **foggier, foggiest.**

foothill A low hill near the lower part of a mountain or mountain range. The cabin was in the *foothills* of the Blue Ridge Mountains.
foot•hill (fŭt′hil′) *noun, plural* **foothills.**

foul Very unpleasant or dirty. The water in the old well looked *foul. Adjective.* —A violation of the rules. The basketball player committed a *foul. Noun.*
▲ Another word that sounds like this is **fowl.**
foul (foul) *adjective,* **fouler, foulest;** *noun, plural* **fouls.**

fowl One of a number of birds used for food. Chicken, turkey, and duck are kinds of *fowl.* We always eat *fowl* for Thanksgiving dinner.
▲ Another word that sounds like this is **foul.**
fowl (foul) *noun, plural* **fowl** *or* **fowls.**

fowl

fragrance A sweet or pleasing smell. Roses have a beautiful *fragrance.*
▲ **Synonym:** smell
fra•grance (frā′grəns) *noun, plural* **fragrances.**

fray To separate into loose threads. Many years of wear had *frayed* the cuffs of the coat.
fray (frā) *verb,* **frayed, fraying.**

freeze 1. To harden because of the cold. When water *freezes,* it becomes ice. 2. To cover or block with ice. The cold weather *froze* the pipes.
freeze (frēz) *verb,* **froze, frozen, freezing.**

at; āpe; fär; câre; end; mē; it; īce; pîerce; hot; ōld; sông; fôrk; oil; out; up; ūse; rüle; půll; tûrn; chin; sing; shop; thin; **this;** hw in white; zh in treasure. The symbol ə stands for the unstressed vowel sound in about, taken, pencil, lemon, and circus.

739

---

fret To suffer emotional distress; irritation. My brother *frets* whenever he gets a low grade on a test. *Verb.* —One of the ridges fixed across the fingerboard of a stringed instrument such as a guitar. The notes get higher each time I move my finger up a *fret. Noun.*
fret (fret) *verb,* **fretted, fretting;** *noun, plural* **frets.**

Gg

gallon A unit of measure for liquids. A *gallon* equals four quarts, or about 3.8 liters.
gal•lon (gal′ən) *noun, plural* **gallons.**

garbage Things that are thrown out. All the spoiled food went into the *garbage.*
▲ **Synonym:** trash
gar•bage (gär′bij) *noun.*

generation 1. A group of persons born around the same time. My parents call us the younger *generation.* 2. One step in the line of descent from a common ancestor. A grandparent, parent, and child make up three *generations.*
gen•er•a•tion (jen′ə rāsh′ən) *noun, plural* **generations.**

gild To cover with a thin layer of gold. The artist *gilded* the picture frame.
▲ Another word that sounds like this is **guild.**
gild (gild) *verb,* **gilded** *or* **gilt, gilding.**

girth The measurement around an object. The *girth* of the old redwood tree was tremendous.
girth (gûrth) *noun, plural* **girths.**

glint To sparkle or flash. Her eyes *glinted* with merriment.
glint (glint) *verb,* **glinted, glinting;** *noun, plural* **glints.**

glisten To shine with reflected light. The snow *glistened* in the sun.
glis•ten (glis′ən) *verb,* **glistened, glistening.**

glum Very unhappy or disappointed. Every member of the losing team looked *glum* after the game.
glum (glum) *adjective.*

740

---

gourd A rounded fruit related to the pumpkin or squash. Gourds grow on vines and have a hard outer rind. The hollow *gourd* hung above the tub of water.
gourd (gôrd) *noun, plural* **gourds.**

governess A woman who supervises and cares for a child, especially in a private household. The *governess* made sure the children were ready for bed.
gov•ern•ess (guv′ər nis) *noun, plural* **governesses.**

graze 1. To feed on growing grass. The sheep *grazed* on the hillside. 2. To scrape or touch lightly in passing. The branch *grazed* the house when the wind blew.
graze (gāz) *verb,* **grazed, grazing.**

guilt 1. A feeling of having done something wrong; shame. I felt *guilt* because I got angry at a good friend. 2. The condition or fact of having done something wrong or having broken the law. The evidence proved the robber's *guilt.*
▲ Another word that sounds like this is **gilt.**
guilt (gilt) *noun; adjective,* **guilty.**

Hh

harbor A sheltered place along a coast. Ships and boats often anchor in a *harbor. Noun.* —To give protection or shelter to. It is against the law to *harbor* a criminal. *Verb.*
har•bor (här′bər) *noun, plural* **harbors;** *verb,* **harbored, harboring.**

haul To pull or move with force; drag. We *hauled* the trunk up the stairs. *Verb.* —The act of hauling. It was an easy *haul* by truck. *Noun.*
▲ Another word that sounds like this is **hall.**
haul (hôl) *verb,* **hauled, hauling;** *noun, plural* **hauls.**

at; āpe; fär; câre; end; mē; it; īce; pîerce; hot; ōld; sông; fôrk; oil; out; up; ūse; rüle; půll; tûrn; chin; sing; shop; thin; **this;** hw in white; zh in treasure. The symbol ə stands for the unstressed vowel sound in about, taken, pencil, lemon, and circus.

741

haze Mist, smoke, or dust in the air. The bridge was hidden in the *haze*.
haze (hāz) *noun, plural* **hazes.**

headlong 1. With the head first. The runner slid *headlong* into second base. **2.** In a reckless way; rashly. I rushed *headlong* into buying the bicycle.
head•long (hed'lông') *adverb.*

healthy Having or showing good health. She has a *healthy* outlook on life.
health•y (hel'thē) *adjective,* **healthier, healthiest.**

heave 1. To lift, raise, pull, or throw using force or effort. I *heaved* a rock across the stream. **2.** To utter in an effortful way. I *heaved* a sigh of relief.
heave (hēv) *verb,* **heaved, heaving.**

hilltop The top of a hill. From the *hilltop*, the hikers could see the smoke from the campfire.
hill•top (hil'top') *noun, plural* **hilltops.**

horizon 1. The line where the sky and the ground or the sea seem to meet. The fishing boat headed out to sea just as the sun rose above the *horizon*. **2.** The limit of a person's knowledge, interests, or experience. You can widen your *horizons* by reading books.
hor•i•zon (hə rī'zən) *noun, plural* **horizons.**

huddle To gather close together in a bunch. The scouts *huddled* around the campfire to keep warm. *Verb.*—A group of people or animals gathered close together. The football players formed a *huddle* to plan their next play. *Noun.*
hud•dle (hud'əl) *verb,* **huddled, huddling;** *noun, plural* **huddles.**

742

Ii

iceberg A very large piece of floating ice that has broken off from a glacier. Only the tip of the *iceberg* is visible above the surface of the water.
ice•berg (is'bûrg') *noun, plural* **icebergs.**

identify To find out or tell exactly who a person is or what a thing is; recognize. Can you *identify* this strange object?
▲ **Synonym:** recognize
i•den•ti•fy (ī den'tə fī') *verb,* **identified, identifying.**

ignorant 1. Not informed or aware. I wasn't wearing my watch, so I was *ignorant* of the time. **2.** Showing a lack of knowledge. The young cowhands were *ignorant* at first of how to brand cattle, but they learned quickly.
ig•no•rant (ig'nər ənt) *adjective.*

image 1. A person who looks very similar to someone else. That girl is the *image* of her mother. **2.** A picture or other likeness of a person or thing. A penny has an *image* of Abraham Lincoln on one side of it.
im•age (im'ij) *noun, plural* **images.**

importance The state of being important; having great value or meaning. Rain is of great *importance* to farmers, since crops can't grow without water.
im•por•tance (im pôr'təns) *noun.*

ingredient Any one of the parts that go into a mixture. Flour, eggs, sugar, and butter are the main *ingredients* of this cake.
in•gre•di•ent (in grē'dē ənt) *noun, plural* **ingredients.**

injury Harm or damage done to a person or thing. The accident caused an *injury* to my leg.
in•ju•ry (in'jə rē) *noun, plural* **injuries.**

inning One of the parts into which a baseball or softball game is divided. Both teams bat during an inning until three players on each team are put out. Our team won the game by scoring five runs in the last *inning*.
in•ning (in'ing) *noun, plural* **innings.**

at; āpe; fär; cåre; end; mē; it; īce; pīerce; hot; ōld; sông; fôrk; oil; out; up; ūse; rūle; pull; tûrn; chin; sing; shop; thin; this; hw in white; zh in treasure. The symbol ə stands for the unstressed vowel sound in about, taken, pencil, lemon, and circus.

743

inspect To look at closely and carefully. The official *inspected* our car and declared it safe to drive.
▲ **Synonym:** examine
in•spect (in spekt') *verb,* **inspected, inspecting.**

inspire 1. To stir the mind, feelings, or imagination of. The senator's speech *inspired* the audience. **2.** To fill with a strong, encouraging feeling. Success in school *inspired* me with hope for the future.
▲ **Synonym:** encourage
in•spire (in spir') *verb,* **inspired, inspiring.**

instance An example; case. There are many *instances* of immigrants becoming famous Americans.
in•stance (in'stəns) *noun, plural* **instances.**

instinct A way of acting or behaving that a person or animal is born with and does not have to learn. Birds build nests by *instinct*.
in•stinct (in'stingkt') *noun, plural* **instincts.**

Jj

jagged Having sharp points that stick out. Some eagles build nests on *jagged* cliffs.
jag•ged (jag'id) *adjective.*

Kk

keel To fall over suddenly; collapse. The heat in the crowded subway caused two people to *keel* over. *Verb.*— A wooden or metal piece that runs along the center of the bottom of many ships and boats. When we sailed through the shallow waters, the *keel* scraped along the bottom of the lake. *Noun.*
keel (kēl) *verb,* **keeled, keeling;** *noun, plural* **keels.**

744

knapsack A bag made of canvas, leather, nylon, or other material that is used for carrying clothes, books, equipment, or other supplies. A knapsack is strapped over the shoulders and carried on the back. Because she left her *knapsack* on the bus, she couldn't turn in her homework assignment.
▲ **Synonym:** backpack
knap•sack (nap'sak') *noun, plural* **knapsacks.**

knowledge 1. An understanding that is gained through experience or study. I have enough *knowledge* of football to be able to follow a game. **2.** The fact of knowing. The *knowledge* that the car could slide on the icy road made the driver more careful.
knowl•edge (nol'ij) *noun.*

Ll

labor To do hard work. The two women *labored* over the quilt, hoping to finish it in time for the birthday party. *Verb.*—Hard work; toil. The farmers were tired after their *labor. Noun.*
la•bor (lā'bər) *verb,* **labored, laboring;** *noun, plural* **labors.**

launch To start something. The company *launched* its store with a big sale. *Verb.*—The act or process of launching. We watched the rocket *launch* on television. *Noun.*
launch (lônch) *verb,* **launched, launching;** *noun, plural* **launches.**

league 1. A number of people, groups, or countries joined together for a common purpose. Those two teams belong to the same *league*. **2.** A measure of distance used in the past, equal to about three miles. The army's camp was only two *leagues* from the city.
league (lēg) *noun, plural* **leagues.**

at; āpe; fär; cåre; end; mē; it; īce; pīerce; hot; ōld; sông; fôrk; oil; out; up; ūse; rūle; pull; tûrn; chin; sing; shop; thin; this; hw in white; zh in treasure. The symbol ə stands for the unstressed vowel sound in about, taken, pencil, lemon, and circus.

745

Glossary

linger To stay on as if not wanting to leave; move slowly. The fans *lingered* outside the stadium to see the team.
> lin•ger (ling′gər) *verb*, **lingered, lingering.**

lodge A small house, cottage, or cabin. The hunters stayed at a *lodge* in the mountains. *Noun.*—To live in a place for a while. People *lodged* in the school during the flood. *Verb.*
> lodge (loj) *noun, plural* **lodges;** *verb,* **lodged, lodging.**

loft 1. The upper floor, room, or space in a building. The artist cleaned his *loft*. 2. An upper floor or balcony in a large hall or church. The choir sang in the choir *loft*.
> loft (lôft) *noun, plural* **lofts.**

loosen 1. To make or become looser. *Loosen* your necktie. 2. To set free or release. The dog had been *loosened* from its leash.
> loosen (lü′sen) *verb,* **loosened, loosening.**

lurk 1. To lie hidden, especially in preparation for an attack. Snakes *lurk* under rocks. 2. To move about quietly; sneak. Thieves *lurk* in the shadows.
> lurk (lûrk) *verb,* **lurked, lurking.**

Mm

machine 1. A device that does a particular job, made up of a number of parts that work together. A lawn mower, a hair dryer, and a printing press are *machines*. 2. A simple device that lessens the force needed to move an object. A lever and a pulley are simple *machines*.
> ma•chine (mə shēn′) *noun, plural* **machines.**

malachite A green mineral that is used for making ornaments.
> mal•a•chite (mal′ə kit′) *noun.*

mammal A kind of animal that is warm-blooded and has a backbone. Human beings are *mammals*.
> mam•mal (mam′əl) *noun, plural* **mammals.**

marine Having to do with or living in the sea. Whales are *marine* animals. *Adjective.*—A member of the Marine Corps. She joined the *Marines* after she graduated. *Noun.*
> ma•rine (mə rēn′) *adjective; noun, plural* **marines.**

marketplace A place where food and other products are bought and sold. In old towns the *marketplace* was often in a square.
> mar•ket•place (mär′kit plās′) *noun, plural* **marketplaces.**

marvel To feel wonder and astonishment. We *marveled* at the acrobat's skill. *Verb.*—A wonderful or astonishing thing. Space travel is one of the *marvels* of modern science. *Noun.*
> mar•vel (mär′vəl) *verb,* **marveled, marveling;** *noun, plural* **marvels.**

mature Having reached full growth or development; ripe. When a puppy becomes *mature* it is called a dog. *Adjective.*—To become fully grown or developed. The tomatoes are *maturing* fast. *Verb.*
> ma•ture (mə chùr′ *or* mə tùr′) *adjective; verb,* **matured, maturing.**

maze A confusing series of paths or passageways through which people may have a hard time finding their way. I got lost in the *maze* of hallways in my new school.
> maze (māz) *noun, plural* **mazes.**

at; āpe; fär; câre; end; mē; it; īce; pîerce; hot; ōld; sông; fôrk; oil; out; up; ūse; rüle; pùll; tûrn; chin; sing; shop; thin; **this; hw** in white; zh in treasure. The symbol ə stands for the unstressed vowel sound in about, taken, pencil, lemon, and circus.

memorize To learn by heart; fix in the memory. You can *memorize* the poem by reciting it over and over.
> mem•o•rize (mem′ə riz′) *verb,* **memorized, memorizing.**

merely Nothing more than; only. Your explanations are *merely* excuses.
> mere•ly (mîr′lē) *adverb.*

messenger A person who delivers messages or runs errands. The *messenger* was delayed by traffic.
> mes•sen•ger (mes′ən jər) *noun, plural* **messengers.**

method 1. A way of doing something. Speaking on the telephone is a *method* of communicating. 2. Order or system. I could not find what I wanted because the books had been shelved without *method*.
> meth•od (meth′əd) *noun, plural* **methods.**

microscope A device for looking at things that are too small to be seen with the naked eye. It has one or more lenses that produce an enlarged image of anything viewed through it.
> mi•cro•scope (mi′krə skōp′) *noun, plural* **microscopes.**

microscope

mingle 1. To put or come together; mix; join. This stream *mingles* with others to form a river. 2. To move about freely; join; associate. We *mingled* with the other guests.
> min•gle (ming′gəl) *verb,* **mingled, mingling.**

molar Any one of the large teeth at the back of the mouth. *Molars* have broad surfaces for grinding food.
> mo•lar (mō′lər) *noun, plural* **molars.**

moonscape View of the surface of the moon.
> moon•scape (mün′skāp′) *noun, plural* **moonscapes.**

mound A slightly raised area. The pitcher stands on the *mound* to pitch the ball. *Noun.*—To pile in a hill or heap. I like to *mound* ice cream on top of my pie. *Verb.*
> mound (mound) *noun, plural* **mounds;** *verb,* **mounded, mounding.**

mug A large drinking cup with a handle, often made of pottery or metal. I drink tea out of my purple *mug*. *Noun.*—To attack and rob someone. A lady was *mugged* of all her belongings. *Verb.*
> mug (mug) *noun, plural* **mugs;** *verb,* **mugged, mugging.**

mutter To speak in a low, unclear way with the mouth almost closed. I *muttered* to myself. *Verb.* —Oral sounds produced in a low, unclear way. There was a *mutter* of disapproval from the audience. *Noun.*
> mut•ter (mut′ər) *verb,* **muttered, muttering;** *noun.*

Nn

native Originally living or growing in a region or country. Raccoons are *native* to America. *Adjective.* —A person who was born in a particular country or place. One of my classmates is a *native* of Germany. *Noun.*
> na•tive (nā′tiv) *adjective; noun, plural* **natives.**

natural 1. Found in nature; not made by people; not artificial. *Natural* rock formations overlook the river. 2. Existing from birth; not the result of teaching or training. Is your musical talent *natural*, or did you take lessons?
> nat•u•ral (nach′ər əl) *adjective.*

neighbor A person, place, or thing that is next to or near another. Our *neighbor* took care of our dog while we were away.
> neigh•bor (nā′bər) *noun, plural* **neighbors.**

newsletter A small publication containing news of interest to a special group of people. Our chess club publishes a monthly *newsletter*.
> news•let•ter (nüz′let′ər) *noun, plural* **newsletters.**

at; āpe; fär; câre; end; mē; it; īce; pîerce; hot; ōld; sông; fôrk; oil; out; up; ūse; rüle; pùll; tûrn; chin; sing; shop; thin; **this; hw** in white; zh in treasure. The symbol ə stands for the unstressed vowel sound in about, taken, pencil, lemon, and circus.

Glossary

nip 1. To bite or pinch quickly and not hard. The parrot *nipped* my finger. 2. To cut off by pinching. The gardener *nipped* the dead leaves off the plants.
nip (nip) *verb,* **nipped, nipping.**

nursery 1. A baby's bedroom. The baby's *nursery* was painted pink and blue. 2. A place where young children are taken care of during the day.
nurs•er•y (nûr′sə rē) *noun, plural* **nurseries.**

occasion 1. An important or special event. The baby's first birthday was an *occasion.* 2. A time when something happens. I have met that person on several *occasions.*
oc•ca•sion (ə kā′zhən) *noun, plural* **occasions.**

opponent A person or group that is against another in a fight, contest, or discussion. The soccer team beat its *opponent.*
▲ **Synonym:** enemy
op•po•nent (ə pō′nənt) *noun, plural* **opponents.**

orchard An area of land where fruit trees are grown. We picked apples in the apple *orchard.*
or•chard (ôr′chərd) *noun, plural* **orchards.**

organization 1. A group of people joined together for a particular purpose. The Red Cross is an international *organization.* 2. The act of organizing. Who is responsible for the *organization* of the school dance?
or•gan•i•za•tion (ôr′gə nə zā′shən) *noun, plural* **organizations.**

original Relating to or belonging to the origin or beginning of something; first. The *original* owner of the house still lives there. *Adjective.* —Something that is original; not a copy, imitation, or translation. That painting is an *original* by Monet. *Noun.*
o•rig•i•nal (ə rij′ə nəl) *adjective; noun, plural* **originals.**

750

orphan A child whose parents are dead. The little *orphan* was raised by her grandparents. *Noun.* —To make an orphan of. The war *orphaned* many children. *Verb.*
or•phan (ôr′fən) *noun, plural* **orphans;** *verb,* **orphaned, orphaning.**

overalls Loose-fitting trousers with a piece that covers the chest and attached suspenders.
o•ver•alls (ō′vər ôlz′) *plural noun.*

overcome 1. To get the better of; beat or conquer. The tired runner couldn't *overcome* the others in the race. 2. To get over or deal with. I *overcame* my fear of small spaces.
▲ **Synonym:** defeat
o•ver•come (ō′vər kum′) *verb,* **overcame, overcome, overcoming.**

overflow To be so full that the contents spill over. The bathtub *overflowed. Verb.*— Something that flows over. We mopped up the *overflow. Noun.*
o•ver•flow (ō′vər flō′ *for verb;* ō′vər flō′ *for noun*) *verb,* **overflowed, overflowing;** *noun.*

oxygen A colorless, odorless gas that makes up about one fifth of our air.
ox•y•gen (ok′si jən) *noun.*

 Pp

pathway A course or route taken to reach a particular place. This *pathway* leads to the rose garden.
path•way (path′wā′) *noun, plural* **pathways.**

patient A person under the care or treatment of a doctor. The pediatrician had many *patients* to see. *Noun.*—Having or showing an ability to put up with hardship, pain, trouble, or delay without getting angry or upset. I tried to be *patient* while I waited in the line at the post office. *Adjective.*
pa•tient (pā′shənt) *noun, plural* **patients;** *adjective.*

at; āpe; fär; câre; end; mē; it; īce; pîerce; hot; ōld; sông; fôrk; oil; out; up; ūse; rüle; püll; tûrn; chin; sing; shop; thin; this; hw in white; zh in treasure. The symbol ə stands for the unstressed vowel sound in about, taken, pencil, lemon, and circus.

751

peddler One who carries goods from place to place and offers them for sale.
▲ **Synonym:** vendor
ped•dler (ped′lər) *noun, plural* **peddlers;** *verb,* **peddled, peddling.**

percent The number of parts in every hundred. The symbol for *percent* when it is written with a number is %.
per•cent (pər sent′) *noun.*

permit To allow or let. My parents will not *permit* me to play outside after dark. *Verb.*—A written order giving permission to do something. You need a *permit* to fish here. *Noun.*
per•mit (pər mit′ *for verb;* pûr′mit *or* pər mit′ *for noun*) *verb,* **permitted, permitting;** *noun, plural* **permits.**

Word History
Permit comes from the Latin word *permittere,* "to let through."

pesky Troublesome or annoying. If that *pesky* fly does not stop buzzing in my ear, I'll swat it.
▲ **Synonym:** annoying
pes•ky (pes′kē) *adjective,* **peskier, peskiest.**

plantation A large estate or farm worked by laborers who live there. Before the Civil War, cotton was grown on *plantations.*
plan•ta•tion (plan tā′shən) *noun, plural* **plantations.**

pod A part of a plant that holds a number of seeds as they grow. Beans and peas grow in *pods.*
pod (pod) *noun, plural* **pods.**

poisonous Containing a drug or other substance that harms or kills by chemical action. Many household chemicals are *poisonous.*
poi•son•ous (poi′zən əs) *adjective.*

poncho A cloak made of one piece of cloth or other material, with a hole in the middle for the head.
pon•cho (pon′chō) *noun, plural* **ponchos.**

752

portable Easy to carry from place to place. *Portable* computers are very popular.
port•a•ble (pôr′tə bəl) *adjective.*

portfolio 1. A case for carrying loose pictures, pamphlets, or papers. I placed all the pictures in my *portfolio.* 2. A set of drawings or pictures bound in a book or a folder. I must get my *portfolio* ready for the meeting.
port•fo•lio (pôrt fō′lē ō′) *noun, plural* **portfolios.**

pottery Pots, bowls, dishes, and other things made from clay. I made a bowl in *pottery* class.
pot•ter•y (pot′ə rē) *noun.*

pouch 1. A bag; sack. The mail carrier took the letters out of her *pouch.* 2. A pocket of skin in some animals. Kangaroos and opossums carry their young in *pouches.*
pouch (pouch) *noun, plural* **pouches.**

prairie Flat or rolling land covered with grass, and with few or no trees.
prai•rie (prâr′ē) *noun, plural* **prairies.**

prairie

praise An expression of high regard and approval. The teacher had nothing but *praise* for the student's drawing. *Noun.*—To worship. The minister *praised* God in her sermon. *Verb.*
praise (prāz) *noun, plural* **praises;** *verb,* **praised, praising.**

prance 1. To spring forward on the hind legs. The colt *pranced* and leaped about the field. 2. To move in a proud, happy way. The children *pranced* around the house in their fancy costumes.
prance (prans) *verb,* **pranced, prancing.**

at; āpe; fär; câre; end; mē; it; īce; pîerce; hot; ōld; sông; fôrk; oil; out; up; ūse; rüle; püll; tûrn; chin; sing; shop; thin; this; hw in white; zh in treasure. The symbol ə stands for the unstressed vowel sound in about, taken, pencil, lemon, and circus.

753

prejudice Hatred or unfair treatment of a particular group, such as members of a race or religion. *Noun.*—To cause to have prejudice. Being hurt once by a dentist *prejudiced* me against all dentists. *Verb.*
prej•u•dice (prej′ə dis) *noun, plural* **prejudices;** *verb,* **prejudiced, prejudicing.**

preserve To keep from being lost, damaged, or decayed; protect. It is important that we *preserve* our freedoms. *Verb.*—An area set aside for the protection of plants and animals. Rare birds and mammals breed in that nature *preserve. Noun.*
pre•serve (pri zûrv′) *verb,* **preserved, preserving;** *noun, plural* **preserves.**

pressure The force exerted by one thing pushing against another. The *pressure* of his foot on the gas pedal caused the car to go faster. *Noun.*—To urge strongly. The salesperson tried to *pressure* me into buying something I didn't need. *Verb.*
pres•sure (presh′ər) *noun, plural* **pressures;** *verb,* **pressured, pressuring.**

previously Before; at an earlier time. We had been introduced *previously.*
▲ **Synonym:** earlier
pre•vi•ous•ly (prē′vē əs lē) *adverb.*

quibble A minor dispute or disagreement. It's foolish to have a *quibble* over nothing. *Noun.* To engage in petty arguing. The two sisters *quibbled* for half an hour about who would take out the garbage. *Verb.*
quib•ble (kwi′bəl) *noun, plural* **quibbles;** *verb,* **quibbled, quibbling.**

racial Of or relating to a race of human beings. *Racial* prejudice is prejudice against people because of their race.
ra•cial (rā′shəl) *adjective; adverb,* **racially.**

ramp A sloping platform or passageway connecting two different levels.
ramp (ramp) *noun, plural* **ramps.**

754

reef A ridge of sand, rock, or coral at or near the surface of the ocean. We like to swim near the beautiful *reefs.*
reef (rēf) *noun, plural* **reefs.**

reference 1. A person or thing referred to; source of information. The encyclopedia was the *reference* for my report. **2.** A statement that calls or directs attention to something. The authors made a *reference* to their book.
ref•er•ence (ref′ər əns *or* ref′rəns) *noun, plural* **references.**

reflect 1. To give back an image of something. I saw myself *reflected* in the pond. **2.** To turn or throw back. Sand *reflects* light and heat from the sun.
re•flect (ri flekt′) *verb,* **reflected, reflecting.**

rein One of two or more narrow straps attached to a bridle or bit, used to guide and control a horse. The jockey held tightly to the horse's *reins. Noun.*—To guide, control, or hold back. The rider tried to *rein* in the galloping horse. *Verb.*
rein (rān) *noun, plural* **reins;** *verb,* **reined, reining.**

related 1. Belonging to the same family. You and your cousins are *related.* **2.** Having some connection. I have problems *related* to school.
re•la•ted (ri lā′tid) *adjective.*

at; āpe; fär; câre; end; mē; it; īce; pîerce; hot; ōld; sông; fôrk; oil; out; up; ūse; rūle; pull; tûrn; chin; sing; shop; thin; this; hw in white; zh in treasure. The symbol ə stands for the unstressed vowel sound in about, taken, pencil, lemon, and circus.

755

release To set free; let go. The hostage was *released* after being held prisoner for ten days. *Verb.*—The act of releasing or the state of being released. The criminal's *release* from prison made headlines. *Noun.*
re•lease (ri lēs′) *verb,* **released, releasing;** *noun, plural* **releases.**

relieve 1. To free from discomfort or pain; comfort. The doctor gave me medicine to *relieve* my cough. **2.** To free from a job or duty. The lifeguards stayed on duty until they were *relieved.*
re•lieve (ri lēv′) *verb,* **relieved, relieving.**

reptile One of a class of cold-blooded animals with a backbone and dry, scaly skin, which move by crawling on their stomachs or creeping on short legs.
rep•tile (rep′təl *or* rep′til) *noun, plural* **reptiles.**

require 1. To have a need of. We all *require* food and sleep. **2.** To force, order, or demand. The law *requires* drivers to stop at a red light.
re•quire (ri kwir′) *verb,* **required, requiring.**

research A careful study to find and learn facts. I did *research* in the library for my report. *Noun.*—To do research on or for. I *researched* my speech by reading many books on the subject. *Verb.*
re•search (ri sûrch′ *or* rē′sûrch′) *verb,* **researched, researching;** *noun, plural* **researches.**

resemble To be like or similar to. That hat *resembles* mine.
re•sem•ble (ri zem′bəl) *verb,* **resembled, resembling.**

resound 1. To be filled with sound. The stadium *resounded* with cheers. **2.** To make a loud, long, or echoing sound. Thunder *resounded* in the air.
re•sound (ri zound′) *verb,* **resounded, resounding.**

restless 1. Not able to rest. We got *restless* during the long speech. **2.** Not giving rest. The patient spent a *restless* night.
rest•less (rest′lis) *adjective; adverb,* **restlessly;** *noun,* **restlessness.**

756

rhythm A regular or orderly repeating of sounds or movements. We marched to the *rhythm* of drums.
rhythm (rith′əm) *noun, plural* **rhythms.**

roadblock A barrier or obstacle that prevents people or cars from passing through.
road•block (rōd′blok′) *noun, plural* **roadblocks.**

robot A machine that can do some of the same things that a human being can do.
ro•bot (rō′bət *or* rō′bot) *noun, plural* **robots.**

sacrifice The giving up of something for the sake of someone or something else. The parents made many *sacrifices* in order to send their children to college. *Noun.*—To offer as a sacrifice. Ancient peoples *sacrificed* animals to their gods. *Verb.*
sac•ri•fice (sak′rə fis′) *noun, plural* **sacrifices;** *verb,* **sacrificed, sacrificing;** *adjective,* **sacrificial.**

sage A very wise person, usually old and respected. *Noun.*— Having or showing great wisdom and sound judgment. My grandparents often give me *sage* advice. *Adjective.*
sage (sāj) *noun, plural* **sages;** *adjective,* **sager, sagest.**

sagebrush A plant that grows on the dry plains of western North America.
sage•brush (sāj′brush′) *noun.*

scamper To run or move quickly. The rabbit *scampered* into the woods.
scam•per (skam′pər) *verb,* **scampered, scampering.**

at; āpe; fär; câre; end; mē; it; īce; pîerce; hot; ōld; sông; fôrk; oil; out; up; ūse; rūle; pull; tûrn; chin; sing; shop; thin; this; hw in white; zh in treasure. The symbol ə stands for the unstressed vowel sound in about, taken, pencil, lemon, and circus.

757

Glossary

G9

scribble To write or draw quickly or carelessly. I *scribbled* a note to my friend. *Verb.*—Writing or drawing that is made by scribbling. The paper was covered with messy *scribbles. Noun.*
scrib•ble (skrib′əl) *verb,* **scribbled, scribbling;** *noun, plural* **scribbles;** *noun,* **scribbler.**

scuba (Self-Contained Underwater Breathing Apparatus) Equipment used for swimming underwater.
scu•ba (skü′bə) *noun.*

sediment 1. Rocks, dirt, or other solid matter carried and left by water, glaciers, or wind. 2. Small pieces of matter that settle at the bottom of a liquid. There was *sediment* at the bottom of the bottle.
sed•i•ment (sed′ə mənt) *noun.*

segregation The practice of setting one group apart from another.
seg•re•ga•tion (seg′ri gā′shən) *noun.*

settlement 1. A small village or group of houses. During the 1800s, pioneers built many *settlements* in the American West. 2. The act of settling or the condition of being settled. The *settlement* of Jamestown took place in 1607.
set•tle•ment (set′əl mənt) *noun, plural* **settlements.**

shanty A small, poorly built house; shack. During the Depression, many poor families lived in *shanties.*
▲ **Synonym:** shack
shan•ty (shan′tē) *noun, plural* **shanties.**

shoreline The line where a body of water and the land meet. My friend has a house near the *shoreline.*
shore•line (shôr′līn′) *noun.*

shortcut 1. A quicker way of reaching a place. I took a *shortcut* to school. 2. A way of doing something faster. Don't use any *shortcuts* in your science experiment.
short•cut (shôrt′cut′) *noun, plural* **shortcuts.**

shriek A loud, sharp cry or sound. The child let out a *shriek* of laughter. *Noun.*—To utter a loud, sharp cry or sound. We all *shrieked* with laughter at her jokes. *Verb.*
shriek (shrēk) *noun, plural* **shrieks;** *verb,* **shrieked, shrieking.**

758

shutter 1. A movable cover for a window, usually attached to the frame by hinges. *Shutters* are used to shut out light 2. The part of a camera that snaps open and shuts quickly to let light onto the film when a picture is taken.
shut•ter (shut′ər) *noun, plural* **shutters.**

siren A device that makes a loud, shrill sound, used as a signal or warning. Ambulances and police cars have *sirens.*
si•ren (sī′rən) *noun, plural* **sirens.**

sketch A rough, quick drawing. The artist made several *sketches* of the model before starting the painting. *Noun.*—To make a sketch of. I *sketched* an old barn for my art class. *Verb.*
sketch (skech) *verb,* **sketched, sketching;** *noun, plural* **sketches.**

> **Word History**
> *Sketch* comes from the Dutch word *schets* and the Italian word *schizzo,* meaning "splash." A sketch is often a rough drawing, a splash of an idea that will later become a detailed finished product.

skill The power or ability to do something. *Skill* comes with practice and experience.
skill (skil) *noun, plural* **skills.**

skillet A shallow pan with a handle. A *skillet* is used for frying.
skil•let (skil′it) *noun, plural* **skillets.**

skim 1. To remove from the surface of a liquid. The cook *skimmed* the fat from the soup. 2. To read quickly. *Skim* the paper for the scores.
skim (skim) *verb,* **skimmed, skimming.**

at; āpe; fär; câre; end; mē; it; īce; pîerce; hot; ōld; sông; fôrk; oil; out; up; ūse; rüle; pûll; tûrn; chin; sing; shop; thin; <u>th</u>is; hw in white; zh in treasure. The symbol ə stands for the unstressed vowel sound in about, taken, pencil, lemon, and circus.

759

smog A combination of smoke and fog in the air. *Smog* is found especially over cities where there are factories and many cars.
smog (smog) *noun.*

> **Word History**
> The word *smog* was made using the first two letters of *smoke* and the last two letters of *fog.*

snout The front part of an animal's head, including nose, mouth, and jaws. My dog has a cute *snout.*
snout (snout) *noun, plural* **snouts.**

soapsuds Water that is bubbly with soap. I like my bath to be filled with *soapsuds.*
soap•suds (sōp′sudz′) *plural noun.*

soggy Very wet or damp; soaked. The soil was *soggy* after the rain.
sog•gy (sog′ē) *adjective,* **soggier, soggiest.**

soot A black, greasy powder that forms when such fuels as wood, coal, and oil are burned. The old chimney was caked with *soot.*
soot (sút *or* süt) *noun; adjective,* **sooty.**

spice The seeds or other parts of certain plants used to flavor food. Pepper, cloves, and cinnamon are spices. *Noun.*—To flavor with a spice or spices. I *spiced* the hamburgers. *Verb.*
spice (spīs) *noun, plural* **spices;** *verb,* **spiced, spicing;** *adjective,* **spicy.**

spike 1. Any sharp, pointed object or part that sticks out. Baseball shoes have *spikes* on the soles. 2. A large, heavy nail used to hold rails to railroad ties. It was difficult to hammer in the railroad *spike.*
spike (spīk) *noun, plural* **spikes.**

sponge A simple water animal that has a body that is full of holes and absorbs water easily. The dried skeletons of some *sponge* colonies are used for cleaning and washing. *Noun.*—To clean with a sponge. We *sponged* and dried the dirty walls. *Verb.*
sponge (spunj) *noun, plural* **sponges;** *verb,* **sponged, sponging.**

760

squall A strong gust of wind that arises very suddenly. Squalls often bring rain, snow, or sleet. We were forced indoors by a *squall* of snow.
squall (skwôl) *noun, plural* **squalls.**

> **Word History**
> The word *squall* first appeared in the English language in 1699. It is probably based on the Swedish word *skval,* which means "rushing water."

squeal To make a loud, shrill cry or sound. The little pigs *squealed* with excitement. *Verb.* —A loud, shrill cry or sound. The *squeal* of the brakes hurt my ears. *Noun.*
squeal (skwēl) *verb,* **squealed, squealing;** *noun, plural* **squeals.**

stake A stick or post pointed at one end so that it can be driven into the ground. The campers drove in *stakes* and tied the corners of the tent to them. *Noun.* — To fasten or hold up with a stake. The gardener *staked* the beans. *Verb.*
▲ Another word that sounds like this is **steak.**
stake (stāk) *noun, plural* **stakes;** *verb,* **staked, staking.**

sterilize To make free of bacteria and microorganisms. The nurse *sterilized* the scalpels before the operation.
ster•il•ize (ster′ə līz′) *verb,* **sterilized, sterilizing.**

stitch To make, fasten, or mend with stitches; sew. I *stitched* up the tear in my shirt. *Verb.*—One complete movement made with a needle and thread. *Noun.*
stitch (stich) *verb,* **stitched, stitching;** *noun, plural* **stitches.**

strew To spread by scattering. I have to clean my room because my clothes are *strewn* all over the place.
strew (strü) *verb,* **strewed, strewn, strewing.**

at; āpe; fär; câre; end; mē; it; īce; pîerce; hot; ōld; sông; fôrk; oil; out; up; ūse; rüle; pûll; tûrn; chin; sing; shop; thin; <u>th</u>is; hw in white; zh in treasure. The symbol ə stands for the unstressed vowel sound in about, taken, pencil, lemon, and circus.

761

stroll To walk in a slow, relaxed way. We *strolled* through the park. *Verb.* —A slow, relaxed walk. After dinner we took a *stroll. Noun.*
stroll (strōl) *verb,* **strolled, strolling;** *noun, plural* **strolls.**

sturdy Strong; hardy. Heavy trucks can drive on the *sturdy* bridge.
stur•dy (stûr′dē) *adjective,* **sturdier, sturdiest;** *adverb,* **sturdily;** *noun,* **sturdiness.**

success 1. A result hoped for; favorable end. The coach was pleased with the *success* of the game. **2.** A person or thing that does or goes well. The party was a big *success.*
suc•cess (sək ses′) *noun, plural* **successes;** *adjective,* **successful.**

sunrise The rising of the sun. We went to the beach to watch the *sunrise.*
sunrise (sun′rīz′) *noun, plural* **sunrises.**

swamp An area of wet land. The *swamp* looked scary and creepy. *Noun.* —To fill with water. High waves *swamped* the boat. *Verb.*
swamp (swomp) *noun, plural* **swamps;** *verb,* **swamped, swamping.**

swamp

talker One who exchanges spoken words in conversation. The two friends were great *talkers.*
talk•er (tôk′ ər) *noun, plural* **talkers**

teammate A person who is a member of the same team. We're basketball *teammates.*
team•mate (tēm′māt′) *noun, plural* **teammates.**

threat 1. A person or thing that might cause harm; danger. The outbreak of flu was a *threat* to the community. **2.** A statement of something that will be done to hurt or punish. The trespassers heeded our *threat.*
threat (thret) *noun, plural* **threats.**

ton A measure of weight equal to 2,000 pounds in the United States and Canada, and 2,240 pounds in Great Britain.
ton (tun) *noun, plural* **tons.**

tractor A vehicle with heavy tires or tracks. *Tractors* are used to pull heavy loads over rough ground.
trac•tor (trak′tər) *noun, plural* **tractors.**

tradition A custom or belief that is passed on from one generation to another.
tra•di•tion (trə dish′ən) *noun, plural* **traditions;** *adjective,* **traditional.**

travel To go from one place to another; to make a trip. We *traveled* through England. *Verb.* —The act of traveling. Camels are used for desert *travel. Noun.*
trav•el (trav′əl) *verb,* **traveled, traveling;** *noun, plural* **travels;** *noun,* **traveler.**

tube A container of soft metal or plastic from which the contents are removed by squeezing. I need a new *tube* of toothpaste.
tube (tüb *or* tūb) *noun, plural* **tubes.**

tusk A long, pointed tooth that sticks out of each side of the mouth in certain animals. Elephants and walruses have *tusks.*
tusk (tusk) *noun, plural* **tusks.**

waddle To walk or move with short steps, swaying the body from side to side. The duck *waddled* across the yard. *Verb.* —A swaying or rocking walk. The audience laughed at the clown's *waddle. Noun.*
wad•dle (wod′əl) *verb,* **waddled, waddling;** *noun, plural* **waddles.**

at; āpe; fär; câre; end; mē; it; īce; pîerce; hot; ōld; sông; fôrk; oil; out; up; ūse; rüle; pûll; tûrn; chin; sing; shop; thin; <u>th</u>is; hw in white; zh in treasure. The symbol ə stands for the unstressed vowel sound in about, taken, pencil, lemon, and circus.

weary Very tired. The carpenter was *weary* after the day's hard work. *Adjective.* —To make or become weary; tire. The long walk *wearied* the children. *Verb.*
wea•ry (wîr′ē) *adjective,* **wearier, weariest;** *verb,* **wearied, wearying;** *adverb,* **wearily;** *noun,* **weariness.**

weird Strange or mysterious; odd. A *weird* sound came from the deserted old house.
▲ **Synonym:** peculiar
weird (wîrd) *adjective,* **weirder, weirdest;** *adverb,* **weirdly;** *noun,* **weirdness.**

wharf A structure built along a shore as a landing place for boats and ships; dock. We had to unload the boat once we reached the *wharf.*
wharf (hworf *or* wôrf) *noun, plural* **wharves** *or* **wharfs.**

whicker To neigh or whinny. The horse began *whickering* at the kids. *Verb.* —A neigh or whinny. The horse let out a *whicker. Noun.*
whick•er (hwi′kər) *verb,* **whickered, whickering;** *noun, plural* **whickers.**

whinny A soft neigh. We heard the *whinnies* of the horses. *Noun.* —To neigh in a low, gentle way. My horse *whinnied* when he saw me. *Verb.*
whin•ny (hwin′ē *or* win′ē) *verb,* **whinnied, whinnying;** *noun, plural* **whinnies.**

wildlife Wild animals that live naturally in an area. My favorite part of hiking is observing the *wildlife.*
wild•life (wīld′līf′) *noun.*

windowpane A framed sheet of glass in a window. I placed my candles by the *windowpane.*
win•dow•pane (win′dō pān′) *noun, plural* **windowpanes.**

wondrous Extraordinary; wonderful. The local theater put on a *wondrous* performance.
▲ **Synonym:** marvelous
won•drous (wun′drəs) *adjective;* *adverb,* **wondrously;** *noun,* **wondrousness.**

wrestle 1. To force by grasping. The champion *wrestled* his opponent to the mat. **2.** To struggle by grasping and trying to force and hold one's opponent to the ground, without punching. The children *wrestled* on the lawn.
wres•tle (res′əl) *verb,* **wrestled, wrestling.**

wriggle 1. To twist or turn from side to side with short, quick moves; squirm. The bored children *wriggled* in their seats. **2.** To get into or out of a position by tricky means. You always try to *wriggle* out of having to wash the dishes.
wrig•gle (rig′əl) *verb,* **wriggled, wriggling;** *adjective,* **wriggly.**

Word History
The word **wriggle** comes from the Old English word *wrigian,* which means "to turn."

at; āpe; fär; câre; end; mē; it; īce; pîerce; hot; ōld; sông; fôrk; oil; out; up; ūse; rüle; pûll; tûrn; chin; sing; shop; thin; <u>th</u>is; hw in white; zh in treasure. The symbol ə stands for the unstressed vowel sound in about, taken, pencil, lemon, and circus.

Cover Illustration: Terry Widener

The publisher gratefully acknowledges permission to reprint the following copyrighted material:

Autobiographical piece by Matt Christopher from PAUSES: AUTOBIOGRAPHICAL REFLECTIONS OF 101 CREATORS OF CHILDREN'S BOOKS by Lee Bennett Hopkins. Copyright © 1995 by Lee Bennett Hopkins. Used by permission of HarperCollins Children's Books, a division of HarperCollins Publishers.

Autobiographical piece by Robert Ballard from TALKING WITH ADVENTURERS by Pat and Linda Cummings. Copyright 1998 by Pat Cummings and Linda Cummings. Used by permission of the National Geographic Society.

"Beezus and Her Imagination" from BEEZUS AND HER RAMONA by Beverly Cleary. Copyright © 1955 by Beverly Cleary. Used by permission of Dell Publishing, a division of The Bantam Doubleday Dell Publishing Group, Inc.

"The Biggest Problem (Is in Other People's Minds)" from FREE TO BE ... YOU AND ME AND FREE TO BE ... A FAMILY by Don Haynie. Copyright © 1997, 1987, 1974 by the Free to Be Foundation, Inc. Used by permission of Running Press.

"Birdfoot's Grampa" from ENTERING ONANDAGA by Joseph Bruchac. Copyright © 1978 by Joseph Bruchac. Used by permission.

"Dakota Dugout" from DAKOTA DUGOUT by Ann Turner. Copyright © 1985 by Ann Turner. Reprinted with the permission of Simon & Schuster Books for Young Readers, an imprint of Simon & Schuster Children's Publishing Division.

"The Dentist" from ANOTHER FIRST POETRY BOOK by Judith Nicholls. Copyright © 1987 by Judith Nicholls. Used by permission of Oxford University Press.

"Don't Make a Bargain with a Fox" from THE KING OF THE MOUNTAINS: A TREASURY OF LATIN AMERICAN FOLK STORIES by M. A. Jagendorf and R. S. Boggs. Copyright © 1960 by M. A. Jagendorf and R. S. Boggs. Copyright renewed 1988 by Andre Jagendorf, Merna Alpert and R. S. Boggs. Used by permission of Vanguard Press, a division of Random House, Inc.

"Earth Day Rap" by Doug Goodkin. Copyright © 1995. Used by permission of The McGraw-Hill Co., Inc.

"8,000 Stones" from 8,000 STONES: A CHINESE FOLKTALE retold by Diane Wolkstein. Text copyright © 1972 by Diane Wolkstein. Used by permission.

"Evergreen, Everblue" by Raffi. Copyright © 1990 Homeland Publishing, a division of Troubadour Records Ltd. Used by permission.

ACKNOWLEDGMENTS

The publisher gratefully acknowledges permission to reprint the following copyrighted material.

"Amelia's Road" by Linda Jacobs Altman, illustrated by Enrique O. Sanchez. Text copyright © 1993 by Linda Jacobs Altman. Illustrations copyright © 1993 by Enrique O. Sanchez. Permission granted by Lee & Low Books Inc., 95 Madison Avenue, New York, NY 10016.

"August 8" by Norman Jordan. From MY BLACK ME: A Beginning Book of Black Poetry, edited by Arnold Adoff. Copyright © 1974. Used by permission of Dutton Books, a division of Penguin Putnam, Inc.

"Baseball Saved Us" by Ken Mochizuki, illustrated by Dom Lee. Text copyright © 1993 by Ken Mochizuki. Illustrations copyright © 1993 by Dom Lee. Permission granted by Lee & Low Books Inc., 95 Madison Avenue, New York, NY 10016.

"Final Curve" by Langston Hughes from MY BLACK ME: A Beginning Book of Black Poetry, edited by Arnold Adoff. Copyright © 1974. Used by permission of Dutton Books, a division of Penguin Putnam, Inc.

"The Fox and the Guinea Pig" / "El zorro y el cuy" A traditional Folk Tale translated by Mary Ann Newman, illustrated by Kevin Hawkes. Copyright © 1997 Macmillan/McGraw-Hill, a Division of the Educational and Professional Publishing Group of the McGraw-Hill Companies, Inc.

"The Garden We Planted Together" by Anuruddha Bose from A WORLD IN OUR HANDS. Reprinted with permission of A WORLD IN OUR HANDS by Peace Child Charitable Trust, illustrated by Sanjay Sinha ($15.95). Copyright © 1995 Tricycle Press (800-841-BOOK).

"Gluskabe and the Snow Bird" from GLUSKABE AND THE FOUR WISHES retold by Joseph Bruchac. Copyright © 1995 Cobblehill Books/Dutton.

"Grass Sandals" / "The Travels of Basho" by Dawnine Spivak, illustrated by Demi. Text copyright © 1997 by Dawnine Spivak, illustrations copyright © 1997 by Demi. Reprinted by permission of Atheneum Books for Young Readers.

"The Hatmaker's Sign" by Candace Fleming, illustrated by Robert Andrew Parker. Text copyright © 1998 by Candace Fleming. Illustrations copyright © 1998 by Robert Andrew Parker. All rights reserved. Reprinted by permission by Orchard Books, New York.

"How to Tell the Top of a Hill" by John Ciardi from THE REASON FOR THE PELICAN. Copyright © 1959 by John Ciardi. Reprinted by permission of the Estate of John Ciardi.

"I Ask My Mother to Sing" by Li-Young Lee. Copyright © 1986 by Li-Young Lee. Reprinted from *Rose* with the permission of BOA Editions, Ltd., 260 East Ave., Rochester, NY 14604.

"Just a Dream" is from JUST A DREAM by Chris Van Allsburg. Copyright © 1990 by Chris Van Allsburg. Reprinted by permission of Houghton Mifflin Company.

"Justin and the Best Biscuits in the World" is from JUSTIN AND THE BEST BISCUITS IN THE WORLD by Mildred Pitts Walter. Copyright © 1986 by Mildred Pitts Walter. Published by Lothrop, Lee & Shepard Books and used by permission of William Morrow & Company, Inc. Publishers, New York.

"Leah's Pony" by Elizabeth Friedrich, illustrated by Michael Garland. Text copyright © 1996 by Elizabeth Friedrich. Illustrations copyright © 1996 by Michael Garland. Used by permission of Boyds Mills Press.

"The Lost Lake" by Allen Say. Copyright © 1989 by Allen Say. Reprinted by permission of Houghton Mifflin Company. All rights reserved.

"The Malachite Palace" by Alma Flor Ada, translated by Rosa Zubizarreta, illustrated by Leonid Gore. Text copyright © 1998 by Alma Flor Ada, illustrations copyright © 1998 by Leonid Gore. Reprinted by permission of by Atheneum Books for Young Readers.

"Meet an Underwater Explorer" by Luise Woelflein. Reprinted from the June 1994 issue of RANGER RICK magazine, with the permission of the publisher, the National Wildlife Federation. Copyright © 1994 by the National Wildlife Federation.

"Mom's Best Friend" by Sally Hobart Alexander, photographs by George Ancona. Text copyright ©1992 by Sally Hobart Alexander. Photographs copyright © 1992 by George Ancona. Reprinted with permission of Simon & Schuster Books for Young Readers, Simon & Schuster Children's Publishing Division.

"My Poems" by Alan Barlow. From RISING VOICES: WRITINGS OF YOUNG NATIVE AMERICANS selected by Arlene B. Hirschfelder and Beverly R. Singer. Copyright © 1992. Published by Scribner's. Used by permission.

"On the Bus with Joanna Cole" excerpt from *On the Bus with Joanna Cole: A Creative Autobiography* by Joanna Cole with Wendy Saul. Copyright © 1996 by Joanna Cole. Published by Heinemann, a division of Reed Elsevier Inc. Reprinted by permission of the publisher. Illustration on page 447 by Bruce Degen from THE MAGIC SCHOOL BUS INSIDE THE HUMAN BODY by Joanna Cole. Illustration copyright © 1989 by Bruce Degen. Reprinted with permission of Scholastic, Inc. THE MAGIC SCHOOL BUS is a registered trademark of Scholastic, Inc.

"Pat Cummings: My Story" reprinted with the permission of Simon & Schuster Books for Young Readers from TALKING WITH ARTISTS compiled and edited by Pat Cummings. Jacket illustration copyright ©1992 Pat Cummings. Copyright © 1992 Pat Cummings.

"A Place Called Freedom" by Scott Russell Sanders, illustrated by Thomas B. Allen. Text copyright © 1997 by Scott Russell Sanders, illustrations copyright © 1997 by Thomas B. Allen. Reprinted by permission of Atheneum Books for Young Readers.

"The Poet Pencil" by Jesús Carlos Soto Morfín, translated by Judith Infante. From THE TREE IS OLDER THAN YOU ARE: A Bilingual Gathering of Poems and Stories from Mexico, selected by Naomi Shihab Nye. Copyright © 1995 Simon & Schuster Books for Young Readers.

"The Rajah's Rice" from THE RAJAH'S RICE by David Barry, illustrated by Donna Perrone. Text Copyright © 1994 by David Barry. Art copyright © 1994 by Donna Perrone. Used with permission of W. H. Freeman and Company.

"Sarah, Plain and Tall" text excerpt from SARAH, PLAIN AND TALL by Patricia MacLachlan. Copyright © 1985 by Patricia MacLachlan. Reprinted by permission of HarperCollins Publishers. Cover permission for the Trophy Edition used by permission of HarperCollins Publishers.

"Scruffy: A Wolf Finds His Place in the Pack" by Jim Brandenburg. Copyright © 1996 by Jim Brandenburg. Published by arrangement with Walker Publishing Company, Inc.

"Seal Journey" From SEAL JOURNEY by Richard and Jonah Sobol. Copyright © 1993 Richard Sobol, text and photographs. Used by permission of Cobblehill Books, an affiliate of Dutton Children's Press, a division of Penguin USA, Inc.

"Teammates" from TEAMMATES by Peter Golenbock, text copyright © 1990 by Golenbock Communications, reprinted by permission of Harcourt Brace & Company.

"To" by Lee Bennett Hopkins from BEEN TO YESTERDAYS: Poems of a Life. Text copyright © 1995 by Lee Bennett Hopkins. Published by Wordsong/Boyds Mill Press. Reprinted by permission.

"The Toothpaste Millionaire" by Jean Merrill. Copyright © 1972 by Houghton Mifflin Company. Adapted and reprinted by permission of Houghton Mifflin Company. All rights reserved.

"Tortillas Like Africa" from CANTO FAMILIAR by Gary Soto. Copyright © 1995 Harcourt Brace & Company, Inc.

"Familiar Friends" from ON THE FARM by James S. Tippett. Compilation copyright © 1991 by Lee Bennett Hopkins. Used by permission of Little, Brown and Company.

"Follow the Drinkin' Gourd," Words and Music by Ronnie Gilbert, Lee Hays, Fred Hellerman and Pete Seeger TRO- © Copyright 1951 (Renewed) Folkways Music Publishers, Inc., New York, New York. Used by permission.

"Fossils" from SOMETHING NEW BEGINS by Lilian Moore. Copyright © 1982 by Lilian Moore. Reprinted with the permission of Atheneum Books for Young Readers, an imprint of Simon & Schuster Children's Publishing Division.

Four haiku from CRICKET NEVER DOES: A COLLECTION OF HAIKU AND TANKA by Myra Cohn Livingston. Text copyright © 1977 by Myra Cohn Livingston. Used by permission of Margaret K. McElderry Books, an imprint of Simon & Schuster Children's Publishing Division.

"Whales" excerpt from WHALES by Seymour Simon. Copyright © 1989 by Seymour Simon. Reprinted by permission of HarperCollins Publishers.

"Yeh-Shen: A Cinderella Story from China" is from YEH-SHEN: A CINDERELLA STORY FROM CHINA by Ai-Ling Louie. Text copyright © 1982 by Ai-Ling Louie. Illustrations copyright © 1982 by Ed Young. Reprinted by permission of Philomel Books. Introductory comments by Ai-Ling Louie and used with her permission.

"Your World" by Georgia Douglas Johnson appeared originally in HOLD FAST TO DREAMS selected by Arna Bontemps. Extensive research has failed to locate the author and/or copyright holder of this work.

Cover Illustration
Terry Widener

Illustration
Roberta Ludlow, 16-17; Jean and Mou-Sien Tseng, 128-129; David Ridley, 130-131; Elizabeth Rosen, 252-253; J. W. Stewart, 254-255; Bruno Paciulli, 372-373; Stefano Vitale, 408-419; Amy Vangsgard, 482-483; Susan Leopold, 484-485; Yoshi Miyake, 612-613; David Catrow, 666-687; B. J. Faulkner, 724-725; George Thompson, 728, 749; Rodica Prato, 732, 739; John Carrozza, 745, 759, 763.

Photography
18-19: c. Fine Art Photographic Library, London/Art Resource, NY. 42-43: c. The Bridgeman Art Library International Ltd. 66: c. Superstock. 94-95: c. Shelburne Museum. 118-119: c. E. A. Barton Collection, England. 132-133: c. Jerry Jacka. 158-159: c. MPTV. 190-191: c. The Museum of Modern Art, New York. 216-217: c. The Bridgeman Art Library International Ltd. 242-243: c. The Bridgeman Art Library International Ltd. 256-257: c. Richard Estes. 282-283: c. Superstock. 298-299: c. The Bridgeman Art Library International Ltd. 332-333: c. The Phillips Collection. 360-361: c. Cordon Art B. V. 406-407: c. The Heard Museum. 374-375: c. 424-425: c. Corbis/Bettman. 444-445: c. Private Collection. 472-473: c. The Bridgeman Art Library International Ltd. 486-487: c. Christies Images. 516-517: c. Millenium Pictures. 536-537: c. Art Resource. 568-569: c. Omni-Photo Communications. 600-601: c. The Bridgeman Art Library Ltd. 614-615: c. Jonathan Green. 632-633: c. Chester Beatty Library, Dublin. 664-665: c. Motion Picture and Television Archives. 692/693: c. Superstock. 714-715: c. The Bridgeman Art Library Ltd.

"Hats Off to the Cowboy" from HOME ON THE RANGE: COWBOY POETRY by Red Steagall. Copyright © 1989 by Texas Red Songs. Used by permission of Dial Books, a Division of Penguin Books USA, Inc.

"How It All Began" from THE STORY OF BASEBALL by Lawrence S. Ritter. Copyright © 1983, 1990 by Lawrence S. Ritter. Used by permission of William Morrow and Company, Inc., and Raines and Raines.

"Indians of the Plains" from WORLDS I KNOW AND OTHER POEMS b1y Myra Cohn Livingston. Text copyright © 1985 by Myra Cohn Livingston. Reprinted with the permission of Macmillan Publishing Company, an imprint of Simon & Schuster Children's Publishing Division.

"Jackie Robinson" from FOLLOWERS OF THE NORTH STAR: RHYMES ABOUT AFRICAN AMERICAN HEROES, HEROINES, AND HISTORICAL TIMES by Susan Altman and Susan Lechner. Copyright © 1993 Childrens Press ®, Inc. Used by permission of Childrens Press.

"The Needle in the Haystack" from CRICKET MAGAZINE by John Hamma. Copyright © 1982 by John Hamma. Used by permission of Doris Hamma.

"Pack" text copyright © 1995 by Lee Bennett Hopkins from BEEN TO YESTERDAYS by Lee Bennett Hopkins. Reprinted by permission of Wordsong/Boyds Mills Press, Inc.

"The Paper Garden" from BREAKING THE SPELL: TALES OF ENCHANTMENT by Tony Ramsay. Text copyright © Sally Grindley 1997. Illustrations copyright © Susan Field 1997. Used by permission of Larousse Kingfisher Chambers.

"Rhodopis and Her Golden Sandals" from MULTICULTURAL FABLES AND FAIRY TALES by Tara McCarthy. Published by Scholastic Professional Books. Copyright © 1993 by Tara McCarthy. Reprinted by permission of Scholastic, Inc.

"Seal" from LAUGHING TIME by William Jay Smith. Copyright © 1990 by William Jay Smith. Used by permission of Farrar, Straus & Giroux, Inc.

"Spider in the Sky" by Anne Rose. Copyright © 1978 by Anne Rose. Used by permission of Harper Collins Publishers.

"Super-Goopy Glue" from THE NEW KID ON THE BLOCK by Jack Prelutsky. Text copyright © 1984 by Jack Prelutsky. Used by permission of Greenwillow Books, a division of William Morrow & Company, Inc.

"What's the Big Idea, Ben Franklin?" by Jean Fritz. Text copyright © 1976 by Jean Fritz. Illustrations copyright © 1976 by Margot Tomes. Used by permission of Coward, McCann & Geoghegan.

"When Whales Exhale (Whale Watching)" from WHEN WHALES EXHALE AND OTHER POEMS by Constance Levy. Text copyright © 1996 by Constance King Levy. Used by permission of Margaret K. McElderry Books, an imprint of Simon & Schuster Children's publishing Division.

"Windows of Gold" from WINDOWS OF GOLD AND OTHER GOLDEN TALES by Selma G. Lanes. Text copyright © 1989 retold by Selma G. Lanes. Illustrations copyright © 1989 by Kimberly Bulcken Root. Used by permission of Simon and Schuster Books for Young Readers.

"The Wolf" from THE RANDOM HOUSE BOOK OF POETRY FOR CHILDREN by Georgia Roberts Durston. Copyright © 1983. Used by permission of Random House.

Acknowledgments

Notes

Backmatter Contents

Jackie Robinson

1919–1972
First black major league baseball player

by Susan Altman and Susan Lechner

For many years,
Across the nation,
Baseball upheld
Segregation.

Black men couldn't
Make their mark
At Wrigley Field
Or Fenway Park.

The Brooklyn Dodgers
Changed all that
When they signed Robinson
To bat.

He hit 'em low.
He hit 'em high.
He made that baseball
Really fly!

With Robinson
On second base,
The Dodgers moved
Up to first place.

He scored the runs,
Was MVP,
And led the team
To victory.

With Brooklyn's Dodgers
(Now L.A.)
He paved the way
For blacks to play.

'Cause segregation
Is not fair
In baseball, school,
Or anywhere.

And Robinson made millions shout
When he struck
Segregation out.

Windows of Gold

retold by Selma G. Lanes

Once upon a time at the bottom of a high hill, there lived a widow and her small son Harry. They were poor as church mice, but the mother did fine sewing and, in this way, earned money enough to keep a cottage roof over their heads and simple food on their table.

Whenever the sun shone, Harry played outside the cottage, while his mother worked at her sewing indoors. Though he had no toys, still Harry managed with sticks and stones to amuse himself quite well. Best of all, Harry liked to gaze up to the top of the high hill.

There he saw a cottage much like his own. It had just one difference: the cottage at the top of the hill had windows all made of gold! How they gleamed in the mid-morning sunlight, and how Harry wished that he and his mother might live in such a grand place themselves.

One bright and cloudless day, when Harry and his mother were just finishing their lunch of bread and milk, the boy had an idea. Instead of playing outside the cottage as usual this afternoon, he would go exploring. Harry decided to make a long trip up the high hill. He would visit the house with the windows all made of gold.

His mind made up, Harry stepped into the dirt road not far from the cottage door. If he turned to the right, the boy knew that the road led into town. He had made this trip with his mother many times. But, if he turned to the left, the road wound round and round the high hill until, at last, it reached the very top. Harry had never made that trip. None the less, he was determined to do so now.

Harry walked, and walked, and walked until at last he came within sight of the cottage at the top of the hill. Outside of it, Harry could see a girl his own size playing with a rag doll. When the child caught sight of Harry, she ran towards him. Visitors were few so far from town, and the girl, whose name was Sally, was overjoyed to see a boy her own age.

"She must be a princess," thought Harry to himself, "to live in such a house with windows all made of gold." But where were the golden windows he had come so far to see? Now that he was here, Harry saw only that the cottage looked even more like his own: Its windows were not made of gold, but of glass—exactly like his own!

"Who are you?" asked Sally. "From where do you come?"

"I'm Harry," he told her. "And I come from the cottage at the bottom of the hill."

The little girl's eyes opened wide as she pointed down towards Harry's cottage. "From the house with the windows all made of gold?" she asked.

Harry thought she might be making fun of him, but he turned toward his own house, far off in the distance. There, at the bottom of the hill it was, much like the one where he now stood. It had just one difference: Harry's cottage had windows all made of gold!

How could that be? What magic took place while Harry was walking from the bottom of the hill to the top?

Sun magic. Every morning when Harry looked up the high hill, he saw the sun's golden rays reflected in the windows of the cottage at the top. And every afternoon when Sally looked down the high hill, she saw the sun's golden rays reflected in the windows of the cottage at the bottom.

If Sally was a princess, then Harry was a prince! The sun had crowned them both. But Harry and Sally became something else that day—friends. Now, they took turns visiting one another. And, whether they were at the bottom of the hill or at the top, they could always look off into the distance and see a house with windows all made of gold!

Super-Goopy Glue
by Jack Prelutsky

Permit me to present to you
my famous SUPER-GOOPY GLUE,
by far the finest glue on earth,
one dollar for a penny's worth.

It's rumored that my glue adheres
for easily a thousand years,
my glue's the glue you surely seek,
it's guaranteed for one whole week.

My SUPER-GOOPY GLUE can glue
a carrot to a caribou,
a feather to a ferret's feet,
a pickle to a parakeet.

No other glue is half as good,
it works on metal, glass, and wood,
I'd demonstrate it for you, but
my glue has glued my gluepot shut.

When Whales Exhale
(Whale Watching)
by Constance Levy

There's a horn sound
from the blowhole
and a high-speed spout
when a whale at sea
blasts the old air out.
It breathes up a geyser,
a flare of fizz,
a white cloud that shows you
where it is
in the endless waves
of the great green sea.
Oh, whales exhale
magnificently!

Birdfoot's Grampa
by Joseph Bruchac

The old man
must have stopped our car
two dozen times to climb out
and gather into his hands
the small toads blinded
by our lights and leaping,
live drops of rain.

The rain was falling,
a mist about his white hair
and I kept saying
you can't save them all,
accept it, get back in
we've got places to go.

But, leathery hands full
of wet brown life,
knee deep in the summer
roadside grass,
he just smiled and said
they have places to go to
too.

Annotated Workbooks

Cause and Effect

Name_____ Date_____ Practice **186**

One event can cause another to happen. This kind of relationship is called **cause and effect**. Read the passage below. Then read each cause. Write the effect each event causes. **Answers will vary.**

Her fans called her FloJo. She was fast. She had style. She is considered one of the great track and field athletes of all time.

Florence Griffith Joyner was born in 1959, the seventh of 11 children. Like many great athletes, Florence learned discipline when she was young. Her mother had strict rules for keeping her children out of trouble and doing their very best. No one was allowed to watch television during the week. Even in high school, the children had to be in bed by 10:00. Florence followed her mother's rules, and she made more rules for herself. She set goals and then worked to achieve them. Florence liked school and books, especially poetry. She also showed talent in creating hair styles and clothing. In her diary, she wrote about her plans and everything she hoped to accomplish.

From the time she was seven years old Florence liked running. She easily won a race for the Sugar Ray Robinson Youth Foundation. Florence never stopped racing. Her mother encouraged her to compete, and she did. In the 1988 Olympics in Seoul, Korea, she won three gold medals. That wasn't enough for her. She has also designed and modeled clothing and has developed a series of books to help children. FloJo was a winner in every way.

Cause

1. Florence followed her mother's strict rules.
2. Florence liked books and writing in her diary as a child.
3. As a young girl, Florence was interested in hair and clothes styles.
4. Florence's mother urged her to compete in track and field.
5. FloJo entered the 1988 Olympics.

Effect

Florence learned discipline when she was young.

As an adult she developed a series of books for children.

As an adult she designed and modeled clothing.

She never stopped racing.

She won three gold medals.

5 Book 4/Unit 6
Teammates

At Home: Have students describe the causes and effects that setting goals has on their lives.

186

Vocabulary

Name_____ Date_____ Practice **187**

Use context clues to write a definition of the underlined word in each question.

1. Is a rainbow an <u>extraordinary</u> or an unexciting sight?
   remarkable, exciting

2. Would a public notice be <u>circulated</u> or kept hidden?
   passed around

3. Do people in <u>organizations</u> work against each other or together for a common cause? groups with special aims

4. If you launched a new program at school, would the program be <u>starting</u> or ending? starting

5. Is your <u>teammate</u> a member of your own team or a fan?
   member of the same team

6. Would <u>opponents</u> be on the same side or opposite sides of a contest?
   persons on opposite sides

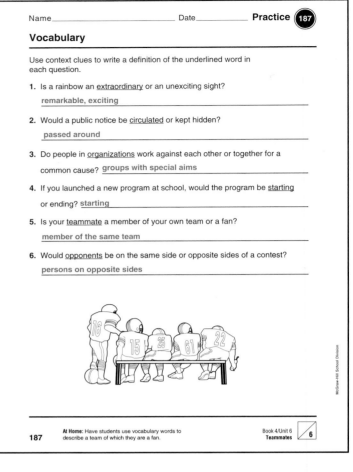

187 **At Home:** Have students use vocabulary words to describe a team of which they are a fan.

Book 4/Unit 6
Teammates 6

Ordinary and Extraordinary

Clancy was an ordinary girl. At least that's how she saw herself. Her schoolwork could be better. It could also be worse. There was one thing, though, that made Clancy *extraordinary*. She could run like the wind. She ran all the time. Soon Clancy began spending time with another girl and boy in her neighborhood. They could run fast, too. Clancy started a neighborhood track team. Each friend signed up as a *teammate*. Clancy and her team *launched* a campaign for more members. They asked business *organizations* nearby to post advertisements about the team in their store windows.

Clancy *circulated* a handout asking other kids to join the team. Ten kids joined. Then the team looked for *opponents* to race. Soon they were part of a league, racing other teams. The team worked hard. Clancy trained five days a week. Clancy began applying discipline to her school work. Clancy's ordinary school work became extraordinary, too.

1. What was ordinary about Clancy and what was <u>extraordinary</u>?
   She was an ordinary student, but an extraordinary runner.

2. Who were the first two <u>teammates</u> to sign up for the track team?
   a girl and boy in her neighborhood

3. What did business <u>organizations</u> have to do with Clancy's racing team?
   They put advertisements for new team members in their store windows.

4. What kind of paper had Clancy <u>circulated</u>, and how did it affect the team?
   It was a handout asking for more team members.

5. Why do you think Clancy's school work became <u>extraordinary</u>?
   She applied discipline to her schoolwork.

5 Book 4/Unit 6
Teammates

At Home: Have students write to describe how they are extraordinary in some way.

187a

Story Comprehension

Name_____ Date_____ Practice **188**

Complete the story chart about "Teammates."
Answers will vary. Possible answers are given.

CHARACTERS

1. Branch Rickey
2. Jackie Robinson
3. Pee Wee Reese

SETTING

4. the world of American baseball in the 1940s

PROBLEMS FACED BY CHARACTERS

5. Branch Rickey: wanted to integrate the major leagues by hiring a talented African American player.

6. Jackie Robinson: faced pain, humiliation, and anger caused by other people's prejudices.

7. Pee Wee Reese: was saddened by the way people treated his teammate.

HOW EACH CHARACTER SOLVED HIS PROBLEM

8. Branch Rickey: hired Jackie Robinson.

9. Jackie Robinson: exercised courage and performed well on the baseball field.

10. Pee Wee Reese: stood up for his teammate; put his arm around Jackie Robinson in front of a crowd of prejudiced fans.

Teammates • PRACTICE

Page 189

Name_____ Date_____ Practice **189**

Use the Card Catalog: Subject Card

Suppose you are looking for a book about board games. You can look under B in the **card catalog**, or you can enter the words board games on the computer. You may find a **subject card** like the one below. Suppose you know the name of an author who wrote a book about board games? You can find that person in the card catalog drawer or on the computer.

Use the subject card to help you answer the questions.

```
SUBJECT CARD
J 794 D   Making and playing board games    call number/subject
          Doney, Meryl                       author
          Games                              title
          New York: Franklin Watts, ©1996    publisher/date
          32 pages illustrations
```

1. What is the first line of information on the subject card? _Call number and subject of book._

2. What is the subject of the book? _Making and playing board games._

3. Who is the author? _Meryl Doney_

4. How many pages does the book have? _32_

5. Is the book illustrated? _Yes_

6. What is the call number of the book? _J 794 D_

Page 190

Name_____ Date_____ Practice **190**

Cause and Effect

Recognizing **cause and effect** can help you understand a story's plot. Review "Teammates." Then add the missing causes and effects to the chart.

Cause	Effect
1. _Laws against segregation didn't exist in the 1940s_	In the 1940s African American baseball players were not allowed to compete in the same league as white players.
2. Branch Rickey, the general manager of the Brooklyn Dodgers, thought segregation was unfair.	_He decided to hire an African American ball player._
3. _Branch Rickey wanted a talented player who had the courage not to fight back._	Branch Rickey hired Jackie Robinson, a talented African American baseball player.
4. _Jackie Robinson was the first African American player to try out for a major league team._	When Jackie Robinson arrived for spring training with the Brooklyn Dodgers, crowds of African Americans met him.
5. When Pee Wee Reese heard fans yelling hateful things at Jackie Robinson, he decided to take a stand.	_He showed support for Jackie by putting his arm around him and silenced the crowd._

Page 191

Name_____ Date_____ Practice **191**

Make Judgments and Decisions

Characters in stories **make judgments and decisions** based on what they see. Read each passage, and then answer each question.
Answers will vary.

Mr. Garcia, the principal, brought the new student to the fourth grade classroom around 10:00. The class was in the middle of a math test. The whole class looked at Mr. Garcia when he said, "Please help me welcome your new classmate, Charlie Cable." Everybody turned back to their math test. The new student looked scared.

1. What judgment did the storyteller make about Charlie Cable? ___
He was scared.

In gym, teams were chosen for baseball. Everyone was chosen except for Charlie. He went with the last team. Up at bat, Charlie looked nervous. It was obvious that Charlie had never held a bat before. To no one's surprise, Charlie struck out. Matt Carlson remembered when he was the new kid. After gym, he walked back with Charlie, but Charlie didn't talk.

2. What judgment did the storyteller make about Charlie's baseball abilities?
He thought Charlie wouldn't be able to get a hit.

3. Why did Matt decide to walk back with Charlie? _He remembered what is was like to be new and he wanted to show support for Charlie._

The next day, everyone chose partners for the field trip. Everyone wanted to be Matt Carlson's partner. Matt chose Charlie Cable. This time Charlie talked a little to Matt on the bus. Everyone could hear Matt laughing like crazy. Everyone was curious. What was so funny? A couple of the kids turned around to listen to Charlie. Pretty soon, they were laughing, too.

4. What judgment did Matt make about Charlie's humor? ___
He thought Charlie was funny.

5. What decision did some of the kids make? ___
to listen and talk with Charlie and Matt

Page 192

Name_____ Date_____ Practice **192**

Context Clues

Many words have more than one meaning. The **context clues** can help you to define a word. Read each sentence below. Then circle the letter of the meaning for each underlined word.

1. The rough and tough coach was really a very <u>sweet</u> man.
   a. good-tempered   **b.** sugary tasting

2. Each team player <u>trains</u> several hours a day to throw, catch, and hit.
   a. practices   **b.** railroad cars

3. The umpire <u>called</u> several times to the first baseman.
   a. telephoned   **b.** shouted

4. The high <u>fly</u> ball went over the fence and onto the street.
   a. without touching the ground   **b.** insect with wings

5. There was only a <u>light</u> rain so the teams kept on playing.
   a. not very much   **b.** lamp

6. The pitcher and first baseman talked in the <u>bullpen</u>.
   a. writing instrument   **b.** dugout

7. The player faced a <u>mountain</u> of criticism for bad sportsmanship.
   a. large amount   **b.** steep hill of great height

8. The catcher slapped the ball into the <u>palm</u> of his hand.
   a. tropical tree   **b.** center portion of a hand

9. On a baseball team, <u>race</u> makes no difference among the players.
   a. a group of mankind   **b.** a running contest

10. Jackie Robinson was a <u>star</u> baseball player.
   a. heavenly body visible at night   **b.** a person famous for achievement

Teammates • RETEACH

Cause and Effect

> Noticing **cause and effect** relationships in a story can help you understand the story better. A cause is why something happens. An effect is what happens as a result.

Read the paragraph below. Then answer the questions that follow.

One cause of segregation in the South goes back to the years following the Civil War. The Civil War ended slavery in the United States. However, later some southern states wrote laws that denied African American citizens equal rights. Blacks could not go to the same schools, restaurants, or even drinking fountains as whites. African Americans were prevented from voting in elections and running for office.

1. What was one effect of the Civil War? The Civil War ended slavery in the United States.

2. What did some southern states do after slavery ended? The states passed laws that denied African Americans equal rights.

3. What was one specific effect of the segregation laws? Answers will vary: Possible answer: Black students could not attend the same schools as white students.

4. Why couldn't African American citizens in the South vote or hold office after the Civil War? Segregation laws prevented them from doing so.

Book 4/Unit 6
Teammates 4

At Home: Have students tell about something that happened in school and then have them identify the cause of the event.

186

Vocabulary

Read each clue. Then find the vocabulary word in the row of letters that best fits the clue and circle it.

circulated opponents	extraordinary organizations	launched teammate

1. very special   l o q e x t r a o r d i n a r y m z c
2. sent off   k l a u n c h e d m d r s w t
3. the other team   z r t y u o p p o n e n t s y
4. someone on your team u y r t e a m m a t e v c d r
5. groups of people   e g h t o r g a n i z a t i o n s d g
6. passed around   u h c i r c u l a t e d s w v b

6

Story Comprehension

Write a ✔ next to every sentence that tells something about the story "Teammates."

1. ✔ Segregation was legal in the 1940s.
2. ✔ Only white players were in the major leagues in the 1940s.
3. ___ Most Americans fought against racial prejudice in the 1940s.
4. ✔ Branch Rickey was the general manager of the Brooklyn Dodgers.
5. ✔ Jackie Robinson was a star Negro League player.
6. ___ Opposing players treated Robinson like any other player.
7. ___ Jackie Robinson argued with Mr. Rickey about his right to fight back.
8. ✔ Pee Wee Reese was a friend to Jackie Robinson.

At Home: Have students use some of the vocabulary words to tell what they know about Jackie Robinson.

187–188

Book 4/Unit 6
Teammates 8

Use the Card Catalog: Subject Card

> When you want to find books in the library about a particular topic, use the **card catalog**. The **subject card** will lead you to books that may be useful when you're researching a general subject like baseball or the Civil War.

Baseball, fiction
JS   Slote, Alfred   **Author**
        Finding Buck McHenry   **Title**
        New York: Harper Collins, 1991   **Publisher**
Number of pages   187   Illustrations
1.   Baseball   2. Negro Leagues
Summary: Eleven-year-old Jason, believing the school custodian to be Buck McHenry, a famous pitcher from the old Negro League, tries to enlist him as coach for his Little League team by revealing his identity to the world.

Use the subject card to answer the questions.

1. What is the subject of the book? Baseball, fiction
2. What is the title? Finding Buck McHenry
3. Who is the author? Alfred Slote
4. How many pages does the book have? 187 pages
5. What does the **S** in the call number stand for? the first letter of the author's last name, Slote
6. When is it good to use a subject card? when you are researching a general topic

Book 4/Unit 6
Teammates 6

At Home: Have students identify three subjects for which they would like to find books at the library.

189

Cause and Effect

> As you read, it is important to distinguish between causes and effects. A **cause** is why something happens and an **effect** is what happens as a result.

Read each paragraph below. Then say if each of the following statements is the **cause** or the **effect**.

Jackie Robinson was a great base runner. Even when he didn't steal a base, he helped the Dodgers win in other ways. Robinson would dance off first base, almost daring the pitcher to try to get him out. Then the pitcher would get mixed up and then make bad pitches to the batter.

1. Jackie Robinson would dance off the base and almost dare the pitcher to try to get him out. Cause
2. The pitcher would get mixed up and make bad pitches. Effect

Jackie Robinson made the Brooklyn Dodgers a great team. Jackie played for the Dodgers for nine years, from 1947 to 1956. Before 1947, the Dodgers had only played in one World Series in the last 20 years. With Jackie leading the Dodgers, Brooklyn won the National League pennant five times. In 1955, they won the World Series against the New York Yankees.

3. The Dodgers won five pennants and the World Series. Effect
4. Jackie Robinson played for the Dodgers for nine years. Cause

At Home: During their leisure-time reading, have students look for cause and effect relationships.

190

Book 4/Unit 6
Teammates 4

Teammates • RETEACH

Make Judgments and Decisions

> Characters in stories **make judgments and decisions**. Readers make judgments and decisions about what characters decide to do or not do.

Read the paragraph. Then answer the questions.   Student's answers may vary.

> Jackie Robinson was a proud man who hated to lose. He was the kind of athlete who never gave up. That's what makes what he did in his first years with the Dodgers so unusual. Branch Rickey told Jackie he wanted him to promise he would not fight back. When people called Robinson, names, threw things at him, or tried to block him, Rickey wanted Robinson just to walk away. Rickey told Robinson that walking away would make the other fellow look bad. To Robinson, walking away felt like backing down. But he knew by not fighting back he would help the cause of black baseball players.

1. What decision did Jackie have to make? He had to decide if he could keep a promise to not fight back.

2. Was it fair of Branch Rickey to ask this of Robinson? Rickey probably felt strongly that Robinson could keep his promise, which would help all the players.

3. Why was the decision hard to make? Robinson was a proud man. Walking away felt like backing down to him.

4. Did Robinson's decision turn out to be a good one? Why? Yes. People saw Robinson as a wonderful athlete, not just an African American. He opened the doors for other African American players.

Book 4/Unit 6
Teammates
4

At Home: Have students discuss a difficult decision they have made.

191

Context Clues

> Remember: **Context clues**, or words and sentences nearby in the text, can help you figure out unfamiliar words.

Read the story, and each of the context clues in the box below the story. Then write the bold-faced word and the letter of the clue that helped you understand the word on the lines provided.

> This game had a little of everything. Garcia put down a perfect **bunt**. She ran her hands up the bat and just tapped the ball in front of home plate. Logan, the pitcher, was **southpaw**. As a left-handed thrower, she had to turn completely around to throw to first base. Logan then made a bad pitch to Zimmerman, and the **slugger** hit it out of the park. The **umpires** would not have to make a decision about that play! Logan recovered and struck out Lee. In the last inning, the final **score** was 5 to 2 in our favor.

> a. would not have to make a decision about that play
> b. She ran her hands up the bat and just tapped the ball in front of home plate.
> c. made a bad pitch to; hit it out of the park
> d. As a left-handed thrower
> e. 5 to 2 in our favor

1. to tap the ball without swinging bunt; b

2. officials who rule on plays umpires; a

3. someone who is left-handed southpaw; d

4. record of points made in a game score; e

5. powerful hitter slugger; c

192

At Home: Encourage students to use context clues to help them figure out the meaning of unfamiliar words that they find in a magazine or newspaper article.

Book 4/Unit 6
Teammates
5

Teammates • EXTEND

Name_____ Date_____ **Extend** ◈186

Cause and Effect

One of the first things we learn as children is **cause and effect**. If you drop a china plate, it will break. If you kick a sand castle, it will crumble. Later, we learn that if we don't study, we may not do well in school. If we treat someone unkindly, we may hurt their feelings.

A cause is something that produces an effect, or a result. Make a list of causes and effects that occur during your day.   **Answers will vary.**

Cause	Effect
Example:	
I threw the baseball too close to the house.	The ball broke a window.

1. _____   _____

2. _____   _____

3. _____   _____

4. _____   _____

5. _____   _____

6. _____   _____

7. _____   _____

8. _____   _____

At Home: Have students identify causes and effects in newspaper articles.

Name_____ Date_____ **Extend** ◈187

Vocabulary

circulated	launched	opponents
extraordinary	organizations	teammate

Write a sentence using each vocabulary word. Then read your sentences aloud to a partner, leaving out the vocabulary word. Have your partner choose the correct word to complete the sentence. Then fill in your partner's sentences.   **Answers will vary. Possible answers are given.**

1. The popular book circulated many times.

2. Her talent for playing the piano was extraordinary.

3. The cruise ship was launched in July.

4. Many volunteer organizations came to the aid of the flood victims.

5. The team beat all of their opponents to become state champions.

6. Each football teammate was equally important.

Extend ◈188

Story Comprehension

Think about Pee Wee Reese's courageous and kind acts in "Teammates." Write about how his actions may have affected others.

Answers will vary. Possible answers may include: By openly accepting Jackie Robinson as his teammate, he may have changed the way some other people thought about African Americans.

At Home: Have students name the effects of one of their actions today.

Name_____ Date_____ **Extend** ◈189

Use the Card Catalog: Subject Card

A **card catalog** helps you find books in the library. You can look up books in the card catalog by author, title, or subject. Subject cards help you find books by topic. For example, if you were interested in reading about Jackie Robinson, you would look for his name on a subject card.

Subject Card

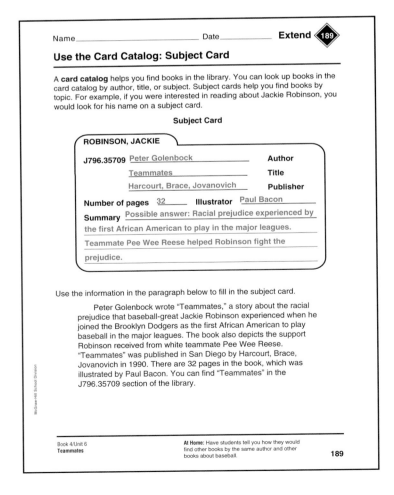

ROBINSON, JACKIE

J796.35709	Peter Golenbock	Author
	Teammates	Title
	Harcourt, Brace, Jovanovich	Publisher

Number of pages 32   Illustrator Paul Bacon

Summary Possible answer: Racial prejudice experienced by the first African American to play in the major leagues. Teammate Pee Wee Reese helped Robinson fight the prejudice.

Use the information in the paragraph below to fill in the subject card.

  Peter Golenbock wrote "Teammates," a story about the racial prejudice that baseball-great Jackie Robinson experienced when he joined the Brooklyn Dodgers as the first African American to play baseball in the major leagues. The book also depicts the support Robinson received from white teammate Pee Wee Reese. "Teammates" was published in San Diego by Harcourt, Brace, Jovanovich in 1990. There are 32 pages in the book, which was illustrated by Paul Bacon. You can find "Teammates" in the J796.35709 section of the library.

At Home: Have students tell you how they would find other books by the same author and other books about baseball.

Name_____ Date_____ **Extend** ◈190

Cause and Effect

As you read the story "Teammates," you will see that each thing that happened to Jackie Robinson caused him to do something else. Sometimes those effects become causes themselves.

For example:

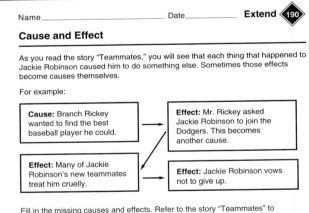

Cause: Branch Rickey wanted to find the best baseball player he could. → **Effect:** Mr. Rickey asked Jackie Robinson to join the Dodgers. This becomes another cause.

Effect: Many of Jackie Robinson's new teammates treat him cruelly. → **Effect:** Jackie Robinson vows not to give up.

Fill in the missing causes and effects. Refer to the story "Teammates" to help you.

Cause	Effect
1. Robinson was the first African American player to try out for a major league team.	At spring training, Jackie Robinson was mobbed by African American fans.
2. Jackie Robinson faced abuse and hostility throughout the baseball season.	Often he felt very alone.
3. Only white players were allowed in hotels in the towns where the team played.	Jackie Robinson had to live by himself while on the road.
4. He heard the fans yelling at Jackie Robinson	Pee Wee Reese decided to take a stand.
5. Pee Wee put his arm around Robinson and stood next to him.	The crowd gasped, then there was silence.

At Home: Have students tell about a time they stood up for something they believed in.

T10 *Annotated Workbooks*

Teammates • EXTEND

Make Judgments and Decisions

We make many **judgments and decisions** every day. Some are so easy we make them automatically. Others are more difficult and require careful thought.

Read the sentences or paragraphs below. Write what decision you would make in each situation. Be sure to explain your thinking.   Answers will vary. Possible answers are given.

1. You see two classmates teasing and scaring a younger child on the playground.
   If a parent is present, you alert the parent. If not, you go up to the child
   and help the child.
   _____

2. You promise you will rake the yard before dinner. You are halfway done when your best friend rides up on her bicycle and asks you to go for a ride.
   You ask your friend to wait or help you. If the friend declines, you
   continue raking.
   _____

3. A friend tells a joke that makes fun of certain people. It makes you uncomfortable.
   You tell your friend you don't like jokes that make fun of people.
   _____
   _____

4. You really want to buy a new baseball glove. You have saved $10 so far. You are invited to go to the video arcade for the afternoon. You know you'll spend at least $5 there, but it sounds like fun.
   The decision depends on how soon you need the glove. If you need it
   soon, you don't go; if you won't need it for a while, you'll probably go
   and plan to continue saving.

McGraw-Hill School Division

At Home: Have students keep a list of some of the decisions they have to make in one day.

Context Clues

Sometimes you can determine what an unfamiliar word means by looking at the words around it. **Context clues** give you hints about the meaning of a word or a series of words.

Find the following words in the story "Teammates." Tell which context clues helped you understand what each word means. Then write your definition.

Word	Context Clues	Definitions
leagues	baseball, players	groups of teams
prejudice	racial, wrong, unfair	unfair treatment of a particular group
racial	white, black, skin color	having to do with race
segregation	black people not allowed to go to the same schools, restaurants as white people	separation of a particular group
vigilante	Ku Klux Klan, violently, reacted	people who use violence to make a point
apathetic	few dared, feared, it was dangerous to object	do nothing
humiliations	cruel, nasty names, threats	cruelty, hostile intentions
audible	gasp, rose, then silence	able to be heard

McGraw-Hill School Division

At Home: Have students use context clues to figure out two unfamiliar words in a news article about an athlete.

Teammates • GRAMMAR

Grammar 161 — LEARN

Name_____ Date_____

Adverbs That Tell How

- An **adverb** is a word that tells more about a verb.
- Some adverbs tell how an action takes place.
- Most adverbs that tell how end in *-ly*. They are formed by adding *-ly* to an adjective.

A. Underline the adverb in each sentence.

1. In the 1940s, few Americans <u>openly</u> opposed racial segregation.

2. People were <u>generally</u> willing to let things stay as they were.

3. Many people believed that everyone should be treated <u>equally</u>.

4. They might have acted on their belief without stating it <u>publicly</u>.

5. There were groups that reacted <u>violently</u> to the idea of equality.

B. Add *-ly* to the bold faced word before each sentence to form an adverb that completes the sentence.

6. **significant** Branch Rickey changed baseball <u>significantly</u>.

7. **strong** He felt <u>strongly</u> that his team should have the best players, regardless of color.

8. **careful** He looked <u>carefully</u> for just the right player.

9. **exact** He found <u>exactly</u> the man he was looking for in Jackie Robinson.

10. **successful** He believed Jackie would <u>successfully</u> break the color barrier.

Grade 4/Unit 6
10 Teammates

EXTENSION: Ask students to write three sentences that include -ly adverbs.

161

Grammar 162 — LEARN & PRACTICE

Name_____ Date_____

Adverbs That Tell When or Where

- Some **adverbs** tell *when* or *where* an action takes place.
- Adverbs that tell *when* include *first, always, next, after, tomorrow, soon, early, today, then, yesterday*.
- Adverbs that tell *where* include *there, outside, up, here, nearby, ahead, around, far, away, everywhere*.

A. Rewrite each sentence by adding an adverb that tells *when*, and then underline the adverb you include. Students' answers may vary.

1. Jackie Robinson played with the Dodgers' farm team, the Montreal Royals.
   Jackie Robinson <u>first</u> played with the Dodgers' farm team, the Montreal Royals.

2. He was moved up to play with the Brooklyn Dodgers.
   He was <u>then</u> moved up to play with the Brooklyn Dodgers.

3. No matter with happened, Jackie Robinson remained calm.
   No matter with happened <u>after</u>, Jackie Robinson remained calm.

4. He earned the respect of his fellow players.
   He <u>soon</u> earned the respect of his fellow players.

B. Rewrite each sentence by adding an adverb that tells *where*, and then underline the adverb you include. Students' answers may vary.

5. Negro League teams traveled in their own cars and buses.
   Negro League teams traveled <u>everywhere</u> in their own cars and buses.

6. Their fans were loyal and would travel to see a game.
   Their fans were loyal and would travel <u>around</u> to see a game.

7. Hotels would tell them they couldn't stay.
   Hotels would tell them they couldn't stay <u>there</u>.

8. At restaurants they would hear, "You can't eat."
   At restaurants they would hear, "You can't eat <u>here</u>."

Extension: Ask students to identify and write three sentences from the selection that include adverbs. Have them decide if each adverb tells how, when, or where.

162

Grade 4/Unit 6
Teammates 8

Grammar 163 — PRACTICE AND REVIEW

Name_____ Date_____

Adverbs

- An **adverb** is a word that tells more about a verb.
- Some adverbs tell *how* an action takes place.
- Some adverbs tell *when* an action takes place.
- Some adverbs tell *where* an action takes place.

Underline the adverb in each sentence. Then tell if the adverb tells *how*, *when*, or *where* the action takes place.

1. Jackie Robinson ran <u>out</u> onto the field. <u>where</u>

2. What happened next hurt him <u>deeply</u>. <u>how</u>

3. Some fans were <u>enthusiastically</u> cheering for him. <u>how</u>

4. Some fans were booing at him <u>loudly</u>. <u>how</u>

5. <u>Soon</u> the players on the other team started calling him names. <u>when</u>

6. His teammates stood <u>by</u> and said nothing in his defense. <u>where</u>

7. Jackie Robinson <u>calmly</u> took it all without getting angry. <u>how</u>

8. His dignity <u>quickly</u> earned him his teammates' respect. <u>how</u>

9. Pee Wee Reese <u>bravely</u> set the example. <u>how</u>

10. He walked <u>over</u> and put his arm around Jackie's shoulders. <u>where</u>

11. <u>Then</u> the jeering crowd was silent. <u>when</u>

12. <u>Afterward</u> the Dodgers became a team in the true sense. <u>when</u>

Grade 4/Unit 6
12 Teammates

Extension: Have students write three sentences: one with an adverb that tells how, one with an adverb that tells when, and another with an adverb that tells where.

163

Grammar 164 — MECHANICS

Name_____ Date_____

Using Good and Well

- *Good* is an adjective and is used to describe nouns.
- *Well* is an adverb that tells *how* about a verb.
- Do not confuse the adjective *good* with the adverb *well*.

A. Read each sentence below and find the word *good* or *well* used incorrectly. Then write what the correct word is on the line provided

1. Pee Wee Reese proved himself a courageous man and a well friend.
   <u>good</u>

2. Jackie Robinson played good in spite of the abuses he suffered. <u>well</u>

3. Pee Wee Reese was a well man who believed in doing the right thing.
   <u>good</u>

4. Reese's action is a well example of fairness and sportsmanship. <u>good</u>

5. He said if Jackie played good enough to take his job, he deserved it.
   <u>well</u>

B. Complete each sentence by writing the word *good* or *well* on the line provided.

6. Branch Rickey wanted <u>good</u> players on the Dodgers.

7. If a man played <u>well</u>, the color of his skin didn't matter.

8. He thought Jackie Robinson would handle himself <u>well</u> on the field.

9. Reacting to the insults or fighting back would not be a <u>good</u> thing.

10. For Jackie, behaving <u>well</u> was the best revenge.

Extension: Have students write two sentences using the adjective good and two sentences using the adverb well.

164

Grade 4/Unit 6
Teammates 10

Teammates • GRAMMAR

Adverbs

Read each sentence. Then using the clue in the parenthesis, circle the letter before the adverb that completes each sentence.

1. The Dodgers played ____ . (when?)
   a. here
   b. yesterday
   c. enthusiastically
   d. the Reds

2. Jackie Robinson changed the game of baseball ____. (how?)
   a. then
   b. there
   c. permanently
   d. everywhere

3. His success was a victory for black athletes ____. (where?)
   a. today
   b. forever
   c. then
   d. everywhere

4. He gave black athletes the opportunity to compete ____. (how?)
   a. equally
   b. today
   c. anywhere
   d. nearby

5. There are African-American heroes in all sports ____. (when?)
   a. today
   b. everywhere
   c. internationally
   d. successfully

6. Some of the fans treated Jackie Robinson ____. (how?)
   a. next
   b. later
   c. cruelly
   d. before

McGraw-Hill School Division

Grade 4/Unit 6
Teammates
6

165

Adverbs

- An **adverb** is a word that tells more about a verb.
- Some adverbs tell *how* an action takes place.
- Most adverbs that tell *how* end in *-ly*. They are formed by adding *-ly* to an adjective.

Mechanics

- *Good* is an adjective and is used to describe nouns.
- *Well* is an adverb that tells how about a verb.
- Do not confuse the adjective *good* with the adverb *well*.

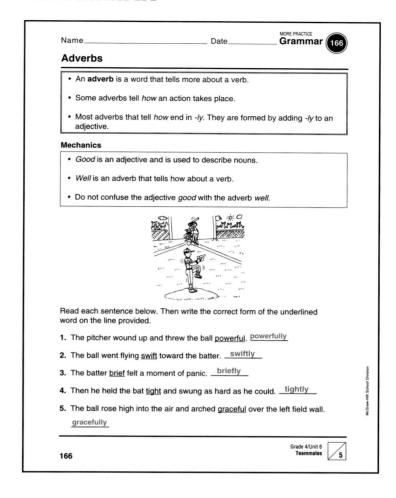

Read each sentence below. Then write the correct form of the underlined word on the line provided.

1. The pitcher wound up and threw the ball <u>powerful</u>. ___powerfully___

2. The ball went flying <u>swift</u> toward the batter. ___swiftly___

3. The batter <u>brief</u> felt a moment of panic. ___briefly___

4. Then he held the bat <u>tight</u> and swung as hard as he could. ___tightly___

5. The ball rose high into the air and arched <u>graceful</u> over the left field wall.
   ___gracefully___

McGraw-Hill School Division

166

Grade 4/Unit 6
Teammates
5

T13

Teammates • SPELLING

Page 161

Name_____ Date_____

Words with Silent Letters

Pretest Directions
Fold back the paper along the dotted line. Use the blanks to write each word as it is read aloud. When you finish the test, unfold the paper. Use the list at the right to correct any spelling mistakes. Practice the words you missed for the Posttest.

To Parents
Here are the results of your child's weekly spelling Pretest. You can help your child study for the Posttest by following these simple steps for each word on the word list:

1. Read the word to your child.
2. Have your child write the word, saying each letter as it is written.
3. Say each letter of the word as your child checks the spelling.
4. If a mistake has been made, have your child read each letter of the correctly spelled word aloud, and then repeat steps 1–3.

1.	_____	1. knew
2.	_____	2. climb
3.	_____	3. calm
4.	_____	4. although
5.	_____	5. knight
6.	_____	6. writer
7.	_____	7. knob
8.	_____	8. numb
9.	_____	9. delight
10.	_____	10. wren
11.	_____	11. knead
12.	_____	12. plumber
13.	_____	13. chalk
14.	_____	14. midnight
15.	_____	15. wreck
16.	_____	16. stalk
17.	_____	17. kneel
18.	_____	18. sought
19.	_____	19 thorough
20.	_____	20. wrestle

Challenge Words

_____ circulated
_____ extraordinary
_____ launched
_____ opponents
_____ organizations

Page 162

Name_____ Date_____

Words with Silent Letters

Using the Word Study Steps

1. LOOK at the word.
2. SAY the word aloud.
3. STUDY the letters in the word.
4. WRITE the word.
5. CHECK the word.

Did you spell the word right? If not, go back to step 1.

Spelling Tips
Silent letters may come at the beginning of a word, in the middle of a word, or at the end of a word. For example,
At the beginning: knob
In the middle: delight
At the end: numb

Find Rhyming Words
Rhyming words have the same last sound. Circle the word in each row that has the same last sound as the spelling word on the left.

1. knew	kneel	(few)		11. chalk	chart	(walk)
2. climb	(rhyme)	limb		12. wreck	(deck)	wrench
3. although	(grow)	enough		13. kneel	knot	(wheel)
4. knight	(bright)	knit		14. sought	(bought)	laughed
5. writer	written	(brighter)		15. thorough	(sorrow)	tough
6. knob	knee	(job)		16. calm	calf	(palm)
7. numb	(plum)	number		17. plumber	(summer)	plus
8. delight	(write)	delay		18. midnight	(white)	middle
9. wren	wrote	(when)		19. stalk	step	(hawk)
10. knead	(seed)	nod		20. wrestle	wring	(nestle)

To Parents or Helpers
Using the Word Study Steps above as your child comes across any new words will help him or her learn to spell words effectively. Review the steps as you both go over this week's spelling words.
Go over the Spelling Tip with your child. Help your child find the silent letters in each of this week's spelling words.
Help your child complete the spelling activity.

Page 163

Name_____ Date_____

Words with Silent Letters

knew	knight	delight	chalk	kneel
climb	writer	wren	midnight	sought
calm	knob	knead	wreck	thorough
although	numb	plumber	stalk	wrestle

Pattern Power!
Write the spelling words with these spelling patterns.

words with silent k
1. knew
2. knight
3. knob
4. knead
5. kneel

words with silent b
6. climb
7. numb
8. plumber

words with silent l
9. calm
10. chalk
11. stalk

words with silent gh
12. although
13. delight
14. midnight
15. sought
16. thorough

words with silent wr
17. writer
18. wren
19. wreck
20. wrestle

Page 164

Name_____ Date_____

Words with Silent Letters

knew	knight	delight	chalk	kneel
climb	writer	wren	midnight	sought
calm	knob	knead	wreck	thorough
although	numb	plumber	stalk	wrestle

What's the Word?
Complete each sentence with a word from the spelling list.

1. This book was written by my favorite ____writer____.
2. His hiking boots helped him ____climb____ the steep hill.
3. The jacket still fits, ____although____ I've grown a bit.
4. She turned the ____knob____ of the door.
5. My fingers became so cold, they felt ____numb____.
6. A tiny ____wren____ built a nest in the bird house.
7. We had to call a ____plumber____ to come and fix the leak.
8. A cat will first ____stalk____ a mouse before catching one.
9. Tom is learning to ____wrestle____ in the gym after school.
10. They ____sought____ to find a way to solve the problem.
11. The ____chalk____ broke when he used it on the chalkboard.
12. When I heard the phone ring, I ____knew____ it must be you.

Opposites
Write the spelling word that is opposite in meaning to the words below.

13. nervous ____calm____   16. build ____wreck____
14. sadness ____delight____   17. stand ____kneel____
15. noon ____midnight____   18. incomplete ____thorough____

Challenge Extension: Write a fill-in sentence for each challenge word. Exchange papers with a partner and complete each other's fill-in sentences.

Teammates • SPELLING

Words with Silent Letters

Proofreading

There are six spelling mistakes in the paragraph below. Circle the misspelled words. Write the words correctly on the lines below.

"Oh, no!" coach said, as he twisted the (nob) turn off the water. "The sink in the team bathroom is leaking again." My Aunt Mary is a (plummer.) So we called her to come fix the sink. It was hard to find the leak. Aunt Mary had to (neal) on the hard tile floor until her knees were (nubm.) After finding the leak, she went to the store to buy a new pipe. Aunt Mary had to (restle) with the new pipe to get it in place. "There!" Aunt Mary said, smiling with (delite.) "The sink is fixed."

1. ___knob___
2. ___plumber___
3. ___kneel___
4. ___numb___
5. ___wrestle___
6. ___delight___

Writing Activity

What team sport do you like to play or to watch? Write a few sentences about your favorite sport. Use four spelling words in your writing.

_____

_____

_____

_____

Words with /ou/ and /oi/

Look at the words in each set below. One word in each set is spelled correctly. Use a pencil to fill in the circle next to the correct word. Before you begin, look at the sample sets of words. Sample A has been done for you. Do Sample B by yourself. When you are sure you know what to do, you may go on with the rest of the page.

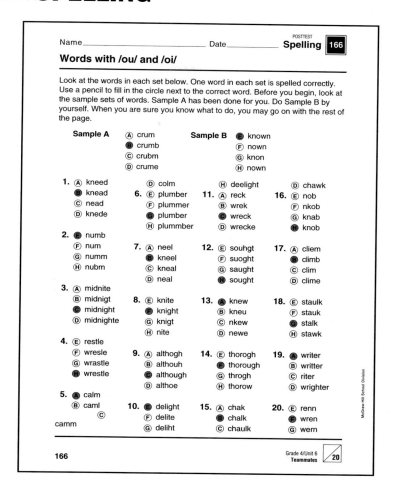

Sample A
- Ⓐ crum
- Ⓑ crumb ●
- Ⓒ crubm
- Ⓓ crume

Sample B
- Ⓔ known ●
- Ⓕ nown
- Ⓖ knon
- Ⓗ nown

1.
- Ⓐ kneed
- Ⓑ knead ●
- Ⓒ nead
- Ⓓ knede

2.
- Ⓔ numb ●
- Ⓕ num
- Ⓖ numm
- Ⓗ nubm

3.
- Ⓐ midnite
- Ⓑ midnigt
- Ⓒ midnight ●
- Ⓓ midnighte

4.
- Ⓔ restle
- Ⓕ wresle
- Ⓖ wrastle
- Ⓗ wrestle ●

5.
- Ⓐ calm ●
- Ⓑ caml
- Ⓒ camm

6.
- Ⓔ plumber
- Ⓕ plummer
- Ⓖ plumber ●
- Ⓗ plummber

7.
- Ⓐ neel
- Ⓑ kneel ●
- Ⓒ kneal
- Ⓓ neal

8.
- Ⓔ knite
- Ⓕ knight ●
- Ⓖ knigt
- Ⓗ nite

9.
- Ⓐ althogh
- Ⓑ althouh
- Ⓒ although ●
- Ⓓ althoe

10.
- Ⓔ delight ●
- Ⓕ delite
- Ⓖ deliht

11.
- Ⓐ reck
- Ⓑ wrek
- Ⓒ wreck ●
- Ⓓ wrecke

12.
- Ⓔ souhgt
- Ⓕ suoght
- Ⓖ saught
- Ⓗ sought ●

13.
- Ⓐ knew ●
- Ⓑ kneu
- Ⓒ nkew
- Ⓓ newe

14.
- Ⓔ thorogh
- Ⓕ thorough ●
- Ⓖ throgh
- Ⓗ thorow

15.
- Ⓐ chak
- Ⓑ chalk ●
- Ⓒ chaulk

16.
- Ⓔ nob
- Ⓕ nkob
- Ⓖ knab
- Ⓗ knob ●

17.
- Ⓐ cliem
- Ⓑ climb ●
- Ⓒ clim
- Ⓓ clime

18.
- Ⓔ staulk
- Ⓕ stauk
- Ⓖ stalk ●
- Ⓗ stawk

19.
- Ⓐ writer ●
- Ⓑ writter
- Ⓒ riter
- Ⓓ wrighter

20.
- Ⓔ renn
- Ⓕ wren ●
- Ⓖ wern

The Malachite Palace • PRACTICE

Problem and Solution

In many stories, the main character will often have a **problem** to overcome. There may be more than one **solution** to the problem. Read the short story below. Write what the problem is. Then write three possible solutions to the problem, and choose the final solution.

A long time ago, Pierre was hungry. He was always hungry, and the people in the local village were tired of feeding him. "Why don't you get a job, and they can pay you with food," someone said.
"Why don't you grow a garden," said another.
"Why don't you ask the king to feed you," said someone else.
Pierre thought someone else would feed him as usual, but this time no one did.
The next day, Pierre was really hungry. He knew what he would do. He got a pot almost as big as himself and filled it with water. Then he hauled it to the town square and built a fire under it. Soon everyone wanted to know what he was doing. "Well," said Pierre. "I'm making soup for my friends. I put in my secret ingredients, and my soup is very delicious. I wish to share it with the village."
"Ah, how wonderful," said the people.
"I just need a few more things for my soup," said Pierre. "Please, give me some meat, a few carrots, and beans. Oh yes, potatoes would be good, too."
Everyone brought something. When the soup was done, the villagers declared the soup delicious. They asked Pierre to make the soup every day. Pierre was never hungry again.

What was the problem?

1. Pierre was hungry.

What two solutions that were presented to Pierre by the villagers?

2. He could get a job and be paid with food.

3. He could grow a garden.

What solution to his problem did Pierre choose?

4. Pierre filled a pot with water and got all the people in town to bring

   ingredients to make soup for everyone.

Vocabulary

Choose the correct word from the box to complete each sentence.

cultured	feeble	fragrance	mingled	resembled	scampered

1. One bird was strong and healthy, and the other was weak and feeble_____.

2. They smelled the wonderful fragrance_____ of the rose bushes and other flowers.

3. After the shows, the actors walked around, talked, and mingled_____ with the people.

4. He is known as a very intelligent, cultured_____, and well-mannered boy.

5. The two sisters resembled_____ each other because of their similar hair and clothing.

6. The kindergartners scampered_____ up the hill after the puppies.

Write two sentences that use two vocabulary words in each sentence.
Answers will vary but should make correct use of the vocabulary.

7. _____

8. _____

Andrew's Father

Everyone said Andrew's father was the most *cultured* man in town. He was a gentleman. Andrew's father had studied hard as a boy. He knew about music and paintings. He had read many books.
Andrew's father had something else he was known for. It was his beautiful flower garden. People could enjoyed the *fragrance* of his flowers as their scents *mingled* in the air. People brought their dying and *feeble* plants to Andrew's father. He told the people what to do. Soon the plants were strong again. As a small boy, Andrew *scampered* in and out of the garden as his father weeded and planted. Now that he was older, Andrew worked alongside his father, learning everything he could. When Andrew grew up, people remarked about how much he *resembled* his father. That made Andrew feel proud.

1. What makes a person *cultured*?
   Answers will vary, but may include that they are educated;
   that they enjoy the arts; or that they have manners.

2. What were the two things Andrew's father was known for?
   Possible answers: being cultured; growing a beautiful
   flower garden; bringing feeble plants back to help.

3. How did the *fragrance* of the flower garden affect people?
   The fragrance of the flowers mingled in the air and people enjoyed it.

4. What kinds of plants did people bring to Andrew's father?
   feeble and dying plants.

5. How do you think Andrew felt about his father?
   Answers will vary, but may include that he felt pride and admiration.

Story Comprehension

Read each statement. Write **T** if the statement describes "The Malachite Palace." Write **F** if it does not describe "The Malachite Palace."

1. __T__ The princess is the only child living in the palace.

2. __T__ The queen and the governess do not understand that the princess is lonely.

3. __F__ The princess has fun with her governess and the lady-in-waiting.

4. __F__ The governess admires the children who live near the palace.

5. __T__ The princess thinks the children sound happy as they play outside.

6. __F__ The bird only likes rich foods, caviar, and chocolate.

7. __F__ The bird can not sing because of an illness.

8. __T__ The princess turns the cage into a kind of bird feeder, and the birds come and go as they wish.

Refer to "The Malachite Palace" to help you answer each question.

9. How did the princess prove to be wiser than her governess and lady-in-waiting? Answers may vary, but should include:
   The princess knew the bird needed to be free because it was
   lonely, just as she needed to play with the children.

10. Describe how the little bird and the princess are alike.
    Possible answers: The bird wanted to have the freedom to be
    with other birds. The princess wanted to play with other children.
    Both the princess and the bird were lonely.

The Malachite Palace • PRACTICE

Use the Card Catalog: Author and Title Card

There are three kinds of cards in the **card catalog**: the **title card**, the **author card**, and the **subject card**. Below are a title and an author card for books by Alma Flor Ada. Look at the cards and answer the questions.

	TITLE CARD
Call Number	Pic A
Title	The Malachite Palace
Author	Ada, Alma Flor
Summary	A tiny yellow bird helps a lonely princess learn the truth about freedom and the children beyond the palace gates.
Translator	Translation by Rosa Zubizarreta. Illustrations by Leonid Gore.
Publisher/Date	New York: Atheneum Books for Young Readers, ©1998
Number of Pages	32 pages

	AUTHOR CARD
Call Number	J B Ada
Author	Ada, Alma Flor
Title	Where the Flame Trees Bloom
Summary	In this biography, Alma Flor Ada tells 12 stories about her early life in Cuba. The stories are of her great-grandmother and other relatives, Samone, their kindly hired hand, and the land and hacienda where she lived.
Translator	Rosa Zubizarreta. Illustrations by Antonio Martorell.
Publisher/Date	New York: Atheneum, ©1994
Number of Pages	75 pages

1. Suppose you can't remember the author's name of "The Malachite Palace." Which card could you use? title card

2. What is the name of the second book written by Alma Flor Ada? "Where the Flame Trees Bloom"

3. Suppose you wanted to find out if your library has any other books by the same author. Where would you look? author card

4. Which book might be for older kids and which would be better suited for younger kids? Why? "The Malachite Palace" would be useful for younger children because it is a picture book and is shorter. "Where the Flame Trees Bloom" is a biography with 75 pages, making it more suited to older children.

Problem and Solution

Stories often have **problems** and **solutions**.
Read the problems below. Think about different ways the problems can be solved. Write ways you might solve the problem. Then tell how a similar problem was solved in "The Malachite Palace."
Answers will vary. Possible answers are given.

A. Problem: A child is lonely because she has no one to play with.

Three possible solutions:

1. She might invite children from the neighborhood to visit.

2. She might get a pet.

3. She might join a play group or athletic team.

Author's solution in the story:

4. The princess notices children playing outside the palace and decides to join them.

B. Problem: You want a pet that is wild and is not suited as an indoor companion for a child.

Three possible solutions:

5. You choose a pet like a cat or dog.

6. You set up an outdoor feeder so you can admire the animal from a far.

7. You set the pet free.

Author's solution in the story:

8. The princess sets the bird free and turns the cage into a feeder.

Cause and Effect

Events in a story can often be organized by **cause and effect**. One event causes another to happen. Fill in the missing cause or effect of each event listed in the chart below. Answers will vary. Possible answers are given.

Cause	Effect
1. The governess thought the children outside the palace were rude, ignorant, and common.	The princess had no friends.
2. The princess kept the palace windows tightly closed.	The princess couldn't hear the children laughing and playing.
3. A singing bird flew into the room.	The princess and the governess tried to catch the singing bird and put it in a cage.
4. The lady-in-waiting and the governess give the bird in the cage caviar and chocolate	The bird would not sing.
5. The children were peeking through the iron fence.	The queen planted thick and tall vines so the children couldn't peek in.
6. On a colder day, the princess could hear the children laughing through the vines, so she did something for the bird.	The princess opened the cage and let the bird fly out.
7. The princess made a bird feeder out of the old cage by cutting off the door.	The little bird returned with other birds.
8. The laughter of children playing outside seemed more joyful than ever.	The little princess opened the gate and ran out to play with the children.

Synonyms and Antonyms

Synonyms are words that mean the same or almost the same thing.
Antonyms are words that mean almost the opposite.

Write a synonym from the list that could replace the underlined word.

rude	joyful	governess	malachite

1. Luis felt so happy in his new school. joyful

2. The prince had a teacher who lived in the palace with him. governess

3. There is never a bad-mannered student in Mrs. Oakley's class. rude

4. The girl wore a copper-colored bracelet on her wrist. malachite

Write an antonym for the underlined word or words to complete the sentences.

rude	interesting	relaxed	ignorant

5. The queen said one person was cultured, and the other person was ignorant.

6. One person was kind and thoughtful, and the other person was rude.

7. One movie was boring, but the other one was interesting.

8. Before the test, many people felt anxious, but after, everyone felt relaxed.

The Malachite Palace • RETEACH

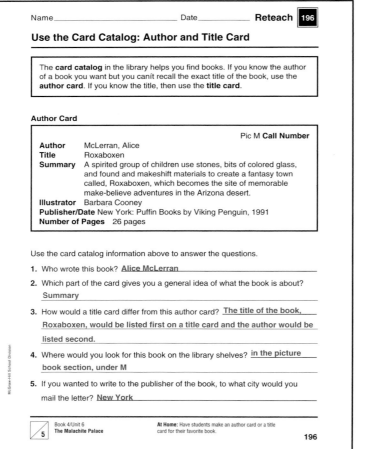

Problem and Solution

Many times a character in a story will have a **problem**. What he or she does to correct the problem is called the **solution**.

Read each of the following stories. Then fill in the charts by identifying the problem and solution in each story.

Olga wanted to have her friend Jin visit after school. But Olga's little sister Jessica was always such a pest. Jessica would play tricks and spy on the older girls. Then Olga had an idea. She asked her mom if Jin's little sister Lei could come to the house, too. Jessica and Lei had a great time, and the older girls were able to talk and visit in peace.

Problem	Solution
1. Jessica is a pest when Olga's friends come over to visit.	2. Olga invites Jin's little sister Lei to come to play with Jessica, so she won't bother Jin and her.

Mickey loves baseball, and he is a good hitter. But since he joined the school team, he hasn't made a hit. He knows everyone is watching him when he comes up to bat. Mickey tried extra practice, but that didn't help. Then he asked his brother for advice. Tim told Mickey to picture himself at bat in the backyard, with no one watching. At the next school game, Mickey made a hit.

Problem	Solution
3. Mickey can't make hits since joining the school team. He gets nervous.	4. Mickey asks his brother for advice. Following it, Mickey pictures himself alone at bat, with no one watching. He makes a hit in the next game.

Book 4/Unit 6
The Malachite Palace 4

At Home: Have students reread a familiar story to identify the problem and solution.

193

Vocabulary

Write a word from the list to complete each sentence.

mingled	feeble	scampered	cultured	fragrance	resembled

1. The girl is <u>cultured</u> because she knows about art, music, and dance.
2. The woman was too <u>feeble</u> to go out in the storm alone.
3. The <u>fragrance</u> of the flowers in spring is wonderful.
4. The voices of the children <u>mingled</u> with the music.
5. The children <u>scampered</u> happily across the lawn.
6. The figure on the painting <u>resembled</u> her father.

6

Story Comprehension

Write the answers to the following questions about "The Malachite Palace." You may look back at the story.

1. Why wasn't the princess allowed to play with the other children? <u>The adults around the princess thought the children were not good enough.</u>
2. Why did the princess want the little bird caught? <u>She wanted a friend, or something to keep her company.</u>
3. Why did the little bird stop singing? <u>Caged, the bird missed the outdoors, the children, and freedom.</u>
4. What did the princess make the birdcage into? <u>She made it into a birdfeeder, a place where birds could eat and fly away.</u>

At Home: Have students write about their favorite part of "The Malachite Palace."

194–195

Book 4/Unit 6
The Malachite Palace 4

Use the Card Catalog: Author and Title Card

The **card catalog** in the library helps you find books. If you know the author of a book you want but you can't recall the exact title of the book, use the **author card**. If you know the title, then use the **title card**.

Author Card

Pic M **Call Number**

Author	McLerran, Alice
Title	Roxaboxen
Summary	A spirited group of children use stones, bits of colored glass, and found and makeshift materials to create a fantasy town called, Roxaboxen, which becomes the site of memorable make-believe adventures in the Arizona desert.
Illustrator	Barbara Cooney
Publisher/Date	New York: Puffin Books by Viking Penguin, 1991
Number of Pages	26 pages

Use the card catalog information above to answer the questions.

1. Who wrote this book? <u>Alice McLerran</u>
2. Which part of the card gives you a general idea of what the book is about? <u>Summary</u>
3. How would a title card differ from this author card? <u>The title of the book, Roxaboxen, would be listed first on a title card and the author would be listed second.</u>
4. Where would you look for this book on the library shelves? <u>in the picture book section, under M</u>
5. If you wanted to write to the publisher of the book, to what city would you mail the letter? <u>New York</u>

Book 4/Unit 6
The Malachite Palace 5

At Home: Have students make an author card or a title card for their favorite book.

196

Problem and Solution

Sometimes in a story more than one character has a problem. Read carefully to identify each **problem** and its **solution**.

Read the following story. Then answer each question below.

Brendan's mom was worried. It was the first day she let Brendan walk home from school alone. It was 3:30 P.M., and he was 20 minutes late. Finally she went to look for him. She found him cheerfully talking to some friends. Brendan didn't understand why his mom was so worried. He was afraid she wouldn't let him walk home alone again.

Later, Brendan told his mom that walking home alone was important to him. They agreed that he would wear a watch to keep track of time. He would be home each day by 3:20 P.M.

1. What is Brendan's mother's problem?
   a. She lost her watch in the neighborhood.
   b. (She doesn't know why Brendan is late.)
2. How does she solve her problem?
   a. She calls the neighbors.
   b. (She goes to look for Brendan.)
3. What is Brendan's problem?
   a. (He wants to be able to talk with friends on the way home.)
   b. He doesn't want to walk home alone.
4. What solution do Brendan and his mother agree upon?
   a. Brendan will buy a watch on the way home.
   b. (Brendan will wear a watch and get home by 3:20 P.M.)

At Home: Have students express their feelings about the two characters' problems and solutions.

197

Book 4/Unit 6
The Malachite Palace 4

Cause and Effect

> Many readers look for **cause and effect** relationships as they read. They ask themselves "what is happening?" and "why?"

Read each story below. Then write the missing cause or effect on the lines provided.

Every year in April we see many snow geese flying overhead. They head north because it is their migration time. This year the cornstalks had just been cut in a nearby field and corn seed was scattered on the ground. This made the field an ideal place for the geese to stop to eat and rest.

1. **Cause:** It is migration time for snow geese.

   Effect: We see many snow geese flying overhead.

2. **Cause:** Cornstalks had just been cut in a nearby field and corn seed was scattered on the ground.

   Effect: The field was a good stopping place for the geese to eat and rest.

Rachel is upset. Rachel wants to play soccer, but her mom wants her to play the piano. Rachel likes to wear jeans, but her mom keeps buying her dresses. Rachel wants to stop her mom. She also wants to make a strong statement. She packs and tells her mom she is going to stay with her grandmother.

3. **Cause:** Rachel and her mother disagree about many things.

   Effect: Rachel is upset.

4. **Cause:** Rachel wants to make a strong statement.

   Effect: Rachel packs and tells her mom she will go to stay with her grandmother.

198

Synonyms and Antonyms

> **Synonyms** are words that have the almost the same meaning.

Write the letter of the proper synonym for each numbered word on the line provided.

e	**1.** permitted	**a.** small
a	**2.** tiny	**b.** labor
h	**3.** rare	**c.** placed
g	**4.** came	**d.** watched
f	**5.** sounds	**e.** allowed
b	**6.** work	**f.** noises
c	**7.** positioned	**g.** arrived
d	**8.** observed	**h.** unusual

> An **antonym** is a word that has the opposite meaning.

Write the letter of the proper antonym for each numbered word on the line provided.

e	**1.** nothing	**a.** closed
h	**2.** captured	**b.** polite
d	**3.** friend	**c.** slowly
b	**4.** rude	**d.** enemy
g	**5.** heavy	**e.** everything
c	**6.** quickly	**f.** under
a	**7.** opened	**g.** light
f	**8.** over	**h.** released

199

The Malachite Palace • EXTEND

Problem and Solution

Many different kinds of **problems and solutions** exist. Different people may often choose different solutions for the same problem.

Read each problem below. Write your solution. Then compare your solutions with a partner. How are the solutions the same? How are they different?   Answers will vary. Possible answers are given.

1. It's your first day at a new school. At lunch time, the cafeteria is crowded with unfamiliar faces. What would you do? I would walk to a table with an empty seat and ask if I could join the people sitting there.

_____

2. You have three homework assignments tonight, and you have to study for tomorrow's spelling test. You feel overwhelmed. What would you do?
I would study for the test first. Then I would start to work on the other assignments.

3. You and four friends are going to a movie. Your mother is driving all of you. Another friend asks to join you, but there is no more room in the car. What would you do?
I would ask if someone else's parent could take two of us.

_____

4. You and two classmates are working on a project that has four parts to it. How do you divide the work in a way that is fair to everyone?
I would give each person one part and have all three work jointly on the fourth part.

Vocabulary

cultured	feeble	fragrance	mingled	resembled	scampered

Work with a partner. Each of you choose three words from the vocabulary list and write down the definitions. Then make up false definitions for each of your three words. Read your partner both definitions for each word, and have him or her guess which is correct.   Answers will vary.

_____

_____

_____

_____

_____

Story Comprehension

After feeling lonely and frustrated for a long time, the princess in the story "The Malachite Palace" solved her problem for herself. What kinds of judgments or decisions did the princess make in order to solve her problem?

Answers will vary. Possible answer: After watching the bird and seeing that it wasn't happy being caged and isolated from the children, the princess realized that her own situation was the same. She decided to set the bird free and to end her loneliness by playing with the other children.

Use the Card Catalog: Author and Title Cards

A **card catalog** helps you find books in the library. Subject cards help you find books by subject. Author cards help you find books written by a certain author. Title cards help you find books by title. The card catalog is arranged alphabetically. The call number in the upper left-hand corner of the card tells you where to find the book on the library shelves.

Title Card
Fill in the title card with the information listed below.

• 26 Pages
• After the dragon burns down the kingdom and captures Prince Ronald, Princess Elizabeth uses her wits to outsmart the dragon and rescue the prince.
• Toronto: Annick Press, 1980
• Illus. by Michael Martchenko
• JL M
• Musch, Robert N.
• The Paper Bag Princess

Call Number:
1. JL M

Title   2. The Paper Bag Princess

Author   3. Munsch, Robert N

Summary: 4. After a dragon burns down the kingdom and captures Prince Ronald, Princess Elizabeth uses her wits to outsmart the dragon and rescue the prince.

Publisher/Date: 5. Toronto: Annick Press, 1980

Number of Pages/
Illustrations: 6. 26 pages; illus. by Michael Martchenko

7. When would you find this card helpful? When you know the title and author of the book.

Problem and Solution

The princess in the story "The Malachite Palace" used her imagination to find a **solution** for the **problem** of the captured bird's loneliness. By experimenting with tools she had never used, she found a way to make his cage into a home from which the bird could come and go as it pleased.

Suppose your school needs a new playground, but it cannot afford to buy expensive equipment. Think about how you might solve this problem, and design the playground so that it meets the needs of all the students in your school. Write about your plan for the new playground and why you think it will work.

Answers will vary. Accept all reasonable solutions.

_____

_____

_____

_____

_____

_____

_____

_____

_____

The Malachite Palace • EXTEND

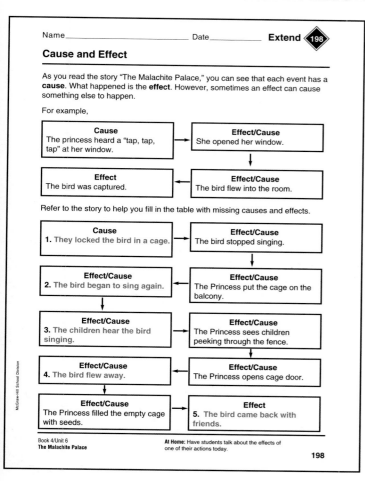

Cause and Effect

As you read the story "The Malachite Palace," you can see that each event has a **cause**. What happened is the **effect**. However, sometimes an effect can cause something else to happen.

For example,

Cause	Effect/Cause
The princess heard a "tap, tap, tap" at her window.	She opened her window.

Effect	Effect/Cause
The bird was captured.	The bird flew into the room.

Refer to the story to help you fill in the table with missing causes and effects.

Cause	Effect/Cause
1. They locked the bird in a cage.	The bird stopped singing.

Effect/Cause	Effect/Cause
2. The bird began to sing again.	The Princess put the cage on the balcony.

Effect/Cause	Effect/Cause
3. The children hear the bird singing.	The Princess sees children peeking through the fence.

Effect/Cause	Effect/Cause
4. The bird flew away.	The Princess opens cage door.

Effect/Cause	Effect
The Princess filled the empty cage with seeds.	5. The bird came back with friends.

Book 4/Unit 6
The Malachite Palace

At Home: Have students talk about the effects of one of their actions today.

198

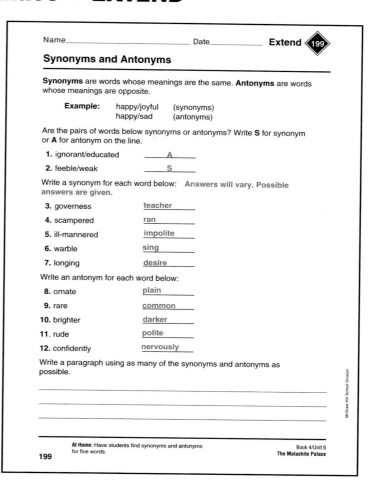

Synonyms and Antonyms

Synonyms are words whose meanings are the same. **Antonyms** are words whose meanings are opposite.

Example: happy/joyful   (synonyms)
happy/sad   (antonyms)

Are the pairs of words below synonyms or antonyms? Write **S** for synonym or **A** for antonym on the line.

1. ignorant/educated   A
2. feeble/weak   S

Write a synonym for each word below: Answers will vary. Possible answers are given.

3. governess   teacher
4. scampered   ran
5. ill-mannered   impolite
6. warble   sing
7. longing   desire

Write an antonym for each word below:

8. ornate   plain
9. rare   common
10. brighter   darker
11. rude   polite
12. confidently   nervously

Write a paragraph using as many of the synonyms and antonyms as possible.

_____

_____

_____

At Home: Have students find synonyms and antonyms for five words.

199

Book 4/Unit 6
The Malachite Palace

T21

The Malachite Palace • GRAMMAR

Name _____ Date _____ **Grammar** 167

Adverbs That Compare

- An **adverb** can compare two or more actions.
- Add *-er* to short adverbs to compare two actions.
- Add *-est* to short adverbs to compare more than two actions.

Add *-er* or *-est* to each boldfaced adverb to complete the sentences below. Remember to drop final *e* or change *y* to *i* when necessary before adding *-er* and *-est*.

1. **near** She walked _nearer_ to look into the silver cage.

2. **close** The _closer_ she came, the sadder the yellow bird appeared to be.

3. **early** The princess rose _earlier_ than the rest of household.

4. **low** The lady-in-waiting bowed low, but the governess bowed _lower_.

5. **high** Of all the birds in flight, the little yellow one flew _highest_.

6. **loud** When it sang, it sang _loudest_ and best.

7. **straighter** The princess stood _straighter_ after she defied the queen.

8. **deeper** She breathed _deeper_ and laughed more.

9. **fast** Sliding over the snow, the princess went _fastest_ and farthest.

10. **soon** The _sooner_ people learn to enjoy simple things, the better they will be.

Name _____ Date _____ **Grammar** 168

Adverbs That Compare

- Use *more* or *most* to form comparisons with adverbs that end in *–ly* or with longer adverbs.
- Use *more* to compare two actions.
- Use *most* to compare more than two actions.
- When you use *more* or *most*, do not use the ending *-er* or *-est*.

Use *more* or *most* with the underlined adverb in each first sentence, to complete the two sentences that follow.

1. A lark sings <u>sweetly</u> in the morning.
   Some think a nightingale sings _more sweetly_ in the evening.
   But the princess's little yellow bird sang _most sweetly_.

2. The children laughed <u>joyfully</u> as they played in the snow.
   They laughed _more joyfully_ when they saw the yellow bird.
   However, they cheered and laughed _most joyfully_ when the princess came out to play with them.

3. The lady-in-waiting spoke <u>harshly</u> about the other children.
   The governess spoke _more harshly_ about them.
   The queen spoke of them _most harshly_ of all.

4. The princess told the lady-in-waiting <u>firmly</u>, "That's not true."
   She told the governess _more firmly_, "That's not true."
   She told the queen _most firmly_, "That's not true."

5. The iron fence <u>effectively</u> separated the princess from other children.
   Vines _more effectively_ shut her off from the children.
   They isolated her _most effectively_ after they had grown tall and thick.

Name _____ Date _____ PRACTICE AND REVIEW **Grammar** 169

Adverbs That Compare

- An **adverb** can compare two or more actions.
- Add *-er* to short adverbs to compare two actions.
- Add *-est* to short adverbs to compare more than two actions.
- Use *more* or *most* to form comparisons with adverbs that end in *–ly* or with longer adverbs.
- Use *more* to compare two actions.
- Use *most* to compare more than two actions.
- When you use *more* or *most*, do not use the ending *-er* or *-est*.

Write the comparative form of the adjective given to complete each sentence.

1. sadly
On the balcony the bird sang again, but _more sadly_ than it had before.

2. brightly
Whenever the children laughed, the bird would sing _more brightly_ than before.

3. beautifully
The bird sang _more beautifully_ than other birds.

4. thickly
When summer came, the vines covered the iron fence _more thickly_ than in the winter.

5. loud
The more the children laughed, the _louder_ the yellow bird sang.

6. loud
The bird sang _loudest_ when the princess laughed.

7. clumsily
At first the princess worked _most clumsily_ with the tools.

8. confidently
But after a while, she began to work _more confidently_.

Name _____ Date _____ MECHANICS **Grammar** 170

Using *More* and *Most*

- Never add *-er* and *more* to the same adverb.
- Never add *-est* and *most* to the same adverb.

Write the correct adverbs on the lines provided.

1. Children live more happilier in the company of others. _happily_

2. The princess spoke most confidentliest when she said, "That's not true!".
   confidently

3. At the end, the yellow bird sang more louder than before. _loudly_

4. She opened the window more wider, and the yellow bird flew in. _wider_

5. When the children laughed, the bird sang more brightlier. _brightly_

6. Nobody worked with tools more clumsilier than the princess. _clumsily_

7. She developed her skills more sooner than most. _sooner_

8. She removed the door so that the bird could come and go more freelier.
   freely

9. Now the cage more closelier resembled an archway. _closely_

10. The yellow bird returned most willingliest and brought his friends. _willingly_

The Malachite Palace • GRAMMAR

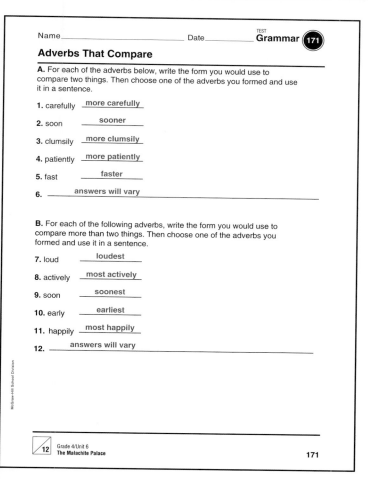

Adverbs That Compare

A. For each of the adverbs below, write the form you would use to compare two things. Then choose one of the adverbs you formed and use it in a sentence.

1. carefully __more carefully__

2. soon ____sooner____

3. clumsily __more clumsily__

4. patiently __more patiently__

5. fast ____faster____

6. ____answers will vary____

B. For each of the following adverbs, write the form you would use to compare more than two things. Then choose one of the adverbs you formed and use it in a sentence.

7. loud ____loudest____

8. actively __most actively__

9. soon ____soonest____

10. early ____earliest____

11. happily __most happily__

12. ____answers will vary____

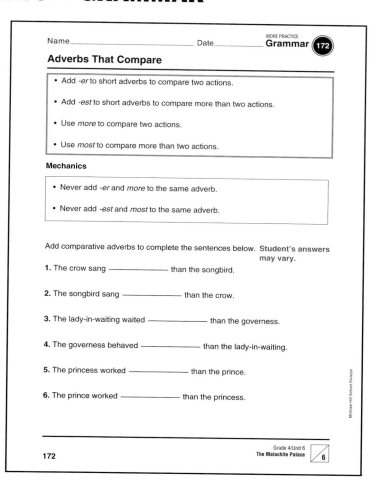

Adverbs That Compare

- Add *-er* to short adverbs to compare two actions.

- Add *-est* to short adverbs to compare more than two actions.

- Use *more* to compare two actions.

- Use *most* to compare more than two actions.

Mechanics

- Never add *-er* and *more* to the same adverb.

- Never add *-est* and *most* to the same adverb.

Add comparative adverbs to complete the sentences below. **Student's answers may vary.**

1. The crow sang _____ than the songbird.

2. The songbird sang _____ than the crow.

3. The lady-in-waiting waited _____ than the governess.

4. The governess behaved _____ than the lady-in-waiting.

5. The princess worked _____ than the prince.

6. The prince worked _____ than the princess.

T23

The Malachite Palace • SPELLING

Homophones and Homographs

Pretest Directions

Fold back the paper along the dotted line. Use the blanks to write each word as it is said aloud. When you finish the test, unfold the paper. Use the list at the right to correct any spelling mistakes. Practice the words that you missed for the Posttest.

To Parents

Here are the results of your child's weekly spelling Pretest. You can help your child study for the Posttest by following these simple steps for each word on the word list:

1. Read the word to your child.
2. Have your child write the word, saying each letter as it is written.
3. Say each letter of the word as your child checks the spelling.
4. If a mistake has been made, have your child read each letter of the correctly spelled word aloud and then repeat steps 1–3.

1. _____	1. seen
2. _____	2. great
3. _____	3. light
4. _____	4. beat
5. _____	5. lean
6. _____	6. scene
7. _____	7. beet
8. _____	8. bowl
9. _____	9. grate
10. _____	10. fan
11. _____	11. peak
12. _____	12. post
13. _____	13. pail
14. _____	14. bury
15. _____	15. punch
16. _____	16. pale
17. _____	17. grave
18. _____	18. berry
19. _____	19. peek
20. _____	20. dates

Challenge Words

_____ feeble
_____ fragrance
_____ mingled
_____ resembled
_____ scampered

Homophones and Homographs

Using the Word Study Steps

1. LOOK at the word.
2. SAY the word aloud.
3. STUDY the letters in the word.
4. WRITE the word.
5. CHECK the word.

Did you spell the word right? If not, go back to step 1.

Spelling Tips

Homophones are English words that sound alike but are spelled differently, depending on the meaning of the word in a sentence. For example: Jill looked pale as she tumbled after Jack while holding her pail

Homographs are English words that are spelled the same, even when they mean different things. For example, This lamp is light to carry and can light up the room.

Find and Circle

Where are the spelling words?

l	g	r	a	t	e	r	m	g	l		p	o	s	t	b
a	r	b	e	r	r	y	e	r	p	a	i	l	o	r	
d	a	t	e	s	c	e	n	e	p	l	i	g	h	t	
l	v	p	s	a	e	r	w	a	f	e	m	o	s	b	
p	e	e	f	t	t	e	r	t	u	b	e	c	k	u	
j	i	a	a	l	p	u	n	c	h	o	c	k	a	r	
a	z	k	n	e	r	l	i	e	b	o	w	l	m	y	

To Parents or Helpers

Using the Word Study Steps above as your child comes across any new words will help him or her spell well. Review the steps as you both go over this week's spelling words.

Go over the Spelling Tip with your child. Help him or her think of sentences using each of this week's spelling words.

Help your child complete the spelling activity.

Homophones and Homographs

seen	lean	grate	pail	grave
great	scene	fan	bury	berry
light	beet	peak	punch	peek
beat	bowl	post	pale	dates

There are six pairs of spelling words that are homophones. They sound the same, but are spelled differently. Sort the homophones into pairs. Find the pair of words that sound the same. Write the words on the lines below.

1. seen, scene
2. great, grate
3. beat, beet
4. peak, peek
5. bury, berry
6. pail, pale

Eight spelling words are homographs. Homographs are words that are spelled the same, but that have different meanings. Write two different meanings for each spelling word below.

1. _____

meaning 1._____

meaning 2._____

2. lean

meaning 1._____

meaning 2._____

3. bowl

meaning 1._____

meaning 2._____

4. fan

meaning 1._____

meaning 2._____

5. post

meaning 1._____

meaning 2._____

6. punch

meaning 1._____

meaning 2._____

7. grave

meaning 1._____

meaning 2._____

8. dates

meaning 1._____

meaning 2._____

Homophones and Homographs seen

seen	lean	grate	pail	grave
great	scene	fan	bury	berry
light	beet	peak	punch	peek
beat	bowl	post	pale	dates

Complete each sentence below with a spelling word.

1. Close your eyes and don't _____ peek _____.
2. Have you _____ seen _____ the movie that just opened?
3. Please _____ grate _____ the carrots for the salad.
4. I say three lines in _____ scene _____ one of the play.
5. She likes to eat dried, sweet _____ dates _____ for dessert.
6. That carton is _____ light _____ enough for me to carry myself.
7. They climbed to the _____ peak _____ of the mountain.
8. I use suntan lotion because I have _____ pale _____ skin.
9. Let's _____ bury _____ the treasure in the back yard.
10. Mix the batter in a large, mixing _____ bowl _____.
11. He carried the water in a large _____ pail _____.
12. I am a big _____ fan _____ of the Dallas Cowboys football team.

Word Meaning: Analogies

Write the spelling word that fits the analogy.

1. _____ great _____ is to terrific as bad is to awful
2. vegetable is to _____ beet _____ as meat is to steak
3. _____ grave _____ is to serious as happy is to glad
4. tall is to short as fat is to _____ lean _____

Challenge Extension: Challenge Extension: Write a fill-in sentence for each Challenge Word. Exchange papers with a partner and complete the sentences.

The Malachite Palace • SPELLING

Homophones and Homographs

Proofreading

There are six spelling mistakes in the paragraph below. Circle the misspelled words. Write the words correctly on the lines below.

Though Jason was a prince, he had never (scen) the top of a mountain before. This day, he decided to climb a mountain. He stood on the (peke) saw the whole country. The (lite) of the sun shone on the valleys below. It was very beautiful. After a while, Jason became hungry. He munched on some delicious (dats) drank some sweet (punche). When the sun began to set, Jason started down the mountain toward home. That night, in bed, Jason thought about the (grat) time he'd had that day. He promised himself that he would climb the mountain again soon.

1. ____seen____   3. ____light____   5. ____punch____
2. ____peak____   4. ____dates____   6. ____great____

Writing Activity

Think of a place you would like to see. Write a few sentences about what you would see or do there. Use four spelling words in your writing.

_____

_____

_____

_____

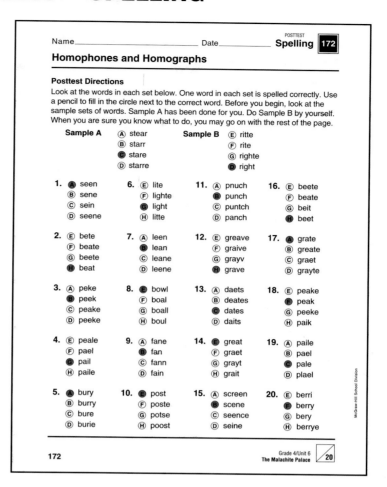

Homophones and Homographs

Posttest Directions

Look at the words in each set below. One word in each set is spelled correctly. Use a pencil to fill in the circle next to the correct word. Before you begin, look at the sample sets of words. Sample A has been done for you. Do Sample B by yourself. When you are sure you know what to do, you may go on with the rest of the page.

Sample A
- Ⓐ stear
- Ⓑ starr
- ● stare
- Ⓓ starre

Sample B
- Ⓔ ritte
- Ⓕ rite
- Ⓖ righte
- ● right

1. ● seen
   Ⓑ sene
   Ⓒ sein
   Ⓓ seene

2. Ⓔ bete
   Ⓕ beate
   Ⓖ beete
   ● beat

3. Ⓐ peke
   ● peek
   Ⓒ peake
   Ⓓ peeke

4. Ⓔ peale
   Ⓕ pael
   ● pail
   Ⓗ paile

5. ● bury
   Ⓑ burry
   Ⓒ bure
   Ⓓ burie

6. Ⓔ lite
   Ⓕ lighte
   ● light
   Ⓗ litte

7. Ⓐ leen
   ● lean
   Ⓒ leane
   Ⓓ leene

8. ● bowl
   Ⓕ boal
   Ⓖ boall
   Ⓗ boul

9. Ⓐ fane
   ● fan
   Ⓒ fann
   Ⓓ fain

10. ● post
    Ⓕ poste
    Ⓖ potse
    Ⓗ poost

11. Ⓐ pnuch
    ● punch
    Ⓒ puntch
    Ⓓ panch

12. Ⓔ greave
    Ⓕ graive
    Ⓖ grayv
    ● grave

13. Ⓐ daets
    Ⓑ deates
    ● dates
    Ⓓ daits

14. ● great
    Ⓕ graet
    Ⓖ grayt
    Ⓗ grait

15. Ⓐ screen
    ● scene
    Ⓒ seence
    Ⓓ seine

16. Ⓔ beete
    Ⓕ beate
    Ⓖ beit
    ● beet

17. Ⓐ grate
    Ⓑ greate
    Ⓒ graet
    Ⓓ grayte

18. Ⓔ peake
    ● peak
    Ⓖ peeke
    Ⓗ paik

19. Ⓐ paile
    Ⓑ pael
    ● pale
    Ⓓ plael

20. Ⓔ berri
    ● berry
    Ⓖ bery
    Ⓗ berrye

T25

Name_____ Date_____ **Practice** 200

Make Judgments and Decisions

Making **judgments and decisions** about characters is a part of reading.
Read the following story. Then answer each question.
Answers will vary. Possible answers are given.

> Karen ran around the backyard picking up the toys her little twin brothers had left out on the grass. Karen's friend, Sara, would be coming by to pick her up in a half hour. "These twins are a lot of work," thought Karen.
>
> Back in the house, Karen's mother asked her to watch the twins while she took care of the laundry. "They can stay by themselves for one minute while I change," thought Karen. Suddenly, the twins were screaming.
>
> Karen raced into the living room. Karen's mother ran into the room, too. The twins were fighting over Karen's red magic marker. They had red marks on their faces and arms. Karen decided to tell the truth. "I left them alone for a minute while I changed clothes," said Karen.
>
> Karen's mother thought for a moment and said, "You'd better finish changing, Sara will be here any minute."

1. As she was picking up toys in the yard, what opinion does Karen have of the twins? <u>She thinks the twins are a lot of work.</u>

2. What does Karen decide to do when her mother asks her to watch the twins?
<u>She decides to leave the room for a minute and change clothes.</u>

3. What was Karen's decision about what to tell her mother?
<u>She told the truth which was that she had left the room.</u>

4. What was Karen's mother's opinion about what Karen did?
<u>Karen has a lot of responsibility and usually handles it well.</u>

5. What is your opinion of Karen and her mother?
<u>Answers will vary, but may include that Karen's mother</u>
<u>is fair and understanding and that Karen is honest.</u>

5 Book 4/ Unit 6
The Toothpaste Millionaire

At Home: Have students write about judgments and decisions they make when hurrying to do something before they leave home.

200

Name_____ Date_____ **Practice** 201

Vocabulary

Answer each question using the vocabulary word in your response.
Answers will vary. Sample answers are shown.

1. **brilliant** — Why are some people called brilliant?
<u>Brilliant people are very smart and usually make good decisions.</u>

2. **successful** — What do you need to do to be a successful rope jumper?
<u>To be a successful rope jumper you need to practice a lot.</u>

3. **gallon** — How many quarts are there in a gallon?
<u>There are four quarts in a gallon.</u>

4. **expensive** — What do you think is an expensive item?
<u>A house is an expensive item.</u>

5. **ingredient** — What is the most important ingredient in lemonade?
<u>The most important ingredient in lemonade is lemon juice.</u>

6. **commercials** — What type of television commercials do you like best?
<u>Dog food commercials are fun to watch.</u>

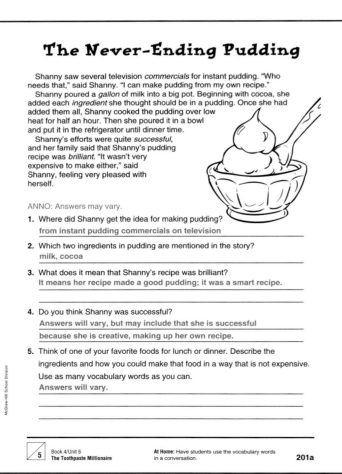

201 **At Home:** Have students write a television commercial.

Book 4/Unit 6
The Toothpaste Millionaire 6

The Never-Ending Pudding

Shanny saw several television *commercials* for instant pudding. "Who needs that," said Shanny. "I can make pudding from my own recipe."

Shanny poured a *gallon* of milk into a big pot. Beginning with cocoa, she added each *ingredient* she thought should be in a pudding. Once she had added them all, Shanny cooked the pudding over low heat for half an hour. Then she poured it in a bowl and put it in the refrigerator until dinner time.

Shanny's efforts were quite *successful*, and her family said that Shanny's pudding recipe was *brilliant*. "It wasn't very expensive to make either," said Shanny, feeling very pleased with herself.

ANNO: Answers may vary.

1. Where did Shanny get the idea for making pudding?
<u>from instant pudding commercials on television</u>

2. Which two ingredients in pudding are mentioned in the story?
<u>milk, cocoa</u>

3. What does it mean that Shanny's recipe was brilliant?
<u>It means her recipe made a good pudding; it was a smart recipe.</u>

4. Do you think Shanny was successful?
<u>Answers will vary, but may include that she is successful</u>
<u>because she is creative, making up her own recipe.</u>

5. Think of one of your favorite foods for lunch or dinner. Describe the ingredients and how you could make that food in a way that is not expensive. Use as many vocabulary words as you can.
<u>Answers will vary.</u>

5 Book 4/Unit 6
The Toothpaste Millionaire

At Home: Have students use the vocabulary words in a conversation.

201a

Name_____ Date_____ **Practice** 202

Story Comprehension

Read statements 1 to 6 below. Write **T** for true if the statement describes "The Toothpaste Millionaire." Write **F** for false if it does not.

1. <u>F</u> Rufus started making toothpaste because he wanted to buy a boat.

2. <u>F</u> Joe Smiley is one of Rufus's best friends.

3. <u>T</u> Kate was with Rufus in the drugstore when he decided to make toothpaste.

4. <u>T</u> The main ingredient in toothpaste is baking soda.

5. <u>T</u> Mr. Conti's math class was very helpful to Rufus.

6. <u>F</u> When Rufus's business got bigger, he didn't have to pay rent because he made the toothpaste at home.

Write to tell why the following statements are not true. Answers may vary.

7. If Rufus sold one billion containers of toothpaste charging a dollar for each jar, he could make a million dollars. <u>Rufus would make a profit of one penny per container resulting in ten million dollars.</u>

8. If you are a stockholder in a soap company, you are part of the sales team.
<u>A stockholder gets a share of the profits of a company.</u>

202 **At Home:** Have students describe a company they would like to have.

Book 4/Unit 6
The Toothpaste Millionaire 8

The Toothpaste Millionaire • PRACTICE

Conduct an Interview

An **interview** is a meeting between an interviewer who asks questions and a person who is being interviewed. That person has information or an interesting story that the interviewer wants to know more about.

Read the interview plan below. Then answer the questions.
Answers will vary but should be in the correct context.

> **a.** Choose a person to interview who you think is interesting.
> **b.** Think about the person you will interview and what he or she knows. Write good questions to ask that person.
> **c.** Begin the interview by stating your purpose for interviewing.
> **d.** Ask polite, clear questions that use words such as *what? why? where? when? how?*
> **e.** Listen carefully to the answers to your questions and take good notes.

1. On each blank line below write the name of someone you would like to interview:

   Family member: _____ Famous person:_____

   Neighbor: _____ Owner of a business: _____

2. Choose one person from above. Write what you think would be the most interesting question you could ask that person.

   Person:_____

   Question:_____

3. Write three questions you would like to ask this person in your interview.

   _____
   _____
   _____

4. State your purpose for interviewing this person.

   _____

Make Judgments and Decisions

Making judgments and decisions about characters is an important part of reading a story.
Think about "The Toothpaste Millionaire" as you answer the questions below. Answers may vary. Accept all reasonable responses.

1. What did you think of Rufus's decision to make his own toothpaste while he was talking with Kate in the drugstore? _Some students may feel that Rufus was getting in over his head before even finding out how to make toothpaste._

2. Was Rufus right? Is toothpaste very simple to make? _Yes, it has very few ingredients, and the main one is baking soda._

3. What did you think of Mr. Conti's decision to devote time to Rufus's business in the math class? _Students may say that it made the class interesting and realistic, and it helped Rufus._

4. What did you think of Rufus's idea to get his math class involved? _Students may note that it was a good idea because the class already knew about the business and they were interested in it._

5. Why did Rufus's friends deserve to be stockholders? _They worked hard and should enjoy some of the profits._

6. It was the intention of the author, Jean Merrill, to entertain readers but also to help them understand how some businesses are run. In your judgment, do you think the author helped you understand how a business can be run? Explain your answer. _Answers will vary._

   _____
   _____
   _____

Problem and Solution

A story usually has at least one **problem and solution**. There were many problems in "The Toothpaste Millionaire." Rufus solved every one of them.

Read "The Toothpaste Millionaire" again. Then write the solution for each problem.

Problem	Solution
1. Rufus thought the price of toothpaste was too high.	Rufus made a gallon of toothpaste for under a dollar.
2. Rufus needed a name for his toothpaste.	Rufus called it Toothpaste.
3. Rufus had so many customers that he couldn't keep up.	He got his math class to help out.
4. The people in the math class working hard for nothing.	Rufus gave them stock in his company.
5. Kate realized they needed tubes.	Kate goes to an auction and buys a gross of tubes.
6. Rufus's company became so big he needed a machine and a factory.	Rufus rented a machine, a building, and hired a man named Hector.
7. Rufus and the stockholders needed $15,000.	Rufus and Kate went to a bank to borrow money.
8. The bank wouldn't lend money to Rufus because he was too young.	Hector became a stockholder and borrowed the money Rufus needed.

Synonyms and Antonyms

Synonyms are words with the same or almost the same meaning.
Antonyms are words with the opposite meaning.

Write a synonym from the list that could replace the underlined word in each sentence.

expensive	business	fantastic	germ-free	clever

1. His ideas for new games are always wonderful. _fantastic_

2. She is a brilliant chess player. _clever_

3. The baby bottles and dishes are all sterilized. _germ-free_

4. The Green's grandfather started a successful enterprise many years ago. _business_

5. The new clothes for the entire family were costly. _expensive_

Write an antonym for each underlined word from the list.

expensive	initiative	celebrity	upstage	minuscule

6. Some shoes are so _cheap_, and others are so _expensive_ .

7. One actor was an _unknown_, and the other was a famous _celebrity_ .

8. The girl walked _downstage_, and the boy walked _upstage_ .

9. The elephant was _gigantic_, but the ant was _minuscule_ .

10. In doing the project, one girl took the _initiative_ while another girl _gave up_.

The Toothpaste Millionaire • RETEACH

Make Judgments and Decisions

> As you read, put yourself in the position of the main character. Look at the choices that face him or her. Think about the **judgments and decisions** you would make if you were the character in the story.

Read the story below, and write your responses on the lines provided. Then help Lamont by finishing his list of reasons to choose whether he should play in the game or go to the workshop.   Answers will vary. Possible answers are shown.

Lamont is on the school basketball team. He's a good player, but not the team star. The team has worked hard all season and has just won a game. Now the team has a shot at winning the next big game.

Lamont's teacher chose him to represent the school at a leadership workshop. It is a great honor. His parents would be so proud. But, Lamont would have to miss the next basketball game. He knows his team is counting on everyone playing and playing well. Lamont would hate to disappoint his friends and his coach.

1. What decision does Lamont have to make? He has to decide between going to the leadership workshop or playing in the basketball game.

Take Part in Game	Go to Workshop
I want to be part of a winning team.	2. **It is an honor to represent the school.**
I don't want to let down friends and coach.	I am only a good player, not the team star.
	3. **My parents would be proud.**

4. What do you think Lamont will decide? Why? Possible response: Lamont will play the game. Lamont will feel that more people are counting on him to play. Most of them are his friends.

Book 4/Unit 6
The Toothpaste Millionaire   4

At Home: Encourage students to make a list similar to Lamont's for an important decision they have to make.

200

Vocabulary

| commercials | expensive | successful | gallon | brilliant | ingredient |

Write the correct word from the box next to its meaning.

1. four quarts gallon
2. advertisements commercials
3. something added to a mixture ingredient
5. costly; having a high price expensive
6. having achieved something successful

6

Story Comprehension

Write a ✔ next to every sentence that tells something about "The Toothpaste Millionaire."

_____ 1. Rufus saw that toothpaste in the store was inexpensive.

___✔___ 2. Baking soda was the main ingredient in Rufus's toothpaste.

___✔___ 3. Rufus made a one-cent profit on each jar of his toothpaste.

_____ 4. Rufus called his new toothpaste "Sparkle and Shine."

_____ 5. Rufus paid all his friends to work for him.

___✔___ 6. Rufus gave his friends stock in the toothpaste company.

___✔___ 7. It was decided that tubes made better containers than jars.

_____ 8. The bank gave Rufus a loan to get the tube-filling machine he needed.

___✔___ 9. The kids made a commercial to sell more toothpaste.

_____ 10. The toothpaste sold out and Rufus closed his company.

201–202

At Home: Have students discuss two decisions Rufus made in running his business.

Book 4/Unit 6
The Toothpaste Millionaire   10

Conduct an Interview

> The purpose of an **interview** is to gather information about a person. The person who asks the questions is the *interviewer*. The person who answers the questions is the *interviewee*.

Below are some words to remember when preparing to interview someone.

> **Key Words for Conducting an Interview:**
> **Purpose**—Know It
> **Prepare**
> **Questions:** *Who? What? Where? When? Why? How?*
> **Listen**
> **Take Notes**

A famous Olympic skating champion is coming to your school. You have been chosen to interview her at a school assembly. Answer the following questions about your interview with the champion.

1. How would you begin the interview? Introduce myself and the skater to the audience. Tell the purpose of the interview.

2. What would be the purpose of the interview? Possible responses: to learn how the skater became a champion; to learn about her training and experience; to inspire others to work towards their goals.

3. Write three questions you could ask in the interview. Possible responses: When did you start to skate? Who has helped you in your career? What is the most important thing you have learned from skating?

4. If the skater mentions the jumps and turns she does, but you don't understand the skating terms, what should you do? Possible answer: Ask her to explain more in a follow-up question.

Book 4/Unit 6
The Toothpaste Millionaire   4

At Home: Have students think of someone they would like to interview, and then have them write four questions for the interview.

203

Make Judgments and Decisions

> Characters make **judgments and decisions**. You do, too, every day.

Circle the letter beside what you would do in each of the following situations. Then explain your decision.

1. You see smoke coming from a building. You are in a part of the neighborhood your parents have told you to stay away from.
   a. You call the fire department.
   b. You return home, hoping someone will call about the fire.
   Reason: possible answer: I would rather get in trouble than risk someone getting hurt.

2. It is your little sister's birthday. For at least a month, she has been playing practical jokes on you and your family.
   a. You plan a special birthday joke to get even.
   b. You make her a card and a little gift.
   Reason: possible answer: Birthdays are special, and I would want my sister to give me a card and a present if it was my birthday.

3. You know you can't have a pet dog. Your mom is allergic to dogs. You see a cute stray on your street.
   a. You put up signs to find the dog's owner and call a shelter.
   b. You think the dog is small enough to hide and take it home.
   Reason: possible answer: I would make sure the dog was safe until its owner was found.

4. You find an empty wallet, except for a name and address card. It is the kind you always wanted.
   a. You keep the wallet, since it is empty anyway.
   b. You call the owner and return it.
   Reason: possible answer: I wouldn't want someone to lose such a nice wallet, and if I lost my wallet, I would want someone to return it to me.

204

At Home: Have students explain the reasons for deciding what they did in a situation.

Book 4/Unit 6
The Toothpaste Millionaire   8

Name_____ Date_____ **Reteach** 205

Problem and Solution

Noting characters' **problems and the solutions** they find will help you better understand a story.

Read the story below. Then write your responses on the lines provided.

The sixth-grade class wanted to see live whales in the ocean. Nate called for information about a whale-watching trip. It cost $35 per person. For 20 students, one teacher, and four parents, the cost would be $875. The PTA offered to pay $300. The students said they could each afford $10. That left $375 to be raised.

The students decided to hold a car wash and bake sale. A nice day brought a long line of cars. While waiting for their cars, customers bought the delicious baked goods. At the end of the day, the students had raised all the money they needed for the trip.

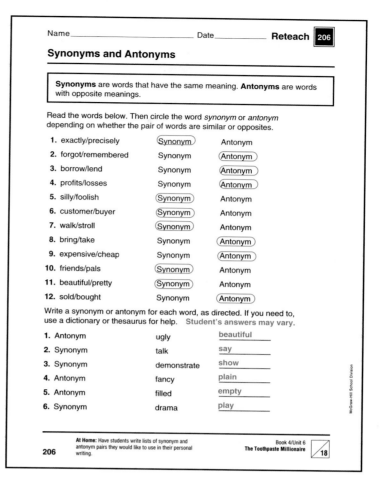

1. What is the students' problem? <u>They need $875.</u>

2. Rate the problem on a scale of 1 to 4. A 4 means it is hard to solve. Explain your rating. <u>Possible answer: 3. There was a lot of money to be raised and it would require hard work on everyone's part.</u>

3. In what two ways do the students solve the problem? <u>They contribute their own money; they have a car wash/bake sale.</u>

4. Rate the solution on a scale of 1 to 4. A 4 means it was a great solution. Explain your answer. <u>4. Everyone gave up some personal money, and everyone helped raise the rest of the money they needed.</u>

Book 4/Unit 6
The Toothpaste Millionaire
4

At Home: Have students explain how they would solve the problem of needing money to buy something important to them.

205

Name_____ Date_____ **Reteach** 206

Synonyms and Antonyms

Synonyms are words that have the same meaning. **Antonyms** are words with opposite meanings.

Read the words below. Then circle the word *synonym* or *antonym* depending on whether the pair of words are similar or opposites.

1.	exactly/precisely	(Synonym)	Antonym
2.	forgot/remembered	Synonym	(Antonym)
3.	borrow/lend	Synonym	(Antonym)
4.	profits/losses	Synonym	(Antonym)
5.	silly/foolish	(Synonym)	Antonym
6.	customer/buyer	(Synonym)	Antonym
7.	walk/stroll	(Synonym)	Antonym
8.	bring/take	Synonym	(Antonym)
9.	expensive/cheap	Synonym	(Antonym)
10.	friends/pals	(Synonym)	Antonym
11.	beautiful/pretty	(Synonym)	Antonym
12.	sold/bought	Synonym	(Antonym)

Write a synonym or antonym for each word, as directed. If you need to, use a dictionary or thesaurus for help. Student's answers may vary.

1. Antonym   ugly   <u>beautiful</u>
2. Synonym   talk   <u>say</u>
3. Synonym   demonstrate   <u>show</u>
4. Antonym   fancy   <u>plain</u>
5. Antonym   filled   <u>empty</u>
6. Synonym   drama   <u>play</u>

206

At Home: Have students write lists of synonym and antonym pairs they would like to use in their personal writing.

Book 4/Unit 6
The Toothpaste Millionaire
18

Make Judgments and Decisions

We are always making choices. Making choices requires us to **make judgements** and **decisions** about what we want to do. Different people might make different decisions about the same choice.

Read the problems below. Write the decision you would make in each situation. Compare your decisions with a partner's. How are they alike? How are they different?   Answers will vary. Possible answers are given.

1. You have arranged to celebrate your birthday party on the same day as the art fair at school. Many of your friends are taking part in the fair.
   I would call my friends and have the party on another day.

2. You promised your mother you would practice the piano before dinner. You have just started practicing when your best friend calls and asks you to come over.
   I would finishing practicing and tell my friend that I'll be over in an hour.

3. You studied hard for a test. A classmate who didn't study asks you on the day of the test to help him study very quickly.
   I would help him if there was time and suggest that we study together next time.

4. You really want to join the tennis team at school, but you're not sure you are a good enough player.
   I would practice hard and try to make the team anyway.

Book 4/Unit 6
The Toothpaste Millionaire

At Home: Have students tell about how they decide what books to read or what movies to see.

200

Vocabulary

brilliant   commercials   expensive   gallon   ingredient   successful

Write an advertisement for a new product using as many of the vocabulary words as you can.
Answers will vary, but should make correct use of the vocabulary.

Story Comprehension

What do you think was the most important decision Rufus made in "The Toothpaste Millionaire"? What caused him to make the decision? What was the effect of Rufus' decision? Explain.

Answers will vary. Possible answer: to make toothpaste that costs less than the store brands. He thought the prices in the store were much too high. His toothpaste cost very little and his friends helped him see that he could make a huge profit. They went into business with him and by keeping costs low built a profitable business.

Conduct an Interview

In an **interview** usually one person asks another person questions to gain information. To conduct a good interview, it is important to plan carefully before you begin. It's also important to be polite and listen carefully during the interview. Taking notes during it will help you organize what you learn from the interview.

Work with a partner. Suppose you were a talk show host who wanted to do a profile, or a short biography, of a guest. What would you want to know? Write a list of questions on an index card. Then interview your partner in the role of guest. Take notes on a separate sheet of paper. Use the notes to write a paragraph telling what you found out about your guest.

Questions:
Answers will vary but should give a clear biographical profile.

Paragraph:
Answers will vary.

Make Judgments and Decisions

Everyone looks at problems differently. People bring their own values and experiences with them when they **make judgments and decisions**.

Suppose that you were Rufus in "The Toothpaste Millionaire." Choose one decision in the story that you would make differently. Explain your choice, and tell why you would do things in a different way. How does your choice affect the outcome of the story?

Answers will vary but should include a judgement or decision with supporting arguments.

The Toothpaste Millionaire • EXTEND

Problem and Solution

In the story "Toothpaste Millionaire," Rufus had a **problem**: The bank turned him down for a loan. What was the **solution** to Rufus' problem? He asked an adult to approach the bank for the loan.

Suppose your class wants to raise money for a class trip. Think of a way to solve the problem. List the steps in your solution clearly. Try to persuade your teachers and classmates that your solution will work. Be convincing!

Answers will vary but should include a reasonable solution.

_____
_____
_____
_____
_____
_____
_____
_____
_____
_____
_____
_____
_____
_____
_____
_____

Book 4/Unit 6
The Toothpaste Millionaire

At Home: Have students tell how they might solve a problem they are having at home or at school.

205

Synonyms and Antonyms

Synonyms are words whose meanings are the same. **Antonyms** are words whose meanings are opposite.

Examples: *Brilliant* and *bright* are synonyms.
               Downturn and *upturn* are antonyms.

Write a synonym and antonym for each word below. Then write a paragraph using the synonyms and antonyms. Draw a picture to illustrate a detail from your paragraph.

Word	Synonym	Antonym
1. successful	doing well	failing
2. sterilized	clean	dirty
3. portable	moveable	not movable
4. expensive	costly	cheap
5. fantastic	wonderful	ordinary
6. celebrity	star	unknown

Paragraphs and pictures will vary.

_____
_____
_____
_____

```
(blank box for picture)
```

206

At Home: Choose three words from a magazine or newspaper article. Have students name a synonym and antonym for each.

Book 4/Unit 6
The Toothpaste Millionaire

T31

The Toothpaste Millionaire • GRAMMAR

Negatives

- A **negative** is a word that means "no," such as *not, never, nobody, nowhere,* and contractions with *n't*.
- Do not use two negatives in the same sentence.
- You can fix a sentence with two negatives by removing one.

Correct each sentence by removing one of the negatives. Then rewrite the sentence.   Student's answers may vary

1. "I wouldn't never pay a dollar and eighty-nine cents for toothpaste."

   "I would never pay a dollar and eighty-nine cents for toothpaste."

2. "Toothpaste isn't made of no expensive ingredients."

   "Toothpaste isn't made of expensive ingredients."

3. Rufus wasn't trying to make no money.

   Rufus wasn't trying to make money.

4. He thought people shouldn't never have to pay a lot for toothpaste.

   He thought people should never have to pay a lot for toothpaste.

5. He didn't use no secret ingredients.

   He didn't use secret ingredients.

6. His toothpaste didn't have no special name.

   His toothpaste didn't have a special name.

7. He didn't put no printing on the box.

   He didn't put printing on the box.

8. "I don't have no profits to pay you yet."

   "I don't have any profits to pay you yet."

Extension: Have students work with a partner to write and correct sentences with two negatives.

173

Negatives

- You can correct a sentence with two negatives by changing one negative to a positive word.

| no ——— any | nothing ——— anything | no one ——— anyone |
| never ——— ever | nobody ——— anybody | nowhere ——— anywhere |

Correct these sentences by changing one negative word to a positive word.

1. "I don't think nobody should pay a lot for toothpaste."

   "I don't think anybody should pay a lot for toothpaste."

2. The main ingredient isn't nothing but baking soda.

   The main ingredient isn't anything but baking soda.

3. No one would never think three cents was too much for toothpaste.

   No one would ever think three cents was too much for toothpaste.

4. You can't find cheaper toothpaste nowhere.

   You can't find cheaper toothpaste anywhere.

5. No one never turned down a chance to be a stockholder.

   No one ever turned down a chance to be a stockholder.

6. Kate had never seen nothing more beautiful than that machine.

   Kate had never seen anything more beautiful than that machine.

7. "We don't exactly lend money to just nobody," said Mr. Perkell.

   "We don't exactly lend money to just anybody," said Mr.Perkell.

8. Our toothpaste doesn't have nothing like a fancy name or a fancy box.

   Our toothpaste doesn't have anything like a fancy name or a fancy box.

Extension: Ask students to work with partners to write sentences including the negatives *no, never, nothing, nobody, no one,* and *nowhere.* Have them exchange their sentences with a partner, who will correct the sentence by changing the negative to a corresponding positive word: *any, ever, anything, anybody, anyone,* and *anywhere.*

174 Grade 4/Unit 6
The Toothpaste Millionaire 8

Negatives

- Do not use two negatives in the same sentence.
- You can fix a sentence with two negatives by removing one.
- You can correct a sentence with two negatives by changing one negative to a positive word.

Rewrite each sentence below by dropping a negative or changing one negative to a positive word.

1. There isn't no profit yet.

   There isn't any profit yet.

2. *Toothpaste* doesn't make no fancy claims.

   Toothpaste doesn't make fancy claims.

3. It doesn't do nothing but clean your teeth.

   It does nothing but clean your teeth.

4. They never waste no money making it.

   They never waste money making it.

5. Rufus doesn't have no new ideas yet.

   Rufus doesn't have any new ideas yet.

6. Rufus never had to pay his classmates nothing.

   Rufus never had to pay his classmates anything.

7. They never worked for nothing but stock.

   They never worked for anything but stock.

8. There couldn't have been no better deal.

   There couldn't have been a better deal.

Extension: Have students review the strategies they used to correct the sentences on this page. Then have students try to correct each sentence by using the other possible strategy.

175

Contractions

- A **contraction** is a shortened form of two words.
- A contraction can be formed by combining a verb with the word *not.*
- An apostrophe (') shows where one or more letters have been left out.

can't = cannot	*didn't = did not*	*aren't = are not*
don't = do not	*haven't = have not*	*couldn't = could not*
doesn't = does not	*wasn't = was not*	*wouldn't = would not*

Fix the following sentences with two negatives by removing the contraction of the word *not.*

1. He can't see no reason for it.

   He can see no reason for it.

2. He wouldn't never spend a lot for toothpaste.

   He would never spend a lot for toothpaste.

3. Doesn't he have no more good ideas?

   Does he have no more good ideas?

4. You aren't going nowhere.

   You are going nowhere.

5. We couldn't do nothing to stop him.

   We could do nothing to stop him.

6. Compared with the usual price, three cents wasn't nothing.

   Compared with the usual price, three cents was nothing.

7. You haven't finished none of your work.

   You have finished none of your work.

8. She didn't nothing of the kind.

   She did nothing of the kind.

Extension: Have students identify and list the contractions formed with *not* found in the selection, *The Toothpaste Millionaire.*

176 Grade 4/Unit 6
The Toothpaste Millionaire 8

Page 177

Negatives

A. Circle the letter next to the sentence that best revises each sentence with two negatives.

1. Rufus wasn't trying to make no money.
   - a Rufus was trying to make money.
   - **b Rufus wasn't trying to make money.**
   - c Rufus was not trying to not make money.
   - d Rufus was trying not to make money.

2. We don't have no profits to pay anybody yet.
   - a We have profits for pay people yet.
   - b We have no profits yet to pay nobody.
   - c We don't have profits to pay nobody yet.
   - **d We have no profits to pay anybody yet.**

3. *Toothpaste* doesn't make no fancy claims.
   - **a *Toothpaste* doesn't make any fancy claims.**
   - b *Toothpaste* makes any fancy claims.
   - c *Toothpaste* never makes no fancy claims.
   - d *Toothpaste* doesn't make any claims.

4. We didn't have no other kids working with us.
   - **a We didn't have any other kids working with us.**
   - b We did have other kids working with us.
   - c We had other kids working with us.
   - d We never worked with other kids.

5. Isn't this not the most beautiful machine ever?
   - a Is this the most beautiful machine never?
   - b This isn't the most beautiful machine, is it?
   - **c Isn't this the most beautiful machine ever?**
   - d Is this a beautiful machine?

6. They don't use no expensive ingredients.
   - a They use not expensive ingredients.
   - b They use expensive ingredients.
   - c They don't use any ingredients.
   - **d They don't use expensive ingredients.**

Page 178

Negatives

- Do not use two negatives in the same sentence.
- You can fix a sentence with two negatives by removing one.
- You can correct a sentence with two negatives by changing one negative to a positive word.

Mechanics

- A contraction is a shortened form of two words.
- A contraction can be formed by combining a verb with the word *not*.
- An apostrophe (') shows where one or more letters have been left out.

Correct the sentences, remembering the rules above, to make them describe this picture:

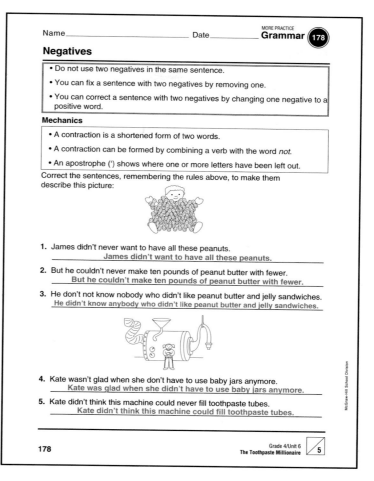

1. James didn't never want to have all these peanuts.
   _____James didn't want to have all these peanuts.____

2. But he couldn't never make ten pounds of peanut butter with fewer.
   _____But he couldn't make ten pounds of peanut butter with fewer.____

3. He don't not know nobody who didn't like peanut butter and jelly sandwiches.
   He didn't know anybody who didn't like peanut butter and jelly sandwiches.

4. Kate wasn't glad when she don't have to use baby jars anymore.
   _____Kate was glad when she didn't have to use baby jars anymore.____

5. Kate didn't think this machine could never fill toothpaste tubes.
   _____Kate didn't think this machine could fill toothpaste tubes.____

T33

The Toothpaste Millionaire • SPELLING

Page 173 (Pretest)

Name_____ Date_____ PRETEST **Spelling** 173

Words with Suffixes

Pretest Directions
Fold back the paper along the dotted line. Use the blanks to write each word as it is read aloud. When you finish the test, unfold the paper. Use the list at the right to correct any spelling mistakes. Practice the words that you missed for the Posttest.

To Parents
Here are the results of your child's weekly spelling Pretest. You can help your child study for the Posttest by following these simple steps for each word on the word list:

1. Read the word to your child.
2. Have your child write the word, saying each letter as it is written.
3. Say each letter of the word as your child checks the spelling.
4. If a mistake has been made, have your child read each letter of the correctly spelled word aloud, and then repeat steps 1–3.

1. _____
2. _____
3. _____
4. _____
5. _____
6. _____
7. _____
8. _____
9. _____
10. _____
11. _____
12. _____
13. _____
14. _____
15. _____
16. _____
17. _____
18. _____
19. _____
20. _____

1. useless
2. entertainment
3. construction
4. adjustable
5. darkness
6. motionless
7. description
8. measurement
9. adorable
10. breathless
11. fairness
12. government
13. protection
14. dependable
15. sickness
16. hopeless
17. production
18. enjoyable
19. greatness
20. encouragement

Challenge Words
_____
_____
_____
_____
_____

brilliant
commercials
expensive
ingredient
successful

20 Grade 4/Unit 6
The Toothpaste Millionaire
173

Page 174 (At Home Word Study)

Name_____ Date_____ AT HOME WORD STUDY **Spelling** 174

Words with Suffixes

Using the Word Study Steps

1. LOOK at the word.
2. SAY the word aloud.
3. STUDY the letters in the word.
4. WRITE the word.
5. CHECK the word.

Did you spell the word right? If not, go back to step 1.

Spelling Tip
Learn how to spell suffixes you use often in writing.

Word Scramble
Unscramble each set of letters to make a spelling word.

1. slussee — useless
2. treamnentien — entertainment
3. stronctioun — construction
4. jablauste — adjustable
5. knesards — darkness
6. slimontose — motionless
7. prescintod — description
8. mensurteame — measurement
9. bladoare — adorable
10. thasbleres — breathless
11. afrnies — fairness
12. merntevong — government
13. oprictnote — protection
14. plabdedeen — dependable
15. sniksecs — sickness
16. shlopese — hopeless
17. upictonrod — production
18. jabloyeen — enjoyable
19. sesterang — greatness
20. cenroumagneet — encouragement

To Parents or Helpers
Using the Word Study Steps above as your child comes across any new words will help him or her learn to spell words effectively. Review the steps as you both go over this week's spelling words.
Go over the Spelling Tip with your child. Ask your child if he or she can think of some words with suffixes
Help your child complete the spelling activity.

174
Grade 4/Unit 6
The Toothpaste Millionaire 20

Page 175 (Word With Suffixes)

Name_____ Date_____ WORD WITH SUFFIXES **Spelling** 175

Explore the Pattern

useless	darkness	adorable	protection	production
entertainment	motionless	breathless	dependable	enjoyable
construction	description	fairness	sickness	greatness
adjustable	measurement	government	hopeless	encouragement

Pattern Power
Sort each spelling word by writing it under the correct suffix.

–less
1. useless
2. motionless
3. breathless
4. hopeless

–ness
5. darkness
6. fairness
7. sickness
8. greatness

–ment
9. entertainment
10. measurement
11. government
12. encouragement

–tion
13. construction
14. description
15. protection
16. production

–able
17. adjustable
18. adorable
19. dependable
20. enjoyable

20 Grade 4/Unit 6
The Toothpaste Millionaire
175

Page 176 (Practice and Extend)

Name_____ Date_____ PRACTICE AND EXTEND **Spelling** 176

Words with Suffixes

useless	darkness	adorable	protection	production
entertainment	motionless	breathless	dependable	enjoyable
construction	description	fairness	sickness	greatness
adjustable	measurement	government	hopeless	encouragement

Word Meaning: Suffixes
A suffix is added to the end of a word to give the word meaning. Different suffixes have different meanings. (examples: "happiness" means "the state of being happy" "readable" means "able to be read")

-less	=	without
-ment	=	the act of
-able	=	able to be
-ness	=	the state of being
-tion	=	the act of

Write the spelling word that fits each meaning below.

1. without use — useless
2. the act of constructing — construction
3. able to be adjusted — adjustable
4. being dark — darkness
5. without breath — breathless
6. the act of describing — description
7. the act of measuring — measurement
8. without motion — motionless
9. able to be adored — adorable
10. the state of being fair — fairness

Challenge Extension: Challenge Extension: Have you ever seen an ad on TV? Think of an ad that you like and write about it using the Challenge Words.

176
Grade 4/Unit 6
The Toothpaste Millionaire 10

The Toothpaste Millionaire • SPELLING

Words with Suffixes

Proofreading

There are six spelling mistakes in the paragraph below. Circle the misspelled words. Write the words correctly on the lines below.

I set to work to invent a time machine. Everyone said it was (hopeless) But I did it! I designed the machine myself. Then I got the materials I needed and began on the machine's (construktion) Time travel is not like "real" travel. You and the machine are absolutely (moshunless) When the machine stops and you get out, what you see is beyond (diskription) Just yesterday, I visited some (adorible) dinosaurs. Tomorrow, I think I'd like to go to the future. Do you think the (govinment) would be interested in buying one of my machines?

1.	hopeless	3.	motionless	5.	adorable
2.	construction	4.	description	6.	goverment

Writing Activity

What would you like to invent or produce? Write a few sentences about what your invention would be like. Use four spelling words in your writing.

_____

_____

_____

_____

Words with Suffixes

Posttest Directions

Look at the words in each set. One word in each set is spelled correctly. Use a pencil to color in the circle in front of that word. Before you begin, look at the sample sets of words. Sample A has been done for you. Do Sample B by yourself. When you are sure you know what to do, you may go on with the rest of the page.

Sample A
- (A) developmint
- (B) devellopmunt
- ● development
- (D) divelopmunt

Sample B
- (E) clooliss
- ● clueless
- (G) clooless
- (H) cluliss

1.
- ● adjustible
- (B) adjustable
- (C) adjustble
- (D) adjustable

6.
- ● useless
- (F) usless
- (G) useles
- (H) ussless

11.
- (A) dependible
- (B) dependble
- ● dependable
- (D) dipendable

16.
- ● protection
- (F) protectin
- (G) protetion
- (H) prutection

2.
- (E) construcsion
- (F) constructin
- ● construction
- (H) construkton

7.
- (A) measurment
- ● measurement
- (C) measuremint
- (D) mesurement

12.
- (E) discription
- ● description
- (G) descriptoun
- (H) deskription

17.
- (A) adorble
- ● adorable
- (C) adorabel
- (D) adorible

3.
- ● fairness
- (B) fairnes
- (C) fairnese
- (D) fareness

8.
- (E) enjoiable
- (F) enjoyble
- (G) enjoyible
- ● enjoyable

13.
- ● motionless
- (B) motonless
- (C) motionles
- (D) motunless

18.
- (E) hopless
- (F) hopeliss
- ● hopeless
- (H) hopeles

4.
- (E) breathles
- (F) breatheless
- ● breathless
- (H) brethliss

9.
- (A) darknes
- (B) darkniss
- ● darkness
- (D) darkniss

14.
- (E) gretness
- (F) grateness
- ● greatness
- (H) graitness

19.
- ● sickness
- (B) sickniss
- (C) sicknes
- (D) siknes

5.
- (A) producsion
- (B) producton
- ● production
- (D) priduction

10.
- (E) encouragment
- ● encouragement
- (G) encouragemint
- (H) encuragement

15.
- (A) intertainment
- ● entertainment
- (C) entertanment
- (D) entertanment

20.
- (E) goverment
- ● government
- (G) governmnt
- (H) govenmint

T35

Whales • PRACTICE

Compare and Contrast

To understand information you may want to **compare and contrast** two things to see how they are alike and different. Compare and contrast as you read the passage below. Then answer the questions.

In 1964, four divers lived in a structure beneath the Atlantic Ocean near Bermuda. This structure, or laboratory, was placed upon an old volcano 192 feet below the surface of the water. The structure was called "Sealab I." The four divers lived, slept, and worked for 11 days and nights in Sealab I. The men used power tools and poured concrete. They wanted to know what it would be like to build a permanent structure under the ocean. During this time, the men were away from their families, but mail was delivered to them every day. Their mail carrier was a trained dolphin, Tuffy.

Sealab II was planned for the following year. Ten men would live and work 205 feet below the ocean. Sealab II was much bigger than Sealab I. It had hot showers and a galley where the men could cook their meals. New technical advances made it easier to breathe without the necessity for using helium. Tuffy didn't work for Sealab II.
Answers will vary. Sample answers are shown.

1. Compare Sealab I and Sealab II. How were their purposes alike?
   Both were designed so that people could live beneath the sea for
   many days and nights.

2. Contrast the two Sealabs in terms of the number of people they could carry.
   Sealab I was built for four people, and Sealab II was built for ten
   people.

3. How might Sealab II have been more comfortable for the people
   to live and work in? New technical advances made it easier to breath
   and the building was larger and more comfortable.

4. Compare how the two Sealabs received mail. Sealab I had Tuffy, the
   dolphin, to deliver mail. It is not known how mail delivery was
   handled for Sealab II.

Vocabulary

Complete each sentence with a vocabulary word.

mammals	preserve	related	marine	identify	pods

1. A _marine_ biologist is a person who studies plant and
   animal sea life.

2. Whales, seals, and other marine life live in groups
   called _pods_ .

3. Warm-blooded animals, such as dogs, lions, and whales, are
   mammals .

4. My friend is _related_ to our baseball coach.

5. The girl put a leaf in a scrapbook to _preserve_ it for
   a long time.

6. Some people can _identify_ every kind of flower and
   leaf in their yards.

Whale Watch Adventure

Nelson Washington stood on the long dock next to the sign that said: "WHALE WATCH! OBSERVE *MARINE* LIFE UP CLOSE." Nelson and his parents watched as the people got off the boat. A man and a woman smiled and said to the Washington family, "You're in for a wonderful adventure! We saw two different *pods* of whales. Two whales were close to our boat–such enormous *mammals*!"

Nelson understood how they felt. He had seen many whales with his parents. He could even *identify* some kinds of whales by name–like orca or baleen. Nelson felt almost *related* to the whale watchers.

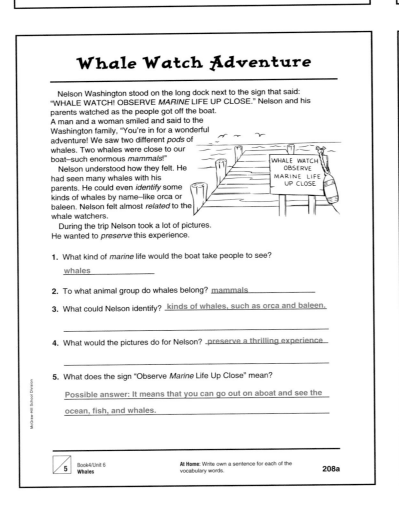

During the trip Nelson took a lot of pictures. He wanted to *preserve* this experience.

1. What kind of *marine* life would the boat take people to see?
   whales

2. To what animal group do whales belong? mammals

3. What could Nelson identify? kinds of whales, such as orca and baleen.

4. What would the pictures do for Nelson? preserve a thrilling experience

5. What does the sign "Observe *Marine* Life Up Close" mean?
   Possible answer: It means that you can go out on aboat and see the
   ocean, fish, and whales.

Story Comprehension

Think about what you've learned about whales. Then complete the outline. Refer to "Whales" for help. Some parts of the outline are already filled in.
Answers will vary.

I. TOOTHED WHALES

  A. Three features of toothed whales

    1. feed mostly on fish and squid

    2. have only one blowhole

    3. are closely related to dolphins and porpoises

  B. Three kinds of toothed whales

    4. sperm whale

    5. narwhal

    6. orca

II. BALEEN WHALES

  A. Three features of baleen whales

    7. have a two-part nostril or blowhole

    8. have food-gathering baleen plates

    9. are the biggest whales of all

  B. Three kinds of baleen whales

    10. gray whale

    11. fin whale

    12. blue whale and humpback whale

Whales • PRACTICE

Use an Encyclopedia Index

The last book in a set of encyclopedias is an **index**. Every subject in the entire encyclopedia is listed there. In order to find what you are looking for, you would decide on the key word, or most important word in your subject.

Suppose your key word is **porpoises**. You look under **p** in the index, and you find **porpoises**. The listing tells you to look under **d** for Dolphins and porpoises, so you turn to the listing for d in the index. You find the index section below. Look at it, and then answer the questions.

| Dolphins and porpoises 5:321-325 |
| Common 4:321 |
| Echo 6:291 |
| Locomotion 1:278 |
| Training 5:324 |
| Tuna and dolphins 20:355 |
| See also list of Related Articles in the Whale article. |

1. What is the main entry? <u>Dolphins and porpoises</u>

2. On what pages would you find the most information on dolphins?

   <u>on pages 321 through 325 in Volume 5</u>

3. In which volume and on what page would you find information about dolphins' movements or locomotion? <u>Volume 1, page 278</u>

4. Does "echo" have anything to do with dolphins? How do you know?

   <u>It must have. It is listed under Dolphins and porpoises.</u>

5. Suppose you wanted to write a report with unusual information about

   dolphins. How might using the key word Dolphins and the index help you

   think of an idea? <u>Answers may vary, but may include that entries such</u>

   <u>as Echo, Training, and Locomotion might help you decide what to</u>

   <u>emphasize in your report.</u>

At Home: List which volumes in an encyclopedia might have information about a favorite topic. Compare your list with the encyclopedia listing for the topic.

Compare and Contrast

When you **compare and contrast** you tell how things are alike and how they are different. You have read about two main types of whales, toothed whales and baleen whales. To see how these whales are alike and different, complete each box below. Look back through "Whales" if you need help. Answers will vary.

What do the toothed whales and baleen whales have in common?

1. They are mammals.

2. Their population is shrinking.

3. They live in oceans.

4. They seem friendly to humans they meet.

How would you describe toothed whales?

5. They have teeth.

6. They have only one blowhole.

7. They feed mostly on squid and fish; but can eat larger sea animals.

How are you different from toothed whales?

8. They have food-gathering baleen plates.

9. They have two-part blowhole.

10. They feed mostly on small fish and very small sea animals.

At Home: Have students list ways in which pet dogs and cats are alike and ways in which they are different.

Make Judgments and Decisions

Making **decisions and judgments** about characters in a story is an important part of reading. Read the passage below. Think about what the characters are doing and why. Then answer the questions.

A fourth-grade class was asked to think about their favorite school subject and then make a suggestion for a related field trip. Mrs. Canby said the subject could not be recess or lunch.

The students had lots of ideas. Benjamin wanted to go to the natural history museum to observe carpenter ants. Every other person in the class started groaning. Several students who like reading wanted to go to a play. Other kids had never been to a play, and they weren't interested. They would, however, go to a movie. Soon everyone started arguing. So Mrs. Canby made the decision to go to the natural history museum. Almost everyone enjoyed the field trip.

1. Mrs. Canby decided recess and lunch classes could not be used as

   ideas for a field trip. Why do you think she decided this? <u>Possible</u>

   <u>answer: She wanted students to take the field trip seriously.</u>

2. What would you say to someone who said bugs are boring? <u>Answers will</u>

   <u>vary, but may include examples of bugs that are interesting.</u>

3. What do you think about going to a movie for a field trip? Can you think

   of any movie that might make a good learning experience? Tell why.

   <u>Answers will vary.</u>

4. Are you surprised that everyone enjoyed the museum? Why or why not?

   <u>Answers will vary.</u>

5. Do you think Mrs. Canby should refrain from having students make

   suggestions for field trips in the future? What are your reasons for thinking

   as you do? <u>Answers will vary.</u>

At Home: Have students write about a decision they have made recently.

Context Clues

Sometimes you can figure out an unfamiliar word by looking for clues in the nearby words and sentences. These clues are called **context clues**. Context clues help readers to define unfamiliar words.

Use context clues to fill in the blank line with a word from the box. Then write the context clue.

| sea siren | manatee | migration | krill | orca |

1. The <u>manatee</u> are called sea cows because they have

   chubby bodies and are gentle.

   Context clue: <u>sea cows, chubby bodies</u>

2. The killer whale, or <u>orca</u> has a strong jaw and teeth shaped

   like cones.

   Context clue: <u>killer whale, teeth shaped like cones</u>

3. Like whales, a <u>sea siren</u> has no hind legs and they were mistaken long

   ago for mermaids.

   Context clue: <u>mistaken for mermaids</u>

4. The longest-known annual <u>migration</u> to other waters

   is made by the gray whale.

   Context clue: <u>longest known, to other waters, is made by the gray whale</u>

5. Baleen whales feed on tiny, shrimp-like <u>krill</u>.

   Context clue: <u>tiny, shrimp-like</u>

At Home: Have students use context clues to define unknown words.

T37

Reteach 207

Name_____ Date_____

Compare and Contrast

Writers often **compare and contrast** two or more things in a story or an article to show how things are alike and different.

Read the selection below. Then decide if each numbered statement tells about all the big cats, lions, or leopards. Circle the letter of your answer.

Big cats have many things in common. They all are built for hunting and killing. They have sharp pointed teeth and razor-sharp claws. They also have keen senses.

Lions are the most recognizable of the big cats. The males have distinctive manes. Most lions are a beautiful tawny color. Unlike other cats, lions are social animals. They live in groups called prides.

Leopards are much smaller than lions. They have a yellowish coat with black spots. Unlike other cats, leopards are skillful climbers who lay in wait high in tree branches.

1. They have keen senses.
   a. lions   b. leopards   **c.** all big cats
2. The males have distinctive manes.
   a. lions   b. leopards   c. all big cats
3. They are skillful climbers.
   a. lions   **b.** leopards   c. all big cats
4. They are built for hunting and killing.
   a. lions   b. leopards   **c.** all big cats
5. They live in groups called prides.
   a. lions   b. leopards   c. all big cats

Book 4/Unit 6
Whales
5

At Home: Have students draw a diagram to show the similarities and differences between two animals.

207

Reteach 208

Name_____ Date_____

Vocabulary

Unscramble each word by using the clues for help. Then write the unscrambled word on the line provided.

identify	mammals	marine	pods	preserve	related

1. MALMASM   warm blooded animals   _mammals_
2. SDOP   whale herd   _pods_
3. ENIRAM   relating to the oceans   _marine_
4. DLEATRE   connected to in some way   _related_
5. YFITNEDI   to name   _identify_
6. ERESRPVE   save   _preserve_

6

Story Comprehension

Reteach 209

Circle the letter of the words that complete each statement about the story "Whales."

1. Whales are
   a. fish.   **b.** mammals.
2. Baleen whales have
   a. no teeth.   b. teeth.
3. The blue whale is bigger than the biggest
   a. dinosaur.   b. woolly mammoth.
4. Baleen, or toothless, whales eat.
   a. giant squid.   **b.** tiny fish.
5. There are not many gray whales because of.
   a. over hunting.   b. air pollution.
6. The goal of the International Whaling Commission is to.
   a. limit the hunting of whales.   b. tag whales for identification.

At Home: Have students recall what they have learned about whales.

208–209

Book 4/Unit 6
Whales
6

Reteach 210

Name_____ Date_____

Use an Encyclopedia Index

Just like any other index at the back of a book, an **encyclopedia index** can help you locate information quickly. The encyclopedia index is usually the last volume in the set. The first numbers tells the volume. The second number gives the page the article is on or begins.

Elephant	**6:148** *with picture*
Animal	**1:345** *with picture;* (table) **1:354**
African Animals	**1:246**
Conservation	**4:374**
Endangered Species	**5:201** (table)
India	**10:346** *with picture*
Zoos	**21:232** *with picture*

Use the sample index entry above to answer the questions.

1. What is the main entry? _Elephant_
2. In which volume would you find a picture of an Indian elephant? _10_
3. On what page would you begin reading about African animals? _246_
4. In what volume and on what page would you find information about endangered species? _Volume 5, page 201_
5. Why would you use an encyclopedia index? _Possible answers: To find information quickly, to find related articles, to find pictures and tables, when you aren't sure where to begin looking for information on a topic._

Book 4/Unit 6
Whales
5

At Home: Have students use a home or school encyclopedia index to find references pertaining to dolphins.

210

Reteach 211

Name_____ Date_____

Compare and Contrast

Jotting down likenesses and differences in a chart can make **comparing and contrasting** two or more things easier.

Read the chart below, and then answer the questions.

Crocodiles	Whales
reptiles/cold-blooded	mammals/warm-blooded
good swimmers	good swimmers
air-breathers	air-breathers
swim mostly in fresh water	swim in salty ocean water
can move on land	cannot move on land
lay eggs that will hatch on land	bear live young in water

1. What are two things crocodiles and whales have in common? _They are good swimmers; they are air-breathers._
2. What is different about where the animals swim? _Crocodiles swim mostly in fresh water. Whales swim in salty ocean water._
3. Which animals cannot move on land? _whales_
4. What is different about where the animals give birth? _Crocodiles lay eggs that will hatch on land. Whales give birth to live babies under water._
5. If the crocodile is cold-blooded, which means its body temperature changes according to the temperature of the surrounding air or water, what do you think the body temperature of the mammal does? _Stays the same if the temperature changes._

At Home: Have students compare and contrast two kinds of trees.

211

Book 4/Unit 6
Whales
5

Whales • RETEACH

Make Judgments and Decisions

> As you read, try to use what you know to be right and wrong, wise and unwise from your own experience to help you understand a character's **judgments and decisions**.

Read the following story and then answer the questions.   Answers will vary: Possible answers are shown.

> The royal princess complained to the king. She had requested that the royal carpenter adjust her throne. She had asked that the silver at the top be changed to gold and that the gold at the bottom be changed to silver. The legs of the throne needed to be made shorter, and the arm rests had to be padded with blue velvet. Now her throne was ruined. The carpenter had made the whole throne red velvet and the legs twice as long. She insisted that the old, hard-of-hearing carpenter did everything wrong on purpose. She wanted him put in jail.
>
> The king asked if she had made a list of her requests, so the carpenter would have a record of what to do. "No," she said. "It is not the work of a princess to make lists!"

1. What must the king decide? _whether to jail the carpenter_
   _____

2. Why do you think the king asked if the princess had given the carpenter a list?
   Possible answers: The king probably knew the carpenter was hard-of-
   hearing. He could see that he was old.

3. How do you think the king responded to the princess's statement that lists
   were not her work? _It may have made him more sympathetic to the_
   carpenter and less to the princess.

4. In whose favor will the king decide? _Possible response: the carpenter's_
   favor
   _____

Context Clues

> Remember: **Context clues**, or nearby words, phrases, and sentences can help you to figure out unfamiliar words.

Read the paragraph. Then read each context clue below and write the boldface word it helps to explain on the line provided.

> One kind of dolphin is the **bottlenose dolphin**. It looks like what it is named for. They are amazing animals. A dolphin mother trains her baby, or **calf**, by "talking" to it so it will recognize her sounds. Dolphins use **echolocation** to communicate with each other and to find their way around the ocean. That means they send out a series of squeaks and sounds and then listen for the echo back to figure out where things are. Dolphins eat a lot of fish, **squid**, and other sea animals. Dolphins use **fluking**, or slapping of the tail, to move themselves forward.

1. slapping of the tail
   fluking

2. series of squeaks and sounds; listen for the echo back
   echolocation

3. and other sea animals
   squid

4. looks like what it is named for
   bottlenose dolphin

5. her baby
   calf

Whales • EXTEND

Name_____ Date_____ Extend ◆207

Compare and Contrast

To **compare** is to look at two or more things and tell how they are they same. To **contrast** is to look at two or more things and tell how they are different.

Compare and contrast a horse and a camel. Write three ways the animals are the same and three ways they are different.   Possible answers are given.

Compare:

1. Both animals can be ridden by humans.
2. Both animals can be used to help people work.
3. Both animals have four legs and hooves.

Contrast:

1. Camels live mostly in Africa and Asia, while horses are found on all continents except Antarctica.
2. Camels have humps on their backs. Horses do not.
3. Horses can run very fast while camels usually move at a slow pace.

Book 4/Unit 6
Whales

At Home: Have students compare and contrast themselves with other members of the family.

207

Name_____ Date_____ Extend ◆208

Vocabulary

| identify | mammals | marine | pods | preserve | related |

Suppose you went on a whale-watching trip with your family. Using at least four of the vocabulary words above, write a diary entry about what you saw. Answers will vary, but should include at least four vocabulary words.

Dear Diary,

_____
_____
_____
_____
_____

Extend ◆209

Story Comprehension

Write a paragraph comparing and contrasting two of the types of whales mentioned in the story. Look back at "Whales" for help.

Answers will vary but should cite examples of similarities and differences from the story.
_____
_____
_____
_____

208–209

At Home: Have students compare two rooms in the house or apartment.

Book 4/Unit 6
Whales

Name_____ Date_____ Extend ◆210

Use an Encyclopedia Index

The best way to quickly find a subject in an encyclopedia is to use the **encyclopedia index**. This is the last book, or volume, in the set. It lists all the encyclopedia entries in alphabetical order, and tells you in which volume and on what pages you will find the information you are looking for.

Think of two topics that interest you. Find your topics in an encyclopedia index and then answer the questions below.   Answers will vary.

1. What are your two topics? _____
_____

2. Where will you find information on your topics in the encyclopedia?
_____
_____

3. What entries did you find for each topic? _____
_____
_____

4. Which topic has more information in the encyclopedia?
_____

5. List some additional information—charts, graphs, maps, tables, and so on—that are available for your topics. _____
_____
_____

6. On which topic would you rather write a report? Explain your choice.
_____
_____
_____

Book 4/Unit 6
Whales

At Home: Have students look up subjects in an encyclopedia index and tell where they would find the information in the encyclopedia.

210

Name_____ Date_____ Extend ◆211

Compare and Contrast

Comparing two or more things tells how the things are alike.

   Example: Whales and dolphins are both sea creatures.

Contrasting two or more things tells how the things are different.

   Example: Whales are mammals, and sharks are fish.

Think about yourself and a friend. How are you alike? How are you different? Write a paragraph that compares and contrasts the two of you. Then draw a picture of yourself and your friend.

Answers will vary but should draw appropriate comparisons and contrasts.
_____
_____
_____
_____
_____

At Home: Have students compare and contrast themselves as they were at the age of 6 with themselves today.

211

Book 4/Unit 6
Whales

Whales • EXTEND

Make Judgments and Decisions

The Makah live in the state of Washington. This Native American group has been trying to bring back their ancient tradition of whale hunting. The United States government has decided to allow Makah people to hunt up to 20 gray whales for only two years, however protesters are afraid that this will pave the way for whale hunting all over the world.

Suppose you were the one who had to decide whether Makah should be allowed to hunt gray whales or not. Use your **judgment**. What **decision** would you make and why? Be sure to explain your thinking. Be convincing!

Answers will vary but should include a judgment or decision with
supporting arguments.
_____
_____
_____
_____
_____
_____
_____
_____
_____
_____
_____
_____
_____
_____

Book 4/Unit 6
Whales

At Home: Have students tell about difficult decisions they have made recently. Why were the decisions hard to make?

212

Context Clues

Sometimes you can figure out what an unfamiliar word means by looking at the words around it. This is called using **context clues**. Context clues give you hints about a word or a series of words. These clues are especially important for subjects, such as marine biology or medicine, that have a specialized vocabulary.

Find the following words in the story "Whales." Tell which context clues helped you understand what each word means, and then write your definition. Possible answers are given.

Word	Context Clues	Definition
1. blow hole	nostril	hole to breathe out of
2. frayed	filter, skim, gaps	full of fine threads
3. sediment	stirring up, sea floor	things that have settled on the sea floor
4. skim	open-mouthed, trap	act like a net
5. filter	trap, pour out, frayed	something that separates solid things from water
6. migration	journey, yearly, travel	a trip from one place to another

213

At Home: Read an article about animals. Have students use context clues to figure out three unfamiliar words.

Book 4/Unit 6
Whales

T41

Whales • GRAMMAR

Prepositions

- A **preposition** comes before a noun or pronoun and relates that noun or pronoun to another word in a sentence.
- Common prepositions are *about, above, across, after, around, at, behind, down, for, from, in, near, of, on, over, to, under,* and *with.*

Complete each sentence by adding a preposition.

1. The selection gives information __about__ whales.

2. There are many different kinds __of__ whales.

3. The sperm whale can stay underwater __for__ more than an hour.

4. Narwhals live __in__ the Arctic.

5. Orcas are found all __around__ the world.

6. Baleen plates hang __from__ the whale's upper jaw.

7. Every year, gray whales migrate __to__ warm Mexican waters.

8. Gray whales feed __at__ the bottom of the ocean floor.

9. They fill their mouths, and then they rise __to__ the surface.

10. Fin whales often work __with__ partners to round up fish.

11. A humpback whale's song can be heard __from__ far away.

12. When humpback whales feed, they send out clouds of bubbles __under__ a school of small fish to trap them.

| 12 | Grade 4/Unit 6 **Whales** | **Extension:** Have students select a paragraph in the selection *Whales* and list the prepositions. | **179** |

Prepositional Phrases

- A **prepositional phrase** is a group of words that begins with a preposition and ends with a noun or pronoun.

Underline the prepositional phrases in the following sentences.

1. Every year, gray whales travel about ten thousand miles.

2. Blue whales strain krill through their baleen plates.

3. Toothed whales are closely related to dolphins and porpoises.

4. A narwhal has a tooth that sticks through its upper lip.

5. Orcas, or killer whales, perform in marine parks around the country.

6. Orcas eat fish and other sea mammals, but they are gentle in captivity.

7. Orcas are found in all the world's oceans.

8. Right whales used to be common in the North Atlantic Ocean.

9. In the summer, gray whales feed in cold Arctic waters.

10. In the winter, they travel ten thousand miles to warmer waters.

11. The journey of the gray whales is the longest migration of any mammal.

12. The International Whaling Commission was established in 1946.

| 180 | **Extension:** Have students write five sentences, including at least one prepositional phrase in each sentence, about the selection *Whales.* | Grade 4/Unit 6 **Whales** | 12 |

Prepositions and Prepositional Phrases

- A **preposition** comes before a noun or pronoun and relates that noun or pronoun to another word in a sentence.
- A **prepositional phrase** is a group of words that begins with a preposition and ends with a noun or pronoun.

Circle the preposition and then underline the prepositional phrase in each sentence.

1. There used to be many whales in the world's oceans.

2. Some whales have been hunted almost to extinction.

3. The right whale used to be common in the North Atlantic Ocean.

4. It got its name from early whalers.

5. For them, it was the "right whale" to hunt.

6. It swam slowly, and it had lots of baleen and blubber.

7. Now it is hard to find a right whale anywhere in the world.

8. A right whale has strange bumps, called callosities, on its head.

9. Each whale has its own unique pattern of bumps.

10. Scientists can identify a particular whale by its callosity pattern.

| 10 | Grade 4/Unit 6 **Whales** | **Extension:** Ask students to write three facts about whales and have them include a prepositional phrase in each sentence. | **181** |

Letter Punctuation

- Begin the greeting and closing in a letter with a capital letter.
- Use a comma after the greeting and the closing in a letter.
- Use a comma between the names of a city and a state.
- Use a comma between the day and year in a date.

Add capital letters and commas where they are needed in these letters.

12 Nightingale Lane

Portland, ME 04000

August 26, 2001

dear Robert,   Dear

    I can't wait to see you next week. I am really looking forward to our trip on the whale-watching boat. Do you really think we'll see whales?

        your friend,   Your

        Fred

        8 Prospect Street

        Portsmouth , NH 03000

        September 2 , 2001

dear Fred,   Dear

    I'm looking forward to our trip, too. I hope we see some whales. There's a good chance we will. It's really exciting when it happens. See you soon.

        your friend,   Your

        Robert

| 182 | **Extension:** Have students pretend that they visited a marine park and saw an orca. Have them write a short letter to a friend telling about what they saw. | Grade 4/Unit 6 **Whales** | 8 |

Name_____ Date_____ **Grammar** (183)

Prepositions and Prepositional Phrases

A. Complete each sentence below by writing the missing preposition.

1. Orcas are familiar ___to___ most people.

2. Many people have seen them ___at___ marine parks.

3. They live and perform ___in___ huge tanks of water.

4. They are real crowd-pleasers and are loved ___by___ audiences.

5. People are amazed ___by___ the things an orca can do.

B. Underline the prepositional phrase in each of the sentences below.

6. Baleen whales feed <u>on small fish and krill</u>.

7. The baleen <u>in the whale's mouth</u> acts like a filter.

8. Baleen whales open their mouths and skim <u>through the water</u>.

9. As they swim, krill is trapped <u>by the baleen</u>.

10. The water passes <u>through the gaps in the baleen</u>.

Name_____ Date_____ **Grammar** (184)

Prepositions and Prepositional Phrases

- A **preposition** comes before a noun or pronoun and relates that noun or pronoun to another word in a sentence.
- A **prepositional phrase** is a group of words that begins with a preposition and ends with a noun or pronoun.

Mechanics

- Begin the greeting and closing in a letter with a capital letter.
- Use a comma after the greeting and the closing in a letter.
- Use a comma between the names of a city and a state.
- Use a comma between the day and year in a date.

Add capital letters, commas, and prepositions to correct and complete this letter.

356 Lakeside Road

Orlando, Florida 32899

March 30, 2001

dear Grandma,   Dear

Remember the baby orca we saw when you were here last year? We went ___to___ the marine park and saw it again. It performed ___by___ itself this time ___in___ a special show. It was terrific! I wish you had been ___with___ us.

Love,

Andrea

Whales • SPELLING

Words with Prefixes

Pretest Directions

Fold back the paper along the dotted line. Use the blanks to write each word as it is read aloud. When you finish the test, unfold the paper. Use the list at the right to correct any spelling mistakes. Practice the words you missed for the Posttest.

To Parents

Here are the results of your child's weekly spelling Pretest. You can help your child study for the Posttest by following these simple steps for each word on the word list:

1. Read the word to your child.
2. Have your child write the word, saying each letter as it is written.
3. Say each letter of the word as your child checks the spelling.
4. If a mistake has been made, have your child read each letter of the correctly spelled word aloud, and then repeat steps 1–3.

1. _____	1. redo
2. _____	2. unkind
3. _____	3. disappear
4. _____	4. reread
5. _____	5. nonfat
6. _____	6. inactive
7. _____	7. international
8. _____	8. unlucky
9. _____	9. dislike
10. _____	10. unpack
11. _____	11. nonstop
12. _____	12. refill
13. _____	13. uncertain
14. _____	14. interstate
15. _____	15. incomplete
16. _____	16. rewind
17. _____	17. unsure
18. _____	18. disagree
19. _____	19 reheat
20. _____	20. nonsense

Challenge Words

_____	identify
_____	mammals
_____	marine
_____	preserve
_____	related

Words with Prefixes

Using the Word Study Steps

1. LOOK at the word.
2. SAY the word aloud.
3. STUDY the letters in the word.
4. WRITE the word.
5. CHECK the word.

Did you spell the word right? If not, go back to step 1.

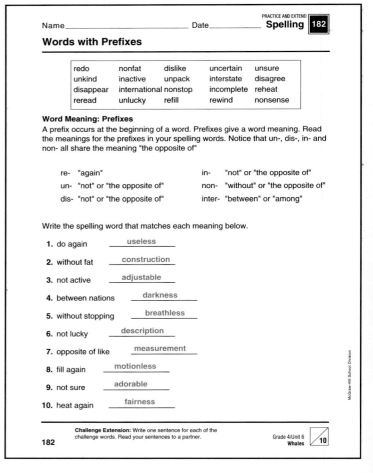

> **Spelling Tip**
>
> Learn how to spell prefixes you use often in writing.
>
> *re- un- in- dis- inter- non-*

X the Word

Put an X on the word that does NOT have the same prefix as the spelling word on the left.

1. **redo**	return	~~red~~	2. **reread**	retell	~~ready~~
3. **refill**	rebuild	~~rental~~	4. **reheat**	reach	refresh
5. **unkind**	untold	~~under~~	6. **unlucky**	unite	unfold
7. **unpack**	unfold	~~uncle~~	8. **uncertain**	uncover	~~unit~~
9. **incomplete**	~~ink~~	incurable			
10. **inactive**	indirect	~~inch~~			
11. **disappear**	~~disease~~	disrespect			
12. **dislike**	~~dish~~	distrust			
13. **international**	interconnect	~~interior~~			
14. **nonfat**	~~none~~	nonviolent			
15. **nonsense**	~~nontheless~~	nonstop			

To Parents or Helpers

Using the Word Study Steps above as your child comes across any new words will help him or her learn to spell words effectively. Review the steps as you both go over this week's spelling words.
Go over the Spelling Tip with your child. Ask you child to name words that start with these prefixes.
Help your child complete the spelling activity.

Words with Prefixes

redo	nonfat	dislike	uncertain	unsure
unkind	inactive	unpack	interstate	disagree
disappear	international	nonstop	incomplete	reheat
reread	unlucky	refill	rewind	nonsense

Pattern Power

Write the spelling words that double the consonant before adding -ed.

words with –re

1. _____redo_____
2. _____reread_____
3. _____refill_____
4. _____rewind_____
5. _____reheat_____

words with –un

6. _____unkind_____
7. _____unlucky_____
8. _____unpack_____
9. _____uncertain_____
10. _____unsure_____

words with –dis

11. _____disappear_____
12. _____dislike_____
13. _____disagree_____

words with –inter

14. _____international_____
15. _____interstate_____

words with –in

16. _____inactive_____
17. _____incomplete_____

words with –non

18. _____nonfat_____
19. _____nonstop_____
20. _____nonsense_____

Words with Prefixes

redo	nonfat	dislike	uncertain	unsure
unkind	inactive	unpack	interstate	disagree
disappear	international	nonstop	incomplete	reheat
reread	unlucky	refill	rewind	nonsense

Word Meaning: Prefixes

A prefix occurs at the beginning of a word. Prefixes give a word meaning. Read the meanings for the prefixes in your spelling words. Notice that un-, dis-, in- and non- all share the meaning "the opposite of."

re-	"again"	in-	"not" or "the opposite of"
un-	"not" or "the opposite of"	non-	"without" or "the opposite of"
dis-	"not" or "the opposite of"	inter-	"between" or "among"

Write the spelling word that matches each meaning below.

1. do again — useless
2. without fat — construction
3. not active — adjustable
4. between nations — darkness
5. without stopping — breathless
6. not lucky — description
7. opposite of like — measurement
8. fill again — motionless
9. not sure — adorable
10. heat again — fairness

Challenge Extension: Write one sentence for each of the challenge words. Read your sentences to a partner.

Whales • SPELLING

Words with Prefixes

Proofreading Activity

There are six spelling mistakes in the letter below. Circle the misspelled words. Write the words correctly on the lines below.

Dear Seth,

Last week I went whale watching. The humpback whales were so beautiful. It makes me so sad to think that one day whales may (disapere.) I think it is (unkinde) for people to hunt them. There is an (internatunal) law against killing whales. Some nations think whaling is not harmful, but I (disagrea.) Experts say that it is (uncertin) if all whale species will survive. In the past, whales have been (unluky.) Today, people all over the world are trying to save them.

1. ___disappear___   3. ___international___   5. ___uncertain___

2. ___unkind___   4. ___disagree___   6. ___unlucky___

Writing Activity

What animal would you like to protect? Write a few sentences about how that animal should be protected. Use four spelling words in your writing.

_____

_____

_____

_____

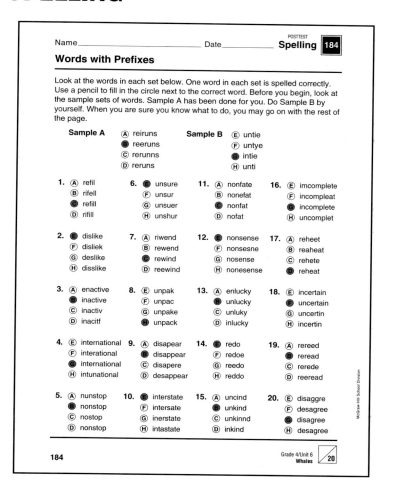

Words with Prefixes

Look at the words in each set below. One word in each set is spelled correctly. Use a pencil to fill in the circle next to the correct word. Before you begin, look at the sample sets of words. Sample A has been done for you. Do Sample B by yourself. When you are sure you know what to do, you may go on with the rest of the page.

Sample A
- Ⓐ reiruns
- ● reeruns
- Ⓒ rerunns
- Ⓓ reruns

Sample B
- Ⓔ untie
- Ⓕ untye
- ● intie
- Ⓗ unti

1.
- Ⓐ refil
- Ⓑ rifell
- ● refill
- Ⓓ rifill

2.
- ● dislike
- Ⓕ disliek
- Ⓖ deslike
- Ⓗ disslike

3.
- Ⓐ enactive
- ● inactive
- Ⓒ inactiv
- Ⓓ inacitf

4.
- Ⓔ international
- Ⓕ interational
- ● international
- Ⓗ intunational

5.
- Ⓐ nunstop
- ● nonstop
- Ⓒ nostop
- Ⓓ nonstop

6.
- ● unsure
- Ⓕ unsur
- Ⓖ unsuer
- Ⓗ unshur

7.
- Ⓐ riwend
- Ⓑ rewend
- ● rewind
- Ⓓ reewind

8.
- Ⓔ unpak
- Ⓕ unpac
- Ⓖ unpake
- ● unpack

9.
- Ⓐ disapear
- ● disappear
- Ⓒ disapere
- Ⓓ desappear

10.
- ● interstate
- Ⓕ intersate
- Ⓖ inerstate
- Ⓗ intastate

11.
- Ⓐ nonfate
- Ⓑ nonefat
- ● nonfat
- Ⓓ nofat

12.
- ● nonsense
- Ⓕ nonsesne
- Ⓖ nosense
- Ⓗ nonesense

13.
- Ⓐ enlucky
- ● unlucky
- Ⓒ unluky
- Ⓓ inlucky

14.
- ● redo
- Ⓕ redoe
- Ⓖ reedo
- Ⓗ reddo

15.
- Ⓐ uncind
- ● unkind
- Ⓒ unkinnd
- Ⓓ inkind

16.
- Ⓔ imcomplete
- Ⓕ incompleat
- ● incomplete
- Ⓗ uncomplet

17.
- Ⓐ reheet
- Ⓑ reaheat
- Ⓒ rehete
- ● reheat

18.
- Ⓔ incertain
- ● uncertain
- Ⓖ uncertin
- Ⓗ incertin

19.
- Ⓐ rereed
- ● reread
- Ⓒ rerede
- Ⓓ reeread

20.
- Ⓔ disaggre
- Ⓕ desagree
- ● disagree
- Ⓗ desagree

Practice 214

Name_____ Date_____

Cause and Effect

Things you read often include **cause and effect**. Why something happened is the cause. What happened is the effect. Read the selection, and then fill in the missing cause or an effect in the following exercise.

The early colonists and later settlers of our country often built their homes near rivers because they needed rivers for travel and to transport goods. Soon rivers became the country's highways, and boats were the trucks transporting goods and people across the country. As more settlers came, towns near rivers developed.

As towns grew, some settlers drained the lowlands near rivers. They also built homes and towns near rivers that flooded often, causing much damage and even death. To solve the problem, some townspeople built dams and dikes. However, the rivers continued to flood.

Today, people continue to ignore the danger of upsetting the balance of nature. Our cities are spreading up mountains and into deserts and remaining forests. As a result, the land where animals can live is shrinking. As wild animals lose their habitats, some are becoming endangered. Now the federal government and other organizations are studying land use and advising people where they should or should not build.

Cause	Effect
1. Colonists and settlers came to this country near rivers.	They built homes near rivers.
2. Rivers became the country's highways.	Boats became the trucks carrying people and goods across the country
3. Settlers built homes and towns near rivers that flooded often.	Rivers flooded, causing much damage, even death.
4. Dams and dikes were built.	Rivers continue to flood.
5. Today people are continuing to upset the balance of nature.	Animals are losing their habitat.

5 Book 4/Unit 6
Saving the Everglades

At Home: Have students describe a cause and effect related to a weather event.

214

Practice 215

Name_____ Date_____

Vocabulary

Choose a word from the list to complete each sentence below.

soggy	compares	importance	lurk	wildlife	instance

1. The trees, plants, and animals in the forest are called **wildlife**.

2. The sponge is **soggy** because it has soaked up all the water.

3. The class **compares** peach seeds to plum seeds to find out how they are the same.

4. The river's **importance** to the land is very great.

5. A frog will hide and **lurk** on the riverbank, waiting for small insects.

6. Some plants, such as moss for **instance**, need little soil to grow.

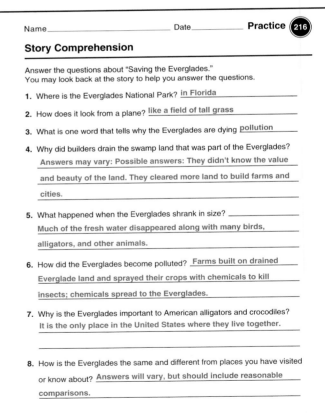

215

At Home: Have students write a paragraph, using vocabulary words, describing their neighborhood in a rainstorm.

Book 4/Unit 6
Saving the Everglades 6

The Slippery Frog

Karen and her mother liked to explore the *wildlife* near the pond behind their house. They always had interesting experiences. For *instance*, one time they decided to catch a frog, keep it in the house overnight, and observe it. They wanted to see how a frog living inside compares to one living in the pond.

Karen and her mother knew the *importance* of providing pond water and leaves for the frog so that it would feel at home in the house. Grabbing two small pails, they went down to the pond. Because it had rained the night before, the ground was *soggy*. Karen slipped at the edge of the pond and fell in. As she began to climb out, she saw a frog *lurk* in the lily pads. Before Karen could catch it, the frog leaped back into the pond. Karen's mother fell in the pond trying to catch a frog, too. Karen's mother laughed. After an hour of trying to catch a frog, the only thing they had to compare was their wet clothes.

1. What did Karen and her mother like to do near the pond? _____ **explore wildlife**

2. Give one *instance* of an interesting thing they did? **try to catch a frog** and keep it overnight in their house.

3. Why was the *importance* of using pond water? **To help the frog feel at** home.

4. What did the rain make the ground? **soggy**

5. Would you trust Karen and her mother with any animals, wild or tame? Why or why not? **Answers will vary, but should include the care they** took of the frog they caught.

5 Book 4/Unit 6
Saving the Everglades

At Home: Have students write a description of an imaginary pond behind their houses, using as many vocabulary words as they can.

215a

Practice 216

Name_____ Date_____

Story Comprehension

Answer the questions about "Saving the Everglades."
You may look back at the story to help you answer the questions.

1. Where is the Everglades National Park? **in Florida**

2. How does it look from a plane? **like a field of tall grass**

3. What is one word that tells why the Everglades are dying **pollution**

4. Why did builders drain the swamp land that was part of the Everglades? **Answers may vary: Possible answers: They didn't know the value and beauty of the land. They cleared more land to build farms and cities.**

5. What happened when the Everglades shrank in size? **Much of the fresh water disappeared along with many birds, alligators, and other animals.**

6. How did the Everglades become polluted? **Farms built on drained Everglade land and sprayed their crops with chemicals to kill insects; chemicals spread to the Everglades.**

7. Why is the Everglades important to American alligators and crocodiles? **It is the only place in the United States where they live together.**

8. How is the Everglades the same and different from places you have visited or know about? **Answers will vary, but should include reasonable comparisons.**

216

At Home: Have students write about why they think the Everglades are important and should be preserved.

Book 4/Unit 6
Saving the Everglades 8

Use the Internet

Name_____ Date_____ Practice **217**

When you want more information about the Everglades or any topic, you can search for it on the **Internet**. You can also find several topics set up just for kids on the internet. Look at the website on the computer screen. Then answer the questions.

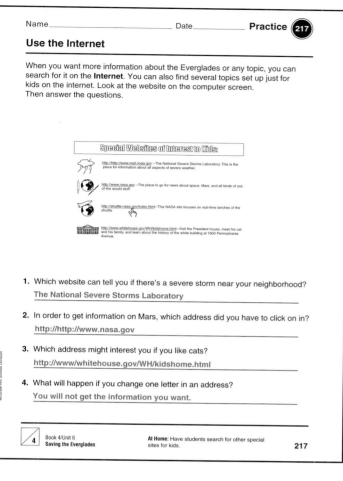

Special Websites of Interest to Kids:

http://www.nssl.noaa.gov—The National Severe Storms Laboratory. This is the place for information about all aspects of severe weather.

http://www.nasa.gov —The place to go for news about space, Mars, and all kinds of out-of-the would stuff.

http://shuttle.nasa.gov/index.html—This NASA site focuses on real-time lanches of the shuttle.

http://www.whitehouse.gov/WH/kidshome.html—Visit the President house, meet his cat and his family, and learn about the history of the white building at 1600 Pennsylvania Avenue.

1. Which website can tell you if there's a severe storm near your neighborhood?
The National Severe Storms Laboratory

2. In order to get information on Mars, which address did you have to click on in?
http://http://www.nasa.gov

3. Which address might interest you if you like cats?
http://www/whitehouse.gov/WH/kidshome.html

4. What will happen if you change one letter in an address?
You will not get the information you want.

4 Book 4/Unit 6
Saving the Everglades

At Home: Have students search for other special sites for kids.

217

Compare and Contrast

Name_____ Date_____ Practice **218**

In "Saving the Everglades," the author **compares and contrasts** what this vast wetland was like at the end of the 1800s with what it is like now. Think about how the Everglades are the same and how they are different. Then answer the questions below.
Students' answers will vary. Possible answers are shown.

1. Compare the feelings many nature lovers of long ago had about the Everglades to the feelings many scientists and nature lovers have today. How are those feelings the same? Both could see and appreciate the wild beauty.

2. Contrast peoples' understanding of what building farms and cities would do to the Everglades. Long ago people did not realize the value of the Everglades. To them it was just swampland. They had part of it drained to build farms and cities. Today, people know that draining part of the land and polluting it destroy a valuable area for animals, plants, and people.

3. Why are scientists today putting rivers back on their winding courses? Straightening the rivers by draining land and building dikes has harmed the Everglades. Scientists are returning the rivers to what they once were.

4. The Everglades used to be huge, but now the area has been reduced to half its size. Why? Land was drained for farms and cities. People thought the Everglades was a useless swamp area.

5. The Everglades has huge numbers of wild plants, cattails, compared to what there used to be. Why is that? Cattails easily absorb the chemicals found in farm fertilizers so they increase in number and strength.

6. How did the animal population change between the 1800s and the 1900s? Animals have less land to live on and find food. Some of the Everglades animals are now threatened and may possibly disappear.

218

At Home: Have students draw and label a two-part picture illustrating the Everglades long ago and today.

Book 4/ Unit 6
Saving the Everglades 6

Context Clues

Name_____ Date_____ Practice **219**

When you are reading, you may come to a word that you do not know. You can look for clues to that word's meaning in other words or sentences nearby. These clues are called **context clues**.

Read each sentence or group of sentences. Use context clues to help you figure out the meaning of each underlined word. Then write the meaning on the line provided. Students' answers may vary.

1. It is thrilling to watch the large, white egret as it flies overhead head displaying its tufts of long, lacy feathers.
An egret is a big white bird with long, lacy feathers.

2. If you stand on the high, human-made banks of a canal during flood season, you can watch the water rising as the canal drains the nearby land.
A canal is like a river made to drain water from nearby lands.

3. Hundreds of people gathered to work on the dikes. These walls that hold in the river water must become higher and higher as the river water rises.
Walls that hold the river back.

4. One town near the river had been flooded last year, but people were hoping that the river water would remain stable. The river water did not stay at the same level. It rose and flooded the same town again.
To remain stable means to stay the same and to have no changes.

5. Some students used charts and sketches to explain the water cycle. They showed that in a water cycle, water evaporates into the sky, forms clouds, rains or snows, and raises lakes and rivers, and then evaporates once again. The water cycle is the pattern that shows how water evaporates, causes rain, which raises water levels on the earth's surface, and then evaporates again.

6. There are many native plants in the Everglades that have always grown in that area. Native plants are those that have always grown in one area.

8 Book 4/Unit 6
Saving the Everglades

At Home: Have students explain context clues to a family member using any of the underlined words above.

219

Synonyms and Antonyms

Name_____ Date_____ Practice **220**

Choose a word from the list that means the same thing as the underlined word. Write your answer on the line provided.

saline	immense	wetlands	migrating	reside

1. Swamps are a kind of wetlands that contain trees, shrubs, and bushes.

2. The huge Everglades make up an immense freshwater marsh measuring at 4,000 square miles.

3. Marshes and swamps can be important rest areas for birds traveling great distances, such as ducks and other migrating birds.

4. Alligators and crocodiles live side-by-side in the Everglades and reside there year around.

5. The salt-filled lands near the ocean are home to animals that need a saline element in their foods.

Choose a word from the list that means the opposite of the underlined word or words. Write your answer on the line provided.

finite	saltwater	nutrients	enhance	endangered

1. Some areas of the wetlands have fresh water while others have saltwater.

2. Changing the course of rivers can enhance the land, or it can take away many important aspects of the area.

3. The Florida Everglades receive many of their nutrients or vitamins from rain water, but they also receive poisons.

4. Some wetland species are endangered, while others are already protected by law.

5. Some rivers of grass seem endless, but they are finite and growing smaller.

220

At Home: Have students use antonyms and synonyms in ten sentences.

Book 4/Unit 6
Saving the Everglades 10

Saving the Everglades • RETEACH

Cause and Effect

> The **cause** is why something happens and what happens is the **effect**.

Read the paragraph below. Then write sentences to answer the questions about causes and effects on the lines provided.

People don't intend to harm our planet, but they cause environmental problems because they don't think about the effects of their actions. A good example is flood prevention on the Mississippi River. For centuries, the great river has overflowed its banks. Billions of dollars have been spent on projects to keep the river from flooding. The river still floods, though. Some experts argue that the flood prevention projects have only made the floods worse. Additionally, wetlands have been filled in. The consequences of this loss of habitat are serious changes in animal and plant life.

1. What is the general cause of environmental problems? The cause is people not thinking about the effects of their actions.

2. What has been the general and disappointing effect of efforts to stop the Mississippi from flooding? It still floods.

3. What cause of flooding do experts argue about? Flood prevention projects are making the effects of floods worse.

4. What are two other effects of the flood prevention program? Wetlands have been filled in. This in turn has changed the animal and plant life in the area.

Vocabulary

Write the letter of the word that matches the numbered definitions on the lines provided.

_d_ 1. to wait in hiding
_c_ 2. is similar to
_f_ 3. an example or case
_a_ 4. very wet
_e_ 5. animals in nature
_b_ 6. significance

a. soggy
b. importance
c. compares
d. lurk
e. wildlife
f. instance

6

Story Comprehension

Write the letter of the word or words that complete each statement about "Saving the Everglades."

1. The Everglades are in the state of _b_.
   a. New York   **b.** Florida
2. Builders tried to _a_ the swamp to get usable land.
   a. drain   **b.** cover over
3. _b_ build canals and dikes to stop flooding.
   a. Home owners   **b.** Engineers
4. Fertilizers and other chemicals changed _b_ in the Everglades.
   a. water temperature **b.** plant life
5. Most people feel strongly that it is _a_ to save the Everglades.
   a. possible   **b.** impossible

Use the Internet

> The **Internet** is a useful research tool on your computer. With a simple point and click, you can find information on just about anything.

Read the following text from a website home page. Then use the menu on the computer to answer the questions.

If you were interested in information about Yellowstone National Park, a good starting place would be the national park home page. You can find it at http://www.nps.gov/yell/. This home page will direct you to many different topics that you can read by moving your pointer to the topic and clicking. Each topic will lead you to other topics. At the end of the home page there is also a link to other pages or websites.

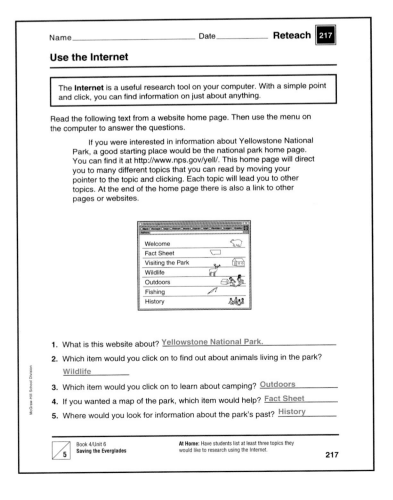

Welcome
Fact Sheet
Visiting the Park
Wildlife
Outdoors
Fishing
History

1. What is this website about? Yellowstone National Park.
2. Which item would you click on to find out about animals living in the park? Wildlife
3. Which item would you click on to learn about camping? Outdoors
4. If you wanted a map of the park, which item would help? Fact Sheet
5. Where would you look for information about the park's past? History

Compare and Contrast

> Writers often **compare and contrast** two or more things. They point out how the things are alike and different.

Read the paragraphs below. Then write your responses on the lines provided.

Some people call lemons the sunny fruit. The bright yellow color reminds them of the sun. Lemons have a thick skin that protects the juice and pulp inside. The zesty tart flavor of lemons is just perfect in cakes, candies, and drinks. Lemons ship well and are available throughout our country.

Peaches are an orange pink color. They have a soft, fuzzy skin. The flesh of a ripe peach is soft, and the flavor is sweet. People often eat peaches out of their hands. They make a great snack. Peaches often turn up in pies in the summertime. Peaches bruise easily and must be shipped with care.

List four ways in which lemons and peaches differ.

1. Lemons are yellow. Peaches are an orange pink color.

2. Lemons have a thick skin. Peaches have a soft, fuzzy skin.

3. Lemons are tart. Peaches are sweet.

4. Lemons ship well. Peaches bruise and must be shipped with care.

5. Although it is not stated, what is one way lemons and peaches are alike? Lemons and peaches are both fruits; they are both juicy.

Saving the Everglades • RETEACH

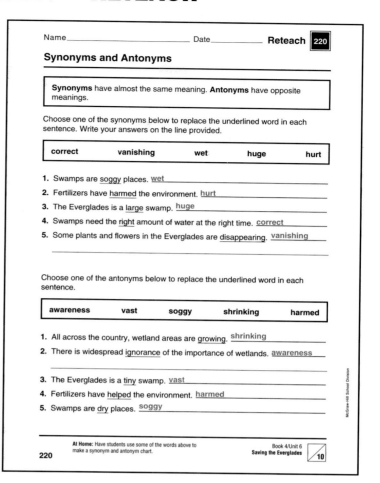

Context Clues

Readers often can figure out unfamiliar words by using **context clues**, or nearby words.

Read the paragraph. Look for context clues to help you figure out the meanings of the words in boldface.

> The Rocky Mountains are important for more than their **soaring** height and rugged beauty. In the middle of the **range**, you come to the Continental Divide. The term means just what it says. The top of the mountains divide the continent's rivers. Those running down the western **slope** end up in the Pacific Ocean. Rivers running down the eastern slope end up in the Atlantic Ocean. Between the peaks and the **tree line** you can find beautiful **alpine**, or mountain, meadows covered with flowers in summer.

Context Clues
a. or mountain
b. height; skyward
c. rivers running down
d. between the peaks and ...are meadows
e. Rocky Mountains; middle of the

Write the letter of the context clue and the word it helped you define next to each word's definition.

Definitions

1. rising upward .... soaring, b
2. slanting surface .... slope, c
3. highest point at which trees grow .... tree line, d
4. chain of mountains .... range, e
5. as in the Alps or Alp Mountain range ... alpine, a

Book 4/Unit 6
Saving the Everglades
5

At Home: Have students use the words in boldface to tell a story.

219

Synonyms and Antonyms

Synonyms have almost the same meaning. **Antonyms** have opposite meanings.

Choose one of the synonyms below to replace the underlined word in each sentence. Write your answers on the line provided.

correct	vanishing	wet	huge	hurt

1. Swamps are soggy places. wet
2. Fertilizers have harmed the environment. hurt
3. The Everglades is a large swamp. huge
4. Swamps need the right amount of water at the right time. correct
5. Some plants and flowers in the Everglades are disappearing. vanishing

Choose one of the antonyms below to replace the underlined word in each sentence.

awareness	vast	soggy	shrinking	harmed

1. All across the country, wetland areas are growing. shrinking
2. There is widespread ignorance of the importance of wetlands. awareness
3. The Everglades is a tiny swamp. vast
4. Fertilizers have helped the environment. harmed
5. Swamps are dry places. soggy

220

At Home: Have students use some of the words above to make a synonym and antonym chart.

Book 4/Unit 6
Saving the Everglades
10

Saving the Everglades • EXTEND

Cause and Effect

A **cause** is something that produces an **effect**, or a result. Work with a partner. Write down causes. Trade lists with your partner and write down the effects. Answers will vary but should include logical cause and effect relationships.

Cause	Effect
Example:	
I was caught in the rain without a raincoat.	I got soaking wet.
1. _____	_____
2. _____	_____
3. _____	_____
4. _____	_____
5. _____	_____
6. _____	_____
7. _____	_____
8. _____	_____

Draw two illustrations, one showing the first cause and the other the last effect.

Vocabulary

compares	importance	instance	lurk	soggy	wildlife

Work with a partner. Each of you choose three words from the vocabulary list and write down the definitions. Read your definitions to your partner. Have him or her guess the words.

_____
_____
_____
_____
_____
_____

Story Comprehension

Human interference and pollution are causing the Everglades to disappear. Write about the causes of the problem. What are the effects of human behavior on the situation? What decisions are being made in order to solve the problem?

Answers will vary, but should include reasonable causes and effects.

_____
_____
_____
_____
_____
_____
_____
_____

Use the Internet

Using the Internet is a good way to find information about many different topics. Once you find a home page on a particular subject, you can usually move into other files by clicking on the topic of your choice.

Welcome to All About Alligators

Did you know that the alligator is the Florida state reptile?
Do you want to learn more about alligators? Just point and click.
- Alligators and their Cousins
- Family Life
- Habitat
- Favorite Foods
- Alligator Facts
- Alligators and You—Safety First

Alligator Facts:

An adult alligator can grow to 12 feet in length and weigh as much as 550 pounds. Their life expectancy is 50 to 60 years.

Use the screens above to answer these questions.

1. What is the name of this website? All About Alligators

2. What would you click to find out about where alligators live? Habitats

3. What would you click to learn more about the feeding habits of an alligator?
   Favorite Foods

4. Is it true or false that alligators can grow to be 12 feet long and weigh 550 pounds? true

5. About how long do alligators live? 50 to 60 years

6. Which button would you click on the All About Alligator home page, and why?
   Answers will vary.

Compare and Contrast

Comparing two or more things tells how the things are alike.
    Example: Alligators and crocodiles are both reptiles.
Contrasting two or more things tells how the things are different.
    Example: Alligators have broader snouts than crocodiles.

Compare and contrast an environmental issue in your community to the disappearance of the Everglades. Do some research on your topic on the Internet or in newspapers. How are the issues alike? How are they different? How are the solutions to your environmental problem and the problem of the Everglades alike? How are they different? Write your findings in the appropriate section of the chart below. Answers will vary.

	Community Issue	Everglades
Comparisons		
Contrasts		

T50 *Annotated Workbooks*

Saving the Everglades • EXTEND

Context Clues

Context clues in a sentence can give you hints about the meaning of an unfamiliar word or a series of words. You can also look at the meaning of an entire passage to figure out words you don't know.

Write a sentence for each word below. Provide context clues for the words. Exchange sentences with a partner. Have them locate the context clues for each word in your sentences.   Answers will vary. Possible answers given.

canals	dikes	egrets	engineers	swampland	wildlife

1. **canals:** The water flowed through the deep canals that ran along the corn fields for irrigation.

2. **dikes:** The rain came so hard that soon the water overflowed the tall walls of the dikes.

3. **egrets:** The egrets took off suddenly, leaving long white feathers behind.

4. **engineers:** The engineers who designed the bridge say it will be open for travel soon.

5. **swampland:** The swampland was a refuge for snakes and alligators who prefer marsh-like areas.

6. **wildlife:** Unlike our tame pets, wildlife of the forest should never be approached without great caution.

At Home: Read an article on an environmental issue. Have students use context clues to determine the meanings of unfamiliar words.

219

Synonyms and Antonyms

Synonyms are words whose meanings are the same. **Antonyms** are words whose meanings are opposite.

Are these pairs of words synonyms or antonyms? Write **S** or **A** on the line.

1. surface/depth   A
2. threatened/protected   A
3. rescuing/saving   S

Write two synonyms for each word below: Possible answers given.

4. soggy   wet; dripping
5. dikes   dams; walls
6. stable   barn; unchanged

Write two antonyms for each word below:

7. native   foreign; tourist
8. winding   straight; unbending
9. flood   drought; dryness
10. broader   narrower; tighter

Write a poem using as many of the synonyms as possible.

_____
_____
_____
_____
_____
_____
_____
_____
_____
_____
_____

At Home: Have students replace words in a magazine article with synonyms and antonyms.

220

T51

Saving the Everglades • GRAMMAR

Combining Sentences with Adjectives and Adverbs

> • Two sentences can be combined by adding an **adjective** or **adverb** to one sentence.

Rewrite the sentences below by adding an adjective or adverb to combine them into one sentence.

1. The Everglades is in trouble. It's serious.
   The Everglades is in serious trouble.

2. Farmers use chemicals. The chemicals are dangerous.
   Farmers use dangerous chemicals.

3. Everglades' animals eat plants. They are native plants.
   Everglades' animals eat native plants.

4. Some plants are invasive. They are pushing out native plants.
   Some invasive plants are pushing out native plants.

5. The Everglades is very beautiful. It is swamplike.
   The swamplike Everglades is very beautiful.

6. Before us is a field of tall grass. It is flat and soggy.
   Before us is a flat and soggy field of tall grass.

7. An egret stands at the water's edge. It is motionless.
   An egret stands motionless at the water's edge.

8. Tree frogs croak. They croak noisily.
   Tree frogs croak noisily.

9. You can tell an alligator from a crocodile. You can easily do it
   You can easily tell an alligator from a crocodile.

10. A crocodile has a tooth that sticks out. It is long.
    A crocodile has a long tooth that sticks out.

Extension: Ask students to write two sentences and have a partner combine them into one sentence by adding an adjective or an adverb.

Combining Sentences with Prepositional Phrases

> • Two sentences can be combined by adding a **prepositional phrase** to one sentence.

Rewrite these sentences below by adding a prepositional phrase to combine them into one sentence.

1. Large numbers of people moved. They moved to Florida.
   Large numbers of people moved to Florida.

2. Engineers tried to stop flooding. They did this in the 1920s.
   In the 1920s, engineers tried to stop flooding.

3. Their efforts had a negative effect. The effect was on the Everglades.
   Their efforts had a negative effect on the Everglades.

4. Engineers are returning the rivers. They are returning the rivers to their original courses.
   Engineers are returning the rivers to their original courses.

5. The Everglades has been called a "river of grass." It is in Florida.
   The Everglades in Florida has been called a "river of grass."

6. The Everglades has been damaged. It's been damaged by people.
   The Everglades has been damaged by people.

7. People saw the Everglades just as swampland. This was true for almost a century.
   For almost a century, people saw the Everglades just as swampland.

8. People's thinking has changed. This has happened in recent years.
   In recent years, people's thinking has changed.

Extension: Ask students to write two sentences for a partner to combine by joining the two sentences with a prepositional phrase.

Combining Sentences

> • Two sentences can be combined by:
>   adding an **adjective** or an **adverb** to one sentence.
>   adding a **prepositional phrase** to one sentence.

Combine the pair of sentences below by adding an adjective, adverb, or prepositional phrase. Then underline what you added to join the two sentences.

1. We spent the day observing nature. We were at Everglades National Park.
   We spent the day observing nature <u>at Everglades National Park.</u>

2. We spotted a tree frog. It was lime-green.
   We spotted a <u>lime-green</u> tree frog.

3. The ibis glided over the water. It glided soundlessly.
   The ibis glided <u>soundlessly</u> over the water.

4. A splash attracted our attention. It happened suddenly.
   <u>Suddenly</u> a splash attracted our attention.

5. A reptile slipped into the water. It was large and greenish-brown.
   A <u>large and greenish-brown</u> reptile slipped into the water.

6. It disappeared before we could get a good look. It disappeared underwater.
   It disappeared <u>underwater</u> before we could get a good look.

7. Then we noticed a tooth sticking out. It was a long tooth.
   Then we noticed a <u>long</u> tooth sticking out.

8. It was a crocodile we saw. We saw it in the water.
   It was a crocodile we saw <u>in the water.</u>

Extension: Ask students to write four more sentences telling about something they think they might see on a visit to the Everglades. Then have them combine two of them using an adjective, adverb, or prepositional phrase.

Using Punctuation Marks

> • Every sentence begins with a capital letter.
> • Use the correct end mark for each sentence.
> • Use a comma to set off a person's name when the person is spoken to directly.
> • Use a comma after introductory words such as *yes, no,* and *well.*

Make corrections to this dialogue between Max and Carrie, who are visiting Everglades National Park, by adding the correct punctuation marks.

Carrie: will we see wildlife if we take this trail
Will we see wildlife if we take this trail?

Max: yes I think we will that's what the map shows
Yes, I think we will. That's what the map shows

Carrie: Max look it's a snowy egret isn't it beautiful
Max, look! It's a snowy egret. Isn't it beautiful?

Max: that's pretty amazing
That's pretty amazing!

Carrie: look at all of those flamingoes have you ever seen a real one
Look at all of those flamingoes! Have you ever seen a real one before?

Max: no I've only seen plastic ones in people's front yards
No, I've only seen plastic ones in people's front yards.

Carrie: well you're seeing the real ones now they look really different from the plastic ones
Well, you're seeing the real ones now. They look really different from the plastic ones

Max: yes I have to agree with you about that Carrie
Yes, I have to agree with you about that, Carrie.

Extension: Have students continue writing the dialogue between the two characters visiting Everglades National Park, being sure to use the correct punctuation.

Saving the Everglades • GRAMMAR

Combining Sentences

Study the sentences below. Then circle the correct choice of what was added to combine the two sentences into one.

1. We stood on the boardwalk. It was wet.
    We stood on the wet boardwalk.
    a. adjective
    b. adverb
    c. prepositional phrase

2. We stared into the water. We stared for a while.
    We stared into the water for a while.
    a. adjective
    b. adverb
    c. prepositional phrase

3. I was certain I could see an alligator lurking. It was below the surface.
    I was certain I could see an alligator lurking below the surface.
    a. adjective
    b. adverb
    c. prepositional phrase

4. Then we spotted another alligator. It was on the bank.
    Then we spotted another alligator on the bank.
    a. adjective
    b. adverb
    c. prepositional phrase

5. The alligator winked an eye. It did it sleepily.
    The alligator winked an eye sleepily.
    a. adjective
    b. adverb
    c. prepositional phrase

6. Then the alligator slithered down the bank. It moved silently.
    Then the alligator slithered silently down the bank.
    a. adjective
    b. adverb
    c. prepositional phrase

Correcting Sentences

- Two sentences can be combined by:
    adding an **adjective** or an **adverb** to one sentence.
    adding a **prepositional phrase** to one sentence.

Mechanics

- Every sentence begins with a capital letter.
- Use the correct end mark for each sentence.
- Use a comma to set off a person's name when the person is spoken to directly.
- Use a comma after introductory words such as *yes, no,* and *well.*

Combine the groups of words below to form one sentence. Then add the correct sentence punctuation.

1. do you see that crocodile   it is on the bank
    _____Do you see that crocodile on the bank?_____

2. yes I see that crocodile   it is sleepy-looking
    _____Yes, I see that sleepy-looking crocodile._____

3. the grass almost hides him   the grass is tall
    _____The tall grass almost hides him._____

4. his snout is almost in the water   it is pointy
    _____His pointy snout is almost in the water_____

5. do you think he sees us up here   we are on this walk
    _____Do you think he sees us up here on this walk?_____

6. well my friend I don't think so   I really don't
    _____Well, my friend, I really don't think so._____

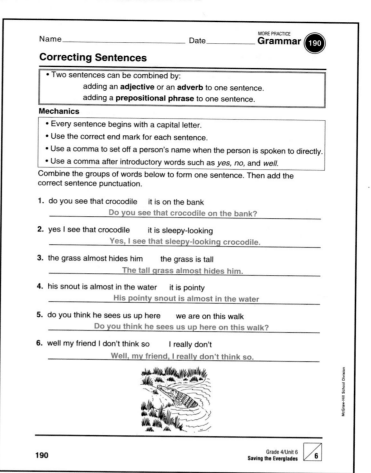

T53

Saving the Everglades • SPELLING

Page 185

Name_____ Date_____

Words from Math

Pretest Directions
Fold back the paper along the dotted line. Use the blanks to write each word as it is read aloud. When you finish the test, unfold the paper. Use the list at the right to correct any spelling mistakes. Practice the words that you missed for the Posttest.

To Parents
Here are the results of your child's weekly spelling Pretest. You can help your child study for the Posttest by following these simple steps for each word on the list:

1. Read the word to your child.
2. Have your child write the word, saying each letter as it is written.
3. Say each letter of the word as your child checks the spelling.
4. If a mistake has been made, have your child read each letter of the correctly spelled word aloud, and then repeat steps 1–3.

1. _____	1. area
2. _____	2. hundreds
3. _____	3. size
4. _____	4. billionns
5. _____	5. weight
6. _____	6. minute
7. _____	7. noon
8. _____	8. cone
9. _____	9. yard
10. _____	10. edge
11. _____	11. amount
12. _____	12. cylinder
13. _____	13. zero
14. _____	14. figure
15. _____	15. calendar
16. _____	16. quart
17. _____	17. decade
18. _____	18. rectangle
19. _____	19 era
20. _____	20. length

Challenge Words

_____	compares
_____	importance
_____	instance
_____	lurk
_____	soggy

Grade 4/Unit 6
Saving the Everglades 20

185

Page 186

Name_____ Date_____

Words from Math

Using the Word Study Steps

1. LOOK at the word.
2. SAY the word aloud.
3. STUDY the letters in the word.
4. WRITE the word.
5. CHECK the word.

   Did you spell the word right? If not, go back to step 1.

Spelling Tip
Become familiar with the dictionary and use it often.

Find Rhyming Words
Circle the word in each row that rhymes with the spelling word on the left. Unscramble each set of letters to make a spelling word.

1. **quart** — (short) quick quail
2. **yard** — yield (hard) board
3. **noon** — none one (balloon)
4. **weight** — though week (date)
5. **size** — maze (rise) breeze
6. **length** — enough eighth (strength)
7. **cone** — soon none (bone)
8. **amount** — among (count) about
9. **edge** — (ledge) egg badge
10. **zero** — cow (hero) true

To Parents or Helpers
Using the Word Study Steps above as your child comes across any new words will help him or her learn to spell words effectively. Review the steps as you both go over this week's spelling words.
Help your child find other math words, and words from other subjects, and list them in a Personal Word List.
Help your child complete the rhyming activity.

186

Grade 4/Unit 6
Saving the Everglades 10

Page 187

Name_____ Date_____

Words from the Math

area	weight	yard	zero	decade
hundreds	minute	edge	figure	rectangle
size	noon	amount	calendar	era
billions	cone	cylinder	quart	length

Syllable Practice
Write the spelling words in alphabetical order.

Numbers
1. hundreds
2. billions
3. amount
4. zero

Shapes
5. area
6. size
7. cone
8. edge
9. cylinder
10. figure
11. rectangle

Time
12. minute
13. noon
14. calendar
15. decade
16. era

Measurement
17. weight
18. yard
19. quart
20. length

Write the spelling words quart, cylinder, zero, and hundreds in alphabetical order.

21. cylinder
22. hundreds
23. quart
24. zero

Grade 4/Unit 6
Saving the Everglades 24

187

Page 188

Name_____ Date_____

Words from Math

area	weight	yard	zero	decade
hundreds	minute	edge	figure	rectangle
size	noon	amount	calendar	era
billions	cone	cylinder	quart	length

What is the Meaning?
Write the spelling word that belongs in each group.

1. triangle, rectangle
2. tens, hundreds
3. millions, billions
4. minute, hour
5. noon, midnight
6. year, decade
7. foot, yard
8. pint, quart

What's the Word?
Complete each sentence with a spelling word.

9. The playground is that whole area behind the school.
10. If you subtract four from four, you'll end up with zero.
11. What size shoes do you wear?
12. We circled her birthday on the calendar.
13. Move the cup away from the edge of the table.
14. What amount of money do you need to buy the car?
15. A three-sided figure is called a triangle.
16. The length of the hallway is about 50 feet.
17. The era of the dinosaurs occurred long ago.
18. I have gained a lot of weight from eating cookies.

188

Challenge Extension: Challenge Extension: Write one sentence for each challenge word.

Grade 4/Unit 6
Saving the Everglades 18

Saving the Everglades • SPELLING

Words from Math

Proofreading Activity

There are six spelling mistakes in the paragraph below. Circle the misspelled words. Write the words correctly on the lines below.

    The Everglades covers an (areah) of about 5,000 square miles in southern Florida. Its (siz) makes it one of the largest wetlands in the world. During the past (decad) a growing population and farming has harmed this wetland. Today, alligators must be protected or they will die out. An alligator's (lenth) can measure 9 feet or more. Their (wayt) can be as much as 250 pounds. If we do not save the Everglades, the (erah) of the Florida alligator may be over.

1. _____area_____   3. _____decade_____   5. _____weight_____

2. _____size_____   4. _____length_____   6. _____era_____

Writing Activity

Write about an animal or a place that you would like to save. Use four spelling words in your writing.

_____

_____

_____

_____

Words from Math

Look at the words in each set below. One word in each set is spelled correctly. Use a pencil to fill in the circle next to the correct word. Before you begin, look at the sample sets of words. Sample A has been done for you. Do Sample B by yourself. When you are sure you know what to do, you may go on with the rest of the page.

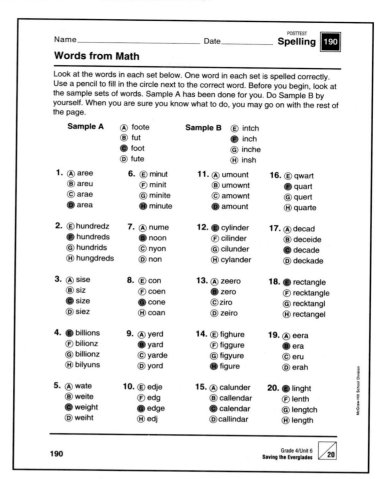

Sample A
- Ⓐ foote
- Ⓑ fut
- 🅒 foot
- Ⓓ fute

Sample B
- Ⓔ intch
- 🅕 inch
- Ⓖ inche
- Ⓗ insh

1.
- Ⓐ aree
- Ⓑ areu
- Ⓒ arae
- 🅓 area

6.
- Ⓔ minut
- Ⓕ minit
- Ⓖ minite
- 🅗 minute

11.
- Ⓐ umount
- Ⓑ umownt
- Ⓒ amownt
- 🅓 amount

16.
- Ⓔ qwart
- 🅕 quart
- Ⓖ quert
- Ⓗ quarte

2.
- Ⓔ hundredz
- 🅕 hundreds
- Ⓖ hundrids
- Ⓗ hungdreds

7.
- Ⓐ nume
- 🅑 noon
- Ⓒ nyon
- Ⓓ non

12.
- 🅔 cylinder
- Ⓕ cilinder
- Ⓖ cilunder
- Ⓗ cylander

17.
- Ⓐ decad
- Ⓑ deceide
- 🅒 decade
- Ⓓ deckade

3.
- Ⓐ sise
- Ⓑ siz
- 🅒 size
- Ⓓ siez

8.
- Ⓔ con
- Ⓕ coen
- 🅖 cone
- Ⓗ coan

13.
- Ⓐ zeero
- 🅑 zero
- Ⓒ ziro
- Ⓓ zeiro

18.
- 🅑 rectangle
- Ⓕ recktangle
- Ⓖ recktangl
- Ⓗ rectangel

4.
- 🅔 billions
- Ⓕ bilionz
- Ⓖ billionz
- Ⓗ bilyuns

9.
- Ⓐ yerd
- 🅑 yard
- Ⓒ yarde
- Ⓓ yord

14.
- Ⓔ fighure
- Ⓕ figgure
- Ⓖ figyure
- 🅗 figure

19.
- Ⓐ eera
- 🅑 era
- Ⓒ eru
- Ⓓ erah

5.
- Ⓐ wate
- Ⓑ weite
- 🅒 weight
- Ⓓ weiht

10.
- Ⓔ edje
- Ⓕ edg
- 🅖 edge
- Ⓗ edj

15.
- Ⓐ calunder
- Ⓑ callendar
- 🅒 calendar
- Ⓓ callindar

20.
- 🅔 linght
- Ⓕ lenth
- Ⓖ lengtch
- 🅗 length

Unit 6 Review • PRACTICE and RETEACH

Name_____ Date_____ **Practice 221**

Unit 6 Vocabulary Review

A. Read each word in Column 1 and find a word in Column 2 that means the same thing. Then write the letter of the word on the line provided.

	Column 1	Column 2
f	1. extraordinary	a. water-filled
d	2. feeble	b. save
e	3. expensive	c. mixed
a	4. soggy	d. weak
b	5. preserve	e. costly
c	6. mingled	f. unusual

B. Answer each question using the underlined vocabulary word in your response. Students' answers will vary.

7. <u>teammate</u>   What is one important quality you like in a teammate for baseball?
A person who plays fair and helps others perform well is a good teammate.

8. <u>organizations</u>   What organizations are there set up especially for kids?
The Boys Scouts and the Girl Scouts are organizations for kids.

9. <u>successful</u>   Why might one student be more successful in spelling than another?
A more successful student might spend more time studying.

10. <u>brilliant</u>   What is the most brilliant idea you ever thought of?
My most brilliant idea was getting my dad to build a tree house.

11. <u>commercials</u>   What two commercials on television do you find most enjoyable?
The commercials I like most are those for video games.

12. <u>gallon</u>   How many quarts of milk are there in a half gallon?
There are two quarts of milk in a half gallon.

Name_____ Date_____ **Practice 222**

Unit 6 Vocabulary Review

A. Read each word in Column 1. Then find a definition for each word in Column 2. Write the letter of the definition on the line.

	Column 1	Column 2
e	1. opponents	a. plants and animals in their habitats
f	2. instance	b. germ-free
d	3. lurk	c. business
a	4. wildlife	d. watch in a sneaky manner
b	5. sterilized	e. people on the opposite team
c	6. enterprise	f. for example

B. Write the correct vocabulary word that completes each sentence.

circulated	fragrance	portable	identify	successful	ingredient

1. I can carry my computer because it is portable_____.

2. In order to make the sauce for the spaghetti, I need one more ingredient_____.

3. Those who did not study were not successful_____ at completing the project.

4. Hank circulated_____ a paper and asked everyone to read it.

5. Emily can identify_____ the name of every car on the road.

6. The fragrance_____ from the baking bread made everyone hungry.

Name_____ Date_____ **Reteach 221**

Unit 6 Vocabulary Review

A. Use the words from the list below to complete each sentence.

fragrance	preserve	teammate	gallon	launched

1. Pee Wee Reese was Jackie Robinson's teammate_____.
2. Scientists launched_____ a search for whales all over the world.
3. The flowers had a sweet fragrance_____.
4. Please buy a gallon_____ of milk at the store.
5. Many people are working to preserve_____ the environment.

B. Unscramble each word and write it on the line provided. Then write the letter of the correct definition of the word from the list below.

circulated	pods	compares	brilliant	feeble

Definitions
a. whale herds
b. weak
c. is similar to
d. passed around
e. very smart

1. REMCOPAS   compares, c_____
2. DOPS   pods, a_____
3. NTAILILRB   brilliant, e_____
4. ELEFEB   feeble, b_____
5. DTEALUCRIC   circulated, d_____

Name_____ Date_____ **Reteach 222**

Unit 6 Vocabulary Review

A. Choose a word from the list to complete each statement.

mammals	opponents	wildlife	cultured	ingredient

1. People who compete with you in a sport are examples of opponents_____.
2. Opera fans, art historians, and drama critics are examples of people who are considered cultured_____.
3. Bears, dogs, and pigs are all mammals_____.
4. Flour, sugar, milk, and eggs are each an example of an ingredient_____.
5. Tigers, giraffes, and zebras are examples of wildlife_____.

B. Choose the correct word from the list to complete the sentences below.

commercials	successful	mingled	resembled	organizations

It was an impressive party. Successful_____ people from many different organizations_____ attended. They mingled_____ with each other for a while. Then they watched the new commercials_____ for their organizations on a huge television monitor. Someone remarked that the party itself resembled_____ a television show.

T56   *Annotated Workbooks*

Name_____ Date_____ **Extend** ◈ 221

Vocabulary Review

Play a matching game with the vocabulary words below and their definition. Cut out each box below. Then write its definition on a separate index card or strip of paper. Turn the cards or paper face down, and scramble. Arrange in four rows of four cards. Turn over two cards at a time. Try to match each word with its definition. Keep any matches you make.

| extraordinary | feeble | marine | portable |
| organizations | resembled | scampered | instance |

extraordinary	feeble
marine	portable
organizations	resembled
scampered	instance

Book 4/Unit 6
Unit 6 Vocabulary Review

At Home: Have students use each vocabulary word in a sentence.

221

Name_____ Date_____ **Extend** ◈ 222

Vocabulary Review

Choose 10 words. Scramble the letters for each word, and write the scrambled words on a separate sheet of paper. Exchange scrambled words with a partner.

brilliant	circulated	compares	cultured	gallon
identify	ingredient	lurk	mingled	opponents
pods	soggy	sterilized	stockholder	
successful	teammate	toothpaste	wildlife	

1. _Answers will vary._   6. _____
2. _____   7. _____
3. _____   8. _____
4. _____   9. _____
5. _____   10. _____

Use each word in a sentence on the lines below.

1. _____
2. _____
3. _____
4. _____
5. _____
6. _____
7. _____
8. _____
9. _____
10. _____

At Home: Have students choose three vocabulary words to use in a paragraph.

222

Book 4/Unit 6
Unit 6 Vocabulary Review

Name_____ Date_____ REVIEW **Grammar** ● 191

Read each passage and look at the underlined sentences. Is there a better way to write or say each sentence? If there is, which is the better way? Circle your answer.

> The most remarkable thing about Jackie Robinson was his ability to take insults without fighting back. <u>Crowds attacked him wordly.</u> (1) <u>Players on the other team might try to hurt him with cleats.</u> (2) Through it all, he never let anger get the better of him.

1. **A** Crowds attacked him words.

   B Crowds attacked him verbally. (circled)

   C Crowds attacked him verbal.

   D No mistake.

2. **F** Players on the other team might try to hurt him physical.

   G Players on the other team might try to hurt him physically.

   H Players on the other team might try to hurt him bad.

   J No mistake.

> The yellow bird sat sadly in its cage, never singing. Then one day, for no reason, the princess let it out. <u>Free again, the bird sang most sweetly than before.</u> (3) <u>But it sang even more joyfully when princess came out to play with the other children.</u> (4)

3. **A** Free again, the bird sang most sweet.

   B Free again, the bird sang more sweeter.

   C Free again, the bird sang more sweetly than before. (circled)

   D No mistake.

4. **F** But it sang joyfully of all when princess came out to play with the other children.

   G But it sang even more joyful when princess came out to play with the other children.

   H But it sang even most joyfully when princess came out to play with the other children.

   J No mistake. (circled)

6 Grade 4/Unit 6
Sorting It Out

191

Name_____ Date_____ REVIEW **Grammar** ● 192

> <u>Toothpaste didn't have no fancy name.</u> (5) Its basic ingredient was baking soda, and it was flavored with a little peppermint oil. People loved it. <u>It didn't do nothing but clean your teeth.</u> (6)

5. **A** Toothpaste didn't have no kind of fancy name.

   B Toothpaste didn't have any fancy name.

   C Toothpaste did have no fancy name.

   D No mistake.

6. **F** It didn't do but clean your teeth.

   G It didn't do anything but clean your teeth.

   H It did do nothing but clean your teeth.

   J No mistake.

> Orcas are also called "killer whales." <u>They can be found over most of the world's oceans.</u> (7) Many people have seen orcas, but not in the ocean. <u>They have seen them around marine parks.</u> (8)

7. **A** They can be found in most of the world's oceans. (circled)

   B They can be found most of the world's oceans.

   C They can be found over most in the world's oceans.

   D No mistake.

8. **F** They have seen them about marine parks.

   G They have seen them at marine parks. (circled)

   H They have seen them from marine parks.

   J No mistake.

> We spent the day observing nature at Everglades National Park. <u>We spotted a tree toad. It was lime-green.</u> (9) We saw a white egret. <u>We saw an alligator sunning itself on the bank.</u> (10) When it heard us, it slipped into the water.

9. **A** We spotted a tree toad and it was lime-green.

   B We spotted a smartly dressed tree toad. It was lime-green.

   C We spotted a lime-green tree toad. (circled)

   D No mistake.

10. **F** We saw an alligator sunning itself and it was on the bank.

    G We saw an alligator lazily sunning itself. It was at the bank.

    H We saw an alligator sunning itself. It was on the bank.

    J No mistake. (circled)

192

Grade 4/Unit 6
Saving the Everglades 10

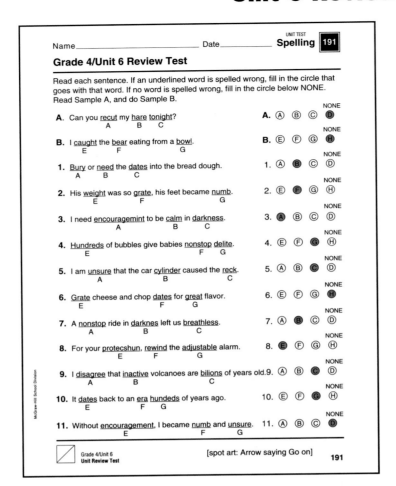

Name_____ Date_____ **Spelling** 191

Grade 4/Unit 6 Review Test

Read each sentence. If an underlined word is spelled wrong, fill in the circle that goes with that word. If no word is spelled wrong, fill in the circle below NONE. Read Sample A, and do Sample B.

A. Can you <u>recut</u> my <u>hare</u> <u>tonight</u>?
      A   B   C
A. Ⓐ Ⓑ Ⓒ ● (NONE)

B. I <u>caught</u> the <u>bear</u> eating from a <u>bowl</u>.
      E   F   G
B. Ⓔ Ⓕ Ⓖ ● (NONE)

1. <u>Bury</u> or <u>need</u> the <u>dates</u> into the bread dough.
    A   B   C
1. Ⓐ ● Ⓒ Ⓓ (NONE)

2. His <u>weight</u> was so <u>grate</u>, his feet became <u>numb</u>.
      E   F   G
2. Ⓔ ● Ⓖ Ⓗ (NONE)

3. I need <u>encouragemint</u> to be <u>calm</u> in <u>darkness</u>.
        A   B   C
3. ● Ⓑ Ⓒ Ⓓ (NONE)

4. <u>Hundreds</u> of bubbles give babies <u>nonstop</u> <u>delite</u>.
    E   F   G
4. Ⓔ Ⓕ ● Ⓗ (NONE)

5. I am <u>unsure</u> that the car <u>cylinder</u> caused the <u>reck</u>.
      A   B   C
5. Ⓐ Ⓑ ● Ⓓ (NONE)

6. <u>Grate</u> cheese and chop <u>dates</u> for <u>great</u> flavor.
    E   F   G
6. Ⓔ Ⓕ Ⓖ ● (NONE)

7. A <u>nonstop</u> ride in <u>darknes</u> left us <u>breathless</u>.
      A   B   C
7. Ⓐ ● Ⓒ Ⓓ (NONE)

8. For your <u>protecshun</u>, <u>rewind</u> the <u>adjustable</u> alarm.
        E   F   G
8. ● Ⓕ Ⓖ Ⓗ (NONE)

9. I <u>disagree</u> that <u>inactive</u> volcanoes are <u>bilions</u> of years old.
    A   B   C
9. Ⓐ Ⓑ ● Ⓓ (NONE)

10. It <u>dates</u> back to an <u>era</u> <u>hundeds</u> of years ago.
      E   F   G
10. Ⓔ Ⓕ ● Ⓗ (NONE)

11. Without <u>encouragement</u>, I became <u>numb</u> and <u>unsure</u>.
        E   F   G
11. Ⓐ Ⓑ Ⓒ ● (NONE)

Name_____ Date_____ **Spelling** 192

Grade 4 Unit 3 Review Test

12. Taste a <u>great</u> <u>bury</u> pie. <u>Knead</u> the crust first!
      E   F   G
12. Ⓔ ● Ⓖ Ⓗ (NONE)

13. He became <u>inactive</u> and lost <u>wait</u> after a train <u>wreck</u>.
      A   B   C
13. Ⓐ ● Ⓒ Ⓓ (NONE)

14. I am <u>breathless</u> with <u>delight</u> to be a part of this <u>era</u>.
      E   F   G
14. Ⓔ Ⓕ Ⓖ ● (NONE)

15. For <u>protection</u> from fire, <u>bury</u> the <u>cylinder</u> of gas.
      A   B   C
15. Ⓐ Ⓑ Ⓒ ● (NONE)

16. "<u>Grate</u> <u>billions</u> of cabbages <u>nostop</u>," I said.
      E   F   G
16. Ⓔ Ⓕ ● Ⓗ (NONE)

17. I <u>disagre</u> that <u>berry</u> pie makes me <u>weight</u>.
    A   B   C
17. Ⓔ Ⓕ ● Ⓗ (NONE)

18. <u>Billions</u> of stars in the sky keep me <u>cam</u> in the <u>darkness</u>.
    E   F   G
18. Ⓔ ● Ⓖ Ⓗ (NONE)

19. <u>Encouragement</u> and <u>protection</u> make a baby <u>calm</u>.
    A   B   C
19. Ⓐ Ⓑ Ⓒ ● (NONE)

20. I'm <u>unshure</u> of how to sell <u>hundreds</u> of <u>adjustable</u> chairs.
      E   F   G
20. ● Ⓕ Ⓖ Ⓗ (NONE)

21. <u>Rewind</u> the <u>enactive</u> toys to <u>delight</u> the children.
    A   B   C
21. Ⓐ ● Ⓒ Ⓓ (NONE)

22. Seeing her <u>berry</u> the gold left me <u>breathless</u> and <u>numb</u>.
       E   F   G
22. Ⓔ Ⓕ Ⓖ ● (NONE)

23. We measured the <u>berry</u> in an <u>adjustabel</u> <u>cylinder</u>.
      A   B   C
23. Ⓐ ● Ⓒ Ⓓ (NONE)

24. In which <u>ira</u> did humans first <u>knead</u> and <u>grate</u> foods?
       E   F   G
24. ● Ⓕ Ⓖ Ⓗ (NONE)

25. I <u>disagree</u> that the toy will <u>wreck</u> if you <u>rewined</u> it.
    A   B   C
25. Ⓐ Ⓑ ● Ⓓ (NONE)

Cause and Effect

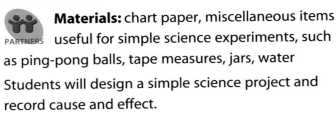

OBJECTIVES Students will demonstrate an understanding of cause and effect by conducting simple science experiments, illustrating appropriate causes, and telling a story based on a given effect.

Alternate Activities

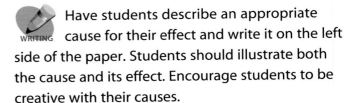

Kinesthetic

SCIENTISTS AT WORK

PARTNERS **Materials:** chart paper, miscellaneous items useful for simple science experiments, such as ping-pong balls, tape measures, jars, water

Students will design a simple science project and record cause and effect.

- Have students choose a partner and select items to be used in creating a simple science experiment.
- Allow students time to prepare and perform their experiment.
- Have students use chart paper to record the cause and effect illustrated by their experiment. Ask student pairs to share their experiments with the class.
  ▶ **Logical/Mathematical**

Visual

WHAT'S THE CAUSE?

ONE **Materials:** sheets of newsprint

Have students write and illustrate causes for an effect.

- Write each of the following effects on the board:

  The countdown stopped, and the rocket was grounded again.

  Sitting at his desk, Bobby was scared stiff.

The snake sat prepared to strike.

Amy walked away with a big smile on her face.

- Have students fold their newsprint sheets in half and label the right half "Effect." Ask students to choose one effect from the board and write it under the heading.

 WRITING Have students describe an appropriate cause for their effect and write it on the left side of the paper. Students should illustrate both the cause and its effect. Encourage students to be creative with their causes.
  ▶ **Linguistic**

Auditory

MYSTERY CAUSE

GROUP **Materials:** one or more copies of the book *The Mysteries of Harris Burdick* by Chris Van Allsburg

Students will orally describe a cause for each picture in the book.

- Organize students into groups of three or four. Assign each group one picture from the book *The Mysteries of Harris Burdick*.
- Have groups study the picture and read the "effect" caption on the facing page.
- Have groups work to develop a story that explains the cause of the effect. Ask students to share their stories with the class.
  ▶ **Linguistic**

See Reteach 186, 190, 198, 214

Library/Media Center

OBJECTIVES Students will apply knowledge of library/media center resources by participating in a scavenger hunt, interviewing a classmate, and playing a media matching game.

Alternate

Activities

Kinesthetic

SCAVENGER HUNT

Materials: list of questions for students to answer in library/media center, pencils

Students will participate in a "scavenger hunt" for answers while learning about resources in the library/media center.

- Organize students into teams of three. Provide each team with a copy of a list of questions that require exploration of and research in the library/media center. Questions should involve using various tools to find the answers, such as: *What is the current temperature in Washington, DC?* (internet); *What is the capital of Alaska?* (encyclopedia or dictionary); *How many magazines does this library subscribe to?* (interview with librarian).

- Have students work with their team to locate the sources of information necessary to answer each question. The first team to find correct answers to all the questions is the winner.

▶ **Logical/Mathematical**

Visual

CLASSMATE COAT OF ARMS

Materials: newsprint, paper, pencils, markers, library resources on heraldry and coats of arms

Have students conduct an interview and use the information to create a graphic representation.

- Work with students to brainstorm a list of interview questions for classmates.

- Have students choose partners and interview each other. Ask students to take notes on their interview.

- Have students create a graphic representation that shows some of the things they found out about their partner. They can check sources for visual ideas. Display their graphics in the classroom.

▶ **Spatial**

Auditory

MEDIA MATCH

Ask students to identify appropriate sources for answering a given question.

- Write the following sources on the board: *Card catalog, Encyclopedia, Internet, Interview.*

- Organize students into four teams. In turn, ask each team a research question. The team has fifteen seconds to confer and then choose the source most likely to provide an answer to the question. In some instances, more than one answer may be appropriate. Challenge teams to justify their answers.

- Allot a point for each correct answer. Total points at the end of the game determine the winner.

▶ **Bodily/Kinesthetic**

See Reteach 189, 196, 203, 210, 217

Judgments and Decisions

OBJECTIVES Students will use a mock trial and real-life scenarios to practice making judgments and decisions. They will apply their knowledge by creating a rubric for creative writing.

Alternate Activities

Kinesthetic

CLASSROOM COURT

Materials: text of a fairy tale with an obvious villain, video camera

Students will conduct a mock trial to practice making judgments and decisions.

- Read aloud a famous fairy tale with an obvious villain. Tell students they will be conducting a mock trial of the story's villain.

- Organize class into two teams. Assign one team the role of prosecutor and the other team the role of defender. Have students work together to create a presentation complete with evidence, charts, and witnesses.

- Videotape the presentation. Have students review the tape and vote as a jury on the guilt or innocence of the villain. Or you may wish to invite another class to serve as the jury. Classroom teacher or a guest, such as the school principal, can serve as the judge.

▶ **Logical/Mathematical**

Visual

WRITING A RUBRIC

Materials: space suitable for recording brainstormed ideas: chart paper, overhead, or chalkboard

Students will develop and utilize a rubric to assess their writing.

- Explain to students that a rubric is a chart describing criteria used to assess a piece of work.

- Provide students with the following list of skills to focus on in developing assessment criteria: *originality, character development, spelling, grammar.*

Ask students to think about each skill and to determine what kind of work would receive Unacceptable, Developing, Acceptable, and Outstanding scores in each category. Have students write criteria for each skill using these four elements as their guide.

- Format student criteria into a rubric. Have students use the rubric criteria they developed to assess a piece of their own writing.

▶ **Logical/Mathematical**

Auditory

WHAT WOULD YOU DO?

Have students participate in a discussion about decision making.

- Present students with a scenario in which a student is faced with a difficult decision.

- Invite students to discuss how they would handle the situation. Explore possible decisions and their outcomes.

- Challenge students to evaluate each situation, determine what course of action they feel would be best, and defend their decision.

▶ **Bodily/Kinesthetic**

See Reteach 191, 200, 204, 212

Context Clues

 OBJECTIVES Students will learn to use context clues to understand difficult content-area and specialized vocabulary by playing a word game, creating mind maps, and learning reading strategies.

Alternate
 **Activities**

Kinesthetic

WHAT'S MY WORD?

GROUP **Materials:** list of difficult vocabulary words from different curricular areas, dictionaries, textbooks

- Organize students into small groups. Assign each person in the group a vocabulary word. Tell students to keep their word secret.

- Have students use the reference materials to write three clues about their word. These clues may include things like what content area it comes from, the word's definition, and a synonym or antonym of the word.

- When all students have written their clues, bring groups together. Provide each student with a list of all the vocabulary words being used in the game as a reference for determining each other's words. Students may also use these lists to write the definitions of each vocabulary word as it is guessed.

- Have students attempt to guess each other's word by asking questions and using the clues given.
  ▶ **Logical/Mathematical**

Visual

MIND MAPPING

PARTNERS **Materials:** chart paper, dictionaries, textbooks, encyclopedias, internet

Students will create a mind map to learn information about a given vocabulary word.

- Pair each student with a partner. Give each pair a content-area vocabulary word and a piece of chart paper. Have students write their vocabulary word in the center of the chart paper and circle it.

WRITING Ask students to use the reference material provided to find out everything they can about their vocabulary word. Have students write the information they find on the chart.

- Have students share their mind maps with the class and display them in the classroom.
  ▶ **Spatial**

Auditory

CONTENT CLUES

GROUP **Materials:** chart paper, markers
Have students brainstorm strategies for remembering difficult vocabulary words.

- Ask students to think of strategies they use to figure out and remember the meanings of particular difficult vocabulary words.

- Have students brainstorm a list of these strategies and record them on chart paper; for example, using picture clues.

- Discuss how each of these strategies can be used to improve student understanding of difficult content words. Display the chart in the classroom for students to use as a reference.
  ▶ **Bodily/Kinesthetic**

See Reteach 192, 213, 219

Problem and Solution

OBJECTIVES Students will examine problems and solutions through skits, games, and class discussions.

Kinesthetic

SATISFYING SOLUTIONS

 Students will perform a skit to demonstrate the solution to a problem.

- Organize students into groups. Provide each group with a problem situation, such as: You and your best friend had an argument at lunch. You feel bad about it, but both you and your friend are very upset. How can you solve this problem?

- Ask groups to think through their problem and brainstorm a list of possible solutions. Have students agree on one solution and present it to the class in the form of a skit.

  ▶ **Interpersonal**

Visual

PLAYING GAMES

 Materials: cardboard or poster board, dice, markers, small items to be used as game pieces

Ask students to create a game involving problems and solutions.

- Have students brainstorm a list of games that involve finding the solution to a problem—for example, Clue, mystery games, logic problems, computer games involving quests.

 Ask students to work with a partner and create their own game. The game should present a problem, and the solution should be

arrived at by playing the game. Students may use a board game format, or any other format they choose. Have students write detailed instructions for playing their game.

- Allow time for students to play all the games. Leave the games in a central location for use during free time.

  ▶ **Logical/Mathematical**

Auditory

CIRCLE TIME

 Students will discuss problems they face at school and strategies they use to solve those problems.

- Have students sit in a circle. Ask students to share some problems they face at school.

- Have students discuss these problems and offer strategies they have used in similar circumstances. This type of circle discussion can be useful as a regular class meeting. It allows students a time to communicate concerns and problems in a supportive environment. It also allows for open discussion and provides opportunities for positive solutions to these problems.

  ▶ **Interpersonal**

See Reteach 193, 197, 205

Antonyms and Synonyms

 **OBJECTIVES** Students will brainstorm synonyms and antonyms for a writing reference, learn to identify synonyms and antonyms, and use them in a word game.

Alternate Activities

Kinesthetic

SYNONYM/ANTONYM MARATHON

 Students will practice identifying antonyms and synonyms for a given word.

- Organize students into four teams. Have each team stand in a line in front of the board. Write a different word at the top of the board in front of each team. If "Go" is written, for example, the first student in that line goes to the board and writes an antonym under that word ("Come").

- The student hands the chalk to the next person on the team and goes to the back of the line. That student must write a synonym for the new word on the board. The next student will then write an antonym, and so on, alternating synonyms and antonyms until the team runs out of ideas. Words may not be duplicated in the list.

- The team that comes up with the longest list of synonyms and antonyms is the winner.
  ▶ **Bodily/Kinesthetic**

Visual

WRITING TOOLS

 Materials: two large pieces of chart paper, markers

Students will brainstorm synonyms and antonyms to use in their writing.

- Label one piece of chart paper "Synonyms" and the other piece "Antonyms."

- Invite students to list pairs of words for the two categories. Write the words on the charts, and display the charts in the classroom. Students can refer to them when writing and use the words to make their work more interesting.
  ▶ **Spatial**

Auditory

THE ANSWER IS. . .

 Materials: cards for each student labeled *Synonym* and *Antonym*, list of word pairs that are either synonyms or antonyms

Students will identify word pairs as either synonyms or antonyms.

- Read a pair of words that are either synonyms or antonyms of each other.

- Have students identify which category the word pair belongs in by holding up either their *Synonym* or *Antonym* card.
  ▶ **Intrapersonal**

See Reteach 199, 206, 220

Compare and Contrast

OBJECTIVES Students will use a writing activity, a mystery box exploration, and a question and answer discovery to compare and contrast different things.

Alternate Activities

Kinesthetic

WHAT'S INSIDE?

Materials: four sets of two items with characteristics that are both similar and different, such as a rock and a nerf softball; a box or bag, chart paper, markers

Students will compare and contrast to identify mystery objects.

- Organize students into four groups. Provide each group with a piece of chart paper, markers, and two boxes or bags each containing a mystery object. Have students divide the chart paper in half and label one side *Compare* or *Same* and the other side *Contrast* or *Different*.

- Invite each student to feel inside the two boxes or bags without peeking and to record on the chart paper how the objects are alike and how they are different.

- When each student has had an opportunity to feel both objects, ask the group to determine what is in each box. Have students look inside to check their accuracy.

  ▶ **Logical/Mathematical**

Visual

JUST LIKE ME

Students will compare and contrast characteristics of themselves with those of selected animals and bugs.

- Write on the board: *bee, goat, lamb, butterfly, owl, ostrich*.

- Discuss the characteristics commonly associated with each of these creatures. Ask students to think about what characteristics they share with each creature, and how they are different.

  Ask students to pick the creature most like them and the one most different, and to write a paragraph explaining their choices.

  ▶ **Intrapersonal**

Auditory

SAME—DIFFERENT

Materials: a pair of similar but different objects, such as a rose and a daisy, a shoe and a boot, a baseball and a golf ball; paper; pencils

Students will work in pairs to discover what is the *same* and what is *different* between two items.

- Organize students into pairs. Display a pair of like but different objects for all students to view.

- Ask each pair of students to create a chart on their paper by dividing the page in half. Have students label the left side "Same" and the right side "Different."

- Working with their partner, ask students to list on their paper things that are the same and things that are different about the two objects.

- When all students have finished, ask pairs to share their results with the class.

  ▶ **Logical/Mathematical**

See Reteach 207, 211, 218

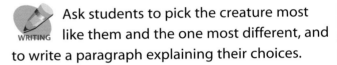

A Communication Tool

Although typewriters and computers are readily available, many situations continue to require handwriting. Tasks such as keeping journals, completing forms, taking notes, making shopping or organizational lists, and the ability to read hand-written manuscript or cursive writing are a few examples of practical application of this skill.

BEFORE YOU BEGIN

Before children begin to write, certain fine motor skills need to be developed. Examples of activities that can be used as warm-up activities are:

- **Simon Says** Play a game of Simon Says using just finger positions.
- **Finger Plays and Songs** Sing songs that use Signed English, American Sign Language or finger spelling.
- **Mazes** Mazes are available in a wide range of difficulty. You can also create mazes that allow children to move their writing instruments from left to right.

Determining Handedness

Keys to determining handedness in a child:

- Which hand does the child eat with? This is the hand that is likely to become the dominant hand.
- Does the child start coloring with one hand and then switch to the other? This may be due to fatigue rather than lack of hand preference.
- Does the child cross midline to pick things up or use the closest hand? Place items directly in front of the child to see if one hand is preferred.
- Does the child do better with one hand or the other?

The Mechanics of Writing

DESK AND CHAIR

- Chair height should allow for the feet to rest flat on the floor.
- Desk height should be two inches above the level of the elbows when the child is sitting.
- The chair should be pulled in allowing for an inch of space between the child's abdomen and the desk.
- Children sit erect with the elbows resting on the desk.
- Children should have models of letters on the desk or at eye level, not above their heads.

PAPER POSITION

- **Right-handed children** should turn the paper so that the lower left-hand corner of the paper points to the abdomen.

- **Left-handed children** should turn the paper so that the lower right-hand corner of the paper points to the abdomen.

- The nondominant hand should anchor the paper near the top so that the paper doesn't slide.

- The paper should be moved up as the child nears the bottom of the paper. Many children won't think of this and may let their arms hang off the desk when they reach the bottom of a page.

The Writing Instrument Grasp

For handwriting to be functional, the writing instrument must be held in a way that allows for fluid dynamic movement.

FUNCTIONAL GRASP PATTERNS

- **Tripod Grasp** With open web space, the writing instrument is held with the tip of the thumb and the index finger and rests against the side of the third finger. The thumb and index finger form a circle.

- **Quadrupod Grasp** With open web space, the writing instrument is held with the tip of the thumb and index finger and rests against the fourth finger. The thumb and index finger form a circle.

INCORRECT GRASP PATTERNS

- **Fisted Grasp** The writing instrument is held in a fisted hand.

- **Pronated Grasp** The writing instrument is held diagonally within the hand with the tips of the thumb and index finger on the writing instrument but with no support from other fingers.

- **Five-Finger Grasp** The writing instrument is held with the tips of all five fingers.

TO CORRECT WRITING INSTRUMENT GRASPS

- Have children play counting games with an eye dropper and water.
- Have children pick up small objects with a tweezer.
- Do counting games with children picking up small coins using just the thumb and index finger.

FLEXED OR HOOKED WRIST

- The writing instrument can be held in a variety of grasps with the wrist flexed or bent. This is typically seen with left-handed writers but is also present in some right-handed writers. To correct wrist position, have children check their writing posture and paper placement.

Evaluation Checklist

Functional writing is made up of two elements, legibility and functional speed.

LEGIBILITY

MANUSCRIPT

Formation and Strokes

☑ Does the child begin letters at the top?

☑ Do circles close?

☑ Are the horizontal lines straight?

☑ Do circular shapes and extender and descender lines touch?

☑ Are the heights of all upper-case letters equal?

☑ Are the heights of all lower-case letters equal?

☑ Are the lengths of the extenders and descenders the same for all letters?

Directionality

☑ Are letters and words formed from left to right?

☑ Are letters and words formed from top to bottom?

Spacing

☑ Are the spaces between letters equidistant?

☑ Are the spaces between words equidistant?

☑ Do the letters rest on the line?

☑ Are the top, bottom and side margins even?

CURSIVE

Formation and Strokes

☑ Do circular shapes close?

☑ Are the downstrokes parallel?

☑ Do circular shapes and downstroke lines touch?

☑ Are the heights of all upper-case letters equal?

☑ Are the heights of all lower-case letters equal?

☑ Are the lengths of the extenders and descenders the same for all letters?

☑ Do the letters which finish at the top join the next letter? (*l, o, v, w*)

☑ Do the letters which finish at the bottom join the next letter? (*a, c, d, h, i, k, l, m, n, r, s, t, u, x*)

☑ Do letters with descenders join the next letter? (*f, g, j, p, q, y, z*)

☑ Do all letters touch the line?

☑ Is the vertical slant of all letters consistent?

Directionality

☑ Are letters and words formed from left to right?

☑ Are letters and words formed from top to bottom?

Spacing

☑ Are the spaces between letters equidistant?

☑ Are the spaces between words equidistant?

☑ Do the letters rest on the line?

☑ Are the top, bottom and side margins even?

SPEED

The prettiest handwriting is not functional for classroom work if it takes the child three times longer than the rest of the class to complete work assignments. After the children have been introduced to writing individual letters, begin to add time limitations to the completion of copying or writing assignments. Then check the child's work for legibility.

Handwriting Models—Manuscript

Handwriting Models—Cursive

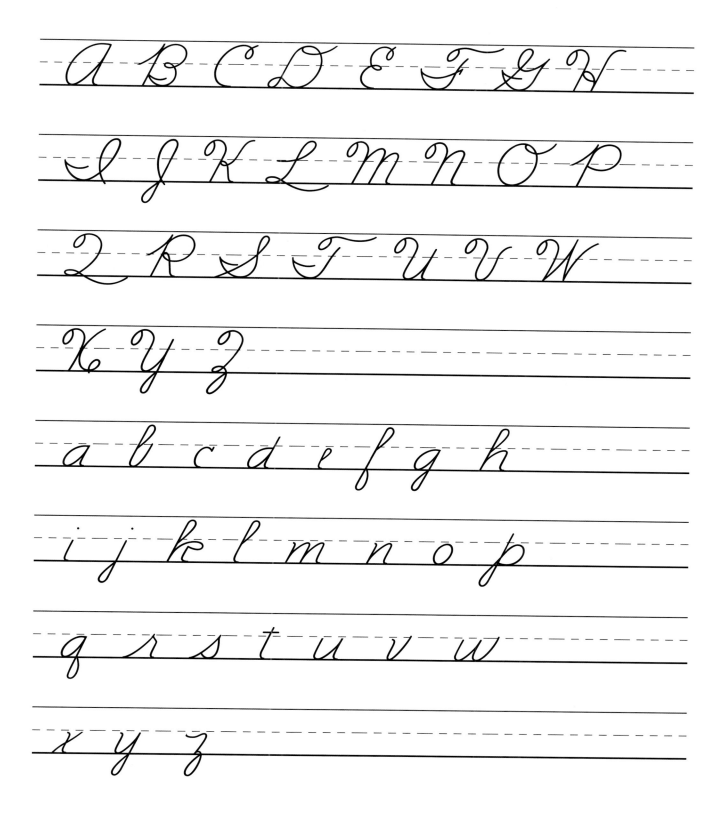

Selection Titles

Honors, Prizes, and Awards

TO
Unit 1, p. 16
by *Lee Bennett Hopkins*

Poet: Lee Bennett Hopkins, winner of Golden Kite Honor Book Award (1995), Christopher Award (1996) for *Been to Yesterday: Poems of a Life*

THE LOST LAKE
Unit 1, p. 20
by *Allen Say*

Author/Illustrator: Allen Say, winner of Christopher Award (1985) for *How My Parents Learned to Eat*; Boston Globe-Horn Book Award (1988), Caldecott Honor, ALA Notable (1989) for *The Boy of the Three-Year Nap*; Caldecott Medal, Boston Globe-Horn Book Award, ALA Notable, New York Times Best Illustrated (1994) for *Grandfather's Journey*

AMELIA'S ROAD
Unit 1, p. 44
by *Linda Jacobs Altman*
Illustrated by *Enrique O. Sanchez*

Illustrator: Enrique O. Sanchez, winner of Parent's Choice Award (1993) for *Abuela's Weave*

SARAH, PLAIN AND TALL
Unit 1, p. 68
by *Patricia MacLachlan*
Illustrated by *Burton Silverman*

Golden Kite Award for Fiction, IRA-CBC Children's Choice, School Library Best of the Best (1985), Newbery Medal, Christopher Award, Scott O'Dell Historical Fiction Award (1986)

SEAL JOURNEY
Unit 1, p. 96
by *Richard and Jonah Sobol*
Photographs by *Richard Sobol*

Outstanding Science Trade Book for Children (1994)

JUSTIN AND THE BEST BISCUITS IN THE WORLD
Unit 2, p. 134
by *Mildred Pitts Walter*
Illustrated by *Floyd Cooper*

Coretta Scott-King Award (1987)
Author: Mildred Pitts Walter, winner of Coretta Scott King Award for illustration (1984) for *My Mama Needs Me*
Illustrator: Floyd Cooper, winner of Coretta Scott King Award (1995) for *Meet Danitra Brown*

JUST A DREAM
Unit 2, p. 160
by *Chris Van Allsburg*

Author/Illustrator: Chris Van Allsburg, winner of ALA Notable, Caldecott Medal (1982) for *Jumanji*; ALA Notable (1984) for *The Wreck of the Zephyr*; ALA Notable, Boston Globe-Horn Book Honor, Caldecott Medal (1986) for *The Polar Express*; NSTA Outstanding Science Trade Book for Children (1988), IRA-CBC Children's Choice (1989) for *Two Bad Ants*; ALA Notable (1994) for *The Sweetest Fig*

Selection Titles | Honors, Prizes, and Awards

LEAH'S PONY
Unit 2, p. 192
by *Elizabeth Friedrich*
Illustrated by *Michael Garland*

National Council of Trade Books Award, Golden Kite Award, Parent's Magazine Best Book of the Year, IRA Teacher's Choice Award (1997), Texas Bluebonnet Award (1997-98)

BASEBALL SAVED US
Unit 2, p. 218
by *Ken Mochizuki*
Illustrated by *Dom Lee*

Parent's Choice Award (1993)

THE HATMAKER'S SIGN
Unit 3, p. 258
by *Candace Fleming*
Illustrated by *Robert Andrew Parker*

Illustrator: Robert Andrew Parker, winner of Caldecott Honor (1970) for *Pop Corn and Ma Goodness*

PAT CUMMINGS: MY STORY
Unit 3, p. 284
by *Pat Cummings*

Boston Globe-Horn Book Award (1992), ALA Notable (1993)

GRASS SANDALS: THE TRAVELS OF BASHO
Unit 3, p. 300
by *Dawnine Spivak*
Illustrated by *Demi*

National Council of Trade Books Award (1998)
Illustrator: Demi, winner of the New York Times Best Illustrated Children's Books of the Year (1985) for *The Nightingale*

A PLACE CALLED FREEDOM
Unit 3, p. 334
by *Scott Russell Sanders*
Illustrated by *Thomas B. Allen*

Notable Children's Book in the Field of Social Studies (1998)

FINAL CURVE
Unit 4, p. 372
by *Langston Hughes*

Poet: Langston Hughes, winner of Witter Bynner Prize (1926); Harmon Foundation Literature Award (1931); Guggenheim Fellowship (1935); American Academy of Arts and Letters Grant (1946); Spingarn Medal (1960)

Selection Titles	Honors, Prizes, and Awards
SCRUFFY Unit 4, p. 376 by *Jim Brandenburg*	**Author/Photographer: Jim Brandenburg,** winner ALA Best Book for Young Adults Award, Orbis Picture Award for Outstanding Non-fiction Honor Book, Minnesota Book Award (1994) for *To the Top of the World: Adventures with Arctic Wolves*; Parent's Choice Award, Outstanding Science Trade Book for Children, John Burroughs List of Outstanding Nature Books for Children (1995) for *Sand and Fog: Adventures in South Africa*; ALA Best Book for Young Adults (1996) for *An American Safari: Adventures on the North American Prairie*
GLUSKABE AND THE SNOW BIRD Unit 4, p. 408 by *Joseph Bruchac* Illustrated by *Stefano Vitale*	**Author: Joseph Bruchac,** winner of the Skipping Stones Honor Award for Multicultural Children's Literature (1997) for *Four Ancestors*
ON THE BUS WITH JOANNA COLE Unit 4, p. 446 by *Joanna Cole with Wendy Saul*	**Author: Joanna Cole,** winner of Washington Children's Choice Picture Book Award, Colorado Children's Book Award (1989) for *The Magic School Bus at the Waterworks*; Parenting's Reading Magic Awards (1989) for *The Magic School Bus Inside the Human Body*
TORTILLAS LIKE AFRICA Unit 4, p. 482 by *Gary Soto*	**Poet: Gary Soto,** winner of Academy of American Poets Award (1975); American Book Award (1984) for *Living Up the Street*; California Library Association's John And Patricia Beatty Award, Best Books for Young Adults Awards (1991) for *Baseball in April and Other Stories*; Americás Book Award, Honorable Mention (1995) for *Chato's Kitchen*; Americás Book Award, Commended List (1995) for *Canto Familiar*; (1996) for *The Old Man and His Door*; (1997) for *Buried Onions*
HOW TO TELL THE TOP OF A HILL Unit 5, p. 484 by *John Ciardi*	**Poet: John Ciardi,** winner of New York Times Best Illustrated Children's Books of the Year (1959) for *The Reason for the Pelican*; (1960) for *Scruffy The Pup*; (1966) for *The Monster Den: Or, Look What Happened at My House—and to It*; ALA Best Book Award (1961) for *I Met a Man*; (1963) for *John Plenty and Fiddler Dan: A New Fable of the Grasshopper and the Ant*; National Council of Teachers of English Award for Excellence in Poetry for Children (1982)

Selection Titles	Honors, Prizes, and Awards
MOM'S BEST FRIEND Unit 5, p. 518 by *Sally Hobart Alexander* Photographs by *George Ancona*	**Author: Sally Hobart Alexander**, winner of Christopher Award (1995) for *Taking Hold: My Journey Into Blindness*
YEH-SHEN Unit 5, p. 570 retold by **Ai-Ling Louie** Illustrated by **Ed Young**	**ALA Notable, School Library Journal Best Books of the Year (1982), Boston Globe-Horn Book Honor (1983)** **Illustrator: Ed Young,** winner of Caldecott Honor (1968) for *The Emperor and the Kite*; Boston Globe-Horn Book Honor (1984) for *The Double Life of Pocahontas*; NCSS Notable Children's Book Award (1989), Caldecott Medal, Boston Globe-Horn Book Award, ALA Notable (1990) for *Lon Po Po*; ALA Notable (1991) for *Mice Are Nice*; ALA Notable (1992) for *All Of You Was Singing*; ALA Notable, Boston Globe-Horn Book Award, Caldecott Honor (1993) for *Seven Blind Mice;* ALA Notable (1994) for *Sadako*; National Council for Social Studies Notable Children's Book Awards (1998) for *Genesis* and *Voices of the Heart*
TEAMMATES Unit 6, p. 616 by *Peter Golenbock* Illustrated by **Paul Bacon**	**Author: Peter Golenbock,** winner of National Council of Trade Books in Social Studies Award; Redbook Children's Picture Book Award (1990)
THE MALACHITE PALACE Unit 6, p. 634 by *Alma Flor Ada* Illustrated by *Leonid Gore*	**Author: Alma Flor Ada,** winner of Christopher Award (1992) for *The Gold Coin*
WHALES Unit 6, p. 694 by *Seymour Simon*	**Author: Seymour Simon,** winner of ALA Notable (1985) for *Moon*; (1986) for *Saturn*; (1987) for *Mars*; (1993) for *Our Solar System* and *Snakes*; Texas Blue Bonnet Master List (1996–97) for *Sharks*; NSTA Outstanding Science Tradebook for Children (1997) for *The Heart*
DECISIONS Unit 6, p. 724 by *Angela Shelf Medearis*	**Poet: Angela Shelf Medearis,** winner IRA-Teacher's Choice Award, Primary Grades (1995) for *Our People*

Trade Books

Additional fiction and nonfiction trade books related to each selection can be shared with students throughout the unit.

TEAMMATES

Alice Ramsey's Grand Adventure
Don Brown (Houghton Mifflin, 1997)

In 1909, Alice attempts to be the first woman to drive across the United States.

A Boy Called Slow: The True Story of Sitting Bull
Joseph Bruchac, illustrated by Rocco Baviera (Philomel Books, 1994)

As Slow approaches manhood, he is determined to perform a brave deed to prove himself worthy of a new name.

In the Year of the Boar and Jackie Robinson
Bette Bao Lord, illustrated by Marc Simont (HarperTrophy, 1986)

Struggling to adjust to her new country in 1947, ten-year-old Shirley Temple Wong discovers baseball and Jackie Robinson.

THE MALACHITE PALACE

Nim and the War Effort
Milly Lee (Farrar, Straus and Giroux, 1997)

Despite the consequences, Nim is determined to be the winner when her school holds a newspaper drive during World War II.

The Crystal Heart: A Vietnamese Legend
Aaron Shepard, illustrated by Joseph Daniel Fiedler (Atheneum, 1998)

The consequences of cruelty and the redemption of compassion are portrayed in the retelling of this Vietnamese legend about a mandarin's daughter and a humble fisherman.

Class President
Johanna Hurwitz, illustrated by Sheila Hamanaka (William Morrow, 1990)

Julio realizes that he possesses leadership qualities when a classmate nominates him for class president.

Technology

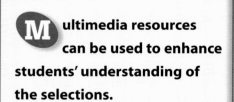

Multimedia resources can be used to enhance students' understanding of the selections.

 Jackie Robinson (SRA/McGraw-Hill) Video, 30 min. A profile of the life of Jackie Robinson.

 Angel and Big Joe (Coronet/MTI) Video, 27 min. The story of an unlikely friendship between a telephone lineman and a young Chicano migrant worker.

 Differences (AIMS Multimedia) Video, 17 min. Two young children of different ethnic backgrounds learn to respect and appreciate each other.

 Broderick (Phoenix/BFA) Video, 10 min. A young mouse decides to become something special, and the path he takes opens up new worlds for him.

 The Superlative Horse (Phoenix/BFA) Video, 36 min. Han Kan, the royal groom, makes a decision that surprises everyone.

 The Wave: A Japanese Folktale (Phoenix/BFA) Video, 9 min. An old villager makes a decision that the village people cannot understand until they realize that it has saved their lives.

THE TOOTHPASTE MILLIONAIRE

WHALES

SAVING THE EVERGLADES

Uncle Jed's Barbershop
Margaree King Mitchell (Aladdin, 1998)

Uncle Jed went through some tough times and showed his determination by not giving up until he had his own barbershop.

The Bobbin Girl
Emily Arnold McCully (Dial Books, 1996)

A ten-year-old girl working in a textile mill in Lowell, Massachusetts, in the 1830s must decide whether she will support the movement to stand united and fight for her rights at work.

A Job for Jenny Archer
Ellen Conford, illustrated by Diane Palmisciano (Springboard Books, 1990)

Jenny's decision to purchase a fur coat for her mother's birthday present leads to a series of money-making adventures.

The Whales' Song
Dyan Sheldon, illustrated by Gary Blythe (Dial Books for Young Readers, 1991)

Enchanted by her grandmother's stories about whales, Lilly dreams of hearing them sing their song to her.

Punia and the King of Sharks: A Hawaiian Folktale
Lee Wardlaw, illustrated by Felipe Davalos (Dial Books, 1997)

A courageous young boy outsmarts several vicious sharks who guard a cave where lobsters can be found.

The Music of Dolphins
Karen Hesse (Scholastic, 1996)

A feral adolescent raised by dolphins is rescued and re-acculturated. Learning what it means to be human, she decides to return to her aquatic family.

Everglades
Jean Craighead George, illustrated by Wendell Minor (HarperCollins, 1995)

Storytelling and beautiful paintings are used to describe the impact of humans on the Florida Everglades.

Sawgrass Poems: A View of the Everglades
Frank Asch, photographs by Ted Levin (Harcourt Brace, 1996)

The beauty and mystery of this unique ecosystem are captured in poetry and stunning photographs.

Marjory Stoneman Douglas: Friend of the Everglades
Tricia Andryszewski (Millbrook Press, 1994)

A biography of the environmentalist who devoted her life to preserving the Florida Everglades.

 Toothpaste Millionaire (GPN) Video, 15 min. A dramatization of the story of Rufus Mayflower, the teenage "toothpaste millionaire."

 Alexander, Who Used to Be Rich Last Sunday. (AIMS) Video, 14 min. In this award-winning film, Alexander's monetary decisions teach him a lesson in the importance of making wise choices about money.

 Uncle Jed's Barbershop (GPN/Reading Rainbow) Video, 30 min. Once Uncle Jed makes a decision to open his own barbershop, he is determined that nothing will keep him from his goal.

 Portrait of a Whale (National Geographic Educational Services) Video or film, 12 min. A portrait of the right whale.

 The Great Ocean Rescue (Tom Snyder Productions) Videodisc, Macintosh, Windows. Scientific experts explore the world of oceans.

 See (Phoenix/BFA) Video, 13 min. A visual journey into the depths of the ocean and a look at the creatures of the sea.

 Protecting Habitats, Preserving Biodiversity (Coronet/MTI) Videodisc. This informative program describes how natural habitats are disappearing and how new solutions are being implemented to save them.

 The Wetlands (AIMS) Video or laserdisc, 13 min. This film examines the wetlands ecosystem and the impact of man on ecosystems.

 Wetlands: Conserving America Series (ESI) Video. An exploration of the wetlands ecosystem and an introduction to Marjory Stoneman Douglas, champion of the Everglades for the last fifty years.

Aladdin Paperbacks
(Imprint of Simon & Schuster Children's Publishing)

Alaska Northwest Books
(Division of Graphic Arts Center Publishing Co.)
3019 NW Yeon Ave.
Box 10306
Portland, OR 97296-0306
(503) 226-2402 • (800) 452-3032
Fax (503) 223-1410
www.gacpc.com

Annick Press
(Imprint of Firefly, Ltd.)

Atheneum
(Imprint of Simon & Schuster Children's Publishing)

Avon Books
(Division of Hearst Corp.)
1350 Ave. of the Americas
New York, NY 10019
(212) 261-6800 • (800) 238-0658
Fax (800) 223-0239
www.avonbooks.com

Bantam Doubleday Dell Books for Young Readers
(Imprint of Random House)

Peter Bedrick Books
156 Fifth Ave., Suite 817
New York, NY 10010
(800) 788-3123 • Fax (212) 206-3741

Beech Tree Books
(Imprint of William Morrow & Co.)

Blackbirch Press
1 Bradley Road, Suite 205
Woodbridge, CT 06525
(203) 387-7525 • (800) 831-9183

Blue Sky Press
(Imprint of Scholastic)

Bradbury Press
(Imprint of Simon & Schuster Children's Publishing)

BridgeWater Books
(Distributed by Penguin Putnam Inc.)

Candlewick Press
2067 Massachusetts Avenue
Cambridge, MA 02140
(617) 661-3330 • Fax (617) 661-0565

Carolrhoda Books
(Division of Lerner Publications Co.)

Cartwheel Books
(Imprint of Scholastic)

Children's Book Press
246 First St., Suite 101
San Francisco, CA 94105
(415) 995-2200 • Fax (415) 995-2222

Children's Press (Division of Grolier, Inc.)
P.O. Box 1796
Danbury, CT 06813-1333
(800) 621-1115 • www.grolier.com

Chronicle Books
85 Second Street, Sixth Floor
San Francisco, CA 94105
(415) 537-3730 • (415) 537-4460
(800) 722-6657
www.chroniclebooks.com

Clarion Books
(Imprint of Houghton Mifflin, Inc.)
215 Park Avenue South
New York, NY 10003
(212) 420-5800 • (800) 726-0600
www.hmco.com/trade/childrens/shelves.html

Crabtree Publishing Co.
350 Fifth Ave., Suite 3308
New York, NY 10118
(212) 496-5040 • (800) 387-7650
Fax (800) 355-7166
www.crabtree-pub.com

Creative Education
The Creative Co.
123 S. Broad Street
P.O. Box 227
Mankato, MN 56001
(507) 388-6273 • (800) 445-6209
Fax (507) 388-2746

Crowell (Imprint of HarperCollins)

Crown Publishing Group
(Imprint of Random House)

Delacorte
(Imprint of Random House)

Dial Books
(Imprint of Penguin Putnam Inc.)

Discovery Enterprises, Ltd.
31 Laurelwood Dr.
Carlisle, MA 01741
(978) 287-5401 • (800) 729-1720
Fax (978) 287-5402

Disney Press
(Division of Disney Book Publishing, Inc., A Walt Disney Co.)
114 Fifth Ave.
New York, NY 10011
(212) 633-4400 • Fax (212) 633-4833
www.disneybooks.com

Dorling Kindersley (DK Publishing)
95 Madison Avenue
New York, NY 10016
(212) 213-4800 • Fax (800) 774-6733
(888) 342-5357 • www.dk.com

Doubleday (Imprint of Random House)

E. P. Dutton Children's Books
(Imprint of Penguin Putnam Inc.)

Farrar Straus & Giroux
19 Union Square West
New York, NY 10003
(212) 741-6900 • Fax (212) 633-2427
(888) 330-8477

Firefly Books, Ltd.
PO Box 1338
Endicott Station
Buffalo, NY 14205
(416) 499-8412 • Fax (800) 565-6034
(800) 387-5085
www.firefly.com

Four Winds Press
(Imprint of Macmillan, see Simon & Schuster Children's Publishing)

Fulcrum Publishing
350 Indiana Street, Suite 350
Golden, CO 80401
(303) 277-1623 • (800) 992-2908
Fax (303) 279-7111
www.fulcrum-books.com

Greenwillow Books
(Imprint of William Morrow & Co, Inc.)

Gulliver Green Books
(Imprint of Harcourt Brace & Co.)

Harcourt Brace & Co.
525 "B" Street
San Diego, CA 92101
(619) 231-6616 • (800) 543-1918
www.harcourtbooks.com

Harper & Row (Imprint of HarperCollins)

HarperCollins Children's Books
10 East 53rd Street
New York, NY 10022
(212) 207-7000 • Fax (212) 202-7044
(800) 242-7737
www.harperchildrens.com

Harper Trophy
(Imprint of HarperCollins)

Henry Holt and Company
115 West 18th Street
New York, NY 10011
(212) 886-9200 • (212) 633-0748
(888) 330-8477 • www.henryholt.com/byr/

Holiday House
425 Madison Avenue
New York, NY 10017
(212) 688-0085 • Fax (212) 421-6134

Houghton Mifflin
222 Berkeley Street
Boston, MA 02116
(617) 351-5000 • Fax (617) 351-1125
(800) 225-3362 • www.hmco.com/trade

Hyperion Books
(Imprint of Buena Vista Publishing Co.)
114 Fifth Avenue
New York, NY 10011
(212) 633-4400 • (800) 759-0190
www.disney.com

Just Us Books
356 Glenwood Avenue
E. Orange, NJ 07017
(973) 672-0304 • Fax (973) 677-7570

Kane/Miller Book Publishers
P.O. Box 310529
Brooklyn, NY 11231-0529
(718) 624-5120 • Fax (718) 858-5452
www.kanemiller.com

Alfred A. Knopf
(Imprint of Random House)

Lee & Low Books
95 Madison Avenue
New York, NY 10016
(212) 779-4400 • Fax (212) 683-1894

Lerner Publications Co.
241 First Avenue North
Minneapolis, MN 55401
(612) 332-3344 • Fax (612) 332-7615
(800) 328-4929 • www.lernerbooks.com

Little, Brown & Co.
3 Center Plaza
Boston, MA 02108
(617) 227-0730 • Fax (617) 263-2864
(800) 343-9204 • www.littlebrown.com

Lothrop Lee & Shepard
(Imprint of William Morrow & Co.)

Macmillan
(Imprint of Simon & Schuster Children's Publishing)

Mikaya Press
(Imprint of Firefly Books, Ltd.)

Millbrook Press, Inc.
2 Old New Milford Road
Brookfield, CT 06804
(203) 740-2220 • (800) 462-4703
Fax (203) 740-2526
www.millbrookpress.com

William Morrow & Co.
1350 Avenue of the Americas
New York, NY 10019
(212) 261-6500 • Fax (212) 261-6619
(800) 843-9389
www.williammorrow.com

Morrow Junior Books
(Imprint of William Morrow & Co.)

National Geographic Society
1145 17th Street, NW
Washington, DC 20036
(202) 828-5667 • (800) 368-2728
www.nationalgeographic.com

Northland Publishing
(Division of Justin Industries)
P.O. Box 62
Flagstaff, AZ 86002
(520) 774-5251 • Fax (800) 257-9082
(800) 346-3257 • www.northlandpub.com

Orchard Books (A Grolier Company)
95 Madison Avenue
New York, NY 10016
(212) 951-2600 • Fax (212) 213-6435
(800) 621-1115 • www.grolier.com

Oxford University Press, Inc.
198 Madison Ave.
New York, NY 10016-4314
(212) 726-6000 • (800) 451-7556
www.oup-usa.org

Penguin Putnam, Inc.
345 Hudson Street
New York, NY 10014
(212) 366-2000 • Fax (212) 366-2666
(800) 631-8571
www.penguinputnam.com

Philomel Books
(Imprint of Penguin Putnam, Inc.)

Pippin Press
Gracie Station, Box 1347
229 E. 85th Street
New York, NY 10028
(212) 288-4920 • Fax (732) 225-1562

Puffin Books
(Imprint of Penguin Putnam, Inc.)

G.P. Putnam's Sons Publishing
(Imprint of Penguin Putnam, Inc.)

Random House
201 East 50th Street
New York, NY 10022
(212) 751-2600 • Fax (212) 572-2593
(800) 726-0600
www.randomhouse.com/kids

Rising Moon
(Imprint of Northland Publishing)

Scholastic
555 Broadway
New York, NY 10012
(212) 343-6100 • Fax (212) 343-6930
(800) SCHOLASTIC • www.scholastic.com

Sierra Club Books for Children
85 Second Street, Second Floor
San Francisco, CA 94105-3441
(415) 977-5500 • Fax (415) 977-5793
(800) 935-1056 • www.sierraclub.orgbooks

Silver Burdett Press
(Division of Pearson Education)
299 Jefferson Rd.
Parsippany, NJ 07054-0480
(973) 739-8000 • (800) 848-9500
www.sbgschool.com

Simon & Schuster Children's Books
1230 Avenue of the Americas
New York, NY 10020
(212) 698-7200 • (800) 223-2336
www.simonsays.com/kidzone

Gareth Stevens, Inc.
River Center Bldg.
1555 N. River Center Dr., Suite 201
Milwaukee, WI 53212
(414) 225-0333 • (800) 341-3569
Fax (414) 225-0377
www.gsinc.com

Sunburst
(Imprint of Farrar, Straus & Giroux)

Tricycle Press
(Division of Ten Speed Press)
P.O. Box 7123
Berkeley, CA 94707
(510) 559-1600 • (800) 841-2665
Fax (510) 559-1637
www.tenspeed.com

Viking Children's Books
(Imprint of Penguin Putnam Inc.)

Voyager
(Imprint of Harcourt Brace & Co.)

Walker & Co.
435 Hudson Street
New York, NY 10014
(212) 727-8300 • (212) 727-0984
(800) AT-WALKER

Warwick Publishing
162 John St.
Toronto, CAN M5V2E5
(416) 596-1555
www.warwickgp.com

Watts Publishing
(Imprint of Grolier Publishing; see Children's Press)

Yearling Books
(Imprint of Random House)

Multimedia Resources

AIMS Multimedia
9710 DeSoto Avenue
Chatsworth, CA 91311-4409
(800) 367-2467
www.AIMS-multimedia.com

Ambrose Video and Publishing
28 West 44th Street, Suite 2100
New York, NY 10036
(800) 526-4663 • Fax (212) 768-9282
www.AmbroseVideo.com

BFA Educational Media
(see Phoenix Learning Group)

Boston Federal Reserve Bank
Community Affairs Dept.
P.O. Box 2076
Boston, MA 02106-2076
(617) 973-3459
www.bos.frb.org

Brittanica
310 South Michigan Avenue
Brittanica Center
Chicago, IL 60604-4293
(800) 621-3900 • Fax (800) 344-9624

Broderbund
(Parsons Technology;
also see The Learning Company)
500 Redwood Blvd.
Novato, CA 94997
(800) 521-6263 • Fax (800) 474-8840
www.broderbund.com

Carousel Film and Video
260 Fifth Avenue, Suite 705
New York, NY 10001
(212) 683-1660 • e-mail:
carousel@pipeline.com

CBS/Fox Video
1330 Avenue of the Americas
New York, NY 10019
(800) 457-0686

Cornell University Audio/Video Resource Ctr.
8 Business & Technology Park
Ithaca, NY 14850
(607) 255-2091

Coronet/MTI
(see Phoenix Learning Group)

Direct Cinema, Ltd.
P.O. Box 10003
Santa Monica, CA 90410-1003
(800) 525-0000

Encyclopaedia Britannica Educational Corp.
310 South Michigan Avenue
Chicago, IL 60604
(800) 554-9862 • www.eb.com

ESI/Educational Software
4213 S. 94th Street
Omaha, NE 68127
(800) 955-5570 • www.edsoft.com

Films for the Humanities and Sciences
P.O. Box 2053
Princeton, NJ 08543-2053
(800) 257-5126 • Fax (609) 275-3767
www.films.com

GPN/Reading Rainbow
University of Nebraska-Lincoln
P.O. Box 80669
Lincoln, NE 68501-0669
(800) 228-4630 • www.gpn.unl.edu

Journal Films and Videos
1560 Sherman Avenue, Suite 100
Evanston, IL 60201
(800) 323-9084

Kaw Valley Films
P.O. Box 3900
Shawnee, KS 66208
(800) 332-5060

Listening Library
One Park Avenue
Greenwich, CT 06870-1727
(800) 243-4504 • www.listeninglib.com

Macmillan/McGraw-Hill
(see SRA/McGraw-Hill)

Marshmedia
P.O. Box 8082
Shawnee Mission, KS 66208
(800) 821-3303 • Fax (816) 333-7421
marshmedia.com

MECC
(see The Learning Company)

National Geographic Society Educational Services
P.O. Box 10597
Des Moines, IA 50340-0597
(800) 368-2728
www.nationalgeographic.com

New Jersey Network
1573 Parkside Ave.
Trenton, NJ 08625-0777
(609) 530-5180

PBS Video
1320 Braddock Place
Alexandria, VA 22314
(800) 344-3337 • www.pbs.org

Phoenix Films
(see Phoenix Learning Group)

The Phoenix Learning Group
2348 Chaffee Drive
St. Louis, MO 63146
(800) 221-1274 • e-mail:
phoenixfilms@worldnet.att.net

Pied Piper (see AIMS Multimedia)

Rainbow Educational Video
170 Keyland Court
Bohemia, NY 11716
(800) 331-4047

Social Studies School Service
10200 Jefferson Boulevard, Room 14
P.O. Box 802
Culver City, CA 90232-0802
(800) 421-4246 • Fax (310) 839-2249
socialstudies.com

SRA/McGraw-Hill
220 Daniel Dale Road
De Soto, TX 75115
(800) 843-8855 • www.sra4kids.com

SVE/Churchill Media
6677 North Northwest Highway
Chicago, IL 60631
(800) 829-1900 • www.svemedia.com

Tom Snyder Productions (also see ESI)
80 Coolidge Hill Rd.
Watertown, MA 02472
(800) 342-0236 • www.teachtsp.com

Troll Associates
100 Corporate Drive
Mahwah, NJ 07430
(800) 929-8765 • Fax (800) 979-8765
www.troll.com

United Learning
6633 W. Howard St.
Niles, IL 60714-3389
(800) 424-0362
www.unitedlearning.com

Weston Woods
12 Oakwood Avenue
Norwalk, CT 06850
(800) 243-5020 • Fax (203) 845-0498

Zenger Media
10200 Jefferson Blvd., Room 94
P.O. Box 802
Culver City, CA 90232-0802
(800) 421-4246 • Fax (800) 944-5432
www.Zengermedia.com

UNIT 1

Vocabulary | Spelling

THE LOST LAKE

Vocabulary				
brand-new				
compass				
darted				
mug				
muttered				
talker				

Words with Short Vowels

drank	hung	lift	swept
rest	trouble	flock	pleasant
ahead	**magazines**	trust	fist
drink	self	cousin	couple
dock	deaf	cannon	wealth

AMELIA'S ROAD

Vocabulary
accidental
labored
occasions
rhythms
shortcut
shutters

Words with long *a* and long *e*

cape	agree	crayon	**rusty**
gray	**teacher**	cable	tray
station	secret	fail	raisin
rail	**family**	tea	bean
freight	cane	zebra	**tidy**

SARAH, PLAIN AND TALL

Vocabulary
eerie
huddled
overalls
pesky
reins
squall

Words with long *i* and long *o*

tiger	crow	tomato	pine
drive	oak	**stove**	**overhead**
reply	iron	below	chose
roll	alike	groan	hollow
note	supply	title	file

SEAL JOURNEY

Vocabulary
assured
horizon
jagged
mature
nursery
squealed

Words with /ū/ and /ü/

ruler	**continue**	**improve**	ruin
avenue	gloomy	beautiful	bugle
raccoon	unit	cube	argue
loose	whose	stool	community
commute	humor	**movement**	tuna

TIME FOR KIDS: OPEN WIDE, DON'T BITE!

Vocabulary
broad
fangs
patients
healthy
reptiles
skills

Words from Health

dentist	**gums**	brain	ache
crown	gland	cavity	**dental**
hospital	joint	disease	clinic
medicine	fever	plaque	oral
diet	**chewing**	vitamin	**molars**

Boldfaced words appear in the selection.

UNIT 2

Vocabulary	Spelling

JUSTIN AND THE BEST BISCUITS IN THE WORLD

Vocabulary
- festival
- guilt
- inspecting
- lingered
- pranced
- resounded

Syllable Patterns

biscuit	cabin	local	**razor**
clover	plastic	mustard	fancy
public	radar	pupil	limit
oven	mitten	sofa	**famous**
bandage	**knapsack**	**welcome**	item

JUST A DREAM

Vocabulary
- bulging
- crumpled
- foul
- haze
- shrieking
- waddled

Words with Consonant Clusters

blank	bridge	brand	credit
daring	**float**	among	darling
claim	plank	flatter	flutter
flour	classified	**clothesline**	clatter
crack	cradle	bridle	cruise

LEAH'S PONY

Vocabulary
- bidding
- clustered
- country
- glistened
- overflowing
- sturdy

Words with Consonant Clusters

thrill	sprint	stern	stung
spruce	spare	spectacle	sparkle
stand	threw	strap	stress
speed	**stranger**	thrifty	special
stretch	springtime	street	steak

BASEBALL SAVED US

Vocabulary
- crate
- ditches
- endless
- glinting
- inning
- mound

Plurals

cities	engines	eyelashes	**sunglasses**
mistakes	**soldiers**	**uniforms**	groceries
foxes	ranches	batteries	loaves
babies	hobbies	calves	**mattresses**
knives	yourselves	**shovels**	ferries

TIME FOR KIDS: WILL HER NATIVE LANGUAGE DISAPPEAR?

Vocabulary
- backgrounds
- century
- communicate
- extinct
- generations
- native

Words from Social Studies

language	accent	folktale	symbol
history	tribe	practice	guide
pottery	human	**relatives**	totem
study	custom	interview	colony
spoken	village	region	**prints**

Boldfaced words appear in the selection.

T81

UNIT 3

	Vocabulary	Spelling

THE HATMAKER'S SIGN

admitted
brisk
displaying
elegantly
strolling
wharf

Words with /ou/ and /oi/

oily	royalty	**aloud**	**however**
annoy	bounce	tower	appointment
around	**bowing**	avoid	scout
growl	moist	employ	powder
disappoint	enjoyment	**lookout**	noun

PAT CUMMINGS: MY STORY

exist
image
inspire
loft
reference
sketch

Words with /u̇/ and /yu̇/

curious	**should**	**would**	woolen
pure	furious	bulldozer	pudding
fully	cure	soot	goodness
sure	handful	tour	pulley
wooden	crooked	butcher	overlook

GRASS SANDALS: THE TRAVELS OF BASHO

chanted
nipped
pouch
restless
scribbled
stitching

Work with Digraphs

changed	south	**cloth**	whittle
watch	chimney	**themselves**	thoughtful
fresh	scratch	crunch	birch
shoulder	shove	batch	switch
whatever	wheat	harsh	theater

A PLACE CALLED FREEDOM

fretted
gourd
plantation
settlement
sunrise
weary

Adding -ed and -ing

freed	**carried**	shedding	varied
hugged	**believed**	sledding	**arrived**
emptied	dimmed	magnified	plugging
figured	studied	wedged	rising
budding	providing	rotting	**celebrated**

TIME FOR KIDS: TWISTED TRAILS

challenge
combine
contained
entertaining
mazes
requires

Words from the Arts

designs	art	assemble	mold
artist	create	craft	easel
building	**master**	express	plaster
activity	poster	arrange	masterpiece
museum	statue	**professional**	exhibit

Boldfaced words appear in the selection.

UNIT 4

	Vocabulary	**Spelling**

SCRUFFY: A WOLF FINDS HIS PLACE IN THE PACK

Vocabulary	Spelling — Words with /ô/ and /ôr/			
affection	awful	**toward**	false	dawn
climate	daughter	already	jaw	hoarse
clinging	roar	brought	offer	war
injury	order	**form**	sauce	board
methods	office	author	**chorus**	cough
threat				

GLUSKABE AND THE SNOW BIRD

Vocabulary	Spelling — Words with /är/ and /âr/			
confusion	**apart**	repair	starve	therefore
freeze	hardly	**careful**	barber	dairy
hilltop	yarn	scare	carnival	hare
lodge	army	somewhere	carpet	**prepare**
messenger	marbles	wear	unfair	pear
praised				

MEET AN UNDERWATER EXPLORER

Vocabulary	Spelling — Words with /îr/ and /ûr/			
connected	fern	mere	**worse**	period
endangered	curve	cheer	swirl	insert
haul	worst	serious	**gear**	purpose
overcome	**shirt**	germ	sincerely	twirling
poisonous	**clear**	burst	volunteer	spear
sponge				

ON THE BUS WITH JOANNA COLE

Vocabulary	Spelling — Compound Words			
abandon	**bedroom**	backyard	**outline**	**whirlwinds**
absorb	**anymore**	railroad	windowpane	loudspeaker
available	everybody	forever	**evergreens**	northwest
original	**classroom**	bathtub	grandparents	thunderstorm
research	anyway	homemade	**photocopy**	bedspread
traditional				

TIME FOR KIDS: EARTH'S FIRST CREATURES

Vocabulary	Spelling — Words from Science			
ancestors	**shells**	**discovered**	mineral	kelp
disaster	**crabs**	cast	dolphin	caterpillar
microscope	liquid	lobster	**systems**	depth
snout	fact	**hatch**	clam	skeleton
spikes	butterfly	expert	imprint	fungus
weird				

Boldfaced words appear in the selection.

UNIT 5

	Vocabulary	Spelling

THE FOX AND THE GUINEA PIG

Vocabulary:
amazement
destroyed
eldest
fowl
stake
strewn

Spelling: **Words with /s/ and /f/**

mess	rough	**laughter**	alphabet
sorry	certain	citizen	triumph
balance	telephone	advice	careless
police	**surprise**	photograph	tough
classic	elephant	cider	**enormous**

MOM'S BEST FRIEND

Vocabulary:
clippers
errands
instinct
memorizing
relieved
sirens

Spelling: **Words with /ər/ and /chər/**

brother	**pictures**	member	anchor
honor	odor	nature	pasture
either	enter	tender	chapter
popular	vinegar	visitor	suffer
number	capture	polar	**furniture**

THE RAJAH'S RICE

Vocabulary:
attendants
awkwardly
celebration
knowledge
released
spice

Spelling: **Words with /əl/ and /ən/**

final	pencil	reason	**medical**
uncle	lion	gentle	evil
several	**taken**	total	listen
model	simple	settle	common
terrible	women	level	cotton

YEH-SHEN: A CINDERELLA STORY FROM CHINA

Vocabulary:
beloved
bid
desire
heaved
marveled
permit

Spelling: **Contractions**

that's	there's	they'll	it'll
he'll	couldn't	weren't	hadn't
wasn't	he'd	here's	they'd
what's	could've	she'd	where's
I'd	let's	who's	wouldn't

TIME FOR KIDS: CAN WE RESCUE THE REEFS?

Vocabulary:
coral
damage
loosened
percent
reefs
ton

Spelling: **Words from Science**

rescue	**dying**	**seaweed**	adapt
survive	shelter	**creatures**	locate
channel	extreme	dissolve	assist
vessel	**danger**	motion	future
expose	protect	feature	**divers**

Boldfaced words appear in the selection.

UNIT 6

Vocabulary	Spelling

TEAMMATES

Vocabulary
- circulated
- extraordinary
- launched
- opponents
- organizations
- teammate

Words with Silent Letters

knew	writer	knead	stalk
climb	knob	plumber	kneel
calm	numb	chalk	**sought**
although	delight	midnight	thorough
knight	wren	wreck	wrestle

THE MALACHITE PALACE

Vocabulary
- cultured
- feeble
- fragrance
- mingled
- resembled
- scampered

Homophones and Homographs

seen	scene	peak	pale
great	beet	post	grave
light	bowl	pail	berry
beat	grate	bury	peek
lean	fan	punch	dates

THE TOOTHPASTE MILLIONAIRE

Vocabulary
- brilliant
- commercials
- expensive
- gallon
- ingredient
- successful

Words with Suffixes

useless	motionless	fairness	hopeless
entertainment	description	government	**production**
construction	measurement	protection	enjoyable
adjustable	adorable	dependable	greatness
darkness	breathless	sickness	

WHALES

Vocabulary
- identify
- mammals
- marine
- pods
- preserve
- related

Words with Prefixes

redo	inactive	nonstop	rewind
unkind	**international**	refill	unsure
disappear	unlucky	uncertain	disagree
reread	dislike	interstate	reheat
nonfat	unpack	incomplete	nonsense

TIME FOR KIDS: SAVING THE EVERGLADES

Vocabulary
- compares
- importance
- instance
- lurk
- soggy
- wildlife

Words from Math

area	minute	**amount**	quart
hundreds	noon	cylinder	decade
size	cone	zero	rectangle
billions	yard	figure	era
weight	edge	calendar	length

Boldfaced words appear in the selection.

Listening, Speaking, Viewing, Representing

☑ Tested Skill

☐ Tinted panels show skills, strategies, and other teaching opportunities

LISTENING	K	1	2	3	4	5	6
Learn the vocabulary of school (numbers, shapes, colors, directions, and categories)							
Identify the musical elements of literary language, such as rhymes, repeated sounds, onomatopoeia							
Determine purposes for listening (get information, solve problems, enjoy and appreciate)							
Listen critically and responsively							
Ask and answer relevant questions							
Listen critically to interpret and evaluate							
Listen responsively to stories and other texts read aloud, including selections from classic and contemporary works							
Connect own experiences, ideas, and traditions with those of others							
Apply comprehension strategies in listening activities							
Understand the major ideas and supporting evidence in spoken messages							
Participate in listening activities related to reading and writing (such as discussions, group activities, conferences)							
Listen to learn by taking notes, organizing, and summarizing spoken ideas							

SPEAKING	K	1	2	3	4	5	6
Learn the vocabulary of school (numbers, shapes, colors, directions, and categories)							
Use appropriate language and vocabulary learned to describe ideas, feelings, and experiences							
Ask and answer relevant questions							
Communicate effectively in everyday situations (such as discussions, group activities, conferences)							
Demonstrate speaking skills (audience, purpose, occasion, volume, pitch, tone, rate, fluency)							
Clarify and support spoken messages and ideas with objects, charts, evidence, elaboration, examples							
Use verbal and nonverbal communication in effective ways when, for example, making announcements, giving directions, or making introductions							
Retell a spoken message by summarizing or clarifying							
Connect own experiences, ideas, and traditions with those of others							
Determine purposes for speaking (inform, entertain, give directions, persuade, express personal feelings and opinions)							
Demonstrate skills of reporting and providing information							
Demonstrate skills of interviewing, requesting and providing information							
Apply composition strategies in speaking activities							
Monitor own understanding of spoken message and seek clarification as needed							

VIEWING	K	1	2	3	4	5	6
Demonstrate viewing skills (focus attention, organize information)							
Respond to audiovisual media in a variety of ways							
Participate in viewing activities related to reading and writing							
Apply comprehension strategies in viewing activities							
Recognize artists' craft and techniques for conveying meaning							
Interpret information from various formats such as maps, charts, graphics, video segments, technology							
Evaluate purposes of various media (information, appreciation, entertainment, directions, persuasion)							
Use media to compare ideas and points of view							

REPRESENTING	K	1	2	3	4	5	6
Select, organize, or produce visuals to complement or extend meanings							
Produce communication using appropriate media to develop a class paper, multimedia or video reports							
Show how language, medium, and presentation contribute to the message							

Reading: Alphabetic Principle, Sounds/Symbols

☑ Tested Skill

Tinted panels show skills, strategies, and other teaching opportunities

PRINT AWARENESS	K	1	2	3	4	5	6
Know the order of the alphabet							
Recognize that print represents spoken language and conveys meaning							
Understand directionality (tracking print from left to right; return sweep)							
Understand that written words are separated by spaces							
Know the difference between individual letters and printed words							
Understand that spoken words are represented in written language by specific sequence of letters							
Recognize that there are correct spellings for words							
Know the difference between capital and lowercase letters							
Recognize how readers use capitalization and punctuation to comprehend							
Recognize the distinguishing features of a paragraph							
Recognize that parts of a book (such as cover/title page and table of contents) offer information							

PHONOLOGICAL AWARENESS	K	1	2	3	4	5	6
Identify letters, words, sentences							
Divide spoken sentence into individual words							
Produce rhyming words and distinguish rhyming words from nonrhyming words							
Identify, segment, and combine syllables within spoken words							
Identify and isolate the initial and final sound of a spoken word							
Add, delete, or change sounds to change words (such as *cow* to *how*, *pan* to *fan*)							
Blend sounds to make spoken words							
Segment one-syllable spoken words into individual phonemes							

PHONICS AND DECODING	K	1	2	3	4	5	6
Alphabetic principle: Letter/sound correspondence	☑	☑	☑				
Blending CVC words	☑						
Segmenting CVC words	☑						
Blending CVC, CVCe, CCVC, CVCC, CVVC words	☑	☑	☑				
Segmenting CVC, CVCe, CCVC, CVCC, CVVC words	☑	☑	☑				
Initial and final consonants: /n/n, /d/d, /s/s, /m/m, /t/t, /k/c, /f/f, /r/r, /p/p, /l/l, /k/k, /g/g, /b/b, /h/h, /w/w, /v/v, /ks/x, /kw/qu, /j/j, /y/y, /z/z	☑	☑					
Initial and medial short vowels: *a, i, u, o, e*	☑	☑	☑				
Long vowels: *a-e, i-e, o-e, u-e* (vowel-consonant-e)		☑	☑				
Long vowels, including *ay, ai; e, ee, ie, ea, o, oa, oe, ow; i, y, igh*		☑	☑				
Consonant Digraphs: *sh, th, ch, wh*		☑					
Consonant Blends: continuant/continuant, including *sl, sm, sn, fl, fr, ll, ss, ff*		☑					
Consonant Blends: continuant/stop, including *st, sk, sp, ng, nt, nd, mp, ft*		☑					
Consonant Blends: stop/continuant, including *tr, pr, pl, cr, tw*		☑					
Variant vowels: including /u/oo; /ô/a, aw, au; /ü/ue, ew		☑	☑				
Diphthongs, including /ou/ou, ow; /oi/oi, oy		☑	☑				
r-controlled vowels, including /âr/are; /ôr/or, ore; /îr/ear			☑				
Soft *c* and soft *g*			☑				
nk		☑	☑				
Consonant Digraphs: *ck*	☑	☑					
Consonant Digraphs: *ph, tch, ch*			☑				
Short *e: ea*			☑				
Long *e: y, ey*			☑				
/ü/oo		☑	☑				
/är/ar; /ûr/ir, ur, er		☑	☑				
Silent letters: including *l, b, k, w, g, h, gh*			☑				
Schwa: /ər/er; /ən/en; /əl/le;			☑				
Reading/identifying multisyllabic words		☑	☑				

Reading: Vocabulary/Word Identification

WORD STRUCTURE	K	1	2	3	4	5	6
Common spelling patterns							
Syllable patterns							
Plurals							
Possessives							
Contractions							
Root, or base, words and inflectional endings (-s, -es, -ed, -ing)							
Compound Words							
Prefixes and suffixes (such as un-, re-, dis-, non-; -ly, -y, -ful, -able, -tion)							
Root words and derivational endings							

WORD MEANING	K	1	2	3	4	5	6
Develop vocabulary through concrete experiences							
Develop vocabulary through selections read aloud							
Develop vocabulary through reading							
Cueing systems: syntactic, semantic, phonetic							
Context clues, including semantic clues (word meaning), syntactical clues (word order), and phonetic clues	☑	☑	☑	☑	☑	☑	☑
High-frequency words (such as the, a, an, and, said, was, where, is)							
Identify words that name persons, places, things, and actions							
Automatic reading of regular and irregular words							
Use resources and references dictionary, glossary, thesaurus, synonym finder, technology and software, and context)							
Synonyms and antonyms							
Multiple-meaning words							
Figurative language							
Decode derivatives (root words, such as like, pay, happy with affixes, such as dis-, pre-, -un)							
Systematic study of words across content areas and in current events							
Locate meanings, pronunciations, and derivations (including dictionaries, glossaries, and other sources)							
Denotation and connotation							
Word origins as aid to understanding historical influences on English word meanings							
Homophones, homographs							
Analogies							
Idioms							

Reading: Comprehension

PREREADING STRATEGIES	K	1	2	3	4	5	6
Preview and Predict							
Use prior knowledge							
Establish and adjust purposes for reading							
Build background							

MONITORING STRATEGIES	K	1	2	3	4	5	6
Adjust reading rate							
Reread, search for clues, ask questions, ask for help							
Visualize							
Read a portion aloud, use reference aids							
Use decoding and vocabulary strategies							
Paraphrase							
Create story maps, diagrams, charts, story props to help comprehend, analyze, synthesize and evaluate texts							

(continued on next page)

☑ Tested Skill

Tinted panels show skills, strategies, and other teaching opportunities

SKILLS AND STRATEGIES

	K	1	2	3	4	5	6
Story details	☑						
Use illustrations	☑	☑					
Reality and fantasy	☑	☑	☑	☑			
Classify and categorize	☑						
Make predictions	☑	☑	☑	☑	☑	☑	☑
Sequence of events (tell or act out)	☑	☑	☑	☑	☑	☑	☑
Cause and effect		☑	☑	☑	☑	☑	☑
Compare and contrast	☑	☑	☑	☑	☑	☑	☑
Summarize	☑	☑	☑	☑	☑	☑	☑
Make and explain inferences		☑	☑	☑	☑	☑	☑
Draw conclusions		☑	☑	☑	☑	☑	☑
Important and unimportant information				☑	☑	☑	☑
Main idea and supporting details	☑	☑	☑	☑	☑	☑	☑
Form conclusions or generalizations and support with evidence from text			☑	☑	☑	☑	☑
Fact and opinion (including news stories and advertisements)			☑	☑	☑	☑	☑
Problem and solution			☑	☑	☑	☑	☑
Steps in a process		☑	☑	☑	☑	☑	☑
Make judgments and decisions				☑	☑	☑	☑
Fact and nonfact				☑	☑	☑	☑
Recognize techniques of persuasion and propaganda					☑	☑	☑
Evaluate evidence and sources of information					☑	☑	☑
Identify similarities and differences across texts (including topics, characters, problems, themes, treatment, scope, or organization)							
Practice various questions and tasks (test-like comprehension questions)							
Paraphrase and summarize to recall, inform, and organize							
Answer various types of questions (open-ended, literal, interpretative, test-like such as true-false, multiple choice, short-answer)							
Use study strategies to learn and recall (preview, question, reread, and record)							

LITERARY RESPONSE

	K	1	2	3	4	5	6
Listen to stories being read aloud							
React, speculate, join in, read along when predictable and patterned selections are read aloud							
Respond through talk, movement, music, art, drama, and writing to a variety of stories and poems							
Show understanding through writing, illustrating, developing demonstrations, and using technology							
Connect ideas and themes across texts							
Support responses by referring to relevant aspects of text and own experiences							
Offer observations, make connections, speculate, interpret, and raise questions in response to texts							
Interpret text ideas through journal writing, discussion, enactment, and media							

TEXT STRUCTURE/LITERARY CONCEPTS

	K	1	2	3	4	5	6
Distinguish forms of texts and the functions they serve (lists, newsletters, signs)							
Understand story structure							
Identify narrative (for entertainment) and expository (for information)							
Distinguish fiction from nonfiction, including fact and fantasy							
Understand literary forms (stories, poems, plays, and informational books)							
Understand literary terms by distinguishing between roles of author and illustrator							
Understand title, author, and illustrator across a variety of texts							
Analyze character, character's point of view, plot, setting, style, tone, mood		☑	☑	☑	☑	☑	☑
Compare communication in different forms							
Understand terms such as *title, author, illustrator, playwright, theater, stage, act, dialogue,* and *scene*							
Recognize stories, poems, myths, folktales, fables, tall tales, limericks, plays, biographies, and autobiographies							
Judge internal logic of story text							
Recognize that authors organize information in specific ways							
Identify texts to inform, influence, express, or entertain							
Describe how author's point of view affects text							
Recognize biography, historical fiction, realistic fiction, modern fantasy, informational texts, and poetry							
Analyze ways authors present ideas (cause/effect, compare/contrast, inductively, deductively, chronologically)							
Recognize flashback, foreshadowing, symbolism							

(continued on next page)

(Reading: Comprehension continued)

☑ Tested Skill

Tinted panels show skills, strategies, and other teaching opportunities

VARIETY OF TEXT	K	1	2	3	4	5	6
Read a variety of genres							
Use informational texts to acquire information							
Read for a variety of purposes							
Select varied sources when reading for information or pleasure							
FLUENCY							
Read regularly in independent-level and instructional-level materials							
Read orally with fluency from familiar texts							
Self-select independent-level reading							
Read silently for increasing periods of time							
Demonstrate characteristics of fluent and effective reading							
Adjust reading rate to purpose							
Read aloud in selected texts, showing understanding of text and engaging the listener							
CULTURES							
Connect own experience with culture of others							
Compare experiences of characters across cultures							
Articulate and discuss themes and connections that cross cultures							
CRITICAL THINKING							
Experiences (comprehend, apply, analyze, synthesize, evaluate)							
Make connections (comprehend, apply, analyze, synthesize, evaluate)							
Expression (comprehend, apply, analyze, synthesize, evaluate)							
Inquiry (comprehend, apply, analyze, synthesize, evaluate)							
Problem solving (comprehend, apply, analyze, synthesize, evaluate)							
Making decisions (comprehend, apply, analyze, synthesize, evaluate)							

Study Skills

INQUIRY/RESEARCH	K	1	2	3	4	5	6
Follow directions							
Use alphabetical order							
Identify/frame questions for research							
Obtain, organize, and summarize information: classify, take notes, outline							
Evaluate research and raise new questions							
Use technology to present information in various formats							
Follow accepted formats for writing research, including documenting sources							
Use test-taking strategies							
Use text organizers (book cover; title page—title, author, illustrator; contents; headings; glossary; index)		☑	☑	☑	☑	☑	☑
Use graphic aids, including maps, diagrams, charts, graphs		☑	☑	☑	☑	☑	☑
Read and interpret varied texts including environmental print, signs, lists, encyclopedia, dictionary, glossary, newspaper, advertisement, magazine, calendar, directions, floor plans		☑	☑	☑	☑	☑	☑
Use reference sources, such as glossary, dictionary, encyclopedia, telephone directory, technology resources		☑	☑	☑	☑	☑	☑
Recognize Library/Media center resources, such as computerized references; catalog search—subject, author, title; encyclopedia index		☑	☑	☑	☑	☑	☑

Writing

MODES AND FORMS	K	1	2	3	4	5	6
Interactive writing							
Personal narrative (Expressive narrative)			☑	☑	☑	☑	☑
Writing that compares (Informative classificatory)			☑	☑	☑	☑	☑
Explanatory writing (Informative narrative)		☑	☑	☑	☑	☑	☑
Persuasive writing (Persuasive descriptive)			☑	☑	☑	☑	☑
Writing a story		☑	☑	☑	☑	☑	☑
Expository writing		☑	☑	☑	☑	☑	☑
Write using a variety of formats, such as advertisement, autobiography, biography, book report/report, comparison-contrast, critique/review/editorial, description, essay, how-to, interview, invitation, journal/log/notes, message/list, paragraph/multi-paragraph composition, picture book, play (scene), poem/rhyme, story, summary, note, letter							

PURPOSES/AUDIENCES	K	1	2	3	4	5	6
Dictate messages such as news and stories for others to write							
Write labels, notes, and captions for illustrations, possessions, charts, and centers							
Write to record, to discover and develop ideas, to inform, to influence, to entertain							
Exhibit an identifiable voice in personal narratives and stories							
Use literary devices (suspense, dialogue, and figurative language)							
Produce written texts by organizing ideas, using effective transitions, and choosing precise wording							

PROCESSES	K	1	2	3	4	5	6
Generate ideas for self-selected and assigned topics using prewriting strategies							
Develop drafts							
Revise drafts for varied purposes							
Edit for appropriate grammar, spelling, punctuation, and features of polished writings							
Proofread own writing and that of others							
Bring pieces to final form and "publish" them for audiences							
Use technology to compose text							
Select and use reference materials and resources for writing, revising, and editing final drafts							

SPELLING	K	1	2	3	4	5	6
Spell own name and write high-frequency words							
Words with short vowels (including CVC and one-syllable words with blends CCVC, CVCC, CCVCC)							
Words with long vowels (including CVCe)							
Words with digraphs, blends, consonant clusters, double consonants							
Words with diphthongs							
Words with variant vowels							
Words with r-controlled vowels							
Words with /ər/, /əl/, and /ən/							
Words with silent letters							
Words with soft c and soft g							
Inflectional endings (including plurals and past tense and words that drop the final e when adding -ing, -ed)							
Compound words							
Contractions							
Homonyms							
Suffixes including -able, -ly, or -less, and prefixes including dis-, re-, pre-, or un-							
Spell words ending in -tion and -sion, such as station and procession							
Accurate spelling of root or base words							
Orthographic patterns and rules such as keep/can; sack/book; out/now; oil/toy; match/speech; ledge/cage; consonant doubling, dropping e, changing y to i							
Multisyllabic words using regularly spelled phonogram patterns							
Syllable patterns (including closed, open, syllable boundary patterns)							
Synonyms and antonyms							
Words from Social Studies, Science, Math, and Physical Education							
Words derived from other languages and cultures							
Use resources to find correct spellings, synonyms, and replacement words							
Use conventional spelling of familiar words in writing assignments							
Spell accurately in final drafts							

(continued on next page)

☑ Tested Skill

Tinted panels show skills, strategies, and other teaching opportunities

GRAMMAR AND USAGE	K	1	2	3	4	5	6
Understand sentence concepts (word order, statements, questions, exclamations, commands)							
Recognize complete and incomplete sentences							
Nouns (common; proper; singular; plural; irregular plural; possessives)							
Verbs (action; helping; linking; irregular)							
Verb tense (present, past, future, perfect, and progressive)							
Pronouns (possessive, subject and object, pronoun-verb agreement)							
Use objective case pronouns accurately							
Adjectives							
Adverbs that tell how, when, where							
Subjects, predicates							
Subject-verb agreement							
Sentence combining							
Recognize sentence structure (simple, compound, complex)							
Synonyms and antonyms							
Contractions							
Conjunctions							
Prepositions and prepositional phrases							

PENMANSHIP	K	1	2	3	4	5	6
Write each letter of alphabet (capital and lowercase) using correct formation, appropriate size and spacing							
Write own name and other important words							
Use phonological knowledge to map sounds to letters to write messages							
Write messages that move left to right, top to bottom							
Gain increasing control of penmanship, pencil grip, paper position, beginning stroke							
Use word and letter spacing and margins to make messages readable							
Write legibly by selecting cursive or manuscript as appropriate							

MECHANICS	K	1	2	3	4	5	6
Use capitalization in sentences, proper nouns, titles, abbreviations and the pronoun *I*							
Use end marks correctly (period, question mark, exclamation point)							
Use commas (in dates, in addresses, in a series, in letters, in direct address)							
Use apostrophes in contractions and possessives							
Use quotation marks							
Use hyphens, semicolons, colons							

EVALUATION	K	1	2	3	4	5	6
Identify the most effective features of a piece of writing using class/teacher generated criteria							
Respond constructively to others' writing							
Determine how his/her own writing achieves its purpose							
Use published pieces as models for writing							
Review own written work to monitor growth as writer							

For more detailed scope and sequence including page numbers and additional phonics information, see McGraw-Hill Reading Program scope and sequence (K-6)

Notes

Scoring Chart

The Scoring Chart is provided for your convenience in grading your students' work.

- Find the column that shows the total number of items.
- Find the row that matches the number of items answered correctly.
- The intersection of the two rows provides the percentage score.

TOTAL NUMBER OF ITEMS

NUMBER CORRECT

Correct \ Items	1	2	3	4	5	6	7	8	9	10	11	12	13	14	15	16	17	18	19	20	21	22	23	24	25	26	27	28	29	30
1	100	50	33	25	20	17	14	13	11	10	9	8	8	7	7	6	6	6	5	5	5	5	4	4	4	4	4	4	3	3
2		100	66	50	40	33	29	25	22	20	18	17	15	14	13	13	12	11	11	10	10	9	9	8	8	8	7	7	7	7
3			100	75	60	50	43	38	33	30	27	25	23	21	20	19	18	17	16	15	14	14	13	13	12	12	11	11	10	10
4				100	80	67	57	50	44	40	36	33	31	29	27	25	24	22	21	20	19	18	17	17	16	15	15	14	14	13
5					100	83	71	63	56	50	45	42	38	36	33	31	29	28	26	25	24	23	22	21	20	19	19	18	17	17
6						100	86	75	67	60	55	50	46	43	40	38	35	33	32	30	29	27	26	25	24	23	22	21	21	20
7							100	88	78	70	64	58	54	50	47	44	41	39	37	35	33	32	30	29	28	27	26	25	24	23
8								100	89	80	73	67	62	57	53	50	47	44	42	40	38	36	35	33	32	31	30	29	28	27
9									100	90	82	75	69	64	60	56	53	50	47	45	43	41	39	38	36	35	33	32	31	30
10										100	91	83	77	71	67	63	59	56	53	50	48	45	43	42	40	38	37	36	34	33
11											100	92	85	79	73	69	65	61	58	55	52	50	48	46	44	42	41	39	38	37
12												100	92	86	80	75	71	67	63	60	57	55	52	50	48	46	44	43	41	40
13													100	93	87	81	76	72	68	65	62	59	57	54	52	50	48	46	45	43
14														100	93	88	82	78	74	70	67	64	61	58	56	54	52	50	48	47
15															100	94	88	83	79	75	71	68	65	63	60	58	56	54	52	50
16																100	94	89	84	80	76	73	70	67	64	62	59	57	55	53
17																	100	94	89	85	81	77	74	71	68	65	63	61	59	57
18																		100	95	90	86	82	78	75	72	69	67	64	62	60
19																			100	95	90	86	83	79	76	73	70	68	66	63
20																				100	95	91	87	83	80	77	74	71	69	67
21																					100	95	91	88	84	81	78	75	72	70
22																						100	96	92	88	85	81	79	76	73
23																							100	96	92	88	85	82	79	77
24																								100	96	92	89	86	83	80
25																									100	96	93	89	86	83
26																										100	96	93	90	87
27																											100	96	93	90
28																												100	97	93
29																													100	97
30																														100

Writing That Compares

Scoring Rubric: 6-Trait Writing

6 Exceptional	5 Excellent	4 Good	3 Fair	2 Poor	1 Unsatisfactory
• **Ideas & Content** crafts a clearly-detailed comparison between two animals; shares fresh observations about the animals and their habitat.	• **Ideas & Content** crafts a cohesive, carefully-detailed comparison of two animals; makes some fresh observations of the habitat.	• **Ideas & Content** presents a solid, clear comparison; details help to bring the main idea into focus.	• **Ideas & Content** attempts to compare two animals; some ideas or details are not clear, or do not fit the task.	• **Ideas & Content** has little control of task to compare, or seems unsure of the topic; ideas are vague; facts and details are few, repeated, or inaccurate.	• **Ideas & Content** does not compare two animals; writer is unfocused, or unsure of what s/he wants to say.
• **Organization** presents a logically-devised sequence of facts and ideas; strong beginning and effective conclusion; carefully-placed details clarify the information.	• **Organization** presents a well-planned strategy, in a sequence that helps the reader follow and understand the comparisons; facts and details are evenly connected.	• **Organization** presents facts and observations in a logical order; has a clear beginning and ending; reader can follow the writer's logic.	• **Organization** tries to structure a comparison, but the logic is sometimes hard to follow; ideas, sentences, and paragraphs may need more transition or connection.	• **Organization** has no clear structure; the order of ideas is hard to follow; few connections are made between ideas; details don't fit where they are placed.	• **Organization** has extreme lack of organization; ideas are not connected; details, if any, are incomplete, irrelevant, or do not fit.
• **Voice** shows originality, and deep involvement with the topic; a genuine personal style enlivens the facts.	• **Voice** shows originality and strong involvement with the topic; personal style helps bring the animal habitat to life.	• **Voice** tries to convey an authentic personal touch to the reader; shows involvement with the topic; message style matches the comparison purpose.	• **Voice** may not be involved with the topic; message comes across, but does not clearly connect to the purpose and audience.	• **Voice** is not involved in sharing observations with a reader; writing may be lifeless, with no sense of who is behind the words.	• **Voice** does not address an audience; does not have a sense of sharing a personal message or style.
• **Word Choice** imaginative use of specific language brings the animal habitat to life; careful choices make the comparisons unusually precise and interesting.	• **Word Choice** thoughtful use of precise, colorful language makes comparisons clear and interesting; explores new words, or uses everyday words in a fresh way.	• **Word Choice** communicates the main idea; uses a variety of words that fit the comparison task; explores some new words, or may try to use everyday words in a new way.	• **Word Choice** compares two animals in an obvious way; may try to use a range of words, but some do not fit; may overuse some words/expressions.	• **Word Choice** does not choose words that paint strong pictures of animals or a habitat; some words are overused, or may confuse the comparison points.	• **Word Choice** uses words that do not compare, or are vague and confusing; no new words are attempted; may overuse familiar words.
• **Sentence Fluency** simple and complex sentences flow in a natural rhythm; writing is easy to follow and read aloud; fragments or other devices, if used, strengthen the comparisons.	• **Sentence Fluency** well-paced simple and complex sentences flow naturally; a variety of lengths, beginnings, and patterns fit together and enhance the text.	• **Sentence Fluency** creates careful, easy-to-follow sentences that vary in length, beginnings, and patterns; uses simple and complex constructions, with stronger control of simple sentences.	• **Sentence Fluency** most sentences are readable, but are limited in lengths and patterns; some rereading may be necessary to follow the meaning; choppy or awkward sentences make the text hard to read aloud.	• **Sentence Fluency** sentences may be choppy or awkward; patterns are similar or monotonous; text may be hard to follow or read aloud.	• **Sentence Fluency** sentences are incomplete, rambling, or confusing, and make the text hard to follow and read aloud.
• **Conventions** is skilled in most writing conventions; proper use of the rules of English enhances clarity, meaning, and style; editing is largely unnecessary.	• **Conventions** shows skills in most writing conventions; proper use of the rules of English enhances clarity, meaning, and style; editing is largely unnecessary.	• **Conventions** may make some errors in spelling, capitalization, punctuation or usage which do not interfere with understanding the text; some editing is needed.	• **Conventions** has basic control of conventions; makes noticeable errors that interfere with an even reading of the text; significant editing is needed.	• **Conventions** frequent errors in spelling, word choice, punctuation and usage make the paper difficult to read; requires extensive editing.	• **Conventions** makes severe errors in most conventions; spelling errors may make it hard to guess what words are meant; some parts of the text may be impossible to follow or understand.

0: This piece is either blank, or fails to respond to the writing task. The topic is not addressed, or the student simply paraphrases the prompt. The response may be illegible or incoherent.

Writing That Compares

Scoring Rubric: 8-Trait Writing

8	7	6	5	4	3	2	1
The writer	The writer	The writer	The writer	The writer	The writer	The writer	The writer
• has used many facts from a variety of research sources, as well as interesting personal observations, to construct a superb comparison of two things.	• has used research sources and personal observation to present a factual, well-organized comparison of two things.	• has used research and some personal observation to construct an organized comparison of two things.	• has used some basic research and articulated a few strong personal observations to construct a fairly well-organized comparison of two things.	• has attempted to compare two things using mostly personal observations.	• may attempt to compare two things, but uses no factual research and limited personal observations.	• has made a poor attempt at comparing two things.	• has not successfully compared two things.
• presents an appealing introductory paragraph or statement, as well as an original conclusion.	• constructs a clear introductory statement and a good conclusion.	• presents introductory and concluding statements.	• presents basic introductory and concluding statements.	• may have constructed an opening or closing statement, but not both.	• includes distracting digressions and demonstrates a lack of strong overall structure.	• has not clearly presented an opening or concluding statement.	• exhibits problems with language serious enough to detract from overall readability.
• consistently and thoroughly constructs comparisons using elaborative details and sophisticated verbs and adjectives.	• has made many colorful comparisons using a variety of elaborative details and well-chosen verbs and adjectives.	• creates comparisons that include strong elaborations and numerous adjectives and verbs.	• creates a few comparisons that may lack elaboration.	• may have failed to develop clear opening and closing statements.	• exhibits serious problems with organization, word choice, and conventions.	• has not demonstrated a grasp of the characteristics of comparative writing.
• has consistently maintained a fluid, logical order of events, linked by a variety of transitional words and phrases.	• maintains a clear sequence of events linked by transition words.	• demonstrates a sound organizational structure with few digressions.	• creates solid comparisons using some elaboration with grade-level adjectives and verbs.	• has not successfully maintained a cohesive organizational structure. The piece contains a few digressions that distract somewhat from its overall readability.	• creates comparisons using few details to elaborate main points.	• has not applied his or her understanding of the genre to the assignment.
			• constructs an overall organizational structure that may include some irrelevant facts and digressions that do not seriously detract from overall readability.				

0: This piece is either blank, or fails to respond to the writing task. The topic is not addressed, or the student simply paraphrases the prompt. The response may be illegible or incoherent.

Notes

Notes

Notes

Notes